Machine Guns

14th Century to Present

Ian V. Hogg

Published by

 **krause publications**

700 E. State Street • Iola, WI 54990-0001
Telephone: 715/445-2214
Web: www.krause.com

Please call or write for our free catalog of publications. Our toll-free number to place an order or obtain a
free catalog is 800-258-0920 or please use our regular business telephone, 715-445-2214.

Library of Congress Catalog Number: 2001091076
ISBN: 0-87349-288-9

PREFACE

One of the problems facing the would-be writer on machine guns is the question of where to stop? Some writers in the past have dredged deep and wide, dragging in things like the Davis recoilless gun (which was a single-shot weapon with no pretensions to 'automaticity' whatever) and intermediate anti-aircraft guns in the 50-60mm caliber range. I think we need to keep a sense of proportion here, otherwise any artillery piece with mechanical handling of the ammunition might be argued as a machine gun. So far as we are concerned in these pages, the upper limit is 16mm or 0.70-inch; anything over that is classed as cannon. (I have made one or two exceptions to this, in cases where an odd caliber of weapon has some feature of interest or is significant in the overall story.) The lower limit is whatever the smallest military caliber weapon turns out to be; miniature Gatling guns firing 22 rimfire, ingenious and admirable as they are, do not qualify. Submachine guns are also excluded, notwithstanding the fact that some optimistic designers have provided such weapons with 1000-yard sights and bipods.

The sections of this book are divided up into historical periods that correspond to particular stages in the development of the machine gun. As each gun or type of gun appears, its mechanical features and method of functioning are discussed; but a few generalized words on methods of operation might not come amiss and these form the basis of Chapter One.

As far as possible I have gone to the fountainhead for information; either asking the manufacturers, or reading their literature, or getting hands on the actual gun, or reading official reports on tests and trials. In the few cases where such first-hand information has not been available, then I have had to fall back upon contemporary journals, both military and engineering, for their reports on contemporary developments. Unfortunately some of the writers were better journalists than they were engineers or soldiers, and consequently they frequently omitted some piece of vital information. You would be told that the barrel was made from Whiplash & Dingbat's Patent Molybdenum Steel, but not how long it was or how many grooves it had. And in the case of modern guns, although it may sound strange, there are still some details that the manufacturers or users will not divulge.

I would like to express my gratitude for the various opportunities afforded to me over the years by such establishments as the U.S Marine Corps Museum at Quantico, the British School of Infantry Museum, the Royal Artillery Museum, the Royal Military College of Science and, of course, the Ministry of Defense Pattern Room, and its curator Mr. Herbert Woodend and his assistant curator, Mr. Richard Jones. Without these facilities my researches would have been severely curtailed. I am also indebted to Colonel Des Radmore of the South African Defense Force, the late Dr. Edward Ezell, Terry Gander, Peter Chamberlain, John Slough and John Walter for information and photographs and, of course, to the various manufacturers who have provided photographs, drawings and details of their products. Without all these helpers, this book would have been a good deal thinner.

Machine Guns
Contents

On the Covers...

What better to show on the covers than a spectacular example of the 1905 Maxim gun on a wheeled Sokolov mount, kindly loaned to us for photography by International Military Antiques, Inc. At some point, this particular gun had the field green military paint removed and the phosphor-bronze water jacket and mount base polished. Obviously a display piece of some prominence, the gun's early history is unknown.

More recently, the New Jersey firm of I.M.A. (International Military Antiques, Inc.) managed to obtain three similar 1905s; this one being the best of the lot. Two are now in new homes; this third Maxim '05 remains with I.M.A. This specimen, like the other makes and models IMA markets, is classified as a 'non-gun' because it has been deactivated per federal regulations. One cannot tell it from the exterior, however.

Author Ian Hogg reports on this early Maxim–and all the others–within this book.

For more information about I.M.A. and their non-gun machine guns, contact them at the following address: International Military Antiques, Inc., Box 256, Millington NJ 07946.
Phone: 908-903-1200;
Website: www.ima-usa.com

CHAPTER ONE

OVERTURE AND BEGINNERS

THE TERM 'AUTOMATIC' is applied to weapons in a fairly loose manner, and it would be as well to begin by clarifying the term. The classic and formal definition of an automatic weapon is *'A weapon which, when the trigger is pressed, will fire and continue to reload and fire so long as the trigger remains pressed and the supply of ammunition is maintained.'* The classic and formal definition of a mechanical machine gun has, so far as I can discover, never been drawn up. For my part, I consider it to be governed by the feed system – how the ammunition is put into the breech. There are a number of weapons put forward as machine guns but which require every cartridge to be loaded into the feedway by hand, whereupon the gunner rotates a crank or pulls a handle to close the breech, fire the round, and eject the spent case *(if any)*. His assistant then throws in another round. I do not consider such a weapon to be a machine gun. A machine gun must have a continuous *(or at least renewable)* store of ammunition and must extract the cartridge from this store and load it by mechanical action.

The sequence of events which take place in the firing of one shot from an automatic weapon is often referred to as 'the loading cycle' or 'the operating cycle', and it will be useful to explain this cycle so that it will have relevance to the mechanisms explained later.

Considering the weapon to be at rest, loaded; the mechanism must first fire the cartridge in the chamber; this must then be followed by unlocking and opening the bolt, extracting the empty case from the chamber and ejecting it clear of the gun. The mechanism must then cock the firing arrangement, obtain a fresh cartridge from the feed system, position it correctly for loading and load it into the chamber. Finally the bolt must be closed and locked so that the weapon is again ready to fire. Apart from the obvious parts of the sequence - e.g. the empty case has to be extracted before a new one can be loaded - the various operations can be performed in varying order, and indeed some operations may be performed simultaneously - for example, as the bolt is ejecting the empty case it can be withdrawing a fresh cartridge from the feed system. Moreover, some operations may not be present - some weapons do not positively extract the empty case but

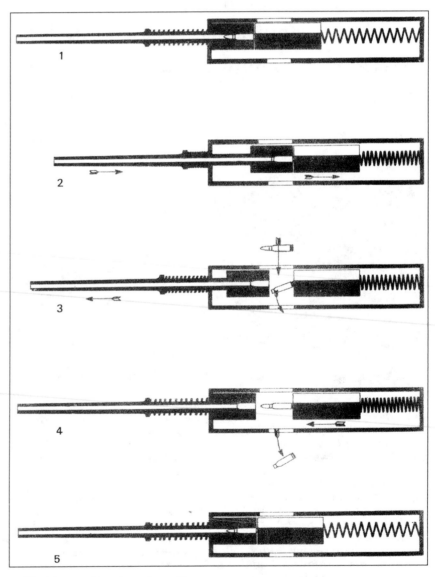

The long-recoil system of operation:
1) Firing pin strikes, cartridge explodes, recoil begins.
2) Barrel and bolt recoil, locked together.
3) Bolt unlocked and held, barrel returns to battery, empty case is extracted.
4) Empty case ejected, new round placed in feedway.
5) Bolt released, runs forward to chamber round, lock breech and fire.

rely upon chamber pressure to blow it out, others do not lock the bolt but merely rely upon its mass to resist being blown open by the exploding cartridge. But, by and large and making allowances for this sort of variation, the sequence can be detected in every automatic weapon, no matter how it may be powered.

How it may be powered is the next question. Strictly speaking, to be called an 'automatic' machine gun, the weapon must develop its own power. If this is not the case, then it becomes a mechanical machine gun or, in modern parlance, an 'externally powered' gun. External power can be anything from a soldier turning a crank handle to a 24-volt electric motor or a 500 horsepower airplane engine. Automatic guns rely, in the last

analysis, upon the power of the propelling charge in the cartridge, since this is the only source of power available inside the gun. Which is why the first round fired from an automatic gun has to be manually loaded and fired in order to start the ball rolling.

Mechanical guns might be expected to encompass merely those historical curiosities such as the Gatling, Nordenfelt and Gardner, Lowell and Ager and so forth. But there is rather more to it than that: the mechanical machine gun is still a force to be reckoned with, though not as an infantry ground gun, and it has enjoyed a resurgence in the last quarter of the 20th century.

Automatic guns are classified according to the broad principle of their operation, as being recoil-,

gas- or blowback-operated. But whatever title is applicable; they all derive the initial impulse from the cartridge. Recoil operation depends upon Newton's law, which says that action and reaction are opposite and equal; here the action is the bullet departing up the bore at high velocity, and the reaction is the mass of the gun barrel and breechblock recoiling in the opposite direction at a much lesser speed but with equal momentum. How far these two components recoil together governs whether the gun is a 'long-recoil' or 'short-recoil' weapon, the latter being in the majority. A 'long-recoil' weapon is one in which the barrel and breechblock (or bolt - the terms are synonymous) recoil locked together for a distance greater than the length of a complete cartridge. They then stop, the bolt is unlocked and held, and the barrel allowed to run forward (or 'into battery') driven by its own spring. During this movement the empty cartridge case is extracted and ejected. As the barrel reaches its in-battery position, the bolt is released and, driven by its own spring, runs forward, collects a fresh round from the ammunition supply, chambers it, closes the breech and locks. A 'short-recoil' gun has the barrel and breechblock recoil together for a distance shorter than the length of a cartridge; the breech is then unlocked, the barrel stops, and the breech-block carries on recoiling, driven by its own momentum, for whatever distance the designer wants. During this phase the case is extracted and ejected and the firing mechanism cocked. The breech-block is then sent back by a spring, chambering a fresh round into the barrel, and locks, whereupon the barrel and breech run into battery. In earlier days, recoil operation was looked upon as the senior and more responsible member of the family; for sustained and accurate fire nothing else was considered, and this attitude lasted until the early 1930s in many quarters.

Gas operation almost always means gas *piston* operation. There have been other ways of applying the expansion of gas behind the bullet to drive the mechanism, but most of them have fallen by the wayside. Perhaps more than the other systems, gas operation really needs a close collaboration between the ammunition designer and the gun designer; and since the gun designer usually comes along many years after the ammunition has been designed, it rarely happens.

A
Start of cycle

B
Bolt unlocked
acceleration starts

C
Acceleration
completed

D
Barrel rebounding
from recoil buffer;
bolt rebounding from
back plate buffer

E
Bolt loading
fresh cartridge

The sequence of events in firing a short-recoil-operated machine gun. These drawings do not represent any specific machine gun, they merely demonstrate the principles of operation.

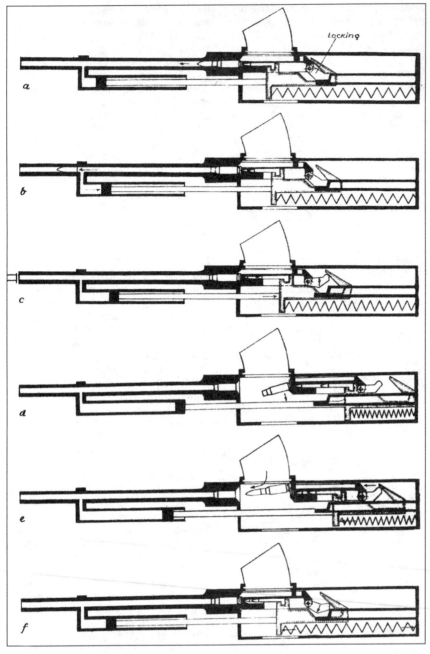

locking

The gas-operated machine gun:
a) Firing pin strikes, cartridge explodes, gas pressure begins.
b) Bullet passes the gas port; piston starts to move back.
c) Bullet leaves muzzle; piston starts to open breech.
d) Empty case ejected.
e) Run-out begins; bolt rests on piston slide cartridge force from magazine.
f) Gun loaded, breech closed. As piston advances further it will depress and lock the bolt and then strike the firing pin.

Hence the problems with gas fouling that are sometimes exacerbated by the ammunition people doing their own thing without reference to the gun designers. The Colt M16 rifle - though not a machine gun - and the 5.56mm cartridge, are a classic example of this. Traditionally, too, if recoil operation was the respectable face of the machine gun, gas-operated weapons were the black sheep of the family. *Everybody* knew that gas-operated weapons gave poor accuracy and poor reliability. The gun makers replied that if you kept the thing clean it was as reliable as any other system, and as far as accuracy went, if you wanted pinpoint accuracy go and buy a sniping rifle. The object of the machine gun is to spread the stuff around, not put all of the shots through the same hole. *(I first heard this argument in 1942 and was still hearing it fifty years later.)* The point at issue here is that for the most part, recoil-operated guns fire from a closed bolt,

while gas-operated weapons usually fire from an open bolt. This is because an open bolt *(a)* simplifies design and *(b)* means that a current of air can pass through the barrel and cool it down in between bursts of firing. Recoil-operated weapons are usually heavier and provide for better dissipation of heat from the barrel by one means or another.

When you pull the trigger of a closed-bolt weapon, the hammer falls or the firing pin is released and the gun fired without movement. When you pull the trigger on an open-bolt weapon the bolt goes rushing down the receiver, hits a cartridge in the feed way, scoops it up, rams it home, locks the breech perhaps, and then fires. All that movement and commotion means the gun moves quite a lot between pulling the trigger and firing the first shot; after which the gunner gets over his initial shock and gets the thing under control. Which is why the first round goes here and the subsequent rounds go there, a phenomenon known as the 'split group' that is inseparable from open-bolt gas operation.

Within these two broad groups of operation, there is a further sub-division, that of whether or not the breech is locked. Indeed, much of the difference between guns within the two groups lies in the method of breech locking; after all, the Maxim and the Browning machine guns look very much alike on the outside, and both work by recoil, but their methods of locking the breech are totally different. Maxim used a toggle lock *(a system which will be explained in detail later)*, Browning used a simple slab of metal moved up and down on a ramp as the working parts recoiled and ran back, others have used a simple pivoting lump of metal holding the breech closed, or have lifted the rear end of the breech-block to wedge into a prepared face in the gun body, or moved the rear end of the block sideways, or lifted the nose; others have based their ideas on the bolt-action rifle and used a bolt which rotates and locks by means of lugs, either into the barrel chamber or into an extension— or even into lugs in the gun body itself. There are rotating rings which are controlled either by barrel movement or gas piston movement so as to clamp barrel and bolt together, there are flaps, wedges, rollers, tappets and pins which move in and out by various agencies... the list is considerable, and if we include all the hare-brained ideas which have appeared in the

No matter who lays claim to what, the fact remains that the Gatling was the first *practical* machine gun. Here it is performing in the hands of the British Naval Brigade at Alexandria, Egypt, in 1881. Just why the bearded three-badge man was trying to tear the wheel off escapes me for the moment.

patent digests for the past hundred and fifty years, the list is virtually endless.

Which is perhaps why exasperated designers have sometimes thrown all the ideas into the trash and settled for a simple solution: no lock at all. Blowback operation might be considered as short-recoil operation without restraint, since the breechblock is not locked to the fixed barrel and the only delay in opening is due to the inertia of the block, which therefore needs to be substantial. In fact pure blowback operation is a rarity in machine guns, since if the gun is to have any tactical value at all it needs to have a powerful and long-ranging cartridge, which argues a breech-block of massive proportions. So what happens in real life is that the blowback becomes a 'delayed blowback' or 'hesitation lock' in which some agency prevents or slows

down the opening of the block until the bullet has left the barrel, so that the subsequent action is not so violent as a pure blowback would have been. Even so, this sort of action is mostly confined to the early days of machine guns, when inventors were feeling their way, and to a more recent period when cartridges have become less powerful and production engineers had more to say than designers.

There are some machine guns that adapt features from more than one system of operation, though sometimes one is inclined to wonder why. An example would be the case where a breechblock is unlocked by the operation of a gas piston mechanism, after which the block is propelled to the rear and the loading cycle completed by simple blowback action. Many of these hybrid designs were put forward in the early days when getting around

restrictive patents was the hardest part of the inventor's task. However, these various aberrations will be dealt with when they appear.

It follows from all this that when you come right down to it there are about half-a-dozen reliable ways of operating a machine gun; the rest is simply icing on the cake. Some designs of the past have been largely smoke and mirrors disguising the fact that, at bottom, they were gas or blowback or some other well-known application. If one studies the patent applications for machine guns since the 1880s, there will be found every conceivable, and many inconceivable, methods of driving a machine gun. Some of them - relatively few - actually worked. But making a mechanism work once is not enough in the machine gun business: you have to make it work at about 1000 times a minute to

Today's machine gun is perhaps more subtle, certainly more deadly. The FN Minimi used as a company support gun.

receive any credit for it. Which is why I have not explored such byways and primer actuation, clockwork spring drive *(oh yes, there was one...)*, hydro-pneumatic pistons instead of return springs, spinning discs which launch bullets by centrifugal force *(assiduously promoted during World War I by more than one hopeful...)*, guns driven by propane gas, diesel oil or compressed air, and similar entertainments. We will have enough to do digesting the ones that have succeeded.

Some readers may be surprised at the relatively small number of machine gun designs, as compared with other types of military weapon. It is, of course, a somewhat restricted market: a machine gun design can only survive if a military force adopts it. No military adoption means no production, since unlike other types of weapon there is no way a machine gun can be adapted to the civilian market. New machine guns do not, therefore, appear in the same quantity as do new pistols, submachine guns or rifles; once an army settles on a good machine gun design it tends to stay with it, and if a change of cali-

ber comes along, then, if possible, the tried and trusted gun is merely modified to suit rather than discarded for an entirely new pattern. The only time this rule does not hold good is where the change of caliber involves a cartridge of such considerably different dimensions that modification would be impractical. As a result, the most recent rash of new machine gun designs came in the 1980s when the 5.56mm cartridge began to achieve respectability as the basic infantry round, and the infantry squads demanded a machine gun firing the same ammunition as their rifles. Since that time one or two designs have appeared in the hope of displacing existing weapons with something a bit better. The only problem is that merely being a bit better is not sufficient of a reason for junking millions of dollars' worth of machine guns. Between 1980 and 2000 half-a-dozen designs of heavy machine gun appeared with the intention of replacing the venerable 50-caliber Browning as the world's standard heavyweight, but none succeeded. This was not because they were unsound designs; they were quite good, even

excellent designs. But nobody was prepared to face the vast expense of re-equipping, particularly since the Russian bear had turned out to be somewhat mangy and toothless. A new design will have to be vastly better than the existing weapon to even be considered today.

All this is by way of explanation for, firstly, the limited number of designs, and secondly for the paucity of information on some of the unsuccessful designs. Machine guns which are not taken up by the military tend to disappear very thoroughly; specimens may remain in military museums or collections but very little of the paperwork survives, and formal manuals were probably never written, so that details of performance, or even how to dismantle some of the more baffling designs, are missing. I know of one museum curator, a man skilled in firearms, who dismantled an obscure machine gun and then spent a frustrating week before he managed to get it back together again. Understandably, requests by researchers to dismantle that particular weapon in order to study its operation are refused.

CHAPTER TWO

MECHANICAL MACHINE GUNS

AS WITH MANY other firearms inventions, the success of the machine-gun revolved around ammunition it fired; and even though a great deal of mechanical ingenuity was displayed, as long as the only round of ammunition was a lead ball, a heap of gunpowder and a sharpened flint the results were never likely to produce a practical weapon. But in fact one of the weapons that is generally quoted as being an early approach to the machine gun in appearance and design, as well as intent, appeared in the flintlock era.

This was 'The Defense', patented by James Puckle in 1718, a sin-

gle-barreled gun with a revolver-like chamber behind it and a flintlock ignition unit on top of the cylinder. A crank at the rear acted as a screw-jack to force the cylinder against the rear end of the barrel. Once screwed tight, the flintlock was tripped, firing the charge in the chamber and discharging a bullet from the barrel. The operator now swung the crank to unlock the cylinder, moved it round to line up the next loaded chamber with the barrel, clamped up and fired again. Once the cylinder was empty - it had six or more chambers - loosening the crank allowed it to be taken off and a fresh one loaded on.

Puckle demonstrated his gun to the English Board of Ordnance in 1717, but they were not impressed and took no further action. He demonstrated it several more times; on one occasion in 1722 it fired 63 shots in seven minutes, which was most impressive performance for the time. But in spite of offering it for sale in a variety of sizes, and even offering a model firing round bullets against Christians and square ones against Infidels, Puckle never prospered with it. The Duke of Montagu is reputed to have purchased two, using them to arm his expedition to colonize the West Indies, but these appear not to have been used and there is no record of their purchase

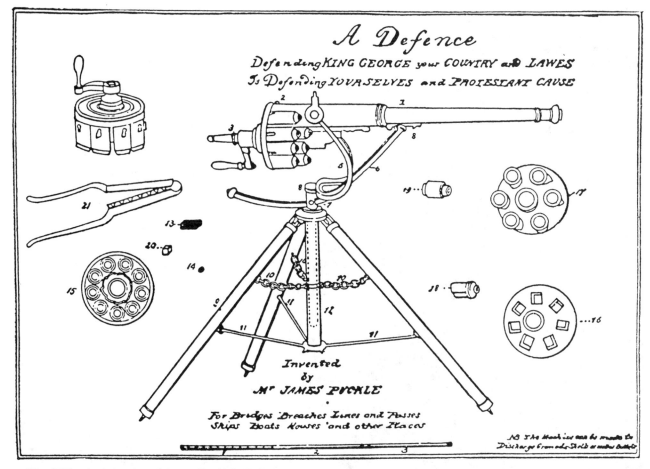

The 1718 patent drawing of James Puckle's 'Defense' gun, generally considered to be the forefather of all machine guns.

Unlike most inventors of his day, Puckle managed to get his invention manufactured; this is the specimen held by the Royal Armouries at the Tower of London (now removed to Leeds, in the north of England).

or of their employment. One of the few existing specimens of Puckle's gun is now in the Tower of London armories.

To be honest, though, one has to admit there is a world of difference between Puckle's gun and a machine gun; he might possibly be said to be the father of the six-shot revolver, but his connection with the machine gun is tenuous, to say the very least.

Other multiple firing systems were put forward at various times. One of the most persistent is the idea of having had a dozen or so touch-holes in a musket barrel, then loading half a dozen charges and balls, each topped by a well-greased wad. A sliding pan and lock is then aligned

A closer view of Puckle's gun; the flintlock ignition system has been folded forward and the cylinder withdrawn. Note the chamfered ends to each chamber, fitting tightly into the coned end of the barrel when the screw handle is tightened. By our standards, not a very practical weapon, but Puckle had studied his subject and done his homework.

with the foremost touch-hole and fired, discharging the foremost charge and ball. The pan is slid back to the second touch-hole, primed and fired, and so on until the last ball is sent on its way and the weapon then has to be re-loaded. When carefully prepared there is a fair chance that this weapon will work as intended, but the slightest carelessness in loading, particularly with the wad separating each charge, and there is a very good chance the first firing will ignite the entire contents in one massive discharge and wreck the musket into the bargain. It would not do the musketeer much good either.

So if one barrel was a difficult proposition, perhaps using multiple barrels might provide the desired firepower. This is probably one of the oldest ideas in firearms design. The first appearance of the 'ribauldequin', as it was then known, comes in 1382, when the men of Ghent, in Belgium, fell out with their neighbors in Bruges and set forth with a number of these weapons to reinforce their argument. They were light, wheeled carts with a number of small-caliber cannon barrels fixed to the bed of the cart. A piece of quickmatch connected all the touch-holes, and by firing the match, the barrels were fired in succession. Or, when things really got tough, a simple train of powder allowed firing them all at once.

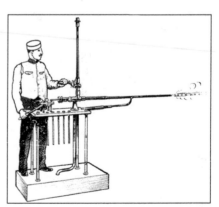

The Perkins Steam Gun, based on a contemporary engraving; not very informative about where the steam came from, but as a 'technology demonstrator' it was quite impressive.

Agar's 'Coffee Mill', the first attempt at using a self-contained 'cartridge' in a rapid-fire weapon.

The *ribauldequin* soon died out; in the early days cannon were more use in firing heavy projectiles against castles than erratically scattering small shot at people, and the multiple-barrel weapon took far too long to reload when half a ton of armored knight on horseback was bearing down on you with drawn sword. The idea occasionally re-appeared, earning itself the name of a 'battery gun' *(because it consisted of a 'battery' of gun-barrels)* but, like every other idea, was constrained by powder, ball, flint and steel.

In the early 19th century Forsyth introduced his percussion system, and with this the would-be designer of a rapid-firing weapon found his task a trifle easier; but only a trifle. Since placing a cap on the nipple of a firearm was difficult to manage by mechanical means, the battery gun underwent a revival, a number of rifle barrels being mounted on some sort of framework and then fired in succession. This produced a fearsome blast of gunfire for a few seconds, but as before, there was then a long pause while the gunner reloaded all the barrels - it was still the muzzle-loading, powder and ball era.

There were, of course, inventors who tried to circumvent the pow-der-and-ball restriction by finding some other way of propelling the bullet. Among the more practical ideas was the Steam Gun of Jacob Perkins, patented in 1824. Perkins was an English engineer who actually started by developing an improved steam generator, which could be made portable but produced a useful pressure without danger of explosions. Casting round for some way of putting this to use, he came up with the idea of a steam gun, which he exhibited to the

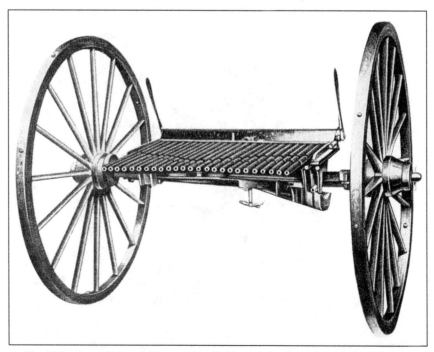

The Billinghurst-Requa battery gun or 'bridge gun' revived the old *ribauldequin* principle but used breech-loading barrels to speed up the reloading.

Board of Ordnance in 1826. In brief, it was a tube with a valve at one end into which steam was piped. Above this was a vertical magazine loaded with lead balls, and there was a simple hand lever to operate the weapon. Having got steam pressure, a tube full of one-ounce bullets was inserted into the top of the weapon, and the operator depressed and released the lever. This first allowed a ball to drop into the breech and then injected a burst of steam at about 200 lb/in^2 which blew the ball down the barrel and out of the muzzle with sufficient force to penetrate twelve one-inch oak planks or quarter-inch thick iron plate at a distance of 35 yards. A skilled operator could easily get 60 shots per minute from the gun and, provided the steam pressure and ammunition supply were kept up, it could go on indefinitely, for there was very little to wear out.

Perkins received no encouragement from the Board of Ordnance so he went to France and sold a gun to the French, which was claimed to fire five-pound balls at 60 shots per minute. He died some time in the 1830s, and his work was continued by A.M. Perkins, possibly his son, who improved things until he could get a pressure of 700 lb/in^2 and much better range and penetration, but in spite of a great deal of favorable publicity in London newspapers in the 1850s he failed

to raise any official interest and no more was ever heard of it.

The American Civil War acted as a spur to inventors in this field, and one of the first weapons to approach the mechanical definition of a machine gun was the 'Ager Coffee Mill Gun' which got its nickname from the appearance of the loading hopper and operating crank. The gun carried a hopper on top, into which steel tubes containing a lead ball, a charge of powder, and a percussion cap already in place, were dropped. Beneath this was a crank, and turning this pushed a tube into the barrel chamber, locked it there and then dropped a hammer onto the cap. The gun fired, and continued rotation of the crank extracted the tube and ejected it, then began feeding in another. The gunner's mate had his work cut out, picking up the ejected tubes, opening them up and re-loading them, then dropping them back into the hopper so as to keep up the fire.

The Ager gun worked and, for its day, worked well. The trouble was that few people were convinced of it. Those with some smattering of mechanical or scientific knowledge avowed that it was quite ridiculous; since according to Ager it should be possible to fire 100 rounds a minute if the ammunition was prepared. *'Nonsense'* said the experts. *'This means you are proposing to explode a pound or so of gunpowder inside*

the barrel every minute. Steel will never stand up to the heating effect.'

There was a good deal of truth in this, of course, but the point would have been better made had they sat down and proposed some system of solving the problem rather than just rubbishing the whole idea. They had, in fact, put their finger on one of the greatest problems facing the machine gun designer, but they preferred to ignore it rather than solve it. Poor Ager, in spite of having a war on his doorstep, never sold more than about 50 guns.

Next on the scene was Dr. Joseph Requa, who invented a 'Battery Gun' and had it made by one William Billinghurst of Rochester, New York. Hence it became known as the 'Billinghurst-Requa Gun' and consisted of 24 rifle barrels mounted on a wheeled carriage. The gun was demonstrated in New York shortly before the Civil War broke out, and several were purchased by both the Union and Confederate sides. They were often referred to as 'bridge guns' since they were ideal for defending a bridge by delivering a sudden blast of fire into an attacking party.

Requa had got over the problem of the long pause for reloading by making his weapon a breechloader; indeed, he had almost gone back to Puckle's system. In the Requa gun a number of cartridges were fitted into a sheet-iron frame and dropped in place so that they mated with the breeches of the barrels. Two levers clamped the frame in place and a single percussion cap in the center of the frame was then fired. The flame from this ignited the nearest cartridges and they, in turn, communicated flame to the remainder, so that the gun fired in a ragged volley. In August 1863 the Ordnance Select Committee in London reported on this weapon. From their report it seems that the whole weapon weighed just over half a ton, was of 60-caliber and fired a 414-grain lead ball. But the Committee members were not impressed, as their reports shows: *'The Committee are of the opinion that none of the rifle batteries could ever be effectually substituted for field guns of any description, and that even as a device for multiplying and accelerating infantry fire from rifle barrels in the field their utility would be very questionable. The Committee see no occasion for having a gun of this nature specially prepared for trial in this country. Should it be hereafter decided to employ them ... such instruments could be readily*

A contemporary engraving of the Montigny Mitrailleuse as used by the French army in the war of 1870. The gunner is holding the breech open while his assistant drops in a loaded plate of cartridges.

The actual Montigny Mitrailleuse tested by Colonel Fosbery and purchased for the British army in 1869. The mounting is not the field carriage but merely a modified artillery carriage for the purpose of display.

devised by our own mechanicians, without applying to the United States for them.'

Short as it is, this extract from the report pinpoints the greatest problem facing the early development of machine guns: how were they to be used? It seemed apparent to everybody at the time that they were some sort of artillery weapon, and that they should be handled in the field in the same way, setting down some distance from the enemy and leisurely taking him under fire. It was this question of method of employment that was to be the greatest brake on the early development.

During the time that these guns were being considered in the USA, a European designer had been busy with his version of a battery gun. In 1851 a Belgian inventor, Captain Fafschamps, had designed a weapon that, in some respects, paralleled the Requa gun. He passed his drawings and ideas to a manufacturer named Montigny, who put them into effect and produced the weapon, which was known in consequence as the 'Montigny Mitrailleuse'. After spending several years on its development and perfection, Montigny managed to interest Napoleon III and in 1869, in great secrecy, the French Army was outfitted with 156 of these guns. They were manufactured in the Meudon Arsenal, and only those officers who were to be concerned in operating the weapons were allowed to see them. But in spite of this attempt at secrecy there were a number of leaks to the press, and the newspapers lost no chance of telling the world what a revolutionary weapon the French now had, a miracle gun that would defeat the Prussians with no effort on the French part. Consequently the Prussians were not surprised when they were confronted with them in the war of 1870.

The *Mitrailleuse* consisted of 25 rifle barrels mounted inside a cylindrical casing so that, externally, the gun resembled a field gun mounted on the usual sort of two-wheeled carriage. A breechblock, fitted with a firing mechanism operating 25 separate firing pins, slid backwards and forwards in the barrel casing when a loading lever was operated by hand. The cartridges were carried in a metal plate which had 25 holes drilled in it corresponding to the

The 37-cartridge plate for the Mitrailleuse and the 37-barrel muzzle.

Doctor Gatling in about 1890, with a late-model Gatling gun.

"The weapon tested had 37 barrels...range 225 metres...target 10 feet by 12 feet. The first few shots struck low, the remainder of the volley struck the upper part of the target or passed over it. " This proved to be due to using a thick layer of India-rubber underneath the gun mounting. It was removed, the wheels sunk unto the ground and the trail supported on a sandbag, after which the shooting showed a remarkable improvement. "Misfires were a frequent occurrence and averaged 10.8 per cent. Dissection of several of the cartridges led to the conclusion that the fault in each case was due to the cartridges. The mechanism of the Mitrailleur worked well without the slightest hitch. Major Fosbery loaded and fired the battery himself several times with great ease and rapidity... On 14 June 1868 a further experiment was made at 400 metres in comparison with shrapnel fired from four rifled breech-loading six-pounder guns. One minute's firing from the Mitrailleur proved superior to 12 rounds from the four guns. 10 plates or 370 cartridges were fired, the first five slowly at about half minute intervals, the remainder in 46 seconds, one man only on the gun. 40 misfires took place, 330 cartridges exploded and 278 bullets struck the target..." Further tests then took place at 600 and 800 meters range, with similarly encouraging results. Fosbery ended by summarizing his views; which were that the idea was sound but the cartridges and the rifling were not of the best design. He then went on to say that "he does not recommend the Mitrailleur as a substitute for artillery but as an addition..... for the defense of roads, bridges or defiles; for the attack of mountain passes; for flanking short faces of

arrangement of the barrels. With the breechblock slid backwards, this plate, loaded with cartridges, was dropped into grooves on the front face of the block. The block was then pushed forward, whereupon the cartridges entered the chambers of their respective barrels and the firing mechanism was cocked. Revolving a crank at the rear of the gun now caused the firing pins to fall in succession, faster or slower according to the speed at which the crank was turned. Normal rate of fire was a quick spin of the crank, which fired all 25 barrels in one second. With a supply of ready-loaded plates handy a three-man crew could keep up a rate of about 250 rounds per minute.

In spite of the French passion for secrecy, most of the world's armies knew all about the Mitrailleuse. The India Office, that branch of the British government which looked after India, sent a report on the weapon to the Director-General of Ordnance, which was an account of a visit to the Belgian test ranges at Braeschaet in August 1868 by none other than Major G.V. Fos-

bery VC, of the Bengal Staff Corps. *(One is tempted to wonder if this was the match which ignited Fosbery's interest in automatic weapons, resulting in the Webley-Fosbery revolver some thirty years later.)* The report makes interesting reading:

The earliest type of Gatling is exemplified by this 1865 model in 50-caliber.

works; for protecting decks of iron-clads; for dealing with an enemy unprovided with artillery; and is of the opinion that we shall seek in vain elsewhere for a weapon which, weighing only 392 pounds and requiring only two men, will prove so destructive."

That was fairly enthusiastic, but he soon had cold water poured all over him:

"Director-General of Ordnance minutes, 14/12/68, that he believed that good infantry and good field artillery are a better investment.... Admiralty, by letter 15/1/69 states that this invention is not likely to prove of service to the Navy." In spite of this, the Comander-in-Chief recommended that one be purchased (for £314) together with various spares and 10,000 cartridges (at 80 francs per 1000). The weapon was duly purchased, and today sits in the Royal Artillery Museum at Wolwich in south-east London.

In addition to the Mitrailleurs, the French had bought a number of Gatling guns *(of which we shall see more)*, and they went to war in 1870 in high spirits. But the war was an unmitigated disaster for many reasons, and one of the least successful areas was the performance of the Mitrailleurs.

The faults lay not with the mechanism of the guns or their operation,

The naval application of the Gatling gun was to place it in the 'fighting tops' and sweep the decks of enemy ships that got too close. Or the decks of your own if the enemy got *that* close.

The actual 42-caliber Gatling gun demonstrated by Dr. Gatling at Woolwich Arsenal, London, on 11 August 1870.

The genuine article; a ten-barrel 65-caliber Gatling on a naval deck mounting.

but with their tactical handling; there was still doubt about whether they were infantry weapons or artillery weapons, and since they looked like artillery they were handled the same way, being brought into action wheel to wheel in open positions. Since the maximum range of the Mitrailleuse was about 1800 yards, and the maximum range of the Prussian artillery about 2500 yards,

the result was a foregone conclusion. As soon as the French unlimbered their machine guns, the Prussian artillery opened up and pounded them into impotence. It could have been the death-knell of the machine gun, but fortunately the fault was recognized as one of employment and not of operation, and the guns survived - just. On the few occasions when they were sited

intelligently and under cover, with a good field of fire, they did great execution, but these occasions were few and far between.

The Austrians had been sufficiently impressed by the mechanical ability of the Mitrailleuse to purchase another design of Montigny gun, with 37 barrels chambered for their 11mm Werndl cartridge. But instead of using

The same ten-barrel, 65-inch model could also appear on a field carriage for use by naval landing parties.

Armies preferred lighter six-barrel models in 45 or 50 caliber; this is Major Owen's Gatling Battery, Royal Artillery, in Zululand in 1879.

them for field operations they reserved them for fortification defense, a role that most military authorities agreed was ideal for such weapons. The guns would be within a protected fort where they could be served and reloaded in safety, while the volume of fire was just what was needed to deal with sudden assaults against the ramparts or incursions into the ditch around the fort.

But the Mitrailleuse was overshadowed by its American contemporary, the Gatling gun, one of the most famous of all machine-guns and certainly the best-known of the mechanical weapons if not the most perfect. Dr. Richard Jordan Gatling invented the Gatling in 1861. Although qualified in medicine he never practiced, and spent most of his life inventing, though of all his inventions only the gun has survived to perpetuate his name, his steam-plough, hemp-breaker and rice-planter having faded from view.

Gatling more or less took the Ager system of loading a cartridge by a forward stroke of a crank and applied it to a metallic cartridge. He also appreciated the point about the heating effect of firing pounds of gunpowder in a barrel, and arranged his gun to have six barrels, which would be fired in turn. Thus if the gun had rate of fire of, say, 300 rounds per minute, any one barrel would only be firing at 50 rpm, and it would have an opportunity to cool down during the time that the other five were being fired. The six barrels were mounted around a central axis, and behind them was the loading and firing arrangement operated by a crank at the side of the gun. The cartridges were placed into a feeding

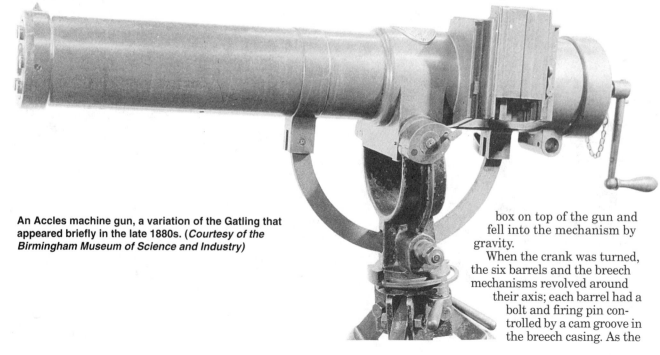

An Accles machine gun, a variation of the Gatling that appeared briefly in the late 1880s. (*Courtesy of the Birmingham Museum of Science and Industry*)

box on top of the gun and fell into the mechanism by gravity.

When the crank was turned, the six barrels and the breech mechanisms revolved around their axis; each barrel had a bolt and firing pin controlled by a cam groove in the breech casing. As the unit revolved, projections in the bolts, riding in the groove, caused the bolts to open and close in the barrel breeches. Taking one barrel as an example, at the topmost position in its revolution the breech was open and a cartridge from the feed column fell in. As the barrel continued to move round, the bolt was closed by the cam groove and the cartridge was forced into the gun chamber.

The bolt was then locked and as the barrel reached the bottom-most position the cam tripped the firing pin and the cartridge was fired. Then as the barrel began to move up the other side of the circle the bolt was unlocked and opened, the cartridge case extracted and ejected, and it arrived once more at the top, empty, ready to be reloaded. It should perhaps be said that this description is of the perfected Gatling; the first models, understandably, were not quite so neat and tidy, although they were quite serviceable. General Ben Butler thought sufficient of them to buy 12 (at $1000 apiece), which he used successfully at the Siege of Petersburg, Virginia, but apart from that the Gatling gun made little headway during the Civil War; it seems that both sides suspected Dr. Gatling's sympathies.

In January 1865 his perfected model was tested by the US War Department, and in the following year it was officially adopted, 50 guns of 1-inch caliber and 50 of

0.50-inch being ordered. With this to sustain him, Gatling began to sell the gun throughout the world. The British Army began to take an interest in the Gatling in 1869, and in 1870 a most comprehensive trial was carried out, in which the Gatling was compared with the Montigny Mitrailleuse, a 12-pounder breech-loader firing shrapnel, a 9-pounder muzzle-loader firing shrapnel, six soldiers firing Martini-Henry rifles and six soldiers firing Snider rifles. The Gatling fired 492 lbs. of ammunition and obtained 2803 hits on various targets; the Montigny fired 472 lbs. for 708 hits; the 12-pounder 1232 lbs. for 2286 hits; and the 9-pounder 1013 lbs. for 2207 hits. This certainly proved the economy of the Gatling gun.

In a test of timed fire, the Gatling fired 1925 rounds in 2.5 minutes to score 651 hits; the Montigny, in the same time, 1073 rounds to obtain 214 hits; the six men firing Martini-Henry rifles got off 391 rounds for 152 hits, and the six with Snider rifles 313 rounds for 82 hits. This trial was fired at various ranges, and the Gatling stood out for its accuracy at 900 yards, managing a far higher percentage of hits at long range than did any of the other competitors.

The Ordnance Select Committee said in their report that "*of the two systems of machine-guns. . . the Gatling has proved to be far supe-*

Two French *matelots* firing a 47mm Hotchkiss revolving cannon some time in the 1890s. At 47mm caliber (1.85 inches) it can hardly be called a machine gun, but no history can omit the Hotchkiss.

rior . "*... and went on to recommend 'The immediate introduction of the small Gatling gun for employment in the field ... for a first installment, 50 guns of the small caliber (0.42-in) for land service, and as many of the small and medium sized (0.65-in) guns as the Lords Commissioners consider requisite for the Navy, to be ordered from Dr. Gatling, pending the preparation of suitable plant either at Enfield or at Woolwich for future production'.*" In the event, manufacture was actually undertaken by Sir William Armstrong & Co., who obtained a license from Dr. Gatling.

And these elegant gentlemen are from a Territorial Yeomanry regiment and showing off their shiny new 303 Gatling in about 1890.

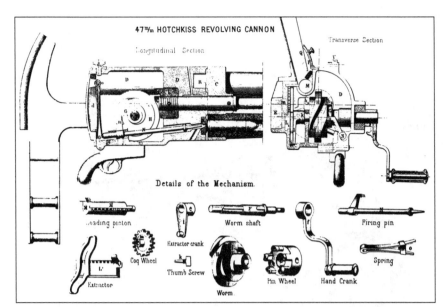

47ᵐ/ₘ HOTCHKISS REVOLVING CANNON

Longitudinal Section

Transverse Section

Details of the Mechanism.

Loading piston

Worm shaft

Firing pin

Extractor crank

Cog Wheel

Thumb Screw

Pin Wheel

Hand Crank

Spring

Extractor

Worm

A contemporary drawing of the Hotchkiss that is more artistic than helpful, but linking up the letters on the components with the two upper drawings will explain quite a lot. The round enters at the top left of the gun, is carried 'round to fire at the six-o'clock position, the case is ejected at 8-o'clock and the chamber is then ready for reloading at about '11:15' or so.

But in addition to their technical report upon the comparative performance of the Gatling gun, in December 1871 the Committee took the opportunity of summing up their opinion on 'Mitrailleurs' in general, and they are worth study as a perfect example of the tactical beliefs and opinions of the time:

"The Committee are of opinion that the mitrailleur should be treated purely as a defensive weapon, capable of considerably increasing the fire of infantry and of delivering, *up to distances proportional to the size of the weapon employed* a more certain and more deadly fire than any field gun.

They entirely agree with the officers who have given evidence, as well as with the officers of the Prussian army, that the field artillery should not be reduced by a single man or horse for the sake of substituting mitrailleurs. At the same time they are satisfied, both from their own experiments and from the evidence adduced, that these weapons, more particularly Gatling guns, possess certain advantages which cannot be ignored, and they are prepared to show not only that there is a place for them in permanent works, but also in the field.

To treat the larger Gatling gun, 0.65-inch, first:

The Committee consider that in addition to its employment on board ships of war, as already recommended, a gun of this caliber would be found excessively useful for the defense of coast batteries against the attack of boats, or for assisting in keeping down the fire of ships engaging forts at close quarters or attempting to force a passage, by pouring an incessant fire into their ports.

Such Gatlings, well served, would effectively put a stop to any attempt at landing, and would be more reliable at short ranges than field guns.

With regard to the small Gatling gun, 0.45-inch:

The proper role for a gun of this caliber and power, appears to the Committee to be the defense of entrenched positions and villages, or for covering roads, defiles, bridges or other narrow places, along which an enemy may be expected to pass.

Looking to the uncertainty of shell fire, even with the best percussion or time fuses, there can be little doubt that a body or troops having to advance to the attack of an entrenched position, *over any distance within 1,200 yards*, would suffer far more from Gatling guns delivering an incessant and wide spread fire of the deadliest *mitraille* than from field guns.

The Committee are unanimously of opinion that a proportion of Gatling guns, worked by the Artillery, and not exceeding the weight recommended in their report of 14/3/70, *viz.*, 18 cwt. *[2,016 lbs.]*, should accompany every army in the field, for the specific purposes above detailed; and that they should be kept with the reserves for the express purpose of increasing infantry fire at critical moments, in precisely the same way that guns of position are used for strengthening the fire of the field artillery.

As a rule, mitrailleurs should invariably be so entrenched as to bid defiance to the fire of field guns, and be kept masked until the attack

This drawing, together with the previous one, will tell you all you need to know about the Hotchkiss revolver.

The Lowell gun, with its ammunition feeder in place and four barrels visible.

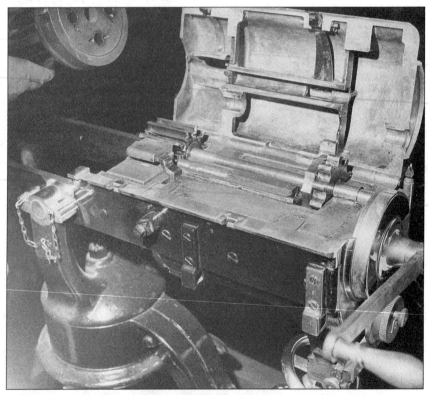

to doubt if they will ever be found so effective for working with cavalry as the horse artillery gun.

Another view of the Lowell. This shows the operating handle at the rear and also shows how the barrel is carried on a revolving disc at the front. The upright handle at the front of the receiver is the barrel release and revolving lever.

is fully developed, and the enemy well within effective distance.

They should be provided with Nolan's rangefinders.

The Committee do not share in the apprehension that great inconvenience would be caused to an army in the field by the addition to the reserves of a limited number of Gatling guns drawn by two horses each.

The results of their experiments show them that in proportion to the weight of ammunition to be carried, the destructive effect against troops in the open of the small Gatling gun *at ranges within 1,400 yards,* is nearly three times that of the 9-pounder rifle muzzle-loading field gun, and there is every reason to expect that this so-called 'small Gatling' can be so materially reduced in weight without detriment to its power and efficiency, as to bring it, with its carriage and ammunition, within the powers of a single cart horse, thus further lessening the objection to it, as inconveniently increasing the *impedimenta* of an army.

The committee are decidedly averse to the employment of mitrailleurs for advancing with infantry, or, indeed, for attacking in any form, except when the enemy is provided with an inferior artillery or no artillery at all.

An exception should be made in the case of mountain batteries, for which the 0.45-inch Gatling gun, reduced in weight to 150lbs, to fire from a tripod, seems eminently adapted as an adjunct to guns notoriously weak in their shrapnel and canister fire.

In the present state of the inquiry in regard to the employment of the larger kinds of mitrailleurs under experiment in Russia and Austria, the Committee recommend no trials, being inclined

The Committee think either description of Gatling gun would be found invaluable at a siege, for purposes of defense, on both side; for the besiegers, in repelling sorties, in protecting the advanced works, particularly at night, or in assisting to keep down the fire of the place; on the part of the garrison, for sweeping the ditches, defending a breach, or for close fighting of any kind.

The ammunition feed of the Lowell gun: cartridges drop from the feed column into the fluted cylinder, which revolves and carries them down to the feedway behind the operative barrel. Note that the barrel group has been raised and the chambers of three of them can be seen.

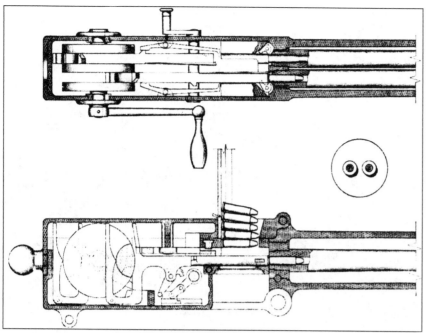

The mechanism of the Gardner gun is very similar to a two-cylinder steam engine, with the two breechblocks coupled to a crankshaft turned by an outside handle.

In coming to the above conclusions, the Committee have given full weight to the opinions of officers, foreign as well as British, who have had experience of the mitrailleur in the late war, and they have not overlooked the fact reported by Major General Walker that a very large majority of the officers of the German Army who have been consulted on the subject, are against the introduction of the mitrailleur as a field gun.

With reference to these opinions, the Committee would call attention to the following circumstances:-

1. That the Gatling gun was very little needed by the French.

2. That the French mitrailleur was almost as heavy, and required as many men and horses, as the French field gun.

3. That the French appear by all accounts to have used their mitrailleurs with little judgment, firing them into all sorts of cover, at very long ranges, and without any special means of ascertaining the distances.

They seem also to have frequently neglected the precaution of covering their mitrailleurs, either naturally or artificially, thus laying them open to destruction by the German artillery.

4. That the Germans had no opportunity of testing the merits of the mitrailleurs for defensive purposes, having almost invariably acted on the offensive.

5. That the Germans have no necessity for considering the question of introducing these weapons, being already well provided with a very large number of French mitrailleurs, which, having recently been tried at Berlin in comparison with Montigny and Gatling mitrailleurs, have been unanimously pronounced superior to either.

With regard to the question of protecting the small Gatling with a light iron shield, the Committee reserve their opinion until the pattern gun has been tried."

At more or less the same time the Russian government, looking to the prospect of another war with Turkey, ordered 400 Gatling guns. Their General Gorloff was sent to America to superintend the preparation of these weapons and he, with considerable astuteness, had nameplates bearing his own name manufactured and fixed to the guns, in place of the original plates bearing the name of Colt's Patent Firearms Company, before they were shipped to Russia. They were thereafter known as 'Gorloff' guns, and an article in the *Journal de St Petersburg* of 27 November 1870 is not without interest as an example of early Russian disinformation:

"*The mitrailleuse adopted in Russia is on a model invented by Major-General Gorloff and based upon the American Gatling system. The Gorloff gun, however, only resembles the Gatling in exterior form and is quite original. In perfecting his arm, Dr Gating has, it appears, been guilty of important plagiarisms on the Gorloff model, which has a just title to the name of the 'Russian mitrailleuse'.*"

Be that as it may, the Russians used the Gatling/Gorloff to good effect when they eventually went to war with the Turks in 1877. The siege of Plevna gave opportunity for using it in position warfare, while some of the operations in Central Asia showed how effective

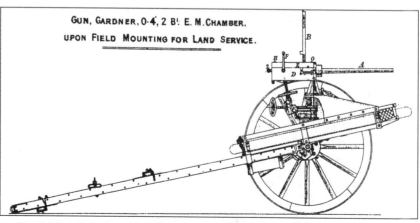

The field carriage for a 40-caliber two-barreled Gardner gun dating from 1887; the odd caliber did not survive long and the guns were converted to 45-caliber in 1889.

Two sailors demonstrate the operation of the Gardner gun. An interesting minor feature of this drawing is the provision of cartridges pre-packed in cartons of 20, ready for insertion into the feed column of the gun.

A five-barrel Gardner being demonstrated by two traveling salesmen.

The Nordenfelt, in three-barrel configuration and mounted on a field carriage.

it could be in dealing with cavalry charges.

The British took a number of Gatlings to various parts of the world, though their initial experience was less than satisfactory because of the ammunition. The first army guns in 45-caliber were chambered for the rolled-brass bottle-necked Martini-Henry cartridge, which tended to come apart and jam the mechanism, particularly when fighting in a sandy or dusty environment. Their experience in the Sudan led to the famous lines in Sir Henry Newbold's poem "Vita Lamnpada":

"The sands of the desert are sodden red
Red with the wrack of a square that broke
The Gatlings jammed and the colonel dead
And the regiment blind with the dust and smoke."

The rolled cartridge was replaced by a solid-drawn cartridge

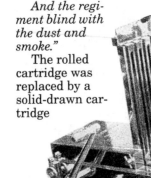

and after that the Gatling's reputation was unassailable.

The original Gatling feed system was simply a straight metal strip with the edges folded over to grip the rims of the cartridges - you could think of it as a giant rifle clip, though the cartridges were dropped in by hand and the feed strip was a gun accessory, not an ammunition one. This was largely replaced in the early 1880s by a feed drum designed by James G. Accles, and known as the 'Accles Positive Feed'. Accles was born in Australia in 1850; his parents moved to the USA in 1861 and Accles was apprenticed to Colt's in Hartford. In 1872 he moved to England and worked in a percussion cap factory near Birmingham, then became a project engineer for Gatling, setting up fifteen Gatling gun and ammunition factories in China and other countries. It was during this period that he developed the 'Accles Positive Feed' drum, which he patented in 1881. In 1888 he returned to Birmingham and joined the Gatling Arms & Ammunition Factory, a company independent of the American Gatling firm and set

up to market Gatling guns for the Eastern hemisphere. The company failed in 1890 and Accles then joined Captain Hubert Grenfell to form Grenfell & Accles Ltd., taking over the Gatling Gun company factory and stock and continuing to sell Gatling guns until this stock ran out. He also patented the Accles machine gun, a derivative of the Gatling and sold this with some degree of success but, as appears to have been the case with most of his enterprises, the firm was under-capitalized and went into liquidation in 1900.

Gatling developed several different models of gun for his various customers, but the differences appear to have lain principally in the caliber or in the carriages - the actual gun mechanism changed very little. The most noticeable change came when calibers began to reduce in the 1890s and countries such as the USA and Britain

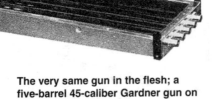

The very same gun in the flesh; a five-barrel 45-caliber Gardner gun on a naval deck mounting.

GUN NORDENFELT. 3 BARREL.
POSITION OF ACTION FOR FIRING, AND EXTRACTING.
COVER REMOVED.

The action of the Nordenfelt gun, showing the three breechblocks lined up behind their respective barrels and *(dotted)* the three hammer mechanisms lined up behind them.

Close-up of the Nordenfelt, showing the operating lever and its safety catch. The plate on the carriage identifies it as No. 19, built by Nordenfelt in 1887.

took up Gatlings in their new service rifle caliber, 30 Krag and 303 Lee Enfield respectively. Now, instead of the naked bunch of barrels rotating in a frame, the barrel cluster was enclosed in a smooth cylindrical jacket giving the weapon a neater appearance but, it would seem, not doing very much for the cooling of the barrels. But perhaps the rate of fire was never high enough for this to become a serious problem.

With the world's armies clamoring for Gatling guns, or so it must have seemed with Accles running round the world throwing up factories (in what must rank as the first 'turnkey' operation in the armaments industry), other inventors decided to get into the machine gun business. Gatling's first serious competitor in Europe was the French Hotchkiss company who developed a revolving cannon of their own, primarily intended for use by naval vessels.

By the 1870s the autonomous torpedo, which could be started up, fired into the sea and left to get to its target, was becoming a considerable threat to navies. The contemporary tactic envisaged a small, light and fast ship carrying perhaps four torpedoes, dashing into an enemy anchorage at full speed, loosing off its missiles and then departing before the surprised crews could retaliate. Moreover, even if the crews were on the alert, their guns were generally too big and cumbersome to deal with such

a fast target, or they could not depress far enough to shoot at a tiny vessel only a few hundred yards away. So Hotchkiss produced his revolver, firing a 37mm high explosive shell, which could spray the enemy with small shells sufficient to do damage or, at worst, put the attacker off his aim, and could

be operated fast enough to cope with the envisaged targets.

It will be seen, in due course, that 37mm was a popular caliber; it equates to 1.456 inches and one might well ask how such a peculiar figure evolved. The answer lies in the Declaration of St. Petersburg of 1868, by which the major powers agreed to prohibit the use of "...*any projectile of a weight below 400 grams which is either explosive or charged with a fulminating substance.*" And at the current stage of technical development, 37mm represented the smallest caliber that could produce a stable projectile weighing 400 grams (14.1 ounces). So 37mm suddenly became popular and has stayed that way for over a hundred years, even though the original reason for it has long been forgotten.

The Hotchkiss used a bunch of revolving barrels just like the Gatling, but that was as far as the resemblance went. The big difference was that the Gatling had a bolt and breech mechanism for each barrel, while the Hotchkiss had only one bolt, which locked and unlocked into each barrel in turn as they rotated past the bolt station. It meant a slower rate of fire, but that was quite acceptable in 37mm caliber. One might well ask what was the point of having six barrels for only one bolt, but, like the

Members of a Rifle Regiment with their new Nordenfelt in the late 1880s. The carriage is definitely non-standard, but many militia regiments in Britain purchased machine guns at their own expense rather than wait for them to be authorized and issued, and they were not necessarily the approved models.

A sunny morning off Constantinople in the 1890s, and the Turkish battleship 'Osmanlieh' is exercising it's machine gun crews and their Nordenfelts.

Gatling, the loading of the fresh round and the extraction of the spent case were performed during the rotational period, and with rounds weighing almost one pound each gradual loading was a desirable feature. And, of course, the barrels never overheated.

Because of these mechanical differences, and because of the large caliber, the Hotchkiss was never considered to be infringing Gatling's patents, and the two co-existed quite happily. The Hotchkiss 'Revolver Cannon' was widely adopted by navies, but its only land army adoption was for arming continental forts. At this time the '*caponier*' had become a popular feature of the contemporary forts being built all over Europe, and the Hotchkiss gun was ideal for employment in it. The *caponier* was a masonry structure of one or two floors that stretched across the ditch surrounding the fort, from the fort itself to the exterior wall of the ditch. In some cases it acted as a passage across the ditch to give access to firing galleries set into the farther wall, but in

all cases the *caponier* had side-firing ports from which rifles, machine guns and light artillery could be fired along the floor of the ditch to deal with scaling parties who were attempting to get into the fort. The Hotchkiss was perfect for this application and became very

popular in European land forts and was also used by the USA in a number of their coast defense forts to defend the work from attack from the land side.

The next contender was the Lowell machine gun, invented by DeWitt Clinton Faringdon who set up the

The rare and mysterious Den Helder 10-barrel machine gun on a field carriage.

Another view of the Den Helder; only the rotating crank and the full-width cartridge hopper distinguish it from a Nordenfelt.

Lowell Manufacturing Company in Lowell Mass., in order to make the gun. At first glance it appears to be another near-Gatling with a cluster of revolving barrels. But the gun is quite different; the barrels do not revolve during firing. There are four barrels held in two discs, the front one of which is slung in trunnions in the trough-like gun frame. The rear disc can be unlocked from the breech mechanism and the rear end of the barrel cluster raised. The cluster can then be rotated a quarter turn to bring a fresh, cool, barrel into line with the chamber and the cluster dropped back into the frame and locked. This solved the cooling problem without treading on Gatling's toes.

The gun fired a 50-caliber cartridge originally developed for the Gatling, and fed from the same sort of vertical strip. It was driven by a hand crank at the rear that rotated the two feed sprockets and also the cam that controlled the operation of the bolt. As the handle was turned a cartridge dropped from the feed strip and was moved by the feed sprocket to a position behind the breech, from where it was rammed by the bolt. The operating cam now held the bolt closed while the striker was released to fire the cartridge, after which the continuing rotation of the handle now drew the bolt open and extracted the empty cartridge case. Once this was clear of the chamber the extractor jaws

opened and the case was collected by the second sprocket and ejected from below the gun at the same time as the first sprocket was bringing the next round into line.

Faringdon demonstrated his gun to the US Navy in October 1876, and instead of, as was usual with inventors, operating the gun himself, he asked the Navy to provide him with two unskilled laborers. He gave these two a crash course in the Lowell gun, after which they fired 2,100 rounds in 8.5 minutes, including time out to do a barrel change. In the course of the day's testing the two men fired over 10,000 rounds, and had one stoppage, which was cleared in 40 seconds by rotating to a fresh barrel.

The return of the Gatling: the US Vulcan Air Defense System (VADS) in its two forms: towed and self-propelled.

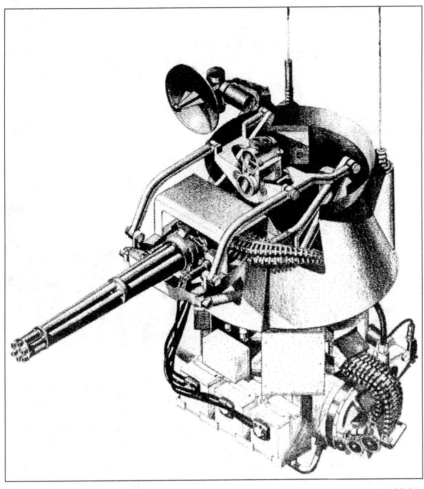

The M163 VADS assembly ready to be dropped into any convenient armored vehicle.

With praise ringing in his ears Faringdon went away, made some small modifications, and returned in July 1877 where another 50,000 rounds were fired without incident. More tests appeared to prove that the gun was a faultless performer. But the US Army and Navy were at peace, there was no cash available for new weapons, and that was that. Faringdon sold a handful to the US Navy, 20 to Russia. and two more handsfull to the California Prison Service and the Cincinnati Police force, and the Lowell company was then closed down. A rare specimen of the Lowell exists in the Royal Artillery Museum at Woolwich, England. Its presence there suggests that it must have been tested in Britain at some time, but I can find no trial reports or other documentary evidence.

The next design to appear had more success. William Gardner was a native of Ohio who went to England some time in the latter 1860s to study law. His antecedents are unknown, but he may have served in the American Civil War, since he was generally referred to as 'Captain', though no details of his military service are known. Of a mechanical turn of mind, he soon abandoned law for the study of firearms and in 1870 offered a magazine pistol to the

The trailer-mounted Vulcan system was the M167, and was adopted by a number of armies.

GEMAG 25+ was a potential replacement for the VADS. It consisted of a 25mm Gatling gun accompanied by four Stinger missiles and the usual suite of detection and fire-control electronics.

British War Office, who refused it. He then developed the Gardner machine gun, which was accepted and entered British service in 1881. He was a prolific patentee of all sorts of improvements to firearms and developed a tubular-magazine rifle in about 1880, specimens of which exist, and also drew up designs for a cartridge-loaded cannon but his sudden death from illness in 1887 prevented further development of these weapons.

The Gardner machine gun was operated by a crank handle at the side of the receiver that drove a reciprocating breechblock to load, fire and extract. The simplest visualization is to think of a motor-cycle engine laid on its side and the crank attached to the flywheel. The piston is the breechblock, the cylinder the chamber. And there you have the Gardner gun. Turn the handle and the flywheel revolves, driving the crank and piston forward to load and fire the cartridge and on the return stroke to extract the spent case. Feed was by the then-standard vertical strip just like the Gatling and Lowell guns. In fact most Gardner guns were two-barreled, with two cranks arranged 180 degrees out of phase so that one barrel was loading when the other was extracting.

Gardner appears to have been a patriotic man, and he first took his gun idea to the USA where he had it built by Pratt & Whitney in Hartford, Conn. He then demonstrated it to the US Navy at Washington Navy Yard in June 1879 and amazed the onlookers by firing 10,000 rounds in 27 minutes and

36 seconds, about 364 rounds per minute – no mean feat for a hand-operated gun. Some 16,000 rounds were fired, with five failures to extract, and during a break Gardner dismantled the gun, filed down a burr on the offending extractor and re-assembled the gun, after which there were no more stoppages.

In spite of this performance the US authorities were not disposed to purchase the gun, so Gardner took it to England and demonstrated it to the Admiralty and then the Army. It is recorded that during the Admiralty tests the gun reached a rate of fire of 812 rounds per minute, which is just over twice as fast as the (later) full automatic Maxim gun. The British were impressed and adopted it in both services, the Royal Navy

using it as a support gun for landing parties. In fact the first British Gardner gun was five-barreled model in 45-caliber, mounted on a heavy wheeled carriage. Then came two-barreled models, one on a pedestal for ship mounting and the other on a tripod for field use, and numbers of the latter were later converted into 303-caliber. Most of these were installed in coast defense forts and were not made obsolete until 1926.

The last of the serious contenders in the mechanical stakes was the Swedish Nordenfelt gun. This was actually designed by a man called Helge Palmcrantz, but Nordenfelt put up the money and his name therefore attached to the gun.

The design was virtually a mechanized battery gun; up to

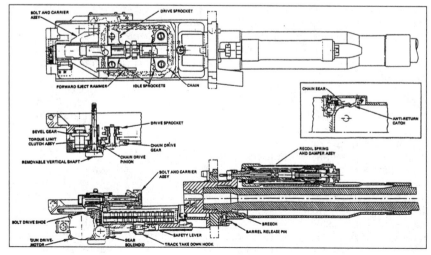

A 7.62mm Hughes Chain Gun, a novel mechanism that has become a highly successful design.

A 7.62mm Hughes Chain Gun, a novel mechanism that has become a highly successful design.

twelve barrels lay side by side in a frame with a feed hopper above. It was operated by pulling and pushing on a reciprocating handle on the right side. This withdrew a large breech block and allowed cartridges to fall from the hopper and onto a carrier block, which was behind the chambers but not aligned with them. Pushing on the lever now moved the carrier block sideways to line up with the chambers, then closed the breechblock, ramming the rounds into place and locked the breech by means of an over-center toggle mechanism. The final movement of the handle lined up 'action block', which carried the firing hammers, with the firing pins in the breechblock and then released the hammers to fire all the barrels.

Nordenfelt was a banker and entrepreneur, and he had a lot of influential friends in banking and business circles. He was also a pretty good salesman and he made sure that the Nordenfelt gun was on view at all times, represented at every military show or exhibition, and presented at every army's door for test whenever the opportunity offered. In 1882 he took a 10-barrel model to Britain and put it through its paces for the Admiralty, demonstrating his ability to fire 3000 rounds in three minutes, which was an astonishing performance for the time. The Admiralty were totally convinced of the efficiency of the Nordenfelt gun and bought a number of the .45-inch five-barrel version for fitting into the fighting tops of warships so as to sweep the decks of enemy ships. They also bought a number of three-barrel guns in one-inch caliber for defense against torpedo-boats. Several other navies followed suit, and the Nordenfelt soon spread across Europe. It was also used on a field carriage, in limited numbers, and, like the Gardner, was not removed from the British Army's inventory until 1926.

One notable defect of the Nordenfelt was that it was not possible to see, at a glance, whether the gun held ammunition or not, or whether it was loaded or empty. This gave rise to some near-disasters such as the following report to the Director of Artillery on a demonstration firing of Nordenfelt guns in June 1884:

"One great danger showed itself on more than one occasion. After 'cease firing' was given the Number 1 [the gun commander] was forgetful to ascertain if there remained any unexploded cartridges in his gun. This was the cause of what might have been a very nasty accident but happily only did damage to a few carriages lying in the line of fire. A zealous person, wishing to make himself familiar with the working of the gun, found himself innocently blazing into the crowd, nearly costing the army its Commander-in-Chief and your department its Assistant Superintendent of Experiments. A similar accident occurred a short time ago and is one difficult to guard against. As a question of drill, however, it would seem more desirable to address 'cease firing' to the man supplying the hopper and not to the Number 1 who should continue to work the lever until the gun is silent." Within a week of this report orders had been given that upon receiving the order 'cease firing' *"the cover is to be raised and all cartridges taken out of the barrels, and the cover to remain open until practice is resumed or the gun secured"* and a similar order was soon made for Gardner guns.

A rare gun, easily confused with the Nordenfelt, is the 'Den Helder', another ten-barrel battery gun on a field carriage. The prime visual difference is the much wider ammunition hopper, which extends the full width of the ten barrels, instead of being a narrower hopper placed in the middle of the barrel group. The second difference, and the more fundamental one, is that the oper-

ating handle is a rotating crank and not a push-pull lever, and in consequence the loading and firing process is somewhat different.

I have only ever seen two of these weapons, and both were made by an otherwise unheard-of company calling themselves the *Gusstahl Waffenfabrik* of Dusseldorf and both had numbers below 20. No army seems ever to have recorded the employment of the Den Helder, nor can I find any army that recorded performing trials of the gun. I can only assume that the guns (both in 45 Martini-Henry caliber) were made for trial and demonstration purposes but failed to attract any customers. This may well have been because it appeared on the scene just as Maxim had demonstrated the automatic principle, which, of course, killed the mechanical machine gun stone dead.

Or at least, it seemed to. For the greatest military complaint against the mechanical guns was not their reliability, or their tendency to jam, or their cumbersome carriages. It was simply their inaccuracy. Once the initial euphoria of spewing out hundreds of bullets was past, a more critical look showed that far too many of those bullets missed their target, and the reason they missed was simply that the actual operation of the gun – winding the crank handle or pushing a lever back and forth – was enough to shake the entire gun from side to side or up and down and scatter the shots accordingly. This is why Nordenfelts and Gardners and Gatlings usually have screw-controlled elevation and traverse mechanisms to try and hold the gun on the point of aim while the brawny gunner heaves away at the handle. Even with those constraints, the energy needed to operate the gun was enough to shake the entire carriage. So an automatic gun, which merely vibrated around its own axis rather than shaking violently from side to side, was bound to be more accurate. Numbers of mechanical guns lingered, almost entirely in fortifications, but their appearance in the field was a rare event by 1890 as the Maxim gun took over. Probably the last appearance of mechanical guns in actual combat was in the Russo-Japanese War of 1904, when numbers of Gorloff-Gatlings were in use by the Russian defenders during the Siege of Port Arthur.

But the inventors were not deterred. Nordenfelt developed a simple, light, hand-operated single-barrel gun; nobody was interested - everybody *knew* that the only way to get firepower from a mechanical gun was by multiple barrels. Dr. Gatling, even later, strapped an early electric motor to one of his rifle-caliber guns and produced a weapon firing 3000 rounds a minute - and with better accuracy than usual due to the absence of a human arm shaking the gun all over the place while turning the crank. That was applauded as a clever trick but totally impractical - how do you carry all those wet-cell batteries into battle? It was a valid argument, and the mechanical protagonists gave up the struggle.

Twenty years went by and then, in 1917, came the problem of how to fire a machine gun through a whirling propeller on the front of an airplane without shooting off the blades. Since the automatic machine gun had one fixed speed of operation - some designs tried varying the speed but there was little practical value in it - and

since the airplane engine varied its speed from minute to minute, there seemed little prospect of harmonizing the two. But wait.... a mechanical gun *driven by the airplane engine* would always be in step, and it would simply be a matter of arranging the timing so as to shoot when the propeller was elsewhere than in front of the muzzle. (Or, alternatively, *not* to shoot when the propeller *was* in front of the muzzle - you could play it either way.) This idea occurred to Ingenieur Ferencz Gebauer, an Austro-Hungarian, and he developed a two-barreled gun driven off the engine's camshaft. Flanged couplings allowed infinitely variable timing so that the guns could be set to fire at the correct position of the propeller, and a friction clutch, operated by the pilot, brought the gun into operation.

The mechanism was simple in its principle - merely a pair of reciprocating bolts, cam-driven, but the actual mechanism was somewhat complicated, and dismantling a Gebauer is not a recommended pastime. But it worked, and worked reliably. The rate of fire, obviously, varied with engine speed but at a maximum speed of 2000 engine revolutions per minute (which had been specified by the Aviation Commission) the gun was firing at 800 rounds per minute from each barrel, giving 1600 bullets per minute or 26 rounds a second, which was a reasonable bullet density for the aircraft speeds of the day.

Unfortunately, like so many wartime ideas, it came along too late to

be really useful. Its first trials took place in June 1918, orders were given for immediate manufacture, guns began coming off the production line in October 1918, and the Austro-Hungarians threw in the towel on 4 November. The gun, known by this time as the *Gebauer-Weich-Motor Maschinen-Gewehr* (Weich having put up the money for Gebauer's first prototypes) was acquired by the Danuvia arms company of Budapest and they made some minor improvements and took out patents in Hungary, Germany and Britain in 1926/7. A single-barrel gun capable of over 1200 rounds/minute was also developed, and in the 1930s, when aircraft armament was becoming a major concern in Europe, the Gebauer was entered into various competitive trials. But by that time synchronization of conventional guns was no longer a problem and the design of aircraft was moving to guns set outside the propeller arc anyway, with the result that the Gebauer was no longer relevant and the design was abandoned.

Anthony Fokker, the Dutch aircraft designer who worked for Germany during the war, also produced a mechanical gun prototype. This was a ten-barreled weapon with the barrels in a ring rather like a Gatling, but the details of the mechanism are scant and do not really explain how he proposed to make it work. It is known that his major feature was that the cartridges were never removed from the belt as it passed

One popular application for the 7.62mm Chain Gun is as a helicopter weapon; others are to be found in various armored vehicles.

King of the Chain Guns is the 25mm M242 Bushmaster, used in the US Army's Bradley Infantry Fighting Vehicles and exported in considerable numbers.

through the gun, but just how he managed to do this is not known.

With a few exceptions, guns with high rates of fire are usually found to be designed for aircraft use and, moreover, designed in the days when the aerial dogfight was the prime tactic. In such a fight the pilot may get his opponent into his sights for no more than a few seconds, and therefore a high rate of fire was vital in order to get as many bullets into the air as possible in the short engagement time. When the jet aircraft promised, in 1944, to increase the speed of fighters and thus decrease the available engagement times, there was a furious search for a faster-firing machine gun. It is also worth noting that when these high rate-of-fire guns began to make their appearance, their advantages to ground attack aircraft soon became apparent. A five-second burst of 30mm APDS shot from the GAU-8/A gun on board the A-10 'Warthog' can make most tanks look quite distressed and can chop a light armored vehicle to pieces.

The US Army Air Corps demanded a gun capable of firing at 1200 rds/minute or better, and with greater hitting power than the existing 50 Browning. Somebody remembered Gatling's experiment of 1890 and acquired an old 45-70 Gatling gun, connected it to an electric motor, and produced short bursts of fire at a rate of about 5000 rds/minute. And with that as a spur the General Electric company set about developing a new-generation, electrically-powered Gatling gun which they called the 'Vulcan'.

Vulcan was actually the code-name of the US Air Force development project, but in 1949, when GE turned up with a 60-caliber six-barreled gun for test, they called it Vulcan and the name stuck. The 60-caliber model proved that the idea - simply taking Gatling's bolt and revolving barrel system and coupling it to an electric motor - was a sound proposi-

tion, and it was soon followed by a 20mm version, the T171, and a 27mm model the T150. But at that early period, the 27mm looked rather like overkill; experience in Korea indicated that 20mm was ample for the task in hand, and so in 1952 all effort was directed to perfecting a production 20mm design, which appeared as the M61 in 1956.

This was purely an aircraft gun, and at that time there was little army interest since there seemed to be no role for such a weapon as a ground gun. But within a very short time it had become apparent that the multiple 50-caliber machine guns used for light air defense were finding it difficult to deal with aircraft that flew faster every week and, into the bargain, were cladding themselves in armor. The army turned a new eye on the Vulcan and by 1956 was developing the 'Vulcan Air Defense System' using a slightly detuned version of the M61 gun. The M61 fired at 6000 rounds per minute to obtain the maximum shell density; the ground gun had rather more time to deal with targets, since it was stationary, and therefore could fire at a slower and more economic rate, and the M168 gun which evolved for the air defense role fired at either 1000 or 3000 rounds per minute.

The first version was the VADS M162, mounted on top of an M113 armored personnel carrier and complete with radar and fire control computer. It was later followed by an M167 towed version, also with all the obligatory bells and whistles for detecting and tracking targets. Thereafter various Gatling-type guns were developed, principally for aircraft use, culminating in the fearsome GAU-8A installation in the A-10 tank destroyer.

The Soviets appeared to have put their money on the missile as the armament of future fighter aircraft, but by the late 1960s they realized this had been a mistake

and, looking to the well-publicized American developments on the Gatling principle, forthwith revived the Gorloff and proceeded to develop multi-barrel guns of their own. However, for a variety of reasons, mostly concerning available space and power supplies, they elected to develop a Gatling gun that, instead of being externally powered, actually drove itself by its own propellant gas. As we shall see, gas operation is common enough in conventional single-barrel guns, but in a revolving gun it is a totally different concept. So far as conventional externally-powered Gatling-type guns went, the only serious Soviet contender was their AO-18 model, adopted by the Navy for close-in air defense. Warships, of course, have more or less unlimited power on tap, so there were no incentives to cleverness.

The principal advantage of a mechanical gun for air forces, if you ignore the high rate of fire, is that a faulty cartridge cannot stop them. A conventional recoil- or gas-operated machine gun or cannon fed with a dud round will misfire and stop dead, which is a trifle embarrassing to the pilot in the middle of a dogfight. A mechanical gun, on the other hand, just carries on churning, flings the misfired round out, loads another and carries on firing. In all probability the gunner would never know that a misfire had taken place. Hangfires - when the primer takes its time about igniting the charge, or the charge takes its time about taking fire, are also discarded by the mechanical gun, but the gunner generally notices when the hangfire finally decides to explode - outside the gun.

Because of this feature, mechanical cannons suddenly began to find favor, and not just the Gatling guns. After all, you need to design the airplane around the gun with some of the 30mm monsters, and where lighter aircraft - helicopters and air defense fighters - were to be armed, the conventional single-barrel gun was easier to fit into an existing aircraft. And so a number of single-barrel mechanical designs appeared,

Probably the first of these was the Hughes Chain Gun, one of the few pieces of original thinking to appear in the firearms world during the second half of the century. It was also one of those ideas that appear to be so obvious that you wonder why nobody thought of it before.

Imagine a shallow square box, in the middle of one side of which is a gun-barrel. In prolongation of the barrel is a trackway upon which a bolt rides back and forth, opening and closing the breech. Beneath the bolt is a transverse bar with a slot in its underside. At the four corners of the box, pivoted on its bottom surface, are four toothed wheels, around which lies a loop of bicycle chain. One link of the chain has an upstanding lug, and this is entered into the slot on the transverse bar beneath the bolt.

Now imagine that the bolt is open, at the far side of the box from the barrel. You now connect a motor to one of the toothed wheels and start it running. The chain will run down the side of the box, and the stud will force the transverse bar, and therefore the bolt, to go with it and close the breech. As the stud turns the front corner of the box the stud slides across the slot; this keeps the bolt closed while the cartridge is fired and the projectile goes up the bore. At the other front corner of the box the lug turns and begins moving back, opening the bolt. As the lug turns the rear corner the bolt stops, the stud rides across, allowing time for air to flow through the barrel and the feed mechanism to position a fresh round. And as the stud turns the fourth corner it starts driving the bolt forward and the whole cycle starts again. That is the simple principle upon which the Chain Gun works; matters like feeding in the ammunition and devising a mounting are minor administrative matters. And the faster you run the motor, the faster the gun fires.

Needless to say this was too simple for people to grasp all at once and it took some time before armies were willing to try the idea out. Whereupon they saw the force of the argument; the US Army adopted in 25mm caliber for the main armament of their Bradley MICVs, the British in 7.62mm caliber as the co-axial machine gun for their Warrior MICV, and more have been sold to other nations. Production commenced in 1981 and within ten years about 10,000 guns had been produced.

With the example of the Chain Gun before them, the French began looking at a mechanical gun in the early 1980s. Being French, the idea of buying a foreign gun was unthinkable, so the engineers of the St. Etienne gun factory came up with a different way of doing the same thing. Imagine a conventional barrel and receiver, with a reciprocating bolt, much the same as the Chain Gun. But extend the transverse bar through a slot in the side of the receiver and end it in a stud. Now place a shaft parallel with the receiver, and with a spiral groove on it into which the stud fits. As you rotate the shaft, so the spiral groove will drive the stud, and hence the bolt, forward and backward. The end product is just the same, the way of arriving at it different. The resulting gun became the Model 811 in 25x137mm caliber, and was then enlarged the Model 781 in 30x150mmB caliber. Both models have been fitted in helicopters and various light armored vehicles. The same cam principle has also been adopted by the South Africans in their EMAK35 35mm anti-aircraft cannon.

Perhaps one of the wildest mechanical projects was the British gun called 'Nutcracker' which appeared in the early 1960s. Designed in a government establishment it relied upon two contra-revolving cylinders which had semi-circular grooves in their outside surfaces; imagine an ordinary revolver cylinder turned down on a lathe until only half the chambers

remained. They were mounted behind a barrel so that when two grooves on the two cylinders came opposite each other they formed the chamber behind the barrel. Behind the two revolving cylinders, in prolongation of the weapon's axis, was an electrical contact.

The cartridge was a brass tube about nine inches long; it had an electric cap at one end, and the other end was open. Inside the tube was a 30mm projectile and, between that and the electric cap, a propellant charge.

A quantity of these cartridges was placed in a feed system above the gun. The two cylinders began revolving inwards, and as they did so a supply of cartridges was dropped into the space between the cylinders so that as two grooves came together they collected a cartridge and carried it into position behind the barrel, whereupon the electric contact fired the cap and the propellant blew the shell up the bore. As the cylinders continued to revolve and brought the next round in, so they discarded the empty case as the two half-chambers opened up once more. The faster you revolved the cylinders, the faster the gun fired.

I gather that the gun got up to a quite phenomenal rate *(for a single-barrel gun)* in the order of 5000 rounds per minute, but it then ran into the single-barrel nightmare - more than one projectile in the barrel at the same time – leading to the barrel bulging and splitting and eventual disintegration. Some useful design lessons had been learned, but Project Nutcracker was abruptly terminated.

The mechanical machine gun, then, is far from dead. In applications where a source of power is available *(and today that invariably means electricity)* it has numerous advantages, among which simplicity, reliability and controllability stand out. It is a pleasant thought that the earliest practical machine gun of all, the Gatling, is sailing into the 21st century in a better position than it has ever been before.

CHAPTER THREE

THE FIRST AUTOMATIC GUNS

THE MECHANICAL MACHINE guns all relied on the input of some sort of effort from outside in order to operate their machinery, usually a man operating a crank or lever of some sort. This seemed quite satisfactory at the time, since the only sources of power other than men were far too complicated or cumbersome to be carried onto the battle-field and set to work to drive a machine-gun. And things might have stayed that way for a long time had it not been for the inquiring mind of one man – Hiram Stevens Maxim.

Hiram Maxim was born in Sangerville, Maine, in 1840 and was apprenticed to a coachbuilder. After that he worked in a machine shop and in a shipbuilding yard.

He had a wide-ranging inventive faculty that embraced such things as electric lights, gas generating plants, steam and vacuum pumps, engine governors and even a steam-driven airplane. In 1882 he attended the Electrical Exhibition in Vienna and, so the story goes, was told by an acquaintance *"Hang your electricity! If you want to make yourself rich, invent something that will enable these fool Europeans to kill each other quicker"*. Whether this tale is true or not, Maxim went to London and set up a small workshop in Hatton Garden where he began to examine the contemporary state of firearms.

He soon put his finger on the vital point - when a gun was fired a vast amount of energy was released, only a small portion of which was used in propelling the bullet. The rest was going to waste, and Maxim resolved to try and adapt this wasted energy to the task of operating the various functions of the gun. Between 1882 and 1885 he analyzed every possible way of using this energy, devised ways of applying the energy to the gun, and patented every conceivable way of operating a gun. Indeed, had Maxim been sufficiently litigious he

could probably, on the strength of his many patents, have stifled every other machine-gun at birth for the next quarter-century, since almost every successful design carries traces of a Maxim patent in it.

He then, the story goes, displayed this to the British army, eventually gained acceptance, and later approached Vickers to manufacture the guns for him, which led to the setting up of Vickers, Son and Maxim Ltd.

Well, up to a point. Some recent research suggests rather that Vickers was actually Maxim's partner and possibly his backer; I have always wondered how Maxim was able to support himself in London for three or four years, working on his machine gun, before it began to make money. The following correspondence, extracted from the *'Proceedings of Department of the*

Director of Artillery' for the middle 1880s, gives a detailed diary of the first few months of the Maxim gun, showing that the initial approach to the British Army came from Albert Vickers, and that the idea of a heavy-weight gun, which appeared years later as the famous 'Pom-Pom', was in Maxim's mind from the very beginning. It also reveals that Maxim had also designed a semi-automatic rifle by the summer of 1884, as well as his machine gun.

Minute 42,131. Mr. Vickers, 26/9/84, writes, as one of the part owners of the patents of the machine gun (Maxim's), stating that he has several machine guns ready for inspection, and asks that the Surveyor-General of Ordnance will detail an officer to witness their trials, and also that he may be supplied with Government Gatling

The original and first Maxim machine gun, as demonstrated on 30th January 1885. The phosphor-bronze water jacket is provided with inlet and outlet valves, the belt box is of polished wood, and the scale and pointer on the side is the adjustment for the rate of fire.

The left side of the original Maxim shows the D-shaped feed aperture and, above and to the right, another aperture that shows the rotating cage of the cartridge feed system.

cartridges of 0.45-inch. He states that a very good description of this gun appeared in *The Times* of 22/9/84.

Surveyor-General of Ordnance, 1/10/84, says that Superintendent Royal Small Arms Factory has been directed to attend these trials and has agreed to the supply of the cartridges.

Superintendent Royal Small Arms Factory, 7/10/84, reports that he attended the works of Mr. Maxim, 30/9/84. The magazine arm is not in a forward state but from what he saw of it he considers that its weight will prevent it from being adopted as a service weapon. The machine gun, he thinks, should be tried, as it appears to possess many advantages over any other gun he has yet seen, but in order to have it properly constructed he recommends that Mr Maxim be supplied with Government ammunition.

Director of Artillery 15/10/84 approves special supply.

Assistant Director of Artillery, 3/2/85, reports that he attended at Mr Maxim's on 30.1.85, together with Quarter-Master-General, Adjutant-General and Inspector-General of Fortifications, Commandant School of Musketry, and others. Mr. Maxim showed first his repeating rifle in which the operations of opening the breech and extracting the old cartridge are performed by the recoil. Then he showed his machine gun, explained its mechanism, and fired several rounds. He reports that everything worked perfectly, and as the working parts are enclosed he does not think they are likely to get out of order.

So there we have the undoubted first demonstration of the Maxim gun firmly dated and with a bevy of worthies watching it. (Although the oft-quoted Duke of Cambridge does not appear to

have been there; I feel sure that the Assistant Director of Artillery would have mentioned the presence of his Commander-in-Chief, and that he is unlikely to have been referred to as *'and others'*.) It is generally accepted that although the gun worked satisfactorily, the audience raised a few points with Mr. Maxim, who then went back to his workbench. Not the least interesting part of this correspondence is the speed at which things happened; notice above that the Superintendent RSAF had actually gone to see Maxim before the Surveyor-General had even reported to the DofA.

The original 'first model' Maxim used a semi-rotary crank mechanism to operate the breech. When the gun was ready to fire, with a cartridge in the chamber, the barrel and breechblock were securely locked together by a large hook engaging in the block.

When fired, the two units recoiled together for about half an inch, whereupon the hook was lifted and the barrel stopped. The breechblock was then free to continue recoiling; extracting and ejecting the spent case as it traveled back. The block was attached to a connecting rod and crank, and the recoil stroke caused the crank to revolve through three-quarters of a turn. As it reached the rear dead center position the striker was cocked, and the momentum of the crank carried it past this dead point, reversing the movement of the block so as to load a fresh round and close the breech. The next shot fired would rotate the crank in the opposite direction until it stopped, with the breech closed once more, in the position from which it had begun the recoil for the previous round. One might ask why not simply put a crank in and allow it to make a complete revolution for every shot, but Maxim realized that if he built it that way there would be a 'flywheel effect' and the crank would revolve faster and faster until, sooner or later, something would break. By restricting the movement and alternating its direction he prevented this and kept the rate of fire steady.

Ammunition was delivered by a belt to a 12-chambered rotary feed block, from which the rounds were fed to the breech. This allowed a gradual removal from the belt and a more reliable feed, which Maxim probably adopted because of the

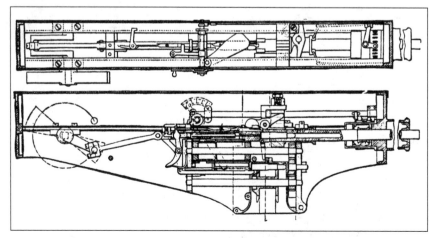

The internal arrangements of the original Maxim, showing the operation of the crank controlling the breechblock.

somewhat delicate state of the current Martini-Henry cartridges; these had been designed for hand-loading into a single-shot weapon and were a mixture of wrought iron base, paper wadding and a wrapped brass body carrying a lead bullet. The final refinement was a hydraulic buffer mechanism connected to the crank. This not only absorbed various mechanical stresses but was also adapted to act as a rate-of-fire controller. Adjusting the hydraulic valve regulated the movement of the crank, and the gun could be set to fire at any desired rate up to a maximum of 600 rounds per minute.

Maxim wasted no time in modifying his gun; indeed, he did more than modify it, he entirely redesigned it. And the astonishing thing is that it took him barely three months to do it:

Minute 42,519: Superintendent Royal Small Arms Factory, 3/3/85, reports that in accordance with instructions, he visited Mr. Maxim's workshop on 2/3/85 and there inspected a third gun of Mr. Maxim's manufacture which is, in his opinion, an enormous improvement over the original design, from which it differs entirely in construction. It is extremely simple and compact, very much shorter and lighter than the first guns, and not so liable to get out of order. Two are under construction. One of these is being made to fire 1-inch Nordenfelt ammunition and the other to fire the 0.45-inch Gatling gun ammunition. He adds that Mr. Maxim is working solely for Her Majesty's Government and that he does not intend to take any foreign orders.

Maxim Gun Company, 9/4/85, write that they have now fired the 1-inch gun and that Mr Maxim is satisfied with the results obtained; that they have persuaded him not to take out any foreign patents for it at present, in order that Her Majesty's Government may have the option of purchasing the secret of its construction, should they desire to do so. The gun is very simple and fires to perfection. They ask that a time may be appointed for the gun to be inspected

Director of Artillery, 10/4/85. replies that Lt. Colonel Ellis and Colonel Arbuthnot will visit the works officially on 13/4/85.

Colonel Arbuthnot (*Superintendent Royal Small Arms Factory*) 21/4/85, reports that, in company with Lt. Colonel Ellis he visited the Maxim Gun Company's works, and saw the gun fired, and as it appeared to be satisfactory it was arranged

that it should be sent to Enfield. It was received at Enfield on 20/4/85 and the preliminary trial was most satisfactory. He recommends that a small committee should be formed to report on the gun after trial.

The Director of Artillery then set about forming a small committee, chaired by Colonel Arbuthnot and including a naval officer:

Superintendent, Royal Small Arms Factory, 11/5/85, reports that the Committee met on 5/5/85 and experimented with the 1-inch gun submitted by the Maxim Gun Company. The gun is submitted simply to show the working of the principle and to show that it is possible to construct a gun on this principle, and not as a finished gun. The examination of this gun, and the trials which were subsequently carried out, lead the Committee to believe that trials on a more extended scale should be carried out and that Mr. Maxim should

receive a definite order to construct guns of different calibers, to fulfill certain conditions. The Committee do not recommend any more trials with the 1-inch gun being carried out as the Naval member states that no more guns of this nature will be required by the Navy; the smallest gun that they will require in the future for torpedo-boats being the 2-pounder. The Committee therefore recommend that Mr. Maxim should be requested to submit for trial *(1)* a gun on his principle to fire Gatling ammunition, and *(2)* a 2-pounder gun. Should this proposal be approved, the Committee are prepared to submit the conditions that they consider the gun should fulfill.

Director of Artillery, 14/5/85, after conferring with the Surveyor-General of Ordnance, telegraphs to the Maxim Gun Company that there is no intention of asking them not to patent

The cover of the first sales brochure issued by the Maxim Gun Company.

The production version of the improved pattern gun had a larger water jacket. The inscription on the fuzee spring cover reads 'Maxim-Nordenfelt Gun & Ammunition Co. Ltd. Maxim's Patent 1339'.

the invention abroad, and that they will receive a further written communication on this subject.

And 22/5/85 informs the Committee that he approves of their proposals.

Superintendent RSAF, 8/6/85, forwards a copy of the conditions drawn up by the Committee, which have been discussed with Mr. Maxim and accepted by him. They recommend that he be supplied with a cone mounting for a 2-barrel Gardner gun and with a drawing and specimen of a 3-pounder Hotchkiss cartridge, which is, on approval of Director of Artillery, ordered to be done 10/6/85

Director of Artillery, 11/6/85, writes to the Maxim Gun Company, ordering supply of two guns to fulfill the following conditions:

(a) A gun on their proposed principle to fire the ammunition employed in Her Majesty's Service for 0.45-inch machine gun.

(b) A 2-pounder gun.

Conditions for the manufacture of the 45-caliber gun:

1.To fire the Gatling ammunition.

2.The barrel to be rifled on the Henry principle, or to give results in range, accuracy and penetration

equal to those obtained with the Martini-Henry rifle.

3.To be capable of firing at least 400 rounds per minute.

4.To be capable of firing 1000 rounds continuously in four minutes.

5.Weight of gun complete, without mounting, not to exceed 100 lbs.

6.Simplicity of construction to be aimed at as far as possible. The mechanism to be such as to ensure freedom from jams due to faults of construction.

Maxim Gun Company, 15/6/85, acknowledging the order for two guns made to the conditions supplied, say that they would prefer to say that the cost of the guns should compare favorably with that of any other description of machine gun firing an equal number of shots per minute, instead of naming a price, and that the matter be left for arrangement after the efficiency of the guns has been tested under the conditions supplied.

Superintendent RSAF, 27/6/85, in reply to Director of Artillery 22/6/85, considers that the request is a reasonable one. No price, he says, that the company could quote could possibly repay them for the outlay in plant and machinery at Hatton Garden, which fact must of necessity make the cost of turning out the first few guns enormous.

He considers, however, that some arrangement should be made with the company that, in the event of their gun not being adopted, they should not expect to receive more for it than has been paid for other guns of a similar nature already adopted in the Service.

Director of Artillery, 2/7/85, informs the Maxim Gun Company to this effect.

The involvement of the Department of the Director of Artillery with the Maxim gun appears to have come to an end shortly after this exchange of correspondence, and the subsequent minutes of that department make no mention of the Maxim, although they continue to report on various matters concerning the Gardener, Gatling and Nordenfelt guns. This is due to a departmental re-organization which led to the setting up of the Small Arms Committee, removing the responsibility for new small arms from the D of A's Department. It is also probable that an elementary form of security fell on the subject, since the Proceedings of the Small Arms Committee were never so widely published as had been those of the D of A. And doubtless Maxim had his own problems, since 1886 was largely taken up with the introduction of drawn-brass cases for 45-caliber ammunition and he would have had to modify his design to accommodate this. Indeed, it is highly likely that he would never have achieved the stipulated 1000 shots in four minutes had he been restricted to using the wrapped-brass Boxer-cased ammunition originally supplied for the Martini-Henry rifle.

(It is worth noting that this 1000 rounds in four minutes stipulation was due to experience with earlier designs of battery and machine guns in which the barrel rapidly overheated. Any gun that

Maxim's improved pattern guns; the larger of the two is in 303-caliber and the smaller is in 32-revolver caliber. It was used to demonstrate the Maxim gun when only an indoor rifle range was available, and could be carried in a small suitcase by salesmen.

Two early 303 Maxims, the nearer one with the original phosphor-bronze water jacket, the further with a replacement painted steel jacket.

could fire 1000 rounds in four minutes without jamming due to overheating would obviously be worth further consideration. A gun that couldn't, wasn't.)

Having spent the intervening time in improving and perfecting his design, Maxim produced his first 45-caliber gun for test by the Small Arms Committee in March 1887. Three guns were supplied, all of which fell well inside the stipulations of the Committee; one gun, in fact, fired its thousand rounds in ninety seconds. The guns were submitted to the usual sand and rust tests, which they passed without any defects, whereupon the Committee pronounced itself satisfied and the guns were accepted and paid for; though the records do not show what price was eventually agreed. There then followed a series of severe comparative tests.

The first test was against the Gardner, which weighed 200lbs, plus a further 100lbs for the tripod. The Maxim gun itself weighed just 50lbs and the tripod and traversing head another 60lbs. Four trained soldiers operated the Gardner – one to turn the crank, one to point the gun and two to attend to the feeding of the two barrels. They fired 300 rounds in 61 seconds; they

then attempted to fire faster and merely jammed the gun, which took 15 minutes to dismantle and clear. One man then fired the Maxim, delivering 334 rounds in 35 seconds. Tests against targets at ranges up to 1300 yards then demonstrated the superior fire power and accuracy of the Maxim.

A similar test against the 5-barrel Nordenfelt and the 2-barrel Gardner took place, with the same results, the Maxim firing 400 rounds in 40 seconds while the best the other two could do was 200 rounds in 25 seconds from the Nordenfelt. The overheating problem also made its appearance with the two mechanical guns, while the Maxim brought its water jacket to the boil after 600 continuous rounds had been fired, and evaporated the water at a rate of approximately 1.5 pints per thousand rounds thereafter.

The new model still used recoil as the driving force

The barrel, barrel extension and lock of the Maxim, with the toggle fully to the rear and the empty cartridge case gripped by the T-slot in the front of the breech-block.

but did away with the cumbersome locking hook, replacing it with a toggle joint. An extension frame attached to the barrel carried the 'lock' – or breechblock – which was kept firmly closed by a toggle joint anchored to a cross-shaft at the rear of the extension.

The action of the toggle joint can best be imagined by thinking of the human leg, which it closely resembles. Both the leg and the toggle unit consist of two solid sections: the shin and the thigh - connected by a joint - the knee. Imagine the leg as the toggle in the Maxim gun. The hip is the joint at the end of the barrel extension, while the sole of the foot is the breechblock. If the toggle - or leg - is extended in a straight line, any pressure on the foot - such as the explosion of the cartridge - will pass straight up the leg and be resisted by the anchorage of the hip bone to the barrel extension. But if someone were to tap the underside of the knee joint, then there would no longer be any resistance and the

Another view of the Maxim lock with a 45-caliber Martini-Henry round and an empty case in the T-slot.

leg would fold up; in other words, the toggle would fold and the breechblock would be able to move away from the barrel.

In Maxim's toggle joint the operation was downward. As the whole unit - barrel, barrel extension and toggle - recoiled to the rear, the barrel and breech block were securely locked together so that the full force of the exploding cartridge was driving the bullet from the gun and there was no danger of the breech opening while the chamber pressure was high. After about half an inch of movement a crank handle on the end of the cross-shaft struck a fixed roller, and this gave the toggle a downward impulse which broke the joint and accelerated the breech block backwards while the barrel remained still. At the same time, rotation of the shaft wound a spring.

A Chinese delegation in 1890, inspecting a tree chopped down by the Maxim gun. Hiram Maxim at the right, holding his hat.

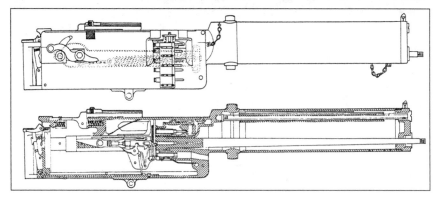

The perfected Maxim mechanism.

When the toggle came to a halt, this spring reversed the movement and drove the block forward, loading a fresh round and lifting the toggle once more until it resumed its locked position. With the abandonment of the part-rotational crank system the hydraulic buffer and rate of fire controller was also dropped, and the gun now had only two options - single shots or 600 rpm.

The first recorded combat use of the Maxim was in the British colony of Sierra Leone on 21 November 1888. A small punitive expedition under General Sir Francis de Winton was sent out to deal with a tribe who had been raiding various settlements and among the armament was a 45-caliber Maxim gun, purchase privately by de Winton. The contemporary report in the *Daily Telegraph* read:

"Governor Hay, at Sierra Leone, found himself compelled to dispatch an expedition under the command of Sir Francis de Winton, with orders to advance through the dense jungle to the fortified villages, and bombard and destroy them if possible. This jungle was so thick that nothing

could be transported through it excepting what two coolies could carry at a time; besides this, the enemy had cut down trees, and they lay in ambush at these obstacles to fire from their long guns, and in this way killed several of the soldiers of the West India Regiment. Our troops had to march in single file, the coo-

lies carrying the guns and ammunition being placed in the center. General Sir Francis de Winton took with him the Maxim gun, 45-caliber, and a small 7-pdr. The Maxim gun was carried by two coolies, and its tripod by two more, while a few others followed in single file, bearing the boxes of ammunition. Sir Francis was accompanied by the Hon. J. S. Ray, C.M.G., Governor of the Gambia, each having to carry his rifle as a private soldier, and make frequent use of it. After crossing the jungle the country became more open, and the stronghold Robari was seen. On coming in view of this fort, in the absence of Field Artillery, a pause was made, and the whole column of 200 men of the West India Regiment, fifteen Naval Brigade, and fifty of the Sierra Leone Police, assembled. A commanding position was assumed for the Maxim gun and 7-pdr. rifled gun, at a range of 450 yards. The enemy were in swarms in the wooden towers on the walls. The 7-pdr. opened fire, but the shells stuck in the mud wall and were of little use. Sir Francis de Winton, meantime, had the machine gun ready and, working it himself, poured in a tremendous volley into the nearest tower. The bullets rained in through the portholes and in-between the planks, killing numbers of the enemy. The breastwork and other towers were treated in the same manner, and in a few minutes it was seen that the garrison were issuing from the fort and flying for their lives. Such was the consternation created by the rapid and accurate shooting of the gun that the chief war town was evacuated, as well as the other villages of the same nature, and the chiefs surrendered, and are now in prison."

Apprentice armorers under training at Woolwich Arsenal in 1895, showing the range of machine guns then in service with the British army: 2-barrel Gardner, Maxim and 3-barrel Nordenfelt.

The machine gun was originally handled as an adjunct to artillery using similar types of carriage. A 45-caliber Maxim at practice in 1895.

Wittingly or unwittingly, General de Winton had applied the machine gun correctly to his tactical problem, but he was an exception. The principal brake upon the adoption of the Maxim gun was the simple question of how it was supposed to be used. The failure of the French *mitrailleuse* during the war of 1870 was still fresh in many minds, and if the French, who were supposed to be the foremost military brains in Europe, couldn't make a success of the machine gun, who could? And if the army was to adopt complicated modern weapons it would have to do something about its soldiers; in the 1870s barely ten percent of the private soldiers were literate and most could scarcely comprehend the workings of a machine gun.

After due consideration the Maxim was accepted as an infantry weapon, though most armies placed it on a wheeled carriage as they had done with the Gatling and other mechanical guns. But by this time the age-old practice of standing up in serried ranks to face the enemy had been blasted out of existence by the breech-loading magazine rifle, and a row of prone soldiers, doing their best to conceal themselves while keeping up an effective fire, were not helped by the presence of two machine guns on their flank, towering above them and advertising their presence for miles around and drawing any fire that was going. The wheeled carriage fairly rapidly fell into disuse and was replaced by the more sensible tripod.

The artillery-style of handling survived into the South African War of 1900. This is a 303 Maxim with muzzle booster, firing from behind a stone breastwork.

Another example of how the wheeled Maxim gun advertised the presence of otherwise concealed riflemen.

The success of the Maxim gun soon led other inventors to look at the possibilities of driving an automatic gun by using the gun's own energy. Among the first was another notable American gun designer, John Moses Browning. Browning had already made a name for himself by

Sometimes they just didn't bother to even try to conceal them; what sort of tactical situation this maneuver was meant to meet is open to doubt.

But before the end of the South African War the wheeled carriage had given way to the tripod and the machine gun was as well concealed as anybody else on the battlefield.

And instead of horses and wheels, manpower shifted the Maxim. German soldiers with their M1900 Maxim gun.

The other side of the South African War - Boer troops with their one-pounder Maxim Pom-Pom.

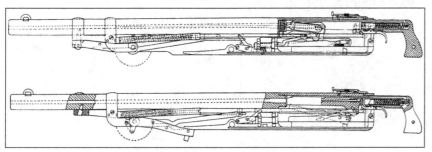

The internals of the M1895 Colt, showing the action of the swinging piston.

adopted into service as the Model 1895.

These guns are almost always called the 'Potato Digger' guns due to their unusual action. The gas is tapped off just before the muzzle, but instead of driving a piston in a cylinder, it blasts straight down onto the tip of an arm hinged beneath the barrel. Thus the arm described an arc, swinging down and back, and it is coupled to a lever that thus drives the gun mechanism. While this is an unusual system, it is also a very efficient one in that it delivers the force of the gas very gently, absorbing shock and keeping the rate of fire down to a practical figure, and there is every likelihood that Browning adopted this for that very reason, so as to avoid a too-violent extraction of the cartridge. Extraction is best divided into two phases, primary and secondary; primary extraction is a slow but powerful leverage to loosen the case in the chamber and ease it slightly outward. In a bolt-action rifle this is generally done during the rotation of the bolt on the opening movement. Secondary extraction is faster and requires less power since it is merely a matter of flicking the loosened case out of the chamber and bouncing it off the extractor. So Browning's leverage system would, by its geometry, exert this powerful but slow thrust to start the bolt moving backwards and loosening the cartridge case from its grip on the chamber, after which, as the swinging arm came down to the vertical, the bolt speed would have accelerated and given the secondary extracting impulse. In a similar manner the closing stroke would have rapidly stripped a round from the belt, after which the movement would have slowed down to ease the cartridge into the chamber and then lock the bolt.

The actual locking system is of interest as it foreshadows his later BAR design. The rear end of the operating rod has cam surfaces that lift the rear end of the bolt out of its locked position, braced against a recess in the receiver. The rod then carries the bolt back, and at the end of its stroke the bolt strikes a cylindrical hammer, carried in the top of the pistol grip, and drives it back to cock it. This also acts as a buffer spring to cushion the final movement of the bolt.

designing repeating rifles and shotguns, and in 1889 he began working on a machine gun. While he fully understood Maxim's use of recoil, he was of the opinion that muzzle blast was an equally fruitful source of energy, and his first models were based on the use of a plate to trap the excess gas after the exit of the bullet and, through the medium of levers, operate the breech. He then drilled a hole in the gun barrel, close to the muzzle, and led the gas out to a port below the barrel, where it propelled a piston that in turn carried out the various functions of loading, firing and extracting. This was the first true gas-operated gun. By 1890 he had perfected his design and offered it to the Colt company; a prototype model was made and tested by the US Navy in 1892-3, being

The Colt M1895 machine gun, designed by John M. Browning.

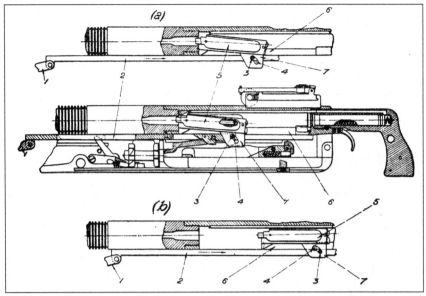

The bolt of the M1895 was locked by its rear end being cammed down into a recess in the floor of the receiver. The upper picture shows the bolt and operating rod alone; the center picture shows the same thing but in the context of the complete gun; and the bottom picture is a top view with the bolt fully open.

A driving spring then forced the operating rod back into the forward position, which returns the swinging arm to contact with the hole in the barrel. During this movement the rod carries the bolt forward, loading a fresh round, and then cams the rear end down, back into the locking recess. Pressing the trigger releases the hammer, which flies forward and strokes the rear end of the firing pin, carried in the bolt.

The principal drawback to this system was that the gun had to be used on a tripod or other high-set

mounting, otherwise the swinging arm would dig into the ground – which is where the 'Potato Digger' name came from. But as the tacticians of the day had not yet got around to thinking about men crawling around the battlefield with machine-guns, there was little notice taken of that side of things. Nevertheless, Browning, as was his habit, wasn't satisfied with the weapon and sat down to develop a fresh design as a low-priority ongoing project. Colt, who had purchased the license from Browning, produced the weapon in various calibers and sold it in various places around the world. The only people they could never sell it to were the U.S. Board of Ordnance and the US

The Skoda machine gun of 1909 with its odd belt feed. This gun is also provided with a rather ornate optical sight for use in indirect fire.

Army. They were quite content with the mechanical Gatling and refused to even test the Browning gun, being quite sure that such a mechanism had no place on the battlefield. Somehow, I discern the hand of the autocratic Chief of Ordnance General Crozier in there somewhere.

In Europe, the first local design of an automatic gun came from Austria. In 1888 Field-Marshal the Archduke Karl Salvator and Count George von Dormus patented a gun operating on a delayed blowback system. In this system the breech-block was never positively locked to the barrel, but was held closed by its own inertia, plus that of a pivoting block and the force of a powerful spring. As a result the bullet was out of the short barrel and the gas pressure had dropped to a reasonably safe level before the breech had begun to open.

Being a mechanically simple design it was, for its day, quite reliable; it is commonly said that due to its construction only 'relatively weak' cartridges could be used, but the normal chambering was for the 8x50R Mannlicher, which generated 2243 foot-pounds at the muzzle - scarcely 'weak' by anybody's reckoning - the contemporary 7.92mm Mauser delivered 2220 foot-pounds and nobody ever called that weak. The weak point in its design lay in the ammunition feed, which was a form of a slanting guide, generally called a 'hopper' for the want of a better descriptive term. The cartridges were fed into the top by hand and slid down the guide to be delivered to the breech area. Careless loading of the hopper could cause cartridges to jam, though since the guide was open-sided, jams were fairly easy to rectify. Being a blowback weapon firing a powerful bottle-necked cartridge, the empty cases were inevitably going to stick in the chamber, and therefore it is to Salvator and von Dormus that we owe the idea of oiling cartridges on their way into the gun, an oil tank being attached to the side of the feed hopper and, using felt pads, gave each round a film of oil as it passed. A last refinement was the attachment of an adjustable pendulum to the trigger mechanism that, by pushing the weight up or down the pendulum, allowed the rate of fire to be adjusted between 180 and 250 rounds per minute. This latter is an exceptionally slow figure, even for those early days, and is no doubt due to the breech mechanism that demanded the movement of a heavy component compressing a powerful spring.

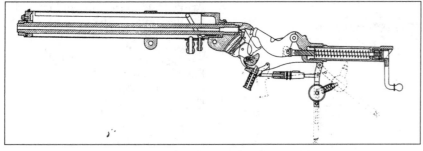

The workings of the Skoda, a delayed-blowback weapon. A hinged breechblock pivoted just below the chamber, is held in place by a large locking piece propelled by the horizontal spring. Their interface is so designed that the rearward pressure of the cartridge will gradually force the locking piece down and allow the breechblock to open. The pendulum mechanism acts on the trigger and controls the rate of fire, adjusted by sliding the weight up or down.

The first production Hotchkiss was this Model 1897, and the design never changed very much thereafter.

This, then, was the Skoda Mitrailleuse Model 1893, and it was adopted by the Austro-Hungarian Army, the Skoda armaments company having licensed the patents from Salvator and von Dormus, and was principally used in fortifications. A later model, the 1902, made some improvements to the feed hopper but few of these appear to have been made.

The Model 1909 was a considerable improvement, since it adopted a belt feed; but what a belt feed! It went in at the bottom left side of the receiver and came out on the top left side, having made a 180° turn enroute. This peculiar arrangement *(which was very similar to Maxim's first design)* was necessary because the design of the breech closure system made a side-to-side through belt an impossibility. The last of the series came in 1913, which exhibited a strengthening of the general design and an improvement in the tripod mount, but retained the same general system of feed and operation. But by that time the Austro-Hungarian Army had settled on

another design, the Schwarzlose, and the Skoda M1913 was turned down. Its day was yet to come; in the initial setbacks suffered by the Austro-Hungarians in 1914-15 machine gun losses were serious, and Skoda were

ordered to produce the M1913 in a desperate search for replacements.

In France the Hotchkiss Company was now directed by another American, Lawrence V. Benet, and in 1893 he was approached by another Austrian, Captain Adolf Odkolek, with the design of a gas-operated gun. Benet could see that the design had some useful features, but he could also see that it was going to take some hard work before it became a practical gun, and he bought the design and patents from Odkolek for a fixed sum, refusing any sort of royalty deal.

This was rather rough on Odkolek, although Benet in later years claimed that he had been *'amply recompensed'*, and certainly Odkolek worked with Hotchkiss in the development and improvement of his design for many years, which he would hardly have done had he not been satisfied with his contract. The heart of Odkolek's design was a gas cylinder beneath the barrel in which a piston operated to drive the gun mechanism. The breech was locked by a pivoting locking flap controlled by the movement of the gas piston, and the ammunition was carried in a pressed metal strip that was inserted into the gun on the right-hand side. As the bolt operated, so rounds were pulled from the strip and the strip moved across until it fell, empty, from the left side of the gun.

The Hotchkiss was adopted by the French Army in 1897; it proved to be moderately reliable but was prone to overheating, in spite of massive brass cooling fins on the barrel. It was succeeded by a Model 1900 in which the barrel

had been redesigned with integral steel cooling fins in the hope of improving matters. This was slightly better. It was not, though, good enough for the French Army. Moreover, they were annoyed at having to pay a commercial firm for their machine gun when all their previous arms had come from government arsenals, and so they set themselves the task of

Apart from having a hand-grip rather than a shoulder-piece the 1914 Hotchkiss was much the same as the 1897 model.

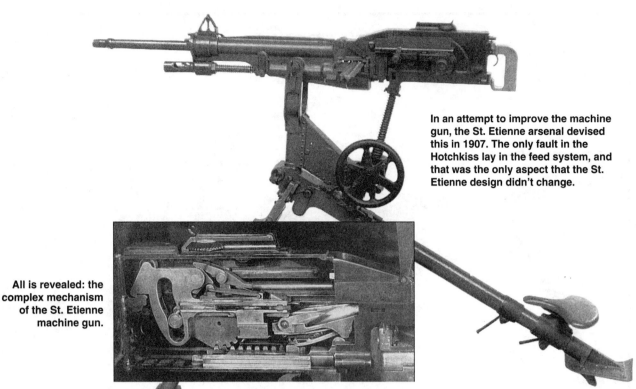

In an attempt to improve the machine gun, the St. Etienne arsenal devised this in 1907. The only fault in the Hotchkiss lay in the feed system, and that was the only aspect that the St. Etienne design didn't change.

All is revealed: the complex mechanism of the St. Etienne machine gun.

developing an improved Hotchkiss gun, though without going so far as to consult Hotchkiss in the matter.

The results were disastrous. The first attempt was introduced as the 'Puteaux' or Model 1905 gun; it was more or less the 1900 Hotchkiss with a lot more brass fins on the barrel and a variable rate-of-fire device of questionable utility. The gun proved to be a failure and it was withdrawn from line units and put into fortifications as a fixed defense gun. The next attempt was the 'St. Etienne', or Model 1907, which can best be described as a Hotchkiss with almost everything changed around simply for the sake of changing. It used the same gas piston – but now the piston was blown forward, instead of back, and so there had to be a rack-and-pinion system to reverse the movement and make sure that the breech block went back

as the piston went forward. The well-tried Hotchkiss bolt lock was thrown out and a peculiar over-center device, resembling the Maxim toggle, was put in. The gas cylinder had an adjustable volume so that the rate of fire could be altered by slowing or speeding up the action of the piston. The return spring was mounted close beneath the barrel and this, allied with the well-known propensity of the design for overheating, more or less guaranteed that the spring would lose its temper *(in the metallurgical sense)* before much firing had been done. In fact the only thing the designers failed to alter was the strip feed system, which most people agreed was the only really faulty feature of the original Hotchkiss design. After numbers of these guns had been built, World War I

broke out and soon exposed them for the hopeless mechanical oddities that they were. The French Army were then very glad to get back to the original Hotchkiss and sent the St. Etienne guns off to the Foreign Legion as quickly as possible.

The Hotchkiss was bought by several nations, among them the Japanese, who used them in considerable numbers in the Russo-Japanese War. The Russians were using Maxim and Madsen guns, and this war was the first real testing ground for the machine-gun. It was the first time that two major powers, each armed with machine guns, had come face to face and the results were watched very closely by other nations. The Russians first used their Maxims at the Yalu River, where eight guns beat off

(Continued on Page 48)

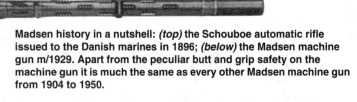

Madsen history in a nutshell: *(top)* the Schouboe automatic rifle issued to the Danish marines in 1896; *(below)* the Madsen machine gun m/1929. Apart from the peculiar butt and grip safety on the machine gun it is much the same as every other Madsen machine gun from 1904 to 1950.

THE MADSEN GUN

The typical Madsen gun, a design virtually unchanged for half a century.

The late Major Frank Hobart, instructor in small arms at the British Army's Royal Military College of Science in the 1960s, famously said that the amazing thing about the Madsen gun was not that it worked well; it was that it worked at all. It is, in effect, the Peabody dropping-block breech mechanism, designed for single-shot rifles and patented in the USA in 1862. Mechanizing this to obtain repetitive fire involved machining a 'switch plate', a series of interwoven cam tracks, in the side of the receiver so that during the recoil and run-out movements of the barrel and breech, lugs riding in the switch plate would control the movement of various items. Since the bolt does not move backwards and forwards, the insertion and ramming of the round has to be done by a separate mechanism, as does the extraction of the

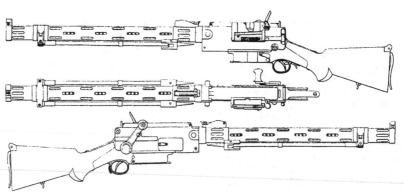

Plan and elevation drawings of the Madsen. Note that the return spring is around the barrel, and that the magazine housing is offset to the left of the receiver so as not to interfere with the sight line.

DATA	(Model 1950)
Caliber	7.92 x 57mm Mauser and others
Operating system	Short recoil, selective fire
Locking system	Tilting block
Feed system	30-round overhead box
Overall length	45.9 in (1166mm)
Weight, empty	22.0 lbs (10kg)
Barrel	18.8in (478mm)
Muzzle velocity	2700 ft/sec (822 m/sec)
Muzzle energy	3194 ft/lbs (4316J)
Rate of fire	400 rds/min
Effective range	600m

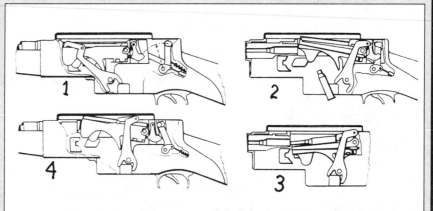

The sequence of events inside the Madsen; 1) the gun fires; 2) the bolt is lifted and the case extracted beneath it; 3) the bolt now drops and the fresh round is rammed across the top; 4) the bolt moves up to close the breech ready for firing.

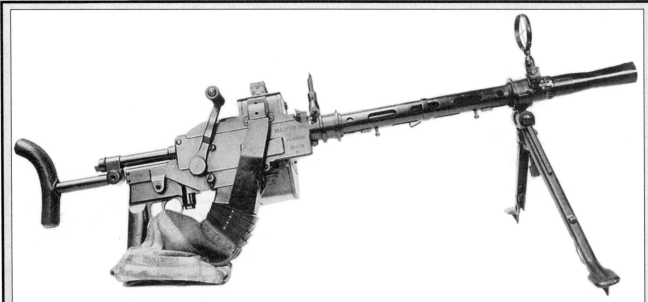

A belt-fed Madsen for aircraft use; note the two bags, one underneath for empty cases and the other on the side for collecting links.

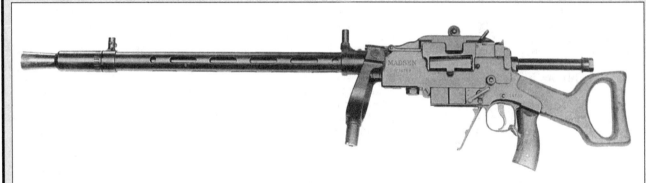

Another belt-fed aircraft gun; the tube at the rear of these belt-fed guns is a stronger buffer to withstand more powerful

empty case - but all is powered by the recoil movement and controlled by the switch plate. Because of this, the path described by the cartridge during loading is actually a curve, which merely adds another complication, since some cartridges do not take kindly to being warped in that way.

It is often said that the Madsen has been used by many armies but never taken into use by a first-class power; this is not quite true, since the Russian cavalry used it, and the British used it in tanks during World War I. But it is certainly true that no major army ever adopted it as its primary machine gun. The Madsen is most usually seen as an infantry gun, magazine fed; but it was also supplied in belt-fed form as an aircraft observer's gun, though comparatively few were ever adopted.

Field Stripping:

Set the change lever to 'Unl' - the unloading position - and remove the magazine. Press the trigger, recock, set the change lever to 'F' and press the trigger once more. Turn the locking-bolt lever upwards to the vertical and pull it out to the left. Push the butt forward and to the right, supporting the receiver in the left hand.

Hook the forefinger around the feed arm axis bar and draw back the barrel and breech mechanism. Withdraw the barrel with care, ensuring that the ring at the muzzle does not foul any of the internal components as it passes through. Depress the spring catch and unscrew the flash-hider from the muzzle.

Remove the breech-block bolt. Turn the feed arm to the rear, raise the front and depress the rear of the breech-block, ease the feed arm forward and lift the block out of the piston slide. The firing pin is held by a retaining screw which, when unscrewed, allows the pin and its spring to be removed.

To re-assemble.

Reverse the sequence given above. When replacing the barrel and breech mechanism, be careful not to allow the muzzle to strike the distributor arm as you ease it into the jacket; see that the feed arm is fully forward, place the thumb behind the feed arm axis bar and slide the barrel and mechanism home in one smooth movement. Hook the butt into the receiver, raise it into position and push in the locking bolt.

A typical Madsen light machine gun; this carries the badge of the Siamese Navy on the receiver.

(Continued from Page 45)

several Japanese assaults and the Japanese, used to attacking en masse, were decimated. They, in their turn, used their Hotchkiss guns with great boldness, carrying them forward in the attack so as to provide fire whenever it was needed. They became adept at giving cover to an assault by firing over the heads of the attacking troops to keep down the defenders. As a result of their experiences the Japanese were well satisfied with the Hotchkiss design and, having acquired a license to manufacture them in Japan, they gradually improved the design by incorporating their own ideas.

The Russian cavalry were armed with the Danish Madsen gun, which was one of the most remarkable machine guns ever built. It was the first that would be called, by modern standards, a light machine gun, and it was produced in almost the same model for over 50 years. It was used as an infantry gun,

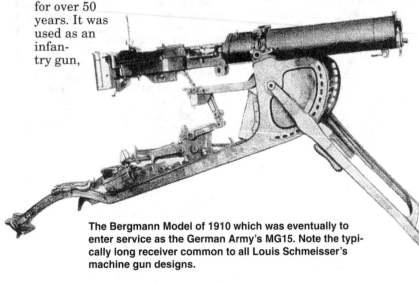

The Bergmann Model of 1910 which was eventually to enter service as the German Army's MG15. Note the typically long receiver common to all Louis Schmeisser's machine gun designs.

a tank gun and an aircraft gun, and it was probably one of the most complicated mechanisms ever to achieve success.

The Madsen gun was designed by a Danish officer called Jens Schouboe, and was probably the only one of his many weapon designs that was a success. It first appeared as an automatic rifle design in the mid-1890s, and a number - possibly a thousand - were bought by the Danish Marines and issued as the 'Rekylkarabinen M/1896', making them the first military force ever to adopt automatic rifles. It didn't do them much good, however. The rifles proved to be failures, constantly breaking, and within a very few years they were scrapped. Schouboe went back to his drawing board and changed the design into a machine gun, which was adopted by the Danish cavalry in about 1902 and named after Madsen, the then-Danish Minister of War who was particularly enthusiastic about the weapon and had pressed hard for its adoption by the army. *(It is some-*

times called the 'Rexer' machine gun in early documents, since it was offered to a number of foreign governments by the Rexer Gun Company of London in the 1900s.)

The mechanism of the gun is recoil-operated and is best described as the adaptation of the Martini pivoting breechblock to automatic action. When a round is fired the breechblock is aligned with the barrel, and pins in the front end of the block are riding in the forward end of a groove in the 'Switch Plate', a track cut in the side of the gun body. As the barrel and bolt recoil, the pin on the bolt is drawn through the groove on the switch plate, and the angle of the groove lifts the breechblock clear of the chamber. A separate extractor, driven by a cam on the barrel, now extracts and ejects the cartridge case.

As the barrel and block move back, a firing hammer is cocked and a recoil spring placed under compression. When the rearward movement stops, the spring begins to force the moving parts forward again. The bolt pin, riding in the switch plate, is now moved by the switch plate groove so that the bolt is dropped below the level of the chamber, allowing a rammer unit to ram a fresh cartridge from the overhead magazine into the chamber. Then, as the barrel and bolt are about to complete their return, the switch plate moves the bolt up and closes the breech ready for the hammer to fall.

Thus, instead of the bolt moving back and forth and doing everything, in the Madsen the bolt simply swings up and down to open and close the breech. Extraction, feed and ramming are all performed by other pieces of the mechanism. It is one of the most complicated devices ever seen,

A Schwarzlose 8mm gun of the Austro-Hungarian army. Note the large flash hider, necessitated by firing a cartridge designed for a long rifle barrel out of a short machine gun barrel.

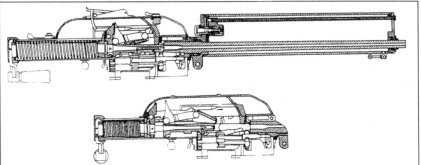

The inside of a Schwarzlose consists mostly of a heavy breechblock and a toggle which never quite locks, coupled to a massive return spring.

gun. This suggests (to me, anyway) that his belt was fundamentally a cloth one since I doubt whether a metallic non-disintegrating belt could have been wound onto a spool small enough for that sort of attachment. It was claimed that this method relieved the bolt of work in lifting the belt (since the feed pawls which moved the belt were driven by a lever driven by the bolt).

This may be connected with one of the noticeable features of the Bergmann, the abnormal length of the receiver. Due to their mechanical systems of operation the Maxim, Schwarzlose, Skoda and Madsen all have receivers that are relatively short when compared with their barrel length. The Bergmann receiver is about the same length as the water jacket from the 1902 model onward, because the bolt is reciprocating straight back, not pivoting or restrained by a toggle as are the others. This needed some space to move and fit the feed and belt mechanism in front of it - hence the length - and this may also have had a bearing on the leverage for the belt feed and the consequent lifting power.

Louis Schmeisser parted company with Bergmann in the mid-1900s, and went off to *Rheinmetall* of Sommerda to develop the

and yet it works without trouble most of the time. It does tend to balk a little at rimmed cartridges, and this is due to the path of the round as it enters the chamber: as the cartridge is forced in, it is slightly bowed or bent. But with rimless ammunition this seems to cause no trouble, and certainly if the Madsen were prone to problems it would hardly have survived as long as it did. A point that is not readily apparent when looking at a picture of a Madsen is that the magazine is not mounted centrally on top of the receiver (although it is always called an overhead magazine) but is actually offset to the left side, so as to leave a clear line of sight over the barrel. The cartridges feed down from the magazine into an oblique feedway to be presented to the rammer.

The next design to appear was the Bergmann that, like almost all Bergmann weapons, was actually designed by Louis Schmeisser. He patented and produced his first prototype in 1901, a recoil-operated weapon using a rising lock plate in the barrel extension that rode on a

ramp and thus dropped during the recoil stroke and rose during the return stroke. (He later used the same type of lock on one or two automatic pistol designs, notably the Bergmann-Bayard.) It was a somewhat unusual mechanism for a recoil-operated weapon, since it fired from an open bolt. The gun was water-cooled, with the usual sort of water jacket, and used a top-mounted magazine that appears to have relied solely upon gravity to propel the cartridges down into the feedway.

After fiddling around with this for some time, Schmeisser redesigned it and produced his 1902 model. This had a shorter barrel, a fatter water jacket and adopted a form of belt feed. What few records there are of this gun describe the belt as 'metallic' but beyond that nobody is prepared to go, and whether it was all-metal or simply metal clips stitched to a canvas belt, we have no way of knowing. In the following year he produced a variation that had the ammunition coiled on a spool inside a box, which could be attached to the side of the

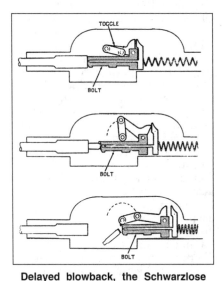

Delayed blowback, the Schwarzlose way: At the top the bolt is closed and the toggle folded; below, the bolt begins to move back, pulling the toggle open but initially at a considerable mechanical disadvantage; finally the bolt is fully opened. Note how the heel of the toggle acts to withdraw the firing pin as the bolt moves back.

Another Schwarzlose, this one with their large condenser can, that is also the storage box for the water hose.

Dreyse machine guns, about which more later. But by that time his son Hugo had begun working for Bergmann *(and in due course was to become their chief designer)* and although there is no definite information, it seems highly probable that Hugo now took over the continuing development of his father's machine gun. In 1908 the German Army, anxious to widen their procurement base, decided to adopt another machine gun in addition to their existing Maxim; for strategic-economic reasons, they wanted it to be a German design. (The Maxim, at that time, was being built in Germany under license from the Vickers-Maxim company in Britain.)

On the face of it, this would appear to have been a shoo-in for Bergmann, but the army put up one stipulation: the new gun had to feed from the existing Maxim type of belt. This made sense, since no army wants to have two different kinds of machine gun belt cluttering up their supply line and, infallibly, getting into the wrong place at the wrong time. The original Bergmann design used 'push-through' belts; in other words, the feed system had a belt in which the round was held by a clip and the bolt pushed the cartridge through the clip and into the chamber. The Maxim used a 'withdrawal' belt in which the mechanism first pulled the cartridge backwards from the loop in the belt, then lowered it in front of the bolt, and finally rammed it into the chamber. Thus there had to be some fundamental changes made to the Bergmann design before it could compete for army adoption.

The re-design seems to have taken place in two stages; firstly the feed mechanism was changed to suit the Maxim belt. This was advertised as the Model 1909 though none seem to have been

produced for sale. Next there was a considerable overhaul of the design, changing it so the gun now fired from a closed bolt, used the recoil of the barrel and barrel extension to drive the belt feed system, and had a bolt accelerator that lifted the rate of fire to about 550 rounds per minute. This became the Model 1910 and it seems that this was accepted in principle by the German Army but that very few were put into service. Numbers were sold abroad - notably to China - but it was not until the outbreak of war in 1914 that the gun went into serious production for the German Army, who confusingly adopted it as their Model 1915.

The Austro-Hungarian Army was far from satisfied with its Skoda machine-gun, and in 1907 it turned to the Schwarzlose design. This was the invention of a German designer, Andreas Wilhelm Schwarzlose (1867-1936), who had served in the Austro-Hungarian artillery and had there been trained as an ordnance mechanic. This seems to have fired his ambition, and after his discharge he went off to Suhl to continue his education and in 1898 designed a self-loading pistol, followed it up with one or two other weapons and then set about designing a machine gun, taking out his first machine gun patents in 1900. Like the Skoda, the Schwarzlose design dispensed with the formality of locking the breech-block before firing the cartridge. Its operation relied entirely on having a massive breechblock, backed up by a form of toggle joint that never actu-

ally locked the block but merely acted to slow down the opening movement. In order to get the breech pressure down quickly, the barrel was short – 20 inches against the Maxim's 28 inches, for example – but, again like the Skoda, due to the rather abrupt functioning of the gun it was necessary to lubricate the cartridges as they were loaded into the chamber so as to allow them to be extracted easily.

The Schwarzlose is always easily recognized by the hump-backed receiver, necessitated by the toggle action, and its bicycle handle-bar grips. The system is actually very simple: there is a barrel with a bolt behind it, running in guides in the receiver, and behind that a massive return spring. Above the bolt is a short barrel extension to which the front end of a simple toggle is attached. The other end of the two toggle arms is attached to the bolt in such a manner that when the bolt is closed the toggle arms are almost completely folded up, the rear pair outside the front arm, and both facing forward and slightly up, over the chamber. As the bolt moves back under the pressure of the propellant explosion, the rear arms are pulled back – they pull on the center hinge of the toggle and this is pulled, at a considerable mechanical disadvantage, up and back so as to unfold the toggle. As the toggle unfolds, so the leverage improves and the opening of the bolt becomes faster, until eventually the bolt is fully open and the toggle almost completely unfolded and lying along the top of the boltway. The powerful return spring then starts the bolt back and this, of course, re-folds the toggle. During the back and forth movement of the bolt, various feed arms have moved the belt across and a fresh cartridge has been extracted, positioned and chambered.

The Austro-Hungarians had a very high regard for the Schwarzlose, largely because it was simple to understand and operate, very robust, and had a respectable rate of fire of 400 rounds per minute, considerably better than the Skoda. It also had the not-inconsiderable advantage of

This peculiar device is actually an SIA machine gun. The four horns at the left-hand end are all that remain of the spade grips. The magazine housing is in the center, over the trunnions,

The Friberg-Kjellman machine gun on tripod mounting.

costing about half the price of a Maxim gun. The Dutch adopted it in 1908 and they were followed by Greece, Serbia, Romania, Bulgaria, Sweden and Turkey - all before 1912. And although Schwarzlose built his prototypes in his own workshop, until 1917 the Steyr factory in Austria manufactured all the production guns. In that year the Dutch *(who were, of course, neutral during World War I)* needed machine guns, could not purchase any worth having, and set up a line to produce the Schwarzlose in their own arsenal at Hembrug. These differed in minor details from the original pattern and remained in production until 1940.

In 1912 came a slightly improved model, with an internal oil tank which permitted firing up to 4500 rounds before it required refilling; the original 1907 design could only fire 2000 before it needed a refill. The new gun (the 07/12 or 08/12, according to who owned it and the adoption year of their original guns) also had the rate of fire stepped up to 500 rounds per minute.

Operation of the Schwarzlose is quite straight-forward, the only unusual feature being to open the top cover before loading the gun and ensuring that the oil tank for the automatic cartridge oiler is full. (It is sometimes stated that the later Schwarzlose guns dispensed with the oil pump; this may have been a proposal, even the subject of a prototype, but no production gun was ever made without one.) Then close the cover and insert the tag end of the belt over the star wheel on the right side. Then rotate the cocking handle to the rear and release it four times; the final movement will put a round into the chamber.

When Louis Schmeisser left Bergmann's employ some time in 1906-7, he moved from Suhl to Sommerda, about 35 miles away to the north, and began working for the *Rheinische Metallwaren und*

Maschinenfabrik H. Erhardt GmbH, a firm which, understandably, shortened its title to *'Rheinmetall'* in later years. This company was highly respected as a manufacturer of artillery, and could give the more famous Krupp company a run for its money any day. In 1902 they purchased the moribund *Waffenfabrik Dreyse*, the company that had produced the German Army's famous needle gun breech-loading rifle, the weapon that introduced the concept of bolt action.

Rheinmetall was located in Dusseldorf, as befitted a heavy engineering concern, but Dreyse were in Sommerda, in the gun-making area around Erfurt in Thuringia. Having bought Dreyse and taken over their factory, they assessed their purchase, realized that it needed a complete shake-up and hired Louis Schmeisser to become the superintendent and chief designer.

By the time Louis had got his eye in and was beginning to reorganize the works, the German Army appeared with their demand for an alternative machine gun, and Louis immediately went to work on a fresh design, taking under his wing a young apprentice designer called Louis Stange, who was to make his mark some thirty years later. Schmeisser took out his first patents applicable to what was to become the Dreyse machine gun in 1907, more in 1909, and finally produced a gun in 1912. Hardly surprising, it had many points of resemblance to the earlier Bergmann weapon, notably in the length of the slender receiver, but beneath the skin it was somewhat different. Instead of a lug rising and falling to lock and unlock the breechblock, the Dreyse used a pivoted bar in the barrel extension. At the front end this had a lug engaging with the bolt, and the other end rode on a ramp machined in the floor of the receiver; as the barrel and extension, with locked bolt, recoiled, so the tail of this bar rode up the ramp, forcing the nose end down and withdrawing the locking lug. Once the bolt was unlocked, the barrel unit stopped just as an accelerator threw the bolt back. The bolt was connected by a lug on its top surface to a spring carried in the receiver cover, so that the rearward movement of the bolt compressed the spring until the bolt was finally arrested by a buffer unit. The spring then drove it back to chamber a fresh round and release the barrel to run forward, and as it did so the bar rode down the ramp and lifted the locking lug into engagement in the bolt. Ammunition was the standard 7.92mm Mauser round, fed by means of the standard Maxim belt, as decreed by the army.

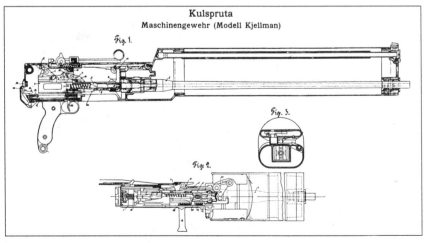

The workings of the Kjellman machine gun, showing Friberg's flap-locked bolt.

As with the Bergmann, the Dreyse was accepted 'in principle' by the army but no major orders followed before the outbreak of war. Although generally called the Model 1912, this is not an official military nomenclature, merely a useful indication of its place in the chronology of the machine gun. It was entirely in the contemporary style, with a water jacket and tripod mount, though the Dreyse tripods (probably due to Schmeisser) seems to be the pioneer of carrying a pair of wheels which allowed the tripod to be folded and used as a transport barrow.

So far all the guns we have considered achieved some success, but by the latter 1900s, when most of the major nations had made their minds up about what gun to adopt, things began to get harder for inventors. Even if they had a good design, they were up against guns that were tried and tested and armies which had already invested money and machinery in the gun of their choice. Sometimes they were hindered by a lack of resolution on the part of the people whom they hoped would buy.

One such designer was an Italian engineer Giuseppe Perino. Perino designed a machine gun in 1900 and offered it to the Italian Army. The gun was a very sound design using recoil augmented by the blast from the muzzle striking a fixed deflector to boost the recoil of the moving parts. Breech locking was done by a bell-crank system, and the recoiling barrel moved in a casing and functioned as a pump, directing a stream of cooling air into the breech area at every stroke. Feed was originally by a belt, but this was soon replaced by a tray system, a box on the side of the gun carrying a number of trays which were, in turn, taken into the gun. This gun was notable for introducing the peculiarly Italian idea of replacing the empty cartridge case into the feed strip instead of ejecting it from the gun, an idea which reappeared many years later but with rather more justification.

By 1911 the gun had been offered to various countries without success - there wasn't a lot wrong with the gun but they already had made up their minds about the guns they wanted and were equipping their armies - but the Italian Army was still undecided. Under conditions of great secrecy they continued to test the gun, trying it against the Maxim, Colt, Skoda and any others they could find. Time went by and still they were unable to come to a decision. While they were still arguing World War I broke out and when, in 1915, the Italians became embroiled in the war they had to go out and buy whatever machine guns they could find, since by that stage there was no time to think of setting up production facilities for the Perino. As a result, the Perino was never heard of again, and the Italians finished up with a handful of designs that were, in many respects, inferior to the Perino.

Another Italian venture is worth recording since it was responsible for an idea which has been used in many designs since. This was the SIA gun, designed by Giovanni Agnelli. The patents were taken up by the *Societe Anonima Italiana G Ansaldo, Armstrong & Company* (SIA) but although they produced one or two guns before 1914 they were unable to make much headway with the design until the 1920s. Eventually a few were sold to the Italian army and air force who used them as training guns in the 1930s. However, the interesting feature of the SIA gun was the method that Agnelli invented to simplify extraction. His design was for a blowback bolt, retarded by the firing pin moving in a helical slot in the breechblock. Like all blowback guns, there was no primary extraction, extraction was violent, and the heads were frequently torn off the cartridge cases, leading to jams and stoppages. Instead of resorting to the accepted method of oiling the cartridges, Agnelli solved it by cutting fine longitudinal grooves in the chamber of the gun, so that when it fired, some of the gas washed around the mouth of the case and entered the grooves. Thus, instead of the pressure on the inside of the case forcing the case tightly against the chamber wall to cause hard extraction, there was now an equal pressure on both sides of the case, and it was virtually floating in the chamber on a layer of gas. This made extraction quite easy, and since that time a grooved chamber has been recognized as the most likely solution to hard extraction with blowback guns.

A good design, which got nowhere, was the Swedish Kjellman - or Friberg-Kjellman as some call it. The basic locking principle used in this gun was actually developed in the late 1870s by a Lieutenant Friberg, who was attempting to develop a mechanical machine gun. Unfortunately he died

Another Kjellman gun on a tripod; the gun made little impression but Friberg's flap-locking bolt was copied and modified by a number of designers in later years.

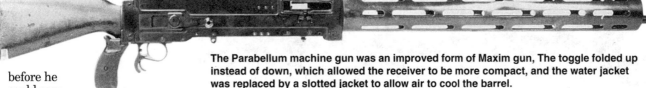

The Parabellum machine gun was an improved form of Maxim gun, The toggle folded up instead of down, which allowed the receiver to be more compact, and the water jacket was replaced by a slotted jacket to allow air to cool the barrel.

before he could complete his plan, and his patents lay forgotten for many years. In the early 1900s a gunsmith named Rudolf Kjellman came across them and set about designing an automatic gun. In the normal course of events, its lack of success would consign it to oblivion, but the locking principle devised by Friberg and perfected by Kjellman was so good that it was used in designs by Degtyarev, Mauser and Rolls-Royce in later years, and thus the originator deserves to have his efforts recorded.

The Kjellman machine gun appeared in about 1907; it was water-cooled, tripod-mounted, and fed by a Maxim-type belt from the right side. Minus water, the gun weighed only 28 lbs. (13kg), which was a good deal lighter than any competition of the day, fired at 500 rounds per minute with the standard 6.5mm Swedish Mauser cartridge, and was so designed that the barrel could be changed in 40 seconds. On firing, the barrel and bolt recoiled - locked together - for about 0.7-inch (18mm). The bolt was locked to the barrel by two flaps, one on each side, and these were cammed out of engagement as the recoil stroke ended. As the flaps unlocked, the firing pin was withdrawn and an accelerator threw the bolt back against its return spring. The bolt withdrew the fired case and carried it back, firmly held in a T-slot in the bolt face. On the return stroke a fresh round was

fed into the T-slot and drove the empty case out to be ejected below the gun. As the bolt chambered the new cartridge so the firing pin moved forward and, due to its shape, forced the flaps back into their recesses, locking the bolt to the barrel. The combined unit then ran forward into battery and the firing pin completed its movement and fired the cartridge.

The Kjellman was tested by the Swedish army and received glowing reports of its efficiency and reliability. But the Swedish army could not see any enemy on the horizon, and the Swedish government had decided on a policy of strict neutrality in the event of any future war that did not directly threaten them, and thus there was no money available for machine guns. Kjellman then tried making a lighter model, calling it his 'machine carbine'; this used the same mechanism but fed from an overhead magazine similar to that of the Madsen gun. Unfortunately he retained the water jacket for cooling the barrel, apparently having no faith in air-cooling. This made the weapon neither a carbine nor a machine gun, according to the thinking of the day, and it failed to arouse any interest. Kjellman returned to commercial gunsmithing and the Kjellman machine guns, of which probably less than a dozen were made, appear to have been scrapped.

By the time the Maxim gun had been in use for 20 years or so, it occurred to various designers that it could stand a little improvement. The first attempt appears to have begun in 1909 when the German Army demanded a machine gun suitable for carrying in aircraft, and therefore lighter than the standard Maxim. The government arsenals could not devote staff or time to such a task, so a commercial company, the *Deutsche Waffen und Munitionsfabrik* of Berlin was given a development contract.

Their designer, Heinemann, spent two years on the project and in 1911 produced the 'Parabellum' machine-gun. This was some 18 lbs. lighter than the Maxim, due to dispensing with the water jacket and redesigning the mechanism so that the toggle broke upwards. This change of direction of the toggle may sound like apple-polishing, with no significant effect, but in fact it saved a good deal of metal since the receiver could now be less deep and the attachment of the water jacket could be greatly simplified. In the case of the Parabellum, though, the barrel was enclosed in a perforated jacket, which allowed air to flow round the barrel to cool it, and the gun was fitted with a shoulder stock and a pistol grip for aircraft observers. It was a very good weapon and saw much service in the air. Had the army had sufficient forethought it would also have made an excellent light machine-gun for the infantry. As it was, when such a weapon was wanted, what the army got was simply the water-cooled Maxim minus its tripod.

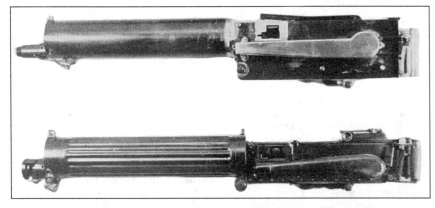

A Maxim gun *(top)* and below it a Vickers gun, showing the differences. Like the German Parabellum of the same period, the Vickers inverted the Maxim toggle and also re-calculated the stresses and safety limits, allowing a considerable saving of weight by reducing the thickness of metal and replacing some steel parts with lighter alloys. Notice the more compact receiver and the inversion of the fuzee-spring (return spring) cover on the side of the receiver. Both guns are chambered for the 303 British.

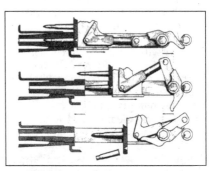

The action of the Vickers lock, showing how the toggle rises.

A late-model Vickers gun with muzzle booster, condensing can, and a panoramic collimating sight for indirect fire.

The other, and more famous, modification to the Maxim was the Vickers gun. This was a fairly simple re-design, involving turning the toggle upside down so that it broke in an upwards direction, and lightening some of the parts by the judicious calculation of stresses and the substitution of lighter metals.

The Vickers gun was introduced in November 1912 and remained in service with the British Army until 1968. It was a firm favorite with the army and performed some notable feats in its time. It had a maximum range of 4500 yards and could be fired, by using an optical dial sight, at targets out of direct view from the gun, the trajectory passing over intervening ground. One famous episode was the barrage fired by ten guns of the 100 Co., Machine Gun Corps on 24 August 1916, when almost one million rounds were fired, One gun fired 120,000 rounds without appreciable pauses and was working as perfectly at the end as it had been at the beginning.

One of the great myths of World War I is that the British Army, hide-bound and reactionary, refused to increase the allocation of machine guns in peacetime and thus entered the war with far fewer machine guns than the German Army. Which is not surprising; the allocation of machine guns in any army was done on a basis of so many machine guns per battalion. So the more battalions you have, the more machine guns you have. And the German Army in August 1914 was a great deal larger than the British Army, had many more battalions and hence many

more machine guns. Its actual allocation - two Maxims per infantry battalion - was exactly the same as the British two Vickers per battalion.

What really bedeviled the British Army's machine gun provision, and delayed its acceleration when war broke out, was the fact that the supply of Vickers guns had been halted once the service battalions of the first line divisions had been equipped in 1912-13. The reason for this goes back to the Lee-Enfield rifle and, while the rifle is not strictly our subject, it is necessary to digress a little in order to get the Vickers supply problem in perspective.

The first issues of the Short Lee-Enfield rifle had been greeted with scorn and abuse by the technical press and, particularly, by the target-shooting fraternity. The sport of rifle shooting had largely been built up in Britain around the military rifle, firstly with the Volunteer Force and then with the Territorial Army, so that there were thousands of men who learned to shoot as civilians but with military weapons and training. To them, the accuracy and target-shooting aspect was uppermost in their minds, and they were not slow to condemn the Short Lee Enfield on these grounds. They wanted something that would deliver bulls-eyes at 2000 yards range; after all, the South African War had shown how vital long-range rifle fire was in modern war.

The War Office finally gave up trying to talk sense into them and set the Royal Small Arms Factory the task of designing a new rifle that would satisfy the critics. This was the 'Enfield Pattern 1914' rifle, and in their search for ballistic perfection, the designers had made it in .276-caliber. Seeing this, the War Office, quite sensibly, said 'If we are

going to have a .276 rifle, then it follows that we will have to have a .276 machine gun. Therefore, cease manufacturing .303 machine guns until such time as this caliber question is settled.' And that was why there was no production of Vickers guns for the year preceding the outbreak of war, and no production line in operation in August 1914. When the war broke out, of course, the rifle project was immediately abandoned and no more was heard of the .276 chambering. But Vickers had to re-start their machine gun production plant and train new workers to run it before they could begin supplying the army with the guns they needed.

[Apropos of nothing in particular, it is an interesting historical oddity that whenever a Committee, Board, Panel or other gathering of the Wise and the Good convenes to determine the Ideal Caliber for a military rifle, they invariably select 7mm or .276. And another interesting historical oddity is that the army in question always ends up with some other caliber.]

By the middle 1900s it was already obvious that the machine gun was falling into a pre-destined mold: it would be belt-fed, water-cooled, mounted on a tripod and probably be given a small, heavy and totally useless shield. But behind the scenes it would seem that there were some people who thought that a machine gun might be more useful if it were to be more easily portable. Among them was Hotchkiss, where Lawrence V. Benet and his chief experimental mechanic Henri Mercié sat down to design what they called their 'Portative' model. The gas piston that they had perfected was retained, but the flap-locking system demanded too much space in the receiver and prevented them from getting the gun down to the compact size they desired. Mercié thought about this for some time and then came up with an elegant solution, the 'fermeture nut' method of locking.

The 'nut' is actually a steel ring, which fits around the rear end of the gun barrel, and has a rim formed into slots and lugs. The

(Continued on Page 57)

VICKERS
(and Maxim-pattern guns generally)

The standard Mark 1 Vickers complete with its regulation water condenser which - nine times out of ten - was, as here, a two-gallon 'Shell' gasoline can with a quick coat of khaki paint.

The Vickers is simply a Maxim in which the toggle joint which locks the breech has been inverted and in which the safety factors have been more exactly calculated and the components made lighter and of more appropriate metals. The result was a more compact and lighter weapon, and the corrugations in the water jacket *(to stiffen a lighter construction)* make the Vickers instantly recognizable. A similar inversion and lightening process produces the German Parabellum at more or less the same time.

The Vickers was produced in 303 and 50 Vickers chambering on a regular basis, and in 30-06, 13.2mm Hotchkiss and sundry other calibers on various occasions. There is an infinity of 'Marks' of different Vickers guns, but the differences are entirely cosmetic – water-cooling or air-cooling, different fittings to suit different aircraft, armored water-jackets for tanks and so forth. Underneath, the basic mechanism is always the same. Once you understand one Vickers, you understand them all.

Because of the unique Maxim operating system, operating a Vickers or Maxim is quite different from operating any other machine gun, and for that reason I append instructions for loading and unloading.

Loading:

Push the belt tag through the feed block from the right, and grasp it with the left hand as it appears on the other side. Hold against the tension, and with the other hand grasp the crank and turn it up and back to its fullest extent. Hold it back while you pull the belt through to the left as far as it will go, then release the crank handle. This will engage the first round in the belt in the extractor claw. Now turn the crank up and back once more, still pulling on the belt. This will extract the first round from the belt and chamber it, and engage the extractor with the second round on the belt. The gun is now ready to fire.

Unloading.

Due to the system of moving the belt by recoil of the gun parts, unloading has to be done in a systematic manner. Without touching the belt, pull back the crank handle as far as it will go, and then release it. This disposes of the round in the chamber and loads the next round. Now pull back the crank and release it once more. This draws out the round in the chamber and ejects it, but since the belt has not been moved, no fresh round is withdrawn to be loaded. Now lift the lower pawls by pressing the fingerplate and at the same time press down the top pawls with the thumb. This will free the belt and allow it to be pulled out from the right side of the gun. The wise man now operates the crank for a third time before lifting the safety latch and pressing the trigger.

Stripping:

Press in the rear cover latch and lift the receiver cover up and forward as far as it will go. Pull back the crank handle on to the roller and lift out the lock and connecting rod. Turn the lock about one-third of a turn clockwise to detach it from the connecting rod. Close the cover.

Go to the front of the gun, remove the split pin retaining the recoil booster to the muzzle, and remove the recoil booster. Using the combination tool, unscrew the muzzle cap and remove it. Lift the front cover latch by pulling it out and turning it counter-clockwise. Lift up the feed block and remove it. Close the cover.

DATA (Vickers Mark 1)	
Caliber	.303 British
Operating system	Short recoil, automatic
Locking system	Toggle lock
Feed system	250-round cloth belt
Overall length	45.5in (1155mm)
Weight, empty	40.0 lbs (18.1kg)
Barrel	28.5in (723mm), 4 grooves, right-hand twist
Muzzle velocity	2450 ft/sec (745 m/sec)
Muzzle energy	2310 ft/lbs (3121J)
Rate of fire	450 rds/min

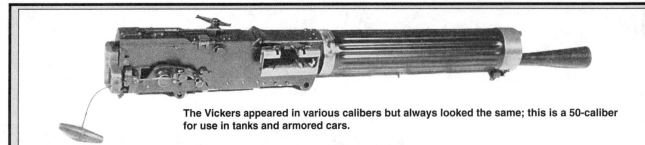

The Vickers appeared in various calibers but always looked the same; this is a 50-caliber for use in tanks and armored cars.

Push forward the fuzee-spring box on the left side of the receiver until the hooks at both ends are free from the studs on the receiver, lift the box clear and disconnect the spring from the fuzee chain. Remove the fuzee and chain to the left.

Lift the rear cover again. Unscrew the large T-head pin in the left rear of the receiver and allow the rear cross-piece to drop to the horizontal position. Now withdraw the left and right slides to the rear. Now pull the crank handle straight to the rear and the remaining components, with barrel, will be withdrawn.

Adjustment of cartridge head-space on these guns is an armorer's job, involving the use of special dummy rounds, various thicknesses of adjusting washers, a spring balance and special tools. It is therefore not described.

Re-assembly is simply a reversal of the stripping procedure.

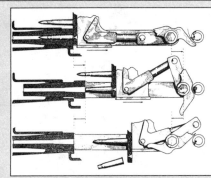

Operation of the Maxim lock in a Vickers gun. In the top picture there is a round in the chamber and one *(actually in the belt)* gripped by the T-slot. Then the barrel extension recoils so that the rear of the toggle hits a fixed roller and folds the toggle up; and finally the lock is fully opened, the empty case ejected, and the fresh round lined up with the chamber ready for the lock to close.

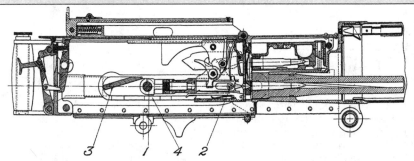

Why the Maxim lock stays locked. In the firing position the center of the crank pin *(1)* is below a straight line drawn between the center of the side-lever axis *(2)* and the crankshaft *(3)*, and the crank rests on the crank stop *(4)*. Therefore any pressure on the lock from the exploding cartridge will tend to force the crank down harder against its stop. Only when the recoiling parts go back far enough for the crank to be lifted by the fixed roller will the lock be permitted to open.

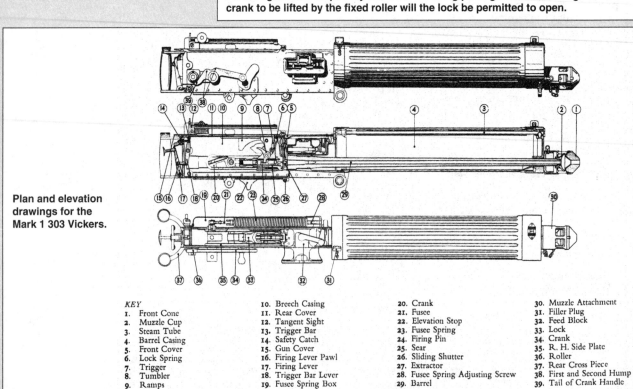

Plan and elevation drawings for the Mark 1 303 Vickers.

KEY			
1. Front Cone	10. Breech Casing	20. Crank	30. Muzzle Attachment
2. Muzzle Cup	11. Rear Cover	21. Fusee	31. Filler Plug
3. Steam Tube	12. Tangent Sight	22. Elevation Stop	32. Feed Block
4. Barrel Casing	13. Trigger Bar	23. Fusee Spring	33. Lock
5. Front Cover	14. Safety Catch	24. Firing Pin	34. Crank
6. Lock Spring	15. Gun Cover	25. Sear	35. R. H. Side Plate
7. Trigger	16. Firing Lever Pawl	26. Sliding Shutter	36. Roller
8. Tumbler	17. Firing Lever	27. Extractor	37. Rear Cross Piece
9. Ramps	18. Trigger Bar Lever	28. Fusee Spring Adjusting Screw	38. First and Second Hump
	19. Fusee Spring Box	29. Barrel	39. Tail of Crank Handle

The MacLean-Lisak 37mm automatic cannon, which was more or less a very large gas-operated machine gun developed in the early 1900s.

(Continued from Page 54)

breechblock - or bolt - has matching lugs formed on its head. The nut also has a lug or stud on the outer surface, beneath the chamber of the barrel. The gas piston has a curved cam path cut into its rear end which rides over the stud on the fermeture nut. As the gas piston is driven back by the pressure behind the bullet, it rotates the fermeture nut so as to bring the slots in its edge opposite the lugs on the bolt. As soon as the two are in alignment, the bolt can be driven backwards by the gas piston, compressing the usual sort of return spring. It then goes forward again, collects a fresh round from the feed system, chambers it and, as the bolt closes, the forward-moving gas piston rod pulls its stud through the cam path once more and rotates the fermeture nut back, so that the lugs on the nut lock behind the lugs on the bolt. The gun is then ready to fire the next round. The feed was by the usual Hotchkiss metal strip.

This was introduced in 1909 as the 'Hotchkiss Portative' and aroused immediate interest, especially from cavalry troops. They had, for some time, been seeking a machine gun, but the essence of cavalry action was speed and mobility, and the contemporary machine guns were not cast in that mold. So something as light as the Portative *(which was offered in some quarters as a 'machine rifle' to emphasize its light weight)* appeared to be the very thing the horsemen had been seeking. French and British cavalry both adopted it as the 'Light Hotchkiss' and the U.S. Army bought a number, calling it the 'Benet-Mercié Machine Rifle M1909'.

The last of the pre-1914 guns we need to consider and, with the Madsen and the Hotchkiss Portative, one of the pioneers of the light machine gun concept, is the Lewis gun.

I have often thought it a cruel trick of fate that MacLean, the man who invented the gun that became the Lewis Gun, is forgotten while Lewis, who did little more than fine-tune MacLean's design, got into the history books. I used to think that Lewis had a hard time of it from the US Ordnance Department, but on mature reflection I think MacLean had the short end of the stick and Lewis was something of an opportunist.

The origin of the Lewis was in a design by Samuel MacLean - who later developed one of the earliest of 37mm automatic cannons - and O.M. Lissak, a highly respected ordnance engineer. The weapon was first developed as the 'MacLean-Lissak Automatic Rifle,' and MacLean took out patents in 1903 and made some prototype guns, examples of which exist today. But for reasons best known to himself, MacLean chose to dispose of his patents to a company who proposed developing the gun. This firm is variously referred to as the Automatic Arms Company, or the Buffalo Arms Company; the only thing that seems settled is that they were in Buffalo, New York. In 1910 they approached Lewis and asked him to develop the MacLean patents into a viable gun, though at this remove of time it is difficult to ascertain exactly what was deficient in the MacLean gun as it stood.

As can be seen from the illustrations, the MacLean gun was a well-finished and compact piece of

(Continued on Page 60)

The rare MacLean machine gun, forerunner of the Lewis Gun. The large cylinder with rounded ends is the water jacket - the muzzle can be seen above a water drain-cock - and the cylinder beneath is the gas piston cylinder. This is one of the few occasions when a gas-operated gun has been cooled by water.

HOTCHKISS PORTATIVE Mle 1909

(and the Benet-Mercié Machine Rifle)

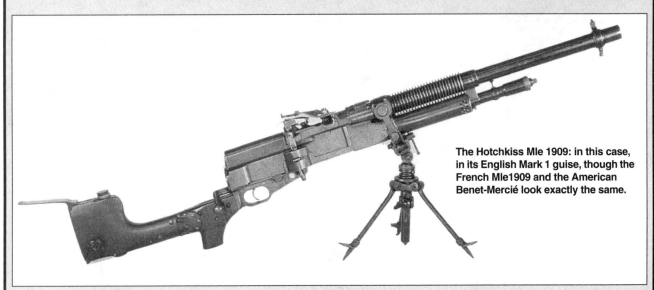

The Hotchkiss Mle 1909: in this case, in its English Mark 1 guise, though the French Mle1909 and the American Benet-Mercié look exactly the same.

Laurence V. Benet, the general manager of Hotchkiss & Cie, of Paris, was among the few people who saw the need for a light machine gun in the first years of the 20th century. After studying the performance of the Danish Madsen gun in the hands of Russian cavalry during the Russo-Japanese war of 1904, he began contemplating scaling-down the standard Hotchkiss gun. He was assisted by Henri Mercié, his head mechanic, who devised the 'Fermeture Nut' system of locking the breech, so making the mechanism more compact. Placed on the market as the 'Portative' in 1909 it was adopted by the U.S. Army as the Benet-Mercié Machine Rifle and by the British as simply the Hotchkiss Mark 1 for cavalry use.

The Benet-Mercié got a bad press during the Mexican war - mostly undeserved - and, outside the ranks of the cavalry, there was really very little interest in the idea of a light gun until the outbreak of war in 1914. Then, overnight, the light Hotchkiss became a hot property. It remained in use until the early 1940s, being brought out of the reserve stores by both British and French armies in 1939 and was not finally declared obsolete until 1946.

Field Stripping:

The Portative *(or the Benet-Mercié as you prefer)* is one of the most instantly recognizable machine guns in history. Its Hotchkiss parentage is advertised by the finned barrel and the strip feed, it usually sits on the most flimsy-looking small tripod, and the butt is a peculiar shape to permit the left *(or disengaged)* hand to grasp it

and thus give better control of the weapon when firing. And if confronted with the task of dismantling it, bear in mind that it is an 1900s design, made in the days when getting it to work well was the primary consideration, and ease of stripping and maintenance came some distance behind.

After removing the feed strip and clearing the gun, turn the cocking handle to the left as far it will go; draw it back about half an inch, and then turn it back to the right about 45 degrees. This disconnects it from the piston and it can be withdrawn to the rear.

Locate the lock screw on the left of the body and unscrew it three turns by means of the attached lever. Hold the gun body in the left hand and the butt in the right, and push forward the butt by about

DATA	
Caliber	8 x 50R Lebel
Operating system	Gas, automatic
Locking system	Fermeture nut
Feed system	30-round metal strip
Overall length	46.75 in (1187mm)
Weight, empty	27.0 lbs (12.25 kg)
Barrel	23.50 in (597mm); 4 grooves right-hand twist
Muzzle velocity	2180 ft/sec (665 m/sec)
Muzzle energy	2090 ft/lbs (2825J)
Rate of fire	500 rds/min
Effective range	500m

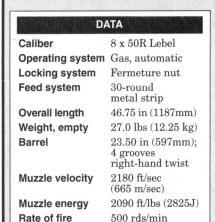

The Mle 1909, with a special cartridge feed strip holder, was the earliest aerial gun to be used by the French.

half an inch until it can be levered down at the rear and removed.

Now take the cocking handle and insert it into the rear of the gas piston, turning it at similar angles to when you removed it, so as to hook it back into the piston. Then turn it to the vertical and pull out the bolt and piston. Then remove the cocking handle from the piston and separate piston and bolt. Remove the firing pin from the bolt.

Open the feed-piece cover on the right side of the gun by pulling the knob outwards. Lift the rear sight leaf and turn it completely on its back. Lift the feed piece as far as possible, then rotate to the left until the feed lever points to the rear; then lift it up and to the rear to remove it.

Using the combination tool, unscrew the ejector cap and remove it.

Using the combination tool, rotate the barrel locking nut *(close to the chamber)* to the right until the left side of the claw aligns with the line inscribed on the gun body; then withdraw the barrel to the front. Turn the barrel locking nut back a little and remove the handguard; then unscrew and remove the barrel locking nut itself. You will now be able to insert a finger into the front of the receiver and extract the fermeture nut.

Putting it all back together again is simply a reversal of the above procedure, but there are, as usual, a few traps for the unwary.

Ensure the fermeture nut is replaced with the flat side to the front.

When screwing the barrel locking nut back into place, allow the claw to pass over the serrated stud *once*. Then stop screwing it

on and proceed with replacing the handguard. The round stud on the barrel locking nut must clear the handguard and then be turned down in order to receive the barrel.

When replacing the bolt and piston into the gun, first ensure the fermeture not is open; put the forefinger through the ejection opening and turn the nut into the slot in the nut lines up with the ejection port.

The firing pin must be rotated to the left in the bolt body before the bolt can be inserted into the receiver. When inserting, it will be necessary to raise the feed-piece to allow the piston to pass.

To replace the butt group, first replace the recoil spring into its recess in the piston. Put the front end of the cocking handle through the hole in the butt plate for about an inch and a half. Grip the cocking handle and butt together and maneuver the two until the head of the cocking handle enters the recoil spring. Grasp the receiver with the other hand and push the butt group forward, hook it into the receiver, and then lift the rear end into engagement and pull it back to lock. Turn the cocking handle lever until it is pointing 45 degrees to the right, push forward until it stops, then turn slightly left of the vertical, push forward again and turn down to the right.

To a generation that thinks little of replacing a camshaft in an automobile engine, the foregoing probably presents few difficulties. But in 1909, when the average soldier regarded the bolt-action rifle as a mechanical marvel, driving that lot into their heads must have been something of a trial for the instructors of the day.

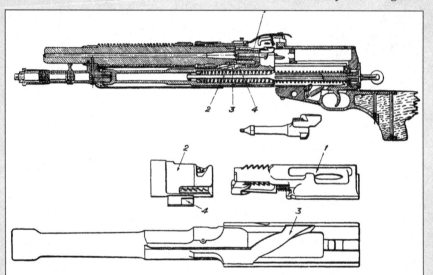

The essential parts of the Mercié design: *1)* the bolt; *2)* the fermeture nut; *3)* the helical groove on the piston slide; *4)* the lug on the fermeture nut. As the piston runs back, so the lug, driven by the groove, rotates the fermeture nut to unlock the bolt.

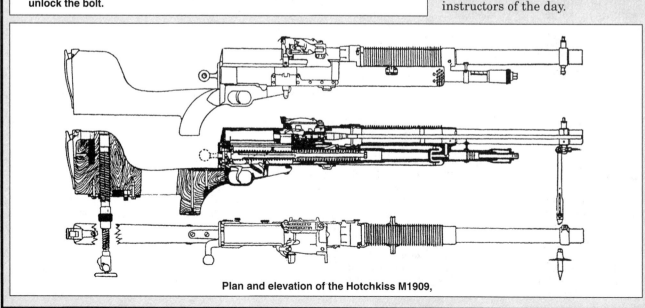

Plan and elevation of the Hotchkiss M1909,

The breech area of the MacLean 37mm cannon, showing the magazine housing, ejection port and cocking handle.

(Continued from Page 57)

work, particularly when you consider its early date. The large, round-ended cylinder is the water jacket, complete with inlet, outlet and safety valve, so that water could either be contained and evaporated or connected into a running supply, or connected to a condenser. The muzzle can be seen just poking out of the front end of this cylinder. Beneath it is the gas cylinder - so that MacLean might claim to being the first of the very few people who have managed to water-cool a gas-operated gun - and above this cylindrical section, at the rear, is the receiver and feed block surmounted by the drum magazine. There are two triggers, one for single shots and one for automatic fire; single shots being fired from a closed breech and automatic from an open breech. The caliber of this gun is 0.30-inch but I am unable to determine whether it is chambered for the 30-40 Krag or the 30-'03 cartridge. It is an impressive piece of work, and given that MacLean was undoubtedly hampered by the

many patents that had been taken out by hopefuls as well as by practical inventors, he seems to have produced a viable solution. It seems that the U.S. Army reported that it was violent in action and somewhat erratic in its stoppages, but this, for the time, was scarcely surprising and I feel that with some more work it could have been a quite serviceable weapon. Whatever led MacLean to dispose of his patents - and it was probably the prospect of a greater and more immediate success with his large-caliber cannon - he certainly deserves more credit that he has hitherto received for his place in the pioneering of the machine gun in the USA.

Lewis, at this time, was a Lieutenant Colonel in the U.S. Coast Artillery and a highly respected technical officer; in 1891 he had invented the Lewis Depression Position Finder, a fundamental fire control device. He later became the Recorder for the Board of Ordnance and Fortification, and in 1904 went to Fortress Monroe Coast Artillery School as an instructor and remained there to become Director, the post he held when approached by the Buffalo company. He accepted their offer - whatever it may have been, and some say cash and others say stock - and presumably spent his evenings and free time fiddling with MacLean's design.

His major modifications and additions appear to have been in the air-cooling system and the coiled return spring, both of which we will examine later. But over and above the mere technical changes, he made a fundamental decision and turned it from being a tripod-mounted, water-cooled medium gun into a shoulder-fired, air-cooled light gun.

He took out patents in 1912, and is said to have made a 'working model' in the same years, which argues an astonishing mechanical ability that one would not expect to find in a senior Coast Artillery officer. I think it more likely that he produced a set of drawings and the Buffalo Company had a gun made. But whichever way it was, it was about this time, and probably a direct result of this prototype, that he ran foul of the autocratic General William Crozier, Chief of Ordnance. The details of their quarrel are lost, but it seems to have been a severe personality clash; Crozier's stated objection was that he felt it wrong that a serving officer of the U.S. Army should receive money, or money's worth, from a private company for doing something in his spare time.

Crozier, it should be pointed out, was the joint patentee of the Buffington-Crozier disappearing gun mounting, which was installed in forts the length and breadth of the USA and its dependencies, and we would be naive to suppose that he did not receive some financial benefit from it. But in the fine Old Army spirit of *'Don't do as I do, do as I tell you.'* Crozier put Lewis under considerable pressure, and in 1913 Lewis resigned his commission *'on the grounds of ill-health'* and became a civilian, though granted the honorary rank of colonel. He continued his development work and submitted four guns to the U.S. Army for trial.

Unfortunately, in those days the development of weapons for the U.S. Army was entirely in the hands of the Ordnance Department: as Crozier announced, the development of guns would be *"conducted by the Ordnance Department, through the instrumentality of Ordnance officers, by the methods of the Ordnance Department, and at the Ordnance Department's place"* and the fighting arms had nothing to do except thank the Ordnance Department when they finally received the weapon. It comes, therefore, as no great surprise to find that the Lewis gun was rejected out of hand with only the most perfunctory trial. It was stated to be too violent in its action, which was probably true, but in other cases this sort of defect had been the subject of examination and recommendations to the inventor, followed by re-testing. Not in Lewis's case.

It is at this point that the story becomes even more clouded. One might have expected the Buffalo company and Lewis to have now gone to Colt or Winchester or some other large US company and tried to interest them in promoting the design. But, instead, Lewis took his guns and his designs and his patents and went off to Belgium, there to set up, with the aid of a Belgian financier, a fresh company called *Armes Automatiques Lewis SA*. Whatever happened to the Buffalo company and its employees and shareholders is a minor mystery; they never appear again in any records of the Lewis gun and its development. And what happened after Lewis arrived in Belgium belongs to the World War I period and will be dealt with in the next chapter.

The Lewis was a gas-operated gun, and Lewis' principal innovations were the cooling system and the unusual method of fitting the return spring. It is well to recall that in the first decade of the 20th century almost all the basic features of the machine gun were securely patented, and the greatest problem confronting a would-be inventor was that of evading these existing patents and still producing a workable gun. B.B. Hotchkiss had the gas piston-operated gun fairly well sewed up, and a simple piston with a concentric return spring or a return spring behind it might have been seen as a patent infringement, although MacLean had used something similar. So Lewis put a clock spring into a little casing, attached it to a gearwheel, and then cut the teeth of a rack into the under-surface of the gas piston. As the piston went back, the teeth of the rack rotated the gearwheel and wound up the spring. There was a simple coiled buffer spring at the back end of the receiver, and the piston struck this and came to a halt, and the wound-up spring then took charge and began to unwind, driving the gear-wheel and thus pulling the piston rod forward. And as it attempted to go forward it was held by the sear and trigger. Pulling the trigger released the sear, the piston went forward, and the gun went into its cycle of operation, driven by the clock spring and gear-wheel.

It follows from this that the Lewis gun has one unusual attribute: you can vary the strength of the return spring and thus compensate for fouling or poor ammunition, or you can increase or decrease the rate of fire within limits. If you pull back the piston for an inch or two, you begin to load the clock spring. If you now lock the pinion and then disengage it from the piston, push the piston back to its forward position, then re-engage the pinion, you have the spring pre-loaded before the piston begins to move, so that there will be more resistance to movement and the piston will be driven forward faster on the loading stroke. If you disengage the pinion, pull back the piston an inch or two, re-engage the pinion and push the piston forward, you have an inch or two of free play before the spring starts to load, reducing the resistance to the gas pressure and speeding up the rate of fire. Not something to be done as a regular pastime, and most instructional texts do not even mention it, but quite a novelty in its way.

The rear end of the piston rod was flattened and carried, rising from this flattened portion, a 'piston post' that terminated in a quite substantial firing pin. The bolt was cylindrical and hollow, with a hole in the front end to allow the tip of the firing pin to pass through, and with lugs at the rear end. The piston post and firing pin were inserted into the bolt through a curved slot in its bottom surface. When the piston was at its rearmost position, held by the sear, the lugs on the bolt rode in pathways cut into the walls of the receiver, which prevented the bolt rotating in any direction. When the trigger was pressed and the sear released, the piston rod ran forward, driven by the clock-spring, and carried the bolt with it. The piston post pressed against one side of the curved slot and consequently drove the bolt forward, the lugs still riding in the receiver grooves and keeping the bolt from turning. The top edge of the bolt now collected a fresh cartridge from the magazine and rammed it into the chamber, and just as the bolt completed this ramming action, so the lugs came to the end of their restraining slots. The piston rod, continuing forward, now pulled the piston post through the curved portion of the slot, so turning the bolt lugs into engagement with locking recesses in the receiver. As the bolt reached the fully locked position, so the curved slot in the bolt became a straight slot and the piston post was now able to run down this at full speed and thrust the firing pin through the bolt face to fire the cartridge.

Having fired, a small portion of the gas passing up the bore behind the bullet was bled off into the gas cylinder beneath the barrel where it started to drive the piston back once more. At the other end of the piston the piston post was now driven back down the straight portion of the slot in the bolt, withdrawing the firing pin, and as it came to the curved part of the slot the post bore against the other side of the slot and caused it to rotate so as to unlock it and align the lugs with the traveling slots in the receiver. Once they were aligned the rearward movement of the piston opened the bolt, the extractor drew out the empty case and ejected it and the bolt ran all the way back to the buffer spring and, if the trigger was still pressed, started back for the next shot. It was all or nothing with the Lewis gun: automatic only, no single-shot mechanism; but the rate of fire was slow enough to let a skilled soldier touch off single shots with some precision.

Now, as we all know by now, firing a machine gun generates heat which has to be got rid of, and here comes the next Lewis gun novelty; the cooling system (*such as it was*). The barrel and gas cylinder were surrounded by a series of aluminum fins that were heated by the

(Continued on Page 64)

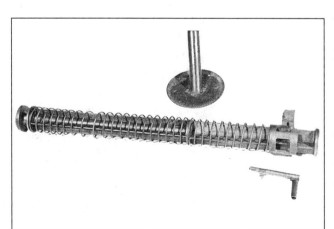

The gas piston, return spring and cocking handle of the MacLean gun *(the round object is the foot of the tripod, left here to show scale)*. The left-hand end of the unit is the gas piston; the right end is cut and shaped to operate the breechblock.

THE LEWIS GUN

The original Lewis, complete with air-cooling jacket, 47-round drum; the bag for spent cartridges was not usual on ground service guns.

The story of the Lewis has been told elsewhere at some length, so we need not repeat it here, but we have room for a couple of diversions

It appears that the last Lewis guns to see service were British, being finally declared obsolete in June 1946. Among the guns listed for scrapping was the 'Gun Machine, Lewis, .303inch SS', and investigation showed that 'SS' meant 'Shoulder Shooting' and it had been instigated by the Royal Navy as an antiaircraft weapon for small ships. It was, in fact, the usual sort of conversion by removing the radiator and its cover and then fitting a steel handguard to protect the gas cylinder from damage.

I have seen, in a serious work on air armament, a story that a World War I pilot flying an airplane with a Lewis gun mounted on the top wing, stood up in his cockpit to change magazines. As he slapped the new magazine into place, his airplane began to roll, and before he could do anything it had rolled far enough for him to slide out of the cockpit, still hanging onto the Lewis magazine strap. He held on while the plane completed its roll and he dropped back into the cockpit, released his

An air service Lewis, with the original cooling jacket removed, 97-round magazine and cartridge bag. Note that this has had an extension butt added to the spade grip and an angle-iron bipod, indicating that it was an emergency issue to the British Home Guard in 1940.

grip and carried on with getting the machine under control again.

Field Stripping

Stripping the Lewis can be something of a nightmare if approached from the wrong direction; one needs to be systematic and break the task down into three distinct groups.

Before starting, of course, remove the magazine and pull back the cocking handle a couple of times to ensure there is no ammunition left in the feedway or chamber and that the gun is empty.

The Piston Group

Press forward the catch on the underside of the butt front; British guns usually have a thumb-piece to press, but some do not, and no American guns have one and thus require the use of a screwdriver, or the nose of a bullet. Rotate the butt counter-clockwise and remove it. Press the trigger and draw back the pistol grip slightly. Pull back the cocking handle and withdraw it side-ways, then pullout the bolt and piston rod. Remove the bolt from the piston post. Unhook the pinion casing (*the 'clock spring' in front of the trigger unit*) and remove it.

The Body Group

Pull back the body cover about half an inch and remove it. Using the nose of a bullet or your Swiss Army Knife, remove the cartridge guide, which is the spring in the curved component in the front of the body cover. Then take out the stop pawl spring and stop pawls, which are the two arms supported by a leaf spring on the underside of the body cover,

Remove the feed arm from the magazine post by moving the arm to the right until it can be lifted off. In British guns it will be necessary to depress the latch on the forward end of the arm in order to move it; American guns do not have a retaining latch. With the feed arm off, it is then possible to remove the feed arm pawl and spring, which lie about half-way along the top of the feed arm.

DATA (U.S. M1917)	
Caliber	.30 M1906
Operating system	Gas, automatic
Locking system	Rotating bolt
Feed system	47 or 97-round drum
Overall length	51.75in (1314mm)
Weight, empty	25lb 4oz (11.45 kg)
Barrel	26.25in (667mm); 4 grooves, right-hand twist
Muzzle velocity	2830 ft/sec (863 m/sec)
Muzzle energy	2640 ft/lbs (3568J)
Rate of fire	500 rds/min
Effective range	600m

A top view of the Lewis Mark 1 gun.

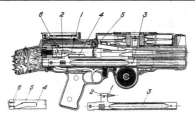

The basic components of the Lewis gun: *1)* the firing pin; *2)* the piston post; *3)* the piston slide; *4)* the helical groove on *5)* the bolt, which carries *6)* the locking lugs.

Now remove the body locking pin, at the lower front of the gun body, by pressing it out with a bullet. Withdraw the pistol grip to the rear and then unscrew the body from the barrel group.

The Barrel Group

The next operation depends upon whether you are stripping a ground gun, with the large barrel jacket and radiator, or an air service gun with exposed barrel and gas cylinder.

With a *ground gun:* Using the gas regulator key, unscrew the locking ring just inside the front end of the jacket, and remove it and the front part of the jacket. Remove the bipod and the gas regulator. Remover the rest of the jacket. Unscrew the gas cylinder and remove it, then remove the muzzle piece *(which has a left-hand thread)* from the barrel.

With *aircraft guns:* remove the gas regulator; unscrew and remove the gas cylinder; unscrew and remove the muzzle brake.

It is possible to go further and strip the pinion and spring and the trigger group, but for normal maintenance there is no need to go to those lengths.

How the piston post, firing pin and bolt fit together and operate.

Firing pin · Locking lugs · Feed stud · Bolt · Piston extension · Piston post · Cam path

And here are two elderly Home Guards being trained in anti-aircraft shooting in 1941.

Re-Assembly

Re-assembly should be tackled by groups, as was the stripping, and in general is simply a reverse of the operations described above. There are, though, one or two points which need to be watched.

When replacing the feed arm, if the piston and bolt are in the gun body, take care to connect the tail of the feed arm to the actuating stud *(the pear-shaped stud on the top rear of the bolt).*

When replacing the stop pawls, make sure that the number on the pawl and the number on the pawl post agree.

When replacing the bolt and piston, ensure that the feed arm is over to the left and the actuating stud fully screwed into the bolt. If there is an obstruction when replacing the piston and bolt into the body, press back the tail of the ejector, lying on the left inside of the body.

After re-assembly, adjust the return spring *(the 'clock spring')* to about 13 lbs pressure, *(measured by a spring balance)* as follows: unlatch the butt and pull the pistol grip slightly back. Then lift the pinion until it connects with the rack on the piston rod and pull back the cocking handle about two inches. This will increase the spring strength by about five pounds. To reduce the strength, disconnect the pinion group, pull back the cocking handle an inch or two, then lift the pinion back into engagement with the rack and push forward the pistol grip. The cocking handle will run forward and the tension on the return spring is reduced. Hook the spring balance to the cocking handle and pull back, observing the reading when the handle begins to move.

Before firing, set the gas regulator to 'No 2' *(on a British gun)* or to the smallest hole *(in an American gun).*

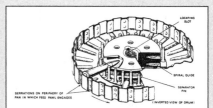

LOCATING SLOT · SPIRAL GUIDE · SEPARATOR PIN · SERRATIONS ON PERIPHERY OF PAN IN WHICH FEED PAWL ENGAGES · (INVERTED VIEW OF DRUM)

The interior of the Lewis drum. To load it, the center is held still and the pan section revolved around as rounds are dropped in, so that they follow 'round the spiral groove until it is full.

(Continued from Page 61)

barrel; these fins were enclosed in a light metal cylindrical casing which was open at the rear end and which extended for a short distance in front of the muzzle. The theory was that the expansion of gases at the muzzle as the gun fired would set up a current of air such that cool air would enter the casing at the rear end, flow over the aluminum fins and cool them down *(and, by transference, cool down the barrel - or at least, conduct heat away from the barrel so that it didn't overheat)* and be drawn out and dispersed at the muzzle.

Well, there is no doubt that the Lewis doesn't overheat, and in the conditions of the trench warfare of World War I, where machine guns tended to fire for relatively long periods of time, it was probably a useful device. But in World War II huge numbers of ex-aircraft Lewis guns, which did not have this elaborate cooling system because they spent their lives out in the slipstream and were well and truly air-cooled, were issued to ground troops in Britain. I had my share of dashing around with one of these guns; they were lighter than the original pattern and a good deal handier to carry, and they never appeared to be seriously affected by overheating. And I think that this was due to the different tactical theories of the time: World War II was a much more mobile and fluid war, and the light machine gun was never called upon to indulge in long periods of continuous fire. Three- to five-round bursts was what we were trained to fire, and with a brief pause between bursts allowing a flow of cool air through the barrel *(for the Lewis fired from an open bolt of course)*, everything worked perfectly well.

The magazine was a flat pan on top of the receiver; again, a bit of a novelty. Other people have used pan magazines since, but none quite the same as the Lewis. That distinctive serrated edge to the Lewis magazine wasn't there for ornament; it was an integral part of the gun mechanism. The magazine consisted of two principal parts, the central core and the cover. The core had a central locating hole that sat on the magazine post of the gun, a spiral groove into which the nose of the bullet fitted, and a series of pegs forming a circle around the core. The cover was simply a flat pan with an indented edge. To load the magazine a special tool was inserted to free the core while holding the cover, and rounds were placed in so that the nose went into the spiral groove, the bullet lay between two pegs and the base of the cartridge fitted into the indents in the edge of the cover. You then fed rounds in, turning the core so that the cartridges gradually passed down the spiral and – eventually – after shoving 47 cartridges in, you had a full magazine.

The magazine was then placed on the magazine post; there was a key on the post and a slot in the hole in the magazine core, so that it could only go on one way and once on, the core remained stationary. Having got the magazine on, the gunner gave it a smack with his hand to rotate it and bring the first cartridge into the feedway. Which hand he used depended on who made the gun; with a British-made Lewis he gave it a 'pull' slap with the right hand; with an American gun he gave it a 'push' slap with the left hand. The reason being that he wanted to use the same hand to both set the magazine and operate the cocking handle, and the handles were on different sides.

The bolt carried a stud at its top rear, and when the bolt moved back and forward this stud moved in a curved slot in a feed arm, pivoted in the top of the receiver. As the bolt moved, so the arm was driven from side to side and a ratchet on its tip engaged with the serrated edge of the magazine and rotated it. A pair of 'butterfly pawls', spring-loaded catches, made sure that the drum only moved round one space and only in the right direction.

A 47-round magazine was considered sufficient for ground use – after all, it weighed four pounds – but when the aerial gunners adopted the gun they asked for more and got a 97-round drum, which worked the same way but weighed twice as much.

As you might have gathered from the foregoing description, the mechanism of the Lewis was quite simple *(which is doubtless why it met with military approval)* and yet it still has a reputation for unreliability and stoppages. Much of this was due to the trench conditions in 1914-18; in my own experience, provided you kept the gun clean and didn't drop it in the mud or sand, it would keep going with no trouble. The 'Immediate Action' drills were few and simple, and the only serious defect would be a broken feed pawl spring or a broken return spring, both of which could be quickly rectified.

And so, as the world entered the second decade of the 20th century, the principal armies were all machine-gun conscious; they had the guns, they had the trained soldiers. Exactly how they were going to use those guns, what tactics they were to employ, how they were to be distributed within the military formations, how they would affect tactical operations... all these were yet to be determined. They were determined in the following four years, and in a very painful manner.

CHAPTER FOUR

WORLD WAR I

BY 1914 THE machine gun was an accepted feature of all armies, though I would not go so far as to say that all armies appreciated the manifold uses to which the machine gun could be put. The 1914-18 war was going to reveal these to them in due course. In general, the purpose of the machine gun was accepted as being the immediate support weapon for the infantry, and the usual disposition was to give two guns to each infantry battalion. Their task was therefore to provide supporting fires during the attack and act as a reserve for the riflemen in the defense, being available to thicken up the fire wherever the attackers were pressing hardest. In some ways they were still treated as a species of artillery; from mediaeval days it had been customary to place artillery on the flanks of the army

where it could rake the approaching enemy with '*enfilade* fire' - where the line of fire was parallel to the enemy's line of advancing troops, so that the cannon could bowl over half a dozen or more men in the line with one shot. Placing a machine gun on the flank and firing across the front would similarly sweep the line of attackers and, similarly, dispose of them far more efficiently than if the gun was in front of them and traversing from side to side.

The ballistic reasoning behind this concept of flanking fire is based upon the '*Dangerous Space*' of the gun, and the *Dangerous Space* is defined as the area between the *First Catch* and the *First Graze*. And if that is not clear, this is because these three phrases have virtually vanished from military textbooks, even if the effects themselves are still in existence.

The *First Catch* and *First Graze* are two points on the end of the trajectory of the bullet; the *First Catch* is the point at which it has descended low enough to strike the head of the average soldier. This is the commencement of the *Dangerous Space*. The bullet then speeds on, getting closer and closer to the ground until it finally strikes the ground at the *First Graze*, which is the end of the *Dangerous Space*. It follows from this that if you have a row of soldiers and you shoot from the front, for any given line of fire you can only hit one man and, should you miss, the remainder of the *Dangerous Space* is wasted. But if you position your gun to a flank and open fire along the whole line, every man between the *First Catch* and the *First Graze* is at risk from every bullet and with any luck you could catch two or possibly three with a single bullet.

Beyond the *First Graze* point there lies a second zone of importance, called the *Beaten Zone* (or sometimes the *Effective Beaten Zone*). To explain this you need to remember that the firing of any weapon is governed by the laws of chance; if you sink a machine gun into a fifty-ton block of concrete, so that no recoil or jump or vibration is going to alter the position of the gun, and you then fire 100 rounds out of it, they will not all go through the same hole at the target. Some will go high, some low, some right, some left – most a little bit of any two. The result can be visualized as a cone of bullets passing through the air and widening as it goes. Of that cone, the lowest bullet will obviously be the first to strike the ground at its particular *First Graze* point. The highest bullet will strike the ground some distance further away from the gun. The most right and most left bullets will also have their individual impact points. And if we draw an ellipse on the ground which includes all the 100 bullets, we have defined the *Beaten Zone* - the

A French machine gun team dashing into action with their M1897 Hotchkiss in 1914. A somewhat unorthodox way of carrying it, but at least it was ready to fire as soon as they dropped it, and in August 19124 speed was of the essence.

By 1915 they were walking into action with their St. Etienne gun separated from its tripod.

zone into which all the bullets fired at a constant elevation will fall; or, looking at it another way, the zone into which any bullet will fall if fired at that particular elevation. The *Dangerous Space* applies to all firing done with a machine gun *(or any other small arm for that matter)* but the *Beaten Zone* is of particular reference to the use of a medium machine gun on a fixed line when firing a defensive barrage so as to deny a stretch of ground to an enemy. If you know the size of the *Beaten Zone* at the particular range at which you are firing *(and this sort of thing is determined during the initial trial firing when the gun is developed)* then all you need do is space your guns so that their Beaten Zones overlap slightly and cover the desired area. Once your guns open fire, nobody entering that area will be safe; the laws of chance will see to it that he will inevitably hit by a bullet.

The allocation of two guns per battalion was an administrative convenience as well as being a tactical disposition. The trouble was, though, that each battalion regarded its two guns as its private property and thus this battalion might well be fighting for its life with two guns, while the next-door battalion, not involved, had two guns doing nothing. The German army put an end to this by placing all six guns of a three-battalion regiment under the command of a Regimental Machine Gun officer, and his job was to dispose of the six guns in the best and most effective manner. Thus when one battalion was attacked, or ran into a defensive position, all six guns could be brought into play at the vital point; it was this flexibility which convinced the British and French that the Germans had far more machine guns than they actually possessed. It's not what you have; it's how you use it that counts. (Another factor, perhaps less obvious, was the readiness of the German soldier to be grouped into *ad hoc* battle groups and small formations, not necessarily of his own regiment and with strange NCOs and officers.)

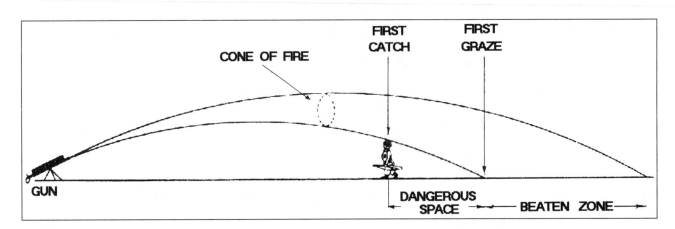

The trajectory of the bullet and the geometry of the target area.

The German Maxim MG '08 on its sledge mount was the German mainstay throughout the war.

The German Army has always been highly flexible in this respect, and not so parochial as are British, French and US soldiers, who seldom perform at their best when divorced from their parent unit.)

A story beloved of those critics who believed that the pre-1914 British army was entirely ignorant of the machine gun's worth, concerns the young officer detailed off to take charge of the machine gun section on a pre-war maneuver. *"Take them off to a flank and hide them,"* growled his superior. This is claimed to show that the superior had no idea of what to do with them and didn't wish to see them on his battlefield. But on reflection, he was perfectly correct: take them to a flank (so that could take the attackers in *enfilade*) and hide them (so that the attackers would be surprised and massacred). Precisely the tactics used so effectively by the Maxim gunners of the German Army in 1915-18.

Conversely, there is another legend of World War I that dies hard, and this is that the machine gun was the supreme killer. Not so. The British army suffered 38.9 percent of its total war casualties from rifle and machine gun bullets; but 51.5 percent from artillery shell splinters or shrapnel balls. Similar figures can be found for every other

combatant, though the difference is not so pronounced for the AEF since a greater proportion of their experience was in the more mobile war of late 1918. But make no mistake; artillery killed far more people than did the machine gun.

Although the makes were different, there was a close similarity between all the machine guns used by the major powers in 1914. They were almost all water-cooled, almost all belt-fed, and carried on tripods or sledge mounts of varying complexity and weight. Many were provided with shields for the gunner and his mate, but these were very soon thrown away or, more usually, removed and used in the parapet of trenches as a bullet-proof screen for the company sniper. A square shield stood out of the battlefield like a sore thumb and simply attracted fire. Far better to get the mounting down as low as possible, lie behind the gun and take your chances. The water-cooling systems also took some modification; several countries neglected to provide steam condensers, with the result that as soon as the gun boiled a plume of steam from the safety valve would signal the position of the gun. The condenser was adopted as much to conceal this tell-tale marker as for economy of water.

The light machine gun, either as a weapon or as a tactical concept was virtually unknown in 1914; the only weapons which could have been classified as *light* were the Madsen, used by the Russian cavalry, the Hotchkiss M1909, used by British and French cavalry, and a handful of Lewis guns held by the Belgian army. Initially they were simply considered as lightweight versions of water-cooled guns and were used in precisely the same tactical manner, providing covering and supporting fire. But shoulder-fired light guns were not the best weapons for sustained fire, and gradually the virtues of lightness were appreciated by other elements of the armies, so that water-cooled guns became the heavy support and light air-cooled guns became the preferred assault infantryman's weapon, easily carried and quickly brought into action to deal with what the old text-books called 'targets of opportunity' - in other words, the odd enemy who poked his head up at the wrong moment.

The British eventually carried it a step further by withdrawing all the Vickers machine guns from infantry battalions and grouping them into an entirely new regiment, the Machine Gun Corps, who then disposed of the guns in batteries, giving massive supportive firepower in either attack or defense, while the infantry conducted their day-to-day affairs with the Lewis – but that was some time off in 1914.

It will be recalled that Lewis had set up a company in Belgium in 1913, and this firm, *Armes Automatiques Lewis,* was vested with the sole rights to produce the Lewis Gun in the Eastern hemisphere. The rights to the Western Hemisphere were licensed to the Savage Repeating Arms Company in Utica, New York. Lewis's next task was to organize production. His original intention was to recruit a number of sub-contractors to manufacture the various parts of the gun, and to set up a factory that would then assemble these parts into complete guns. This proved impossible, since small contractors with the necessary machinery and skills were not to be found, and Lewis went off to Britain to discuss the matter with the Birmingham Small Arms Company (BSA), who were experienced in the manufacture of military

weapons. As soon as they saw Lewis's gun they were enthused; they could see the potential in it and in short order they took over the sole rights from the Belgian firm and began setting up a production line. Lewis remained in Britain to act as consultant and, together with the BSA engineers, made several modifications to the weapon in order to simplify manufacture and improve its performance. This was a fortunate move for Lewis, because in 1914 the German army occupied Liege and *Armes Automatiques Lewis SA* simply vanished overnight.

Lewis now recedes into the background, doubtless living on his license fees, though it is recorded that during World War I he returned every penny of license fees earned from the USA to the US Government. (And even then Crozier tried to have the money refused on the grounds that it constituted bribery.) He seems to have played no further part in the development of the gun, and died in Hoboken in November 1931.

The military service of the Lewis began in 1913 with sales to the Belgian and Russian armies. The British army ordered a handful out of curiosity; recall that in those days the concept of the light machine gun was unknown. Machine guns were big, heavy, water-cooled, and were meant to fire for long periods non-stop. And the wise men in military forces in Europe shook their heads over the Lewis gun, because it was obviously none of those things. To be blunt, in 1913 the Lewis gun was a solution looking for a problem. This, though, changed very rapidly when the German Army invaded Belgium in August 1914 and the Belgians brought their Lewis guns into action; suddenly the Lewis gun made rather more sense and orders began to flow into BSA. Before long the orders were so enormous that an alternative source had to be found and the British Army contracted with Savage in the USA to produce several thousand guns. But it was still slow to get the rate of production the war demanded

Stolen fruit taste the sweetest. An Austrian Schwarzlose machine gun captured by the Russians during the 1914 campaigns and used by them as an air defense gun.

The Hotchkiss Mle 1909 was favored by cavalry because it was light and because they rarely needed much sustained firing.

and although the official British date of approval of the Lewis gun was October 1915 it was actually well into 1916 before everybody was satisfied and production was keeping up with losses.

The American army's initial experience with the Lewis was unfortunate. The four guns that Lewis offered for test in 1913 were to his original design and the slot in the bolt, through which the piston post engaged, was only 0.875-inch long, which gave the gun a particularly violent action. The BSA company, with their considerable experience of firearms design, saw that this was a severe drawback and they lengthened the slot to 1.062-inches. That's a difference of 0.187-inch (three-sixteenths of an inch), but it was the difference between a violent gun, which tore rims off cartridges, and a reliable gun that was built by the million. After seeing the success of the Lewis in Europe the US Army decided to acquire a number for extended troop trials, and bought 350 guns from Savage. These were originally destined for the British army and were therefore chambered and regulated for the 303 cartridge and were supplied together with a quantity of that ammunition, and in operations on the Mexican border in 1915 they performed quite well. Encouraged by this, the US Army then asked Savage to adapt the gun to the standard US 30-06 cartridge and commence production.

Savage did a somewhat hurried conversion once they had completed their contract for the Brit-

ish, and supplied the first guns to the US Army in May 1917. They proved to be a total disaster; they had gone back to Lewis's original design and used the short-length cam slot, and the gas port and piston were designed to work with the British 303 cartridge, which used Cordite propellant. The American 30-06 of the period used 'Pyro Powder', a very fast-burning propellant of very different characteristics and a different pressure-space curve with a higher mean pressure. It was not, as is often claimed, *'far more powerful'* than the 303; the actual increase in power was about nine percent in muzzle energy, and the 303 round had a considerably higher maximum pressure, but burning pattern of the powder and hence the distribution of pressure in the gun barrel was completely different, with the result that the action of the gun was exceptionally violent, ripping rims off cartridges and jamming at the slightest provocation.

Savage reverted to the long slot devised by BSA and re-designed the gas port and piston and the troubles vanished. Eventually the army bought 2,500 M1918 Lewis guns, but a bad reputation once gained takes some living down and the army never entirely trusted the gun, retaining it for training purposes in the USA only and relying *(if that is the right word)* on the Chauchat for field operations in France. The US Navy bought over 4000 for the Marine Corps, who took it to France and had nothing but good to say of it. They retained it in service until the 1930s,

whereas the army couldn't mothball theirs fast enough in 1919.

As an *aircraft* gun, though, the Lewis flourished. Indeed, its possible application to aerial combat had been among the first possibilities to be explored and in both the USA and Britain it had been carried aloft in primitive aircraft and fired at ground targets with moderate success before the outbreak of war; from which one can deduce that the application of machine guns to aircraft was seen, in modern parlance, as an 'air-to-ground weapon' and not as a means of combat between aircraft. But on 22nd August 1914 two British aviators, Lieutenants Strange and Gaskell, took a Lewis gun aloft in a stick-and-string airplane and took a few shots at a German Albatross scouting airplane over Belgium. They reported their success at driving the German off, but they were rapped across the knuckles for their audacity: *How dare they? They might provoke the Germans into shooting back, and then where shall we all be?*

When the fact of aerial combat made itself felt, the Lewis gun was seized upon by the aviators because it had one great advantage over the Maxim and Vickers guns which were the only alternatives: it was a good deal lighter, and the power-to-weight ratio of the 1914-15 airplane was such that every ounce that could be saved was a bonus. It was generally accepted that you could carry a Lewis gun and 300 rounds of ammunition in the early fighter planes, and very quickly one or two aviators began removing the

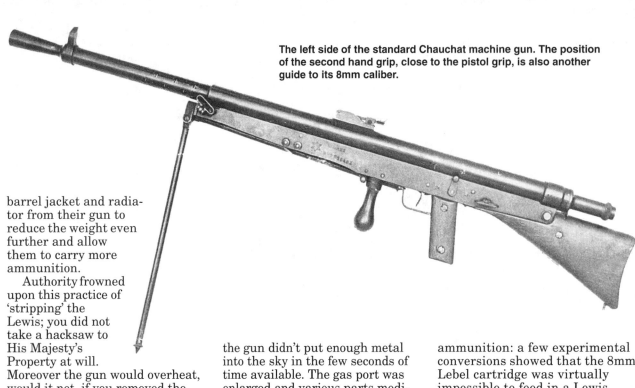

The left side of the standard Chauchat machine gun. The position of the second hand grip, close to the pistol grip, is also another guide to its 8mm caliber.

barrel jacket and radiator from their gun to reduce the weight even further and allow them to carry more ammunition.

Authority frowned upon this practice of 'stripping' the Lewis; you did not take a hacksaw to His Majesty's Property at will. Moreover the gun would overheat, would it not, if you removed the radiator and jacket? Well, no, actually, said the aviators, you see we are traveling at about 100 miles an hour and the wind blowing across the gun.... Yes, well, what about the gas cylinder? The slightest knock on that, it's only thin metal you know, and the gun is out of action. Yes, you have a point; we'll make a wooden protector for that... And so the arguments flew, but the pilots still stripped their Mark 1 Lewis Guns.

Eventually since there seemed no other solution, the Authorities relented and the Mark 2 gun appeared in 1915. This was the Mark 1 with the cooling fins and jacket removed, the gas cylinder strengthened and the butt removed and replaced by a spade grip. In 1916 the 97-round drum was introduced for use with this gun.

Next, the aviators complained because the gun was not fast enough; airplanes were getting faster, so that engagement times – the period during which two airplanes were in shooting distance of each other – were getting shorter, and at 550 rounds per minute the gun didn't put enough metal into the sky in the few seconds of time available. The gas port was enlarged and various parts modified so as to boost the rate of fire to 800 rounds a minute, and that became the Mark 2* gun. The Mark 3, that was simply a brand new gun with all the speed-up modifications built in from scratch, rapidly followed it.

And that was that for World War I. The US M1917 was simply the British Mark 1 re-barreled for the 30-06 cartridge, and the M1918 was the same thing but with vital modifications to the gas system to compensate for the different characteristics of the 30-06 round. The 'Machine Gun. Aircraft, Lewis, Cal 303 M1917' was the British Mark 2 adopted by the US Army Air Corps, while the Machine Gun, Aircraft, Lewis, Cal 30, M1918 was the ground M1918 stripped of its cooling system and fitted with the 97-round drum. The Lewis guns used by the French and Italian forces were generally the British Mark 1 guns, retaining their British ammunition: a few experimental conversions showed that the 8mm Lebel cartridge was virtually impossible to feed in a Lewis drum without generating jams, and the Italian 6.5mm round was ineffectual as an air-to-air round.

Britain was not the only country to be involved in the hunt for a light machine gun. Skillful Belgian use of their Lewis guns during the first few weeks of the war, when things were still fluid and troops could maneuver, opened the eyes of senior soldiers of many nationalities. There were, indeed, calls to arm every soldier with a light machine gun so as to *'drench the enemy with bullets';* this was good rousing stuff for the newspapers, but the prospect of giving every British/French/German soldier a machine gun more or less condemned the entire civilian populations of Britain/France/Germany to working three shifts a day to keep them supplied with ammunition, so it wasn't really a practical proposition.

The infamous Chauchat, or CSRG machine gun. The semi-circular magazine marks this out as the 8mm version for the French army.

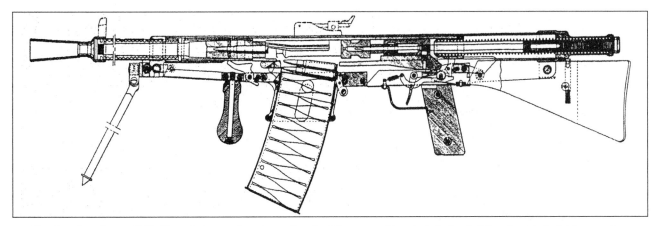

The American issue 30-06 Chauchat, seen here in section, had the second handgrip in front of the almost-straight magazine.

But there were good sound tactical reasons for having light machine guns, even though by the spring of 1915 the war on the Western Front had become bogged down in the trenches, there was always the prospect that next week, or month, or year there would be a breakthrough and mobile warfare would return.

The French military establishment was still smarting from their failure to develop a machine gun 'in-house' and for having to go back to Hotchkiss, cap in hand, for the

An American soldier firing an 8mm Chauchat, issued to units of the AEF before the 30-06 model was in production. His assistant holds a fresh magazine, ready for the change. Note the open-sided magazine, a guaranteed dirt collector in the conditions of the 1918 trenches.

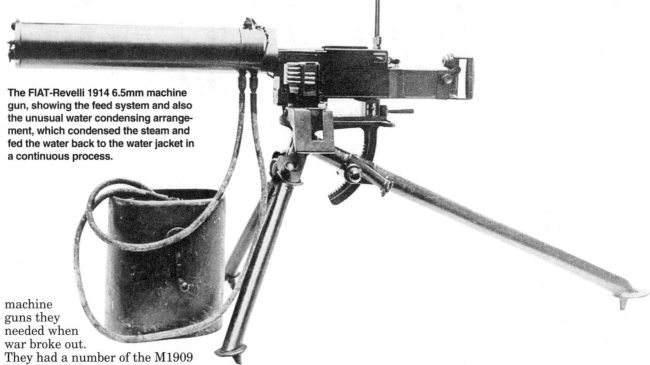

The FIAT-Revelli 1914 6.5mm machine gun, showing the feed system and also the unusual water condensing arrangement, which condensed the steam and fed the water back to the water jacket in a continuous process.

machine guns they needed when war broke out. They had a number of the M1909 Light Hotchkiss guns – the same guns that were in use in the USA as the Benet-Mercié rifle – for their cavalry, but perhaps if the design establishment was to try again, this time for a light gun, they might do better.

The experimental establishments had been fiddling around with machine guns and automatic rifles since about 1900, and a number of tentative designs had appeared in prototype form, none of which had been approved for service. So Colonels Chauchat, Sutter and Ribeyrolle sat down with sharpened pencils and set about designing a light gun. They had to call it something, and instead of the usual French jumble of letters and/or figures, they decided to call it the 'Gladiator', probably on the assumption that it would give every man the powers of one. So the French Army promptly reverted to habit and christened it the C.S.R.G. but everybody else called it the Chauchat, which, over the years, has been corrupted into 'Chauchard' and even 'Shosser'.

There are those - Frenchman, mainly - who will go to their graves maintaining that the Chauchat was a splendid, reliable, robust and accurate weapon. They are probably right, if you specify a hand-made weapon, carefully constructed of the best possible materials. But the mass-produced article of shoddy workmanship and cheap construction which was issued to French and US troops during World War I was a different proposition, and no amount of patriotic argument will alter the facts. I fired one of these about forty years ago, and the memory still lingers; I don't think I have ever felt less confidence in any weapon than I did on that occasion.

The Chauchat was operated by the long recoil system; this means that the barrel and bolt, securely locked together, recoil in the receiver for a distance greater than the length of a complete cartridge. They then stop, and the bolt is unlocked and held in the rearward position while the barrel is released to run forward into its normal firing position. During this forward movement the cartridge case is extracted, being held on the face of the bolt as the barrel moves away from it. It is then knocked clear by a mechanical ejector driven by the movement of the barrel. At the instant the barrel comes to rest, it trips a catch which releases the bolt, which is now driven forward by the usual sort of return spring, collecting a cartridge from the feedway en route and chambering it, after which the bolt locks and the gun is ready to fire once more.

There is nothing inherently defective about the long-recoil method of operation and, in the proper place, it can be quite effective and useful. But a light machine gun is not the proper place; the movement back and forth of the barrel and bolt lead to vibration and oscillation which preclude accurate fire, and the constant movement leads to very rapid wear on the bearing surfaces across which the barrel and bolt move. Lubrication is critical, and long-recoil mechanisms do not generally tolerate dusty or dirty conditions. All this puts them out of court for military adoption, but it is probably fair to say, most of these objections had not been appreciated when the Chauchat was designed. It was, in fact, the Chauchat that was to be the *Awful Example* for future designers.

The other obstacle to efficient operation confronting the Chauchat was the 8mm Lebel cartridge that was the French standard of the period. It was a quite powerful cartridge (2316 ft/lbs with a 198-grain bullet) but had a sharply tapering bottle-necked case with a wide base and prominent rim. It was tolerable

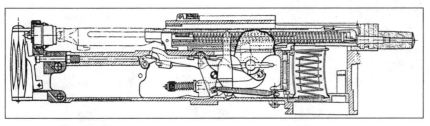

The internals of the FIAT-Revelli; the dotted lines at the upper left show another odd feature of this gun: the bolt came flying out of the back end of the receiver, towards the firer's face, at every shot. Most disconcerting.

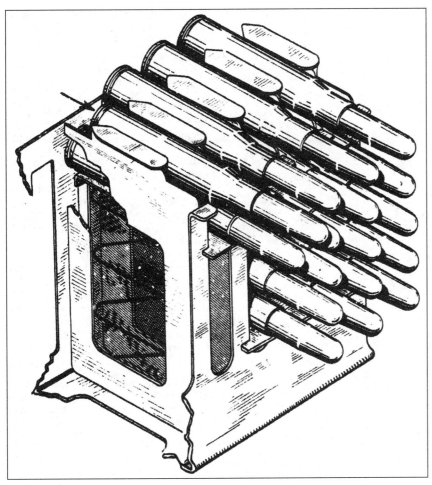

The feed cage for the 6.5mm FIAT-Revelli machine gun. The small arrow indicates the position of the bolt when loading a round into the chamber.

The unfortunate French *poilus* cosseted them, kicked them and cursed them – but soldiered on and fought with them until 1918, though whenever they could get their hands on a Hotchkiss they smartly did so.

Worse was yet to come. As I have observed elsewhere, the French Army unduly influenced the US Army during the early days of the war, and when the French offered to supply the US battalions with machine guns on their arrival in France, the offer was gratefully accepted. What generosity! What *fraternité*! Lafayette, we have arrived! And Lafayette sold them the Chauchat. But in deference to the American supply system, it was redesigned to chamber the US 30-06 cartridge… and therein lay its undoing. For the 30-06 (2385 ft/lbs with a 148-grain bullet) was fairly close to the 8mm Lebel on paper but, due to its powder and internal ballistics, somewhat more abrupt in its action, and it soon shook the Chauchats to pieces. The US Marines soon got rid of them and adopted the Lewis gun, but the army, with its peculiar aversion towards the Lewis, continued to use the Chauchat, even though it used the Lewis for training in the USA.

In fact the 30-caliber Chauchat showed one technical advantage over the 8mm model; because of the more slender rimless cartridge, it could use a more conventional

in a clip-fed rifle but absolutely intolerable in a magazine-fed weapon, which is probably why the Hotchkiss stuck to its peculiar strip feed system for so many years. The magazine for the Chauchat was almost semi-circular, due to the curvature imposed upon its design by the shape of the cartridges; it fitted beneath the receiver where it should have been easy for the moving bolt to slide the cartridge out and into the chamber, but the awkward shape meant that feed jams were common and because the receiver was a drawn steel tube, inside which the barrel and bolt moved back and forth, and because the long recoil system meant that the ejection port was a good distance behind the magazine aperture, if a cartridge jammed going into the chamber, nothing but a complete field-strip would get it out. No amount of fiddling around with a finger in the ejection port or the magazine aper-

ture would have any effect. I know; I can show you the scars.

History tells us that no gun designer ever admits to making a nonsense, and no army willingly admits it has been sold a lemon, so the French Army adopted the C.S.R.G Mle 1915 light machine gun and made the best of it, producing them in a multitude of small factories across the country, with a very poor system of inspection and approval.

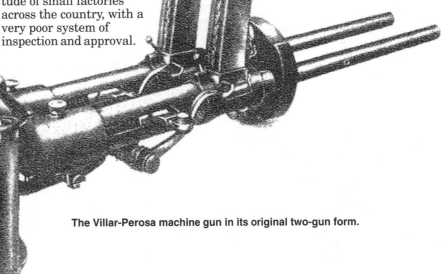

The Villar-Perosa machine gun in its original two-gun form.

The Villar-Perosa could be fitted into an armored shield in entrenched positions or the shield could be fitted to a boat or armored car.

unconfirmed reports that one or two were seen in the Balkans in the latter 1990s.

Having seen their hopes for a light gun from an official source dashed, the French now turned to private enterprise and approached the Darne company. Darne was renowned for their quality shotguns and sporting weapons, and approached the machine gun problem with an open mind. In doing so, they took an entirely different view to that which might have been expected from a traditional gunmaker. Instead of striving for high quality and impeccable finish, they took the entirely practical view that the likely life of a light machine gun in wartime was probably a matter of weeks; a ground gun would probably be destroyed by enemy artillery, while an aerial gun would be shot out of the sky sooner rather than later. So they went for cheap and fast manu-

straight-sided box magazine, and there were fewer feed stoppages. But in the general failure of the gun, that slight bonus tended to be overlooked in the final assessment.

Strangely, the Chauchat managed to survive after 1918. The French, who had tens of thousands of them, handed them out merrily to the various newly-fledged armies they helped to equip in the 1920s, and the weapon was also produced commercially, to a slightly higher standard, and sold to the Greek army under the 'Gladiator' name. But most of the recipients were happy to abandon the weapon once they could afford something better. The chance of a lifetime came in 1936 when the Republican Spanish forces were scouring the world for arms; the Poles and Russians unloaded close on ten thousand Chauchats on to the unsuspecting Spaniards, generously charging them a mere £8 ($40) per gun. I believe other countries also

disposed of their stocks at a profit, though precise figures are not available.

Even after their adoption of better weapons in the 1920s, the frugal French squirreled away a sizable stock of Chauchats in their reserve depots,

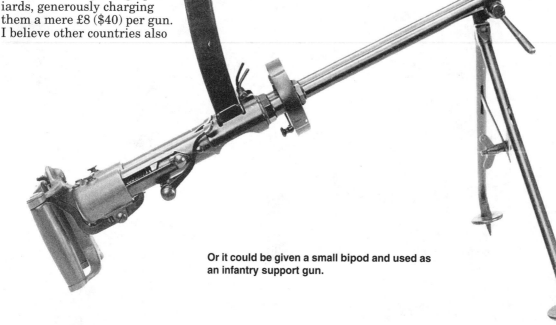

Somebody even tried giving it a wooden buttstock, though how you held it to the shoulder while grasping the spade grips must have been something of a puzzle.

many of which came out of mothballs in 1939 and were issued. More were sent to the various French colonies and tended to be left there when the French departed, which is why the wretched thing popped its head up again in Vietnam. And there are

facture, though not so cheap as to compromise reliability. Their guns were ugly, looked flimsy, were poorly finished where finish was a

Or it could be given a small bipod and used as an infantry support gun.

The eventual solution to the Villar-Perosa was to saw it in half and put each half into a rifle stock, thus producing two quite reasonable submachine guns.

matter of cosmetics but accurately and well made where accuracy and precision were important. They began by making Lewis and Hotchkiss guns under license, after which they applied what they had learned and developed their own designs. Unfortunately it all took time, and while they managed to get a quantity of observer's aircraft guns into use before the war ended, they were unable to perfect their ground guns before 1919.

Italy entered the war in 1915 and were woefully unprepared; fortunately, they had to face the Austro-Hungarian army across the Alps, and the Austrians had taken a considerable hammering from the Russians and Serbians and were in no state to do any immediate damage to Italy. This was to change in

later years when the German army stiffened up the Austrians and the Russians withdrew from the game and thus allowed the combined Austro-German-Hungarian forces to concentrate upon the Italians, but to begin with the Italians had a little time in which to collect their wits and organize their forces. As we have already mentioned, the Italians had been offered a reasonable design, the Perino, for several years, but had been reluctant to come to a conclusion and approve a weapon in case a better one appeared; a phenomenon which later became known as the *'Best is the Enemy of the Good'* syndrome, and has been seen all too often in weapons procurement. In this case the result was that the Italian Army found itself confronted with a

major war and had nothing but a few hundred tired old Maxim guns with which to fight it.

By entering the war in May 1915, the Italians stepped into a marketplace that was already crowded with customers and whose merchants were over-stretched with their order books. Disbarred from dealing with Austria or Germany, they could deal only with Britain, France or the USA as possible suppliers of machine guns, and none of these three were, in mid-1915, in any position to supply them. For some reason, never explained but possibly to do with the manufacturing complexity of the design, it was not possible to set up a production line for the Perino machine gun, but into the breach

An American officer inspecting two Maxim MG '08 guns in a captured German position in 1918. An intriguing feature of this picture is that the two guns are using entirely different feed belts.

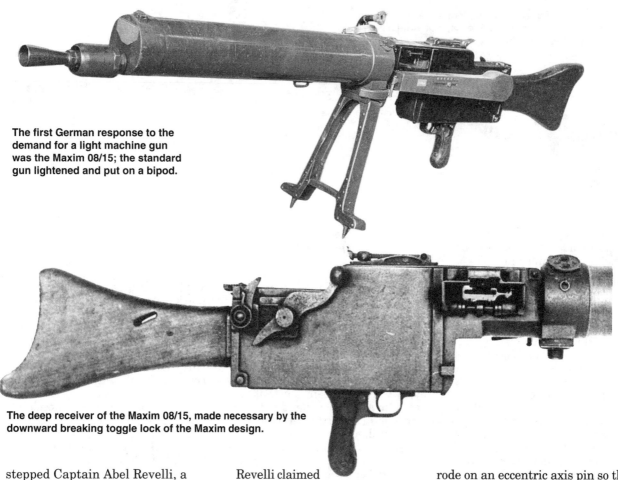

The first German response to the demand for a light machine gun was the Maxim 08/15; the standard gun lightened and put on a bipod.

The deep receiver of the Maxim 08/15, made necessary by the downward breaking toggle lock of the Maxim design.

Another view of the Maxim 08/15; the water jacket was of smaller diameter than that of the MG '08, saving two or three pounds' weight of water.

stepped Captain Abel Revelli, a home-grown gun designer who had first made his mark with the armed forces by developing an automatic pistol known as the Glisenti which was adopted as the official Italian sidearm in 1910. This used a simple swinging wedge to lock the breech; the wedge was pivoted in the pistol frame and extended up, through a hole in the barrel extension and into a recess in the breechblock. When the pistol was fired, barrel, extension and breechblock recoiled, causing the wedge to swing about its axis and so lower itself through the hole in the extension until it was clear of the bolt. The barrel and extension then stopped, the bolt ran back and the operating cycle was duly performed.

Revelli claimed to lock the breech; more critical observers prefer to consider it as a delayed blowback system, which is probably a more accurate assessment. Whatever it may have been, it obviously satisfied Revelli, for in 1908 he began work on a machine gun using a similar system. The only real difference was that in the machine gun design the wedge rode on an eccentric axis pin so that it was possible to make some adjustment to the depth of engagement of the wedge and thus *'tune'* the gun to its smoothest performance.

Revelli spent some years perfecting this design, and worked with the FIAT (*Fabricca Italia Automobiles Torino*) automobile company who built the prototypes; the gun was given frequent trials by the Italian authorities but their indecision precluded anything further than that.

All this changed in 1915, and, looking round for a solution to their machine gun problem, the authorities realized that (*a*) Revelli's gun had done quite well in its trials and (*b*) the FIAT company had the machinery to start making them and the capability of expanding its production. So the FIAT-Revelli M1914 machine gun was approved and put into production forthwith.

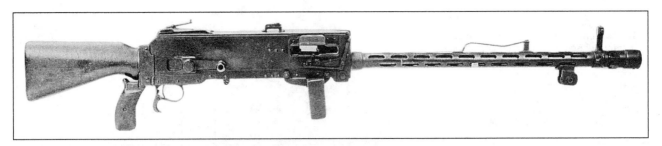

The light-barreled Parabellum was originally developed as an aircraft flexible gun.

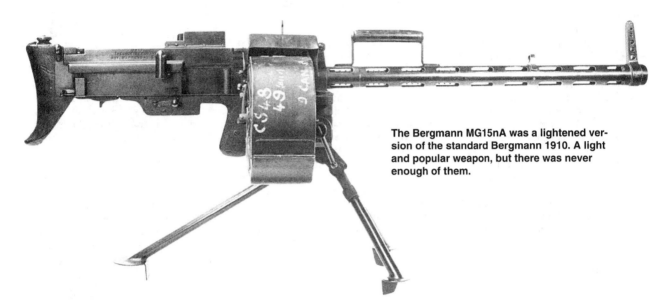

The Bergmann MG15nA was a lightened version of the standard Bergmann 1910. A light and popular weapon, but there was never enough of them.

The M1914 was in the same mold as all the other medium machine guns of the day: tripod-mounted and water-cooled. It was rather lighter than most of the other designs, and it was unique, for its day, in not using a belt feed. Instead it had a most peculiar type of magazine feed system. This consists of a metal cage that held ten columns each of five rounds of 6.5mm cartridges. It was inserted into the gun from the left side and pushed home until it stopped in the feedway. As the bolt moved back and forth it fired the first column of five rounds one after the other, the rounds being pushed up onto contact by a spring. As the fifth round was fired a nib on the cartridge follower contacted a lever in the feed mechanism, which caused an arm to push the cage across until the next column was aligned. And so the gun continued firing each five-round

column in turn until the last round in the last column was fired, whereupon the feed arm ejected the cage from the right side of the gun, while the assistant gunner shoved another in from the left side.

Complicated as it may sound, it worked reasonably well, the only objection being that the magazine cages were not sufficiently robust to stand up to the hurly-burly of life in the front line and the loss rate was far higher than had been anticipated. But the gun was well into production by the time this was realized, and it was cheaper and easier to step up the production of magazines than to change

to a different machine gun.

As noted in the previous chapter, the Italians were also working on the SIA light machine gun, but this failed to come up to expectations and thus the Italian army never had a light machine gun of its own for general infantry use and used Lewis and Hotchkiss guns obtained from its allies. But the Italian Army

Once the aviators had all they needed, the Parabellum was given a rough bipod mounting and was issued to infantry storm troops.

The two-barreled Gast gun, a technical masterpiece that arrived too late to take effect in the air war.

did have one specialist formation which demanded a machine gun of exceptional lightness and fire-power, and that was their crack *Alpini* troops, highly trained mountain troops who could maneuver and fight in the very highest snow-clad peaks where Austria and Italy met. And Captain Revelli had an answer for them, too: the Villar Perosa machine gun.

The Villar Perosa took its name from the factory which made it, the *Officine Villar Perosa*, situated in the town of Villar Perosa in northern Italy some 22 miles southwest of Turin, but it was designed by Revelli and was sometimes known under that name. It was unusual in several respects, not least because in its original form, as the light machine gun for *Alpini*, it was always built as a double gun, two complete guns side-by-side on a single mounting which could be attached to a vehicle or a boat (*not that many appear to have been so used*) but was more often found on a sort of match-seller's tray, slung around the machine gunner's neck. This sounds odd until you understand that the guns themselves were a long way from the ponderous Maxims or even less-ponderous Lewises. The V-P fired a 9mm pistol cartridge and was a delayed blowback weapon with a barrel only 12.5 inches (318mm) long. The overall length of the gun was 21 inches (533mm) and the two guns on their tray weighed just over 14lbs. (6.35kg), so it was not an onerous load to give to a soldier, even though it could be a little awkward to have around your neck when hacking your way up a glacier.

The V-P went into service late in 1915 and proved to be quite effective and popular, and production was parceled out to FIAT and to a Canadian factory (*where it was called the Revelli*). But apart from the *Alpini* the rest of the Italian Army didn't take to it very enthusiastically, largely because a 9mm pistol cartridge (the Glisenti, of the same dimensions but less power than the 9mm Parabellum)

may have been adequate for the short-range antics of the mountain troops but was not much use for the longer ranges between the opposing lines in less perpendicular country. It was even tried as an aircraft gun, in which role it was totally useless. But towards the end of the war the Germans began using their Bergmann submachine guns and some bright spark in Italy realized that by chopping the V-P in half and putting each half into a wooden butt-stock you could have a pretty satisfactory submachine gun. That sealed the fate of the V-P and almost all of them were converted into submachine guns in the early 1920s.

Another design quirk of the V-P is worth noting. The delayed blowback element is subject to some doubt; the bolt carries helical lugs that engage in grooves in the receiver, so that as the bolt is blown open there is a braking effect as the lugs are forced tightly against the rear edges of the grooves and thus have to rotate the bolt. (*One has the feeling that Revelli had been looking over Perino's shoulder when he designed this part of the gun.*) But the shank of the firing pin is shaped in such a way that it can only pass through the bolt and fire the cartridge when the bolt has been rotated into a specific position, at which point the bolt is officially closed, if not locked. Thus, until the bolt is fully closed, any premature release of the firing pin will not result in a discharge, since the pin will not be able to pass through and strike the cartridge cap. The argument is over which was the effect that Revelli was after? Was it the delayed blowback opening, and he thought of the firing pin safety device afterwards? Or did he start with the firing pin safety element uppermost in his mind and took the delayed blowback as an unthought-of bonus? His patent application is a trifle ambiguous. There is also the point that since the weapon is so short and the bolt so light, the delayed blowback element of the bolt's action is also a very useful brake upon the natural firing rate of the combination, keeping the rate of fire down to a mere 1250 rounds per minute from the two guns. Considering that the two overhead-feeding magazines each held only 25 rounds, one supposes that the gunner was followed

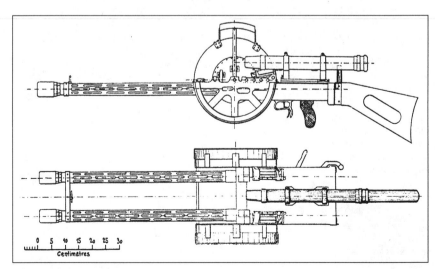

Plan and elevation drawings of the Gast, showing the central stock and sight between the two interconnected guns.

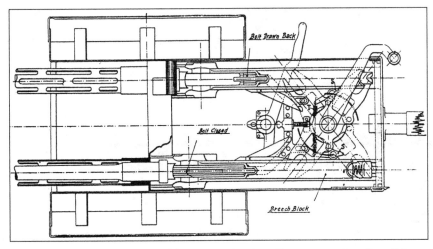

Top view of the Gast machine gun, showing the cross-connecting links between the two bolt mechanisms.

by several men bearing more magazines, since he could empty both in 2.4 seconds.

Of all the combatants, Germany appears to have spent the most time and effort on the provision of machine guns, probably because they were in the position of being besieged on the Western Front and the machine gun was, in those days, seen primarily as a defensive weapon. The official German machine gun was, as we have seen, the Maxim Model of 1908 - or MG '08 - but, as we have also seen, the army had run the rule across the Bergmann and Dreyse 1912 models and marked them down as being suitable for use if the need arose. The need having now arisen, both types were taken into service. At the same time more notice was taken

of the Parabellum derivative of the Maxim, and since this was considerably lighter than the standard MG '08 but of a similar degree of reliability, it was earmarked for the aviation service as soon as that force began considering machine guns.

That took care of the demand for *medium* weapons, but when it came to *light* guns the Germans appear to have lost their touch. Again, this may have been due to their view of their position on the Western Front as being primarily one of defense, in which case the lure of the light machine gun was rather reduced, though one should also remember that they were fighting a highly mobile war with the Russians on the Eastern Front. There was, in fact, very little pressure from the army for a light gun until they cap-

tured their first Lewis guns in 1915. After testing them, it was decided to develop something equivalent, and a military design team was given the job.

Their solution to the problem was simply to take the Maxim MG '08 off its tripod and give it a bipod, fit it with a butt and pistol grip, call it the MG 08/15 and tell the soldiers to get on with it. The gun had been lightened by using thinner walls to the receiver and reducing the diameter of the water-jacket from 10cm to 9cm, which reduced the water capacity from 4 liters to 3 liters – and various other weight-saving modifications were made. The result was to lower the weight from 58 lbs to about 41 lbs when filled with water. It worked well enough, but it could scarcely be called a light gun, and for reasons not entirely clear it had somehow managed to become a good deal less accurate than the original MG '08. However, it was reliable, and unlike most light machine guns it could deliver long bursts of fire without overheating.

The spring of 1915 saw a considerable upheaval in the organization of German machine gun units. Additional four-gun troops were raised within infantry battalions and complete machine gun companies were added to regiments, all of which demanded more and more machine guns. A quantity of Danish Madsen guns was acquired in early 1915 and were first seen at

(Continued on Page 83)

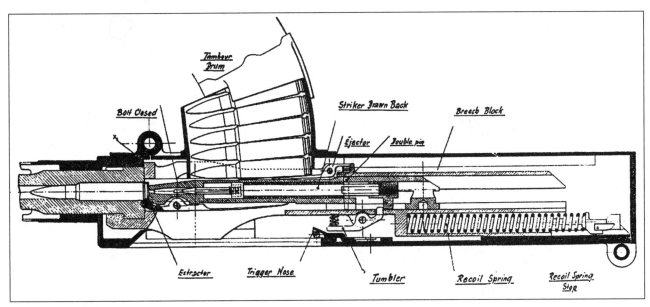

Side view of the Gast mechanism. Bear in mind that the magazine is not a box, but a drum, revolving in the vertical plane alongside the receiver. And the 'recoil spring' acts more as a buffer to smooth out the abrupt action, since it is the firing of one gun that closes the breech of the other - and not the action of the return spring.

BROWNING M1917

Right side of the M1917 Browning, showing the cocking handle and various tripod controls.

The Browning machine gun was first introduced in 1917 that gives it, at the time of writing, 84 years of unbroken service - and it is still being manufactured. This is a record unequaled by any other weapon, and I have every confidence that it will celebrate its centenary still in first-line service with dozens of armies across the world.

The reason for this is simply that nothing has appeared which is suffi-cient of an improvement over the Browning to replace it. Better designs have appeared but the economics of replacing the existing stock of Brownings with a new gun are formidable, and no army is willing to undertake such a change. And the reason for that impasse is that John M. Browning did such a good job in the first place. Like most of his designs it was simple, robust, easy to make and with very little to get out of order. Given that, what more do you want? If it ain't broke...

The M1917 is the basic Browning; understand it and you understand all the 30, 50, 303, 7.62mm and various other caliber guns which appeared in its wake. The gun is recoil-operated, using a barrel and barrel extension that recoil, carrying the breechblock. A vertically-moving lock piece rides down a ramp to unlock the block, whereupon the barrel strikes an accelerator arm and propels the breechblock backward at high speed, while the barrel comes to rest. Movement of the bolt cocks the firing pin and also moves the feed belt. As the bolt goes back, it cocks the firing pin and a claw pulls a cartridge out of the feed belt and forces it into the T-slot in the front of the breech-block, thus pushing out the fired case through the bottom and out of the gun. Returned by the usual spring the bolt moves the feed belt to position the next round, chambers the round in the T-slot, the barrel and block go forward, the lock piece rises and the gun is ready to fire the next shot.

Field Stripping:

Open the receiver cover and remove the belt, pulling it out to the left. Pull back the cocking handle and examine the feedway and chamber to ensure no ammunition remains in the gun. Lower the extractor and release the cocking handle and press the trigger. Leave the cover open.

Using the left hand, pull back the cocking lever as far as it will go and hold it there. This will cause the slotted end of the driving spring guide rod to protrude at the rear of the receiver. Using a cartridge rim, coin, screw-driver or other available implement, push the rod in and rotate it 90° clockwise (until the slot is vertical). Push the cocking handle forward about an inch so that the driving spring rod clears the back-plate of the receiver. Then push forward the cover plate

DATA	
Caliber	30-06
Operating system	Short recoil, automatic
Locking system	Lifting lock
Feed system	250-round cloth belt
Overall length	37.5in (952mm)
Weight, empty	32lb 10oz (14.97 kg)
Barrel	24.0in (610mm), 4 grooves, right hand twist
Muzzle velocity	2800 ft/sec (853mm)
Muzzle energy	2580 ft/lbs (3485 Joules)
Rate of fire	600 rds/minute
Effective range	

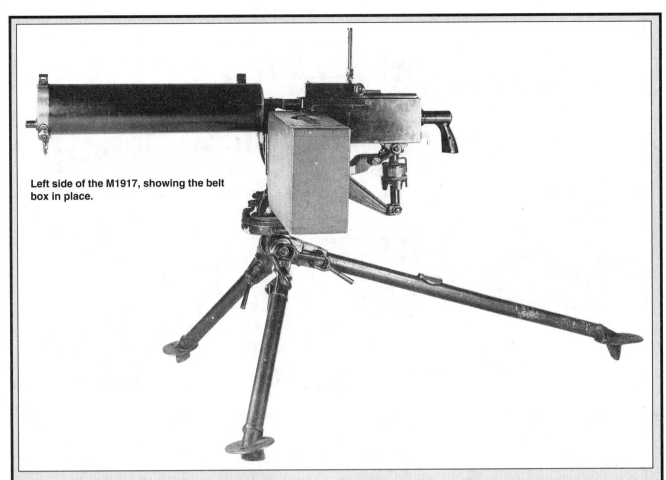

Left side of the M1917, showing the belt box in place.

latch and lift the pistol grip and back-plate out of the slots in the receiver and clear of thegun. Now pull back the cocking handle again, as far as it will go, and withdraw the handle sideways from the bolt. Grasp the driving rod and pull the bolt to the rear and remove it. Using the point of a bullet or some similar tool press in the trigger pin through the hole in the right side of the receiver. Press against the spring pressure and the lock frame and other recoiling parts can be withdrawn to the rear. As the barrel extension comes out and drops below the level of the receiver floor, the entire lock frame, barrel extension and barrel can be withdrawn. Holding the barrel extension, press forward the tips of the accelerator claws and the lock frame will come free from the barrel extension. There is no need to go further than this for normal maintenance.

To re-assemble the gun, insert the barrel and barrel extension into the receiver until the projection beneath the barrel extension rests against the receiver bottom plate. Now assemble the lock frame to the barrel extension: First, place the accelerator claws in front of the T-shaped projection from the barrel extension - insert from beneath. Ensure that the prongs on the lock frame enter the slots in the barrel extension. Now snap the lock frame forwards so that the claws of the accelerator are forced back to compress the barrel plunger spring and thus lock the frame to the extension. Lift the lock and extension and push everything into the receiver until stopped by the trigger pin. Push in the trigger pin against its spring and complete the pushing forward of the lock and barrel unit until the trigger pin engages in the hole in the right side of the receiver.

Now replace the bolt: ensure that the cocking lever is fully forward and the extractor is in place. Rest the front end of the bolt on top of the lock frame

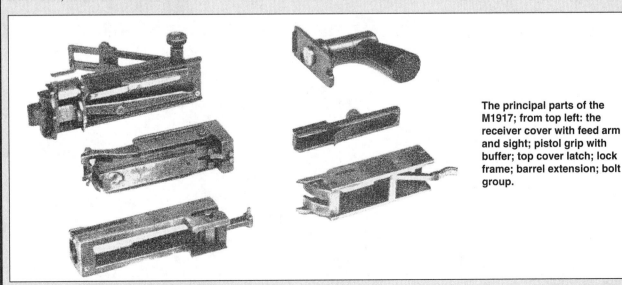

The principal parts of the M1917; from top left: the receiver cover with feed arm and sight; pistol grip with buffer; top cover latch; lock frame; barrel extension; bolt group.

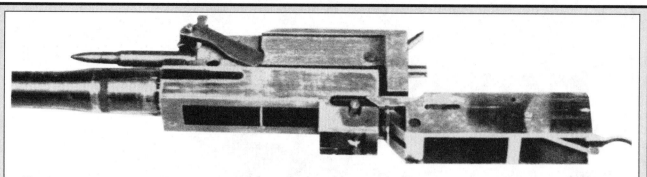

The components assembled; the extractor claw is gripping the next round in the *(absent)* belt; the breech lock is up, the accelerator is forward and the gun is ready to fire.

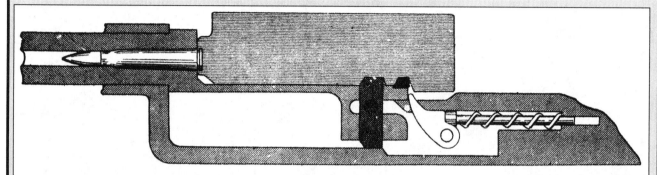

The operation of the bolt lock on the Browning gun; note the accelerator in its forward position. When driven back by the barrel extension, the tip will move more quickly and, hooked into the bolt, will thus send the bolt back faster than the barrel

and push gently forwards until the cocking handle hole appears at the rear of the cutaway section on the right side of the receiver. Then insert the cocking hand through the slot and into the bolt and push forward about an inch or so. Push forward the cover latch and insert the rear plate and pistol grip into the grooves in the receiver; push it firmly home and release the cover latch. Pull back the cocking handle as far as possible, hold with one hand and rotate the slotted end of the driving spring guide rod through 90° counter-clockwise, so that the slot in horizontal. Release the cocking handle. See that the feed slide in the cover is as far over to the right as possible and close the cover.

Cartridge headspace.

All Browning guns need to have the cartridge headspace correctly adjusted after being stripped and re-assembled. The rule-of-thumb method is to screw home the barrel into the barrel extension to the point where the recoiling portions will go fully forward and the breech will just close. Then unscrew the barrel by two clicks, using the combination tool.

Alternatively, with the gun stripped, screw the barrel into the extension until the first click is heard as the barrel lock spring encounters the notches on the barrel. Then insert the bolt, without extractor, into the frame and push firmly against the barrel. From beneath, push up the lock piece so as to lock the bolt to the barrel extension, and, holding it in place, screw up the barrel until resistance is felt. Check to see that the barrel spring is engaged in a notch, and the lock piece is firmly seated. Now let go of the lock; it should drop easily if the adjustment is correct. If it fails to drop, unscrew one click and try again. Once adjustment is correct, remove the bolt and lock piece and continue with re-assembly in the normal way.

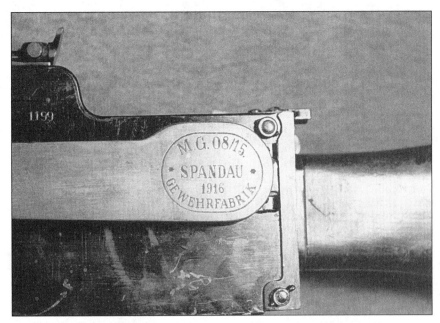

The misleading 'Spandau' marking, in this case on a Maxim 08/15.

(Continued from Page 79)

the front in September; but their 25-round box magazines told against them, since the German troops were accustomed to sustained fire from 250-round belts, and the Madsens were not popular. They were withdrawn by the middle of 1916 and were given to mountain troops, particularly those operating in the Alps with Austrian forces, where they were a good deal more acceptable.

Early in 1915, after discussions with gunmakers and military units, the German High Command instructed the *Rheinische Metall und Maschinenfabrik* to manufacture a new light machine gun for the infantry, and Theodor Bergmann's *Abteilung* to develop a new gun for the air force. In the event, RM&M came up with a modified Dreyse that was a failure, and Bergmann were given orders to change their objective and produce

an infantry gun; the air service was to be satisfied with the Parabellum for the time being.

The Bergmann, as we have seen, went through a number of changes and modifications in the pre-war years, until the final, accepted, version was the M1910. This was water-cooled, feeding from a metal-link belt, and derived its feed power from the recoiling barrel and barrel extension, so that it had ample reserves of power to lift the belt. For the sake of standardization, however, it had then been modified to take the cloth Maxim belt, as used by every other army machine gun. The water jacket was now stripped away and replaced by a slender perforated jacket allowing air-cooling, a shoulder pad and pistol grip were fitted, together with a light tripod and a carrying handle, and the Bergmann now became the MG15nA - '*nA*' meaning '*neuer Art*' or new pattern. The whole thing, gun and tripod, weighed only 35lbs and the rate of fire was an impressive 550 rounds per minute, far better than the Maxim.

The last attempt at a light machine gun for the German infantry came in 1918 with the MG08/18. This was more or less the same thing as the 08/15 - a standard Maxim on a bipod with a shoulder stock and pistol grip - but in this case the water was dispensed with and a slotted small-diameter barrel jacket allowed air-cooling. In fact it was not far

The British relied mainly upon their Vickers, backed up by the Lewis gun.

removed from the air-cooled Maxims, which were used by the air service, and there is little doubt that the origin of the design lay there.

The German air force had, of course, faced the same problem as every other air service - the opposition was moving faster, engagement times were shrinking, so the rate of fire had to go up. By the addition of recoil boosters and the substitution of strong springs the Maxims had been gradually tweaked until they were reaching 500 to 600 rounds per minute, but more speed was needed. As noted in Chapter Two, mechanical guns such as the engine-driven Gebauer were tried, but the one that really succeeded was the Gast.

The Gast MG17 was the invention of Carl Gast, an engineer with the Vorwerk Company of Barmen-Eberfeld. Vorwerk were a general engineering firm and had no background in weapons design or manufacture, but Gast, working from first principles, developed a weapon that eventually reached 1800 rounds per minute and did it with reasonable reliability. Essentially the Gast was actually two guns mounted side-by-side and with their breech-blocks linked by a lever so that as one went forward the other went back, and when one breech was closed the other was open. The bolt was locked to the chamber by a rotating collar; on firing, the barrel and bolt would recoil a short distance, after which a cam turned the collar and unlocked the bolt which was then free to run back in the usual manner. But instead of being resisted by a heavy return spring, it was attached to a pivoted arm which drove the bolt of the other half of the weapon to the closed position,

collecting a round from the magazine and chambering it as it did so. The final movement send bolt and barrel forward, so locking the bolt and, if the trigger was pressed, the sear would automatically release and the cartridge would fire, starting the process in the opposite direction. Feed was by two large drum magazines mounted vertically on each side; these were spring-driven and in consequence they were either right-handed or left-handed, and not interchangeable. This, it would seem, was something of a nuisance in the heat of an aerial dogfight, and the size of the magazines offering resistance to the airflow across the observer's cockpit meant that the gun was not as easily maneuverable as a Lewis or Bergmann. Nevertheless, it delivered a great deal of metal on the target in a very short time, and for that the air service was prepared to overlook a lot of minor deficiencies.

The gun was tested in early 1918 and was forthwith ordered into production, 5000 guns being demanded. But, as we all know, there is a good deal of difference between demanding 5000 guns and getting them, and it has been estimated that no more than 500 were made before the war ended, and not many of those actually got into combat aircraft.

The Allied Control Commission reported the destruction of over 1,300 guns in 1919, but I suspect that many of these had been assembled after the Armistice simply to keep the Vorwerk workers in employment and that some 'guns' were actually no more than the component parts, unassembled. Even so, odd guns kept turning up in peculiar places into the early

1920s. It is doubtful if a dozen exist today, and it is interesting to observe that the most detailed technical study of the Gast ever made was done by the U.S. General Electric Corporation in the late 1940s – during their investigation which eventually produced the Vulcan/Gatling 20mm cannon.

One last note on the German aircraft guns of World War I relates to the 'Spandau'. Spandau was a western suburb of Berlin, in which was located the *Köngliche Gewehrfabrik* or Royal Rifle Factory, more commonly called Spandau Arsenal. It made rifles, as the name implied, and it also manufactured and refurbished other weapons, particularly under the stress of war. As a result, it went into the manufacture of Maxim guns, marking them on the receiver or the return spring cover with 'SPANDAU'. One of their principal Maxim productions was the air-cooled lMG08/15. This terminology leads to confusion; the lower-case 'l' indicates *'luftgekühlte'* or air-cooled; as opposed to LMG with an upper-case 'L' indicating *'Leicht'* for a light machine gun. The lMG08/15 was a full-scale Maxim but with a slotted barrel jacket and with several components lightened both to relieve the load on the airplane and also to lift the rate of fire as far as possible. And, of course, it was marked with the word 'SPANDAU'. So that Allied soldiers with no particular knowledge of machine gun history assumed that this was the Spandau machine gun and the name has stuck ever since. (*I even heard it applied to the MG42 during World War II, which was stretching things a bit.*)

(Continued on Page 89)

The 13mm *Tank und Flieger* (TuF) gun, of which very few were made. As you can see, no more than a beefed-up Maxim '08 design.

The first of a long-lived design was the Browning M1917 machine-gun in 30-06, here seen on an improvised anti-aircraft stand.

BROWNING AUTOMATIC RIFLE

Browning Automatic Rifle M1918A2, with rocker-footed bipod.

Heavy rifle or light machine gun? You can class this weapon in either category and it makes sense. The U.S. Army used it in the squad automatic role from 1918 until the mid 1960s; and due to John Browning's involvement with Fabrique National of Belgium, it was sold into many of the smaller European armies in the 1920s in the same function. In fact, it is difficult to find any army that has ever used it solely as a rifle. Colt, who were Browning's principal licensees for this weapon, produced it as a semi-automatic-only police rifle called the 'Monitor' in the 1920s but the idea failed to catch on and relatively few were so employed.

Perhaps more influential than the weapon was the operating system, which introduced the idea of tipping the bolt up so as to lodge its rear edge

against a hardened face in the top of the receiver. Variations on this theme have appeared in all sorts of weapons, notably the ZB series of Czech machine guns and, since they were Browning's confidants, in the FN-MAG General Purpose Machine Gun. The only serious drawback to the BAR in the squad automatic role was the 20-round magazine, limited to that number because of the space available between the gun breech and the ground in the firing position. The other drawback, the fixed barrel, which tended to restrict prolonged firing, was cured when FN developed a quick-change barrel.

Although it was claimed, at the time of its adoption, that the BAR was an easy manufacturing proposition, anyone who owns a modern automobile will testify that what may be easy to manufacture isn't always easy to maintain or repair... I once had a car on which you had to remove a carburetor before you could change the oil filter. The BAR comes into this category, even though some instruction manuals make field-stripping it sound easy. The official manual, *FM 23-15* of 1940, takes no less than nine pages and 13 illustrations to explain field stripping and re-assembly, though admittedly it goes into such esoterica as how to remove the firing pin without dismantling the rifle, which sounds like good fun on a wet afternoon with not much on the TV. Leaving the more advanced antics to one side, let us look at the basic stripping for everyday cleaning and routine maintenance as referred to the M1918A2:

Begin, as with any weapon, by removing the magazine and clearing the gun, ensuring that there is no ammunition in the feedway or chamber. Leave the gun cocked and lay it down on a table with the barrel pointing to your left. Unscrew the flash hider, remove the bipod. Rotate the gas cylinder retaining spring, on the left front of the receiver, half-a-turn clockwise and remove the pin. Remove the gas cylinder and forend by easing them forward out of the receiver. Now press the trigger with your right thumb while grasping the slide with the left hand so that the middle fingers straddle the gas piston, and allow the working parts to come gently forward.

Turn the trigger guard retaining pin spring a quarter-turn clockwise and remove the pin. Lift out the trigger group. Remove the recoil spring guide rod by pressing in on the checkered end and rotating it so that the inner lugs come free. Pull back the cocking handle about half an inch until the end of the hammer pin can be seen through the hole in the side of the receiver; then, using the end of a dummy round or the recoil spring guide rod, knock out the hammer pin from the cocking handle side. Remove the cocking handle by pulling it straight to the rear and remove the hammer pin. Push the hammer forward, out of its seat in the slide, and lift it out of the receiver.

Push the breech-block as far forward as it will go and then draw the piston forward and out of the receiver, taking care not to strike the gas piston against the gas cylinder bracket. Using

DATA (M1918A2)

Caliber	.30 M1906
Operating system	Gas, selective fire
Locking system	Tilting bolt
Feed system	20-round underslung box
Overall length	47.80in (1214mm)
Weight, empty	19 lb 6 oz (8.80 kg)
Barrel	24.0in (610mm); 4 grooves, right-hand twist
Muzzle velocity	2788 ft/sec (850 m/sec)
Muzzle energy	2593 ft/lbs (3594J)
Rate of fire	450 or 650 rds/min, selectable
Effective range	600m

This BAR M1918A2 was taken from Angolan rebels in the latter 1980s.

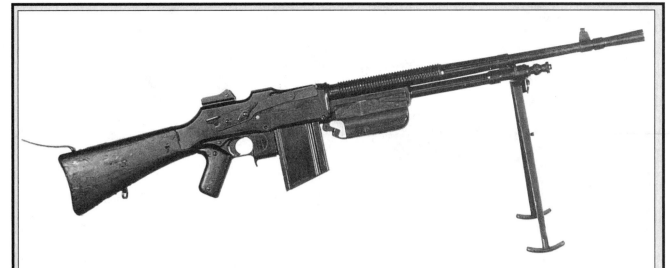

A BAR Model 1930, made by FN of Belgium. Note the finned barrel, adjustable bipod and typical FN gas regulator on the front of the gas cylinder.

the point of a dummy round, force out the bolt guide from inside the receiver, then remove the bolt, bolt lock and link by sliding them to the back of the receiver and lifting them out. The firing pin can then be removed from the breech-block and the extractor can be removed by using the point of a dummy round to press up and forward on the extractor claw.

There is no requirement to go any further; it is possible to dismantle the firing mechanism and trigger unit but there is no need to do so unless something breaks and it is not recommended.

Dismantling a Belgian FN Model D is an entirely different matter. With the magazine off and the gun empty and action forward, withdraw the trigger-guard pin and remove the trigger-guard. Remove the butt locking pin from the receiver, allowing the butt to swing down. Reach into the receiver, grasp the operating spring rod, and pull the entire works out of the gun - gas piston, breech-block, link, slide, hammer and spring guide. *End of routine stripping*.

To reassemble either weapon, the routine is simply to reverse the sequence

of stripping, but there are, as usual, pitfalls for the unwary. With the Model D it is simply a matter of sliding everything back into the rear of the receiver, swinging up the butt and re-inserting the pin. The only point to watch is that when inserting the moving parts, keep the assembly well up in the receiver so that the bolt slides into its guide grooves.

With the M1918A2, begin by replacing the extractor, extractor spring and firing pin into the breech-block and assembling the breech-block, lock and link. Lay the rifle upside down on the table and insert the breech-block

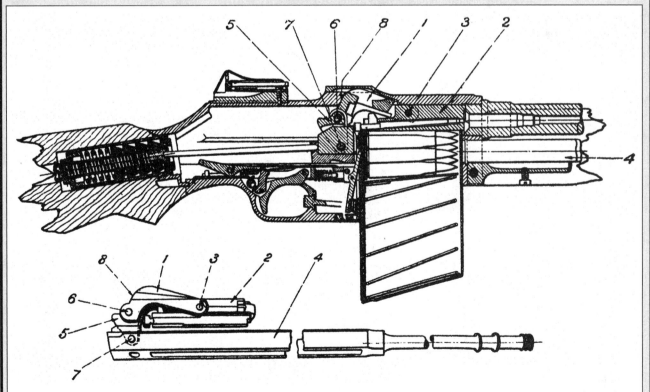

The locking system of the BAR. *1)* bolt lock; *2)* bolt; *3)* connecting pin; *4)* pistol slide; *5)* connecting link; *6, 7)* link pivot pins; *8)* locking shoulder on the bolt lock. When the gun fires, the piston slide moves back and takes the lower end of the link *(5)* with it. This pulls the bolt lock from the locking shoulder. On the return stroke the bolt closes, but the piston continues forward, so taking the link and driving up the bolt lock.

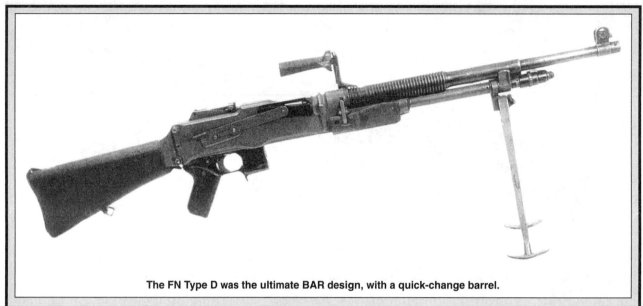

The FN Type D was the ultimate BAR design, with a quick-change barrel.

assembly into the receiver, ensuring that the block engages in its guides. Then press the block down over its spring retaining catch. Push the assembly forward, swing the bolt link down, insert the slide and push it all the way back. Lower the hammer into place in its seat in the slide. Push the breech-block lock fully into its recess and push the slide forward. Now align the holes of the hammer, slide and bolt link with the hole in the receiver, using the recoil spring guide as a probe to get everything lined up. Insert the hammer pin until about a quarter of an inch protrudes from the receiver and then replace the cocking handle. Then drive the hammer pin fully home.

Replace the recoil spring and guide, using a finger on the checkered end of the rod to rotate it half a turn into engagement with its seat. Replace the trigger group and secure it with the locking pin. Cock the gun, and then replace the gas cylinder and forend and lock in place with the relevant pin. Replace the bipod and flash hider. Pull the trigger and allow the working parts to go forward.

The M1917 was accompanied into France by the M 1918 BAR, here seen in its later M1918A2 version.

(Continued from Page 84)

If aircraft could use the machine gun, it could also be used against aircraft, and the infantry became adept at fitting the MG08 to a variety of extemporized mountings and firing at ground attackers. But the aircraft became faster and more strongly built, so that the occasional 7.92mm bullet that struck home failed to do significant damage. And in 1916 the British introduced the tank to the battlefield, and these machines gradually grew in number and also in the thickness of their armor, leading, in the spring of 1917, to a demand for a more powerful machine gun. The designers decided to combine both problems and develop a heavy gun capable of defeating the boilerplate armor of the day and also capable of reaching up to a useful altitude to scare off the ground attackers before they got close enough to do any damage. *(A point, which is frequently overlooked or unappreciated when discussing anti-aircraft fire, is that it is not necessary to destroy the airplane to be successful. If you discourage the pilot from venturing near you, your air defense has worked.)*

Approaching the problem from first principles, the German designers began, in October 1917, by developing a fresh round of ammunition, the 13x92mm semi-rimmed cartridge that became known as the 'Tank-patrone'. This used a

American tanks were to be given this Marlin conversion of the Colt M1895, but these did not reach the troops before the Armistice.

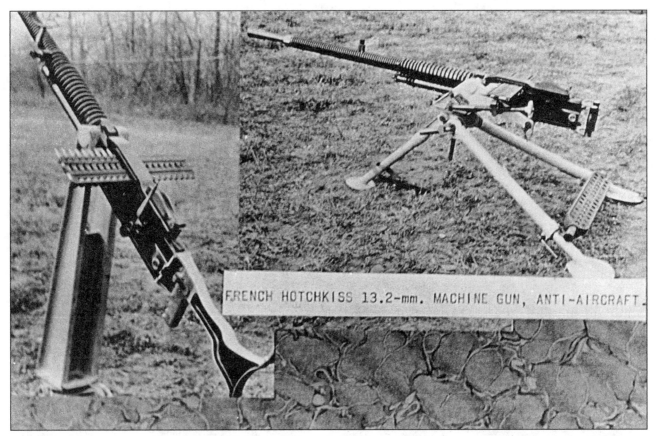

Another late wartime design was this 13.2mm Hotchkiss, originally intended for shooting down artillery observation balloons, but later adapted to more general air defense.

965-grain (2.20 ounces or 62.5 grams) steel-cored bullet capable of defeating 22mm (0.87 inch) of steel armor at 100 yards range. Having got the 'terminal effect' they wanted, now they had to design a gun to fire it. This was too easy: scale up the MG'08 to the new caliber. Designs were accordingly drawn up, but the High Command were somewhat put out to find that the development and setting up of a production line would mean that no guns would appear until the summer of 1918. They had no choice but to agree to this – there was no way of short-cutting the development of such a highly stressed weapon – and in order to provide the infantry with a stopgap, Mauser were instructed to design a single-shot bolt-action rifle to fire the new cartridge. This duly appeared, but not until the late spring of 1918.

The machine gun, now known as the 'Tank und Flieger' or 'TuF' gun, finally achieved production in the final weeks of World War I; it was manufactured by the *Maschinenfabrik Augsburg-Nürnberg* (MAN) and was approved for service on 13 August 1918. A total of 50 pre-production guns were to be delivered by 14 December 1918, and mass production would commence in

January 1919. But this program was overtaken by events, and it is doubtful is as many as a dozen *TuF* machine guns were ever made, none of which entered service, and all of which were destroyed before the Allied Disarmament Commission ever got their hands on them.

All this activity in Europe had not gone unnoticed in the U.S.A., but since they were not, at first, involved in the war it was merely a matter of interest to the military and nobody else. Except John Browning who could see further than most people and who realized that before very long there was going to be a demand for a machine gun. He took out the design he had patented in 1901 after seeing the 'Potato Digger' into production, and began to work on it more seriously. The intention being a medium machine gun for heavy and sustained fire, he decided upon a water-cooled gun, and this more or less dictated that he had to use recoil as the method of operation.

He had, in fact, completed his first design in 1910 and offered it to the US Army, but they were not particularly interested, seeing very little future for the machine gun, and turned it down. Browning was not particularly daunted by this and put the design aside, bringing

it out again in 1916 and making a few minor improvements; Browning never offered a design for test until he was quite satisfied that he had it right, and in a condition to go into production. In February 1917 he demonstrated the gun to military officials but nothing came of it. In April the U.S.A. entered the war, and in May the military were back hammering on Browning's door. He delivered a gun to Springfield Arsenal for test, where it astonished everybody by firing off 40,000 rounds with but two stoppages, both due to defective cartridges. A second gun fired over 28,000 rounds non-stop. Not only was the gun reliable, it was also relatively easy to manufacture, simple to operate and field-strip, accurate and half the price of any competing weapon.

On the 6th April 1917 the US Army's total stock of machine guns consisted of 670 Benet-Mercié machine rifles, 282 M1904 Maxim guns, 353 Lewis guns (chambered for the British 303 cartridge) and 148 Colt M1895 guns. A contract had been given to Colt to manufacture 4125 Vickers guns in 30-caliber under license from the British, but Colt were still setting up their production line for these. Something had to be done. In July 1917

To the victor, the spoils. American troops check out a Maxim '08 as a potential air defense gun....

contracts for the manufacture of 10,000 Browning machine guns and 12,000 Browning automatic rifles were given to Colt, the sole licensees of Browning's patents; since they were already committed to making the Vickers guns, it was obvious that they were being stretched well beyond their capabilities. They set about building a new factory to make the automatic rifles, but eventually agreed to waive their exclusive license for the duration of the war and thus enable the government to shift the machine gun contract to the other companies. By September 1917 contracts had been placed for

...while British troops examine a Maxim pom-pom and wonder what use it might be.

Among the late-comers was the British Beardmore-Farquhar aircraft observer's machine gun, light in weight and light in recoil due to its novel operating system.

15,000 water-cooled Browning machine guns with Remington; 5000 Browning aircraft guns with the Marlin-Rockwell Corporation; and 20,000 Browning automatic rifles also with the Marlin-Rockwell Corporation. Further orders for another 25,000 automatic rifles and 10,000 aircraft guns followed in October and by that time the Browning machine gun had been launched on its illustrious career.

Browning's machine gun design, which went into service in the first instance as the U.S. Machine Gun, Browning, M1917, was a quite conventional water-jacketed gun mounted in a tripod like most its contemporaries; its immediate identifying feature is the pistol grip at the rear of the receiver. It fed from a cloth belt inserted into the left side of the receiver and is operated by the recoil of the barrel and barrel extension. A breech-block, with a front T-slot, slides in the barrel extension, and a locking block is cammed up and down to lock the block to the extension during firing and unlock it for the remainder of the operating cycle. As the lock falls free and the breechblock separates from the chamber, an accelerator, propelled by the barrel extension, drives the

breech-block back at a much faster rate than the barrel is moving. At the same time a claw pulls a fresh cartridge out of the belt, above the chamber, and drops it into the T-slot, forcing the empty case to move down the slot until it falls out through an aperture in the bottom of the receiver. By the end of the recoil stroke, the fresh cartridge is correctly positioned in alignment with the chamber. The bolt strikes a buffer and is then driven forward once more by its return spring, chambering the fresh cartridge. The locking piece is cammed up, locking block and barrel extension together, the barrel goes into battery and if the trigger is pressed the sear will release the firing pin to fire the cartridge.

Like most of John Browning's designs, the M1917 was pretty well right from the start; the only serious wartime fault to be discovered was that the receiver bottom plate was prone to breaking under prolonged firing. This was due to the use of a substitute grade of steel instead of the one that John Browning had specified. Patching cured the defect but in due course the bottom plate was re-manufactured to the original specification and the fault disappeared.

One of my most prized possessions is a small, battered book entitled 'Small Arms Manual' and written by Lt. Col. J.A. Barlow of the West Yorkshire Regiment and the Small Arms School Corps. It was published in 1942 and I bought it to further my military knowledge as a Home Guard, and it is a most down-to-earth volume, full of practical advice. On introducing the Browning Automatic Rifle (BAR) to his readers, Barlow said *"This is a heavy type of automatic rifle or, if you prefer to call it so, a light type of light machine gun"* and I think that just about sums it up.

In 1917 the US Army was heavily - some say far too heavily - influenced by the French Army and its doctrines. What they failed to appreciate at first was that the French simply wanted the US Army trained in their doctrines so that their troops could be fed into the French lines under French command. Fortunately 'Black Jack' Pershing saw through this ploy and made himself thoroughly unpopular with the French by standing out against their ideas of integration. However, he could do little or nothing against the tide of French tactical policies,

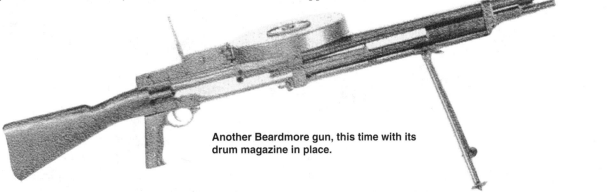

Another Beardmore gun, this time with its drum magazine in place.

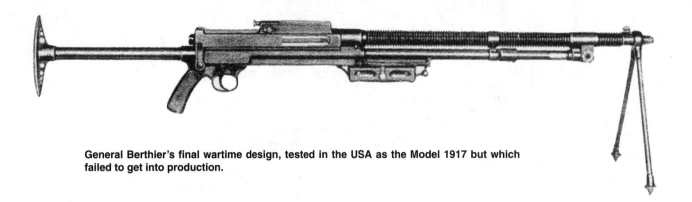

General Berthier's final wartime design, tested in the USA as the Model 1917 but which failed to get into production.

which were assiduously pumped into the US bloodstream, and one of these was *'Walking Fire'*.

The theory here was that every man would have an automatic *(or at least a fast-firing)* weapon slung around his neck so that as he left his trenches and advanced through the mud of No Mans Land (burdened down with some 60 pounds of equipment) he would fire this weapon from the hip, keeping up a stream of fire. If all the men of the company/battalion/regiment in the attack did this, the air would be so thick with bullets that the enemy would never get the chance to man his breastworks and repel the attack.

Like so many military theories of the time, this sounds fine the first time you hear it, but after a while one or two doubts creep in. Like, for example, how does the man carry sufficient ammunition to keep up a stream of fire for perhaps three or four minutes as he staggers through the shell holes and slippery chalky mud? And, of course, there is always the problem that the enemy

might not see things exactly the same way as you. Furthermore there was the question of producing *(and finding the money for)* all these thousands of weapons and their ammunition. No matter. Walking fire was in, and what they needed was a weapon. And at just about the same time John Browning came along with his automatic rifle. He had developed this weapon in response to an open invitation to inventors and engineers from the Machine Gun Board, who had, in mid-1916, arranged for a trial to take place in May 1917 of whatever machine guns anyone might care to put forward. Browning appeared with both his heavy water-cooled gun (which later became the M1917, as discussed above) and a lighter weapon, the Browning Automatic Rifle – or BAR. Both weapons passed their tests with flying colors, and since the automatic rifle appeared to be the answer to walking fire, 12,000 were ordered forthwith.

The first Browning automatic rifles appeared in March 1918 from

the Winchester factory; by the end of June three factories - Winchester, Colt and Marlin-Rockwell - had between them turned out 17,000 rifles, and when the Armistice was declared the total produced stood at 52,238, with orders outstanding for a further 235,000. All US divisions sailing to France after July 1918 had their full complement of Browning machine guns and automatic rifles, and several thousand more were shipped in bulk to outfit units already in France who were using Hotchkiss and Chauchat guns purchased from the French. Some 180,000 guns-worth of contracts were canceled after the armistice and production scaled-down before being terminated in the early 1920s.

The Browning Automatic Rifle M1918, as originally issued, was a gas-actuated weapon using a gas piston moving in a cylinder beneath the barrel and using a link to carry a breech-block in such a manner that as the piston came forward, so it lifted the rear end of

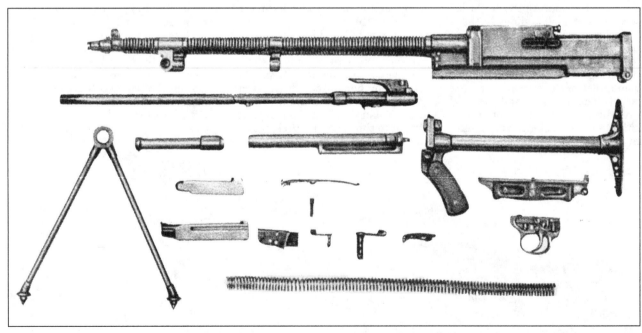

The Berthier Model 1917 gun in its field-stripped condition.

the breech-lock and lodged it against a bearing surface in the roof of the receiver. (Compare this with the M1895 'Potato Digger' in which the bolt was *lowered* into the locking position by cam action of the piston.) It was this lifting of the lock which accounts for the odd 'hump-backed' appearance of the receiver. The rifle could be fired off-hand from the shoulder, but it was far more accurate when used in the prone position with some form of rest. It could fire single shots or automatic fire at a rate of 550 rounds a minute, had a tubular flash hider and fed from a 20-round detachable magazine inserted beneath the receiver. It weighed 16 pounds, which was another good reason for not firing it off-hand from the shoulder.

The two Brownings were unique in that they had been developed, completed, put into production and brought into combat use inside the space of the war years; indeed, upon reflection, it is remarkable how few machine gun designs were put forward - in any country - between 1914 and 1918. Britain, Germany, France and Russia fought the entire war with pre-war guns, modified from time to time to meet present requirements, but pre-war designs nevertheless. This is probably an indication that designing machine guns is a job best left to experts, and the enthusiastic amateurs who bombarded their respective governments with brainwaves for artillery, anti-aircraft guns and shells, hand grenades, and various other warlike stores, viewed the machine gun as beyond even their powers.

There were a few who tried, and perhaps the most persistent, and certainly the only British design to even get close to adoption was the Beardmore-Farquhar aircraft machine gun. This goes down in history as one of the lightest machine guns ever made, since this was the great target - get a light gun and you could carry more ammunition. It achieved this by an unusual method of operation that reduced the stresses and allowed a lighter form of construction and also by eliminating metal that performed no useful function.

The design was due to a Colonel Farquhar, who had spent several years developing rifles and finally an automatic rifle just before the war. Once he saw that aerial warfare demanded a light weapon, he set about his design and he interested the William Beardmore Engineering Company sufficiently for them to join him and do the manufacturing and practical experimentation. Hence the double-barreled name.

At bottom, the Beardmore-Farquhar was a gas-operated gun using a rotating bolt and a drum magazine. But instead of the gas piston operating directly upon the bolt, all it does is to compress a spring.

Once compressed, the front end is held by a catch, while the rear end rests against the bolt carrier. The strength of this spring was carefully designed so that it was not strong enough to open the bolt while the chamber pressure was at an unsafe high level and pressing the bolt locking lugs back against their bearing surfaces. Once the pressure dropped to a safe level, the bolt was freed and the spring could force it to revolve, unlock, and move to the rear against the pressure of a second spring. The bolt extracted the empty case and ejected it, and as it reached the end of its travel, so it operated a lever to unlock the catch holding the front end of the main spring. This removed any resistance to the forward movement of the bolt, and the second spring now drove it forward to chamber a fresh round a close the breech. This forward movement pushed the mainspring back to its first position against the gas piston and the gas piston forward in the gas cylinder.

The result of these springs was firstly to ensure that the breech only opened when the pressure was safe, and secondly to make the action much less violent than was customary with gas-operated guns. The gun vibrated less, was easier to hold on target, and delivered less stress to both its own structure and the mounting that was holding it.

Unfortunately, perfecting this rather unusual design took longer than had been anticipated and a reliably-working specimen did not appear until the summer of 1919. The Royal Air Force tested it, but one feels that it was out of politeness rather than from enthusiasm or any pressing need. Even so, it passed its tests satisfactorily, with only one or two modifications being deemed necessary by the testing officers, and they observed another unique feature - the 77-round drum magazine could be removed and the gun could be fed with the standard five-round charge used with the infantry Lee-Enfield rifle, which would have allowed the weapon to be used as a species of automatic rifle. But in 1919 such matters were purely academic. After all, they had just fought the war to end wars; who cared about machine guns. *Thank you, Colonel; don't call us...*

The American equivalent might be the Berthier machine gun. General Andre V.P.M. Berthier had been busy with weapons design since the early 1900s; he had devised a successful modification to the Lebel rifle, converting it to clip-loading, and in 1908 he displayed a light machine gun which was water-cooled, had a top-mounted box magazine and a bipod, and was operated by a gas piston. The bolt locked by the rear end being lifted into engagement with the receiver, and in general, the mechanism was very much like the later BAR. However, as we have already observed, in the years before 1914 there were considerable reservations about light machine guns and their place on the battlefield, and Berthier got no further with his design.

In 1916 Berthier arrived in the USA; it is far from clear whether he went there in an official capacity to develop his machine gun and get it manufactured for the French army, or whether he was acting in a private capacity, to obtain manufacturing facilities and complete the development of the gun and then try and interest one of the combatants. In any event, he first re-appears with one of his guns being tested by the US Army in May 1917, when the gun was rejected. Tested by the Marines, it was considered suitable for adoption, and with the demand for machine guns clamoring to be satisfied the army changed its opinion and in October 1917 approved a contract for 5000 Berthier M1917 guns and another for 2000 guns for the Marines. Whereupon the whole business went to pieces.

Briefly, what happened was that the contract was placed with the U.S. Machine Gun Company, an offshoot of the Hopkins & Allen company, a well-known firearms manufacturer. Hopkins & Allen got into financial difficulties and were taken over by the Marlin Rockwell Corporation. Marlin-Rockwell had their hands full with orders for guns from various quarters and the Berthier came a long way down their list of priorities, so that they more or less repudiated the contracts. Since there was no other manufacturing plant available, the gun never went into production before the war ended.

And once the war ended, there was no rush to make machine guns; the army had second thoughts and set up some rather more exhaustive tests and canceled the entire business. *Don't call us, General..*

CHAPTER FIVE

BETWEEN THE WARS

WHEN THE HALF-time whistle blew in November 1918 it caused a number of tactical, strategic and development plans to be thrown into the discard. The 1919 Spring Offensive of the Allies was canceled, the great tank-building program was abruptly curtailed, factory construction programs in the USA, Britain and France stopped dead in their tracks and production contracts were canceled by the score. But one or two things survived, because the armies recognized that war had thrown up some problems that were not going to go away and which might cause trouble in the future if they were not addressed. Among these was the question of the machine gun. Everybody, by late 1918, had machine guns, but very few people were entirely satisfied with what they had.

Perhaps the most satisfied were the American forces: the Browning M1917 water-cooled gun had proved its worth, and the air-cooled variation, known as the M1919 would also turn out to be a success, and would eventually replace the M1917 pattern to become the standard medium machine gun. The light machine gun slot was taken by the Browning Automatic Rifle; it may not have been everybody's idea of a light machine gun but it was better than many competitors, immeasurably better that the Chauchat which had infuriated the AEF during the war, and the US Army was perfectly happy with it as their squad automatic. And in the background was John M Browning gilding the lily by developing a fresh model of the M1917 gun but this time with a larger caliber to fire a 0.50-inch cartridge.

The 50-caliber Browning gun had its origins in a demand by General Pershing, Commander of the AEF. Pershing had seen some French 11mm Hotchkiss guns developed as anti-balloon and air defense weapons, and he could see the sense of them and also their

possible application as an anti-tank weapon. And he therefore *minuted* the War Department to the effect that he wanted something along the same lines. Before very much could be done the Armistice came along and everybody had other things to think about, and thus is was not until some months after the war had ended that the heavy machine gun idea was followed up.

By that time several things had come to the attention of the Allies, and among them was the *Tank und Flieger* machine gun and the *Tank-Gewehr* anti-tank rifle; the guns themselves stirred nobody, since the machine gun was just another Maxim and the rifle just an overgrown *Gewehr* 98 bolt action, but the cartridge aroused some interest. John Browning had been handed the heavy machine gun problem and had been given some French 11x59mm ammunition, but this failed to deliver the velocity that was felt to be desirable in this sort of gun. A caliber of half an inch seemed to be a good figure, and the German 13mm *T-Patrone* cartridge, being fractionally above that, was taken as the starting point.

Browning actually built a gun to fire the 13mm cartridge and prove that his ideas were workable, but he realized that the semi-rimmed German cartridge was a potential source of feed problems and the internal ballistics were not well-suited to Browning's ideas, since the German powder had different burning characteristics to the American powders used for military cartridges. [As a general and broad rule, German powders of the time gave a lower breech pressure and higher muzzle pressure than did American or British powders and gun designers had to vary their techniques accordingly.]

Long before this, though, early in 1918, the US Army had seen the Mauser *Tank-Gewehr* bolt-action rifle and decided that something of this nature might be a useful tool

for the AEF. The Winchester company were invited to work upon the problem and they began by developing a rimmed cartridge, also based upon the German 13mm round. Originally they tried it with their off-the-shelf 0.45-inch 500-grain bullets but the ballistics were hopeless, and the caliber was changed to 0.50-inch. Two bullets were tried, one of 508 grains and the other of 707 grains; the former reached 3003 ft/sec and the latter 2596 ft/sec, both of which were considered to be satisfactory for their planned role.

There is some evidence that Winchester had second thoughts about the use of a rimmed cartridge. Others have suggested the design was modified in the light of comments from the Ordnance Department who, aware of Browning's work by this time, thought that a rimless cartridge case would be a better functioning proposition in a machine gun than a rimmed one. In any event, by mid-June of 1918 Winchester had submitted a design of rimless cartridge using a 707-grain bullet and developing just over 2335 ft/sec. This was fine, but the cartridge was considered to be too long; shortening it would make the design of a weapon much easier, thank you. So Winchester shortened it. This reduced the powder space so that the velocity fell too far, and the answer to that was to make the case fatter. This wasn't well liked either, and finally, juggling length and diameter and shoulder position and taper and neck length and bullet intrusion, Winchester produced their final design in October 1918, a design which used a case 4.025 inches long with a 707-grain non-streamlined bullet and developed 2365 ft/sec. And with that Winchester bowed out, having fulfilled their contract.

As the war ended there was a severe pruning of development contracts with commercial companies and the 50-caliber machine gun cartridge now landed in the lap of

Frankford Arsenal. As a first approximation they took the Winchester 50-caliber cartridge and the German 13mm *TuF*, married the two, and the offspring became their proposed 50-caliber round. Both case and bullet were lengthened, the case was semi-rimmed, and the bullet was boat-tailed and weighed 800 grains. Much as the Arsenal liked the semi-rimmed case (because it was strong and had a shape which gave good burning characteristics to the powder) the army was less enthusiastic and demanded a rimless design. So Frankford took the easy way out; they threw everything out and simply scaled up the standard 30-06 cartridge to 50-caliber, and with a few minor adjustments here and there, that became the 'Cartridge .50 M1919.' The case was 3.9 inches long and carried an 804-grain bullet. And with that finally settled, John Browning could draw up his final designs.

Mr. Browning appears to have done his first work using the Winchester rimless rounds, and then altering dimensions so as to change to the Frankfort Arsenal cartridge in 1919. So far as the mechanism went, it was little more than the M1917 gun scaled up to use a bigger cartridge, and the eventual gun was generally similar to the M1917, being water-cooled, belt-fed and tripod mounted. Indeed a photograph of the 50-caliber gun of 1919 is hard to tell apart from the 30-caliber M1917 if there is nothing in the picture by which to judge its size. The first working gun, chambered for the Winchester 707-grain round, was assembled in October 1918 and worked successfully from the very beginning of its life. The rate of fire was just under 500 rounds per minute, but the velocity, at 2335 ft/sec, was below the 2600 ft/sec for which the army was asking. Nevertheless, as a development round the Winchester cartridge was satisfactory and Browning continued his development work with this round until the Frankford Arsenal M1919 cartridge became available. Once he had this, changes in barrel length and spring strengths and various other details produced a velocity and rate of fire acceptable to the army and the 50-caliber machine gun was finally accepted for service as the M1921.

The most significant change in design from the 30-caliber gun was the addition of a hydraulic recoil buffer, necessitated by the powerful Frankford Arsenal cartridge. This was an oil-filled dashpot device, and it was also designed so as to permit some adjustment of the rate of fire, though I doubt if many people ever bothered to use it. The most obvious visual difference in the two guns is that the pistol grip of the M1917 is replaced by double spade grips with a trigger between them, giving the gunner better control over the weapon. Although the gun was standardized as the M1921, shortage of funds meant that none were issued until 1925, and then only in limited numbers; it is doubtful if as many as 100 guns per year reached the service before 1934. Nevertheless, even if the army could not afford to buy many, they could still forward their observations and comments, and (Mr. Browning having died in 1926) the Colt Company could make a few improvements. The first and most useful *(in my opinion, anyway)* was the adoption of the compound cocking handle which, by improving the leverage, made cocking the gun less of a feat of strength. Introduced in 1931, this became the M1921A1, and almost all M1921 guns were retrospectively modified when they came in for routine maintenance or repair.

The water-cooled M1921 was no lightweight and it became the primary all-arms anti-aircraft weapon in the 1930s, issued with a special tripod which permitted firing at high angles of elevation. It was also adopted by the U S Navy in some numbers for shipboard AA applications; many of these were given a new water jacket with large-bore hoses connected to the ship's water supply so that the guns could fire non-stop for long periods without overheating or, indeed, getting very hot at all.

The air-cooled 30-caliber M1919 gun had originally been developed for the cavalry, since they wanted a lightweight weapon for carrying on a horse and were willing to dispense with the weight of the water, since they were rarely called upon to lay down sustained supporting fires; their role was strictly *shoot and scoot* reconnaissance, so an air-cooled weapon was quite feasible. Having got what they wanted in the M1919 model, they now cast their eyes on the 50-caliber M1921 and began thinking–a serious activity for cavalrymen. Every day there was talk of mechanization, and the day was obviously coming when they would have to relinquish their horses and adopt motor vehicles. *Armored* motor vehicles. Not tanks; tanks were only permitted to infantry, by Act of Congress. So the cavalry acquired tanks but called them Combat Cars, and everybody was happy. But Combat Cars could not mount cannon such as the

The original, water-cooled, Browning 50-caliber machine gun in its heyday as the primary air defense weapon of the US Army in the 1930s.

The water-cooled 50 Browning was never used as an infantry support gun in the US forces, but it was marketed with some success in that role by Fabrique Nationale of Belgium.

37mm gun used in the infantry's tanks. So they wanted a 50-caliber machine gun so that they stood a chance of shooting up the armored vehicles that *'The Other Side'* were using. Air-cooled, of course; you couldn't go slinging a gun around in all directions when it had a hose-pipe attached to the water condenser. And who wanted to climb out on top of the Combat Car to fill the water jacket in the middle of a battle?

The Ordnance Department were ahead of them, and when the cavalry made a formal request in 1932 a design was waiting. A handful were built for troop tests, they proved to be highly successful weapons, and in 1933 they entered the Tables of Organization and Equipment as the 'Machine gun, .50, Heavy Barrel, M2'; to be universally known thereafter as the M2HB. The barrel was smooth and tapering, 36 inches long, and was held in place by a short perforated sleeve that screwed into the forward end of the receiver. This served to lock the barrel after the headspace had been adjusted, and also protected unwary hands from the hottest part of the barrel. The M2 also had the ability to be adjusted to feed from either side, though feeding from the left was the usual mode of operation.

In 1936 the 36-inch barrel was replaced by a 45-inch version; this allowed the bullet to develop its maximum power by allowing the powder gas to work on it for an additional nine inches. It improved the accuracy and consistency, though it slightly slowed the rate of fire due to the additional weight, which had to be moved during the recoil operation. From 1936 onwards the 50-caliber Browning began to appear more and more in widely different places; firstly on armored vehicles but then on aircraft, both as a fixed gun and as a flexible or turret-mounted gun; on twin- and quadruple- anti-aircraft mounts; on ground mounts; on ships; and during World War II it was to spread into other armies and countries. But until the 1980s the M2HB remained exactly the same as it was in 1936.

The original M1921 water-cooled weapon had exhibited a defect after some years of service; prolonged firing led to overheating of the muzzle, which protruded beyond the water-jacket, with consequent stripping of the rifling and deformation, leading to inaccurate shooting. Various 'field expedients' were tried, to no avail, and in the end it was decided to redesign the water jacket so as to entirely surround the barrel, in such a way that the muzzle was actually recessed into the jacket. With this change the gun became the 'M2 Water Cooled'. It, too, was given the 45-inch barrel in 1936, which led

firstly to a modification having an extension piece to the original water jacket - recognizable by the nine- or ten-inch front section of the jacket being of smaller diameter than the rest - and then to a completely new water jacket which retained the recessed-muzzle feature but was of the same diameter throughout its length. The M2 Water Cooled was almost entirely used as an air defense weapon by both the army and navy; the army replaced it by M2HB models as soon as they could during World War II, and thereafter only the US Navy used it.

For aircraft use, the Browning 50 underwent more transformations. The US Army Air Corps were quick to demand an air-cooled version of the gun and the M1921 was given a perforated barrel jacket almost as soon as it appeared. The only drawback was that the stick-and-string aircraft of the day were unable to support the recoil force, and therefore after a couple or three trials the gun was shelved while the Air Corps canvassed manufacturers for an airplane strong enough to carry it. Eventually, better aircraft came along and the Air Corps was able to find funds for 1000 M1921 Aircraft guns by the middle 1920s. Two versions were produced, one with spade grips and a trigger for use by air gunners, and one with a mechanical trigger connection for use with

The M2HB 50-caliber Browning was introduced in 1933 but it had to wait until World War II to become universally popular.

synchronizing gear for firing through the propeller arc. But the design of the M1921 gun was such that it could only feed from the left side, which made installation in some kinds of aircraft a difficult task. The Air Corps set about developing a gun that would feed from the right; then they developed a conversion set that permitted a gun to be adjusted to feed from whatever side was required. This became the M1923E gun, and the conversion was then extended to all the M2 guns, as we have already mentioned above. And with that, the M1923E Convertible gun was re-designated to become the M2 Aircraft gun.

The one noteworthy thing about the aircraft family is that they all retained the original 36-inch barrel of the 1921 gun, and did not make the change to the 45-inch barrel in 1936, as did all the ground guns. On the face of it this sounds strange, because the object of the longer barrel was to develop a greater velocity and thus put more punch into the bullet, and one might assume this to be desirable in an aircraft machine gun. So it is, but what is more desirable is a high rate of fire, and the short-barreled M2 provides just that. The recoiling parts of the 45-inch barrel M2 weigh 38.8lbs (17.6kg) and the gun has a rate of fire of from 450 to 575 rounds per minute, depending upon how the oil buffer is adjusted.

The M2 aircraft gun has recoiling parts weighing 19.2lbs (8.7kg) and can reach 850 rounds per minute, putting a lot more metal into the air in the course of a short engagement.

As to the comparative velocities, this is a lot harder to pin down; some of the official figures are, frankly, unbelievable. For example, the Ordnance School Text 'Handbook of Ordnance Materiel', OS9-63, issued by Aberdeen Proving Ground in June 1943, gives the muzzle velocity of the ground M2 with 45-inch barrel as '2500 ft/sec approx.' and the velocity of the M2 Aircraft with 36-inch barrel as '2830-2900 ft/sec', which is obvious nonsense. You do not saw nine inches off a barrel and get an increase of 400 feet a second.

OS-9-18, Ammunition - General, Vol 1, of November 1944 describes the 50-caliber Ball M2 cartridge and says it has a muzzle

velocity of 2935 ft/sec, though without specifying which gun this figure was obtained with. This, though, is a theoretical figure that is deduced from the actual measured velocity of 2900 ft/sec at 78 feet from the gun muzzle. Later in the same text the tracer round M1 is described and has an observed velocity at 78 feet of 2830 ft/sec. Just to compound the mischief, the ball bullet weighed 709.5 grains, while the tracer weighed 681 grains that, if no further figures were available, might suggest that the tracer would have a higher velocity than the ball. Chinn *(Vol 1)* merely observes that *'the caliber .50 ammunition available during this period* (i.e. for the 36-inch barrel M1921 guns) *had a velocity of approximately 2700 feet per second, identical with that of the caliber .30 ammunition'* which doesn't get us much further. A clue appears in *OS-9-18* when it remarks, casually, that *'the Cartridge Tracer M1 is used principally by the Air Corps',* and, elsewhere, that *'the Air Corps no longer uses the M1 Ball cartridge'.* This led me to further digging into records and manuals

The 30-caliber M2 Browning was, like the 50 M2, a slow starter but eventually appeared in every corner of the world.

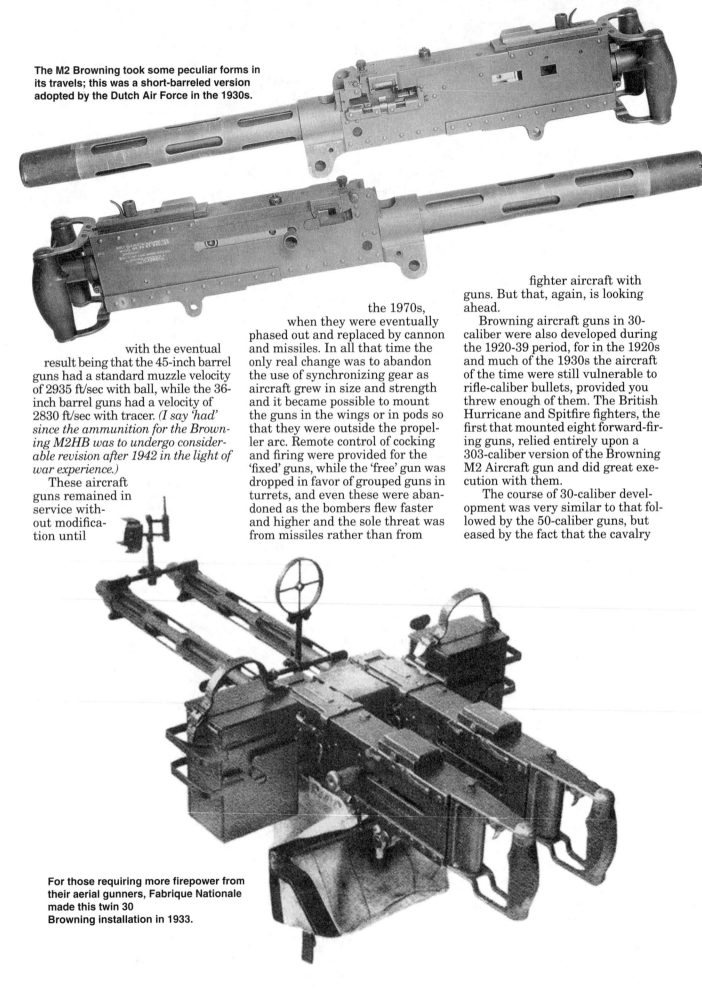

The M2 Browning took some peculiar forms in its travels; this was a short-barreled version adopted by the Dutch Air Force in the 1930s.

with the eventual result being that the 45-inch barrel guns had a standard muzzle velocity of 2935 ft/sec with ball, while the 36-inch barrel guns had a velocity of 2830 ft/sec with tracer. *(I say 'had' since the ammunition for the Browning M2HB was to undergo considerable revision after 1942 in the light of war experience.)*

These aircraft guns remained in service without modification until the 1970s, when they were eventually phased out and replaced by cannon and missiles. In all that time the only real change was to abandon the use of synchronizing gear as aircraft grew in size and strength and it became possible to mount the guns in the wings or in pods so that they were outside the propeller arc. Remote control of cocking and firing were provided for the 'fixed' guns, while the 'free' gun was dropped in favor of grouped guns in turrets, and even these were abandoned as the bombers flew faster and higher and the sole threat was from missiles rather than from fighter aircraft with guns. But that, again, is looking ahead.

Browning aircraft guns in 30-caliber were also developed during the 1920-39 period, for in the 1920s and much of the 1930s the aircraft of the time were still vulnerable to rifle-caliber bullets, provided you threw enough of them. The British Hurricane and Spitfire fighters, the first that mounted eight forward-firing guns, relied entirely upon a 303-caliber version of the Browning M2 Aircraft gun and did great execution with them.

The course of 30-caliber development was very similar to that followed by the 50-caliber guns, but eased by the fact that the cavalry

For those requiring more firepower from their aerial gunners, Fabrique Nationale made this twin 30 Browning installation in 1933.

were anxious for an air-cooled gun, and thus the development of air cooling was applied to both requirements and the eventual results were virtually the same, merely differing in small details which were demanded by the different methods of use. For example, aircraft guns were not provided with sights; fixed guns didn't need sights because they were built into the aircraft and the sighting system was part of the aircraft itself, and flexible guns were merely given sight mounts so that as the techniques of air-to-air gunnery improved and better sights were developed, they could be easily fitted to guns in place of the older pattern.

As with the 50-caliber gun, the principal drawback with the 30-caliber weapons was that they fed only from the left, thus making their installation difficult, and this was the first item to be addressed in the hunt for an aircraft gun. Air-cooling was done by the usual perforated jacket around the barrel, which gave the air access to the hot metal but kept careless fingers off it. Weight was shaved and the mechanism tuned so as to reach a rate of fire of 1000 rounds per minute and an empty weight of about 40 lbs. But one of the basic requirements of an aircraft gun is that it should work in any attitude – pointed sharply up or down, tilted to one side, upside-down, the gun still has to function – and in this respect the first attempts at constructing a specialized aircraft gun fell short of requirements. But by the late 1920s finance was becoming tight, and further development of the gun by the Air Corps was stopped. The ball was punted into the Colt company's yard, and they, with a fine sense of patriotic responsibility, undertook the development of the gun at their own expense. In 1929 they came back with a gun for test, it passed with flying colors - at

all angles - and in 1931 it was standardized as the Gun, Browning, 30 caliber, Aircraft, M2. As with the 50-caliber, it came in fixed or flexible forms, could be synchronized to fire through the propellers, could feed from left or right and could be mounted on open-cockpit Scarff rings or in turrets for free operation.

Having thus sorted all their machine guns out, the Army now turned back to the automatic rifle to see what needed to be done there. As with many other weapons, wartime experience showed that there were a few points that could be improved - not many, it must be said, because like most of John Browning's designs, it was more or less right from the start and just needed some fine-tuning. The first attempt to improve the BAR came with the M1922 model, which was designed specifically as a light machine gun for cavalry use. It was generally similar to the M1918 but had the barrel heavily finned to increase the radiation area and hence keep the barrel cool, had a bipod attached to the barrel, the sight from the Browning M1919 machine gun, and grooves cut into the butt to permit clamping a rear monopod to take the weight during prolonged firing or permit the alignment of the gun for firing on fixed defensive lines. It was never produced in great numbers and is rarely encountered today, having been declared obsolete in 1940.

In 1927 the M1918A1 appeared, with a spike-footed bipod attached to the gas cylinder and a butt-plate that was hinged so that it sat on the firer's shoulder and thus took some of the weight off his wrist. Then in 1939, after more experience, the M1918A2 appeared; this had a skid-footed adjustable bipod attached to the flash hider, the M1919 machine gun sight with windage adjustment, the forend

reduced in depth so as to expose more barrel for cooling and also fitted with a metal heat shield to prevent the recoil spring in the gas cylinder becoming overheated during prolonged firing; and an adjustable rate of fire, either 450 or 650 rounds per minute but with no facility for single shots.

With that, development came to an end and the M1918A2 was the basic squad automatic weapon throughout World War II, finally being removed from service by the arrival of the M60 machine gun in the late 1950s. The final production of M1918A2s took place during the Korean War when the Royal McBee Typewriter Company produced 61,000 rifles.

Which brings us back to Lt. Col. Barlow and his comment on calling it a *heavy* rifle or a *light* light machine gun. What he really meant was that, in truth, it was neither one thing nor the other. It was too heavy and clumsy to be a good rifle, and too light and limited in its abilities to be a good light machine gun. The fact that it stayed in first-line service for forty years or so was not necessarily a testimonial to its efficiency, more a confession of failure to develop anything better in a period when other armies were fielding far superior light machine guns. Its principal drawbacks were the limited magazine capacity, due to feeding from below, and the fixed barrel, which tended to limit the ability to deliver sustained fire due to overheating. But in the eyes of many people these were outweighed by its ease of manufacture and its low cost, compared to other and more exotic guns.

Fabrique Nationale of Belgium, who had long connections with Browning, obtained a license to manufacture in the 1920s and supplied the BAR to a number of countries, notably the newly-emergent countries such as Poland and the Baltic states who needed to equip armies quickly and as cheaply as possible.

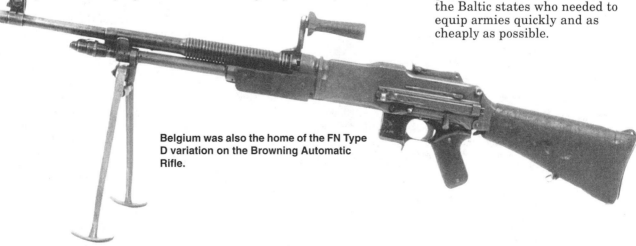

Belgium was also the home of the FN Type D variation on the Browning Automatic Rifle.

The 30-caliber air-cooled Hudson machine gun, tested in 1933. The long tube beneath the barrel casing contains the counter-recoil system.

With the immediate demand satisfied, FN then set about improving the design so as to make it more attractive to potential buyers. Their 'Model 1930' retained the characteristic receiver but used a finned barrel and added a pistol grip. The rocker-footed bipod was attached to the gas cylinder and a peculiar dome-shaped gas regulator crowned the cylinder. Covers were provided for the magazine and ejection openings and the forend was shorter, shallower and with finger grooves instead of the usual checkering. The Model 30 could be supplied from stock in 7mm Spanish, 7.65mm Belgian and 7.92mm German Mauser chambering and would doubtless have been produced in others had there been any demand. A small number were fitted with quick-change barrels locking into the receiver by means of an interrupted thread.

After World War II FN took a harder look at the BAR and did another re-design, producing the result as the 'FN BAR Type D'. In addition to having the quick-change barrel as standard, they also re-arranged the internals, shifting the return spring into the butt, so that the weapon became far easier to field-strip. A mechanical escapement-type rate of fire regulator was fitted, rather than the buffer type used in the US M1918A2, and a monopod was available for fitting into a socket under the butt. But by the time FN had the design perfected, the BAR

was obsolescent and the only quantity purchasers were Egypt and the Belgian army.

The Swedish Army adopted the BAR in 1921, purchasing a number from Colt and having them chambered for their 6.5mm Swedish Mauser cartridge. Generally speaking they are the same as the US M1918 but are easily distinguished by their curved magazine, pistol grip and bell-mouthed flash hider. In the 1930s the Carl Gustav state rifle factory set about re-designing the gun in the light of their experience with it, and produced the Model 37. This had a quick-change barrel and hence had the forend modified to make room for the barrel mounting and locking mechanism, but was otherwise similar to the Model 21, firing the same 6.5mm cartridge.

The last of the distinguishable variants of the BAR is the Polish Model 28; this was in 7.92mm Mauser caliber and was mechanically the same as the M1918A1, distinguishable by the pistol grip and the stock, which is shaped so that the upper surface is longer than the lower surface and the

butt-plate is distinctly curved. Indeed it is quite similar to the US M1919A6 machine gun butt, and in both cases the intention seems to have been to help retain the butt on the shoulder by relieving the firer's wrist of some of the weight.

The BAR was also sold on the commercial market as a police weapon, as the Colt 'Monitor'. It was simply an M1918 with a shorter barrel and capable of semi-automatic fire only. And the final variant was the T34, which was an M1918A2 chambered for the 7.62mm NATO cartridge but which got no further than the prototype stage before the M60 machine gun rendered it superfluous.

The U.S. Navy had adopted the water-cooled 50 Browning, but were not entirely happy with it, feeling that it lacked the range and weight of bullet to deal satisfactorily with torpedo bombers and sundry other types of aerial attack peculiar to navies. Their request for something with more authority than the 50-caliber weapon was formulated in the late 1920s, and a Mr. R.F. Hudson of the Naval Gun Factory in Washington D.C. began studying the problem. The principal difficulty with naval weapons is the 'deck blow', the amount of force delivered to the ship's structure by the recoil force of the weapon; the more recoil force that can be absorbed in the mounting, the better, since this means less 'deck blow'. And with a light weapon such as was being called for, which was liable to be mounted on everything from motor torpedo boats to battleships, the deck blow was still something to be

The next largest Hudson design was this 50-caliber. It worked well enough but the Navy had already decided that the 0.50-inch bullet was not man enough for their requirements, so it got no further.

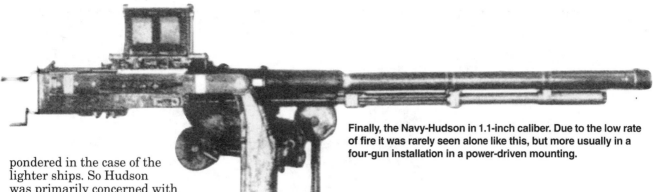

Finally, the Navy-Hudson in 1.1-inch caliber. Due to the low rate of fire it was rarely seen alone like this, but more usually in a four-gun installation in a power-driven mounting.

pondered in the case of the lighter ships. So Hudson was primarily concerned with designing a gun that would have the least possible recoil and thus a deck blow that would be tolerable in even the lightest of craft. His ambition, it seems, was to develop an all-purpose universal mechanism that would fit any caliber from .30 to 3 inches, but he was soon disabused of this idea, and eventually settled on a design, which he drew up in 30-, 50- and 1.1-inch calibers. Since the Navy had already dismissed the 30 and 50 as not being up to their requirements, the 1.1-inch was selected for further development.

Hudson's design relied upon a loose piston moving in a cylinder parallel to and beneath the gun barrel. This cylinder was connected to the gun barrel by a gas port. So far, so good, but the action was not that of a normal gas-actuated weapon. In this case, the gas came out of the barrel and blew the heavy piston *forward*, against a spring, until it struck the solid end of the cylinder. This, obviously, worked in opposition to the recoil force acting on the weapon due to the explosion of the cartridge and the subsequent reactive force against the bolt face. So, in effect, the forward movement of the piston canceled out some of the rearward movement of the gun, so reducing the blow felt by the mounting and, through it, the ship's deck.

When the piston reached its forward point and struck the end of the cylinder, which was carefully timed to occur just before the projectile left the barrel, it uncovered an exhaust port, which allowed the gas to escape to the atmosphere. The spring which had been compressed by the forward movement of the piston now reasserted itself, throwing the piston back, and this movement was communicated to two driving rods which unlocked and opened the breech, then drove the bolt back against a conventional return spring. As the bolt reached its rearmost position a clutch was operated to disengage the main spring (which had propelled the piston) so that the return spring could then drive the

bolt forward, chambering a fresh round, closing and locking the breech and returning the piston to its 'rest' position. The clutch then re-engaged and the mainspring was ready for the next round. It can be seen that the inter-action of the two springs was, in many respects, similar to the balancing act done by the springs in the Beardmore-Farquhar machine gun.

Ammunition was fed from an overhead box magazine holding eight rounds, and the cartridge was specially developed for the gun and never used anywhere else; it used a semi-rimmed case about eight inches long and fired a 14.5oz (416g) shell at 2700 ft/sec (823 m/sec). The shell was fitted with a super-sensitive impact fuze, designed to function on striking the thin fabric of an aircraft wing of the day; this was another reason for the complex mechanism of the gun, that it permitted a controlled rate of fire and a feed system in which the bolt and other component parts were always moving at a controlled speed, independent of any variations which might arise from chamber pressure or sticky cartridge cases.

Due to the system of operation and the frequent need to change magazines, the rate of fire was no more than 120 rounds per minute, and this was not really enough to put the amount of metal into the sky that the Navy felt to be necessary. So for those ships that had the room and strong enough decks, a quadruple mounting was developed and in 1939 the 'Navy-Hudson' 1.1-inch machine gun was formally adopted and installations began. It was not the easiest gun in the world to operate and maintain, but given adequate time to train the crews, good results could be obtained. The Navy were satisfied that they had their low-level air defense under control.

If America was in the best position in 1919, France was probably in the worst; their machine gun

strength was almost entirely made up of elderly Hotchkiss designs, supplemented by the execrable Chauchat and a few Darne guns which, while moderately reliable, were hardly the sort of quality that a peacetime army, with views on the robustness of equipment, would be likely to tolerate. They were, moreover, severely hampered by their standard cartridge, the abruptly tapered and bottle-necked, heavy-rimmed 8mm Lebel. Very wisely, they therefore made their first priority a new cartridge. Once they had that sorted out, a complete new range of infantry weapons could be developed.

To save time they began design of a new machine gun at the same time, and the two came together in 1924 for some practical trials. The cartridge had been developed by taking a good look at the German 7.92x57mm Mauser and the Swiss 7.5mm Schmidt-Rubin rounds and making alterations to suit French preferences; the result was a 7.5x59mm rimless round of considerable power. The gun was a gas-operated weapon using a tilting breech-block locking into the top of the receiver, more or less a copy of the Browning Automatic Rifle system, and first tests appeared to promise a successful combination of weapon and cartridge. The French set about planning mass-production, and also advertised the machine gun for sale to other countries. In 1926 a Romanian delegation were test-firing a gun when a bore explosion occurred which severely injured the firer and several bystanders. Similar explosions took place when the gun began reaching the troops, and very quickly the French soldiers lost whatever confidence they might have had in the weapon. The explosions were officially ascribed to the similarity between the French cartridge and the 7.92x57mm Mauser,

(Continued on Page 103)

CHATELLERAULT Mle 24/29

The Chatellerault Mle 1924/29, a sound if undistinguished light machine gun that served for many years.

Experience in World War II convinced the French that their first post-war task was the development of a decent light machine gun. First, though, they had to develop a modern rimless cartridge, which they did by virtually duplicating the Mauser 7.92mm round - but in 7.5mm caliber. The machine gun followed and was in production in 1924, but the cartridge was badly designed and caused a series of embarrassing accidents, so the whole thing was withdrawn and redesigned, the cartridge being 'de-tuned' in the process and given a shorter case which made it almost a duplicate of the existing 7.5mm Swiss round. The result became the Mle 1929 cartridge and the Mle 1924/29 machine gun.

The resulting gun was a sound if not inspired design that appears to have been influenced by the Browning Automatic Rifle. The Chatellerault *(named after the arsenal which designed it)* was gas operated using a tipping bolt that was locked into a prepared face in the receiver. Variants were developed for fortification and aircraft employment, and although these did not survive World War II, the basic infantry weapon remained in use with the French army until the early 1960s. Numbers can still be found in the armed forces of various ex-French colonies.

Field Stripping

Set the safety catch to 'Safe', remove the magazine and pull back the cocking handle. Inspect the feedway and chamber to ensure no ammunition remains in the gun. Set the safety catch to 'Fire' (upwards), hold the cocking handle and press the trigger, allowing the working parts to go forward under control. Leave the magazine dust cover open.

Unscrew and remove the locking pin at the bottom rear of the receiver. The butt can be lifted off by rotating it upwards, and at the same time the trigger group will come free and swing down; it can be unhooked from its retaining lugs in the receiver by pressing it up and forward slightly, and then removed.

Remove the return spring from the receiver. Pull back the cocking handle to withdraw the bolt and piston assembly. Push out the link pin and separate the bolt from the piston slide. Rotate the lock at the rear end of the gas cylinder to the vertical, swing the rear end of

DATA	
Caliber **Mle 1929**	7.5 x 54mm French
Operating system	Gas, selective fire
Locking system	Tipping bolt
Feed system	26-round box magazine
Overall length	42.60in (1082mm)
Weight, empty	20lb 4oz (9.18kg)
Barrel	19.70in (500mm); 4 grooves, right-hand twist
Muzzle velocity	2700 ft/sec (823 m/sec)
Muzzle energy	2251 ft/lbs (3042 Joules)
Rate of fire	500 rds/minute

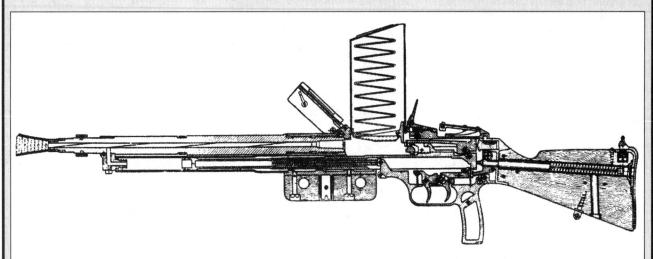

The Mle 24/29 showing the weapon cocked. Note the two triggers for selecting single shots or automatic fire.

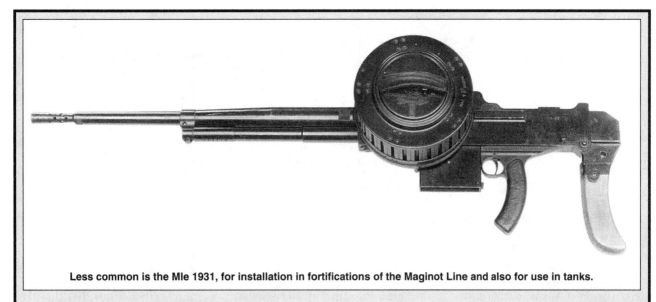

Less common is the Mle 1931, for installation in fortifications of the Maginot Line and also for use in tanks.

the cylinder to the right, and draw it back to separate it from the gas block on the barrel.

This is as far as normal field-stripping goes, but if necessary it is possible to remove the barrel; two wrenches, which fit the flats on the

barrel and receiver, will be needed. Rotate the barrel lock at the left front of the receiver until its index mark points to the 'O' stamped in the receiver. Using the two wrenches, unscrew the barrel counter-clockwise and remove. When refitting the

barrel, screw tight until the two index marks are aligned, then rotate the barrel lock to its former position.

Re-assembly after field-stripping is simply a reversal of the dismantling procedure; there are no hidden traps.

Hotchkiss produced this model in 1922 in an effort to interest the French Army, but they were intent upon developing their own design and left Hotchkiss to sell it on the commercial market.

(Continued from Page 101)

and the likelihood of the wrong ammunition being used with the gun *(since 7.92 German machine guns were being used by the French Army for training at that time).* Whatever the cause, the gun and cartridge were withdrawn, the cartridge re-designed in shorter and slightly less powerful form to become the 7.5x54mm Mle 1929, and the gun, suitably modified, was re-issued as the Mle 24/29, commonly called the Chatellerault from the arsenal in which it had been developed.

The Mle 24/29 was of conventional form, a receiver and butt with an air-cooled barrel and a gas cylinder underneath, plus a top-mounted box magazine, all supported by a bipod. Some can also be found with a telescoping monopod underneath the butt. The barrel is not quick-change-able, but can be removed with the requisite tools, and there are two triggers, the front one giving single shots and the rear one automatic fire at about 500 rpm. A rather unusual item was the short wooden forend

ahead of the trigger guard, which allowed a convenient grip for firing from the hip, the weight being mostly taken by a sling around the firer's shoulder. The wartime concept of 'walking fire' took a long time to die. The rate of fire was rather less than the 'natural' rate of the gun, and was set by means of a rate regulator built into the butt and the rear end of the receiver. Inside the butt is a tube containing a

In an endeavor to widen its appeal, the Hotchkiss 1922 was also made in belt-fed form, but this apparently never got past the development stage.

In an attempt to avoid being 'dated' Hotchkiss changed their system of model numbers; this was the 'Type 2' that succeeded the Model 1922. Fed from a top-mounted magazine it is unusual *(for a Hotchkiss)* in having a forward handgrip similar to that used on the Chauchat, probably in an attempt to fit into the current tactical theories of the late 1920s.

spring and a heavy 'actuator', simply a steel rod. On firing, as the piston and bolt come back they strike the tip of the rod and drive it down the tube, against the pressure of the spring. At the same instant a secondary sear locks the piston and prevents it returning. The actuator goes down the tube, stops and is then flung back by the spring, and when it reaches the end of the butt it strikes a sear release which trips the sear and allows the bolt to go forward to fire the next round. A similar system was to appear many years later on the Czech 'Skorpion' submachine gun of the 1960s.

The Mle 24/29 was fairly quickly augmented by a variation, the Mle 31 that was intended for use in the fortifications of the Maginot Line and also in tanks. It differs from the Mle 24/29 in its feed system; instead of a top-mounted 28-round box it has a side-mounted 150-round drum, and the feed was so designed that the drum could be fitted on either side, whichever was most convenient for its location. Finally, there was a belt-fed version, the Mle 34, for use in aircraft. Of these only the 24/29 survived after 1940, and there were sufficient of them left to outfit the French Army after 1945; its last campaign was in Vietnam in the 1960s in the hands of the Vietcong.

The 24/29 was, of course, classed as a light machine gun. What is surprising is that the French made no attempt to develop a medium or heavy gun to replace the 1914 Hotchkiss, with the result that they were still using it in 1939-40. This can be largely ascribed to their strategic policy: the defense of

France rested on the Maginot Line, and the only purpose of the infantry was to mount rapid offensive patrols and raids, for which the light machine gun was all that was necessary. Unfortunately, it didn't work out that way, but the French collapse in 1940 was so fast that nobody really missed the medium machine gun.

Britain came out of World War I with the Vickers and the Lewis pre-eminent, with the Hotchkiss as a cavalry weapon and a few Madsens in tanks. The Vickers was above reproach. The Lewis was good, but cumbersome. The Hotchkiss would do until something better came along. The Madsen was merely a stopgap and was ditched as soon as the war was over. So far as tanks went, weight was no object and therefore Vickers could make a few modifications to their standard design and produce whatever the *Tin Troopers* wanted. The *Feet*, though, wanted something more convenient than the Lewis if it was to be had. And Vickers had an idea that they could deal with this infantry requirement as well.

In the previous chapter we saw that during 1918 a machine gun designed by the French officer General Berthier had been under scrutiny in the USA under the designation M1917. With the wartime urgency removed, the US Army realized that the design needed more work than they were prepared to fund, and closed down their involvement with Berthier. He then took his design back to

Europe, made a few changes in the light of the experience gained during the American venture, and offered the gun to Vickers in England. Vickers saw that it still needed some work done on it, principally production engineering work to turn it into a reliable and more easily manufactured weapon, something that Vickers could do far better than General Berthier. But they also saw that there was the basis of a good machine gun there, a design that they could, once it was up and running, offer to the British Army as their new light machine gun.

In 1925 Vickers acquired the rights to the Berthier design and began putting their experience to work on it. But the middle 1920s were not a good time to try and sell machine guns - or anything else, for that matter - to the British Army. Money was tight, and getting tighter; the Commandant of the Tank School asked for funds to carry out tests of a new machine gun and was authorized to spend £50 per year - $200 at the then rate of exchange. You didn't get much machine gun for $200, even in the 1920s. So Vickers spent their time refining the Vickers-Berthier until it was just about perfect.

The V-B is often mistaken for the Bren; they both have pistol grips, a flared muzzle, a curved overhead magazine and a bipod. It was Vickers' first venture into

A 6.5mm Hotchkiss supplied to the Greek Army in 1926-28.

The Darne aircraft observer's gun of 1920 used a lifting breechblock driven by a gas piston and could be fed by either Hotchkiss strips or a cloth belt. It was adopted by several of the smaller European air forces and tested by several more.

gas-operated guns and they took their time about getting it right, juggling with the position of the gas port, the diameter of the cylinder, the strength of the return spring and various other factors until they had a very smooth-operating and stress-free gun. The system of bolt locking is similar to the Bren, the rear end of the bolt being driven up by the piston so as to lock into a recess in the roof of the receiver. As well as the tilting bolt, the first models also had a slab-sided wooden forend to allow firing from the hip during the

new light machine gun, and the Indian Army was tired of waiting, so it adopted the Mark 3 Vickers-Berthier, obtained a license from Vickers, and began manufacturing it at the Ishapore Rifle Factory.

The Mark 1 had been introduced in 1928; the Mark 2 appeared in 1929 and was similar to the Mark 1 but with the forend more rounded and extended forward of the receiver to support the gas cylinder. It has a bipod and butt monopod. This was the first gun tested by the

plemented in about 1938 by the Mark 3B, which was almost identical, merely having some minor changes in the gas piston and cylinder to simplify manufacture and improve reliability.

The between-wars years were slow when it came to selling machine guns for ground troops, because armies were more or less static. A far greater potential market lay in the various air forces, because the design of aircraft was proceeding so fast that airplanes

After their success with the aircraft gun, Darne modified it into an infantry light machine gun in 1926, but did less well with it. Infantry demanded a far more robust weapon than did air forces and, although the Darne was reliable, it was far from strong enough for field service.

assault. The principal differences between the early V-B and the Bren were the name engraved on the receiver and the fins on the barrel of the V-B.

Vickers made a few sales, principally to Latvia and some South American states, in the early 1930s, but their big break-through came in 1933 when the Indian Army adopted the gun. It should be explained that although the Indian Army was a British creation and run by the British, it was under no obligation to use the same equipment as the British army; for most of the time it did, but occasionally it lost patience with the dithering and indecision in London, or claimed that its conditions of terrain and climate justified some particular weapon. This was one of those times; the British Army was still trying to make up its mind about a

Indian Army, and after they reported their findings to Vickers, the 'Light Mark 2' was produced. This did away with the monopod, cut away some of the butt, lightened the forend and adopted a smooth barrel without fins. Numbers of these were sent to India in 1931 and were duly put through their paces there. Once again the Indian Army gave its verdict; once again Vickers went back to the drawing board and the result was the Mark 3, which is best described as a beefed-up Light Mark 2, since the only demand was to strengthen some of the parts to withstand the arduous conditions of active service on the North-west Frontier of India.

The Mark 3 equipped the Indian Army during World War II and for several years thereafter, being sup-

were obsolete before they were built, and every new military airplane demanded some form of armament. And, as we saw in World War I, the prime demand was a high rate of fire and a light gun, two things that were not naturally compatible. Vickers, having managed to get a worthwhile contract out of the Vickers-Berthier, now began to look at the aviation market and wonder whether the V-B might have a future in the sky. There was, of course, no hope for it as a fixed and synchronized gun, since the standard Vickers had that aspect fairly well sewed up - or so they thought - but there was room for an observer's free gun. And so they adapted the V-B system to produce a weapon which, to differentiate it

(Continued on Page 108)

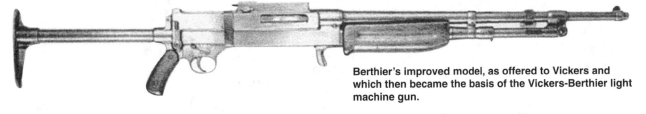

Berthier's improved model, as offered to Vickers and which then became the basis of the Vickers-Berthier light machine gun.

VICKERS-BERTHIER

The Vickers-Berthier Mark 1 of 1928 had a distinctly French flavor to it, with finned barrel, monopod under the butt and short wooden forend.

The basic design of this gun was due to General Berthier of the French Army, and it was tentatively adopted by the US

DATA (Mark 3)	
Caliber	.303 British
Operating system	Gas, selective fire
Locking system	Tilting bolt
Feed system	30-round overhead box
Overall length	45.5in (1180mm)
Weight, empty	22.0 lbs (9.98kg)
Barrel	23.5in (597mm), 5 grooves, right-hand twist
Muzzle velocity	2450 ft/sec (745 m/sec)
Muzzle energy	2310 ft/lbs (3121J)
Rate of fire	600 rds/min
Effective range	600 yards

Army as the M1917 Berthier; but no production was done before World War I ended and the design was promptly dropped. Berthier then sold the rights to Vickers in Britain in 1925; they made some improvements and began manufacture at low volume, principally to keep one of their factories in work during the 1920s. The design was put forward for adoption by the British Army but was beaten at the eleventh hour by the ZB26. However, the Indian Army were not about to wait until the British production of the Bren got going and satisfied the British requirements before they got their chance at it, so they adopted the Vickers-Berthier.

The gun served the Indian Army well, being manufactured in the Ishapore Rifle Factory under license before and during World War II; and it is worth looking twice at any wartime pictures of Indian army troops firing a Bren gun, because it is more likely to be a V-B.

Information has recently come to light of a belt-fed version of the Vickers-Berthier in 13.2mm caliber, on twin and quadruple anti-aircraft mountings. These were proposed in the early 1920s for use on warships, but the idea does not appear to have been developed as far as production. It is probable that the sudden downturn in warship building after the Washington Conference in 1924 led to Vickers abandoning the idea and concentrating on the infantry gun as having a better chance of adoption.

Field Stripping

Remove the magazine, pull back the cocking lever and ensure that the chamber and feedway are empty. Pull the trigger and allow the working parts to go forward into the fired position.

Push out the locking-pin at the front of the trigger guard from left to right. This will allow the butt group, which

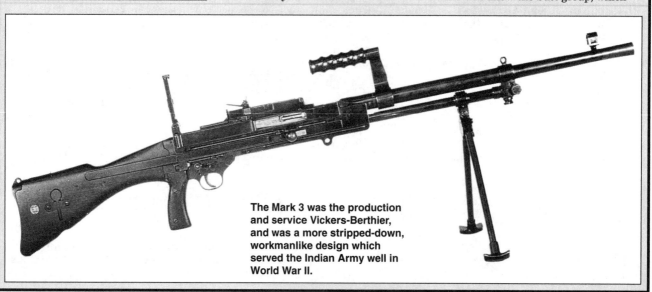

The Mark 3 was the production and service Vickers-Berthier, and was a more stripped-down, workmanlike design which served the Indian Army well in World War II.

After the Indian Army made a few suggestions, this was the 'Indian Light Mark 2' with a not-very-quick-change smooth barrel, a flash eliminator and no monopod.

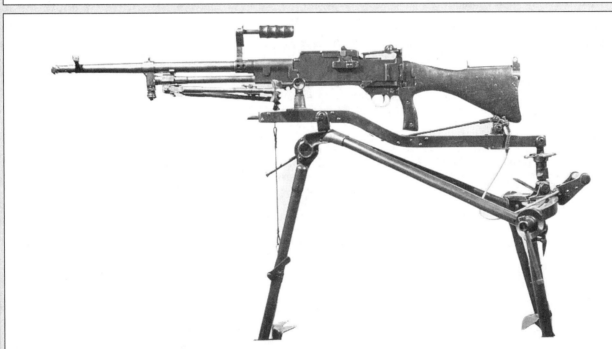

The Mark 3 could be mounted on this tripod for either supporting fire or, more usually, for firing on fixed defensive lines at night.

includes the pistol grip and the trigger mechanism, to be detached by raising the butt at the rear end and unhook the butt group and return spring from the body. Then remove the return spring from the butt.

Pull back the cocking-handle sharply and catch the piston and breech-block as they come out. Remove breech-block from the piston by pulling it forwards and upwards.

To remove the barrel, press in the carrying handle catch button and turn the carrying handle to the vertical. Pull the barrel locking-pin catch to the rear to release the catch from the receiver and turn down and forwards as far as it will go. This will disengage the gas cylinder from the barrel. Holding the carrying handle, rotate the barrel over to the right, disengaging the threaded portion from the receiver, and push the barrel forward and out of the gun.

To remove the gas cylinder pull the barrel locking-pin catch backwards and up into the locked position. This brings the serrated portion of the barrel locking-pin out of engagement with the gas cylinder, and the cylinder - complete with bipod - can be pushed forwards out of the receiver. Now pull the barrel locking-pin catch to the rear, turn it down and forward as when removing the barrel, and withdraw it to the left.

To assemble

Reverse the above procedure. Remember to assemble the breech-block to the piston before putting the piston back into the gun.

The Vickers GO *(Gas Operated)*, or Type K, gun used a drum magazine and was based on the Vickers-Berthier mechanism. An excellent weapon, it appeared just as air forces were changing to belt-fed turret-mounted guns, and it was lucky to be able to sell at all. It made its mark, in later years, as a ground gun with the Special Air Service and the Long Range Desert Group.

(Continued from Page 105)

from the infantry V-B, they called the Vickers Gas Operated, or Vickers G.O. or Vickers Type K.

The principal difference was that the G.O. had a spade grip at the rear end, instead of a wooden butt, had no pistol grip, fed from a round, flat 100-round drum magazine and, most important of all, had a rate of fire of 1050 rounds per minute instead of the V-B's 600. And at 21lbs it was one pound lighter than the V-B, which was quite an achievement in itself.

By the time Vickers got the G.O. perfected, however, it was 1937, at which time open cockpits were going out of fashion and power-operated turrets were all the rage. And a magazine-fed gun had no place in a power-operated turret. Nevertheless they sold a number of various air forces who still retained open-cockpit machines, including the British Royal Air Force.

At about the same time as General Berthier made his journey from the USA to Britain, another inventor made the trip; it was hardly worth his while but it led to an interesting, if minor, digression. General John T. Thompson arrived in Europe in 1920 to promote his

Thompson sub-machine gun and discuss the possibility of co-production with the BSA company in Britain. Since Thompson had very little idea of what the European market might be, BSA were not particularly enthusiastic about the idea and suggested Thompson do his market research first. This Thompson did, but found little interest so soon after the war and returned to the USA.

However, the memory lingered, and in about 1925 the Belgians expressed an interest in the Thompson gun, provided it could be produced in 9mm Parabellum caliber. Thompson contacted BSA who, with a reasonably firm prospect in view, agreed to collaborate. The eventually produced a 9mm version of the well-known sub-machine gun, but by that time the Belgians had a change of heart and the project foundered.

Thompson had also interested the BSA people in his automatic rifle; this is a weapon entirely distinct from the sub-machine gun, and had been developed as a result of Oscar Payne *(Thompson's designer/draftsman)* developing a form of delayed blowback bolt action which relied upon an interrupted-thread lock to the bolt which was so angled that

under high pressure it remained locked but as the breech pressure dropped so the friction of the interfaces was eased and the bolt was able to unlock itself. This was a by-blow of the Blish system of slipping inclined faces, which was the heart of the sub-machine gun, and it proved to be workable with high-pressure rifle ammunition. BSA were attracted by this and, while developing an automatic rifle based on the Thompson/Payne idea, they also developed the 'BSA-Thompson Light Machine Gun' with a view to interesting the British Army - this being the late 1920s, at which time the Small Arms Committee, as we shall see, were hunting for a replacement for the Lewis. But as soon as BSA broached the idea they were rebuffed: there was no way that the SAC would accept a delayed *(or any other form of)* blowback machine gun. A prototype was made, but the project was closed down as soon as the SAC's refusal indicated its lack of future. I photographed the prototype, shown here, in BSA's private collection some forty years ago, shortly before the entire collection was sold at auction, but its present whereabouts are unknown.

The Indians were very happy with the V-B and were not slow in urging the British Army to follow suit. The British had been fiddling with light machine gun designs ever since 1919; indeed, in 1922 it was proposed to adopt the Browning Automatic Rifle as the 'Browning

The Lewis gun continued in service with some air forces well into the 1930s; this is a 1930 model used by the Dutch air force. The all-enveloping slotted barrel jacket is unusual for a Lewis gun.

This exceptionally rare specimen is the short-lived BSA-Thompson, which should probably be classified as a machine rifle. It used the Payne variant of the Blish system of slipping inclined faces to provide a somewhat dubious lock for the interrupted-thread bolt.

Light Machine Gun', but there was never enough money available to carry out this idea and as a result the Small Arms Committee kept trying out various designs as they appeared. Hotchkiss, Madsen, Beardmore-Farquhar, Browning, improved Lewis patterns; all was grist that came to the SAC's mill. In 1924 the Beardmore was rejected; in 1925 the French Mle 24 was given a short trial, and in 1926 a Swiss Fürrer was bought and very rapidly rejected. 1927 saw the McCudden and the Eriksen machine guns under trial, 1928 saw a fresh design from the Madsen company, and in 1929 the McCudden gun re-appeared for a second trip round the arena before vanishing forever.

For 1930 the SAC organized a last, final and definitive trial that, they thought, would sort the sheep from the goats and find *The Gun*. Guns from Browning, Darne, Vickers-Berthier, Kiraly-Ende of SIG in Switzerland, and another Madsen were lined up for a trial to commence in October. And then, at the proverbial eleventh hour, came a letter from the British Military Attaché in Prague, Czechoslovakia. He had just been to see a demonstration of a machine gun manufactured by the *Zbrojovka Brno* (the Brno Armaments Factory) and had been most impressed by its accuracy, simplicity and reliability. Would the Small Arms Committee care to examine one? They would; for the sum of $300 (£75.25) they bought a ZB26; a further $210 (£52.33) bought them 10,000 rounds of 7.92mm Mauser ammunition, and on top of that there was a charge of $30 (£7.60)

for packing and delivery. In fact, what they got was a ZB27, a slightly improved model, and, contrary to legend, the ZB26 was never ever tested in Britain. The gun was then entered into the October trial.

While the Small Arms Committee is testing the ZB27, a short digression on the gun's antecedents would be in order. The commonly accepted legend is that the Holek brothers, designers for the Brno arms factory, sat down and designed the ZB 26 machine gun from scratch, after which it was transformed into the Bren. There is far more to it than that, however.

When the state of Czechoslovakia was founded after World War I, it lost no time in setting up arms factories. On 1 March 1919 the *Ceskoslovenska Zavodi Brno* was set up in a former artillery repair factory with experienced workers and design staff from former Austro-Hungarian arms factories and began manufacturing rifles. And since they looked outwards to the export market in order to make their factories viable, in 1922 they formed the *Ceskoslovenska Zbrojovka Brno* as a commercial arm to deal with foreign sales. Among other factories set up at much the same time was the *Praga Zbrojovka*, employing the two Holek brothers, Vaclav and Emmanuel.

The Czechs, like the Poles and other newly-formed central European nations, were flooded with French 'military advisers' whose primary function, it seems, was to sell French weapons and secondary, to disseminate French organizational and tactical theories. And the French flavor of the year in infantry tactics in the early 1920s was the 'Battle Cluster', a 13-man squad of storm troops, armed with rifles and

grenade launchers and with a light machine gun as the core. So a light machine gun was the Number One priority for the Czech Army.

The first postwar move was to examine Darne and Hotchkiss designs; neither gun entirely fitted in with the Czech tactical ideas but eventually a license was taken out to make a limited number of Hotchkiss guns, simply to have something with which to train the soldiers. The Brno factory undertook this. Meanwhile, in 1921 the Praga firm offered a light machine gun to the army; it was designed by a man called Rudolf Jelen and featured a 'forward-moving barrel' according to the surviving records, though it is difficult to determine exactly how it worked. In any event, the army threw it out, and the Praga works went back to try again. Eventually, by 1923 they had four guns that worked more or less, at least sufficiently for the military testing commission to report that they considered the design was worth supporting. The only problem was that the facilities at the Praga factory were somewhat limited, and even if they designed the bugs out of their gun they were in no condition to mass-produce it. So the government suggested that they should license their patents to the Brno factory, who could not only complete the development but were also equipped to manufacture in quantity.

At this point the whole picture is clouded by politics, dissent and suggestions of partisanship, if not outright bribery, but the eventual result was that in November 1923 the Brno factory took over the responsibility for future development of the Praga I-23 machine gun, whereupon it became the ZB24. In fact the arrangement was three-sided; Praga, with the Holek brothers, were still the design

The left side of the BSA-Thompson. It was offered to the British Army in the late 1920s but rejected on the grounds of small magazine capacity, a non-removable barrel and a dubious breech lock.

agency, while manufacture was to be divided between the Brno factory and the Skoda works.

Under the guidance of the Holek brothers, *Zbrojovka Brno* spent the next two years refining the gun to the point of production, whereupon it became the ZB26. It used gas operation, locked the breech by tilting the bolt up into the top of the receiver, had a most ingenious quick-change barrel *(which was finned for cooling)* and a top-mounted magazine. By the time of the British trials it had already been adopted by the Czech army and sold in large numbers abroad, notably to Yugoslavia, Lithuania, Brazil, Siam, Ecuador and Persia.

When the October 1930 trials ended the Small Arms Committee were in little doubt that the ZB27 was the best gun they had ever seen and everything the Military Attaché had said. It had fired over 10,000 rounds and displayed 'negligible' wear. The only trouble was that it fired the rimless 7.92mm Mauser cartridge, while the British army was equipped with the rimmed 303 Lee-Enfield round. Given the chance, the army would willingly have gone over to the rimless round, for they had a 7.92mm

A Madsen observer's gun; a design that was submitted to several air forces during the early 1930s but without seeing much success.

automatic rifle under trial at the time, but the Treasury vetoed the idea; the magazines were stuffed with zillions of rounds of 303 and there was a great deal of capital invested in machinery for making it. No chance. *(Exactly the same arguments were deployed against General MacArthur when he attempted to change the US Army's standard caliber from 30-06 to 276 with the Pedersen rifle at much the same time.)*

In April 1931 the SAC ordered another ZB27, but this time it was to be chambered for the British 303 cartridge. But by then Holek and his crew had been at work and the gun was now the ZB30, more small improvements having been incorporated into the design. And since it was being chambered for the British cartridge, it became the ZGB30.

A comparative trial was now set up between the ZGB30, the Vickers-Berthier and the Darne (which had not arrived in time for the 1930 trials). The trial program included accuracy shooting over varying ranges up to 2500 yards and a 30,000-round endurance test. The final report (which ran to 88 pages) reported that the ZGB30 was *"...of such outstanding design, workmanship and material as to warrant further serious consideration.."* The only defects were excessive fouling due to the position of the gas port not being suited to the use of cordite propellant, and occasional faulty ejection due to the hasty conversion of the gun to cope with rimmed ammunition. In May 1932 the gun went back to Brno and was modified, moving the gas port back towards the chamber and making the necessary changes to the gas piston and cylinder. Vaclav Holek himself brought the modified gun back to England and under his watchful eye it was put through an endurance test; it fired 18,936 rounds, and had 90 stoppages, of which 61 were due to loose primers in the ammunition.

The Small Arms Committee now asked for a 30-round magazine instead of a 20-round model and ordered ten guns complete with spare parts and spare barrels, costing $700 (£175) each, and shortly after that Holek suggested a modification whereby the piston buffer absorbed some 2mm of recoil of the gun body and barrel as well as

(Continued on Page 114)

A Czechoslovakian ZB26 machine gun in 7.92mm Mauser caliber. This model is identifiable by the long finned barrel and the long gas cylinder having the gas port and regulator very close to the muzzle. This particular specimen turned up in Angola in the 1980s, still shooting well.

THE BREN GUN

The first stage in the Bren story is the ZGB33, which was the original ZB26 with the gas port moved down the barrel to suit the British Cordite cartridge.

As detailed elsewhere, the Bren gun was evolved from the ZB26 through a series of steps. The principal visual difference is the smooth barrel of the Bren, with a gently flared muzzle acting as a flash hider, as compared with

the ZB 26 ribbed barrel and short, angular flash hider; and, of course, the characteristic curved magazine of the Bren, necessitated by the rimmed 303 cartridge. Modern Brens, chambered for the rimless 7.62x51mm NATO round, and wartime Brens made in Canada and chambered for the 7.92x57 Mauser round, for the Chinese Army, used straight magazines. There was also a 100-round drum magazine for anti-aircraft use, but most British soldiers never saw it. It was easy to maintain - all recruits were expected to be able to strip and reassemble a Bren inside three minutes while blindfolded, after their initial six weeks' training. And although not exactly a lightweight, it was quite possible to shoot from the hip with some accuracy.

The basic operating system - a gas piston carrying a bolt and listing it up into a recess in the receive to lock - has been widely copied, and the Bren also has a four-position gas regulator which can be used to fine-tune the operation or produce more gas to combat fouling when there is no time to strip and clean

the gun. The 'Immediate Action' drill used when the gun fails to fire was simple and instinctive, and the Bren was perhaps one of the easiest machine guns to master that any army of World War II had.

Stripping

Begin by removing the magazine and pulling back the cocking handle. Look into the magazine housing the see that the feedway and chamber are empty. Pull the trigger and allow the working parts to go forward and into the fired position.

Push body locking-pin, at the top rear corner of the receiver, out to the right as far as it will go. With left hand holding the receiver across its top, pull back the butt group as far as possible with the right hand. The return spring rod will then be seen protruding forwards from the butt through the buffer.

Holding the return spring rod to the left with the thumb of the left hand, pull the cocking-handle backwards sharply. This will slide the piston and

DATA (Mark 1 gun)

Caliber	.303 British
Operating system	Gas, selective fire
Locking system	Lifting bolt
Feed system	30-round overhead box magazine
Overall length	45.25in (1150mm)
Weight, empty	22lbs 5oz (10.15kg)
Barrel	25.0in (635mm), 6 grooves, right-hand twist
Muzzle velocity	2400 ft/sec (731 m/sec)
Muzzle energy	2238 ft/lbs (3024 Joules)
Rate of fire	500 rds/minute
Effective range	875 yds (800 m)

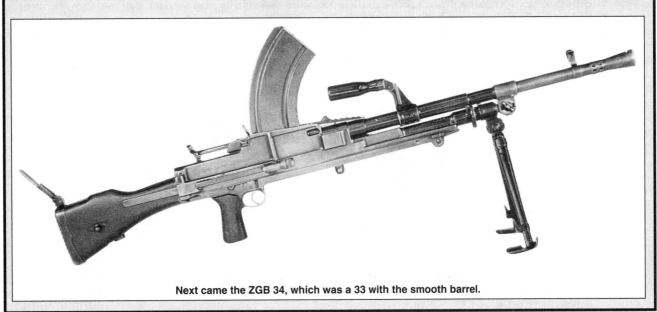

Next came the ZGB 34, which was a 33 with the smooth barrel.

Finally the Bren Mark 1, with the flash hider integral with the barrel, butt strap and handle, drum sight and adjustable bipod.

breechblock out of the back of the receiver. These can then be grasped and removed as one unit. Slide the breech-block to the rear until the claws at the front disengage from the grooves on the piston slide.

The barrel locking lever is on the left of the gun, just in front of the magazine opening. Press in the spring catch on the underside of this lever and raise

it as far as possible. This frees the barrel, which may now be removed by using the carrying handle to move it forward until it can be lifted free.

Raising of the barrel locking lever also allows the butt group to be pulled farther back and removed from the receiver

To remove the bipod, lift the front of the receiver with the right hand,

and with the left hand pull the left leg of the bipod towards you as far as possible and then slide the bipod sleeve off the front end of the gas cylinder. *(Note that the bipod of the Mark II gun cannot be removed.)*

To remove the barrel locking nut, lift the lever as far as it will go and depress the small stud just in front of the magazine opening cover. *(This is most easily*

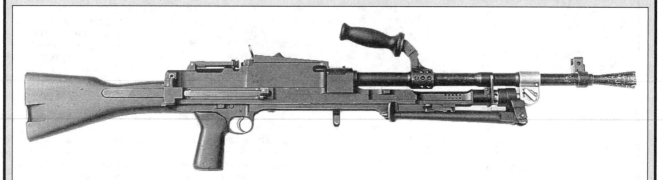

Wartime demands led to some ruthless pruning: this is the Mark 3 with shorter barrel, plain butt with no trimmings, non-adjustable bipod and simple folding tangent sight.

And 65 years after its introduction the Bren still serves: the L4A1 version in 7.62mm NATO caliber, distinguishable only by its slotted flash eliminator instead of the old bell-mouthed flash hider.

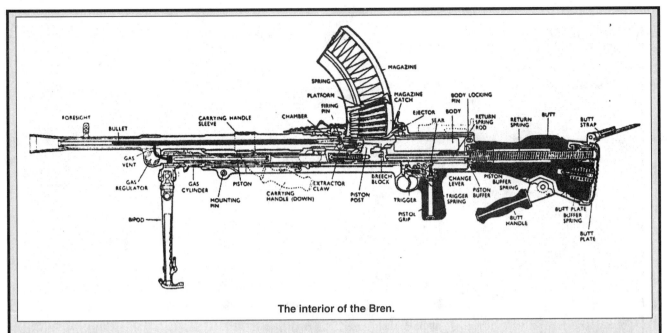

The interior of the Bren.

done by easing the magazine cover forwards so that it depresses the stud.) The barrel nut can then be lifted straight up and out of the receiver.

To strip and assemble the bolt, pry the extractor stay away from the extractor until it jumps out, being careful not to lose it. The extractor will then slide out. To replace, insert the extractor first and then the extractor-stay and spring, pushing the head of the stay well up behind the extractor.

With the nose of a bullet push out the firing pin retainer from right to left, having first put a finger behind the tail of the firing pin to prevent it springing out. The firing pin and spring will then be free to slide out. When replacing, note that the groove cut across the tail of the striker must be upwards to enable the retainer to be pushed back. Push the firing pin forward against its spring until the retainer can be pushed home.

To remove and replace the gas regulator, use a punch or the nose of a bullet to push in the sliding catch in the regulator retainer on the right-hand side of the barrel until it is flush with both ends of the retainer.

Turn the gas regulator until the retainer is opposite the slot in the gas block; the regulator can then be removed to the left.

When replacing, see that the sliding catch is flush with the ends of the retainer, insert regulator into the gas block, turn slightly and push out the sliding catch. Then adjust the regulator so that the correct hole is in operation. This should be indicated by punch-marks on the regulator and gas block. Also check that one of the two cuts on the left side of the regulator is lined up with the horizontal cut on the gas block. *(If this is not done the projection on the receiver will foul the regulator when you try to replace the barrel).*

To assemble

Reverse the above, being careful to note the following points:

To replace the barrel locking nut, push it down into place with the lever as high as possible. It may be necessary to press down the stud in the magazine housing when doing this.

See that the small stop on the left at the forward end of the butt group is in

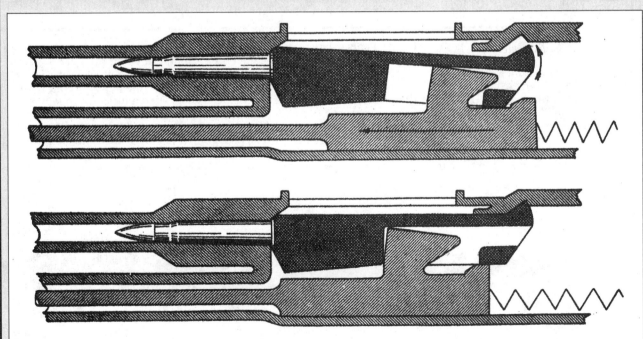

The working of the Bren bolt, standard for all the ZB series of guns. As the slide goes forward it lifts the rear end of the bolt into a recess in the roof of the receiver *(top)*. As the piston slide goes back, so the shaped rear end of the the piston post will pull it down again after a short free travel.

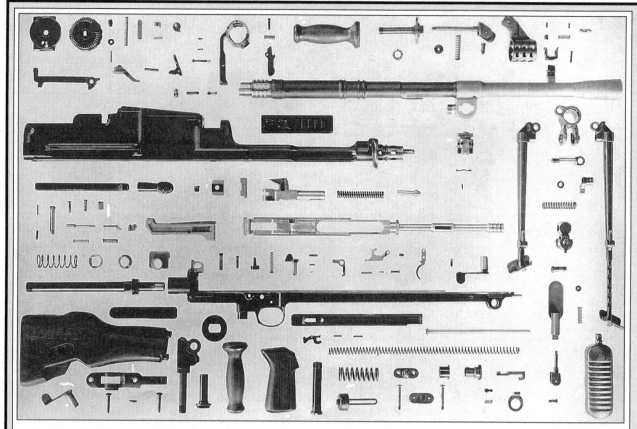

How the Mark 1 came to pieces. This illustrates the complexity of the 'old-fashioned' guns: except for pins and springs, almost every component has been milled or turned from solid steel.

front of the barrel nut lever before lowering the lever.

When replacing the barrel ensure that the long groove underneath, between the gas block and the carrying-handle, engages with the stud on the top of the receiver.

See that the barrel locking lever is fully home and that the catch has engaged on the rib on the receiver

Replace the bolt on the piston slide by sliding the claws down into the grooves on the piston and as far forward as possible, and then letting the tail of the bolt drop.

When replacing the piston and bolt together see that the butt group is fully to the rear, that the bolt is fully forward on the piston, and that the bolt and piston are pushed right into

the receiver before attempting to push forward the butt group.

When pushing forward the butt group, make sure that the return spring rod engages in the recess made for it in the back of the piston slide.

To test correct assembly, cock gun, set change lever at *A* and press trigger.

(Continued from Page 110)

cushioning the piston, a step which reduced the felt recoil. These ten guns were known as the ZGB32 and during 1933 they went through an exhaustive series of tests in England, resulting in further changes. The ejector was modified so that as the bolt closed on the car-

tridge a chisel-like edge struck the base of the cartridge and peened a small amount of brass over the edge of the primer, so preventing the primer blowing out. The rate of fire was reduced from 600 rounds per minute to 480, making the gun steadier and more accurate. The barrel was slightly shortened and the fins removed; trials showed

that oil and dirt collected between them and when the barrel got hot, the fumes and smoke interfered with the line of sight. And in any case, with a quick-change barrel, who needed cooling fins? The free movement of the piston, before the bolt began to open, was lengthened to delay the opening of the breech by a few micro-seconds, thus

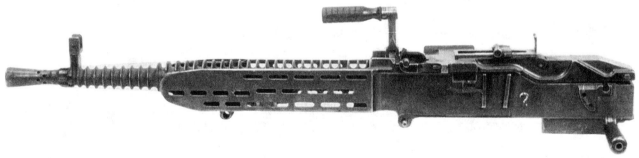

Another Czechoslovakian product of the 1930s was this vz/37 (Model 37) medium machine gun, an attempt by *Zbrojovka Brno* to wean armies away from the water-cooled gun. It was accepted by the Czech army - then by the German - and numbers found their way into Central Africa in the postwar years.

The Besa was the British-made version of the Czech vz/37 and was adopted solely for use in tanks and armored cars. By limiting its use to one particular arm of the service, it could retain the original 7.92mm caliber instead of having to convert to 303.

allowing the pressure to drop even lower. The cocking handle was made to fold forward, and various small modifications to the butt and furniture were requested. The resulting weapon became the ZGB33; two were ordered, with six spare barrels, and when delivered, they were put through three tests: firstly a 1,000 round 'acceptance test'; then a series of accuracy and functioning tests using 50,000 rounds per gun and, finally, a 150,000 round endurance test.

The tests took place in January 1934 and each gun fired at least 140,000 rounds before any defect occurred. Still there were people who remained unconvinced, so two more guns, now called the ZGB34 were purchased and a 50,000 round endurance trial in competition with a new heavy-barreled Vickers-Berthier was arranged in August 1934. This finally convinced the doubters and the Small Arms Committee recommended that the ZGB34 be adopted for service with the British army.

A license was obtained from Brno, and arrangements were made to produce the guns at the Royal Small Arms Factory at Enfield Lock, in north-east London. Since it was designed in *BR*no and to be built at *EN*field, somebody dreamed up the name for it - the Bren gun. The engineering drawings, in metric dimensions, had to be re-drawn into Imperial dimen-

sions, a task that was finished in January 1935. Gages and inspection tools had to be manufactured and staff had to be trained. Manufacture was by conventional techniques: milling, shaping, turning and grinding–and the receiver alone demanded some 270 separate machining operations. The first gun was completed in September 1937 - three years almost to the day from the date of acceptance - and by July 1938 production was running at 300 guns per week, rising to 400 per week in 1939. By June 1940 30,000 guns had been made and issued.

I have dwelt at some length on the acceptance trials of the Bren gun since it is extremely well documented, and serves as a perfect example of the great pains to which it is necessary to go in order to iron out the wrinkles in any design and ensure that every conceivable source of trouble has been identified, studied and eradicated. What becomes obvious is that it cannot be done overnight, and it cannot be done on the cheap; it takes time, it takes money, and it takes highly-skilled specialists to plan, conduct and analyze the testing and make recommendations as to the solutions to be applied. It then takes highly skilled ordnance engineers to devise a method of applying the solution and incorporating it into the gun without upsetting anything else. Laymen frequently look at the

development time of a weapon and assume that the delay is due to reactionary elements in the army, hidebound Colonel Blimps, refusing to countenance modern technology, or bureaucracy shuffling paper from desk to desk for years on end. There are times when these elements crop up but they are rare, and easily overcome; it is the testing, analysis and modification that takes the time. Short cuts and slip-shod work in peacetime procurement means weapons that fail at a critical moment in war. The five years which the British spent in modifying the ZB26– already a widely-used and successful weapon in its own right–until it met their very stringent criteria paid off in 1939-45 when the Bren gun gained a reputation for reliability never equaled by any other light machine gun before or since. And, re-barreled in 7.62mm caliber, it is still in use today, 65 years after its final British approval. No other light machine gun has survived so long in first-line service.

The medium machine gun also came under some scrutiny in the British Army, not in its infantry role but in its application to tanks. In spite of armored jackets, the water-cooled gun was still vulnerable and involved all sorts of plumbing problems inside the tanks to supply the jacket with water.

The Maxim-Tokarev was the first Russian attempt at a light machine gun. It was much the same as the German Maxim 08/15, but air-cooled. It went into production in the mid-1920s since there was ample machinery available for the Maxim mechanism. The guns were later disposed of to Republican Spain, and this specimen was found in the Military Museum in Lisbon, Portugal.

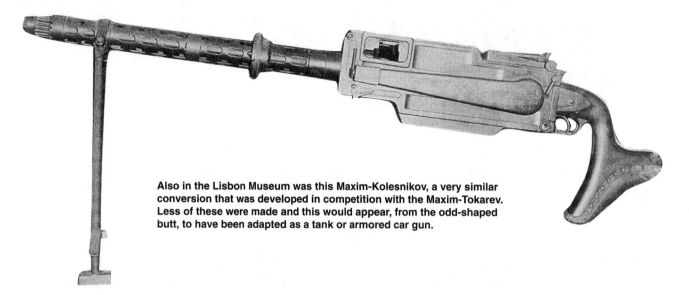

Also in the Lisbon Museum was this Maxim-Kolesnikov, a very similar conversion that was developed in competition with the Maxim-Tokarev. Less of these were made and this would appear, from the odd-shaped butt, to have been adapted as a tank or armored car gun.

Moreover the Vickers, particularly in 50-caliber, was a bulky weapon. Various alternatives were considered, but the astute gentlemen from Brno, on discovering the British were looking for a suitable machine gun, sent along their medium machine gun, the weapon known variously as the ZB53 or vz/37. This was a gas-operated, belt-fed, air-cooled weapon that proved to be compact, reliable and highly accurate. And by 1938 the British army was anxious to settle on a design and get it into production. They accepted the ZB53, obtained a license to manufacture it, and gave the BSA company the job of mass-producing it. It thus acquired the name of the 'Besa' gun and became the standard rifle-caliber machine gun for all British tanks thereafter. The most remarkable thing was that unlike the Bren gun, the army did not insist upon redesigning it to take the standard British 303 rimmed cartridge, but to save time accepted the 7.92mm Mauser cartridge into service. Since the gun was to be used only by armored regiments, the

supply of special ammunition was not an insuperable problem and, in fact, never caused any problems during the war. Moreover, of course, it meant that captured German stocks of ammunition could be used.

The 7.92mm Besa was followed very quickly by a second model in 15mm caliber, which the British adopted as the primary armament of their armored cars and light tanks. This was simply a larger version of the rifle-caliber weapon. Both guns were unusual, for their day, for firing as the working parts were still moving forwards, a fraction of a second before the barrel reached its in-battery position. This meant that the force of the exploding cartridge had to arrest the moving parts before it could drive them back, thus absorbing much of the recoil force and aiding the accuracy. Another unusual feature was the lack of a cocking handle; the guns were cocked by grasping the pistol grip and pulling it back until the bolt caught on the sear. The grip was then pushed back, which re-engaged the trigger mechanism ready for firing.

When Germany occupied Czechoslovakia in 1938 they looked at these two weapons and very quickly adopted the ZB53 into their own service, calling it the MG37(t) and issuing it widely to infantry units. They also adopted the 15mm as the Flak-MG 39(t), using it as a light anti-aircraft gun, but in relatively small numbers.

Because the Tsar's army had bought its machine guns from other countries and then manufactured them under license, Russian machine gun design and development had to start from scratch after the Revolution and took some time to produce results.

The Russians took stock in 1920 so as to assess what was needed to get the army into a reasonable shape. And the obvious top priority was a light machine gun, because all they had were Lewis, Hotchkiss, Madsen and Chauchat left-overs. These were a dwindling asset because there were no spare parts, and since most of them fired foreign calibers of ammunition which were not made in Russia and were almost all used up, they were not going to last very much longer. One

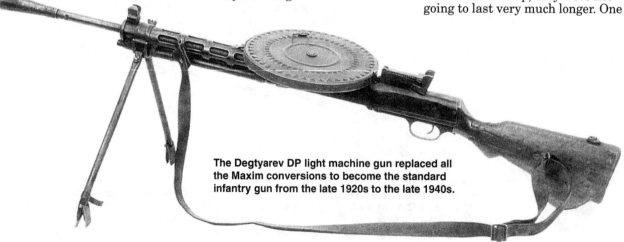

The Degtyarev DP light machine gun replaced all the Maxim conversions to become the standard infantry gun from the late 1920s to the late 1940s.

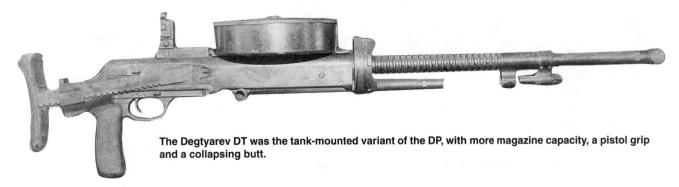

The Degtyarev DT was the tank-mounted variant of the DP, with more magazine capacity, a pistol grip and a collapsing butt.

thing they did have was a large number of water-cooled Maxims, and plant for making more, and their first move was to develop a lightweight Maxim; as a senior Soviet general said, it would take them three years to develop an entirely new machine gun, whereas they could produce a converted Maxim in six months or so. He had the right idea, but he was hopelessly off in his timing.

Two engineers, Kolesnikov and Tokarev were handed the job, each working independently of the other, the theory being that with two separate projects on the go there would be a spirit of competition between the designers and, of course, a chance that if one failed the other would succeed. In any event, they both produced designs, but Kolesnikov vanished into the mysteries of the Soviet Union while Tokarev became a renowned gun designer.

The two designs were fairly similar, which is understandable given that they both started with a Maxim gun. There was the normal Maxim receiver with its crank handle on the right-hand side, and in front of that both designers had placed a slender slotted jacket

around the barrel to produce a light air-cooled weapon. A rifle butt and a pistol grip more or less completed the basic design, and after that there were some minor differences. Kolesnikov, for example, had a quick-release device that allowed the barrel to be changed a good deal faster than was normal with a Maxim. Both men produced working guns in 1924, both were tested and approved, and orders were given to manufacture ten of each for comparative trials. Even this modest order was beyond the capability of the manufacturing plant existing in 1925 and had to be scaled back to three of each.

The guns were tried and appeared to be equally effective, so the testing commission voted and the majority preferred the Maxim-Tokarev, which was formally approved in May 1925 as the future light machine gun. The troops, however, complained that it was still too heavy to be really called a 'light' machine gun, and Tokarev made some changes, shortening the barrel and lightening the receiver, making a lighter bipod and so forth. Eventually, mass production of the gun began in Tula arsenal in November 1926.

Even though the Maxim-Tokarev was accepted, the higher command were under no illusions about its defects. They knew perfectly well that it was simply an extension of life for what was really an outmoded design, and that simpler guns - such as the ZB26, and the German light Dreyse and the Lewis - were loose in the big world outside the Russian borders. So they rounded up another designer and gave him the job of producing a proper light machine gun.

The man they chose was V.A. Degtyarev, an up-and-coming young designer who had learned his trade under Federov in the days of the Tsar. Federov was best known for his automatic rifle designs and thus Degtyarev had a good grounding in the principles of automatic weapons. Even so, he made a few false starts before getting it right.

His first successful machine gun was the DP (*Degtyarev Pulyemet*), which appeared in 1926. This was an air-cooled light gun for infantry use, fed from a flat drum, with a stock and trigger like a rifle and a spindly bipod. Quite honestly, it looks as if a puff of wind would blow it away. But it did the business as far as the Soviet Army was concerned and it went into mass production in 1931. In 1929 the DT (*Degtyarev Tankovii*) was perfected, a version which, as the title suggests, was designed for fitting into tanks. Both weapons saw some use in Spain in 1937-39 and it was discovered that the placing of the return spring around the gas piston beneath the barrel led to the spring overheating and failing. The easy answer to this was to perforate the jacket around the rear half of the barrel with larger

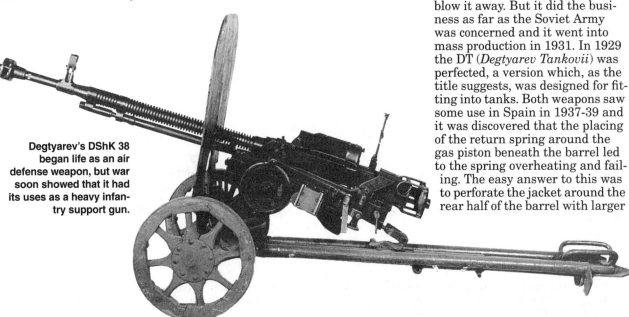

Degtyarev's DShK 38 began life as an air defense weapon, but war soon showed that it had its uses as a heavy infantry support gun.

A rarely-seen variation on the well-known Degtyarev DP was this DA model for use by air gunners.

oval slots so as to allow the heat to escape. The change was made and the two guns went on to become the principal squad and tank automatics for most of World War II.

The DP machine gun contains only 65 component parts and was designed with mass production by unskilled labor in mind. The original model had a finned barrel that could be replaced, but not quickly, and fired from a 49-round drum. The magazine gave some trouble and it was reduced to a 47-round pattern that proved successful; the capacity of the magazine is stamped on its upper surface. In 1940 the method of fixing the barrel was simplified so that the barrel could be more quickly changed in the field, and the fins were dispensed with. The DT differed in using a deeper 60-round magazine and a telescoping skeleton butt which could be thrust up close against the receiver and thus avoid cluttering up the interior of the tank turret when not in use. Neither the DT nor the later DTM were equipped with quick-change barrels.

Both guns used a flap-locking system derived from the Friberg-Kjellman patents of the early 1900s and fired from an open bolt. When the trigger is pressed the gas piston goes forward, carrying the bolt with it to collect a round from the magazine and thrust it into the chamber. The bolt is square in section and has two flaps or plates set into the sides; the bolt closes on the cartridge in the chamber and stops, but the piston is still moving forwards, carrying the firing pin with it. The firing pin is a substantial piece of metal and is designed so that as it goes forward through the bolt, it strikes shoulders on the inner rear end of the two side flaps and so drives the rear ends outward so that they engage with recesses in the walls of the receiver and thus act as locking struts, since their front ends are firmly lodged in the bolt body. The cartridge is fired and the gas piston moves back; now cam surfaces in the piston slide strike studs on the bottom rear of the two flaps and force them back into the bolt body, so unlocking the bolt, whereupon the piston carries

the bolt back to begin the next cycle of operation.

Having finally got the light machine gun settled, the Soviets next looked at their medium support gun, the Maxim 1910 model. As part of the first Five-Year Plan for re-equipping the Soviet Army, in 1930 the gun was modified by some small changes to the firing and safety mechanisms and the fitting a new optical sight for indirect fire with a new heavy-bullet cartridge. A new type of mounting was also developed. Until then the standard mounting was the 'Sokolov' type with two wheels and a box trail and shield. In 1931 the Vladimirov mounting was approved, which kept the same general wheeled form as the Sokolov but used three tubular legs that could be rapidly transformed into an anti-aircraft mount when the need arose. The only drawback was that it weighed 86lbs (39kg), 8kg more than the Sokolov mount, and was therefore not popular.

The second improvement to the M1910 Maxim came in 1941 just before the German attack.

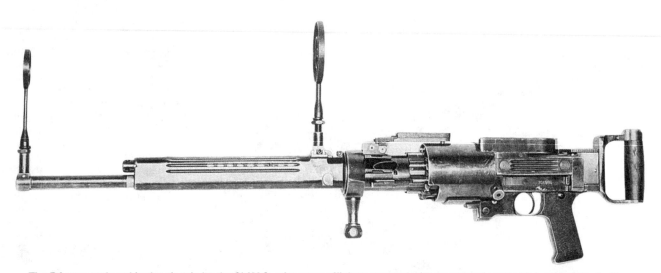

The DA was replaced in the air role by the ShKAS, a far more efficient gun and with an exceptionally high rate of fire for its day. The cylindrical receiver conceals a 'squirrel-cage' mechanism which extracts the cartridge from the belt in a series of steps, giving the gun a very smooth action at high speed.

The sight was simplified, but the most prominent change was the adoption of a very large flap-type filler cap for the water jacket, which allowed faster filling and also allowed handfuls of snow and ice to be used in winter conditions, a modification which had been arrived at as a result of the 1939/40 Winter War in Finland.

But to return to the 1920s, a demand for a replacement for the Maxim had been put forward in 1928, and it had been a somewhat strict specification:

1. To ensure uniformity of training, it must use similar mechanism to the DP and DT guns.

2. It must be air-cooled.

3. It must feed from a 150-round belt.

4. It must have a rate of fire of 500 rounds per minute.

5. The weight, complete with its mount, was not to be more than 66 lbs (30kg).

6. The mounting had to be a tripod, with or without wheels, weighing not more than 33lbs (15kg).

Since they specified a Degtyarev-type gun it made sense for Degtyarev to develop one, and he produced his design in 1930. He had been assisted by G.S. Shpagin, another designer, who developed the belt feed system, and the result was a tripod-mounted gun, using the same gas piston and flap lock system as the DP and DT guns, but with belt feed and a very heavily-finned barrel. This was now called the DS for *'Degtyarev stankovy'* or *'Degtyarev, mounted'*. It went through a prolonged series of trials and modifications to iron out the various defects that appeared, but in September 1939 it was formally adopted as the 7.62mm Model DS. Manufacture for issue commenced in June 1940, and before the year was out the complaints began to come in: it ripped cartridges to pieces when withdrawing them from the belt; it jammed in dusty conditions and froze up in cold weather. After

studying the complaints and the design of the gun it became obvious that there was no quick fix possible and that a complete re-design would be required. Production was stopped in the summer of 1941, after 10,315 DS guns made been made, and production of the Maxim 1910/30 was re-started. By which time the Soviet Union was at war with Germany and things were beginning to look desperate, and we shall examine the future of the 7.62mm medium gun again in the next chapter.

The Soviet Army was among the first to recognize the need for a heavy machine gun capable of being used against aircraft, light armor, anti-tank guns and similar hard targets and as early as 1927 had asked for a heavy anti-aircraft machine gun in which 'the capability to deal with other targets would not be detrimental'. Nothing much happened until the summer maneuvers of 1929, when ground attack aircraft were used for the first time and the lack of air defense machine guns became painfully obvious. Not surprisingly, V. A. Degtyarev was once more called into action, even though he was still busy with his 7.62mm gun, this time to devise a gun for a 12.7mm (0.50-inch) cartridge.

Once more, Degtyarev used his locking flaps and gas piston system; a drum magazine fed the gun. The bolt action was given spring buffers to soften its movements and a muzzle brake was fitted to the finned barrel in order to reduce the recoil force. The result looked more or less like a scaled-up DS gun- which, in most respects, it was - and in 1933 it was officially designated the DK (*Degtyarev krupnokalibernyy* - Degtyarev heavy caliber) and production of a trial batch of 250 guns was approved. The first of them was subjected to troop trials in the summer of 1934, and while the gun performed well and reliably, the users complained that the cyclic rate of fire of 350

rounds a minute was too low, and since the drum magazines were heavy and awkward, the practical rate of fire was very poor. On the credit side the muzzle velocity was 2657 ft/sec (810 meters per second) and the AP bullet would go through 16mm of tank armor at 300 meters range. But the general consensus of opinion was that it would be a better weapon if it was belt fed. Production was stopped and Degtyarev once more called in G.S. Shpagin who had made a particular study of feed systems. Shpagin threw out the drum and designed a 'squirrel-cage' mechanism using a pair of revolving sprockets on top of the receiver that lifted the belt securely and smoothed the process of loading, so that the rate of fire was considerably improved to 575 rds/minute. One of the more notable features of this feed system was that Shpagin managed to design and fit it without significant changes to the rest of the gun; there was merely one lever connecting the piston slide to the new feed system.

This new model was put through the usual tests in the summer of 1938 and was universally praised for its simplicity and reliability, and in February 1939 it was formally approved as the 12.7mm DShK 38. As well as becoming the infantry heavy support gun, it became the universal air defense machine gun throughout the Soviet Army, and by the beginning of 1944 over 8,000 were in use.

One of the advantages of the Soviet system was that by imposing on the general population a standard of living which was barely above subsistence level the state had plenty of money to spread around on armaments, and although Stalin's First Five-Year Plan was ostensibly about heavy engineering, it was actually about building up a massive military force. Much of this effort was directed into two areas where the Soviets felt that, since both were

The German MG13 was descended from Louis Schmeisser's Dreyse machine gun and used the same action but with an air-cooled barrel and generally lighter construction. The gun originally fed from a side-mounted 30-round box magazine, but the odd 75-round double-drum magazine seen here was designed to fit into the side-feed magazine aperture and allow longer effective bursts against aircraft.

new, the older industrial nations need not necessarily hold any advantage over them - tanks and aircraft, the two most modern military technologies. As a result by the early 1930s they had thousands of tanks, more than the rest of the world put together, and thousands of aircraft. And all these needed arming. Which gave rise to an entirely independent group of machine guns, those devised solely for aircraft use and which had no connection with the weapons being produced for infantry and tanks.

The need had been seen in the early 1920s; the Soviet air force was equipped with machines using ex-British 303 Vickers and Lewis aircraft guns, and since there was no manufacturing facility for these, and the supply of spares had long since been exhausted, their replacement was somewhat urgent. So the quick and simple method was taken of modifying the Russian-built Maxim along the lines of the British aircraft Vickers - convert it to air cooling and lighten various parts, put in a recoil booster and reduce the spring tensions so as to speed up the rate of fire and convert the feed mechanism to handle a metal link belt. The resulting weapon, after being thoroughly tested, was approved for service as the PV-1 in 1928 and was adopted widely as a synchronized gun, and models capable of feeding from either side were developed.

The design then took an interesting twist when the designer of the PV-1 (A.V. Nadashkevich) decided to produce an even lighter weapon by making much of the gun from Duralumin alloy. The results can be judged by the remarks of the Testing Commission in their report of April 1925: *"we have not yet produced aluminum alloys with the mechanical properties which steel possesses, not to mention the fact that these alloys have been too little studied...."* Research into the substitution of alloys for steel in machine gun design was forthwith terminated.

As might be expected, V. A. Degtyarev was not slow in entering the aircraft gun field. While developing his DP and DT designs he had appreciated the need for the air force to have a lightweight observer's gun to replace the Lewis. Broadly speaking he took his existing DP and replaced the butt by a backplate with a pistol grip and an upper hand-grip, stripped away the bipod and handguard, and fitting the receiver with a new faceplate with suitable mounting points for aircraft fitting. The drum magazine was made into a three-tier model to hold 63 rounds, and special brackets were fitted on the receiver and the muzzle to accept various patterns of sight. In 1928 this was approved for service and went into production as the DA (*Degtyarev aviatsionnyy*) and after some initial teething troubles with gas regulators set wrongly at the factory and the heavy grease recommended for lubrication freezing at high altitudes, the gun eventually became as well liked and reliable as Degtyarev's ground guns.

But as the designers of guns worked, so did the designers of aircraft, and overnight - or so it sometimes seemed - the speed and general performance of aircraft increased in leaps and bounds. All of which brought up the question of shortening times of engagement, fewer bullets fired, and hence the need to step up the rate of fire and get more metal into the air during the few seconds available. The first solution was simply to increase the number of guns; the DA-2 was simply two DA guns side by side on a ring mount around the observer's cockpit, but at the same time as this was begun, the Air Force instructed F.V. Tokarev to go to work and produce a faster-firing gun within 12 months. He was not slow to point out that developing an entirely new gun was not something that could be done on schedule; in a memorandum to the Director of Tula Arsenal he pointed out that *"Cases exist where difficulties arise and can be overcome by concentrated thought; but on the other hand there are cases where 99 percent of the work is done for nothing because the remaining one percent is either unsolved or agonizingly difficult to find a practical solution for..."* In the event it was to be three years before he produced his final design. It was given a rigorous testing and rejected for unreliability, premature firing, jamming, failure of the synchronizer and, worst of all, inadequate rate of fire.

It was apparent to the Aviation Commission that asking designers of ground guns to design aircraft guns was a forlorn hope; they were too wedded to what they knew. So they looked around for some young designers who had a spark of originality and might be expected to explore new approaches to the problems. Their eye fell upon Boris Shpitalny and Irinarkh Komaritsky. Shpitalny had been itching to develop a fast-firing machine gun since his apprentice days, while Komaritsky, some ten years older, had a solid technical background and had been an instructor in fire-arms design for some years. Shpitalny was entirely responsible for the design, while Komaritsky, with his longer experience of manufacturing and production and what was mechanically feasible, turned the design into a workable weapon capable of being mass-produced.

The ShKAS (*Shpitalny Komaritsky, Aviatsionnyi, Skorostrelnyi* - Shpitalny Komaritsky, Aviation, fast-firing) is a conventional gas-operated gun using a bolt that is cammed up by the gas piston to unlock and then cammed down again as the piston makes its return stroke. The high rate of fire - 1800 to 2000 rounds per minute - is made possible by a very smooth revolver-type feed system.

The cartridge is the 7.62x54R rimmed round, a powerful old-style rifle cartridge dating from 1891

(Continued on Page 123)

The MG34, the first General Purpose machine gun, capable of being used in any role by any service.

MG 34

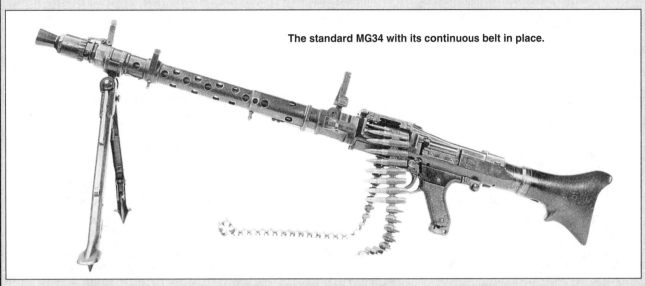

The standard MG34 with its continuous belt in place.

The MG34 was developed in 1932-33 and issued to service units in 1935. It was the standard machine gun of the German army from 1935 to 1943 when it was officially replaced by the MG42, but such were the demands of war on three fronts that it had to remain in service until 1945.

The origins are mixed; as might be inferred from the shape, Rheinmetall had a hand in it, and the manufacture was done by Mauser, but the actual design stimulus came from the Army Ordnance Office, who were hell-bent on having a general purpose machine gun and could not satisfy their desires with any of the designs on offer from Rheinmetall or Mauser. So they took the Rheinmetall MG30 to the Mauser factory and asked them to make some modifications in line with various features they had suggested in the design they had submitted. Things like belt feed and a quick-change barrel. Mauser went back to Rheinmetall, the two put their heads together, and the result was the MG34.

Some commentators have said that it turned out not to be so good as the German army had expected, and therefore they replaced it with the MG42. That is not so; it was every bit as good as the army had expected, and was a superb combat weapon. The only trouble was that it could not be manufactured fast enough to meet wartime demands, and even thought the MG42 was supposed to replace it, the MG34 soldiered on until 1945 with the German Army and a lot longer with the Portuguese and a few others who acquired them in 1945.

Field stripping:

Open the cover, removing any belt and pulling back the cocking handle to ensure that the gun is empty. Release the cocking handle and press the trigger. Lift the cover to the vertical position, press on the right-hand end of the cover hinge-pin and lift off the cover, taking care not to let the feed block slide off.

Press up the catch on the under side of the receiver (about 3 inches behind the pistol grip), twist the butt one quarter turn counter-clockwise and allow the return spring to force it out of the back of the receiver under control. Remove the return spring. The buffer can be removed from the butt by pressing the catch on the underside of the

DATA	
Caliber	7.92mm (7.92 x 57mm Mauser)
Operating system	Recoil, selective fire
Locking system	Rotating bolt
Feed system	50-round continuous link belt or 75-round saddle magazine
Overall length	48.2in (1224mm)
Weight, empty	26lb 7oz (12.0kg)
Barrel	24.75in (629mm), 4 grooves, rh twist
Muzzle velocity	2475 ft/sec (755 m/sec)
Muzzle energy	2695 ft/lbs
Rate of fire	900 rds/minute
Maximum effective range	(Bipod) 600yds (550m); (tripod) 2000yds (1850m)

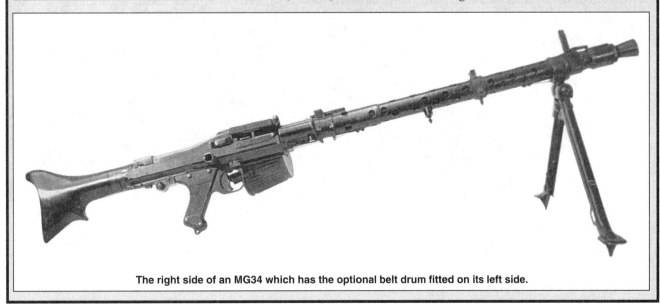

The right side of an MG34 which has the optional belt drum fitted on its left side.

German troops practicing air defense in maneuvers in 1936, using the MG34. The man holding the tripod would do well to close his mouth before he gets a cartridge case in it.

butt and twisting the buffer group a quarter turn in either direction.

Pull the cocking-handle back sharply, taking care that the bolt and bolt carrier do not fly out of the back of the body. Remove bolt and bolt carrier. To separate the bolt from the bolt carrier twist the bolt so that it slides into the carrier and so that the trigger lever (just in rear of the right-hand pair of rollers on the bolt) is tripped and the firing-pin spring released. (The trigger lever is tripped by being driven over a sloping surface on the bolt carrier and forced outwards.) Now pull back the grips on the cocking piece and unscrew it from the firing-pin. The bolt and carrier may now be separated.

Depress the catch below the left rear of the rear sight, and twist the receiver counter-clockwise out of alignment with the barrel. Remove the barrel from the barrel jacket.

To remove the receiver from the barrel jacket, take the receiver in the right hand and with the left hand press up the hinge-pin catch (which is on the underside of the jacket), twist the receiver counter-clockwise until it has rotated 18° from the fully closed position and withdraw it.

To remove the recoil booster, lift the catch in front of the front sight and unscrew. Remove the bell mouth and the cone inside it.

To remove the bipod: raise the front sight and then press up the catch on the underside of the barrel jacket just behind the bipod and twist the latter in either direction until the semi-circular slide is free of the guides.

Re-assembly

Reassembly is simply a matter of reversing the stripping sequence, but there are three points that need to be watched:

In attaching the receiver to the barrel jacket hold the receiver upside-down, press in the hinge-pin catch and push the hinge-pin fully home, then release the catch and, eas-ing the hinge-pin slightly out of its socket, turn the receiver clockwise until the catch snaps home.

When assembling the bolt and carrier be sure that the cocking-piece is fully home and then twist the bolt until the rollers are in line with the lugs on the carrier and that the ejector is forward before inserting into the receiver. Press the trigger and ease the bolt and carrier forward. The ejector is a pin, running through the bolt, at an angle from the face of the bolt to a position just above the right hand pair of rollers.

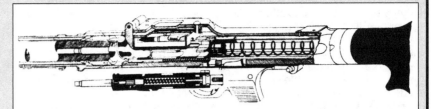

A section from a German army training poster on the MG34, showing the internal arrangements. The gun has just fired, there is an empty case in the chamber, a fresh round in the feed tray, and recoil is about to begin. The smaller drawing shows the bolt and firing pin.

Stupid as it may sound, don't forget to insert the barrel before twisting the receiver home into line with the barrel casing. It has been done!

Once the gun is reassembled, it can be 'tuned' to fire smoothly by screwing in or out the bell mouth of the muzzle booster. This varies the size of the internal expansion chamber and thus the force of the barrel recoil. It acts in much the same way as the gas regulator in a gas-operated machine gun, compensating for fouling or lack of lubrication during an action.

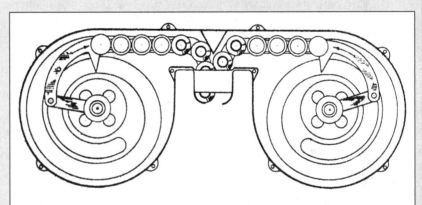

The 75-round saddle-drum magazine, which feeds alternately from each side so as to preserve the balance of the gun as the ammunition weight dwindles.

(Continued from Page 120)

and generating about 2750-ft/sec velocity. As the feed belt enters the receiver of the gun it meets a revolving drum surrounded by a sleeve with a fixed cam track on its inner surface. The body of the cartridge enters a recess in the drum - rather like the flutes in a revolver cylinder - and thus begin to move the round in a circular path; at the same time the rim enters the cam groove which smoothly but rapidly withdraws the cartridge from the belt. There is thus not the usual *snatch and pull* of a claw dragging a cartridge out of a stationary belt nor then the acceleration and deceleration shocks as the belt indexes forward for the next round. The withdrawal of the cartridge is spread over 10 operating cycles and not concentrated into the interval between shots as in a conventional feed system. As the drum brings the round down to the six-o-clock position it is presented in front of the bolt and rammed into the chamber. The breech is locked and the final movement of the piston drives a hammer against the rear of the floating firing pin and fires the round. The gas piston is then driven back, unlocks the breech by camming the bolt upwards and out of engagement with a face in the receiver floor, and the cartridge is extracted from the chamber. It is

The MG15 was preferred by the Luftwaffe for its higher rate of fire. It was derived from the Solothurn MG30, as were most of the German machine guns of the 1930s in one way or another.

then carried back until the mouth of the case clears the chamber, whereupon a mechanical ejector, cam-driven by the gas piston, lifts it up and to the left, clear of the feedway. On the return stroke of the gas piston assembly, a shoulder on the piston strikes the case and drives it forward through a tube to eject forward and left of the barrel.

Apart from the rotary feed system, therefore, the ShKAS displays nothing more than a collection of well-tried principles and mechanisms; the gas piston and lifting bolt was well known and widely employed by that time, and thus there was nothing there to baffle any armorer. Once examined, the feed system was quite a simple mechanism, but that is not to decry Shpitalny, who deserves the highest compliments for devising such an elegant and effective system. Although the ShKAS was highly stressed, there was nothing very hazardous about the design and it worked very well and very reliably; as might be expected it went through a number of minor variations as various defects or drawbacks showed themselves and were corrected, and the rate of fire improved slightly during its development.

The ShKAS was approved for service in July 1932 and the first guns were installed in the Polykarpov I-16 fighter in 1933, but it soon became apparent that there was a price to be paid for the high rate of fire: a barrel life of no more than 2000 rounds. In March 1933 Shpitalny and Komaritsky were told to do something and increase the barrel life to at least 5000 rounds. They managed to do this, making a number of other improvements at the same time, and produced what was virtually a new model of the gun. This went into production late in 1933, and soon introduced a new problem; the recoil force of the gun was too much for the mountings that had been developed for the Degtyarev guns, and thus all the observer's mountings and turret mountings had to be re-designed.

Perhaps the most remarkable variation of the ShKAS was the synchronized version; it is virtually

an immutable law that gas-operated guns firing from an open bolt cannot be synchronized, but the Russians achieved it with the ShKAS in 1936. Just how they did it is far from clear but it is probable that the high rate of fire and the relatively short operating stroke were major factors in their success.

However, even 2000 rounds per minute failed to satisfy the Soviet Air Force, and they looked for an even faster weapon. In 1935 I.K. Savin and A.K. Norov produced a remarkable machine gun, which could reach 3000 rounds per minute with a single barrel. They achieved this by a novel design, the full details of which have never been made public; but the basic principle was that gas was tapped from the barrel in the usual way and directed to a gas chamber where it drove a piston. The piston rod carried a toothed rack that engaged a gearwheel, which in turn drove another rack in the opposite direction. Now comes the tricky bit: the piston drove the barrel forward, and the other rack drove the bolt carrier backwards at the same time. So that instead of the bolt moving, say, four inches back and forth, it moved only two, and the barrel simultaneously went two inches in the opposite direction, so obtaining the full four-inch separation in half the time. Feed was from a belt, a round being delivered into the feedway as the two units slid apart and rammed into the chamber as they closed. Altogether a most unusual weapon that has never been duplicated anywhere and, to the best of my knowledge, was never seen outside the USSR. It was approved as the 7.62mm SN (Savin-Norov) aircraft gun in the summer of 1937, but it does not appear to have been produced in any great quantity.

This may have been due to the fact that Shpagin and Komaritsky had, in May 1937, produced their 'Ultra-ShKAS' machine gun, which pushed the rate of fire to above 2800 rounds per minute by adopting a similar forward-moving barrel as that of the SN. Both the Ultra-ShKAS and the SN were used during the 1939/40 Winter War against Finland, and

during that war it became apparent that rifle-caliber aircraft machine guns were reaching the end of their usefulness and that heavier weapons were needed to cope with modern metal aircraft with self-sealing fuel tanks and armor around vital parts.

This had been foreseen some ten years before, and by 1931 instructions had gone out to design teams that a 12.7mm caliber (0.50-inch) machine gun based on the Shpitalny system of operation was required. This resulted in the ShVAK - *Shpitalny-Vladimirov Aviatsionny Krupnokalerny* (aviation, heavy caliber). The man behind it was S.V. Vladimirov, whose principal contribution appears to have been to turn the Shpitalny design upside down, placing the gas cylinder below the barrel instead of above it, and reverting to a Browning-style tipping bolt-locking system. Shpitalny's rotating feed mechanism was, of course, retained.

A handful of 12.7mm guns were built in 1934/5 and tested during the summer of 1935. The gun was a success, but during the trials somebody pointed out that the base size of the 12.7mm cartridge was not far from that of a 20mm cartridge and that with no more than increasing the size of the barrel and bolt face the gun could be turned into a 20mm cannon. From that moment the 12.7mm ShVAK was a dead number and the designers set about making it into a 20mm weapon.

Another, less publicized, defect of the 12.7mm ShVAK was that it could not be satisfactorily synchronized to fire through the propeller arc, all of which left a hole in the 12.7mm gun program which had to be filled, and after much argument the call went out in the summer of 1938 for a new 12.7mm synchronized gun design. There now appeared M.Y. Berezin, a young designer who had worked since 1935 on a 12.7mm gun entirely different to any previous Soviet design. A gas-operated gun, in some ways it resembled the Maxim or Browning weapons in using a bolt with a T-slot in the face, into which the rim of the cartridge slid

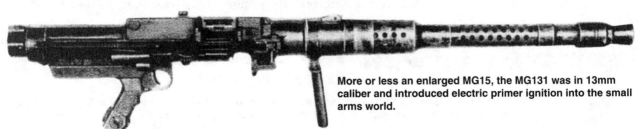

More or less an enlarged MG15, the MG131 was in 13mm caliber and introduced electric primer ignition into the small arms world.

The Mauser MG 81Z, a twin aircraft gun which armed most of the Luftwaffe's bombers by 1939.

during the feed movement. But what made Berezin's gun different was that instead of the cartridge being extracted from the belt above the chamber and forced down into the T-slot, it was extracted and presented to the *side* of the bolt, which had a lateral T-slot. As the bolt moved forward so an angular cam plate, riding in a slot in the bolt, forced the cartridge across until it was lined up with the chamber, after which the further movement of the bolt loaded and fired it. The gas piston then drove the bolt back, extracting the spent case, and retaining it during the recoil stroke; then, as the new cartridge was thrust into the left side of the T-slot and cammed across during the forward stroke, so the empty case was pushed out of the right end of the T-slot and cleared it just as the bolt came opposite the ejection port. A four-position gas regulator allowed a small adjustment of the rate of fire between 700 and 800 rounds per minute to aid in synchronizing the gun to different engines.

This was approved for service in 1939 as the BS (Berezin Synchronized) gun but in the event few of this model were made, because during the testing and pre-production phases of development Berezin had been busy and had developed a universal design, which, with minor accessory changes, could be optimized for synchronized mountings, wing mountings *(firing outside the propeller arc)* and flexible *(or turret)* mountings. This produced three versions: the UBS *(synchronized)*; the UBK *(wing mounted)* and the UBT *(flexible)* and these completely replaced the original BS. The Universal design was given prolonged testing and was finally approved for service in April 1941; how many had actually been fitted into aircraft when, two months later, the Germans invaded, is questionable, but it

became one of the major air weapons of the Red Air Force for the rest of the war.

The German Army in the 1920s was a mere shadow when the politicians of the victorious powers had finished with it. Reduced to 100,000 officers and men, with no mobile anti-aircraft artillery, no tanks, no submachine guns permitted and precious little of anything else, it was hoped, notably by the French, that its teeth had been drawn permanently. The Germans had other ideas. Under the inspired guidance of General von Seekt, and in the absence of hardware, the army steeped itself in theory, studied the lessons of World War I with far more concentration than did the victors, and trained so that eventually every man in the army was qualified for a rank two, three or even four grades higher than that which he held. The object behind this was simple: one day Germany would raise a new army, and the 100,000 men of the *Reichsheer* (as the army was known under the Weimar Republic) would be the leaders and trainers of the new recruits. Moreover their studies would have made them masters of tactics and strategy and would perhaps lead them into some new mode of warfare, which would rapidly vanquish their enemies. Meanwhile, while planning tactics they also had a number of departments who were looking closely at technical questions, such as what weapons would be needed in the future.

The infantry's machine guns were a prime target for reform. The basic weapon was still the Maxim MG '08, augmented by the MG 08/15, the Dreyse MG13 and the

Bergmann MG15nA. All of these were obsolete, and the army was beginning to question the need for a water-cooled gun at all. Their tactical studies were pointing towards a more mobile form of warfare where the hours and hours of sustained fire of World War I would no longer be required. Designs were invited.

The provisions of the Versailles Treaty had caused convulsions in the German gunmaking industry. Factories had been dismantled, production machinery confiscated and scrapped, combines broken up and companies forced out of business. The production of military small arms was virtually prohibited, and only a limited amount of refurbishment and repair, sufficient to maintain the limited armament of the *Reichsheer*, was permitted. But the Treaty said nothing about *designing* weapons, nor had it done anything to break up the pre-war links, agreements and licensing arrangements which spread like an invisible net across the world's armaments manufacturers. So Krupp sent most of their design staff off to Bofors in Sweden, and also manufactured 'agricultural tractors' which they exported to Russia, whereupon various members of the military donned civilian clothing and visited Russia as tourists to learn how to drive 'tractors'.

Rheinmetall set up a sales agency in Holland where it made a small profit by selling off war surplus weapons and also offered designs for more modern equipment. It also purchased a majority shareholding in a Swiss firm,

The Knorr-Bremse. In 6.5mm Swedish it was passable, but in 7.92mm it was over-stressed.

Solothurn A.G., and, by its older links with the *Osterreichische Waffenfabrik Steyr* set up a three-way operation by means of which the Rheinmetall design office in Germany drew up designs, Solothurn in Switzerland built the prototype, tested it, perfected it, and drew up production specifications and schedules, and Steyr of Austria manufactured the weapon. A fresh company, Steyr-Solothurn A.G. of Vienna then offered the product in the export market. So that when the army let it be known that a new machine gun was wanted, the Rheinmetall-Steyr-Solothurn axis was ready and waiting with a suitable design.

The first weapon to appear under the Solothurn name in a matter of months after the firm's purchase by Rheinmetall was the Solothurn S2-100 machine gun. This had been developed in the old *Rheinische Metallwaren und Maschinenfabrik* factory at Sömmerda in the early 1920s under the guidance of Louis Stange, who had succeeded Louis Schmeisser as the company's chief small arms designer. Stange had taken the 'fermeture nut' of the Benet-Mercié machine gun as his starting point, but then dispensed with the gas piston and arranged for the recoil of the barrel to revolve the nut. In doing this he - inadvertently perhaps - introduced the concept of the *'straight line'* layout in which the force of recoil is delivered in a straight line down the axis of the gun to the shoulder of the firer.

In the majority of shoulder-fired guns the butt is cranked in order to bring the barrel up so that the sights fall conveniently to the firer's eye. As a result, the recoil force passes down the axis of the gun on a line

that, if extended, passes above the firer's shoulder. There is thus a turning force about the junction of the shoulder and the butt, which tends to lift the muzzle of the weapon when it is fired. In Stange's design - which was originally known as the Rh29 - the barrel jacket and receiver are a single tubular unit, with a shoulder butt-plate attached at the rear end. The barrel is capable of recoiling inside the jacket. Attached to the barrel is a hollow sleeve with lugs. Passing through the sleeve is the bolt, with the usual sort of return spring behind it. When the bolt is closed, the sleeve lugs, engaging with mating lugs on the bolt, lock the bolt securely to the barrel. The sleeve also carries lugs on its outer surface, which move in spiral pathways cut into the interior surface of the receiver. When the gun is fired, the barrel recoils inside the jacket and thus forces the sleeve back; the sleeve outer lugs, moving in the curved tracks, rotate the sleeve until the bolt is unlocked. At that point the barrel and sleeve stop, and the bolt is free to carry on moving back, compressing the return spring. Finally arrested by a buffer, the bolt then runs forward again, collecting a cartridge from the side-mounted box magazine, and rams it into the chamber. The whole assembly - bolt, sleeve and barrel - then run forward into battery, and in the process the sleeve is revolved so as to lock the breech once more.

The Rh29 became the Solothurn 29 and then, as noted above, the Solothurn S2-100, and was then slightly improved into the S2-200, since Solothurn adopted an entirely different nomenclature system to disguise the origin of their designs. But comparatively few were sold under that designation and it was principally a demonstrator for Stange's design and a hint of future things to come. Usually found in 7.92mm Mauser chambering,

some were sold to El Salvador in 7mm Spanish Mauser, and sales samples were made in other calibers.

However, under the designation MG30 it was taken into service in considerable numbers by the Austrian army, and as the MG31M by the Hungarian army, both models being chambered for the Austrian 8x56R cartridge. The only significant difference between these two models and the original S2-200 lies in the shape of the magazine; the rimmed cartridge demands a more severe curvature.

The German army were offered the MG30 and examined it closely. But while it had some good points, it did not have sufficient of the good points that the army wanted to see. They wanted a quick-change barrel; they didn't like the side-mounted magazine and wanted a weapon that would use either a saddle magazine or a belt, interchangeably. They were, remember, after a universal machine gun, one which would do every task it might be called upon to do, from simple covering fire to sustained fire to anti-aircraft fire, to a tank co-axial gun to even an aircraft gun. So it required a range of accessory mountings, sights, magazines, belt boxes and so forth, none of which were on offer with the MG30. So the German army took an MG30 to the Mauser factory and asked them to cooperate with Rheinmetall and produce a gun along similar lines - they liked the straight-line construction - but incorporating the various bells and whistles which they considered vital.

Mauser called on Louis Stange and suggested some changes to his bolt; they then sat down and designed a quick-change barrel system and a belt-feeding mechanism. After which they got to work on the accessories and tooled up for production.

The resulting weapon was the MG34, a magnificent weapon that went a very long way to being the ideal machine gun that the army wanted. It looked very much like the earlier MG30, so that the two are easily confused, but the internal operation is

The FIAT M1926 was unusual, for a light gun, in having a small tripod rather than the more usual bipod. It was also an early pioneer of the folding butt.

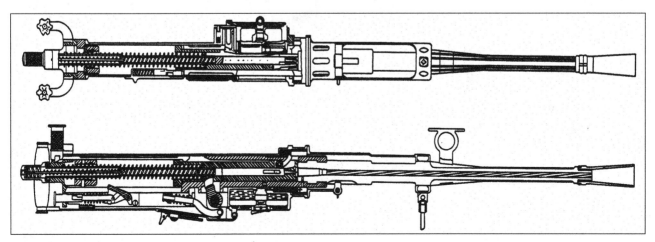

A top view of the FIAT 1926 with the butt folded and tripod removed.

rather different. The sleeve of Stange's Rh29 design is replaced by a two-piece bolt with a revolving head which locks into the chamber by lugs and carries rollers which ride in curved cam tracks in the inside of the receiver. The gun fires: the barrel recoils, very quickly because it is assisted by a muzzle recoil booster, for a very short distance with the bolt locked. As the bullet leaves the muzzle and the gas pressure in the barrel drops, so the recoiling parts meet the cam tracks and the rollers begin to follow the track and unlock the bolt. Once the bolt is unlocked, the barrel stops; cams on the rotating bolt strike two shaped lugs on the rear end of the barrel and accelerate the bolt away from the barrel. The bolt goes back against the usual spring, then comes forward again and collects a fresh cartridge from above, either from a belt or from a dual magazine which straddles the receiver and fed alternately from a drum on each side. The round was chambered and the bolt was rotated by the rollers and cam tracks until it was again locked and both bolt and barrel were in the firing position once more.

Changing the barrel was easily and quickly done, and the recommended interval was after a complete 250-round belt or four 75-round magazines had been fired off either in continuous fire or in a rapid succession of bursts. The gunner merely pulled back the cocking handle to hold the bolt to the rear; he then depressed a catch at the

front end of the receiver and rotated the entire receiver and butt unit through 180° about a pivot point in the top of the barrel jacket, so that he finished up with the rear half of the gun upside-down. By lifting the muzzle of the gun, the barrel simply slid out backwards and was pulled clear by the gunner's assistant (wearing an oven glove) and a new barrel was slipped into place. The gunner swung the receiver back down to lock into its proper place, and all he had to do to recommence firing was pull the trigger. The trigger, it might be added, was a twin-curved affair; pulling back on the upper part of the trigger fired single shots, pulling the lower part fired automatic, at about 800 rounds per minute.

The MG34 went into production in 1935 and was to remain in production for ten years; it was intended that it should be replaced in 1943 but the exigencies of war meant that its replacement could never be produced fast enough to make it possible to withdraw the MG34. It did, though, undergo some minor changes to facilitate quicker manufacture in the course of the war. It was also modified to become a tank gun, but adoption by the Luftwaffe was turned down because, they claimed, it was too heavy.

The Luftwaffe had its own machine gun by that time, the MG15, which it preferred to the MG34. In fact they both stemmed from the same father, since they

both owed something to Stange and his Rh29 gun and the MG15 actually made its debut as the Solothurn T6-220. The bolt was locked by the Stange sleeve system, as described for the MG30, but the rate of fire was pushed up to 1000 rounds per minute by the addition of a muzzle recoil booster. Feed was from a 75-round saddle drum magazine, which fed cartridges alternately from right and left sides so as to preserve the balance of the weapon irrespective of the quantity of ammunition in the magazine. It might also be noted that the ammunition fired from this gun was not the same as that fired by infantry guns: the aircraft gun 7.92mm Mauser cartridge used a slightly lighter bullet and a more powerful charge to produce a higher velocity and, due to the greater recoil force, a fast rate of fire. The use of ball bullets was abandoned shortly before the outbreak of war in 1939, and aircraft guns thereafter fired AP-T (armor-piercing tracer) or API-T (armor piercing incendiary tracer) as their standard projectile.

While the MG15 was satisfactory as a flexible gun, it was less so as a fixed weapon; it fired from an open bolt, which made it difficult to synchronize, and had to be manually cocked before it could be fired. In order to provide a gun for mounting remote from the pilot or observer, such as around an engine or in a wing, the design was modified to become the MG17. This was somewhat heavier than the MG15,

The interior of the FIAT 1926 reveals that it was little more than the FIAT-Revelli of 1914 lightened and converted to air-cooling.

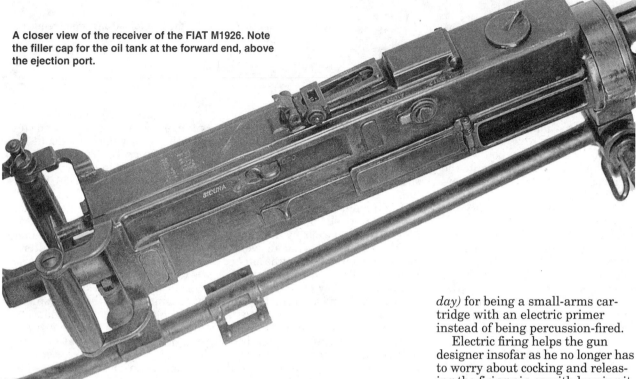

A closer view of the receiver of the FIAT M1926. Note the filler cap for the oil tank at the forward end, above the ejection port.

was cocked by a compressed air piston controlled by a solenoid valve, and fired by a solenoid that released the firing pin. In the case of synchronized installations, this firing solenoid received its signal from the synchronizing apparatus driven by the engine. In the case of unsynchronized guns - those mounted outside the propeller arc - the impulse came from the pilot's firing switch. The unsynchronized gun fired at about 1200 rounds per minute; the synchronized gun was a little slower since the synchronizer sometimes delayed the firing.

In common with other air forces, the Luftwaffe were watching the improvement in protection and the general increase in the robustness of aircraft, and had realized that the day of the rifle-caliber cartridge for aircraft employment was fast approaching its end. In 1933, therefore (before the Luftwaffe officially existed) Rheinmetall were approached for a machine gun of larger caliber and Louis Stange sharpened his pencil. The first stage was to develop a suitable cartridge, which duly appeared as the 13x64mm; it was large enough to be capable of using explosive-filled shells as well as solid armor-piercing shot, and was unique (in its

day) for being a small-arms cartridge with an electric primer instead of being percussion-fired.

Electric firing helps the gun designer insofar as he no longer has to worry about cocking and releasing the firing pin or withdrawing it before the bolt is opened. The pin, insulated from the remainder of the gun (which, admittedly, does present a minor engineering problem) is spring-loaded and permanently forward. As the bolt closes the pin immediately contacts the primer cap but nothing happens until an electrical impulse is delivered from the pin to the cap. The actual contact point is insulated from the rest of the primer assembly so that the current must pass through the primer to ground itself on the cartridge case and thus to the body of the gun, so completing the electrical circuit.

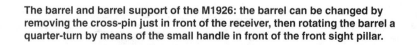

The barrel and barrel support of the M1926: the barrel can be changed by removing the cross-pin just in front of the receiver, then rotating the barrel a quarter-turn by means of the small handle in front of the front sight pillar.

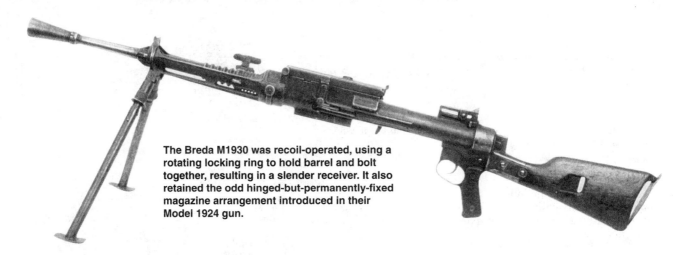

The Breda M1930 was recoil-operated, using a rotating locking ring to hold barrel and bolt together, resulting in a slender receiver. It also retained the odd hinged-but-permanently-fixed magazine arrangement introduced in their Model 1924 gun.

How the primer works is the secret of the whole affair and it was the successful shrinking of an electrical primer into the space of a small arms primer that was the real breakthrough in this gun. Electrical firing of artillery cartridges had been in use since the 1890s in many countries, and the primer operated by having a thin filament wire surrounded by guncotton, which in turn was surrounded by gunpowder. As might be imagined, this meant some tricky assembly, and the electrical primers for 6-inch guns were substantial pieces of brass that could be assembled by hand, have their filaments soldered into place, and have the guncotton hand-wrapped around them. This was obviously a non-starter for a 13mm cartridge. The German ammunition experts developed an entirely new principle; they took the usual sort of primer composition and mixed it with graphite, so making it a conducting substance. By simply loading the cap with this mixture and passing an electric current through it, the resistance of the graphite mixture cause the substance to heat up instantly and ignite the cap composition and so fire the cartridge.

With that little problem solved, the gun was designed around this new cartridge. The gun was a further application of Stange's rotating sleeve locking system, but in addition, in order to absorb a portion of the recoil forces, it was arranged to fire a few microseconds before the barrel and bolt reached the fully forward position. Thus the force of the exploding cartridge had to arrest the forward movement of the heavy components before it could reverse the

motion and begin driving them back again to begin the next firing cycle. This 'Advanced Primer Ignition' became relatively commonplace in later years, but this gun, which went into service as the MG131, was one of the first weapons outside the submachine gun world to employ it.

The gun was belt-fed, and could be adjusted to feed from the left or the right, according to its location in the aircraft. The short recoil stroke, governed by exceptionally heavy return springs and buffers, meant that the manual cocking lever was a ratcheting device requiring several strokes to cock the gun, but the more usual application of the MG131 was as a fixed gun, and the usual air-cocking controlled by an electric solenoid was used. Firing was simply a matter of providing the firing pin with a supply of electricity; there was no need for solenoid releases for the firing pin or any other form of linkage. The maximum rate of fire was about 950 rounds per minute, and the 2.6-ounce (74.5 gram) high explosive shell had a velocity of 2370 ft/sec (722 m/sec), giving it 14,360 ft/lbs (19,400 Joules) of muzzle energy. For 1937, when this gun was adopted, this was startling performance, and the existence of the MG131 was to remain unknown to the rest of the world until 1940.

The ultimate rifle-caliber aircraft machine gun of the 1930s was the

Mauser MG81, which was approved for service in 1938. A recoil-operated gun, using a bolt with rotating head controlled by rollers running in cam tracks in the receiver, it produced a rate of fire of 1600 rounds per minute - over 25 rounds per second - and in an endeavor to deliver as much metal on the target as possible, it was further developed into the MG81Z, a twin-gun assembly controlled by a single trigger and thus delivering 3,200 rounds per minute - 53 rounds per second. Astonishingly compact, each gun fed from its own belt, the left gun feeding from the left, the right from the right. Fired cases were ejected downwards, and a special curved chute was fitted to guide the empty links back across the gun and eject them on the same side as the belt. Had this not been fitted there would doubtless have been a spectacular jam as two guns spewed out 25 empty links per second into the gap between the two receivers.

The MG81 was to become the primary armament of German bombers in the early part of the war. The Heinkel HE111 carry no less than nine of them, five MG81 and two 81Z, and it was widely adopted in a pod, carrying four or five guns, which could be fitted to most German combat aircraft. And

The right side of the Breda M1930 with the magazine closed and in the firing position.

The Breda Model 1937, an excellent design apart from the usual Breda fascination with oddball feed systems.

when the Luftwaffe no longer required the rifle-caliber gun, the MG81 took on a new lease of life as an infantry weapon.

With all the hustle and bustle of German re-armament, it was scarcely surprising that one or two entrepreneurs thought they discerned the chance of making a quick profit in the armaments business. It was obvious that the sudden expansion of the German armed forces, once Hitler had repudiated the Versailles Treaty and announced his intention to build the Thousand-Year Reich, was going to result in soldiers waiting for weapons production to catch up, and if it was possible to acquire suitable weapons elsewhere and sell them on, at, of course, a suitable profit, to the weapon-hungry army, there was bound to be a *Reichsmark* or two to be made.

Such noble thoughts stirred the directors of the Knorr Bremse GmbH of Berlin, a manufacturer or automobile brake components. They looked about and found an inventor in Sweden who had demonstrated a light machine gun, the LH33, in the hopes of selling it to the Swedish army. The Swedes had declined his offer, and Lauf, the inventor, had gone away and made some improvements and was now offering it as the LH35. A gas-operated, magazine-fed light machine gun, it seemed to be the very thing the German army needed, and

Knorr Bremse bought the patents and rights from Lauf and began tooling up to make the gun. It was demonstrated to the German army who refused it; not dismayed, Knorr Bremse, who knew how the system worked, took it around to the back door and offered it to the SS. At that time the SS were still something of the poor relations of the regular forces and consequently at the back of the line when it came to allocation of new weapons. So they were only too pleased to get hold of something, even if the army had refused it. The gun now became the Knorr-Bremse MG36 and several hundred were made and supplied to the SS troops.

Unfortunately, there was one slight flaw; Lauf had designed his machine gun around the 6.5mm Swedish Mauser cartridge; Knorr-Bremse had re-scaled it to chamber the 7.92x57mm German Mauser, which was a good deal more powerful than the 6.5mm Swedish. The result was that the

gun shook itself to pieces under prolonged firing; it was not unknown for the butt to fall off in the middle of firing a burst, which is, to say the very least, disconcerting for the gunner. Once wear began to set in, it became grossly unsafe, capable of releasing the sear when the safety catch was pushed from *safe* to *fire*. One way and another, the MG36 was not the success that the manufacturers had hoped. It received no more contracts and returned to the brake business. The guns were relegated for use as training weapons as soon as supplies of the MG34 began to flow to the SS, and they eventually finished up in the hands of some of the ethnic Waffen SS Legions; I heard some very colorful observations on this weapon from an ex-sergeant of the Latvian SS Legion several years ago.

Italy, having learned the hard way in 1915, was not going to get caught again and spent the inter-war years industriously

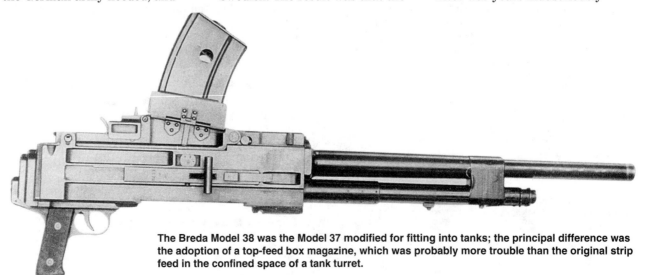

The Breda Model 38 was the Model 37 modified for fitting into tanks; the principal difference was the adoption of a top-feed box magazine, which was probably more trouble than the original strip feed in the confined space of a tank turret.

developing a number of machine guns for both land and air warfare, and in the process it produced some quite eccentric designs. One thing, which appears to have defeated Italian designers of the time, was the concept of *primary* and *secondary* extraction. Somehow or other, the Italians chose to overlook, forget or ignore the primary phase and go straight for the secondary, largely as a result of the locking systems they elected to use in their machine guns. Which meant that unless something was done, the extractor would tear the case rim and the gun would jam. Although, as we have seen, Agnelli had invented the idea of grooving the chamber to float the case on a layer of high-pressure gas to prevent it sticking, this was also ignored (*and not only by the Italians I might add*) and they fell back on the old faithful - oiling the ammunition.

Another source of irritation when considering Italian machine guns is their nomenclature; because of changes in company organizations and sometimes of manufacturers, some machine guns appear under various names according to when or where they were being made at the time. Much of this confusion can be explained very simply: during World War I the principal machine gun manufacturer was Fiat - *Fabricca Italiana de Automobiles Torino* - the well-known carmaker. So great were their orders that they set up a special company, with its own separate factory, to do nothing but make machine guns, the *Societe Anonyma Fabricca d'Armi Torino* or SAFAT. Since their guns were marked with the manufacturer, some had FIAT on them and some had SAFAT, and some people called them one or the other, while some hedged their bets and called them the Fiat-Safat. In the late 1920s Fiat decided their future lay in automobiles and not machine guns

When FIAT were asked to improve their old M1914 medium machine gun, they more or less scaled-up their Model 1926 gun's air-cooled barrel arrangement and grafted it on to the receiver of the 1914 gun. The resulting Model 35 was worse than the 1914 that they had set out to improve.

and put the Safat factory up for sale. At more or less the same time the Breda engineering company, who had also got into machine gun manufacture during the war, decided that they rather fancied their chances as machine gun designers, so they bought the Safat factory. Because they used the same title for the factory, their machine guns became known as Breda-Safats, or just plain Breda. And, of course, since Abel Revelli had designed one or two of the weapons, his name comes into it as well, from time to time.

Italy emerged from World War I with only one Italian-designed machine gun in service, the Fiat-Revelli M1914. Their light machine gun was the Lewis, and they also employed the Vickers, both built under license at the Vickers-Terni factory.

The first new design to appear came from Tempini of Brescia, a firm that had come into the machine gun business by way of a sizable wartime contract to make the Fiat-Revelli M1914 gun. Tempini staff had looked at the M1914 with a critical eye and had identified some of the weak spots in the design, and had set about a design

that removed most of them. Once the war ended and the contracts were run down, the company set about turning their ideas into hardware and produced the Brixia M1920 machine gun.

Not surprisingly it bears some resemblance to the Fiat M1914 pattern but the receiver is a good deal more substantial and a great deal of care was taken to ensure that all the recoiling parts were contained within the receiver, and not, as in the M1914, emerging into the open air and carrying dust and dirt back into the receiver with each shot.

The actual receiver is cylindrical, surmounted by a rectangular casing which contains the trigger mechanism and a somewhat complex and not very successful rate-of-fire regulator. The gun was water cooled, and the principal and most significant change was the adoption of a box magazine feeding obliquely into the lower right side of the receiver, with ejection from the upper left side. The capacity of the magazine is variously reported as either 25 or 50 rounds, and it would seem probable that the field, water-cooled, version used a 25-round magazine while an

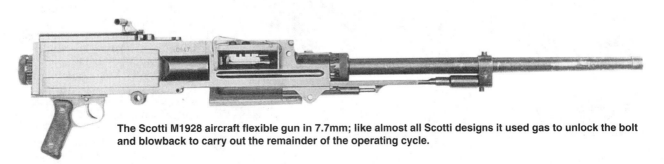

The Scotti M1928 aircraft flexible gun in 7.7mm; like almost all Scotti designs it used gas to unlock the bolt and blowback to carry out the remainder of the operating cycle.

This is the Scotti 7.7mm M1938 aircraft gun, somewhat sleeker than the 1928 design but still using the same method of operation.

air-cooled model, intended for use in aircraft, had the 50-round magazine. It is also noticeable that in the interests of saving weight and also keeping the gunner informed of his ammunition state, the curved magazine was perforated with a series of holes through which the contents could be checked. Which rather negated the efforts made to keep the working parts free of dust.

In any event, the Italian army were not in the mood, either financially or strategically, to spend large sums of money on machine guns immediately after the War to End Wars, and the Brixia never got further than a handful of prototypes. It was hawked around central Europe for some years in the 1920s, but found no takers, and by the early 1930s the design had been abandoned.

But within a very short time the Italian army re-assessed the situation and soon realized that, whether they liked it or not, a new machine gun was necessary, since the way the world was shaping up made it apparent that war was still an option. So they issued a specification calling for a design which could be fabricated either as a light machine gun for infantry or as a flexible observer's gun for use in aircraft. The first to respond were the Breda company, who produced their Tipo 5C in 1924. This introduced a peculiarly Italian novelty in the shape of a permanently-attached magazine on the right side of the receiver. The

whole magazine could be swung forward on a hinge, so as to expose its mouth to the gunner, who then inserted a horse-shoe shaped clip and rammed 20 rounds into the magazine; in default of the special clip the magazine could also be loaded from ordinary rifle clips. Having been loaded, the magazine was then swung back into position and firing continued.

The advantages of this system are that the magazine is never lost, spare magazines are not required, and the feed lips, the most delicate and easily-damaged part of a conventional magazine, can be machined in the receiver body and thus be stronger and more durable. The disadvantages are that the magazine has limited capacity, and if anything damages or distorts or jams it, the gun is out of action until repairs can be done. But the Italian army seemed quite happy with it, although it only bought a small number of the Tipo 5C, calling it the Modello 1924. So far as the dual-purpose requirement went, Breda fitted the rear end of the cylindrical receiver with spade grips and a trigger, for use as an aircraft flexible gun, and also with a wooden stock that could be fitted to the rear end of the receiver and a bipod to fit the weapon for the infantry role. Attempting to use the spade grips when the stock is fitted is not the most convenient method of controlling a machine gun.

The mechanism of the Breda resembled that of the Stange-designed Solothurn guns, using a locking ring attached to the rear end of the barrel. The bolt enters this ring and then bolt, barrel and ring all move forward for about three-eighths of an inch. During this movement a lug on the ring rides in a cam path in the receiver and give the ring a partial rotation, which locks it around lugs on the head of the bolt. The gun fired, recoils for the same short distance, so unlocking the bolt, and the high chamber pressure then blows the case out and drives the bolt back to commence the operating cycle. It is arguable whether this rates as a locked breech or as a delayed blowback system; one thing is certain - the opening of the locking ring does not rotate the bolt, so that once the ring has freed the bolt it comes back violently, without any primary extraction movement, jerking the case from the chamber. Which is why there is an oil reservoir and pump in the upper part of the receiver, lubricating the cartridges as they are fed into the chamber. However, one advantage of this method of construction was that it made it easy to fit the gun with a quick-change barrel, something of a novelty in the early 1920s.

Fiat now appeared on the scene, producing their Modello 1926, which was very little more than the 1914 Fiat-Revelli converted to air-cooling

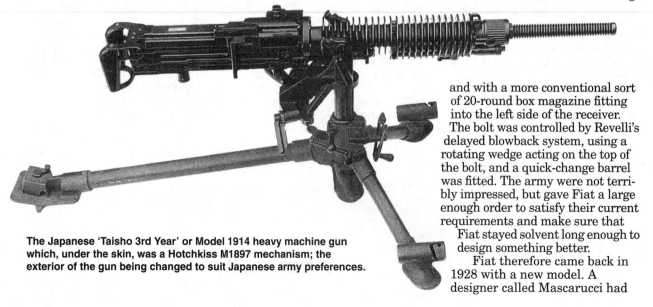

The Japanese 'Taisho 3rd Year' or Model 1914 heavy machine gun which, under the skin, was a Hotchkiss M1897 mechanism; the exterior of the gun being changed to suit Japanese army preferences.

and with a more conventional sort of 20-round box magazine fitting into the left side of the receiver. The bolt was controlled by Revelli's delayed blowback system, using a rotating wedge acting on the top of the bolt, and a quick-change barrel was fitted. The army were not terribly impressed, but gave Fiat a large enough order to satisfy their current requirements and make sure that Fiat stayed solvent long enough to design something better.

Fiat therefore came back in 1928 with a new model. A designer called Mascarucci had

The Japanese Type 96 (1936) was based on an earlier design but adopted a more conventional box magazine instead of the peculiar hopper system of feeding.

The Type 96 could also be fitted with a bayonet if things got really desperate.

developed this in the SAFAT factory, and the only real difference between this and the 1926 model lay in the shape of the locking wedge. Instead of being merely a lump of metal on a pivot which was simply swept back as the bolt moved rearwards, it was re-shaped into a form of hook, so that the bolt did remain positively locked during the first half-inch or so of movement. This meant that the chamber pressure had dropped by the time the bolt was free, and thus the difficulties in extraction experienced with previous designs disappeared. The oil pump and reservoir vanished. The feed system remained a detachable box, and it could now be quick-filled using the same charger device as that used with the Breda gun. The army were impressed and accepted the design into service as the Modello 1928, although the eventual number purchased was not great.

Fiat, encouraged by this, now set about developing a 12.7mm gun using the same mechanism and feed system; it turned out to be a

failure and nothing more was seen of it. This seems to have decided Fiat that their destiny did not lie in the armaments field and that their orders for machine guns could be quite easily satisfied by the production capacity of their normal factory. They therefore disposed of the Safat works to Breda, who were, by this time, definitely showing signs of talent and were about to blow Fiat out of the race.

In 1930 Breda (or Breda-SAFAT) came back with a new model of light machine gun, which was little more than their Model 1924 tidied up and optimized as a ground gun rather than being capable of air or ground applications. The spade grips went and were replaced by a more secure butt and a pistol grip and trigger, but the operating system was the same and the peculiar hinged magazine was retained. It became the Modello 1930

and was produced in considerable numbers in 6.5mm caliber for the Italian army for some years. Numbers were also made in 7mm Spanish Mauser and 7.92mm German Mauser calibers, the former being sold in some numbers in South America, and the latter being bought by the armies of Latvia, Lithuania and Estonia.

Having got the Modello 1930 off to a good start, Breda next introduced an entirely new weapon, the 13.2mm Modello 1931. This was gas operated, using a rising block breech cammed up into a recess in the receiver by lugs on the gas piston rod, but there was still no primary extraction and the cartridges still had to be oiled as they were fed from the top-mounted magazine. The cartridge was a powerful one, which had originated with the French Hotchkiss machine gun in 1920, and it is perhaps useful to point out that in 1931 a 13.2mm machine gun was not an auxiliary

The Type 97 was a notable step forward in design, having been copied from the Czech ZB26 guns captured from the Chinese in Manchuria.

Nambu's Type 99 light machine gun of 1939 was much the same as his earlier Types 11 and 96, but was chambered for a more powerful 7.7mm cartridge

to the main armament, as it would be on a present-day tank: it *was* the main armament on a whole range of light tanks which were then being produced by the Fiat and Ansaldo companies for the Italian army and for export to various countries.

The tank market, though, was a small one and in fact, 13.2mm was considered a bit over the top for some of the two-man 'tankettes' of the period, and Breda were persuaded to down-scale the 13.2mm Model 1931 and chamber it for a new 8x59mm cartridge to make a more acceptable and adaptable tank gun. This took some time and it was not until 1935 that the new cartridge was approved and a further two years went by before the machine gun appeared.

The Breda Modello 1937 used the same rising block system of breech locking as had its 13.2mm predecessor, was quite a substantial weapon *(which proved to be very reliable in service)* but it had one peculiarity; its feed system. It fed from a metal strip into which 20 cartridges were clipped, much the same as the sort of strip used for years by various Hotchkiss machine guns. The strip was fed into the left side of the gun; the movement of the bolt, driven by the gas piston, removed a cartridge from the strip, fed it into the chamber, fired it, extracted the empty cartridge case and then replaced the empty case in the strip from whence it had been removed. The strip was then indexed across one notch and the returning stroke of the bolt now loaded the next round. After the 20th shot the strip, loaded with 20 empty cases, was ejected from the right side of the gun as the gunner's mate inserted a fresh strip into the left.

It will be recalled that this system of replacing the empty cartridge case in its clip in the feed strip was employed by the Perino in pre-1914 days, and it would appear that Breda adopted the idea from there. But Breda at least had a reason for doing it, which can scarcely be seen in the Perino; it was intended as a tank gun, and tanks of those early days were fairly agricultural vehicles, and had a lot of their operating machinery exposed inside the hull, and a carelessly ejected cartridge case could easily find its way onto some of this machinery and cause a mechanical breakdown by jamming some vital component in the heat of battle. So collecting the empties and keeping them under control made a good deal of sense. What didn't make sense was to retain the same system when the gun was adopted as the standard infantry heavy machine gun in 1938, because what it meant in practice was that the gunner's mate had to hurriedly rip the empties out and re-load the strip with fresh cartridges ready for re-use.

What happened next defies rational explanation. In 1938 a fresh model, the Modello 1938, appeared for tank use. This was the same gun, but with a somewhat heavier barrel the better to withstand sustained fire, and with feed from an overhead removable box magazine. Ejection was below the gun, and presumably into a bag clipped to the underside of the receiver. The two features of this change what make no sense are firstly the adoption of a top-mounted magazine for a tank gun, where overhead clearance is always a problem, and secondly, why was the peculiar strip feed with the empties replaced retained

for the ground guns - which, incidentally, were to stay in use until the 1950s.

While all this had been going on, Fiat had been asked to overhaul the design of the 1914 Fiat-Revelli machine gun and put it into production. One is inclined to wonder whether their hearts were really in it, because their overhaul consisted of little more than taking out the water-cooling and replacing it with an air-cooled barrel similar to that of their 1924 light gun and calling the result the Modello 1914/35. The barrel, though, was heavier and chambered for the 8mm cartridge. The mousetrap feed system was retained, there was still no primary extraction, and the cartridges still had to be oiled, so that all the disadvantages of the 1914 gun were retained and, indeed, made worse by the adoption of a more powerful cartridge. However, some time after the gun had been introduced, possible 1938 or 1939, somebody remembered Agnelli and the SIA gun and how he had overcome his extraction problem by fluting the chamber so as to float the case on a layer of high-pressure gas. The production was halted for the necessary change, and the guns began to appear with fluted chambers, and without their oil pump and reservoir. The design does not appear to have been well thought out though, and the fluted-chamber guns never seem to have worked properly, only doing so when the cartridges were wiped with an oily rag before inserting into the feed box. The modification was canceled and production reverted to plain chambers and oil pumps for the remainder of the gun's production life.

In 1938, the Italian army introduced a new 7.35mm cartridge in an attempt to improve the efficiency

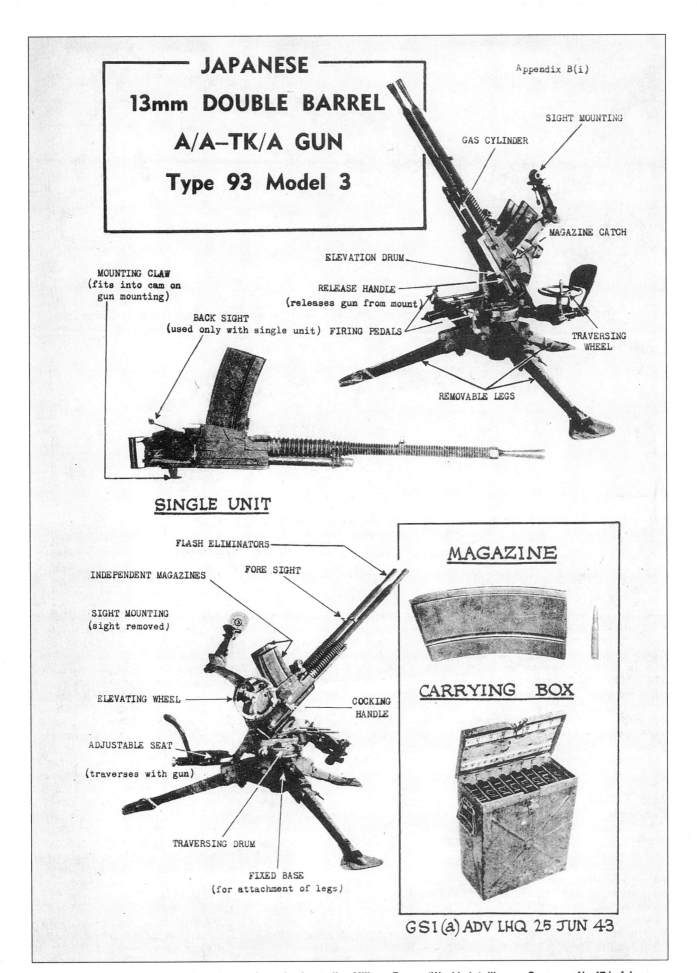

JAPANESE 13mm DOUBLE BARREL A/A–TK/A GUN Type 93 Model 3

GAS CYLINDER

SIGHT MOUNTING

MAGAZINE CATCH

ELEVATION DRUM

RELEASE HANDLE (releases gun from mount)

MOUNTING CLAW (fits into cam on gun mounting)

BACK SIGHT (used only with single unit)

FIRING PEDALS

TRAVERSING WHEEL

REMOVABLE LEGS

SINGLE UNIT

FLASH ELIMINATORS

FORE SIGHT

INDEPENDENT MAGAZINES

SIGHT MOUNTING (sight removed)

ELEVATING WHEEL

COCKING HANDLE

ADJUSTABLE SEAT (traverses with gun)

TRAVERSING DRUM

FIXED BASE (for attachment of legs)

MAGAZINE

CARRYING BOX

GSI (a) ADV LHQ 25 JUN 43

How you get the word in wartime: A page from the Australian Military Forces 'Weekly Intelligence Summary No 47,' of June 1943, announcing the discovery of the Type 3 13mm gun, which was simply the 13.2mm Hotchkiss under a new name.

From the right side, the Swiss Model 26 looks reasonably conventional apart from the side-feeding magazine.

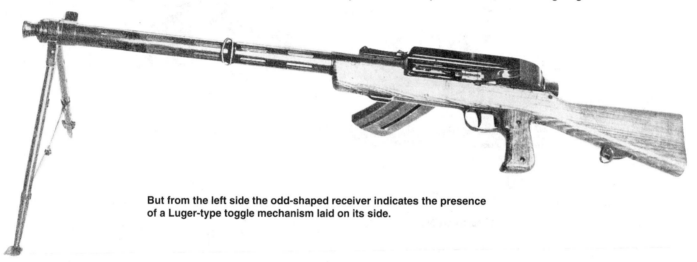

But from the left side the odd-shaped receiver indicates the presence of a Luger-type toggle mechanism laid on its side.

of their rifles; at the same time, they took the opportunity of rechambering some of the Breda Model 30 guns for the larger round, and the Model 38 was the result. The 6.5mm and 7.35mm cartridge cases were almost identical except for the size of the case-mouth, so apart from the barrel, few changes were necessary to execute the conversion.

Breda's last pre-war venture was the 1935 development of a heavy aircraft machine gun in 7.7mm, 7.92mm and 13.2mm calibers; the 7.7mm rimmed cartridge was the British 303 and allowed the use of the British round which the Italians produced for use in their Vickers and Lewis guns. The 7.92mm was principally aimed at the export market, but saw little success, while the 13.2mm version became very popular with the Italian air force in both fixed and flexible installations. The gun was designed in the Safat factory and used a Mascarucci locking system similar to the Fiat 1928 light machine gun,

with the addition of a bolt accelerator and a muzzle booster to speed up the rate of fire. Belt-fed, and capable of feeding from either side, it was given a pistol grip for flexible use, and a hydraulic cocking mechanism with electric solenoid firing for wing mounting.

One more name associated with pre-1939 machine gun development in Italy is that of Alfredo Scotti, a free-lance engineer whose designs were manufactured principally by the Isotta-Fraschin automobile company. Scotti was a prolific patentee of all sorts of automatic weapons, including some far-out conversions of bolt-action rifles into gas-operated weapons that, though they worked, could scarcely be regarded as the cutting edge of 1920s technology. Those aberrations aside, he produced a number of excellent machine gun and cannon designs, many of which were tested by the major European forces, and some of which were adopted by the Italian air force for aircraft armament.

Scotti took a not-very-original system of operation and brought it to a pitch of perfection that nobody else had managed. His guns worked on the principle of using a gas piston to unlock a rotating bolt, after which the residual chamber pressure took over and the remainder of the operating cycle was on the blowback system. The only drawback to this system is that it really has to be designed separately for every different cartridge the gun is intended to use, since the balance between chamber pressure, gas pressure and spring pressure has to be very precise to ensure that the chamber is opened just at the right moment. Not so soon as to release a blast of excessive high pressure and violent recoil, not so late as to fail to deliver sufficient power to complete the recoil stroke. This a gun designed for, say, the 8mm Italian round would not function well if it was simply rebarreled into 7.92mm Mauser without adjusting spring pressures and gas port dimensions. But once properly designed around a specific cartridge the Scotti system proved quite reliable, although, of course, the blowback action demanded lubricated ammunition. A 7.7mm gun *(using the rimmed 303 British round)* was introduced into the Italian air service as the Modello 1928 and continued in use throughout most of World War II, and a 12.7mm gun, using the 12.8x81mmSR Breda cartridge, was also adopted in limited numbers.

Japan had a very minor involvement in World War I and thus had made little or no changes in its weapons. But in the 1920s, as it made further inroads into Manchuria and flexed its muscles, it took time to look at what the other armies of the world were up to and what conclusions might be drawn from the war years. And, inevitably, this brought up the uncomfortable fact that their machine guns were virtually obsolete, being no more than bought-in or licensed copies of early Hotchkiss designs.

The original Hotchkiss design, adopted in 1897, were known as the 30th Year Pattern; the Japan-built version, which differed in some minor details of the tripod, became the 38th Year Pattern having been adopted in 1905. After the Russo-Japanese War, Major Kirijo Nambu, who had developed an automatic pistol, decided to try his hand at a machine gun and, taking the Hotchkiss as his starting point, set about developing a heavy support machine gun. Known as the Taisho 3, in essence it was still a Hotchkiss, using the same flap locking system, and with cooling rings around the barrel, but it was given spade grips instead of a pistol grip–and various other cosmetic details were changed. However, it was, of course, chambered for the 6.5mm Arisaka rifle cartridge, and the manufacture was not as precise as it might have been.

The original French guns had been chambered for the French 8mm Lebel cartridge, a sharply tapered round which gave no problems in either loading or extraction. The Arisaka cartridge was almost straight-walled and had a high operating pressure. The violence of the explosion led to very rapid recoil and consequently rapid opening of the breech, before the pressure had dropped to s safe level. This, coupled to the imprecise manufacture meant a variable headspace and a variable delay in opening the breech, with the result that cartridges were being stretched and had their heads torn off by the extractor. Feed was still by the Hotchkiss metal strip, now holding 30 6.5mm cartridges, and eventually a reduced-charge cartridge, known as the Taisho 3 cartridge, had to be developed in order to reduce the recoil force *(and rate of fire)* so as to get some degree of reliability from the gun. This introduced an unwelcome complication into the supply chain, but, as later events proved, this didn't seem to bother the Japanese as much as it might have bothered other armies. Nevertheless, it was not liked, and the eventual solution was, as you might expect, oiling the cartridge, and an oiling system was incorporated into the receiver. With that, the Taisho 3 seems to have settled down *(perhaps there were some sharp words spoken to the manufacturing plant as well)* and it went on to serve quite effectively until 1945.

That took care of the heavy machine gun; now it was time to produce a light machine gun for use by the infantry section. Once more the Hotchkiss was the point of departure, and the only real change from the Hotchkiss design lay in the feed system. The main objection to the Hotchkiss strip was the need to have some spare hands around the gun to keep stuffing cartridges into the strips

as fast as the gun could fire them. And if, by some freak of fortune you ran out of - or wrecked - all your strips, the gun was silenced. So Major Nambu came up with a system which would allow the infantry rifleman to contribute to the machine gun in time of need - or vice versa. On the left side of the receiver was a hopper into which six five-round chargers of 6.5mm Arisaka cartridges, as issued to the rifle squad, could be dropped. As the bolt opened, so it withdrew a round from the clip, aligned it with the chamber and, on the return stroke, rammed it home. A spring-loaded arm in the hopper now pushed the next round into place. After the fifth round had gone, the empty charger was ejected and the next one was lined up and began feeding. The hopper could be topped up at any time there was less than five chargers in it, and the machine gun crew could, in emergency, give chargers to the riflemen. At least, that was the theory. In fact, the gun suffered from the same headspace and extraction problems as the Taisho 3, and therefore became the recipient of the special reduced-charge round, which was not much use to the riflemen.

This became the Type 11 machine gun, so-called because it appeared in 1922, the 11th year of the Taisho Era. It was never entirely satisfactory; even the reduced-charge cartridges needed to be oiled to ensure some degree of reliability. But it stayed in service until 1945, principally because the Japanese rate of production was never such as would allow it to be entirely replaced by something better.

In the late 1920s the Japanese changed their system of nomenclature; instead of dating a weapon by the year of the emperor's reign, henceforth they would be designated by the year of introduction in the Japanese calendar. This did not correspond to any other calendar,

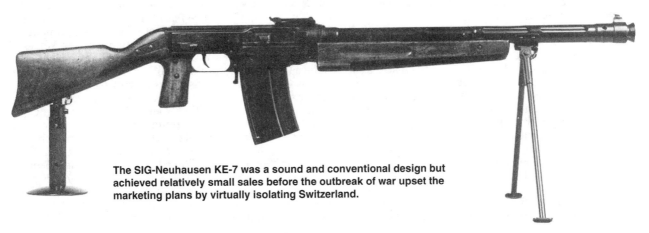

The SIG-Neuhausen KE-7 was a sound and conventional design but achieved relatively small sales before the outbreak of war upset the marketing plans by virtually isolating Switzerland.

Complications. The inside of a Gebauer aircraft machine gun, a temperamental device that could deliver 2000 rounds per minute - 33 rounds a second - when it felt like it.

also, in many cases, a long telescope sight. They can hardly have been popular in the infantry role since they were heavier than any other Japanese 'light' machine gun and no more effective.

Another variation of the Type 11 (which actually appeared before the Type 91) was the Type 89 aircraft flexible gun. Realizing that the 6.5mm round was scarcely effective against aircraft structures, this was enlarged to take a 7.7mm semi-rimmed cartridge based on the British 303 round, and used a 70-round drum based upon the drum magazine of the Lewis gun. It seems that the changed internal ballistics of the new cartridge were more suited to the gun design, since there appears to have been little complaint about the reliability of this weapon and the 7.7mm round, or variants thereof, began to replace the 6.5mm cartridge in new gun designs.

Nambu eventually retired, with the rank of Lt. General, and in 1928 he set up the Nambu Rifle Factory and began designing all sorts of weapons. His first task was to develop a new heavy machine gun as a replacement for the Taisho 3, and this duly arrived and went into service in 1932 as the Type 92. It used the same semi-rimmed 7.7mm cartridge as the Type 89 gun (in fact the cartridge was known as the Type 89 as well) but apart from that, and a few cosmetic changes, it was more or less the same as the Taisho 3. The most astonishing feature was that Nambu had made no effort to cure his extraction problems and the Type 92 still had to use oiled ammunition.

The Type 89 round was semi-rimmed and for reasons, which doubtless seemed good at the time, it was decided to change to a rimless 7.7mm round, which became the Type 99. The Type 92 gun was fortunate in being able to fire both kinds, and it became one of the most widely used guns in the Japanese Army during World War II. The rate of fire was low, and because of a curious stuttering effect in the firing, the gun was nicknamed the 'woodpecker' by Allied troops. Examples of the Type 92 to remain in use with some armies in the Far East until the early 1970s.

The effectiveness of the 7.7mm cartridge, proved in actions in China and Manchuria, led to a decision to convert all small arms to this caliber, and in the mid-1930s

but by a happy coincidence the final digit matched the final digit of the Christian calendar used by western nations. All you need to remember is that 1940 produced the Type 0 of anything, and using that as your base, count back or forward. So the next machine gun, which appeared in 1931, was known as the Type 91.

It was no more that the tank version of the Type 11. It differed very little from the earlier gun except for the feed: the tank gunner needed more than 30 rounds

at one filling of the hopper and so this was enlarged to almost twice the original size. This cannot have been much of an advantage, as the gunner still had to refill it with clips in the confined space of the turret, and since he didn't have any convenient infantrymen, he probably spent his spare time filling the clips up again. The Type 91 does not appear to have stayed in service for long, although some were converted to infantry use by fitting a bipod and

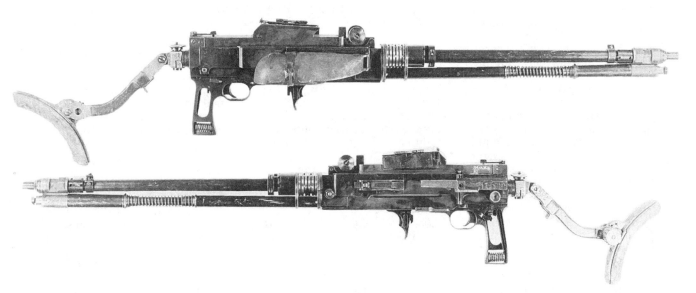

A Hungarian Model 34/37, without its bipod. This was a conversion from an aircraft flexible gun into a ground gun when open-cockpit two-seater fighter airplanes went out of service and left hundreds of perfectly sound machine guns available.

four agencies - the Nambu Rifle Factory, the Tokyo Gas and Electric Company, Nagoya Arsenal and Kokura Arsenal - were each given a development contract for a 7.7mm light machine gun. There can be no doubt that the Nambu factory had the edge here; the other three firms had done some manufacturing but had little or no design experience; moreover it would appear that General Nambu handed over the task to his design office to play with, since he was already busy with the design of a replacement for the Type 11.

This appeared in 1936 as the Type 96 in 6.5mm caliber, firing the same reduced-charge cartridge, and the principal change was in the abolition of the peculiar hopper feed system and the adoption of a more conventional overhead box magazine holding 30 rounds. The cartridge oiler was also abolished, but the necessity for oiling remained, the task being moved to a magazine-loading machine that automatically oiled the cartridges as they went into the magazine. One advantage of getting rid of the oil pump was that the barrel was easier to change, which was a distinct advantage, but apart from these small advances, the Type 96 was little better than the Type 11 which it was meant to replace. In fact it never did replace the 11 because Japanese arms manufacture could not possibly satisfy the demands made upon it. The two versions therefore existed alongside each other for the whole war.

One feature of the Type 96 rarely found on other machine guns was the sight, for in many cases a low-power telescope sight was fitted. The exact reason for this is no longer clear, since the inherent lack of consistent accuracy in the gun makes the use of a telescope quite superfluous.

The next design to appear should have swept every other Japanese machine gun into the scrap pile but, as usual, lack of manufacturing capacity meant that it could never even fulfill its first role, which was to replace the existing Type 91 tank machine gun. I have been unable to discover exactly who designed the Type 97 tank machine gun, but whoever it was, he simply obtained a Czechoslovakian ZB26 light machine gun, doubtless captured from the Chinese army who had purchased a large number, and copied it. The same gas-operated tilting bolt was used, the same overhead magazine, the same quick-change finned barrel, and it was chambered for the 7.7mm rimless round, though it was also possible to fire the semi-rimmed version. And as the breech mechanism had been properly designed and accurately copied, there was no trouble with extraction, no need for oilers, and the Japanese finally had a reliable machine gun. Eventually enough were made to allow them to be fitted with bipods and used as infantry guns, which must have been a revelation to the Japanese soldier used to the Hotckiss-Nambu weapons. In my opinion they were probably better as infantry weapons than as tank weapons, since changing a top-mounted magazine in a tank can be difficult, and tank guns usually want a more sustained type of fire than can be man-

aged with constant magazine changing.

In 1938 the Nambu factory submitted its prototype 7.7mm light machine gun for test; it performed quite well, the second, modified, model did better, and a third model proved acceptable. The other contestants also produced prototypes but all failed their initial tests and the Nambu design was adopted as the Type 99 light machine gun in the summer of 1939. It resembles the Type 96, which came from the same stable, but with significant changes in the mechanism to accommodate the more powerful cartridge (the rimless 7.7mm round) but with the incorporation of primary extraction and provision for the adjustment of the cartridge headspace, so that the bugbear of the oiled cartridge was completely removed. As with other guns, the intention was to replace the earlier models but production never reached its goal and the older weapons continued in use alongside the new ones. One of the less desirable consequences of this was that the Japanese army now had three different 6.5mm and four different 7.7mm cartridges in their supply system simply to keep their machine guns fed.

Since 1931 the Japanese Kwangtung Army in Manchuria had been sporadically fighting the various Chinese warlords who held sway in the area, but more importantly it was also involved in a fairly constant, but usually low-key, sparring match with the Russians, across the Manchurian/Siberian border. First one side would push the other's outposts in, then there would be a small local counter-attack to put the border back where it had been. There would be relative quiet for a week or a month, or even more, and then one side or the other would try it again, at a different point. As time went on these skirmishes became more serious, as local commanders lost their sense of proportion and tried to escalate the conflict, and it all came to a head in the summer of 1939 when the Russians, exasperated with this constant needling by the Japanese, launched a major operation at Nomonhan and virtually destroyed an entire Japanese field army. Not many people in the West noticed, because on the same few days that the battle of Nomonhan took place, the Germans invaded Poland and pushed everything else off the front pages.

But one result of this constant needle match was that the Japanese felt the lack of a machine gun that could keep up a sustained fire for long periods, a weapon with which their border posts could be armed to give solid defensive fire against Russian border forays. In November 1938, therefore, the army demanded a 7.7mm water-cooled, heavy-barreled gun, belt fed, and capable of being fired in enclosed spaces (such as concrete pillboxes) without enveloping the gun crew in powder fumes. The best that the designers could do was to take the existing Type 89 fixed aircraft machine gun, put a heavier barrel on it and wrap a water-jacket around it. Now, the Type 89 Fixed was no more than the British Vickers air-cooled aircraft gun, which the Japanese had bought from Britain in 1929, so that the modification into the Type 96 Heavy Machine Gun was no more than converting it back into the water-cooled Vickers gun (or Maxim) that it had originally been. But somehow, in the process, the Type 89 managed to gain weight and eventually turned the scales at 115lbs (52kg), which was a ridiculous figure for a field army machine gun, even if it was to be fixed in pillboxes. A small number were made in 1939 and issued to the Kwangtung Army, and so far as is known they never appeared in any other theater of war.

As a general observation, therefore, it would be fair to say that in spite of several new designs appearing between 1919 and 1939, at the start of World War II the Japanese were, technically, very little ahead of where they had been in 1918. Only the Type 97 Tank gun showed any real technical advance,

and there was very little evidence of original thought or design talent.

As well as those major powers that were fated to become the major players in World War II, there were a few other countries where machine gun designers were at work. Switzerland, for example, although steadfastly neutral for centuries, has a strong gunmaking tradition, and between the wars produced a cluster of designs. Perhaps the best-known name from this period is Oerlikon, famed for its automatic cannon, but in smaller calibers the *Schwizerische Industrie Gesellschaft*, now more usually know as SIG, produced a number of weapons under their 'brand name' of Neuhausen, and the Swiss National Arsenal at Bern was also actively designing weapons ranging from pistols to anti-tank guns.

Until 1920 the Swiss had only the Maxim machine gun, in various models according to in which year and from whom they had been purchased. After World War I the Swiss army decided they needed a light machine gun and the Arsenal at Bern was asked for a design. The Commandant of this establishment was a Colonel Fürrer, and he had, in 1918, organized a production line to manufacture the Parabellum (Luger) pistol for the Swiss army, since they were unable to obtain the pistols from Germany. In the process of setting up this line, Fürrer had delved deep into the theory of the toggle mechanism which operated the pistol's bolt, and he became - there is no other word - infatuated with the toggle-operated breech lock, applying it to everything up to and including a 37mm anti-tank gun.

The toggle as used in the Parabellum pistol and the Schwarzlose machine gun is a simple two-armed device, folding in the middle; but Fürrer decided that this would not work very well in a light machine gun, since the length of the toggle arms would be excessive. Moreover, in order to keep a low profile for the gun, he tipped the whole mechanism on to its side, so that the toggle opened to the right side rather than straight up. So to keep the toggle arms short he introduced a third arm, anchored to the receiver, pivoted on the barrel extension, and ending in the pivot for the central arm. The movement of the barrel extension, as the barrel and extension recoiled, gave an enormous increase in leverage to the toggle, so allowing it to move sufficiently to eject the empty case (to the right of the gun) and collect a

fresh round from the left-side magazine on its return stroke, all without excessive protrusion of the toggle.

To reduce the recoil, and keep the weapon light, Fürrer then adopted the differential recoil principle: the system is so arranged as to fire the weapon while substantial portions of the recoiling mass are still moving forward, so that the recoil force of the exploding cartridge is largely absorbed in bringing the mass to rest, and then reversing its direction of motion. Most applications of this system are in the blowback weapons in which firing takes place while the heavy bolt is still moving. In the Fürrer, however, the breech toggle is closed and locked while the entire barrel and action unit are still moving forward into battery. The sear is released during this movement, so that the entire mass of the barrel and bolt must be stopped before recoil can begin. Although a very efficient system, it demands careful and expensive manufacture - that is why the Fürrer never achieved any success outside Switzerland. Indeed, although adopted as the M1925 light machine gun by the Swiss Army, I would not even go so far as to say it enjoyed much success in Switzerland. Fürrer also made an expensive and complex submachine gun, using the same three-link toggle system, which the Swiss adopted as the M1941 model, and it is generally felt that it was just as well that Switzerland remained neutral, since combat would undoubtedly have shown up the deficiencies in these two designs.

Whether the engineers at the SIG company looked at the M1925 and decided they could do better for the army, or whether they simply thought that there was a market for a light machine gun waiting to be satisfied is a question lost in the mists of time, but whatever way it was, in the early 1930s SIG decided to design a light machine gun. At that time SIG had among their engineers and designers Pal Kiraly, a wandering Hungarian who worked for them for several years, and Gottard Ende, a more permanent employee of the firm, and these two collaborated in designing a light machine gun which appeared in 1936 as the 'Neuhausen KE-7'

The KE-7 was an attempt to produce a practical light machine-gun at a realistic price. However, it had only limited success in overseas sales although China took several large consignments, and it was not manufactured after 1945. It was an interesting recoil-operated design, and although few light machine-guns have used this system, it has some advantages over gas, particularly in barrel changing, less fouling of the working parts and simplicity. Recoil operation is less successful in that the power of the mechanism cannot be easily altered to compensate for ammunition of varying characteristics. The KE-7 was very light for a full-power light machine-gun - even lighter than the Browning Automatic Rifle - and it was probably difficult to control in continuous fire but, as the magazine only held 20 rounds, there would not be many bursts before it would be necessary to change it. A good point was that the gun fired from an open bolt at all times and had remarkably few parts in its construction. A light bipod was attached to the forend, and there was an optional large tripod not unlike that provided for the MG34 or the Bren. This tripod gave the weapon a measure of stability for fixed fire tasks, but the construction of the gun would not really allow it to be employed in support fire roles since the barrel was too light. Another inconvenience would have been the constant replacement of the small magazines.

Kiraly's involvement in the KE-7 was something of an aberration for him, because his claim to fame lay in a 1912 patent for a two-part bolt, and he employed this quite successfully in a variety of submachine guns and automatic rifles until the 1960s. The KE-7 appears to have been his only venture into the machine gun world, but he had plenty of friends and acquaintances back in Hungary who were only too anxious to design machine guns if they got the chance, people such as Engineer Ferencz Gebauer of the Danuvia Arms Company of Budapest, whom we have met before as the designer of the Gebauer-Weich power-driven aircraft machine gun. Gebauer went to work for the Danuvia company and began designing a recoil-operated gun

which would give a high rate of fire. In the late 1920s he achieved his aim, producing a gun capable of reaching 2000 rounds per minute on a good day and 1800 rpm for most of the time, but it was fearsomely complex, delicate and temperamental. I only know of one specimen in captivity, and the owners refuse to dismantle it for detailed inspection since they are far from sure they can get it back together in working order. It was recoil operated, and it appears that a relatively small number were virtually hand-built for the Hungarian Air Force in the early 1930s.

In 1931 the Hungarians adopted the Solothurn M30, chambering it for a new 8mm cartridge and calling it their M31M. They also converted numbers of elderly Schwarzlose machine guns to the new cartridge, calling them the Model 7/31. The Danuvia company then developed a new aircraft machine gun, again firing the new 8mm cartridge, and called this the Model 34AM. It was a conventional gas-operated, magazine-fed flexible gun and was adopted in some numbers by the Hungarian Air Force.

The MG31M was probably the better gun of the two, but the M34AM was less expensive and also a local product, and so when, in 1936, the Hungarian army began checking its inventory and decided on a new machine gun, the chosen solution was to take the M34AM aircraft gun, put a butt and bipod on it, call it the M34/37 and give it to the infantry. All three of these guns, the MG31M, 34AM and 34/37, can be encountered in either 8mm Hungarian or 7.92mm Mauser chambering; when Hungary threw in its lot with Germany during World War II they decided to standardize of the German service 7.92mm cartridge so that they could work more easily within the German supply system, and from 1943 onwards these guns were either manufactured in, or converted to, the 7.92mm Mauser standard.

As I have noted above, in 1931 the Japanese Army in Manchuria

started their own private war against China, and this marks the start of the slide into general warfare that culminated in Hitler's invasion of Poland in 1939. 1932 saw the Gran Chaco War, between Bolivia and Paraguay. 1936 saw the start of the Spanish Civil War and also the Italian invasion of Abyssinia. In 1939 Italy invaded Albania, and Russia and Japan had two major battles on the Manchuria/Siberia frontier. In all of these, of course, machine guns made their appearance, but there was nothing new in either their design or their employment. Most were World War I guns being commanded by men steeped in World War I tactics, and there was little to comment on. Perhaps the only aspect of the Spanish Civil War which relates to machine guns and is sufficiently unusual as to be worth comment is the astonishing collection of weapons which the Republican forces acquired from every quarter of the globe.

Recent research into original Soviet documents (fully detailed in 'Arms for Spain; The Untold Story of the Spanish Civil War' by Gerald Howson, published 2000 by St. Martin's Press, New York) show the most amazing collection of obsolete and virtually scrap weapons sold by the Soviet government at greatly enhanced prices to their socialist comrades in Spain. The Chauchat turned up, acquired from Poland and other places; old Maxims dating from the 1890s, experimental Maxim-Kolesnikov and Maxim-Tokarevs discarded by the Soviet army, Bergmann 15nA taken from the Germans in 1917, Schwarzlose M1912, purchased from Poland for $68 each and re-sold to Spain for $328.... the list goes on for several pages and is virtually a catalogue of expensive leftovers. After reading this it is less of a surprise to find that the memoirs of Spanish combatants are littered with complaints about ancient machine guns that jammed at the critical moment.

CHAPTER SIX

WORLD WAR II

IN THE SUMMER of 1939 the world's armies, for all their past twenty years of testing and trials and for all their sudden and suddenly-affordable rearmament of the past three years, were still heavily dependent upon World War I weapons so far as the infantry were concerned, particularly in machine guns. There was a mixture of the old and the new even in the German Army, who still fielded a large number of MG'08 Maxim guns, though they were being rapidly replaced by MG34s in all the first-line formations and relegated to the second-line and the reserve. There were numbers of

German troops training in pre-war days with their well-tried Maxim MG '08. Of interest is the man in the foreground, using an optical rangefinder, a common instrument in medium machine gun units throughout Europe.

Knorr-Bremse, Dreyse MG13 and ZB26 in use, the latter being largely the result of the absorption of Czechoslovakia into the Greater German Reich; the Knorr-Bremse was confined to Waffen-SS units, and, together with the MG13 were gradually replaced by the MG34 and were kept as training weapons and later were used to arm the various Waffen-SS ethnic Legions.

The presence of the elderly 'Spandau' or Maxim '08 camouflaged the fact that the German Army was about to inaugurate an entirely new tactical philosophy for the machine gun. As the Maxim was phased out, replaced by the MG34, it would be followed by the phasing-out of the Dreyse, the Knorr-Bremse and any other odds and ends that might still be lying around in the inventory. The only other gun that would be retained would be the ZB26 and that merely until they wore out. Eventually there would be but one machine gun throughout the German army; no more division into 'medium and 'light', no more statements that this machine gun would be for sus-

tained firing in the battalion support role, while that machine gun would be fired in short bursts in the squad automatic role. One machine gun would do all the tasks; given a tripod it would be the sustained-fire weapon; given a bipod it would be the squad automatic. And in either role it would be belt-fed. And while they were at it, the same gun would arm tanks and armored cars and even be used by the navy for air defense on light craft and submarines. The age of the 'General Purpose Machine Gun' was about to dawn, although nobody had yet coined the term.

The Soviet Army relied upon huge numbers of Maxim 1910 guns on their characteristic wheeled mounting, while the basic squad automatic was the Degtyarev DP. For heavy support they also had the 12.7mm DShK which was just beginning to reach regiments in quantity. Misgivings were being felt about the adoption of the medium DS gun and within a very short time production would cease and a frantic search for a replacement would begin.

The British army had their 1912 Vickers as the battalion support weapon, and the Bren as the infantry squad weapon, but they still had a fair number of Lewis guns awaiting replacement by the Bren, while the ex-Czech 7.92mm and 15mm Besa guns were replacing the heavy Vickers in armored cars and tanks. Their principal worry at the outbreak of war was that the entire production of Bren guns was concentrated in one place - the Royal Small Arms Factory - and one good air raid could have wiped the whole production line out of existence; something had to be done to ensure against that happening. On the eve of war they had contracted with John Inglis & Company of Canada to manufacture a batch of 500 Bren guns, but Inglis had to set up production lines, gauges and jigs had to be sent from England, and one way and another there was little prospect of seeing any results from that direction for a year or more. And shortly after war had been declared the Australian Small Arms Factory at Lithgow, New South Wales, was also

But wartime brings a more Spartan attitude; no rangefinder is apparent for this air sentry and his MG34 on the Atlantic coast in 1940. One hopes he inserted a belt before the enemy appeared.

The long-serving Russian Maxim M1910; this shows the wartime modification to the water jacket filler cap, enlarging it to permit handsful of snow to be dumped into the jacket in default of water.

proposed as the source of Bren guns for the Australian and New Zealand armies, and more gauges and drawings had to be produced and dispatched.

The US Army relied mainly upon two World War I veterans, the Browning M1917 water-cooled gun and the Browning M1918 automatic rifle. The 30-caliber air-cooled M1919 was provided for the cavalry, since they were not expected to have much requirement for laying down sustained fire, and the infantry were beginning to eye this weapon with some envy, since it seemed very likely that any future war was going to be one of movement instead of a re-run of 1917. The 50-caliber Browning had

appeared since the war but its only ground application at this time was as an anti-aircraft weapon, and there were not many of them; all the production of air-cooled 0.50-inch guns was going into aircraft. The US Navy, having plunged for the Hudson 1.1-inch machine gun, were installing them in their various ships, but experience was beginning to suggest that they might have been a little premature in their enthusiasm.

France had equipped her infantry with the Chatellerault Mle 24/29 and the Maginot line forts were well-provided with the 1931 fortress version of the same gun. But that was all. Nothing had been done about a sustained-fire battal-

ion gun to replace the 1914 Hotchkiss because the Maginot Line was the impermeable defense of France and the infantry were merely there to carry out reconnaissance patrols and nuisance raids against the enemy as he sat impotently outside the forts. So they didn't need a heavy support gun because the fortress guns would always be covering them. Well, that was the theory, anyway.

The Hotchkiss also featured prominently in the Japanese equipment tables, though not, of course, under that name. Nevertheless the majority of Japanese guns in 1939 were still derivatives

(Continued on Page 147)

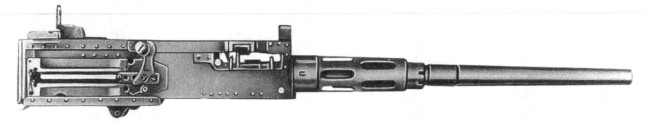

The 50 HB Browning as used by the US Army Air Force: top, the *fixed* gun and below it the *flexible* gun – both use the 36-inch barrel.

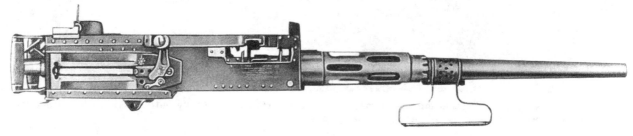

DShK 38

The DShK 38 gun on the wheeled mounting which unfolds to make a tripod.

The DShK was originally conceived as an air defense weapon for infantry and other ground troops to defend themselves against ground attack aircraft, and its subsequent employment in this role in World War II and Korea certainly proved that the concept was valid. But it was also rapidly seen as a very useful heavy support machine gun, with a lethal capacity out to almost a mile and a half range. Moreover, when confronted with light German tanks and armored cars in 1941-45 the DShK, with a tungsten-cored armor-piecing bullet, soon made short work of them.

It is therefore hardly surprising to find it still in use around the world; the Russians themselves retain it in their reserve stocks, not having superseded it in the first line until some time in the 1980s. Like other Russian designs it has been copied by China and North Korea and became the standard tank air defense weapon for the Warsaw Pact armies. The original 'squirrel cage' ammunition feed system was an elegant engineering solution which gave very smooth loading, but was something of a production bottleneck and was eventually replaced by a less elegant but simpler system, becoming the DShK 38/46.

Field Stripping

Although a large and rather complicated gun, stripping is quite simple. First, of course, open the top cover, remove the belt and examine the feed drum or feedway and chamber to ensure no ammunition remains in the gun. Leave the cover open.

Push out the locking pin at the rear of the receiver and remove the backplate. Remove the sear through the back of the receiver.

Grasp the knurled portion of the gas cylinder, push the cylinder as far forward as possible and rotate it clockwise to free it. Pull back the cocking handle and remove the bolt and piston from the rear of the receiver. Then remove the gas cylinder.

On the Model 38/46 unscrew the barrel lock securing nut at the top front of the receiver, pull the barrel lock out to the side and remove the barrel.

DATA	
Caliber	12.7 x 108mm Russian
Operating system	Gas, automatic
Locking system	Kjellman flaps
Feed system	50-round metal link belt
Overall length	62.30in (1582mm)
Weight, empty	73lb 8oz (33.33m)
Barrel	39.37in (1000mm); 8 grooves, right-hand twist
Muzzle velocity	2800 ft/sec (855 m/sec)
Muzzle energy	13,820ft/lbs (18,676J)
Rate of fire	575 rds/min
Effective range	2000m

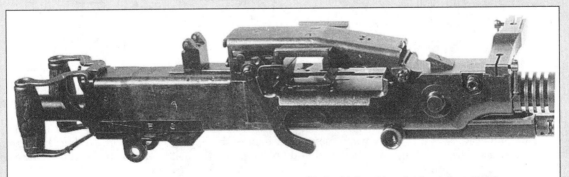

The feed cover of the DShK 38/46 which did away with the high-set 'squirrel-cage' mechanism.

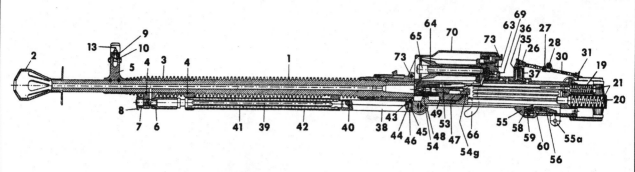

1. Barrel
2. Muzzle brake
3. Cooling flange
4. Retaining pins
5. Front sight base
6. Gas regulator
7. Gas regulator nut
8. Cotter pin
9. Front sight guard
10. Front sight guard base bolt
11. Front sight
19. Bolt buffer spring
20. Barrel extension/locking frame buffer spring

21. Spring housings
26. Rear sight housing
27. Rear sight slide
28. Rear sight
30. Rear sight leaf
31. Rear sight elevation knob
35. Rear sight leaf retaining pin
36. Rear sight spring
37. Rear sight spring cap
38. Slide
39. Gas piston rod
40. Dowel pin
41. Gas piston rod spring

42. Gas cylinder tube
43. Roller
44. Roller press
45. Roller press spring
46. Container base
47. Sear notch
48. Operating handle
49. Bolt
53. Jector
54. Firing pin
54g. Firing pin housing
55. Trigger housing
55a. Ear

56. Trigger release lever
58. Sear
59. Sear spring
60. Safety
63. Receiver base
64. Knob
65. Knob shaft
66. Feed lever
69. Feed base catch
70. Feed cover
71. Feed cover catch
73. Feed cover bolt

The mechanism of the DShK 38 in section.

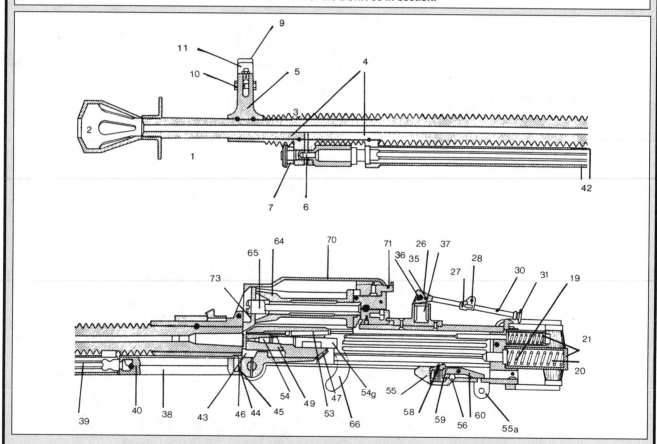

Re-assembly

On the 38/46 replace the barrel, slide the lock into place and replace the securing bolt.

Replace the gas cylinder, aligning it with the receiver, but not locking it in place.

If the bolt has been dismantled, replace the firing pin and spring and the two locking flaps. Place the bolt on the slide, pushing it as far forward as possible, ensure the flaps are closed and flush against the bolt body. Then insert the gas piston and bolt assembly into the receiver.

Now push the gas cylinder forward and rotate counter-clockwise to couple it to the barrel.

Slide the sear unit into the receiver, replace the backplate and replace the locking pin.

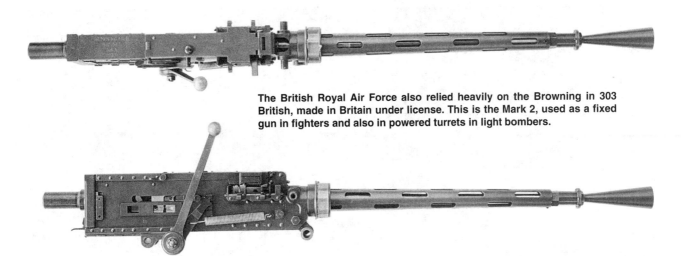

The British Royal Air Force also relied heavily on the Browning in 303 British, made in Britain under license. This is the Mark 2, used as a fixed gun in fighters and also in powered turrets in light bombers.

(Continued from Page 144)

of the Hotchkiss, though the fighting in China and Manchuria had caused the Japanese to have second thoughts about their choice of caliber, and some Czech weapons captured from the Chinese had given them some ideas.

Italy was not immediately embroiled in the war, Mussolini preferring to wait until he could see who was likely to win and where he could make the best pickings. But their machine guns were principally the Fiat-Revelli improvement, the light Fiats and the heavy Breda, all of which had some idiosyncrasy or other, either demanding oiled ammunition or using some eccentric feed system.

The *Blitzkrieg* that demolished Poland in 1939 caused some consternation and tooth-sucking in various War Departments around the world, but did nothing to the machine gun, except perhaps to cause production to be stepped up slightly. The *Sitzkrieg* or 'Phoney War' of 1939/40 in France also did nothing for the forces nominally at war there, but the Russians, intent upon expanding their borders at the expense of Finland, came in for some rude shocks when the Finns had other ideas. One of these shocks was that while their machine guns had passed all their proving ground cold tests, the more authentic test of combat in sub-zero temperatures suggested that some modification was required in such matters as belt design, lubrication in cold conditions, and protecting water-cooled guns against freezing.

The German invasion of Norway, Denmark, the Low Countries and France in the early summer of 1940, which left Britain opposing Germany alone, led to some rapid concentrations of thought. Although much British heavy equipment had been abandoned in France, most troops had brought their small arms home, but the rate of production would barely suffice to equip the rapidly expanding

Italian *Alpini* (mountain troops) with a Breda Model 30 machine gun.

More Italian troops, this time in Eritrea with a Breda Model 37 gun.

army and weapons for the Home Guard, the defense force made up of those too young or too old to serve in the army, had to be acquired from the USA, which was how the British forces became acquainted with the Browning 30-caliber M1917 and the Browning Automatic Rifle. In the same way numbers of Lewis and Marlin guns, moth-balled since 1918, were also shipped across, largely to arm fishing trawlers and coastal ships against dive-bombing attacks.

In order to insure against interruptions to the production of the Bren gun at Enfield, BSA were asked to design a simple machine gun which could be manufactured by the most basic of machine shops in an emergency. They put their designer, a Mr. Faulkner, on to the job and he came up with a gas-operated gun, which used the Bren magazine, so that it looked like a poor relation of the Bren, but was largely of commercially-available tubing and steel plate with a mini-

mum of forged and machined parts. The body and gas cylinder were simple stampings, the trigger mechanism is basic in the extreme, and the piston and breechblock - devoid of any frills - were of square section. The block locked by two lugs which were forced by a ramp into recesses cut in the receiver, and the return spring was contained in the piston and retained by a removable pin pushed up from underneath. Cocking was achieved by pulling the pistol grip to the rear. The gas regulator was a finned cylinder providing four sizes of port, which could be changed by rotating the unit with a bullet nose. A handle projected from the left side of the barrel and was used as a handgrip when changing the barrel unit: it was of little value as a carrying handle as it did not rotate. The rear sight had two positions only, and the legs of the bipod were not adjustable for height, but the Besal was, nevertheless, an impressive gun, and on trial, it shot well

with few stoppages. Once it had been approved, a handful of pilot models were made, detailed production drawings and schedules were prepared, and the whole thing was then put on the shelf against the day of need. Which never came; although Enfield was a massive sprawling collection of machine shops and factory buildings in north London, it was never seriously damaged and production of the Bren gun was never affected.

The Royal Air Force was satisfied with their Vickers-Armstrong-Colt-Browning guns in 303-caliber (*this being the name for the 30 Browning M2 when manufactured under license from Colt by Vickers-Armstrong of Britain*). In the early days of the war their eight-gun fighters did the business quite successfully, and four of these guns in a power-driven turret were seen as the future armament of the heavy bombers then in the process of development. But others were looking ahead and contemplating

One of Scotti's last designs was this 12.7mm gun for aircraft use.

England, in 1940, was a place where desperate measures were everyday currency; this was the air defense of a military headquarters - two rifles and a Bren gun.

the day when the 303, even in multiples of four, would not be capable of dealing with faster and tougher targets, The apparent solution would be to adopt the Browning 0.50-inch as the new standard, but since there were not enough of these as yet to provide all that the American air forces required, there was not much hope of acquiring any for Britain for some time to come.

The Rolls-Royce company, celebrated for their automobiles and for their aero-engines, do not generally figure on anyone's list of weapon manufacturers, but they were (*and still are*) a far-seeing firm, and in 1941 they began to develop a machine gun for use in aircraft turrets. It was intended to fire the standard 0.50-inch Browning cartridge. In order to reduce weight and size to a level suited to aircraft use, the barrel was some 5 inches (126mm) shorter than that of the Browning 50-caliber M2, and the body and cover of the gun were to be made from RR50 aluminum alloy. As finally developed, the gun was recoil-operated and used a breech-locking system based on the

Friberg-Kjellman-Degtyarev flap system with refinements by Rolls-Royce. As the barrel and breechblock recoiled, a pair of accelerator levers carried back a wedge-like 'balance piece' and retracted the striker. The withdrawal of this balance piece allowed the bolt-lock arms to fold in and unlock the breech, after which, the accelerators threw the block back at high speed to strike an oil buffer at the rear of the body. At the same time, a feed claw withdrew the next round from the belt and this was guided down and back to rest on guide lips ready to be rammed into the chamber. The barrel returned into battery under the power of its own return spring, while the bolt was returned not by a spring, but by the pressure of the oil in the buffer, collecting the fresh round enroute and loading it. As the mechanism went forward, the balance piece opened out the breech locks and then carried the firing pin on to the cap to fire the round.

The gun faced its first tests in March 1941. Owing to the short barrel, a long flash-hider had to be

used—which rather detracted from the original idea of compactness— and the trial was bedeviled by minor stoppages, culminating in the breaking of the extractors. A month later, Rolls-Royce decided to redesign the gun around the high-velocity belted 0.55-inch cartridge from the Boys anti-tank rifle, a proposal that would have produced a very formidable weapon. The Ordnance Board agreed that the idea showed promise, and provided 2000 rounds for use in preliminary trials, but shortly after this the demands for Rolls-Royce engines for both aircraft and tanks made it obvious that the company would have its hands full enough without taking on the additional task of perfecting and producing a machine gun. Moreover, by early 1942 the supply situation for the Browning 50-caliber gun had eased, and there was no real reason for Rolls to devote any further time or effort to the project. I believe only two specimens now exist.

As is usual in wars, all the usual suspects appeared with their pet machine gun project under their arm, certain that this time they would succeed. The Beardmore-Farquhar was offered to the Ordnance Board but since it had been offered with various improvements off and on since 1917, and since the gun - primarily intended as a flexible gun for aircraft use - was no longer viable, the Board turned it down without hesitation; and reading between the lines of their brief report, one senses that they were glad to be rid of the thing at last.

Complete strangers also turned up with guns, and some of them managed to get them into production. The Ductile Steel Company of Short Heath, a suburb of Birmingham, developed their own machine gun and submitted it for test in June 1940.

It was basically a modified Lewis action, simplified to facilitate rapid manufacture. The bolt used only one locking lug; a slightly altered Bren drum magazine was fitted beneath the gun, and instead of the clock-spring and rack of the Lewis a conventional return spring was contained in a tube projecting behind the receiver. On trial, it was noted that this return spring housing tended to bruise the cheek of the firer, and with the gun resting on bipod and butt, there was only a bare half-inch clearance beneath the magazine.

Although these faults weighed against it when considered for use as an infantry squad weapon, the Director of Naval Ordnance - who was desperate for anti-aircraft machine guns for small coastal vessels - felt that the simple design was of value in view of the production capacity available at that time, and he recommended its adoption. The Director General of Munitions Production, however, suspended all work on the gun for some months because there was no factory available to make the rifled barrels. Capacity was eventually found, and the Hefah Company of Wednesfield went into production for the Royal Navy. The gun was formally approved for service as the 'Gun, Machine, Hefah V, .303in Mark I' in May 1942. By that time, though, the Royal Navy had found other sources of supply for machine guns and the actual number of Hefah guns manufactured seems to have been relatively small. It was declared obsolete in November 1944, which in itself is something of a condemnation - you don't get rid of a machine gun during a war unless it is a completely hopeless case.

After 1942 there was no development of new machine guns in Britain. The Vickers, Bren and Besa provided all the machine gun power that was needed, they were reliable, they were in mass production, so what more did anyone want? There were far more important things to spend development time and energy upon. There were, from time to time, modifications to existing weapons where combat had shown up some short-coming. The Bren gun, for example, had originally been produced to a very high standard of finish and equipment; the original Bren was finished in a deep brown with the muzzle flare matt bare metal, the sight was a drum and arm pattern, the butt had a hand grip underneath and a shoulder strap on top... it was a really luxurious product. The first thing that went was the drum sight, and a much simpler screw-set folding sight was adopted. The butt fittings went, the finish became baked black enamel, and the surface of the metalwork was somewhat rougher than before.

The threat of airborne landings was uppermost; British Home Guards patrolling a river with Lewis guns at the ready.

And if the Panzers came, the Mobile Reserve was ready: a Home Guard Lewis gun team being inspected by the Secretary of State for Air in August 1940.

The gun still worked just as well, but the production time had been shortened and the demands for highly-skilled machinists had been reduced. Then the barrel was shortened to make it more convenient for paratroops, the bipod became non-adjustable for length, the cocking handle no longer folded, and the drum magazine was more or less abandoned, being retained only for specialist anti-aircraft weapons and for use by the Special Air Service and similar 'private armies'. For all that it was still the same basic gun, and a cynic could well argue that all the changes were simply stripping away the cosmetic trimmings.

With virtually the whole of Europe, with the exception of Spain, Sweden and Switzerland, having been removed from the board by the summer of 1940, European machine

The Bren gun appeared in some peculiar places; here it is attached to the barrel of the 3.45-inch, 25-pounder field gun, with the trigger connected to the gun's firing lever. A cheaper way to teach anti-tank gunnery.

The fear of an air raid stopping Bren production led to the Besal machine gun, a design that could be made by any small machine shop with the minimum of specialist tools. Note the square-section gas cylinder on this first model.

gun development became virtually a German monopoly until the summer of 1945. The arms factories of France and Belgium and the national arsenals of Denmark, the Netherlands and Norway were all under German supervision, and those countries of eastern Europe which were not already under German or Russian occupation were preparing to choose which of the two evils they preferred - if they got any choice at all.

Spain spent the war years slowly recovering from the effects of their Civil War, which ended just before World War II began. For some time in the early part of the war it was assumed that Spain would join the Axis forces, but Franco was a good deal more astute than is generally realized, and although he was willing to trade with Germany (*after they had occupied France*) he was in no mood to let the Germans take over his country and he stayed nominally neutral. This threw the country back on its own resources so far as armament went, since the combatants were in no position to supply neutrals with weapons. During the Civil War Spain had acquired a number of Czech ZB26

light machine guns, and during the war years they began producing a copy of this at the *Fabrica de Armas* at Oviedo, one of their principal arsenals. For this reason it became known as the FAO machine gun. In 7.92mm caliber it is externally indistinguishable from the original Czech model, apart from its Spanish markings.

A heavier machine gun was required, for both infantry and tank purposes, and the Oviedo arsenal set about designing one, issuing it as the Alfa 44. Externally it resembles the Breda Model 38, but internally it is somewhat different. A conventional gas-operated gun, belt-fed and air-cooled, it uses a rising block to lock the bolt and barrel together, controlled by the movement of the gas piston. A sound - if uninspired - design, it proved to be perfectly serviceable and reliable and numbers remained in use well into the 1970s, re-chambered for the 7.62mm NATO cartridge. The Spanish also exported it to Egypt and one or two other Middle Eastern destinations in the immediate post-war years.

Sweden made no advances in machine guns during the

war years, retaining the pre-war armament of Browning guns in 8mm caliber, and adding a number of LH 33 (Knorr-Bremse) guns during the early war years.

Switzerland was another country which rested securely on its pre-war equipment, retaining the Fürrer Model 1925 and adding some SIG KE7s; for the most part their fortifications relied entirely upon Maxim guns, the light weapons being used by the mobile elements of their army.

Which leaves us with Germany, who had started the war with the MG34 as their preferred standard but with a heterogeneous collection of guns old and new that, it was intended, would be gradually replaced by the MG34 and the one-gun-fits-all philosophy. Unfortunately, however, the demands made upon the German army by Hitler's incessant campaigning meant that the supply of MG34s was never going to catch up with even the loss rate of machine guns in battle, never mind replacing existing weapons.

Examination of the problem showed that, not for the first time, the Best had been the Enemy of the

The second and final version of the Besal was slightly more elegant but still simple to make, and tests showed it to be accurate and reliable. But it was never put into production since Bren manufacture was never seriously interrupted.

A prospective beach defense system: twin Mark 1 Bren guns with 100-round magazines, fired from a prepared concrete foxhole.

far too slow to ever permit enough weapons to be made to meet the plans even with five factories working three shifts a day. So the army went back to Mauser in 1941 and asked for a simplified design, quicker and cheaper to make, but no less reliable and no less robust than the MG34.

Mauser thought about this for a while, played with some ideas and then, when they had a firm proposal they went to see Dr. Grunow, a design engineer with the Johannes Grossfuss Metal-und-Lackierwarenfabrik of Dobeln. Dr. Grunow knew nothing about machine guns, but there was nobody who knew more than he did about stamping, pressing, forming and generally maltreating metal to make it take up peculiar shapes. After Mauser had shown what they wanted, Grunow, it is said, took himself off for six weeks and attended an army machine-gunner's course in order to familiarize himself with the actual combat handling of such a weapon and see

Good. In their enthusiasm to make the MG34 the finest machine gun possible, the designers had gone over the top and demanded a far higher quality of finish and precision of manufacture than was really necessary, and the consequent manufacturing process was

And if they came by air instead of sea… well, the mounting could deal with that, too.

Twin Vickers guns on the back of a three-quarter ton truck were a means of protecting troops on the move.

trolled the movement of a belt feed arm in the top cover that in turn operated the feed and locking pawls to control the movement of the cartridge belt.

This, then, was the MG42, one of the finest machine guns of all time. An unexpected bonus of the re-work was the raising of the rate of fire to 1200 rounds per minute, far higher than any other field-employed machine gun and one that gave the MG42 the most characteristic 'tearing calico' sound on the battlefield; you were never in doubt when one of those opened fire within earshot. On the debit side of the ledger, this high rate of fire meant rapid heating and the need to change barrels more often, but this was a simple task in the MG42. The perforated jacket had one long slot on its right side instead of a series of perforations, and to change barrels it was merely necessary to release the breech end from the receiver, swing it out sideways through the long slot and withdraw it to the rear; the new barrel went in in the reverse mode, was slammed in and locked, and the whole process took five seconds with a pair of trained soldiers. The other complaint, which arose because of the rate of fire, was that during prolonged bursts the gun developed a tendency to creep away from the firer due to the vibration. But once on its tripod that little difficulty evaporated and it was the perfect sustained fire support weapon. Once more the one gun for all roles had arrived, and this, it was hoped, would eventually replace everything else, MG34 included. (*It did; but not in the way that had been anticipated.*)

While the MG42 was being developed, work had also gone on - as a form of insurance in case the MG42 fell flat on its face - on improving the MG34. Two prototype models appeared, the MG34S and the MG34/41. The MG34S appears to have been no more than an interim step between the 34 and the 34/41, since the only known example is almost identical to the standard MG34 and may have been no more than an exploratory model using different manufacturing techniques. The MG34/41, though, was radically altered—to the extent that it was no longer capable of using the spare parts provided for the original MG34 and was, therefore, an entirely new gun. The principal change lay in the design of the bolt, which locked by means of simple lugs rather than by an interrupted thread, thus allowing the bolt to open faster and (in conjunction

exactly what the users thought was important. He then returned to his drawing office and designed a machine gun to go around Mauser's operating system, a gun of which most of the component parts could be shaped by stamping and pressing and which could then be assembled by welding and riveting.

This form of construction was a considerable novelty in the gun-making world of 1941 and doubtless caused pain to the older production staff of Mauser when they saw the result, but it brought the price of the gun down from 310 Reichsmarks ($107.30 at the then-rate of exchange) to 250RM ($88.55), a considerable saving when you consider the quantities which would be made, and, perhaps more important, cut the manufacturing time and man-hours by about 35 percent.

The internal arrangements had also been changed from the MG34. The bolt was now a non-rotating unit, which locked into the barrel extension by two rollers that were forced outwards by cam surfaces in the receiver. Unless these rollers were in the fully locked position the firing pin could not pass through to strike the cartridge cap, thus ensuring absolute firing safety. It is this feature - the inability of the firing pin to pass through unless the bolt is locked - which gives the system its similarity to the Kjellman and Degtyarev systems of flap locking. On firing, barrel and bolt recoiled together until the cam tracks in the receiver moved the rollers back into their recesses in the bolt and thus freed the bolt from the barrel extension. Furthermore, the movement of the bolt back and forth in the receiver con-

with a shorter barrel) so increase the rate of fire. Other small changes, largely matters of speeding up manufacture or strengthening components, were made. But by the time the design was completed and tested the MG42 had made its appearance, and since the MG34/41 was not interchangeable with the MG34 and since the modifications did not produce an increase in performance or reduction in manufacturing time and costs comparable with the MG42, the design was abandoned.

That more or less marked the end of field machine gun development in Germany during World War II, and army small-arms designers thereafter were mostly concerned with assault rifles. However, the Luftwaffe were still hunting for the perfect aircraft weapon, though their search had now taken them out of the small arms field and into the realm of cannons. This did, though, have one knock-on effect for the army; several discarded aircraft weapons were given butts and bipods or fitted to tripods and adopted as stopgap machine guns for the army. An example was the MG131, surplus numbers of which were handed over to the army in mid-1944, together with the electrically-primed ammunition, and they were employed as anti-aircraft weapons, usually mounted in pairs on improvised pedestal mounts in fixed positions around vulnerable points. The Mauser MG151, a similar gun to the Rheinmetall MG131 but firing electrically-primed 15mm ammunition, was also used in a similar manner. There are well-known photographs of this weapon on a two-wheeled carriage for field use, but no specimen of that particular application has ever been seen and it is doubtful if any other than the one pilot model were ever made.

German weapon development since 1936 had demonstrated that the traditional methods of making firearms by machining, milling, turning and other time-consuming and skilled operations - once described by a British ordnance engineer at Enfield as *'taking a block of steel and cutting away everything that doesn't look like a rifle'* - was no longer the preferred or even the best method. The use of steel stampings, synthetic materials, the adoption of metal instead of wood for the furniture or the adoption of laminated and treated wood instead of the time-honored - and scarce - seasoned walnut, all these were not only possible, but under the stress of war they were preferable methods. Throughout the war years there was a constant tendency in all sorts of war materiel to short-cut, replace traditional and expensive slow methods by modern technology, materials and assembly techniques. By 1944 this pressure was spreading and as part of this movement Mauser were asked to go further down the road they had pioneered with the MG42 and develop a cheaper and quicker-made machine gun to become the future MG45.

Mauser took up the challenge and began development, but the project was terminated by the defeat of Germany in May 1945, before a prototype gun could be demonstrated. What little is known of this project suggests that it was more or less an MG42 but with the locking bolt mechanism replaced by a delayed blowback mechanism relying upon a two-part bolt with two rollers which, wedging into recesses in the receiver, delayed the opening of the bolt long enough to permit the bullet to leave the barrel and the chamber pressure to fall. Upon closer examination, this would appear to be virtually the same mechanism as the roller-locked breech used in the MG42, but with the critical angles of the interacting faces changed. Just what advantage this conferred upon the MG45 over the MG42 is something that was never made clear. In any event the MG45 was still-born, but, as related elsewhere,

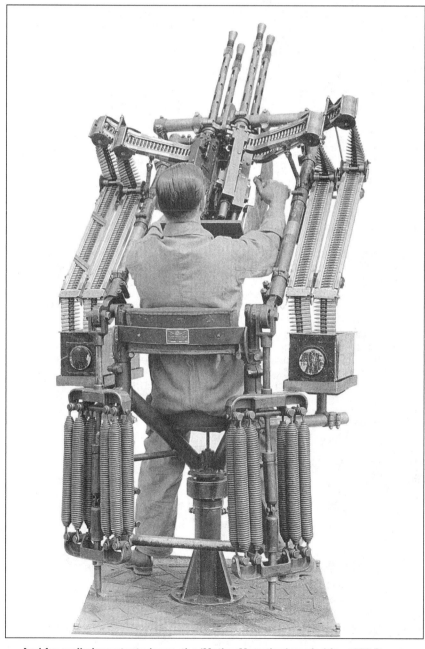

And for really important places, the 'Motley Mounting' carried four 303 Browning M1919 pattern guns.

The Rolls-Royce 50-caliber machine gun with light alloy body and short barrel in order to save weight in aircraft turret installations.

the designers decamped to Spain when Germany fell apart and the delayed blowback system was perpetuated in the CETME automatic rifles, then in the Heckler & Koch rifles and then in the Heckler & Koch machine guns. It also slipped across the Rhine and surfaced in Switzerland in a SIG machine gun. A good idea knows no boundaries.

The only other German development that had a machine gun flavor was actually a highly specialized automatic rifle, but it finds a place here because of its special tactical purpose. The Germans were the first to use parachute and airborne forces in war, and their early record was of success after success. It was not until the battle for Crete, in 1942, that they ran into hard opposition; in the event they succeeded in taking Crete, but they also took far too high a percentage of casualties, and they were never used as airborne troops again, merely as assault infantry. But one of their complaints was that far too many of their men were armed with nothing more than a submachine gun. They demanded an automatic rifle which could be fired from the hip like a submachine gun during the assault but which could also be fired from a bipod as their light machine gun, so combining two weapons in one. They were, in fact, proposing what

might be called the predecessor of the modern selective-fire assault rifle.

The trouble was that they insisted on the 7.92mm Mauser cartridge, and a specification was circularized to gun makers asking for suitable designs. Rheinmetall put Louis Stange on to the job, and he produced a weapon, which could be a single-shot rifle firing from a closed bolt, or an automatic machine gun firing from an open bolt, either being selectable by the flick of a lever. The bolt mechanism was virtually the Lewis bolt and gas piston, the magazine was a box feeding from the side, the gun was laid out in a straight line, and it fired the 7.92mm Mauser cartridge.

The army rejected it out of hand; they saw problems with firing the powerful Mauser cartridge full-automatic off the shoulder from such a light weapon and, moreover, they were busy cooking up their own lightweight assault rifle firing a smaller cartridge. But the paratroops were not army; the Luftwaffe controlled them, and they were Hermann Goering's blue-eyed boys. Whatever his boys wanted, they would have, and he insisted that the *Fallschirmjägergewehr* (parachutist's rifle) 42 would be theirs. Rheinmetall, somewhat intimidated by the army, backed down, so Goering ordered the

Krieghoff company to build the rifle. (Heinrich Krieghoff of Suhl was an experienced arms maker who also produced numbers of MG81 and MG 131.)

Against all the odds, the FG42 was a success, although by the time it finally appeared the parachutists were grounded. It was used in Italy and Western Europe, and although no more than 6,000 were ever made, they turned up so often on those two fronts in late 1944 that the Allies were convinced that far more of them existed. The design was not perpetuated, however; the German Army's objection, that the 7.92mm Mauser round was too much for automatic fire in a 14lb. weapon, proved perfectly correct, and only highly-trained soldiers could extract the best from the FG42. The army's effort - the MP43 or, later, the *Sturmgewehr* 44 - fired a shortened 7.92mm round with less power and produced a more easily controlled weapon which led directly to the modern assault rifle. The FG42 had been a side-turning, which led to a dead end.

The Japanese Army showed a surprising amount of development activity, though considering the guns they had in 1939 there was certainly room for improvement. The first new gun to appear was a highly modified Type 99 light

A second version of the Rolls-Royce with an even shorter barrel; this has the electric firing solenoid unit fitted into the rear of the receiver.

Built to fit into multiple mountings, the Hefah machine gun had no stock or handgrip, and fed from a 100-round Bren magazine fitted underneath the receiver.

machine gun, which was re-designed so that it could be quickly dismantled into its major components for carriage by parachute troops. It is not entirely clear whether this was done so that the gun could be put into a compact container, or whether a single paratrooper carried the various parts distributed around his body, or whether individual men carried various parts in the hopes of meeting up on the ground and assembling a complete gun between them. Whatever the intention, it passed its trials in 1941 and was officially approved, after which it went into production at Nagoya Arsenal. The quantity produced is not known, but specimens are uncommon.

Next came a re-design of the heavy Type 92, which had proved too heavy in actual use and the army demanded a replacement weighing under 88 pounds (40kg) and mounted in a sledge type of mounting similar to the German MG08 mount, capable of being carried by two men. The first prototype appeared in 1940 and tests showed that the designers had gone too far in their search for lightness, resulting in an unstable mounting and an inaccurate gun, which overheated rapidly. A second prototype was tested in July 1940 and appeared to be more robust, but the Infantry School objected to the sledge mounting and the whole project was suspended. It was revived in the summer of 1942 when the demands for a lighter gun became more strident, and a revised version of the second prototype with an improved version of the Type 92 mount was hurriedly sent for test. This proved satisfactory, and in November 1942 it was

standardized as the 7.7mm Type 1 heavy machine gun. It was hoped that this would completely replace the Type 92, but production was slow and never reached a sufficient quantity to completely supplant the earlier gun.

Having watched the progress of the war in Europe, in early 1941 it was decided that the existing Type 97 tank machine gun was not good enough, and that a weapon firing at least 1000 rounds per minute was necessary. The easiest way to get this rate of fire appeared to be a double gun, and a Rheinmetall design was purchased from Germany. A prototype was built but was not a success, and the idea of a double gun was dropped. The next idea was to take an existing aircraft gun that was, in fact, a copy of the US 30-caliber Browning aircraft gun, and modify it for use in a tank. The caliber was changed from the existing 7.92mm to 7.7mm and the modified weapon proved to be highly successful. Approved as the 7.7mm Type 4 Tank Machine Gun in the summer of 1944, that was as far as it ever got, since no manufacturing capacity was available and it could not be put into production.

Mention of the Browning copy above brings us to the last major design project in Japanese machine guns. The 30-caliber aircraft Browning had been copied in 7.92mm Mauser caliber by 1943, and it was followed, in 1944, by a copy of the 50 Browning– but firing the 12.7mm Breda cartridge. Plans were projected to use this as a basis for an infantry heavy machine gun, and the 7.92mm gun would be rebuilt into 7.7mm and replace the Type 92 and Type 1 guns. Apart from the earliest copies, which were all taken by the Japanese Air

Force, none of these plans came to anything, for the same reason as the failure of the Type 4 tank gun: American bombers had made sure that there were no factories capable of manufacturing these guns in the quantity required.

The Soviet Army were fairly certain that they had the machine gun business firmly settled; as noted above, they had a mix of medium Maxims and light Degtyarevs, with the new DShK coming along nicely to replace the Maxims. On that high note they attacked Finland in the winter of 1939 and discovered that what behaves itself well in carefully arranged cold weather trials doesn't always perform the same way in real life cold conditions. Most of their problems were transient ones, cured by more attention to correct lubrication and maintenance, but when the Germans invaded in the summer of 1941 the prolonged use of light machine guns began to show up the defects once more. The DP and DT guns had their return springs wrapped around the gas piston, beneath the barrel and when the barrel got hot from prolonged firing *(for they were not changeable in the field)* the heat communicated itself to the springs and drew the temper so that they lost their power of recuperation and, eventually, the bolt failed to come forward after recoiling. This had been discovered in Spain in 1937-38 and the gun had been modified by simply putting air holes in the sleeve around the gas cylinder

The increased use in the World War II showed that this quick fix to prevent the spring overheating might have been satisfactory for the limited use the gun saw in Spain, but was not

The Spanish 7.92mm Alfa was produced in 1944 at their Oviedo Arsenal and laid the foundations for a series of advanced designs in later years.

the answer for the more continuous use it saw on the Eastern Front. Field replacement of the spring was no great task, but the demand for new springs was a nuisance and, of course, the spring always failed at the wrong moment. So the design was radically changed, shifting the spring into a tube behind the receiver. This had a knock-on effect: placing the tube in prolongation of the bolt movement prevented the firer from holding the butt like a rifle, as he had done since 1928, so a pistol grip had to be fitted. This, in turn, altered the attitude of the gun when at the shoulder, and the bipod had to be altered, so at the same time it was made heavier and given a more secure anchorage on the barrel casing. Fitting the pistol grip also changed the safety system from a grip safety to a more con-ventional safety catch. All this led to the new model being called the DPM *(DP Modernized)*, after which similar changes were applied to the DT to produce the DTM, and both designs were approved for adoption in August 1944.

Throughout the war years attempts were being constantly made to improve the performance of the Degtyarev guns by converting them to belt feed. Some conversions were made and tested in action in 1942 but the soldiers reported unfavorably. The conversion had almost doubled the weight of the gun, and the long flapping belt was a nuisance when the gunner wanted to sprint to a new position.

One of the benefits of the Soviet system was that there was never any shortage of weapon design engineers and design teams, so much so that several parallel lines of development could be pursued at the same time. While the belt-fed Degtyarev gun was being developed and re-developed *(and finally dropped)* others were at work trying to meet a specification for a new 7.62mm light machine gun. Such designers as Degtyarev, Simonov and Kalashnikov *(his first appearance as a designer)* all worked on this project from 1942 onwards. Degtyarev offered two gas-operated guns: one belt-fed, the other using a top-mounted box magazine, both using a rising block breech mechanism; Simonov offered a gas-operated weapon with the gas piston on top of the barrel and using a rotating bolt in a bolt carrier and fed by a box magazine below the receiver. Kalashnikov's offering was a short-recoil design, the barrel recoiling inside a jacket and the bolt locked and unlocked by a cam track engaging with a lug in the receiver.

The test commission had demanded a weight of not more than 15.5lbs. (7kg), practical aimed fire at not less than 100 rounds a minute, and utter reliability. After initial trials they selected the Simonov, but further development revealed a lack of durability and poor accuracy, and the 20-round magazine was not considered sufficient.

By the middle of 1943 the Soviets had developed a new short cartridge - the 7.62x39mm - and this led to a complete re-think of the light machine gun design question. The new short cartridge was originally intended solely for assault rifles, but tests showed it was effective out to 800 meters range, and since war experience had shown that this was perfectly adequate for the squad light automatic, designs for a suitable machine gun were requested. Once more all the famous names paraded their wares, plus a few newcomers; we need not go into the details of the eight or nine designs that were submitted, and simply note that the design finally selected, after some very rigorous testing, was once more from Degtyarev. It was approved in 1944 as the RPD *(ruchnyy pulyemet systema Degtyarev* - light machine gun by Degtyarev).

The RPD was the logical development of the earlier DP and DPM and its principal feature was the adoption of belt feed, made possible by the reduction in the size of the cartridge. For the first time it was possible to pick up a machine gun with a 100 round belt in a box attached to the side and run with it. The design was progressively improved

Air defense the hard way: firing an MG34 off the shoulders of a convenient soldier on the Eastern Front.

The MG42 in the squad automatic role.

during its life. The original model used a cup-type piston head, had a straight cocking handle, which oscillated back and forth as the gun fired, and was without a dust cover. The piston was then modified to the more usual plunger pattern and the dust cover added, and then came a change in the cocking handle to a folding type, which remained still as the gun was fired. The fourth modification had a longer gas cylinder, and a recoil buffer incorporated in the butt—measures intended to improve stability, which was always a problem with this somewhat light weapon, and also to try and improve the reserve of power available to lift the feed belt.

The final version was very slightly changed, having a combined magazine bracket/dust cover, and a sectional cleaning rod housed inside the butt. The RPD was belt-fed from a drum clipped beneath the gun at the center of gravity. The mechanism had therefore to lift the belt up to the breech, and there is evidence that the power available to do this was barely sufficient even after the changes incorporated in the fourth modification, giving rise to malfunctions under adverse conditions.

The barrel was fixed and it became a matter of drill and training for the gunner to avoid firing more than 100 rounds in one minute to prevent overheating the barrel. The remainder of the mechanism was similar to the DP, suitably scaled down for the smaller ammunition and, like its predecessor, the RPD was capable of automatic fire only.

It will be recalled that in 1939 the Soviets had approved the Degtyarev DS medium machine gun for production, and that it had proved a failure in service. Production was halted in 1941 and reverted to the Maxim M1910 model. And since the Germans attacked in that same month, this meant that the supply situation for medium machine guns was in a very sorry state. There were two choices: either build more factories and train more workers to make the Maxim, or find a fresh design that was simpler, quicker and cheaper to manufacture. In a desperate gamble, they went for the second option.

As it happened, a design team led by Pyotr Goryunov had already begun working on a medium machine gun and in June he demonstrated his design to the military. It appeared to be sound and he was given the facilities to produce three pilot models. These passed their tests satisfactorily but in order to avoid another blunder like the DS gun, the test commission had fifty guns made and sent for test, some to a front-line unit and some to the Infantry School. Generally the reports were favorable, merely requesting some minor detail changes to make field operations more convenient. After more tests, in May 1943, the design was finally approved as the 7.62mm SG43 machine gun and put into production.

The SG43 was gas-operated and locked the breech by shifting the rear end of the bolt sideways into a recess in the side of the receiver. It was a simple and robust system, which rarely gave trouble. Feed was by a belt, and the gun was usually mounted on a wheeled carriage similar to that used with the Maxim 1910 gun. The barrel was air-cooled and massive in construction, thereby contributing to the fairly high overall weight. The bore was chromium-plated and able to withstand continuous fire for long periods, although the barrel could be easily changed by releasing a simple barrel lock and the carrying handle allows a hot barrel to be lifted clear without difficulty. The wartime version of the gun had a smooth outline to the barrel, and the cocking handle was between the spade grips. This gun was produced in some quantity before 1945, but it never entirely replaced the Maxim.

The demands of war brought the heavy 12.7mm DShK into much

(Continued on Page 162)

MG42

The MG42 on its standard tripod; the pads on the front leg are to rest against the back of the man who carries the tripod.

The MG42 was intended as the replacement for the MG34, not because it was much better but because it was easier and quicker to manufacture. It also saved $18.50 per copy, so you could build four MG42s for the price of three MG34s and three MG42s in the time it took to build one MG34.

Mauserwerke designed it in collaboration with Grossfüss of Dobeln, who were the foremost experts in metal pressing and stamping at that time. In order to fit the design to the production methods, as well as watching cost and manufacturing time, the internal work-

DATA	
Caliber	7.92mm (7.92 x57mm Mauser)
Operating system	Recoil, automatic only
Locking system	Rotating bolt
Feed system	50-round continuous link belt or 50-round drum magazine
Overall length	48.0in (1220mm)
Weight, empty	23lbs 12oz (10.77kg)
Barrel	21.75in (552mm), 4 grooves, rh twist
Muzzle velocity	2475 ft/sec (755 m/sec)
Muzzle energy	2695 ft/lbs (3649 Joules)
Rate of fire	900 rds/minute
Maximum effective range	(Bipod) 200yds (500m); (tripod) 600yds (1850m)

An MG42 team in action: Italy, 1944.

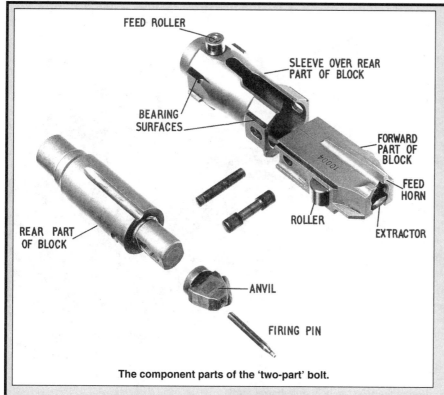

FEED ROLLER

SLEEVE OVER REAR
PART OF BLOCK

BEARING
SURFACES

FORWARD
PART OF
BLOCK

FEED
HORN

ROLLER

EXTRACTOR

REAR PART
OF BLOCK

ANVIL

FIRING PIN

The component parts of the 'two-part' bolt.

immense psychological effects upon the people faced with it.

The weapon was a great success and was put back into production in the middle 1950s for the *Bundeswehr* and also for the Austrian, Italian and Yugoslavian armies. The feed system - a reciprocating arm inside the receiver cover, driven by a roller on top of the bolt, has also been widely copied in other machine guns

Field stripping:

Stripping the MG42 *(and its modern-day descendants)* is quite simple. After removing any belt and checking that the gun is empty, allow the bolt to go forward. Press the cover latch and raise the cover. Press the catch below the receiver and rotate the butt through 90° to withdraw it and the buffer spring from the receiver. Pull back the cocking handle and remove the bolt. Push forward the retaining latch at the right side of the barrel jacket, swing the barrel out to the right and remove it.

The bolt can be separated by holding the bolt head stationary, with the rollers fully out, and then rotating the bolt body. The two parts of the bolt can then be separated and the ejector and spring removed.

Re-Assembly

The reverse of stripping; there are no hidden traps.

ing was changed from Stange's rotating bolt to a two-part bolt locked by rollers which were lodged partly in the bolt and partly in the receiver to lock. The re-design lightened the recoiling parts and lifted the rate of fire to 1200 rounds per minute, which was somewhat high for a ground machine gun, but had

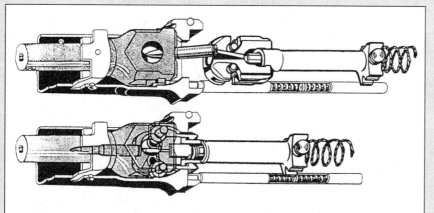

How the MG42 bolt functioned: *top,* the feed horn pushes a round from the belt into the chamber; *bottom,* the bolt is closed and the locking rollers have been squeezed out by the anvil and into their locking recesses.

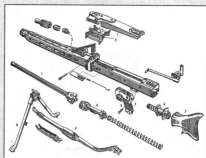

The major components of the MG42: *1)* barrel; *2)* recoil booster; *3)* feed tray and top cover; *4)* bolt; *5)* pistol grip and trigger; *6)* buffer; *7)* butt; *8)* bipod; *9)* sling.

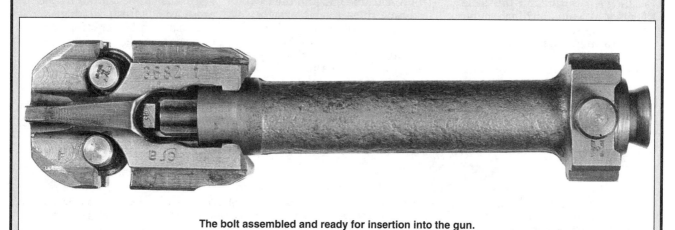

The bolt assembled and ready for insertion into the gun.

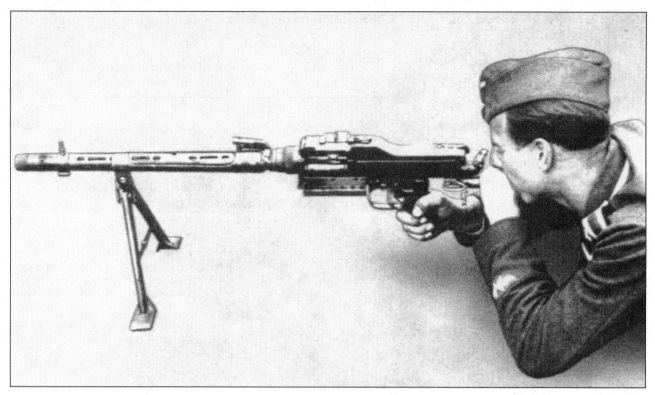

Firing the MG81 in its single-barrel form.

(Continued from Page 159)

greater use than had been antici-pated at the time of its adoption; then it was merely seen as an anti-aircraft weapon, but by 1943 it was in wide use in the basic infan-try support role, and this increased use led to complaints of breakages and feed problems. The revolving feed system developed by Shpagin was removed, and a simpler sys-tem, using a claw to pull the car-tridge out of the belt and present it in front of the bolt, was installed in its place. Various other parts were strengthened, making the gun eas-ier to manufacture, more reliable and less liable to stop firing in the middle of an action. The new model became the DShKM 38/46, the 'M' indicating 'modernized'.

In 1941 the Soviet Army began issuing a powerful anti-tank rifle, firing a 14.5mm (0.57-inch) bullet with a tungsten core, capable of penetrating 25mm (one inch) of armor steel at 500 meters range. The most powerful of all this class

of weapons, it stayed in service throughout the war, long after every other nation had discarded theirs. In 1942, concerned that the DShK was incapable of seriously damaging armor *(the Soviets claimed it could defeat 0.6-inch (15mm) of armor at 500 meters; the contemporary US .50 M8 AP round, with 1200 foot-pounds more muzzle energy than the Soviet bullet, could only defeat 0.6-inch (15mm) at 200 meters – you can work that out for yourself)*, it was suggested that an anti-tank machine gun firing the 14.5mm cartridge might be a good investment.

A designer called Semyon Vladimirov was given the job; he had made something of a name for himself prior to the war in design-ing aircraft cannon, and had also had some sort of a hand in the DShK machine gun and the two anti-tank rifles, though exactly what his contribution was is far from clear in the official Soviet accounts. He set to work and devel-oped what became the KPV

14.5mm machine gun - KPV for *krupnokalb.erny pulyemet Vladim-orova* - large-caliber machine gun by Vladimirov.

The KPV is unusual for a Soviet design in being short recoil oper-ated, and it uses a turning bolt that locks onto two projections on the exterior surface of the breech. The bore of the gun is chrome-plated to increase its life, and the barrel can be quickly changed. It fired from a 40-round belt, and the feed mecha-nism can be adjusted so as to accept the belt from either side. Another unusual feature is the absence of an ejector; the empty case is pulled out by the bolt in the usual way and is ejected by the next cartridge being placed in the feedway. The last round in the belt is ejected by an additional move-ment of the cartridge feed arm, since it is not restrained by the presence of a fresh cartridge and thus makes a longer stroke which ejected the case.

(Continued on Page 165)

The FG42 parachutist's rifle-*cum*-machine gun came in two forms; this is the original design, with steeply-raked pistol grip and a metal butt. Note that the magazine is behind the trigger; there is a good case for crediting this with being the first military bullpup rifle.

GORYUNOV SG43/SGM

An early model of the SG-43 machine gun with finned barrel.

air-cooled weapon. Various designs were tried, and one by Degtyarev was approved and put into production. However, Degtyarev was no John Browning and he got it wrong as often as he got it right; this was one of the 'wrong' times, and the design was canceled and production stopped in 1941. Fortunately Pyotr Goryunov and a small team had been quietly plugging away with their own design of gun and this was put through some severe testing before being approved and put into production in the spring of 1943.

The Goryunov SG-43 was a brilliantly simple design, using a bolt that shifted its rear end sideways to lock into the receiver. It had a heavy quick-change barrel, was belt-fed, and fitted on the same wheeled mount that carried the Maxim 1910 gun. It was later modified to become the SGM; the visual difference lies in the barrel, smooth on the SG-43, longitudinally ribbed on the SGM, and in the cocking handle, a vertical handle between the spade grips at the rear of the receiver in the SG-43 and in the conventional right side position on the SGM. There were also slightly modified types for use as tank and air defense guns.

In the 1930s the Soviet army began looking for a medium machine gun to replace the Model 1910 Maxim; the Maxim was sound enough but the manufacture was a slow business and demanded dedicated machinery and highly skilled machinists. Moreover, the soldiers were getting tired of carrying all that water around the battlefield and wanted an

DATA (SG 43)	
Caliber	7.62 x 54R Russian
Operating system	Gas, automatic
Locking system	Tilting bolt
Feed system	250-round metal belt
Overall length	44.09in (1120mm)
Weight, empty	30lb 7oz (17.80 kg)
Barrel	28.35in (720mm); 4 grooves, right-hand twist
Muzzle velocity	2832 ft/sec (863 m/sec)
Muzzle energy	3295 ft/lbs (4452J)
Rate of fire	650 rds/min
Effective range	1000m

A later SG-53 gun with smooth barrel on the wartime design of wheeled mounting.

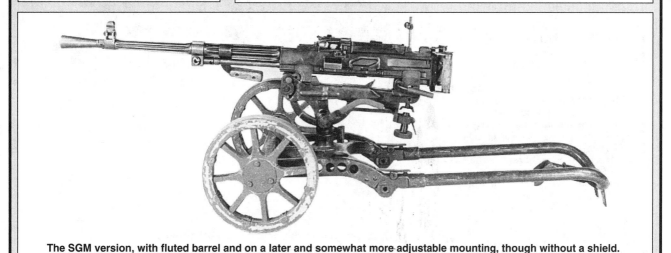

The SGM version, with fluted barrel and on a later and somewhat more adjustable mounting, though without a shield.

The SGM in use as an air defense gun on an armored personnel carrier.

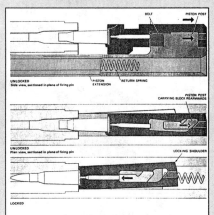

The bolt locking system of the SG-43; the lower pictures are top views, showing the sideways shift of the bolt.

Field Stripping

Open the top cover, remove the belt; inspect feedway and chamber to ensure no ammunition is in the gun. Leave the cover open.

With an SG-43 pull out the locking pin in the lower right corner of the receiver and remove the back-plate. With the SGM and its derivatives depress the detent in the latch at the top center of the back-plate. Slide the latch back, rotate the backplate clockwise and remove it. Remove the return spring.

With the SGM group, slide the sear housing out from the rear of the receiver. With all types, pull the cocking handle to the rear and remove the bolt and slide, lifting the bolt off the slide. Pull the belt feed slide out to the right of the receive,

Grasp the cartridge gripper and slide it rearwards until it can be lifted free from the cut-outs in the lower feed cover. No further dismantling is necessary for routine maintenance.

To re-assemble, the procedure is the reverse of the above, but a few points need to be watched. When replacing the cartridge gripper, make sure the lug at the rear projects downwards.

When assembling the bolt, push the ejector forward and pull the bolt itself as far forward over the piston post as possible. Put the cocking handle in the forward position before inserting piston and bolt into the receiver. Then slide the sear housing into place on the SGM type guns. Insert the return spring into the piston slide and then insert the guide rod into the spring. Finally replace the back-plate and close the covers.

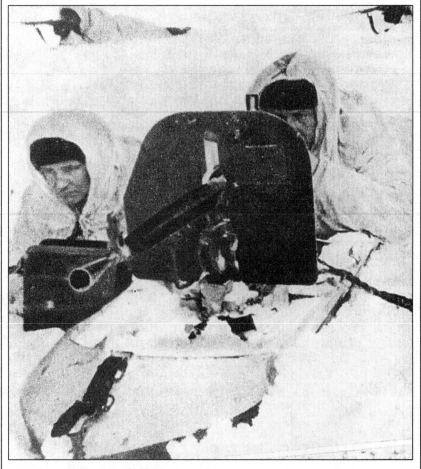

A photograph from the winter of 1944 showing the SG-43 with its shield but mounted on a sled for easier movement over the snow.

The second version of the FG42, which became the production model, had wooden furniture and a less-raked grip.

(Continued from Page 162)

Originally issued with a tripod for infantry use in the closing weeks of the war *(manufacture commenced in February 1945)* it was later realized that the modern tank had grown to be too hard a target for any machine gun, and it was withdrawn. It was then re-developed on wheeled and tracked mountings as a multiple anti-aircraft machine gun and in this guise re-appeared in the middle 1950s.

The United States fought the machine gun war entirely with Browning guns, and there was very little advance in their design during the war years. This was not for the want of trying; machine gun designs were offered on all sides, but none of them proved worthy of being adopted or showed any tactical or technical improvement on the Brownings. The army had realized the shortcomings of the Browning Automatic Rifle during the 1930s, having seen what was happening elsewhere in the light machine gun world, and put forward a specification in November 1939 asking for something lighter and more handy than the M1919 air-cooled gun but with more firepower than the BAR. Several manufacturers responded - Colt, Auto-Ordnance, Sedgely and Shirgun from the commercial world, Springfield Armory and Rock Island Arsenal from the government establishments - and a comparative trial was held in September 1941. The Colt and Springfield Arsenal submissions were recoil-operated and were little more than revamped Browning M1919s; the others were gas-operated and somewhat flimsy in their appearance. All were rejected as being unsatisfactory as they stood, but it was thought that some were worth further development. The most likely of the designs was that put forward by the Auto-Ordnance Corporation and which had been designed by a William Ruger, a man who was little-known at that time but who made a considerable impact in later years. It was taken up by the Army as the Light Machine Gun T10, and further models were built, each improving upon its predecessor. But other tasks appeared to be more urgent and the project was shelved in early 1942.

By the middle of 1943 the Army had sufficient combat experience under its belt to realize that it really needed a good light machine gun, and the T10 project was hurriedly revived. The original design was now so modified that it bore little resemblance to the first T10, and the gun now became the T23. Gas-operated, it used a lifting bolt similar to that of the BAR and was belt-fed from a circular drum on the left side of the receiver. It proved to be a successful design, but by the time it had been perfected the M1919A6 conversion had been tried and approved. This, it was claimed, filled all the requirements for a light machine gun, while the T23 was not sufficient of an improvement over the M1919 pattern to warrant setting up production and introducing an entirely new weapon into the supply system. So the T23 project was closed down.

The M1919A6 that took its place was, probably, the worst interpretation of the phrase 'light machine gun' ever built, and how it was held to have met the requirements baffled most onlookers. It was no more than the M1919A4, the standard tripod-mounted, air-cooled, belt-fed support machine gun, given a shoulder stock (attached to the recoil buffer above the pistol grip), a flash hider, a bipod and a carrying handle. The resulting weapon was 53 inches long and weighed 32.5 lbs. By comparison the Bren gun was 42.6 inches long and weighed 19.3 lbs, and the German MG42 was 48 inches long and weighed 25 lbs.

After specimens of the MG42 had been captured and shipped back to the USA, they were tested; the army was so impressed that it gave the Saginaw Gear division of General Motors a contract to manufacture a few copies. Not satisfied with merely making a copy, Saginaw, who had never made a gun in their lives, decided on a few

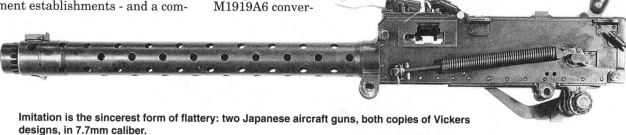

Imitation is the sincerest form of flattery: two Japanese aircraft guns, both copies of Vickers designs, in 7.7mm caliber.

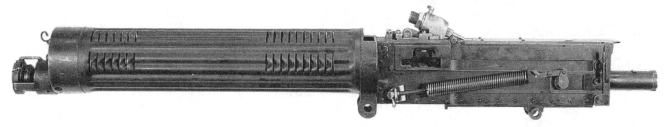

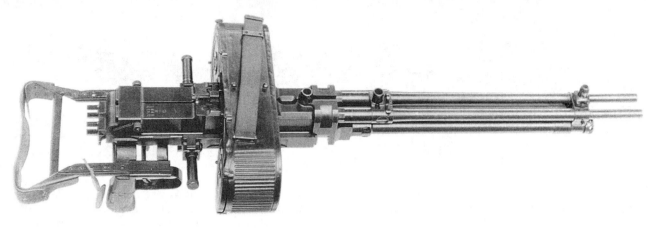

Based on a German design, the Japanese Type 100 aircraft gun was a twin gun firing the 7.92mm Mauser cartridge.

improvements so as to produce the T24 machine gun. In doing so they overlooked the fact that the German 7.92mm cartridge was 80.5mm long while the US 30-06 round was 84.8mm long. The result was that the bolt did not recoil far enough to permit clean ejection of the spent case, and the gun would fire three or four rounds and then stop. Much time and energy was expended on trying to cure the defect before the cause was found, whereupon the two prototypes were dispatched to a museum and the project was closed.

The amazing thing is that while all this nonsense with the T23 and T24 was being perpetrated, a quite good light machine gun had been developed, put into production and supplied to a combatant nation by private enterprise. I refer, of course, to the Johnson machine gun.

Melvin M. Johnson was an officer in the US Marine Corps Reserve, and a lawyer by profession, but his real goal in life was the perfection of automatic weapons. He had begun work in the early 1930s and eventually produced a recoil-operated rifle in 1941. His aim was to have it adopted by the US Army, but by that time he was too late, the M1

Garand had been adopted and the Johnson was not sufficiently better to make an expensive change-over a practical possibility. However it was taken by the US Marines in some number, bought by the Netherlands East Indies Army and eventually used by the Office of Strategic Services (*though what a supposedly clandestine organization needed with a full-size service automatic rifle has always puzzled me*).

Johnson had, alongside his rifle, been developing a machine gun that was really not much more than a heavy-barreled version of his rifle. The US Army refused it because of its recoil action, with the barrel moving back and forth and ingesting all sorts of grit and dirt to wear away its bearing surfaces and promote inaccuracy. It also fed from a side-mounted magazine, and the army wanted a belt-fed light machine gun. But, again, the Dutch East Indies Army, desperate for weapons in the face of Japanese invasion, contracted for several thousand. By the time Johnson had set up full-scale production and begun to ship the guns, it was too late. The Japanese had made their move and the Dutch East Indies had ceased to be Dutch. The contract was completed, the US Gov-

ernment stepping in to rescue Johnson, and the US Marine Corps used the guns for some time until they had all the Brownings they needed, and then disposed of. Several finished up in the hands of the Brazilian Army battalion fighting in Italy alongside US troops.

The Johnson M1941 was quite a good design and had some ingenuous and practical features. The magazine could be topped up through the action at any time without removing it; the gun fired single shots from a closed bolt but fired automatic from an open bolt; and the rate of fire could he altered by changing the tension in the buffer spring, and was theoretically variable between 300 and 900 rounds per minute. The mechanism was quite simple; a rotating bolt that locked into the breech by eight lugs and was controlled by two cams at its rear end, which were driven by cam tracks in the receiver. The barrel and bolt recoiled locked together until the breech pressure had fallen, after which the cams rotated the bolt and unlocked it, the barrel halted and the bolt continued to the rear. The usual return spring then sent it back, stripping a round from the left-side magazine as it did so, and once the bolt had closed the barrel

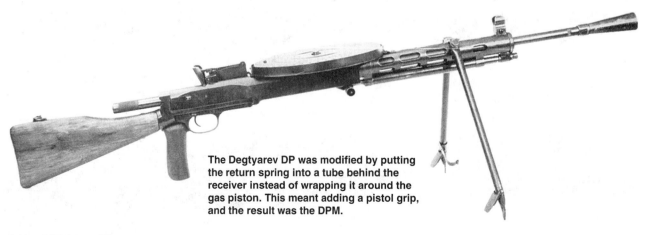

The Degtyarev DP was modified by putting the return spring into a tube behind the receiver instead of wrapping it around the gas piston. This meant adding a pistol grip, and the result was the DPM.

Degtyarev's final design was this RPD, which was more or less his DP adapted to fire the modern 7.62x39mm short cartridge.

The world's most potent machine gun: the 14.5mm KPV fires a cartridge originally developed for use in antitank rifles.

The wartime US standard was this Browning M1919A4 on the Tripod M1917A1. The tripod was later superseded by the simpler M2 model.

The eventual solution to the US Army's search for a light machine gun was the Browning M1919A6. Undoubtedly a machine-gun, but *light*?

But the air-cooled M1919 had not completely replaced the water-cooled M1917; seen here in a ruined house in Karlsruhe in 1945.

and bolt ran forward and the bolt was rotated to lock once more.

Johnson made some small improvements to the design and in 1944 produced a fresh model, the M1944. This was more or less the same weapon but had a curious monopod instead of a bipod and had a buttstock made of two tubes superimposed and carrying a butt plate on the rear end. This failed to raise any interest, but in post-war years the design was taken by the Israeli Army and, modified to feed from a bottom-mounted magazine, became the 'Dror'.

At first sight, it is perhaps surprising that there was so little development of machine guns during the war years, but a moment's reflection will reveal the reasons. Most of the combatants had settled on their machine gun standard before war broke out. Subsequent work was generally in the direction of improving the designs so as to make them easier and quicker to manufacture or attend to some defect that

A US Marine with his M1919 Browning, somewhere in the South Pacific.

The Combination Gun Motor Carriage M15A1 carried a single 37mm cannon flanked by two 50-caliber HB Browning machine guns and was a very effective method of deterring low fliers.

Sometimes the 76mm gun is just a little over the top, so the 50HB comes into its own. A US tanker makes his point, firing across the Rhine in 1945.

only made its presence known under the stress of actual warfare. And in the area where one might have expected to see most development - in aircraft armament - the war very soon showed that the rifle-caliber machine gun was outmoded and even the heavy guns had reached the limits of their ability in that particular field. The future of the aerial machine gun lay with the cannon, and that is where the engineering effort and development was principally directed.

The Johnson M1941 machine gun was a light and elegant recoil-operated weapon, but it failed to gain acceptance until the Dutch East Indies army ordered some. Since the Japanese got to the East Indies first, most of the guns ended up with the US Marines.

Johnson followed up with this M1944 model, which was much the same gun but with more attention paid to production engineering, making it easier and cheaper to manufacture. There were no takers in the USA in 1944, although it is said to have served as the inspiration for a later Israeli design.

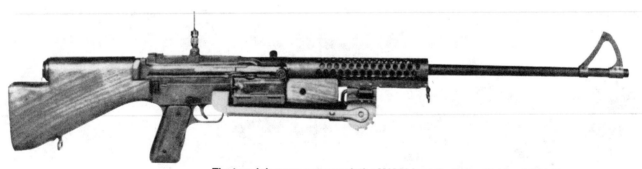

The two Johnsons compared; the M1941 is at the top, with bipod folded.

CHAPTER SEVEN

THE COLD WAR YEARS

The General Purpose Machine Gun (or GPMG)

DURING THE 1939-45 war, as we have seen, the German army used whatever machine guns it could lay its hands on, but its declared policy, to which they would have adhered in less fraught circumstances, was to have but one type or model of machine gun and employ it for whatever role was required. The MG42 was the perfection of that policy; it was carried over the soldier's shoulder as the squad automatic, mounted alongside tank guns as a coaxial weapon, fitted on to vehicle roofs and tank turrets as a protection and air defense gun, mounted on a tripod for sustained fire, locked onto a frame for firing on fixed lines... whatever you wanted to do with a machine gun, the MG42 could do it. From the planner's, the strategist's, the quartermaster's points of view, it was perfect. From the viewpoint of the man who had to carry it, it was perhaps less than perfect: It was rather heavier than the competition (25lbs as opposed to the Bren's 19lbs) and it was belt-fed which was a damned nuisance when you were dashing across an exposed piece of ground to a fresh firing position festooned with shining metal. But as far as reliability and effectiveness went, the German soldier had no complaint.

Every other combatant nation, and all the non-combatants too, for that matter, divided their guns, as we have seen, into medium and light. The medium was belt-fed and usually water-cooled, the light was magazine-fed and usually with a quick-change barrel. [We can leave the heavies out of this discussion because in 1945 they were confined to air defense and the armament of armored vehicles; they were rarely seen in the hands of the infantry.]

In the immediate postwar years the Wise and the Good gathered together to study The Lessons of The War, and, sooner rather than later, somebody raised this point about having one machine gun instead of two or three or even more. And the more they studied it, the better it looked. One gun to manufacture, to train on, to supply spare parts for. It seemed too good to be true, but it was obviously sound - after all, the Germans had done it for the best part of six years and shown that it worked. And so the rush to the General Purpose Machine Gun began.

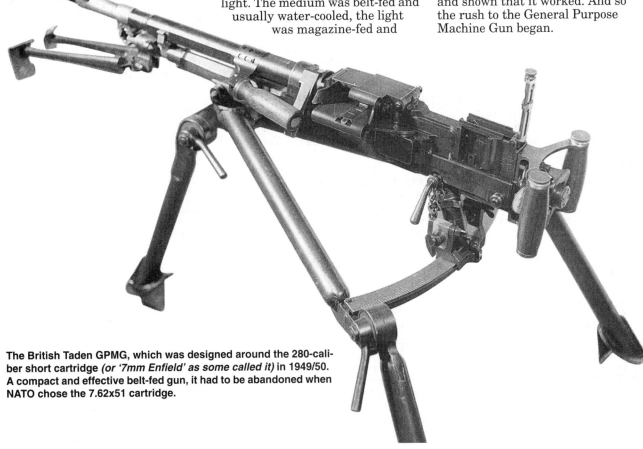

The British Taden GPMG, which was designed around the 280-caliber short cartridge (or '7mm Enfield' as some called it) in 1949/50. A compact and effective belt-fed gun, it had to be abandoned when NATO chose the 7.62x51 cartridge.

The FN MAG, which captured half the world market for a general-purpose machine gun.

'The trouble was that apart from the MG42s, most of which were distinctly shop-worn by that time, there wasn't a gun available that fitted the specification. And while this was being contemplated, NATO came into being and one of its first priorities was to settle the question of a standard small arms cartridge. Until that question was answered, it was no good asking about a general-purpose machine gun. In fact the British had gone ahead and developed a good design, variously known as the Taden or XE5, which fired a short 7mm cartridge they had developed. It was belt-fed and air-cooled, could be fitted with a butt and fired from a bipod or fitted with spade grips and fired from a tripod and generally appeared to be just the answer to the machine gun question. Unfortunately, nobody ever managed to find out because the 7mm cartridge was Not Invented Here and could not therefore be accepted by the US forces. Instead, after a great deal of argument, NATO got the 7.62x51 round as their standard, and it was 1954 before anyone could really begin to think about the GPMG.

By which time it was too late for anyone to begin thinking, because Fabrique Nationale of Belgium had already done their thinking, taken a gamble, and were about to scoop the pool. Standing on the sidelines and watching the furor over the future NATO cartridge, they had weighed up the politics of the affair and had seen that they were of greater importance than mere ballistics or tactical effects, and they had, even before the NATO members had gathered to consider it, realized that the 7.62x51mm cartridge was likely to be the winner. Whereupon they had gone ahead and developed a GPMG based on that cartridge. So that when the

NATO members rubbed their hands together and said 'Well, chaps, that's settled, now let's find a machine gun' there was an FN salesman at the door with a sample GPMG in his bag.

This was the FN MAG: MAG for *Mitrailleuse d'Appui Generale* (General Purpose Machine Gun) and not *'Mitrailleuse a Gaz'* as is often claimed. A gas-operated and belt-fed weapon, it relied upon the well-tried rising bolt, which Browning had bequeathed to Fabrique National with the license to make the BAR. It could be fitted with a butt and bipod to become the squad automatic, or with spade grips and a tripod as the company support machine gun. It could be mounted in armored vehicles or on boats, and it later years was to appear in helicopters and other types of aircraft.

The British, finding that their Taden machine gun was incapable of being re-jigged to fire the NATO standard cartridge, had begun a fresh design, the X11E2. This used the same breech mechanism and gas system as the Bren but was belt-fed and larger and more robust so as to stand up to long periods of sustained fire. It was, of course, air-cooled and adopted the Bren method of changing the barrel. The infantry and the designers cooperated closely and the weapon was capable of firing off a tripod or from a bipod with equal accuracy. But the feed system was driven from the gas piston and involved shafts and gears to get the movement from the bottom of the gun to the top, so that there were friction losses and a lack of belt-lifting power which tended to slow the rate of fire. The other severe defect was that the gun was designed to be built in the good old way, by machining large lumps of steel into complicated shapes.

Nevertheless it was tinkered with and got as far as the X11E4 by 1958, when it was decided to run some comparative trials against the M60, the AA-52, the FN-MAG, the SIG 710 and the Madsen-Saetter. After a long and searching trial the British bought the MAG and put it into service as the General Purpose Machine Gun L7A1. It was one of the first British weapons to adopt this new form of nomenclature, which appeared in the late-1950s to replace the old system of 'Mark 1, Mark 2' and so on. The 'L' stands for Land Service and the 7 is the identifying model number. Subsequent modifications gave rise to the L7A1, L7A2 and so on. The troops invariably called it their 'GPMG'; they never called it the 'Jimpy', a nickname invented, I believe, by a TV scriptwriter.

After that the MAG was adopted by some 57 different countries - most of which had previously adopted the FN FAL rifle - usually in 7.62mm NATO caliber even if they were not NATO members, though it was also available in other calibers. There were, though, a few hold-outs.

After the formation of NATO, Federal Germany was permitted to rebuild its armed forces, and the Federal German Army - the *Bundeswehr* - was initially provided with American weapons. The Germans, with perhaps more excuse than anyone else, had their own views on weaponry and promptly set about obtaining what they wanted. And high on the list was the General Purpose Machine Gun, for which the only possible solution was the MG42. The original engineering drawings had vanished in the end-of-war chaos, so an original

Continued on Page 176)

THE FN-MAG

The FN MAG in the squad automatic role.

The Fabrique Nationale of Herstal, Belgium, have never been backward at looking forward, and when the newly-emergent NATO governments were arguing about their future standard small-arm cartridge, FN took careful note of the options, weighed up the political clout wielded by the various proposers, and placed their bet. They won handsomely, having rightly deduced that the 7.62x51mm cartridge would be the winner. By the time this had been settled, FN had a General Purpose Machine Gun waiting for them.

This design had been developed by Ernest Vervier, FN's Chief Designer, who had begun work on it immediately after World War II ended, having fore-seen that the GPMG concept was going to be the next phase in machine gun development. Various calibers were tested, but the 7.62x51mm version became the standard once NATO had given it the seal of approval. Minor differences will be found between the models adopted by various countries - eg, finned or smooth barrels - but the underlying mechanism remains the same. At the turn of the century the MAG was in use by at least 81 countries.

DATA	
Caliber	7.62 x 51mm
Operating system	Gas, selective fire
Locking system	Tilting bolt
Feed system	Metal link belt
Overall length	49.20in (1250mm)
Weight, empty	22lb 4oz (10.15kg)
Barrel	21.50in (546mm); 4 grooves, right-hand twist
Muzzle velocity	2800 ft/sec (853 m/sec)
Muzzle energy	2611 ft/lbs (3429J)
Rate of fire	850 rds/min
Effective range	1200 m

HEAVY

LIGHT

An early model of the MAG came with two types of barrel, both finned for half their length. The fins were later removed and the heavy barrel dropped from the menu.

The tripod-mounted company support MAG.

A Swedish infantryman starting on a barrel change on his MAG.

Firm believers in mechanical simplicity, FN used the piston and linked bolt gas system similar to of the Browning Automatic Rifle but modified so that the actual bolt does not move up or down, but a separate bolt lock lever is moved down, by the piston link, to lock against a shoulder in the receiver. The feed system has some resemblance to that of the German MG42, using the reciprocation of the bolt, which carried a roller on its top so as to engage with a feed arm. Feed can be from a disintegrating link belt or a continuous link belt; but be warned - the two types cannot be interchanged and there is no indication on the gun as to which belt it uses. The only way to find out is to try one.

Field Stripping

Lift the top cover, remove the belt, pull back the cocking lever and ensure the feedway and chamber are empty. Pull the trigger and allow the working parts to go forward to the *fired* condition.

Remove the butt by depressing the butt catch and lifting the butt upwards. Remove the return spring by pushing the rear end of the return spring rod forward and then lifting it. The spring and rod can then be pulled out of the rear end of the receiver.

Pull back the cocking handle and remove the piston, piston slide and breech-block. Remove the axis pin and separate the bolt from the slide.

Press in the barrel locking nut *(on the rear left side of the barrel)* and while holding it in, rotate the carrying handle to the vertical. Pull the barrel forward out of the gun.

Remove the trigger group locking pin *(behind the pistol grip),* lower the pistol grip and unhook from the receiver.

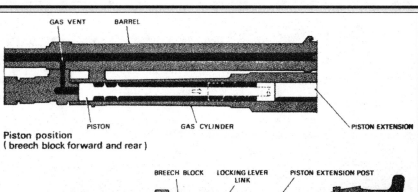

Piston position
(breech block forward and rear)

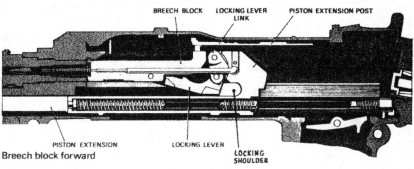

Breech block forward

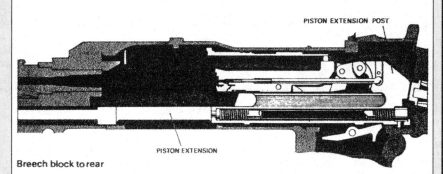

Breech block to rear

The locking system of the MAG. Compare this with the drawings of the BAR system; a similar linkage is used but the methods of locking are entirely different.

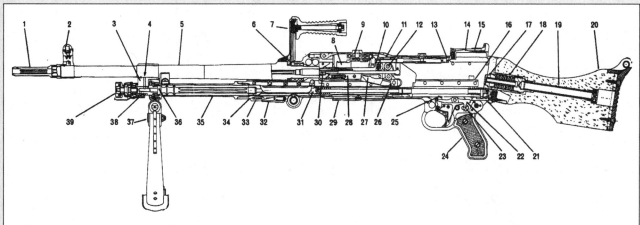

Key for Figures

1. Flash Hider
2. Foresight
3. Gas Block
4. Gas Vent
5. Barrel
6. Barrel Nut
7. Carrying Handle
8. Cartridge Stop
9. Feed Pawls Assembly
10. Roller
11. Feed Arm
12. Link
13. Top Cover Catch
14. Rear Sight Ramp
15. Rear Sight (Folded down)
16. Breech Block Guide
17. Buffer Plate
18. Buffer Assembly
19. Securing Screw
20. Butt
21. Butt Catch
22. Sear
23. Safety Catch
24. Trigger Grip
25. Sear Tripper
26. Locking Shoulder
27. Locking Lever
28. Breech Block
29. Ejection Opening Cover
30. Firing Pin
31. Piston
32. Bipod Retainer
33. Slot (for bipod leg)
34. Dust Cover
35. Gas Cylinder
36. Piston Head
37. Bipod Assembly
38. Gas Plug
39. Gas Regulator

What goes where inside the FN MAG.

The British L37A1 is their tank version of the FN MAG, with pistol grip and special barrel locking arrangements.

To re-assemble.

Engage the slot in the front of the trigger group with the front edge of the aperture in the receiver, lift the rear end of the group and insert the locking pin.

Place the barrel on top of the gas cylinder, line it up with the hole in the receiver, depress the barrel locking but and with the carrying handle vertical ease the barrel into its seating. When fully home, rotate the carrying handle down, releasing the locking nut at the same time and ensuring that the barrel engages with the locking nut.

Place the bolt on the pistol slide, align the holes and insert the axis pin. Press the bolt lock (beneath the bolt) against the bolt and pull the bolt as far forward as possible. Align the bolt with the guides in the receiver walls and insert the assembly into the receiver. Insert the driving spring into the slide,

press the trigger and use the spring to push the piston and bolt assembly fully home. Press the driving spring guide rod forward against the spring and seat it into the slot in the bottom of the receiver. Replace the butt by sliding it down the slots at the rear of the receiver.

Pull the cocking handle to the rear and close the cover. Holding the cocking handle, pull the trigger and allow the working parts to go forward under control.

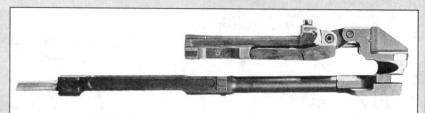

The pistol and bolt assembly of the FN MAG in the unlocked position...

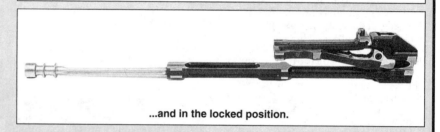

...and in the locked position.

(Continued from Page 172)

gun was acquired, stripped to its smallest part, measured, and the whole gun 'reverse engineered' into a fresh set of manufacturing drawings and specifications. The result was the MG1.

The MG1 differed slightly from the MG42, though the difference is not readily distinguishable; it is almost impossible to tell the two apart when seen on a photograph or from ten feet away. It was developed by Rheinmetall in 1959 and was, therefore, originally known as the MG42/59, the appellation MG1 being the official Bundeswehr designation. It was originally chambered for the 7.92x57mm Mauser cartridge, but this, naturally, had to be changed to the NATO standard 7.62x51mm cartridge, which changed the designation to MG1A1.

The remaining changes were internal and almost entirely concerned with manufacturing techniques, which had changed somewhat since the MG42 had originally been designed.

The MG1A1 used a German continuous metal link belt known as the DM1, and in order to ensure NATO interoperability the feed mechanism was slightly altered so that it was also possible to feed it

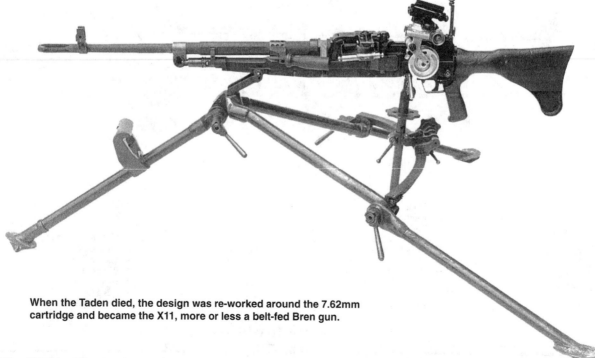

When the Taden died, the design was re-worked around the 7.62mm cartridge and became the X11, more or less a belt-fed Bren gun.

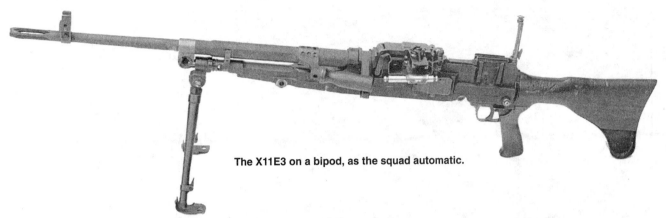

The X11E3 on a bipod, as the squad automatic.

with the standard US Army M13 belt; this version became the MG1A2. Then came the MG1A3, with some more small changes for manufacturing convenience and a new design of muzzle booster, and for some reason or other it reverted to the original feed mechanism and could only fire from the DM1 belt.

During the course of this phase of development, the Bundeswehr had accumulated, from a variety of sources, a fairly large number of original M42 guns that they had used as an interim measure until the new weapons began to enter service. These were all in 7.92mm caliber, and they were now re-barreled and modified as necessary to use the 7.62x51mm NATO cartridge, and the resulting weapon was the MG2.

Development of the new gun continued, and the final alteration, as might be expected, was to change the MG1A3 to accept the US M13 belt and a new German design of disintegrating link belt known as the DM6. This was felt to be a clean break with the older patterns and was formally decreed to become the new army standard, and so in 1968 it was introduced under the title of MG3. This was subsequently adopted by Austria, Chile, Denmark, Greece, Iran, Italy, Norway, Pakistan, Portugal, Spain, Sudan and Turkey. They are, or have been built under license in Greece, Iran, Italy, Pakistan, Spain and Turkey.

The Rheinmetall company also offered the MG42/59 - ie the

7.92mm version - for export and these were sold to a number of armies - notably the Austrian and Italian - and was also manufactured under license in Yugoslavia, originally known as the SARAC 53, later simply as the MG53.

The Heckler & Koch company have also put GPMG designs onto the export market, commencing with the HK21. This was in 7.62x51mm caliber, was derived from their highly successful G3 rifle, and, like all the company's products prior to 1990, relied upon a roller-delayed blowback system of operation, which is worth a closer look because it must rank as the most successful delayed-blowback system ever seen. Like the bolt of the French AA52 described

A day out from the office. British officers and War Ministry officials visit the Royal Small Arms Factory for a spot of 'hands-on' with the X11 machine gun.

The British soldiers, of course, get more than enough 'hands-on' experience with the L7A1 GPMG.

below, it is another variation upon Kiraly's two-part bolt, which we encountered in the 1920s Kiraly-Ende KE7 machine gun and which Kiraly promoted vigorously from 1912 until the 1950s. The essential feature is that the bolt is comprised of two parts, a light head and a very heavy (by comparison) body. The light head is thrust back by the force of the exploding cartridge and has to move the heavy rear body via some method involving a mechanical leverage, which slows down the transfer of impulse and thus delays the movement of the complete bolt. The Heckler and Koch system uses two rollers as the delaying mechanism; it was, in fact devised in the Mauser factory in 1944/45 and stemmed from the roller locking system used in the MG42 machine gun. That was a positively locked system, but by changing the contours of the various interfaces and other subtle tricks of design, it became a delaying system and was put forward for the Mauser Sturmgewehr 45 experimental assault rifle and MG45 machine gun. The war ended before these got past the prototype stage, the design team

split up, some members going to Spain, and the design reappeared in Spain as part of the CETME assault rifle in 7.92mm caliber. This was offered to Germany through the medium of a Dutch firm in the 1950s. The German army accepted the design in principle but then handed it to Heckler and Koch to turn into a practical service weapon. Heckler & Koch were, at that time, working in an old Mauser factory in Oberndorf, so the design had come full circle in a matter of ten years or so.

After successfully developing the G3 rifle and some variant models they then went on to adapt it to the HK21 machine gun, basing the design upon the rifle but with a heavier and changeable barrel and a belt feed system. This would accept the DM1, DM6 or M13 belts interchangeably; moreover, by changing the barrel, bolt and parts of the feed mechanism, the gun could be converted to fire 7.62x39mm Soviet or 5.56mm NATO cartridges, but this facility was dropped due to lack of demand after being offered for a few years. There was a very practical barrel change system, more or less

adapted from that used in the MG34 and MG42, and to crown everything there was an adapter which could replace the belt feed unit and allow feed from a box magazine beneath the receiver. As a result of all this the HK21 could be adapted as a belt-fed light machine gun with bipod, a magazine-fed light machine gun with bipod, a belt-fed tripod-mounted sustained-fire machine gun or a belt-fed tank machine gun.

This was followed by the HK21A, which appeared in the early 1970s. This employed an ingenious feed system in which, instead of feeding the belt into a slot in the side of the receiver, the portion of the receiver underneath the slot was hinged and could be dropped open. This made loading far easier - you simply slap the belt onto the hinged section and lift the whole thing up and close it - and it also made curing stoppages, unloading and maintenance a good deal easier. On the other hand, it meant that the magazine feed adapter would no longer fit and it was no longer an option.

The ultimate variant of the HK21 was the HK21E that had a

The BSA company modified a Bren to belt feed as a potential GPMG in the 1950s.

The MG3 on its sustained-fire tripod; there are some differences in this mounting from that used with the MG42.

Today's German MG3 is practically indistinguishable from yesterday's German MG42.

The L7 is also the roof-mounted close-defense machine gun on British tanks; here some crewmembers stock up on ammunition for their Chieftain tank's gun.

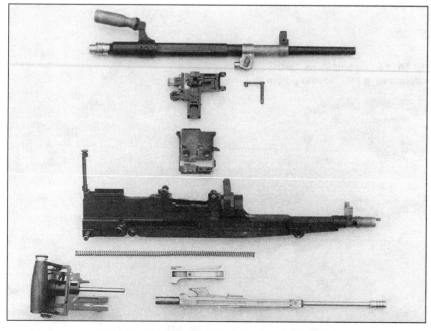

The X11 machine gun reduced to its major parts.

longer barrel and a longer receiver; this allowed a longer bolt travel and thus reduced the felt recoil and improved the accuracy. There was also a completely new trigger mechanism, which in addition to the single shot/automatic options offered on the earlier models added the option of a three-round burst for a single pressure of the trigger. The feed mechanism was improved, as were the barrel change and the sights. Although not adopted by the German army, the HK21A and 21E were both sold successfully in the export market and were used by, among others, Mexico and Portugal.

Taking the HK21E as their model, Heckler & Koch then developed the HK13E as a 5.56mm general-purpose machine gun. Externally the only apparent difference lies in the length of the barrel; the HK21E has about four inches of barrel showing in front of the perforated jacket, while the HK13E merely shows its flash hider. So far as I am aware, a GPMG in 5.56mm caliber appears to be an idea rather in advance of its time, and while a number of armies have conducted trials with the HK13E, none appear to have adopted it in any numbers as yet.

The French entrant into the GPMG field is the *Arme Automatique Transformable 52* or AAT 52. As the title suggests, this appeared in 1952 and thus actually rates as the first post-war GPMG adopted by any major army. One might therefore have expected it to be considered for adoption by other NATO armies during the 1950s when they were looking for a GPMG, but two features counted against it. In the first place it was chambered for the 7.5x54mm Mle 1929 French cartridge, and the French showed little interest or inclination towards changing it to 7.62mm caliber, and in the second place it was a delayed blowback design, a principle of operation which most armies at that time viewed with some suspicion, specially on a machine gun firing a full-power rifle cartridge.

The AA52 uses a two-part bolt to delay the opening of the breech, and the delay is introduced by means of a lever working at a mechanical disadvantage. The complete bolt unit consists of the usual lightweight head and heavy body, and the two are separated by the lever that is carried on the bolt head. The short end of this lever is anchored in a recess in the receiver and the long end bears against the front face of the

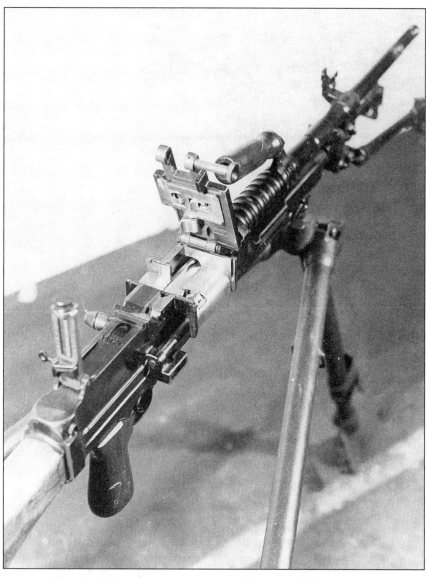

The BSA GPMG with the feed cover opened.

heavy section of the bolt. The chamber is grooved, so as to ease the extraction of the fired case. The case presses the bolt head back; this in turn rotates the lever so as to press back and eventually accelerate the heavy section of the bolt, and as it reaches this point so the short end comes free of the recess and the complete bolt is now free to move back, extract the spent case and commence the firing cycle. On the return stroke the bolt head chambers a fresh cartridge, the toe of the lever enters the recess in the receiver and the continuing pressure of the rear end of the bolt - driven by the usual kind of return spring - causes the lever to flip over and take up its position holding the bolt head firmly against the cartridge.

As one might imagine, this design is highly dependent upon the precision of the cartridge headspace that, in turn, is dependent upon the state of wear in the lever and its bearing surface in the receiver. The gun has been designed so that the bearing surface can be quickly replaced when it becomes worn, but even so the safety margin is just that - marginal. The chamber pressure is around 27 tons per square inch, and the cases are invariably bulged around the head, indicating an excess pressure at the commencement of extraction, and it requires the gunner to be vigilant and send his gun for repair when

Continued on Page 185)

Italian troops firing their MG42/59. This is the commercial model developed by Rheinmetall and is the same as the MG3, which is solely the German Army's designation.

The Yugoslavian M53 machine gun, which is the Rheinmetall MG42/59 built under license in Yugoslavia in the original 7.92x57mm Mauser - making it an MG42 in all but name.

The Heckler & Koch HK21A1in the light machine gun role.

And this is the HK21E on its 'field mount' as the company support gun.

HECKLER & KOCH HK21

The HK21 in the light automatic role, with belt box.

Once the German Army had settled on the MG3 as their new general purpose machine gun, Heckler & Koch realized there was little hope of interesting them in a light machine gun design, and they came up with the idea of a family of weapons which could be made available in three calibers so as to meet most likely demands from export customers; these were 7.62x51mm NATO, 5.56x45mm M193 and 7.62x39mm Soviet M43. Among the first weapons to be developed in this group was the HK21 light machine gun.

So far as the mechanism went it was simply the existing G3 delayed-blowback rifle. What turned it into a machine gun was the heavy quick-change barrel, the bipod, and the

DATA	
Caliber	7.62 x 51mm
Operating system	Delayed blowback, selective fire
Locking system	Roller-delayed two-part bolt
Feed system	Metal link belt
Overall length	40.19in (1021mm)
Weight, empty	16lb 2oz (7.32kg)
Barrel	17.71in (450mm); 4 grooves, right-hand twist
Muzzle velocity	2625 ft/sec (800 m/sec)
Muzzle energy	2297 ft/lbs (3104J)
Rate of fire	750 rds/min
Effective range	1200m

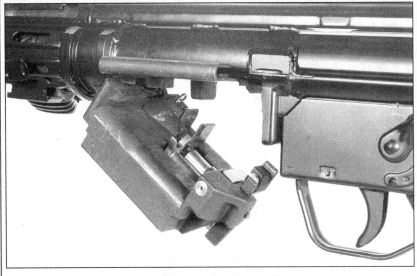

Close-up view of the HK21A1 quick-loading feed tray.

Mounted on a tripod for the sustained fire tasks.

ability to quickly swap between belt and magazine feed by fitting an attachment or removing it. A change of caliber was simply a question of changing the barrel, feed plate and bolt.

It was later improved into the HK21A1, dropping the magazine feed and caliber change options since few customers seemed to be interested in those. It finally became, in 1983, the HK21E by adopting a more robust receiver, a three-round burst facility, a forward handgrip and a quiet bolt-closing device.

Field Stripping:

Note: these stripping instructions are broadly applicable to any H&K rifle or machine gun using their roller-delayed blowback system. Merely make allowances for the obvious differences in procedure between a magazine arm and a belt-fed arm.

Remove the magazine or open the feed cover and remove the belt. Pull back the cocking handle. Examine feedway and chamber to ensure that no ammunition remains in the gun. Pull the trigger and allow the working parts to go forward under control.

Push out the butt retaining pins and withdraw the butt and return spring to the rear. Pull the cocking handle to the rear and remove the bolt.

The HK21 field-stripped, showing the magazine adapter and box magazine.

To remove the feed tray: press down the rear end of the locking plate on the right of the mechanism and at the same time push in the release catch at the left front. The feed tray can then be slid out to the left.

Pull back the barrel locking catch, rotate the barrel arm clockwise and push forwards. Once the barrel clears the receiver, swing the rear end out and withdraw it backwards.

Re-assembly is the reverse of the stripping process. Two points to note

are, firstly, that when replacing the feed tray, only the left side retaining catch should be pressed, and secondly the bolt head should be pushed forward from the bolt body before inserting into the receiver.

It is said by the manufacturers that a trained soldier can strip the HK21 in less than 60 seconds and re-assemble it in less than 90 seconds; which gives you something to aim for.

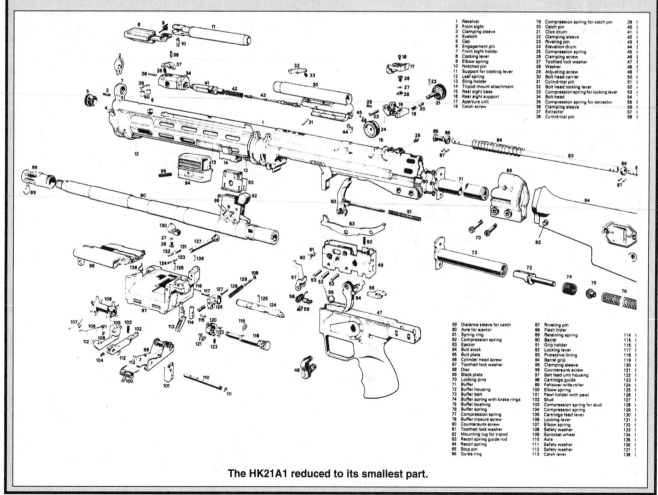

1	Receiver
2	Front sight
3	Clamping sleeve
4	Eyebolt
5	Cap
6	Engagement pin
7	Front sight holder
8	Cocking lever
9	Elbow spring
10	Notched pin
11	Support for cocking lever
12	Leaf spring
13	Sling holder
14	Tripod mount attachment
15	Rear sight base
16	Rear sight support
17	Aperture unit
18	Catch screw
19	Compression spring for catch pin
20	Catch pin
21	Click drum
22	Clamping sleeve
23	Riveting pin
24	Elevation drum
25	Compression spring
26	Clamping screw
27	Toothed lock washer
28	Washer
29	Adjusting screw
30	Bolt head carrier
31	Cylindrical pin
32	Bolt head locking lever
33	Compression spring for locking lever
34	Bolt head
35	Compression spring for extractor
36	Clamping sleeve
37	Extractor
38	Cylindrical pin

59	Distance sleeve for catch
60	Axle for ejector
61	Spring ring
62	Compression spring
63	Ejector
64	Butt stock
65	Butt plate
66	Cylinder head screw
67	Toothed lock washer
68	Disc
69	Black plate
70	Locking pins
71	Buffer
72	Buffer housing
73	Buffer bolt
74	Buffer spring with brake rings
75	Buffer bushing
76	Buffer spring
77	Compression spring
78	Buffer closure screw
80	Countersunk screw
81	Toothed lock washer
82	Mounting lug for tripod
83	Recoil spring guide rod
84	Recoil spring
85	Stop pin
86	Guide ring
87	Riveting pin
88	Flash hider
89	Retaining spring
90	Barrel
91	Grip holder
92	Locking lever
93	Protective lining
94	Barrel grip
95	Clamping sleeve
96	Countersunk screw
97	Belt feed unit housing
98	Cartridge guide
99	Follower with roller
100	Elbow spring
101	Pawl holder with pawl
102	Stud
103	Compression spring for stud
104	Compression spring
105	Cartridge feed lever
106	Locking lever
107	Elbow spring
108	Safety washer
109	Sprocket wheel
110	Axle
111	Safety washer
112	Safety washer
113	Catch lever

The HK21A1 reduced to its smallest part.

Canadian troops with a Browning M1919A2 with a blank-firing attachment on the muzzle, during an exercise in the 1980s. The attachment chokes the muzzle sufficiently to make the gun recoil and thus permit automatic fire with blank cartridges.

US troops with their M60

(Continued from Page 181)

the bulging becomes excessive but before a case actually ruptures.

The gun fires from an open bolt, and uses a disintegrating link belt similar to the US M13 pattern but more flexible. Feed is performed by an arm driven by a lug traveling in a cam groove in the top surface of the rear portion of the bolt. The barrel can be changed when it gets hot, but the design is not a good one; the bipod is attached to the barrel, and thus when the gunner's assistant removes the hot barrel, the gunner is left trying to support a hot gun while he awaits the new barrel. Nevertheless, the French have stuck to it for almost half a century, the only change having come in the late 1960s when they yielded to pressure and reluctantly adopted the 7.62x51mm NATO cartridge. The gun was suitably modified, and the title changed to AA52 F1.

The US Army had actually been contemplating a general-purpose machine gun before World War II had ended. In 1944 work had begun on the T44, a design which was almost entirely based upon elements of various German weapons - the belt feed system was copied from the MG42 machine gun and the piston and the bolt system from the FG42 paratroop rifle. It was not a success but, like many weapons that fail to make the grade, it taught the design teams some useful lessons. The piston and bolt were re-designed to do away with the closed-bolt single-shot capability, and this emerged as the T52. By this time the war was over and the design languished for some time, undergoing a few changes and eventually becoming the T161. The war in Korea underlined the fact that the BAR and the Browning M1919A4, while still sound enough weapons, were not suited to modern tactics involving lightly-equipped troops and helicopters and more effort went into the search for a new machine gun which would replace both these veterans. Eventually the T161, after more modification and development work, became the M60, introduced into service to accompany the M14 rifle, both also serving to introduce the 7.62x51mm NATO cartridge into US Army service.

The M60 was built using a number of steel pressings and plastic components, and was the first US machine gun to have a quick-change barrel. The first model, though, did

(Continued on Page 188)

U.S. M60

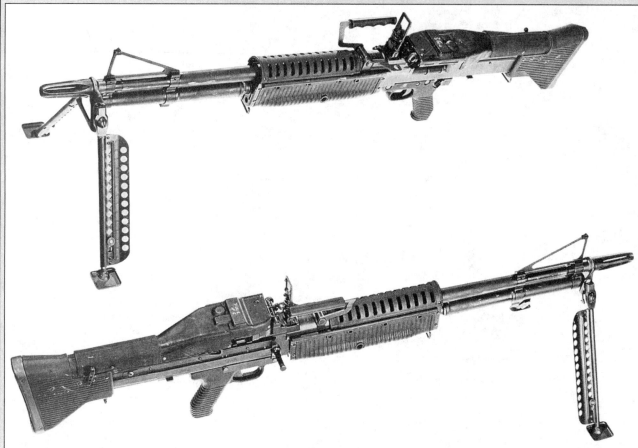

Steps enroute to the M60: the T61 *(top)* and T65 *(below)* machine guns were developmental models in the program which eventually roduced the M60.

The M60 is the American general-purpose machine gun, and much of it stemmed from examination of the German MG42 at the end of World War II. It entered service in 1960 and in one fell swoop replaced not only the M1917 and M1919 families of machine gun but also the BAR, the Thompson submachine gun and the M3 (Grease Gun) submachine gun. The basic M60 can be used as either the squad automatic, with a bipod, or the company support sustained-fire gun on a tripod. In addition, the M60C was developed as an outboard gun for fitting to helicopters, while the M60D became the standard door gun. For turret installations the M60E2 was developed.

Improvements appeared in subsequent years. The M60E3 came in the early 1980s and brought the weight down from 23.16 lbs to 18.75 lbs. Light and heavy barrels were made available so that the barrel could be matched to the tactical role. The most important of the practical innovations was the placing of the bipod on the gas cylinder, so that it was no longer necessary to burden the spare barrel with its own bipod.

The M60E4 appeared in the early 1990s and had a stronger butt, stronger bipod, and a redesigned feed mechanism,

DATA	
Caliber	7.62 x 51mm NATO
Operating system	Gas, selective fire
Locking system	Rotating bolt
Feed system	Metal link belt
Overall length	43.5in (1105mm)
Weight, empty	23lb 3oz (10.51kg)
Barrel	22.04in (560mm) 4 grooves, right hand twist
Muzzle velocity	2838 ft/sec (865 m/sec)
Muzzle energy	2487 ft/lb (3360J)
Rate of fire	550 rds/min
Effective range	Bipod: 850 yards; Tripod: 2000 yards

The M60 field-stripped, showing the barrel, bolt and driving spring.

A 1960 picture of the M60 showing a proposed ammunition feed system from pre-packed cartons.

which improved the belt-lifting ability of the gun. It also introduced a new short 'assault barrel' which makes the gun even more versatile. Nevertheless the basic mechanism, although improved and strengthened in detail, has remained substantially the same - gas-operated with a rotating bolt - throughout the gradual course of improvement.

Field Stripping:

Open the feed cover, remove the belt; draw back the cocking handle, inspect the feedway and chamber to ensure no ammunition remains in the gun. Pull the trigger and allow the working parts to go forward under control. Leave the feed cover open. Procure a live or dummy cartridge, or a suitable punch to use as a dismantling tool.

Lift the butt strap and press the punch or bullet into the hole in the nut-plate to release the latch. Withdraw the butt to the rear. Lift the lock plate vertically to withdraw it, but hold the buffer to prevent it being thrown out by the return spring. Remove the buffer under control.

Withdraw the operating rod, return spring guide and bolt by means of the cocking handle. Press the spring lock at the front end of the trigger housing, and rotate in forward and down to free it from its pin to the left, then push the pistol grip and trigger unit forward to disengage it from the receiver and remove.

Raise the barrel lock lever to the vertical and pull out the barrel from the receiver. It is possible to remove the feed cover and handguard, but there is no need to do so for normal maintenance.

US Marines with an M60 during winter exercises in Norway.

The M60E3 Lightweight machine gun has moved away from the 'general purpose' concept, but is perhaps a more practical weapon.

(Continued from Page 185)

not live up to expectations, several small faults becoming apparent in use - particularly in combat in Vietnam. This, of course, is common to most weapons and the various defects were soon identified and corrected. The most serious design fault, though, was that the interchangeable barrel formed a unit with the gas cylinder and bipod, which were not detachable from the barrel. As a result the spare barrels weighed a good deal more than they really ought to have done, since they incorporated spare cylinders and bipods. More practically, when the gunner called for a new barrel he had either to let the gun lie on the ground or support it in his hands until the new barrel appeared and was fitted by his assistant, since the bipod had gone with the barrel. This was not the easiest of tasks with a hot barrel in the dark. This was cured with the issue of the M60E1, which attached the cylinder and bipod to the gun body, simplified the barrel-change operation, and improved the belt feed system, sights and various other features. Once this gun came into service, the US Army finally had a reliable

GPMG that was as good as anyone could wish.

Nevertheless, the designers did not sit on their hands, and the gun has gone through more changes, some of which appear to have moved away from the original GPMG concept.

The basic M60 design is that of a gas-operated weapon, but it has some interesting and novel features. The gas piston, for example, has a cup-shaped head with a hole drilled through the side of the cup. This hole lines up, when the gun is ready to fire, with the hole in the barrel through which the gas will flow when the bullet passes. When the gas comes through the barrel vent and into the piston, it expands there between the piston and the end of the gas cylinder until it reaches a pressure level which is sufficient to start moving the piston back, driving an operating rod. As the piston moves back, so the hole in the piston wall moves away from the barrel vent and thus cuts off the supply of gas, leaving the expansion of the gas now trapped inside the cylinder to carry out the rest of the operating cycle. Thus instead of, as is usual, having to open up the gas regulator when the

gun gets dirty, so as to overcome the friction by injecting more power, the M60 system is self-regulating; it will accept gas until the pressure is sufficient to overcome any friction, after which it shuts off its supply.

In fact the piston head moves back slightly more than two inches, but that is sufficient to accelerate the operating rod, which ends in a post reaching up into the hollow interior of the bolt. This post carries an anti-friction roller that runs in a cam path in the bolt and so revolves it to lock and unlock; when unlocked, the bolt is driven back by the operating rod, and is constrained by the locking lugs riding in grooves in the receiver. As the return spring drives the bolt forward, so the post will rotate the bolt into the locked position, and this aligns a straight cam path with the roller, so allowing the operating rod and post to go forward and thus carry the firing pin, on the post, into contact with the cartridge primer. As a result, mechanical safety is assured, since the firing pin cannot reach

(Continued on Page 191)

A closer view of the M60; this is the original model with the bipod attached to the barrel, making life difficult when changing the barrel.

A cutaway view of the M60.

The M60E4 carries an auxiliary sight-mounting rail on top of the receiver so that electro-optical and other types of specialist sights can be fitted.

The Russian PK general-purpose machine gun comes in a variety of forms. This is the PKM, with smooth barrel and a receiver assembled from stamped components.

Take away the butt and pistol grip from the PKM, fit it with spade grips, and you have the PKB, which may or may not be accepted as a replacement for the SGM.

The Japanese M74 is a heavy-barrel version of the M62 with spade grips, intended for use as the co-axial turret gun in tanks.

PK

A PKM complete with its belt box and ready to fire.

The PK (*Pulyemet Kalashnikova*) is Mr. Kalashnikov's answer to the general-purpose machine gun problem, and it certainly seems to have been an effective one, since the design was adopted by every Warsaw Pact country and by several countries with no Communist links but who know a good thing when they see one.

The basic mechanism is the same as any other Kalashnikov weapon, a gas-operated automatic with a rotating bolt in a carrier driven by the gas piston. The major change was to adapt the mechanism to the rimmed 7.62x54R Mosin-Nagant cartridge, so as to achieve the greater range and hitting power that this would give. A belt-feed mechanism also had to be devised, and a quick-change barrel, so that the gun could, eventually, replace the SGM as the medium machine gun as well as replacing the RP46 and RPD as the squad light automatic.

The result was a weapon that lends itself to almost any requirement. There are, currently, several versions: the **PK** is the bipod-mounted squad weapon; the **PKS** is adapted to firing from a tripod or as an AA weapon; the **PKT** is modified for use in tanks and armored vehicles generally; the **PKM** id a modernized **PK** with a lighter barrel and most of the feed components made from metal stampings instead of being machined from solid steel; the **PKMS** is a PKM on a tripod; and the **PKB** is the PK with spade grips and tripod mountings.

The **PK** is currently made under license in China as their Type 80, and in Romania and Bulgaria.

Field Stripping:

First clear the gun by opening the top cover, removing the belt and also removing cartridges that may be held in the cartridge gripper or in the feeder. Pull back the cocking handle and inspect the feedway and chamber to ensure no ammunition remains in the gun. Grasp the cocking handle, pull the trigger, and allow the working parts to go forward under control. Leave the top cover open.

Lift the feed tray, which pivots on the same pin as the top cover. Then pull out the barrel lock to the left, grasp the carrying handle and pull the barrel out of the receiver.

The return spring guide protrudes through the rear face of the receiver. Press it in, so that the complete spring and guide assembly can be lifted out of the top of the receiver. Grasp the bolt unit, pull to the rear and upwards to free it from the receiver and lift both bolt and carrier out.

Pull and twist on the bolt head to separate it from the carrier, and remove the firing pin from the carrier. No further dismantling is required for normal maintenance.

DATA	
Caliber	7.62 x 54R Russian
Operating system	Gas, selective fire
Locking system	Rotating bolt
Feed system	30-round box
Overall length	45.67in (1160mm)
Weight, empty	19lb 13oz (9.0kg)
Barrel	25.90 in (658mm), 4 grooves right hand twist
Muzzle velocity	2705 ft/sec (825 m/sec)
Muzzle energy	3010 ft/lbs (4068J)
Rate of fire	700 rds/min
Effective range	1000m

The PKT, for use in armored vehicles, is provided with an electric solenoid trigger.

The PKS is a PK with spade grips and fittings for mounting onto a tripod.

Sudanese irregulars with a PK.

To re-assemble, put the firing pin into its slot in the bolt carrier and then insert the bolt, pushing and twisting so as to engage the rotating lug in the cam path. Replace the bolt and carrier on the piston slide, ensure that the piston head is correctly entered into the gas cylinder, pull the trigger and push the bolt carrier gully forward. Insert the driving spring and guide, sliding it down the rear face of the receiver until the guide protrudes through its hole.

Replace the barrel, slide the barrel lock back into the locked position, lower the feed tray and close the top cover.

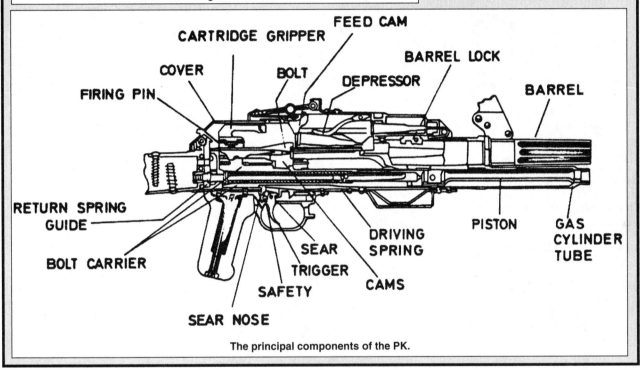

The principal components of the PK.

(Continued from Page 188)

the primer unless the bolt is rotated and locked. Most analysts compare this system with that of the German FG42; in my view it has even stronger similarities with the Lewis Gun.

The feed mechanism in the early developmental designs was lifted from the MG42; as the bolt moved back and forth it drove an operating arm to control the double feed pawls and drag the belt across the feedway. This was progressively simplified to have a single set of pawls that were controlled by a roller on the rear of the bolt driving a grooved arm, pivoted close to its front end, which carries the pawl mechanism. As the bolt goes forward, the arm is swung to position the pawls over the next cartridge in the belt, and as the bolt goes back under the pressure of the operating rod, so the arm swings and drags the belt across.

A last idiosyncrasy is that the front sight is fixed, and thus the sights must be zeroed by adjustment of the rear sight. This means that whenever a new barrel is put on the gun the rear sight has to be re-adjusted to suit. It is, I suppose, possible to zero each barrel for a particular gun in barracks, and identify each barrel with a zero setting which

A pair of Afghan guerrillas pose with a PK 'borrowed' from the Russians.

The Yugoslavian M84 is actually a copy of the PK; this one sports an advanced electro-optical sight to permit night firing.

intention and have become light machine guns. Developed by the Saco company, manufacturers of the M60, these have lighter barrels, forward pistol grips rather than the usual forend, adjustable, zero-able, front sights on each barrel and a lightweight bipod. The E4 variation has an improved feed mechanism with a stronger belt pull, chromed-bore barrels in three lengths, a 'Picatinny Rail' type universal accessory sight mount on top of the receiver and some improvements to the gas system. These two versions have been put into service by the US Marines, Navy and Air Force but the army has not, so far, found it necessary to adopt them.

Those armies which have not equipped themselves with either the FN-MAG, the MG3, the AA-52 or the M60 are almost all using a GPMG of Russian origin, the PK (for *Pulemyet Kalashnikova*). The Russian term for GPMG is 'unified machine gun' and the PK is the only one of this classification to have been adopted by the Russian forces and by the several countries that have adopted Russian equipment.

the gunner can paste inside his helmet and refer to every time he changes the barrel. Possible, but not very practical.

The M60 remains the general-purpose weapon. The M60E2 and M60E4 have diverged from the original

Polish troops with *(center)* a PK machine gun. On the left is a Dragunov sniping rifle; on the right a locally-produced AKM.

Like the PK series, the Czech M59 fires the old Russian 7.62x54R rimmed cartridge from a belt, giving them rather more range and striking power than most of their contemporary GPMGs.

About the only likeness with its predecessors is the finned barrel on the Japanese 62 GPMG. A gas-operated weapon with a tilting bolt, it would be an attractive item on the export market if the Japanese government permitted it.

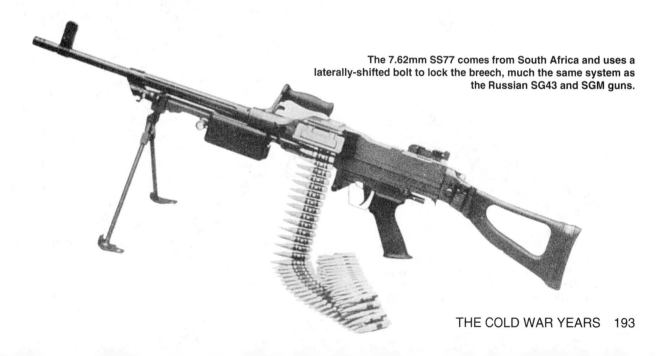

The 7.62mm SS77 comes from South Africa and uses a laterally-shifted bolt to lock the breech, much the same system as the Russian SG43 and SGM guns.

The Swiss MG51 resembles the earlier German MG42 but uses a much different system for locking the bolt. The Swiss also did away with the stamped metal components of the MG42 and replaced them with machined steel parts. These guns will probably last into the 22nd century.

The PK, being a design by Kalashnikov, will obviously be a gas-operated weapon using a rotating bolt inside a carrier, but other features have been taken from other Russian weapons. The barrel changing system and much of the belt feed system comes from the Goryunov SGM, the use of the piston to drive the belt feed is taken from the Czech vz/52, and the trigger mechanism comes from the Degtyarev RPD. The result is a reliable weapon capable of being used from bipod or tripod, with variant models for tank and air defense applications.

Perhaps the most remarkable thing about it is that it still uses the 7.62x54R Mosin-Nagant rifle cartridge, which was first seen in 1891 and is now probably the oldest cartridge still in first-line service anywhere in the world. Old it may be, but it gives the PK more performance than could be achieved with the more modern 7.62x39mm short Russian cartridge and puts it on a more or less equal footing with Western GPMGs.

The PK is the basic gun of the family; it has a fluted heavy barrel and a feed cover assembled from both pressed and machined components. It weighs about 20 pounds. The PKS is the PK mounted in a tripod that is not only suited to sustained support fire but can be extended to make an anti-aircraft mount.

The PKT is the PK modified for use as a coaxial machine gun in tanks. A heavy barrel is fitted; the sights, stock, pistol grip and trigger are removed and an electric firing solenoid is fitted.

The SIG 710-3 from Switzerland, a 7.62mm delayed-blowback weapon of considerable refinement. Note the center picture, showing how to launch a grenade from the muzzle of the gun; this is a *really* general-purpose design.

(Continued on Page 197)

AA 52

The AA52 machine-gun in its squad automatic role.

After 1945 the French Army, having lost virtually all its weapons to the Germans in 1940, was re-equipped with American arms. This affront to French pride put their designers on their mettle, and it must be said that post-1945 French weapon design has been immeasurably superior to the stuff they were using before 1939, from pistols to main battle tanks. They were an early entrant in the General Purpose Machine Gun stakes with this delayed-blowback weapon, which can function with equal facility as the squad automatic or the battalion support gun. The basic weapon comes in two versions, with a light barrel and bipod or with a heavy barrel and tripod, though in fact either weapon can be fitted to either kind of support. The heavy barrel merely means that it can produce longer bursts of sustained supporting fire before the gunner needs to change the barrel, and with the heavier and longer barrel the effective range is pushed out by 400 yards or so.

The delayed blowback system uses the usual two-part bolt but separates them by a lever, which has to be forced back by the light bolt head in order to move the heavy bolt body. The delay is minimal, and ejected cases are invariable bulged in front of the head and have lines of gas markings down the side, indicating the chamber grooves in which high-pressure gas prevents the case sticking. As one authority once said, *"The AA-52 works well - but only just."*

Field Stripping

Pull the cocking handle to the rear, push it forwards as far as it will go, then set the safety catch to *'Safe'* by pushing it to the left. Open the feed cover, remove the belt, and inspect the feedway and chamber to ensure no ammunition remains in the gun. Pull back the cocking handle and, while holding it, press the trigger and allow the working parts to go forward under control.

While pressing firmly down in the butt, unscrew and remove the locking

DATA (Light barrel version)	
Caliber	7.5 x 54mm French Mle 29
Operating system	Delayed blowback, automatic
Locking system	Two-part bolt with delay lever
Feed system	Disintegrating link belt
Overall length	45.08in (1145mm)
Weight, empty	22lb 0oz (9.97kg)
Barrel	19.68in (500mm) 4 grooves, right-hand twist
Muzzle velocity	2700 ft/sec (823m/sec)
Muzzle energy	2250 ft/lbs (3042J)
Rate of fire	700 rds/min

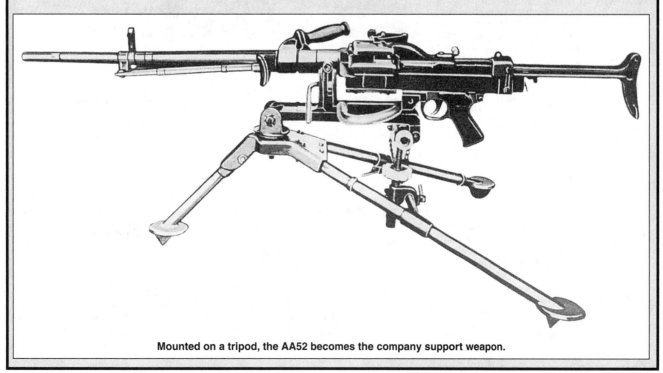

Mounted on a tripod, the AA52 becomes the company support weapon.

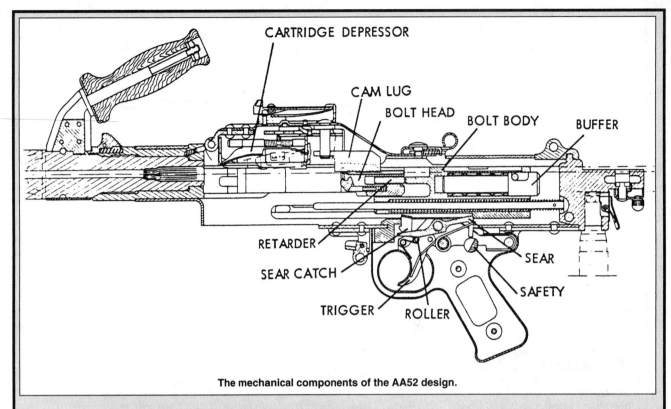

The mechanical components of the AA52 design.

pin on the left rear of the receiver. Once this comes out, spring pressure will tend to force the butt upwards; allow it to rise under control until the spring pressure is released, then continue lifting the butt and remove it together with the receiver back-plate Remove the return spring and its guide rod. Note that some early guns have a telescoping butt that, under a severe blow, can telescope and jam so that it becomes impossible to strip the gun. If confronted with this problem, loop a rifle sling around the shoulder piece, have one man hold the gun and give a sharp pull on the sling to extend the butt.

Using the cocking handle, slide the bolt to the rear until it can be removed. It may come out in one piece, or it may leave the bolt head behind, in which case simply fish the bolt head out. Once the bolt is out it should be separated into its two parts and the firing pin removed.

Behind the pistol grip, beneath the receiver, is the trigger group lock pin. Press in its spring catch, push the pin out and remove the trigger group.

Lift the feed tray up against the open top cover, and pull out the knurled-head feed group locking pin. Lift off the top cover and feed tray. Further dismantling is not recommended.

To re-assemble is merely a matter of reversing the above procedure. The only part demanding explanation is the assembly of the bolt. Insert the firing pin into the head of the bolt so as to leave about an inch and a half protruding. Then fit the head to the body so that the protruding part of the firing pin goes into the hole in the body. Push the two units together until body and head are in contact. It may be neces-

sary to fiddle with the delay lever to get the two parts to fit together.

Having assembled the bolt, slide it into the receiver, pressing the delay lever forward and in to allow the bolt to enter. Press the trigger and push the bolt fully forward. Insert the return spring into the hole in the bolt rear body

Offer up the butt and back-plate to the receiver and seat the return spring guide rod in the recess in the back-

plate. Then hook the lip on the top of the back-plate into the recess under the top of the receiver and swing the butt down against the spring pressure until the locking pin can be inserted and screwed up.

Pull the cocking handle to the rear, close the top cover, grasp the cocking handle, press the trigger and allow the working parts to go forward under control.

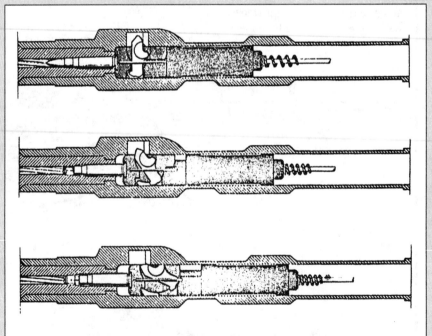

The two-part bolt system of the AA52: *(Top)* bolt closed and locking lever engaged in the recess above it. *(Center)* fired; the case is pushing the bolt head back, which pushes the lever against the heavy bolt body. *(Bottom)* the lever is free of the recess and the entire bolt can now move back. But notice how much of the case has eased out of the chamber while the pressure is still high.

The Brazilian Uirapuru general-purpose machine gun in the bipod-and-butt role.

(Continued from Page 194)

The PKM is an improved PK with lighter, smooth barrel and a feed cover assembled entirely from stamped parts. Excess metal has been trimmed away to bring the weight down to about 18.5 pounds.

The PKMS is simply the PK mounted on the same tripod as the PKS,

The PKB or PKMB is a PKM with the butt, pistol grip and trigger unit removed and replaced with spade grips and the usual sort of trigger that goes with them. This would appear to be a replacement for the SGM, although the latter weapon is still in use.

The bore of the gun is chromed, and the barrel has a quick-change system that is not really as quick as it ought to be. It is necessary to unload the gun and remove the belt before the barrel can be changed, since the feed cover has to be raised to allow the barrel to be unlocked. It is then pulled out forwards (there being no handle on most models, this could be a delicate job with a hot barrel) and the new barrel inserted, after which the gun can be re-loaded.

The gas piston is attached to a slide, upon which the bolt carrier is mounted. The slide has two cam grooves that actuate the belt feed system. As the bolt goes forward two 'grippers' close over the rim of the cartridge lying in the belt. The gun fired, the slide is driven back, and the grippers pull the cartridge from the belt and force it down into feed lips on the bolt face, displacing the empty case that has been extracted. On the return stroke the bolt chambers the new cartridge and the cam path on the slide causes the next round to be indexed across, ready to be gripped as the bolt closes. The cyclic rate of fire is about 700 rounds per minute.

In 1993 a new contender in the unified machine gun field appeared. This was simply known as the '6mm Unified Machine Gun' and was a somewhat optimistic offering from an establishment known as the Institute for Precise Mechanical Engineering situated in Klimobsk, Russia. Little firm information has ever been released about this design, but from what has been seen it appears to be a modified PK with a longer and heavier barrel, firing an entirely new 6mm cartridge. The weight has been reduced to 14.3 pounds (6.5kg) and the cartridge has a "new, improved and more powerful propellant" which, it is claimed, gives a virtually flat trajectory out to an effective range of 1500 meters. But to put this forward at a time when the whole question of small calibers was being debated once more, and when there was a considerable reluctance to reducing the GPMG caliber from 7.62mm in anybody's army, let alone the Russian, does not appear to have helped the 6mm Unified Machine Gun to get a foothold in the market.

Czechoslovakia, with a proven record of producing excellent machine guns before the war, was not best pleased to fall under the Soviet boot, and for a long time it managed to avoid the ignominy of adopting standardized Soviet weapons, although it had to conform to Warsaw Pact standards and adopt Soviet cartridges. It therefore produced a GPMG of its own in 1959, chambered for the Soviet 7.62x54R cartridge, though models were also made in 7.62x51mm NATO for the export market; whether many export sales were actually made is something that has never been divulged.

The vz/59 was, to some degree, a child of the pre-war ZB family, and there are vague similarities in design and operation, though the locking system was quite different. The bolt carries a hinged locking block, which is similar to the locking wedge of the P38 Walther pistol. An upstanding post on the gas piston propels the bolt back and forward; during the closing stroke two wings on the locking piece ride up ramps in the receiver wall and into locking recesses. The piston post then continues forward for a short distance before striking the firing pin. On the rearward stroke there is a brief delay as the piston post moves back and before it contacts the locking piece, forcing it down and out of the locking recesses, after which the

Butt removed and bipod folded, the Uirapuru fits on to this substantial tripod for the sustained fire tasks.

The Chinese Type 67. An interesting and efficient collection of ideas adapted from older designs; just for once, the total is greater than the sum of its parts.

bolt is propelled backwards in the usual manner. Feed is from an open-link belt of Czech design, which permits the rimmed Soviet round to be pushed through the link and into the chamber. Cocking was done by pushing the pistol grip and trigger unit forward to engage with the piston slide, then pulling it back to catch on a sear, a similar system to the vz/37 and the British Besa gun derived from it.

Fitted with a bipod and a 50-round belt box, the M59 was the squad automatic; with a heavier barrel, a tripod and a 250-round box it became the company support machine gun; with the butt, pistol grip and trigger removed and replaced by a firing solenoid it became a co-axial tank gun; and with an extended tripod center post it became the infantry air defense machine gun.

Since the division of Czechoslovakia, it appears that the Slovak Republic had retained the M59 in its original 7.62x54mmR chambering, while the Czech Republic, with one eye firmly on integration into NATO, had converted to the 7.62x51mm caliber, which merely demanded a change of barrel and bolt.

The Japanese Model 62 is another independent design of GPMG, a gas-operated weapon, belt-fed, and using a tilting bolt to lock the breech. In this case, however, and unlike almost every other tilting bolt, the front end of the bolt is lifted instead of the back. The usual gas piston and post actuate the bolt, and as the bolt goes forward it chambers the round and comes to a stop, at which point the continued forward movement of the piston post strikes a cam surface inside the bolt and forces the front end up, so that two wings on the sides of the bolt are lifted into locking recesses in the receiver. The piston post then carries on forward and strikes the firing pin. After firing the piston moves back and a second cam surface carries the front end of the bolt down so as to unlock it before pushing the bolt back.

It will be apparent that until the bolt is locked, the firing pin is not aligned with the cartridge primer; this is put to additional use by so arranging the mechanism of the top cover that once the cover is opened the bolt cannot rise into the locked position. Since it is necessary to open the top cover in order to change the barrel, and since the cover cannot be closed if there is no barrel in place, it becomes impossible to accidentally release the bolt if there is no barrel present. The Model 62 is chambered for the 7.62x51mm NATO cartridge and there is a tank version, the Model 74, which has a heavier barrel and either spade grips with manual trigger or a solenoid firing arrangement, according to its position on the vehicle.

South Africa, due to the long boycott period during which it could not obtain arms from other countries, developed a thriving and highly efficient arms industry, and their GPMG is one of its products. The Vektor SS-77 is gas-operated, air-cooled and belt-fed, and employs a breech-block which is swung laterally in order to lock. As the gas piston carries the bolt forwards, a cam forces the rear end of the bolt sideways so that one edge locks into a recess in the receiver wall. In theory this means that the stresses are concentrated on one side of the receiver, but the Russians made it work for many years with their Goryunov SG43 and SGM guns, so this is merely another of those cases where what it theoretically reprehensible is a practical success. The nomenclature SS-77 is a little misleading; SS refers to the two designers, Smith and Soregi, while 77 marks the inception of the project; but it was then shelved for several years, to be revived in 1984, and the first guns went into service in 1986.

You might think that the success and widespread adoption of the German MG42, and its successor the MG3, would make it proof against improvement; but you would be wrong. The Swiss Army adopted the MG42 in the late 1940s, when low mileage, one-owner specimens were easy to obtain. When this supply dried up,

The British 7mm EM2 machine gun was no more than a heavy-barrel version of the better-known EM2 rifle. Even had the 7mm cartridge survived, it is doubtful it would ever have got into service; souped-up rifles were not considered to be machine guns in 1949.

The Bren lives. A British soldier with a 7.62mm Bren, recognizable by the straight-sided magazine instead of the more familiar curved one, during an exercise in Germany in 1985.

the army arsenal, Waffenfabrik Bern, decided to manufacture them new, but didn't like the stamped metal construction and replaced many of these stamped and pressed parts with machined components. This makes it heavier (by about 8 pounds) and more expensive that the original, but the functioning is faultless and, according to some informants, somewhat smoother than the original; and anyway, that's how the Swiss like to do things. So the resulting M51 machine gun resembles the MG42, though the barrel jacket is rounded rather than squared, and the bolt locking system uses flaps instead of rollers. A variant model is the MG87 tank machine gun, in which the most significant change is that there is a hinge on the bottom front of the receiver, joining it to the barrel jacket, which allows the receiver to be dropped in order to change the barrel. Both these weapons are, of course, chambered for the Swiss 7.5x55mm M11 Schmidt-Rubin cartridge, but by replacement of only four component parts they can be adapted to the 7.62x51mm NATO round.

The SIG company of Switzerland produced a very good general purpose gun in their Model 710; this was originally developed in a number of sub-variants to suit various military-standard calibers but the only one to see volume production was the Model 710-3 in 7.62x51mm.

The MG710-3 is that comparative rarity, a powerful machine gun operating on the delayed blowback system. Not to put too fine a point on it, there are some definite similarities between this gun and the replacement for the MG42 which

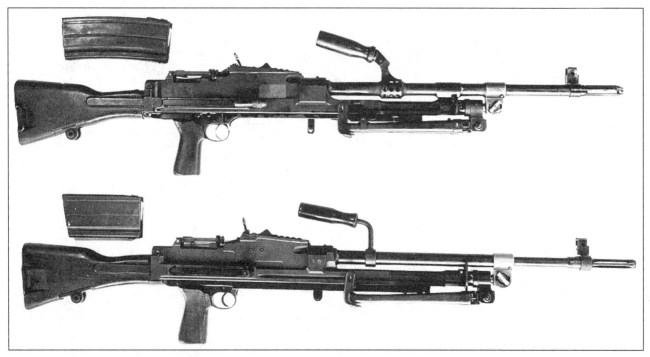

The two 7.62mm Bren conversions which were tested prior to the British adoption of the gun. The upper gun was developed by the Royal Small Arms Factory in Enfield, the lower by Long Branch Arsenal in Canada. The final accepted design used elements of both.

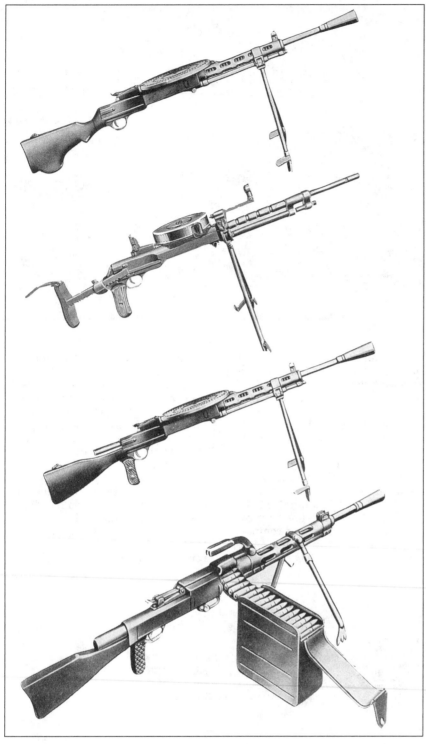

A page from an 1940s Intelligence Summary showing the development path of the Degtyarev machine guns which led to the RP-46.

own way and turn it into a three-piece bolt. The addition of a third piece - the 'anvil' - allows a more certain control of the operation of the rollers and results in a particularly smooth action. The chamber is also fluted with longitudinal grooves that permit some of the chamber gases to get between the chamber wall and the cartridge case, so preventing over-expansion of the case and allowing easy extraction without lubricated ammunition. The remainder of the gun is strongly reminiscent of the MG42, although the perforated barrel jacket is half-length and leaves an equal length of barrel unsupported in front of it. The barrel change is virtually the same as the MG42, though generally more robust, and the stock is no longer wood or plastic but a substantial metal tube carrying a shoulder-piece.

The 710-3 was a superb machine gun and will probably never wear out, but, like all products of such quality, carried a fairly high price tag, and not many armies were willing to pay it. The guns were sold to Chile, Bolivia and one or two other countries in the 1970s, but production ceased in the late 1980s.

In the past the various countries of South America had purchased their small arms from European manufacturers. World War II put a brake on this; some turned to the USA for their supplies, but once the USA became involved in the war, that source virtually dried up, and governments began contemplating manufacturing their own weapons. After the war, European imports resumed but they were soon replaced by license agreements, notably with FN for the production of their FAL rifle and MAG machine gun. Then, in the 1970s, local designers began flexing their muscles with submachine guns, rifles, pistols and, eventually, machine guns.

The most prominent of the GPMG designs to appear, and perhaps the only one to get further than the hand-made demonstrator stage, was the Brazilian 'Uirapuru', which appeared in the late 1970s. It began as a project in the Brazilian army's Military Engineering Institute in 1969, where a design team built three models of a gas-operated gun firing 7.62x51mm cartridges. While the gun worked, it had a number of shortcomings that, it became obvious, only a sustained research program would rectify. Unfortunately the Institute had a number of other, higher pri-

Mauser were developing in Germany in the spring of 1945 and which was abruptly terminated in May of that year, and there seems to be little doubt that the SIG designers took a good long look at the Mauser MG 45 design before they reached for their pencils.

The chief clue to the parentage is the bolt operating system; the weapon is recoil-operated, using a two-part bolt locked - or partially locked - into recesses in the barrel extension by two rollers. These are forced out into their recesses by the rear portion of the bolt moving forward, and are forced out to free the bolt by the lighter forward section of the bolt moving backwards. If this sounds familiar, it is; we are looking at the same roller-delayed bolt which features in the Heckler and Koch designs, as well as in the Spanish CETME rifle and their light machine gun, except that the Swiss, being Swiss, do things their

Left side view of the RP-46, the successful conversion of the wartime DPM into belt feed.

Right side view of the RP-46; also the Chinese Type 58 and the North Korean Type 64.

The Russian RPD, Degtyarev's last design, with belt drum fitted.

The RPD can, of course, be fired without the belt drum.

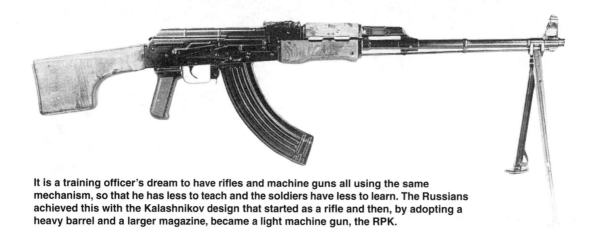

It is a training officer's dream to have rifles and machine guns all using the same mechanism, so that he has less to teach and the soldiers have less to learn. The Russians achieved this with the Kalashnikov design that started as a rifle and then, by adopting a heavy barrel and a larger magazine, became a light machine gun, the RPK.

ority, projects on its hands, so the machine gun was handed over to a private engineering firm in 1972.

No progress was made, and the army reclaimed the guns, and handed them to Olimpio Viera de Mello, one of the original design team, to sort out on his own. In 1976 he produced a gun that worked extremely well, and the army then passed the project over to a commercial firm, *Mekaninka Industria e Comercio*, to do the production engineering and produce pre-production specimens for trial. The army completed these trials and in the late 1980s the gun was approved for production and issue and offered for export.

The Uirapuru was a gas-operated, air-cooled weapon with a quick-change barrel, belt-fed and firing from the open bolt. It could be fitted with a bipod and butt for the light role, or with spade grips and a tripod for the heavy support role. Bolt locking was done by a dropping lever that braced the bolt against a recess in the receiver and was lifted by cam action.

Finally, in this collection of 'independent' GPMG designs, we come to the Chinese Type 67, a native design that is an interesting amalgam of features from previous guns in Chinese service. Belt-fed and gas-operated, the belt feed system has been taken from the Maxim gun, the bolt and gas piston from the Czech ZB26, the trigger mechanism from the Russian Degtyarev DPM, the gas regulator from the Russian Degtyarev RPD and the barrel changing system from the Russian Goryunov SGM. One assumes that there was a certain amount of filing and hammering to get all these to fit together, but the result was a reliable and effective weapon. In its earliest days it was simply the

squad light machine gun, using a butt and bipod and a 50-round belt drum which clamped on to the side of the receiver. After some experience with the gun it was realized that it had more potential; a few modifications were made, particularly a slightly heavier barrel and a 250-round belt box, a tripod was designed, and it became the standard Chinese GPMG in the early 1970s, numbers also being supplied to Vietnam. It fires the standard Soviet 7.62x54R cartridge at about 650 rounds per minute, but it seems now to have been relegated to the reserve and its place taken by the Type 80, which is no more than the Russian PK made in China.

Light Machine Guns

The light machine gun emerged from World War II with its reputation enhanced and, apparently, its position secure. For a while, after the GPMG fever struck, it looked as if its days were numbered, but it

was noticeable that few armies went entirely over to the one-gun GPMG policy. The Germans did, but, of course, they had made their minds up in about 1938, so nobody was surprised at that. The French did, with their AA-52, but since they had practically nothing left of their pre-war inventory, nobody was surprised at that either. The British, in the latter 1940s, were intent upon adopting their .280 or 7mm cartridge, and to accompany the well-known EM2 bullpup rifle they developed the EM2 light machine gun in 280-caliber. It was simply a heavy-barreled EM2 rifle, and without the bipod it could be easily mistaken for the rifle, since the barrel was very little longer and was capable of taking a bayonet. But the adoption of the 7.62mm NATO round pulled the rug from underneath both weapons, so although they adopted the FN-MAG as their L7A2 GPMG, they nevertheless kept the L4 Bren modification (in 7.62x51mm caliber)

The Czechoslovakian vz/52 complete with spare barrel, adapted for belt feed and with the magazine available if needed.

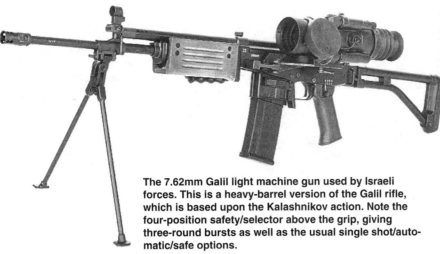

The 7.62mm Galil light machine gun used by Israeli forces. This is a heavy-barrel version of the Galil rifle, which is based upon the Kalashnikov action. Note the four-position safety/selector above the grip, giving three-round bursts as well as the usual single shot/automatic/safe options.

in use as well, while the Soviets, with money to burn on armaments, introduced a range of light machine guns to replace older weapons and reinforce those which survived in service after 1945. With the exception of Russia, it is fairly safe to say that until the middle 1960s the light machine gun used by any army was probably the same one that they had in 1939.

The Russian DPM and DTM designs had served well through the war; they had to, there was nothing else. Although some designers had been working away at fresh designs during the war years, the army saw no necessity to make a change when there were far more important things to think about. But as soon as the war was over they called for new designs, specifying that they be built around the new 7.62x39mm M1943 short cartridge that had been selected as the future standard.

Even so, the first post-war gun to appear still used the old 7.62x54mm rimmed cartridge, largely because it was a design which had begun prior to the arrival of the 1943 cartridge and which was based upon the DP. The Soviet Army had, early in the war, realized their lack of a machine gun capable of a greater rate of sustained fire than the DP but nevertheless light enough to be carried forward in the assault so as to provide

ready defense against the inevitable German counter-attack. A first step was taken in 1942 when two designers, Dubinin and Polyakov, began work on a modified receiver for the DP that allowed the gun to use the standard Maxim machine gun belt. All the modified parts were of stamped metal, the whole thing was cheap and easy to make, and a working machine gun was tested in 1943. Practical tests in the front line showed that while the idea was good, and the feed system worked reasonably well, carrying the gun with a dangling cloth belt was impractical, and the weight of the gun had almost doubled. The practicality of belt feed in light machine guns was still questionable.

At the same time, a competition was opened for a new light machine gun, and such eminent designers as Degtyarev and Simonov began working on designs, as did a young designer named Kalashnikov. Degtyarev produced two gas-operated designs: one belt-fed and the other using a top-mounted box magazine. Simonov also produced a gas-operated weapon, but with the gas cylinder on top of

the barrel, a tipping bolt locking system and a box magazine under the receiver. Kalashnikov's design used short recoil with a rotating bolt unlocked by a cam and fed from a 15-round curved magazine underneath the receiver.

The result of testing these guns led to a specification for a gun weighing no more than 15.5 pounds (7kg) and meeting all the usual requirements for reliability and durability and ease of manufacture. The Simonov design was selected for further development, but more tests of developed models showed several shortcomings and when, late in 1943, the short cartridge was approved for future use, the design demand was dropped and a fresh series of designs, using the new cartridge was demanded. Degtyarev, Simonov, and all the usual names were put to work again; we need not follow their development in detail.

Meanwhile, the modified DP of Dubinin and Polyakov was taken out, dusted, and worked on by another engineer called Shilin. He developed an improved belt-feed mechanism, fitted a slightly heavier barrel so as to provide sustained fire, and submitted the result. It passed its trials and was adopted as the RP-46 (RP - *rotnyy pulyemet* - company machine gun). Apart from the belt feed conversion it was the same gas-operated weapon as the Degtyarev DP, weighing about five pounds more. Instead of the original Maxim cloth belt, it used a metallic link belt that had been developed for the SG43 medium machine gun, a 250-round belt that was carried in

The Stoner 63 system could be configured in several ways. This is the 5.56mm light machine gun version.

The Stoner 63 with a longer barrel and a tripod, becoming perhaps the first attempt at a 5.56mm general-purpose machine gun.

a special box. If, for any reason, belts were not available or the belt feed mechanism failed, the entire feed unit could be quickly removed from the top of the receiver and the standard DP 47-round drum magazine could be fitted.

Although formally adopted, it was never seen very much in Soviet service; most of them appear to have been disposed of to co-religionists. The Chinese adopted it as the Type 58 and later manufactured it in China, while the North Koreans called it the Type 64 and also manufactured their own. So far as the Russians were concerned it was very rapidly supplanted by a short-cartridge design so as to use the same ammunition as the Simonov and Kalashnikov rifles.

The result of the design contest for the short cartridge gun was the Degtyarev RPD which appeared in 1944 but which did not get into full production before the war ended, and which has already been discussed in Chapter Six. The RPD went into volume production and huge numbers were made. It became the Soviet standard light machine gun and was widely distributed among the various Communist satellite armies.

By the middle 1950s it was apparent that the Kalashnikov AK47 rifle was completely replacing the older Simonov and other rifles, as well as all the wartime submachine guns, and it occurred to various authorities that if a machine gun could be developed around the Kalashnikov system a

unified armament could be achieved, with only one basic mechanism to be taught to the soldier. Kalashnikov was therefore called upon to develop a suitable weapon, and he did so by simply putting a longer and heavier barrel and a larger magazine on his basic rifle.

The Kalashnikov rifle mechanism is gas operated, using a cylinder above the barrel in which is piston. The piston is blown back and at its rear end supports the bolt carrier, driving it back against a return spring. The bolt, inside the carrier, locks by rotating so that lugs on the bolt lock into either the receiver or the chamber according to the particular weapon. A cam in the bolt carrier moves through a spiral track on the bolt and thus first revolves it and then withdraws it, ejecting the empty round and then chambering a fresh round on the

return stroke. The firing pin is struck by a hammer and a selector switch, a long pressed-metal lever on the right rear side of the receiver, acts as a selector for single shots or automatic fire and also as a safety lever, blocking the movement of the bolt as well as securing the trigger mechanism.

From this to a machine gun is no great leap; a heavier and longer barrel so as to extract more velocity out of the bullet, a bipod and a larger magazine, and the job was done. This became the RPK and seems to have been introduced in about 1962; it was first seen by Western eyes in 1966, although its existence had been known for some time. Easily recognized by its long thin barrel and hooked butt, it was later supplemented by the RPKS, the same gun but with a folding butt for airborne and similar forces. It was also adopted widely by satellite armies, and was sold to many otherwise uncommitted countries. It has also been widely copied, with or without benefit of license, and variants in 7.62x51mm and

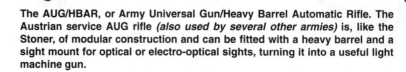

The AUG/HBAR, or Army Universal Gun/Heavy Barrel Automatic Rifle. The Austrian service AUG rifle (also used by several other armies) is, like the Stoner, of modular construction and can be fitted with a heavy barrel and a sight mount for optical or electro-optical sights, turning it into a useful light machine gun.

Heavy-barrel rifles have a respectable background; here a Canadian soldier uses an FN-FAL-HB machine gun version of the FAL rifle to ride shotgun for the Carl Gustav team alongside him.

7.92x57mm calibers were developed for export in Yugoslavia, though that venture seems to have collapsed when civil war broke out in that country.

Among the other useful attributes of the RPK, one unusual one is the commonality of parts with the AK and AKM rifles; practical trials have shown that in five cases out of every six, you can take the bolt out of an AK rifle and drop it into an RPK machine gun and it will work satisfactorily, the cartridge head clearance being sufficiently tolerant. The RPK is provided with two magazines, a box holding 40 rounds and a drum holding 75 rounds; but it will also accept magazines from AK and AKM rifles

The Czech army adopted a light machine gun, the vz/52, in the early 1950s; the first version was chambered for the Czech 7.62x45mm rifle cartridge, but after the country had been gathered into the Communist fold the gun was re-barreled in 7.62x39 Soviet caliber and became the vz/52/57. It had a number of highly ingenious features.

In the first place it would feed from belts or box magazines without the need for any special adapters. The gunner merely opened the feed cover and either put a belt in place across the feed platform or pushed a box magazine into the

The Spanish 5.56mm Ameli in action.

The Minimi can be easily fired from the hip.

prevents spontaneous ignition of the emergent gas and hence flash. This may have worked by day but it certainly did not work by night.

The vz/52 and 52/57 did not survive for long; the Czechs realized they had perhaps over-reached themselves in this design and they went back and tried again, producing the vz/59 general-purpose machine gun that was described in the previous section.

The Finnish Army, for economic and political reasons, uses a good deal of Russian equipment, and adopted the 7.62x39mm cartridge in the 1950s. It then developed a very neat and clean design of light machine gun, basing the mechanism on the pre-war ZB 26 gun, a gas-operated weapon with a tilting bolt lock. Belt-fed from a carrier on the right side of the receiver, it weighed about 22 pounds with a 100-round belt in place and has remained in use by the Finns since 1962.

The last of what we might call the 'full-caliber' light machine guns (as opposed to the 'micro-calibers' dealt with in the next section) appears to have been the Galil 7.62mm ARM model, which appeared in the early 1980s. This is no more than a heavy-barreled version of the Galil 7.62mm rifle, which itself is a thinly-disguised copy of the Kalashnikov, so that the ARM is little more than an RPKS with a shorter barrel and a decent carrying handle.

And with that we have dealt with the post-1945 and current crop of light machine guns using the older rifle calibers. With the arrival of the 5.56mm cartridge in the 1960s and its certification and adoption by NATO in the late 1970s, the way was clear for the wide scale adoption of the 5.56mm rifle as the universally standard infantry arm.

The Micro-Calibers

It was, of course, to be expected that when armies embraced the 5.56mm cartridge as their infantry rifle standard, there would be a call for light machine guns in the same caliber, so that the riflemen could feed the machine gun (or vice versa) in times of need. On the face of it, nothing could be easier; just take any existing machine gun and scale it down. Or, alternatively, take any existing 5.56mm semi-automatic rifle and turn it into a machine gun by giving it a heavier barrel, a larger magazine and a bipod. And several makers chose one or the other of these paths. But there was rather more

aperture in the feed platform, and continued from there. Cocking was done by pushing the pistol grip and trigger unit forward and then pulling it back to cock the bolt. Single shots were fire by pulling on the top section of the trigger, automatic fire by pulling on the bottom section. Changing the barrel was quickly performed by opening the feed cover or removing the magazine if fitted, and then rotating the feed cover to the right until the barrel was freed; it could then be pulled forward by the carrying handle.

Perhaps the strangest thing about this weapon was the flash hider on the muzzle, a conical affair pierced with several holes. The

mouth of the cone closes in to leave a hole only large enough to allow the bullet to pass through. The general effect is to act rather like a muzzlebrake and cut down some of the recoil, but the gases inside the cone are forced out sideways as the emergent bullet briefly blocks the exit hole, with the result that when firing at night there is often a halo-like ring of flame around the flash 'hider'. The theory has been advanced that in spite of its appearance it is solely a muzzle brake, the concealment of flash being done by loading the propellant powder with potassium salts in order to blanket the emergent gases in an inert gas layer which

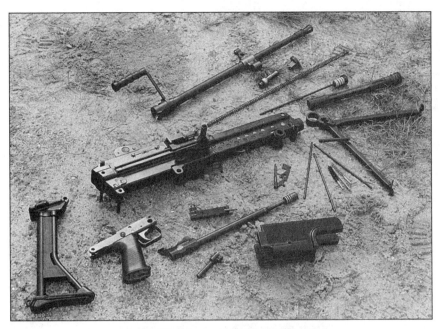

An FN Minimi completely field-stripped.

And the Minimi-Para version with short barrel is compact enough to be handled like an assault rifle.

to it than that. Either course would produce a weapon that worked, but when it came to working for a reasonable length of time, then things fell apart. There seemed to be some crucial point at which muzzle velocity, rate of fire, caliber and temperature all came together to produce a phenomenal rate of wear in these small-caliber barrels. Some early designs had no rifling worth speaking of after firing 5000 rounds. Argument raged between designers and soldiers as to the worth of a weapon which needed a replacement barrel after every 5000 rounds. More research work was done, and eventually, by careful determination of the optimum rate of fire, velocity, tolerances in bullet and bore diameter and other factors, the point was reached where a viable machine gun could be produced, one which would last for a reasonable length of time in battle.

Of the two options – pure machine gun or heavy-barreled rifle – opinion seems to have fallen evenly on each, the rifle solution appearing to have been the easier proposition of the two. Heckler & Koch of Germany were probably the first major manufacturer to adopt the 5.56mm cartridge after Colt introduced it with the M16 rifle, and they produced their HK33 rifle in 1965. They followed it with their HK13 5.56mm machine gun in 1971, and the machine gun was very little more than the rifle with a quick-change heavy barrel, a bipod and a larger magazine. The Stoner 63 machine gun appeared in 1965, also a heavy-barrel variant of the 5.56mm Stoner 63 rifle, and the Steyr-Mannlicher AUG Light Support Weapon, perhaps the most successful of the first-generation 5.56mm weapons, was simply an AUG rifle with heavy barrel, a bipod and a 40-round magazine.

The Heckler and Koch two-part bolt has been described above, when discussing the HK21 general-purpose machine gun; the HK13 was simply the HK21 scaled-down to suit the 5.56mm cartridge. It was quite a reasonable weapon and was bought in small numbers, but the truth of the matter was that H&K were ahead of the market; in 1965 most armies were not even contemplating changing their rifles to 5.56mm caliber, let alone their machine guns, and the HK13 was regarded as something of a curiosity, a weapon which might have an application where light weight was critical, but not a weapon for the run-of-the-mill platoon machine gun.

The FN Minimi in belt-fed mode.

The FN Minimi in magazine-fed mode.

How the trick is performed: sections through the feed tray of the Minimi showing *(left)* the magazine feed position and *(right)* the belt feed position.

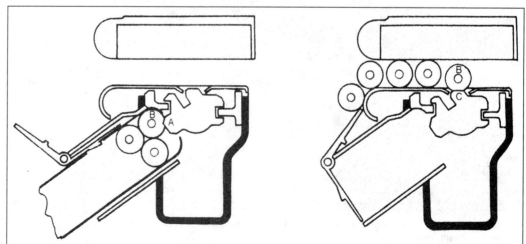

A US soldier with his M249, the US version of the Minimi.

Another view of the M249 light machine gun in use.

The Colt CMG-2 fired a 5.56mm cartridge but it wasn't the same cartridge that every other 5.56mm weapon fired.

Things stayed that way for quite a long time - for almost twenty years in fact, and it was not until the early 1980s that the 5.56mm machine gun began to make any headway. Then, three designs appeared with a rush, just as armies were beginning to think about lightweight weapons once more.

The first to make itself felt was the 'Minimi' developed by Fabrique Nationale of Belgium; then came the Ultimax 100 from Singapore Technologies, and then the 'Ameli' from CETME of Spain. And all three took a different approach to the problem of design.

The Minimi was under development from the mid-1960s; first prototypes were fired in 1974 and the weapon was put into production in 1982. All of which means a long and careful period of design and testing before it was unveiled, and as a result it was very quickly adopted by several major armies across the world. The mechanism is as conventional as you could wish for - a rotating bolt in a carrier, driven by a gas piston - and the exterior design is equally conventional until you look

closer and see one or two ingenious features.

The argument, which was raging among armies at the time of the Minimi's gestation, was whether the squad automatic ought to be fed from a magazine or a belt. So FN simply said *'OK, both'* and designed the receiver and feed system accordingly. A standard M16 rifle magazine can be inserted obliquely from the lower left side; alternatively the dust cover can be flicked over to close the magazine aperture, whereupon it opens the belt-feed aperture and is ready for a 200-round disintegrating link belt to be fed in. As might be expected, the rate of fire changes according to whether the belt

or the magazine is used; when feeding from the belt the rate of fire is about 700 rds/minute; with magazine feed the mechanism no longer has to haul the belt and can reach 1000 rounds per minute. The gun has a quick-change barrel, is normally provided with a bipod - but a tripod can be used if desired - and fixed or folding butts are available. A short-barreled 'Paratroop' model is also manufactured.

For all its virtues - and for all its acceptance by others - when tested by the U.S. Army there was a long list of 'defects'. Many of these were easily dismissed by FN, who pointed out that if you have a dual-feed system, then two rates of fire are inevitable, and that they did not consider that machine guns were intended to put all their shots through the same hole in the target but were supposed to spread them around a little. With these and similar differences of opinion ironed

Another angle on the Colt CMG-2, showing the neatly integrated belt-feed box.

The original Minimi, submitted for the SAWS trials of 1974; it fired the standard US M193 5.56mm cartridge.

The Colt submission for the SAWS contest was this heavy-barrel M16 derivative.

The Maremont XM223 entrant was derived from their earlier 'Universal machine Gun' *(described in Appendix 1)*. It was over the weight limit.

The Philco-Ford XM234 6mm SAWS entrant was an innovative-looking design but failed to make the grade.

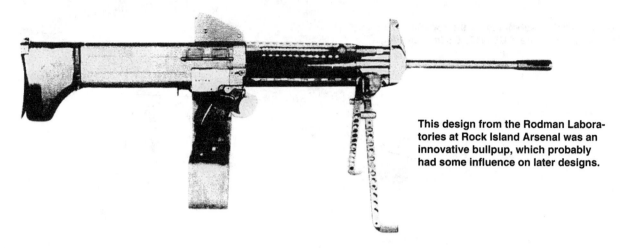

This design from the Rodman Laboratories at Rock Island Arsenal was an innovative bullpup, which probably had some influence on later designs.

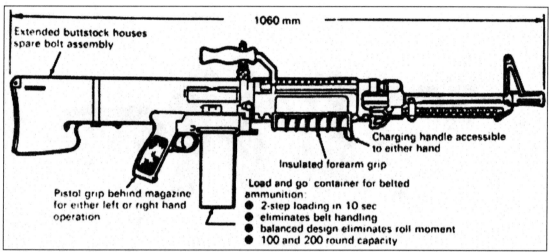

1060 mm

Extended buttstock houses spare bolt assembly

Charging handle accessible to either hand

Insulated forearm grip

Pistol grip behind magazine for either left or right hand operation

'Load and go' container for belted ammunition:
- 2-step loading in 10 sec
- eliminates belt handling
- balanced design eliminates roll moment
- 100 and 200 round capacity

The principal features of the Rodman SAWS entrant, as put over by their promotional material.

out, FN then sat down to modify the Minimi to meet the US Army's demands. The most obvious changes were in the buttstock and the handguard, the addition of a heat shield and a carrying handle. Less obvious were various minor modifications to suit US methods of manufacture and the incorporation of a hydraulic buffer in the butt. The gun was then accepted and became the US M249 Squad Automatic Weapon.

Reaching the Squad Automatic Weapon had been a somewhat traumatic experience for the US Army; a program to produce such a weapon had been inaugurated in the 1960s, and a number of weapons had been designed, built in prototype and thoroughly tested. None had been adopted. A study in 1966

suggested that a machine gun lighter and more portable than the M60 would be an advantage, but it was 1969 before anything came of it. The adoption of the M16 rifle, with its selective fire capability, had inspired a belief that a light machine gun was no longer a necessity and that the automatic fire from the rifles would be just as good. Tests proved otherwise and consequently a formal request for a light machine gun was raised, specifying a weight of not more than 22lbs with 200 rounds of ammunition and an effective fighting range of 800 yards. The weight limit ruled out using the 7.62x51mm NATO cartridge, since 200 rounds would take up too great a proportion of

the 22lbs to permit building a reliable gun. On the other hand, in 1969 the 5.56mm (.223) cartridge was still not totally accepted in the US Army and was regarded with some suspicion in most other armies too. Unfortunately this decision put two quite reasonable designs out of consideration - the Stoner 63 and the Colt CMG

The Stoner 63 was designed by Eugene Stoner, the man who had also designed the M16 rifle and who went on to design a number of other weapons before his untimely death in 1997. It was a weapon system rather than simply a machine gun, since by changing barrels and other components it could be configured into a variety of forms from an assault carbine to a company support machine gun. Gas-operated, and using Stoner's rotating bolt in

This was an entry from Springfield Arsenal, which does not appear to have made it as far as the trials.

When the 6mm program was axed, designs in 5.56mm caliber were solicited. This was the Ford Aerospace XM248 entry.

Another view of the XM248, without its belt box.

A later design from Colt, which has achieved some success, is this 5.56mm M16A2 light machine gun.

The 5.56mm Ultimax 100 from Singapore, with its 100-round drum.

The left side of the Ultimax 100. A sling is not a common accessory.

The Ultimax 100 without its 100-round drum but using a simple 20-round box magazine; there is also a 30-round box available, but both of them are rarely seen.

a carrier, it was a very impressive weapon. But it fired the 5.56mm cartridge and that, in the mid-Sixties, was a trifle advanced for most people, who were reluctant to believe that a 5.56mm bullet had a place on a serious battlefield. (There are people - and I'm one of them - who still have their doubts.)

The Colt CMG-1 was little more than a heavy-barreled version of the M16 rifle and, being magazine-fed, it failed to generate much enthusiasm among the US military. It is worth remarking that the CMG-1 (like the M16 rifle) used a gas system in which the gas was

taken from the barrel and sent down a tube to impinge on the bolt carrier and thus blow it back. This, and a more recent design by Colt, also derived from the M16 and called the Model 715, are the only successful designs ever to use direct gas blast.

Colt then produced the CMG-2 and offered that for trial. This was another 5.56mm gas-operated weapon, belt-fed from a drum-like belt carrier beneath the receiver. It used a rotating bolt, locking via eight lugs, and was cocked in a similar manner to the Czech vz52 and the British Besa guns, by pull-

ing back the pistol grip. The gas system reverted to using a piston, of a similar pattern to that of the M60, which automatically cut off the gas supply once the piston had begun to move. The design was well thought out and the gun was widely demonstrated; but Colt elected to use a special bullet and rifled the gun accordingly: a 68-grain bullet and a twist of one turn in 8.5 inches. This was a tighter twist than the usual US standard of one turn in 12 inches with a 55-grain bullet. The reason

(Continued on Page 221)

An early Ultimax, with non-detachable barrel, field-stripped.

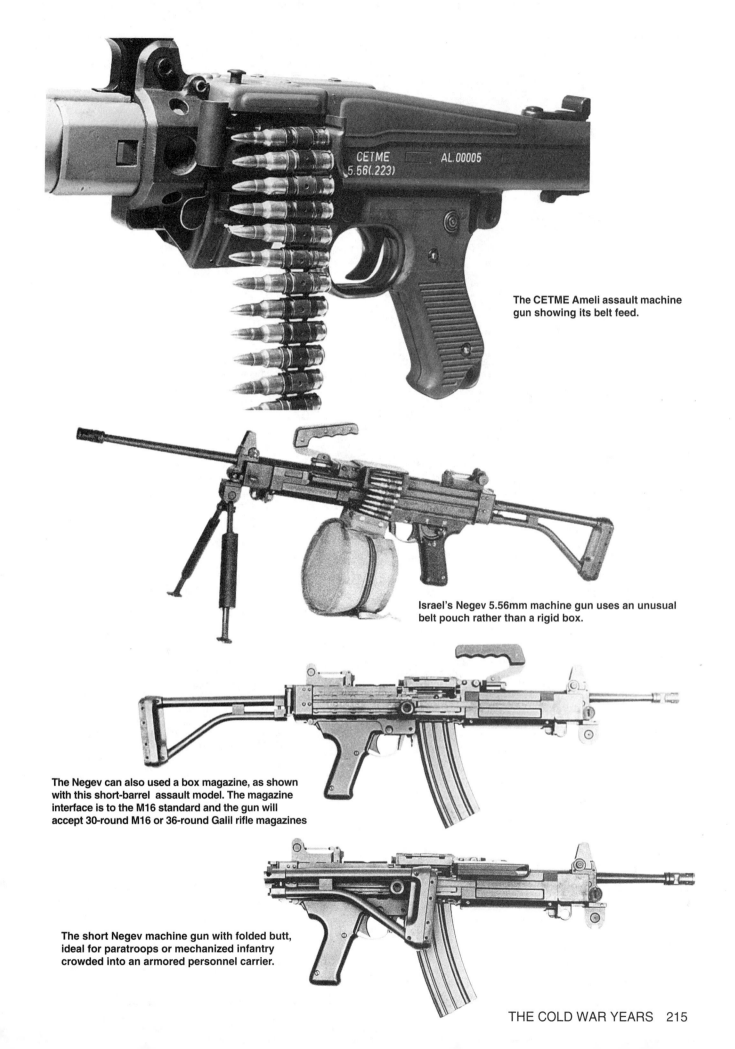

The CETME Ameli assault machine gun showing its belt feed.

Israel's Negev 5.56mm machine gun uses an unusual belt pouch rather than a rigid box.

The Negev can also used a box magazine, as shown with this short-barrel assault model. The magazine interface is to the M16 standard and the gun will accept 30-round M16 or 36-round Galil rifle magazines

The short Negev machine gun with folded butt, ideal for paratroops or mechanized infantry crowded into an armored personnel carrier.

CETME AMELI

The recoil impulse of 5.56mm machine guns being light, they can be fired from the hip with good effect. Notice how the gunner holds the muzzle down to counter the climb, rather than supporting it underneath.

AMELI is a manufactured word derived from '*AMEtralladora LIgera*' for 'Light machine gun.' It resembles a scaled-down model of the German MG42, though the delayed-blowback mechanism is actually derived from the Mauser MG45, an unfinished wartime development project. Firing the NATO-standard 5.56x45mm cartridge, it is officially termed an '*assault*' machine gun, since it is light and com-

pact enough to be carried and used while advancing in the final assault phase of an attack, instead of simply sitting off to a flank and providing covering fire, which is the usual role for the platoon machine gun. Indeed, it is so compact that it is probably the only machine gun in the world which can be carried in a briefcase - broken down, admittedly, but complete and with ammunition.

Ameli was developed by a design team of the *Compania de Estudios Tecnicos de Materiales Especialies S.A.* (CETME) and manufactured by the Spanish state armaments organization, the Empresa Santa Barbara. It was first announced in 1982 and has been in service with the Spanish Army since the late 1980s. Early

guns used a T-shaped cocking handle similar to that of the MG42, but production models adopted a simpler pattern.

Field-stripping:

Press forward the latch at the top rear of the receiver, open the feed cover and remove the belt. Pull back the cocking lever, examine the feed-way and chamber to ensure that no ammunition remains in the gun. Close the cover, pull the trigger and allow the working parts to go forward under control. Procure a live or dummy cartridge for use as a dismantling tool.

Press the point of the bullet into the hole on the underside of the stock,

DATA	
Caliber	5.56 x 45mm
Operating system	Delayed blowback, automatic
Locking system	Two-part bolt with rollers
Feed system	200-round disintgrating link belt
Overall length	38.6 inches (980mm)
Weight, empty	14.0 lbs (6.35kg)
Barrel	18.5in (470mm), 6 grooves, right-hand twist
Muzzle velocity	2870 ft/sec (875 m/sec)
Muzzle energy	1132 ft/lbs (1530J)
Rate of fire	900-125 rds/minute

The Spanish Ameli has a distinct resemblance to the German MG42 but the mechanism is quite different.

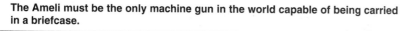

The Ameli must be the only machine gun in the world capable of being carried in a briefcase.

just behind the prominent locking pin, depress the catch and withdraw the pin. The butt can now be removed. Press in the top cover catch and open the top cover.

Grasp the rear of the receiver in the left hand with the thumb on top and, with the forefinger, press in the button underneath the receiver. With the right hand rotate the end of the buffer, in the receiver, a quarter-turn and withdraw it, together with the return spring and bolt. The movement will be halted as the bolt reaches the rear of the receiver due to the feed roller striking a notch in the receiver. Press the bullet tool into the small hole on the right top of the receiver to press down on the roller. Continue withdrawing and the bolt will come out of the receiver.

Pull back the cocking lever until it reaches its removal slot and take it out sideways. Pull back on the barrel lock, which is on top of the chamber, in front of the feed tray and turn the barrel handle clockwise to release the barrel. Pull the rear end of the barrel out to the right side of the weapon and withdraw it.

Close the ejection chute cover, beneath the receiver, then withdraw the lock pin just above the trigger and remove the ammunition box support, beneath the left side of the feed tray. Remove the pin from the top cover hinge and remove the top cover and the feed tray.

Press out the pistol grip pin, just behind the grip. The grip and trigger unit can then be rotated back and down and removed from the receiver. Lift the locking lever of the flash suppressor, just behind the suppressor on top of the jacket, and unscrew the suppressor. Press up the bipod lock, just behind the bipod hinge beneath the jacket, slide the bipod back and tilt it downwards to release it from the front anchorage and remove it.

Re-assembly is the reverse of the above procedure and presents no problems.

Like any good GPMG the Ameli can be tripod-mounted for the sustained-fire role, but in truth the 5.56mm cartridge is not really suited to this task.

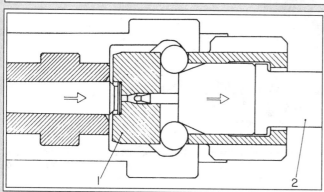

The delay system of the Ameli. 1) the light bolt head; 2) the heavy bolt body. The arrows indicate the direction of the pressure force on the cartridge case; this pressed the bolt head back against the two rollers and has to force the rollers out of their recesses before the pressure can be applied to the bolt body and thus begin the opening movement. Note too that the movement of the case is much less than with the lever system of the AA52 machine gun, so that there is less bulging of the cartridge cases.

The Beretta 70/223, their first 5.56mm machine gun. This was a sound design but it appeared in 1978 when the idea of a 223 (5.56mm) machine gun was something of a novelty. As a result, it didn't make many converts.

The quick-change barrel of the Beretta 70/223: first, grasp the forend and lift the barrel catch with the other hand. . . .

. . . then slide the barrel forward and down. They don't come much easier than this, but even so, sales were poor.

In 1985 Beretta came back with the AR 70/90, accompanying a similar rifle. The Italian Army adopted both in 1990. It's hard to see, but there is a bipod folded up alongside the gas cylinder.

The progress of the British L86 Light Support Weapon. This was the original 1976 design in 4.85mm caliber.

By 1990 more changes, principally an elongated forend to carry the bipod and relieve the barrel of stresses. This was the final production model.

Russia's RPK-74 was simply the AK-74 5.45mm rifle with a heavy and longer barrel and a bipod, with a 45-round magazine.

The Zastava Arms Company of Yugoslavia were the first people to produce the Kalashnikov rifle and its machine gun derivatives in 5.56mm for export to the non-Communist world. This is the Yugoslavian M82A light machine gun, which is no more than an AKM with a college education and firing 'capitalist' ammunition.

The exterior may look different but underneath is the same rotating bolt and gas piston of other Kalashnikov clones; this is the Czech 2000 in 5.56mm, ready for adoption by the Czech army in due course.

The 4.85mm Light Support Weapon stripped and on display at the public introduction of the 4.85mm system in August 1976.

By June 1982 it had been rebuilt into 5.56mm caliber as a result of the NATO decision to standardize on that caliber, and a few other subtle changes had been made.

The one they have to beat; the Russian 14.5mm KPV gun, most powerful machine gun currently in use by any army.

(Continued from Page 214)

for the change was that the faster spin gave the bullet better down-range stability and, being heavier, it also retained its velocity further than the 55-grain bullet. It was possible to fire the US M193 round through the CMG-2 but the results were not the optimum; and while everybody saw the force of Colt's argument, nobody wanted to have to produce an entirely different 5.56mm cartridge solely for the light machine gun. So the CMG-2 went on the shelf and stayed there.

However, although the CMG-2 was turned down because it needed a special cartridge, the more the designers and staff looked at the problem, the more it seemed that in order to get the performance they wanted within the weight limit stipulated, they were going to have to develop a new round whether they liked it or not. Frankford Arsenal undertook this task and produced a 6x45mm round with a 105-grain bullet delivering a muzzle velocity of 2445 ft/sec and muzzle energy of 1394 ft/lbs. This was well below the muzzle velocity of the 5.56mm M193 round (3299 ft/sec) but the heavier bullet gave it a higher muzzle energy (the M193 gave 1252 ft/lbs) and maintained its velocity down range so as to produce a round which outranged the M193 and also had better lethality. Once that was settled the gun designers could get to work.

A number of designs were submitted, mostly from the USA but also some from Europe, but eventually the contest thinned down to six major players: FN of Belgium, Heckler & Koch of Germany, and Colt, Maremont, Philco-Ford, and the Rodman Laboratory of Rock Island Arsenal from the USA.

These were submitted for trials, which were completed in 1974. The FN submission was the design that was later perfected as the Minimi; the Heckler and Koch weapon was the HK23. Both were belt-fed, the Minimi using a gas piston and rotating bolt and the HK23 using Heckler & Koch's roller-delayed blowback system. Both were in 5.56mm caliber, this being permitted since they were commercial entrants; it was assumed that should they be successful, then the question of modifying the designs to 6mm would be addressed.

The Colt entry was a heavy-barreled M16 generally similar to the CMG-1 but in 6mm caliber. The Maremont design was based upon an earlier private venture known as the Universal Machine Gun. This was a 7.62mm NATO-caliber weapon which was unusual in that it could be assembled either as a gas-operated weapon or as a recoil-operated one, a minimum number of parts having to be removed or

added to make the change. (This was obviously a manufacturing option and not a user's field option.) It was belt-fed, from either side, used a rotating bolt, and had a rate of fire of about 600 rounds per minute. It failed to attract any buyers, but Maremont used some of the technology to develop their light machine gun XM233. It was solely gas-operated, the recoil option being abandoned, and fed from a belt drum via the left side of the receiver. But with 200 rounds it weighed 25.3lbs, well over the stipulated limit.

The Philco-Ford XM 234 was also belt-fed and gas-operated, had a somewhat longer barrel than usual, was laid out in a straight line (which meant high-set sights) and turned the scale at 22.4lbs, a mere few ounces over the limit.

The Rodman XM235 design was a bullpup, which is to say that the end of the receiver rested on the firer's shoulder and his face was alongside the action.

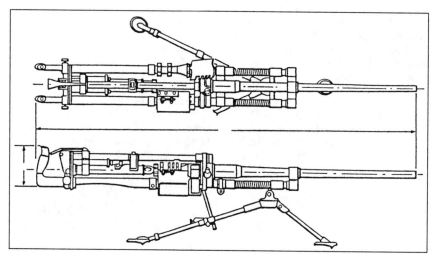

Plan and elevation of the Dover Devil; compare this with the Rodman SAWS design illustrated earlier; particularly the supporting of the barrel between two operating tubes.

The 'Dover Devil' in 50-caliber. You can put a light metal cover over the bolt and feed system but it was not necessary and it was one of the first weapons to adopt a tubular 'chassis' instead of the traditional box-like receiver.

Just to prove it worked. Firing the Dover Devil in a testing range.

This is now fairly commonplace, but in the early 1970s it was regarded as a somewhat radical idea and viewed with some suspicion in many quarters. Gas-operated and belt-fed from the usual sort of underslung belt box, it was a very clean design with two gas cylinders - one above and one below the quick-change barrel - and return springs wrapped around the two gas pistons. The pistons were attached to a bolt carrier holding a rotating bolt, and the barrel had a carrying handle that acted as a handle for changing the barrel in action.

The HK23 and the M16 failed the safety tests; the other four weapons completed the trial and a detailed report was being prepared when the goalposts were suddenly moved.

The Department of the Army now pointed out that introduction of a 6mm caliber cartridge would add complications to the logistic and supply picture, and that future infantry weapons must be built around either the 7.62mm or the 5.56mm NATO cartridges; moreover, the various projects and proposals - not merely the SAWS programs but others as well - ought

to be re-assessed in the light of their implications for NATO standardization and interoperability.

All this, of course, put an abrupt end to the 6mm SAWS program. In an attempt to salvage whatever might be possible, the Rodman Laboratories developed a 5.56mm version of their SAWS contestant. This was then complicated by a proposal to develop two completely new 5.56mm rounds, and that, in turn, was upset by the decision to hold a massive comparative test of 5.56mm and other small calibers to determine the future NATO-standard round.

The 50-caliber General Purpose Heavy Machine Gun developed by the AAI Corporation in the mid-1980s. Note the tubular support for the barrel - everybody's doing it now.

The AAI GPHMG compared with the 'control' - the Browning 50-caliber M2HB.

We could go on, into all the twists and turn of military budget cuts, rival designs, Marines doing this and Army doing that, but the upshot of all the maneuvering was that the FN Minimi was finally settled on as the M249 light machine gun in 1990.

At much the same time as the US Army finally made up its mind and adopted the Minimi, a little-known company called Singapore Technologies suddenly appeared with an entirely new machine gun in 5.56mm caliber. This was the Ultimax 100, which took the number from the fact that it fired from a 100-round drum. And to this day there are some who maintain that had Singapore Technologies been a bit quicker off the mark, they could well have scooped the market, which fell to the Minimi.

The Ultimax was a gas-operated, air-cooled, light machine gun of apparently conventional form, but

it embodies what the makers call 'constant recoil' which really means that the rotating bolt and its carrier have a somewhat longer recoil stroke than normal and are particularly well-buffered. As a result, the felt recoil is very much smaller than any other gun of this class. It can be comfortably fired from the hip, and even fired at arm's length in one hand. I have actually watched this gun fire a complete 100-round magazine, non-stop, balanced on the end of a young lady's nose, and there did not appear to be any damage to her nose afterwards.

You could dismiss this as a gimmick, but the fact remains that this is possibly the smoothest light machine gun ever designed. It uses a 100-round drum magazine, slung beneath the receiver, and the original model was provided with a quick-change barrel. A Mark 2 version had a fixed barrel, and the Mark 3 then came long with an improved method of quick-chang-

ing the barrel. It was adopted by the Singapore armed forces, but because it arrived just too late, it never managed to achieve adoption by a major army, the Minimi having got there first.

The Spanish army adopted the 5.56mm cartridge in the late 1970s, taking the CETME Model L rifle into service at that time. CETME stands for *'Companhia de Estudios Tecnicos de Materiales Especiales'* and is the design agency for the Spanish armed forces. The actual manufacture is done by the Santa Barbara state arsenal organization at their various factories. The rifle was developed from earlier 7.62mm and 7.92mm designs developed by CETME, and their origin lay in the German Mauser Sturmgewehr 45 project, which was terminated by the end of World War II. Many of the Mauser design staff found their way to Spain and were among the original design staff of the CETME organization. The result was the

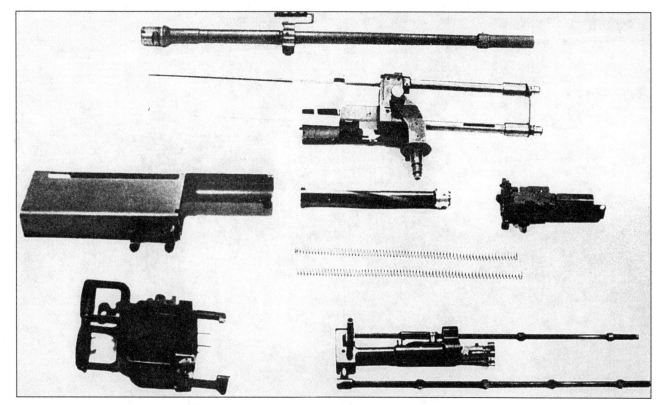

The component parts of the AAI GPHMG.

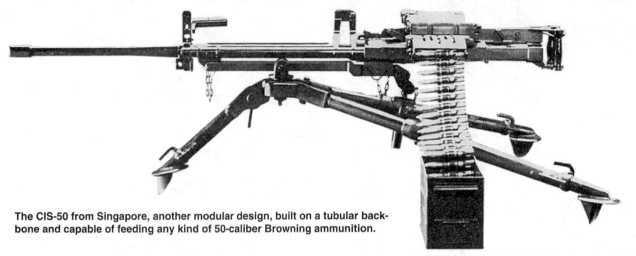

The CIS-50 from Singapore, another modular design, built on a tubular back-bone and capable of feeding any kind of 50-caliber Browning ammunition.

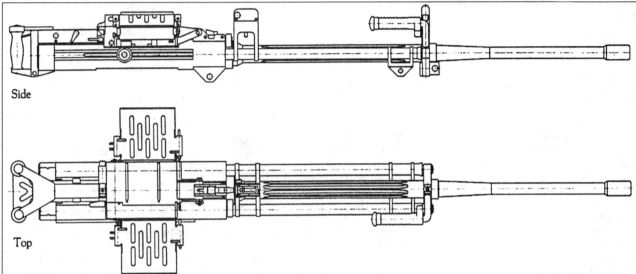

Side

Top

Plan and elevation of the CIS 50 heavy machine gun. Note the double feed - it loads two belts and the gunner can select whichever one he wants at any time. It also sports a really quick quick-change barrel.

The CIS 50 may look rather spindly, but there isn't an ounce of excess weight on it, although the safety margins are still generous.

The CIS 50 mounted on a tank turret. One will have to get used to seeing machine guns with *two* belt boxes.

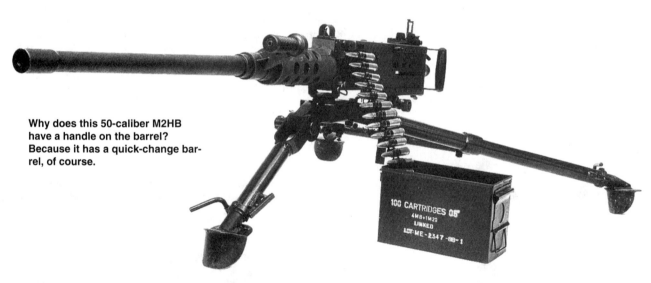

Why does this 50-caliber M2HB have a handle on the barrel? Because it has a quick-change barrel, of course.

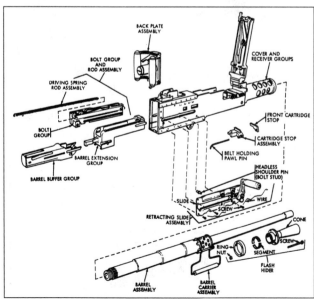

How the 50 M2HB all fits together - an orientation plan.

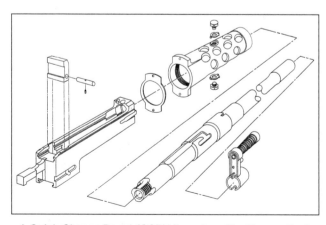

A Quick-Change Barrel *(QCB)* kit produced by Manroy Engineering of England. Compare this with the orientation plan to see how the change is made.

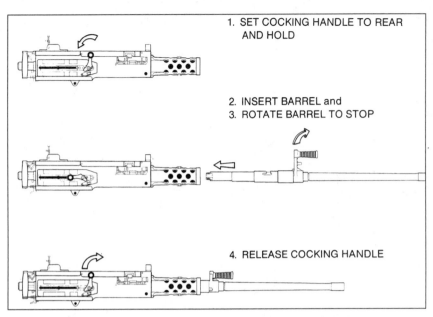

1. SET COCKING HANDLE TO REAR AND HOLD

2. INSERT BARREL and
3. ROTATE BARREL TO STOP

4. RELEASE COCKING HANDLE

Concise instructions on how to change the *QCB*.

roller-delayed blowback two-piece bolt action which we have already explored in the Heckler and Koch 21 and SIG 710 machine guns, This mechanism is at the heart of the CETME rifles and was also adopted for their light machine gun design in 5.56mm caliber called the 'Ameli', a made-up name constructed from the Spanish words for Light Infantry Machine Gun.

It was called an 'assault machine gun' when first introduced, although that title appears to have been dropped in later years. In appearance, it is like a scaled-down MG42, with the same perforated barrel jackets, bell-mouthed muzzle booster and straight-line layout. The only significant difference is the high-set front sight and the rear sight incorporated in a looped carrying handle. It is belt-fed, from a belt box on the left side (or from a free-hanging belt if necessary) and has a maximum rate of fire of about 1200 rounds per minute. Normally fitted with a bipod, it can also be mounted on a tripod and used as a support weapon, though in this caliber the general-purpose concept seems rather limited in its scope. Nevertheless, the Ameli is a very good weapon that had been tried and found satisfactory by various forces, though at present it is only employed by the Spanish army.

The Israeli army, as noted above, had taken a heavy-barreled version of their Galil rifle as their squad automatic, and while this appeared satisfactory in 7.62mm caliber, the 5.56mm version (for the rifle was made in both calibers) was less successful. A 5.56mm machine gun being considered necessary, a fresh design was called for and appeared in 1990. This was the 'Negev' light machine gun and was a very versatile design. In standard form it is belt-fed and the barrel is rifled

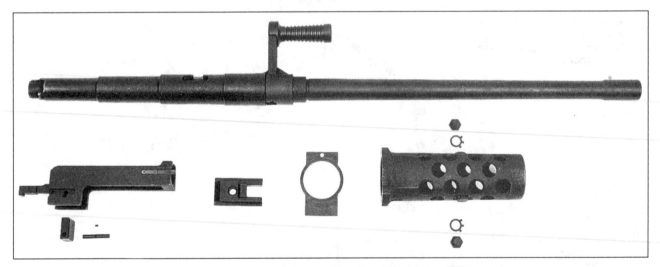

The Manroy kit for converting any 50-caliber M2HB into a QCB gun.

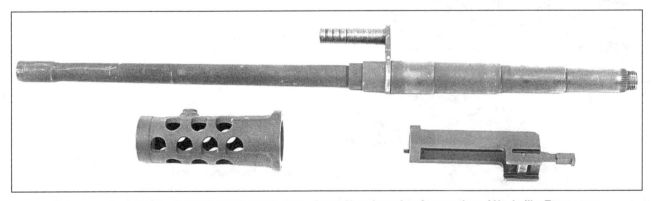

There are others: this is the QCB kit produced by the Ramo Manufacturing Corporation of Nashville, Tennessee.

Another modern adjunct to the 50 M2HB Browning is a cushioned recoil cradle, isolating the operator from the vibration and allowing him better control of the weapon.

The 15mm FN-BRG, original model with smooth quick-change barrel.

A comparison between *(left)* the 15mm FN-BRG and *(right)* the 50-caliber M2HB Browning.

optimally for the 5.56mm NATO round. The barrel can be quick-changed, and operation is by gas piston and a rotating bolt. The gas regulator has three positions: one shuts off the gas completely so that the gun can be used to launch grenades; the second position provides sufficient gas to deliver a rate of fire of 750-850 rounds per minute; and the third position lifts the rate to 900-1000 rounds per minute. The barrel can be quickly changed for one rifled for the 5.56mm M193 round, which has a lighter bullet than the NATO cartridge, for use where the supply of this particular round is easier than the NATO round. The weapon can also be given a short barrel and, by means of an adapter, can use the 30-round box magazines made for either the Galil 5.56mm rifle or the US M16 (which is now, of course, a NATO-standard interface) so that the weapon becomes an assault rifle. Indeed, virtually everything on the rifle is interchangeable so that various non-standard possibilities are open to the user.

The second version of the BRG, in 15.5mm and distinguished by the fluted barrel with flash hider. This was No. 1 on its test mounting at the FN range in Belgium in 1990.

Looking down on the receiver of the FN BRG15; note there are two belt 'gates' only one of which can be in engagement at any time. They are controlled by a lever that moves them, guided by the cam paths that can be seen at the front of each gate. In this case the left-hand belt is feeding, while the right-hand belt is out of engagement.

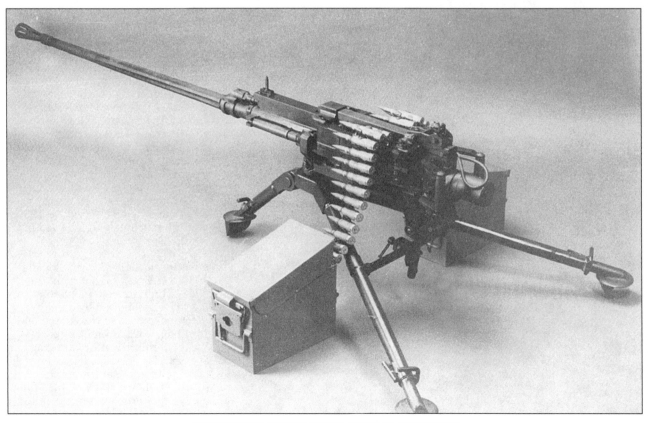

Another view of the FN-BRG15, with both belts loaded.

The receiver of the FN-BRG15 showing the belt paths.

The fieldstripping of the FN-BRG15 requires a certain amount of space.

Italy, as we have seen, had a somewhat uninspiring collection of machine guns during World War II, and not unnaturally set about remedying this in the 1960s. Their first move was to adopt the German MG42/59 as their general-purpose gun, after which they began looking for a light machine gun, principally for their Alpine troops who require the lightest possible equipment. Nothing very much happened until the 5.56mm cartridge appeared, and the firm of Pietro Beretta set about developing a rifle for possible adoption by the Italian army and also for export sales. The rifle duly appeared, after which Beretta developed a heavy-barreled version as a light machine gun, the Beretta AR70-223. This was a neat design that had the gas cylinder above the barrel, and the bipod attached to the cylinder. This allowed a quick-change barrel system, which simply dropped the barrel and forend straight into the gunner's hand when he pressed the release catch. Using a 40-round magazine this appeared to be a very practical weapon but it was before its time and found no takers. Beretta then gave it a heavier, fixed barrel and made a few modifications, re-launching it as the AR70-84, but by that time the rifle, which had been purchased by one or two countries, had revealed a few defects, and the machine gun again found no takers.

Finally, in the early 1980s, Beretta set to and completely redesigned the rifle family, introducing it in 1985 as the AR70-90. The light machine gun version was again a heavy-barrel modification, firing from an open bolt rather than the closed bolt of the rifle family, though the gas operation with rotating bolt was otherwise identical. This family took some time to be developed, largely because the Italian army were having trouble with obtaining funding from their government, but the rifle was finally adopted for service in 1990 and the machine gun followed in 1992.

In 1976 the British army announced their new rifle for the 1980s - SA80 ('Small Arm of the 80s'), a bullpup rifle in 4.85mm caliber. It was followed by a light machine gun or, in the contemporary buzzword, a Light Support Weapon. Shortly afterwards, however, NATO organized a comprehensive trial to determine the future standard rifle and machine gun caliber and everything halted while this took place. The SA80 rifle was entered, but, to nobody's

The most common use of the KPV 14.5mm machine gun is in this ZPU-1 anti-aircraft mount.

The Chinese Type 77 uses gas blast to operate the breechblock and flaps to lock it. It fires the Russian 12.7mm cartridge and has replaced the DShK in Chinese service.

The Russian 12.7mm NSV that is gradually replacing the old DShK in several countries.

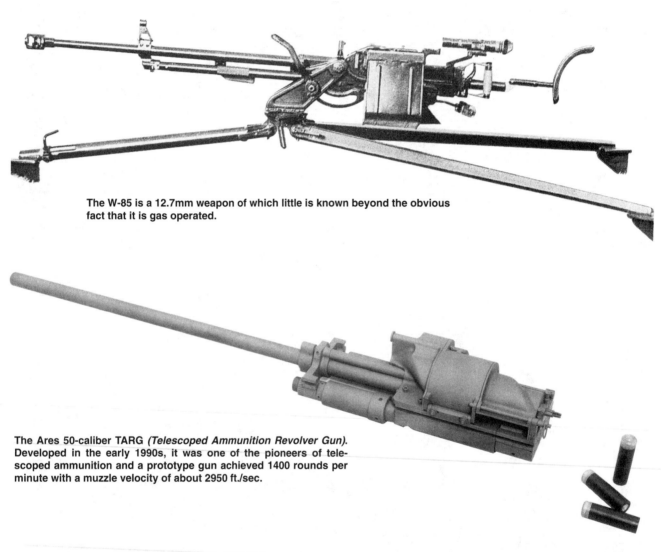

The W-85 is a 12.7mm weapon of which little is known beyond the obvious fact that it is gas operated.

The Ares 50-caliber TARG *(Telescoped Ammunition Revolver Gun)*. Developed in the early 1990s, it was one of the pioneers of telescoped ammunition and a prototype gun achieved 1400 rounds per minute with a muzzle velocity of about 2950 ft./sec.

A 50-caliber Gatling-type gun built by CTA International as a technology demonstrator. It achieved 4000 rounds per minute but it was felt that the many advantages promised by telescoped ammunition were more likely to be achieved in larger calibers and research is now concentrated in the cannon field.

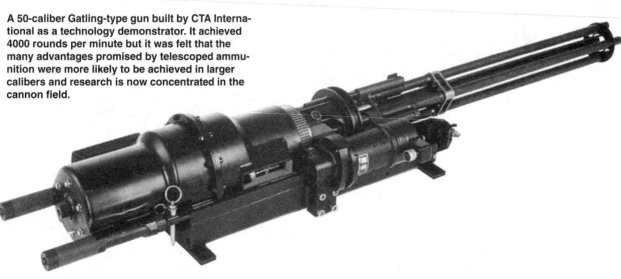

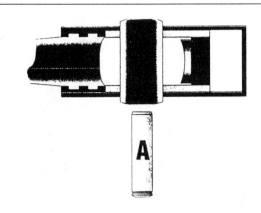

1. Rotating Chamber Open Round "A" Ready to Load

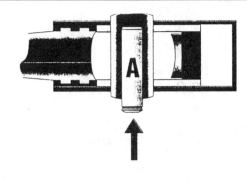

2. Round "A" Loads

3. Rotating Chamber Closes

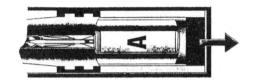

4. Gun Fires, Breech and Barrel recoil and Counter Recoil

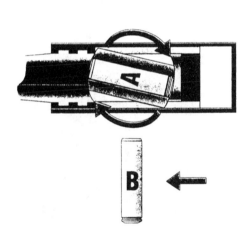

5. Feeder Indexes Round "B" into Position, Chamber Opens

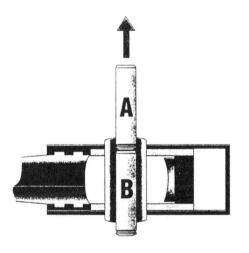

6. Round "B" is Loaded, Pushing Spent Case "A" Out the Side of the Gun

A new method of operation for application to CTA weapons. The chamber can rotate through 90 degrees to be loaded. It then rotates back to fire, and then rotates again to allow the new round to be loaded, so pushing out the spent case. This system has been built and fired, so there is no question about whether it is practical or not.

surprise, NATO did not select the 4.85mm cartridge, the 5.56mm round with a heavier bullet being adopted. Having foreseen this possibility, the British had designed their 4.85mm round using a 5.56mm case, so that modifying the designs to 5.56mm was relatively simple and the two weapons were formally announced in 1985, as the L85 rifle and the L86 light support weapon.

Unfortunately, the weapons started to go into production just as the British government decided to 'privatize' the Royal Ordnance Factories. Production at the old Royal Small Arms Factory at Enfield was stopped, the machinery moved to another ex-Royal Ordnance Factory in Nottingham and re-started under new management. This led to considerable quality control problems and both the rifle and the machine gun acquired dubious reputations.

A Russian soldier prepares to fire his 37mm AGS-17 grenade launcher, which is simply a large blowback machine gun.

Unloading an AGS-17 is a two-man business. The gunner heaves on the cocking lanyard, while his assistant catches the ejected cartridge.

The L86A1 Light Support Weapon is gas-operated and air-cooled, using a rotating bolt in a bolt carrier riding on two rods inside the receiver. The whole lay-out has more than a passing resemblance to Eugene Stoner's 'Stoner 63' rifle design. The barrel is fixed, and the weapon is fed by a box magazine holding 30 rounds and interchangeable with the M16 rifle magazine. The long barrel is supported on a perforated metal forend and there is a vertical grip for the non-firing hand beneath the butt just behind the magazine. The single-shot accuracy is outstanding, and when fitted with the SUSAT optical sight it can almost double as a sniping rifle. Just 22,000 were manufactured for the British armed forces; no other army appeared to be interested and manufacture has therefore ceased.

In about 1978 word leaked out of Soviet Russia that a new rifle firing a new 5.45mm cartridge had been issued to their airborne troops, and shortly after that pictures were seen of the new weapon. It was, quite obviously, a Kalashnikov AK type modified to a new caliber in response to the Western adoption of the 5.56mm cartridge. It was eventually discovered that the weapon was the AK-74, that being the year of initial issue. And it was not long before the inevitable squad machine gun firing the same cartridge made its appearance. The RPK-74 (*Ruchnoii Pulyemet Kalashnikova*) is simply an AK-74 with a longer and slightly heavier barrel, a bipod and a larger magazine.

By the middle 1980s the 5.45mm caliber had become the new Soviet standard for the rifleman and his light machine gun, and was then beginning to spread out to the various Soviet satellite nations. As well as adopting the Soviet weapons, various countries of the Warsaw Pact looked at developing their own weapons around the cartridge, but before very much could be accomplished the collapse of the Soviet Empire freed the satellites from their links and allowed them to make their own decisions about their military equipment. Some have elected to stay with the 5.45mm cartridge, but most countries that began by looking east have turned to look west and have therefore embraced the 5.56mm NATO-standard cartridge. The Yugoslavs, for example, prior to their dissolution, had developed a range of Kalashnikov clones in both rifle and machine gun form, had begun modifying them to 5.45mm caliber and had also developed the same weapons in 5.56mm for export purposes. The Czechs began developing a new machine gun which they called the 'Lada' in 5.45mm caliber (see Appendix 1) but then abandoned it and re-developed it as the CZ2000 in 5.56mm, so that as and when they join NATO they will at least have some measure of standardization in place.

The Heavy Brigade

The Russian adoption of the KPV 14.5mm machine gun in about 1960 caused a good deal of nail-biting among the Western armies. While it might not be much of a threat to main battle tanks, it was certainly a severe threat to the lighter armor that was then beginning to go into service in several countries. Armored personnel carriers and similar vehicles had been designed to keep out the usual rifle-caliber AP bullets, heavier ball bullets and shell fragments, but a tungsten-cored 14.5mm bullet was a very different proposition. The 50-caliber Browning was no competition; a vehicle armed with the 0.50-inch gun would be shot to pieces by the 14.5mm weapon before it got close enough to even scratch the paint on the 14.5mm carrier.

There is a rule of thumb among weapons designers that is generally observed: if you want to improve a weapon, leave it alone and start by improving the ammunition. Raufoss Arsenal of Norway were among the front runners on this occasion and they produced a high-explosive/incendiary/trace round for the 50-caliber Browning which just about doubled its effectiveness, although it didn't improve the effective range by very much. Winchester in the USA, on a military contract, began developing the 50-caliber SLAP (Saboted Light Armor Penetrator) round, to step up the velocity, improve the penetrating ability and extend the effective range by a considerable percentage.

Saboted ammunition was, by this time, a well-accepted system in artillery calibers, but nobody

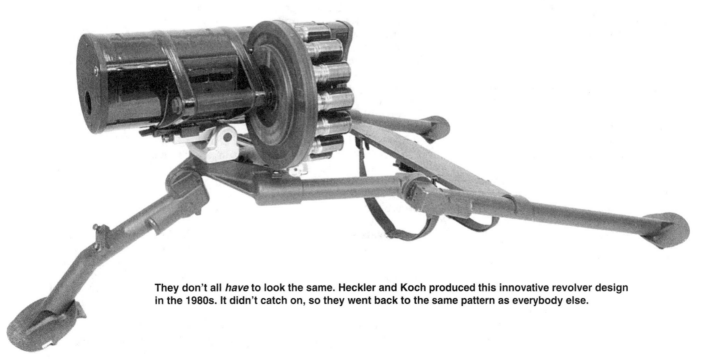

They don't all *have* to look the same. Heckler and Koch produced this innovative revolver design in the 1980s. It didn't catch on, so they went back to the same pattern as everybody else.

A US Marine firing the Mark 19 40mm Machine Gun.

beyond a few dedicated high-velocity enthusiasts had experimented with sabot in small arms calibers, and none of them ever got any consistent results; Winchester had a hard row to hoe. The principle had been first worked on by Edgar Brandt, a French ordnance engineer, in the 1930s, seeking to improve the range of French 105mm howitzer. In brief terms, what he did was to take the existing 75mm gun shell and enclose it in a lightweight support of 105mm diameter. This combination weighed rather less than a 105mm shell, so when it was fired it accelerated faster; therefore, it could be given a heavier propelling charge without exceeding the maximum safe chamber pressure; therefore it left the bore of the gun at a much higher velocity. The enclosing support was designed so that it split apart into a number of segments while traveling up the gun bore, and as soon as it left the muzzle these pieces would be flung outwards - due to the spin of the unit - leaving the 75mm shell, propelled by a souped-up 105mm cartridge, to scream off and reach almost twice the normal range. Brandt was still working on this when the balloon went up in 1940, whereupon most of his research projects fell into the hands of the Germans.

The British had picked up some of this from Brandt, and they took over this development, but with an entirely different aim in view. They wanted velocity and piercing power

for anti-tank weapons, and by re-working the Brandt idea so that the 75mm shell now became a tungsten carbide core, and the surrounding support was made of aluminum alloy, they were able to produce a projectile for their 17-pounder 3-inch antitank gun which left the muzzle at 3950 ft/sec and would go through nine inches of face-hardened steel armor at 1000 yards range. The same gun, firing a conventional steel shot, could only manage 4.3 inches at the same range.

Winchester were now trying to pull the same trick but in 0.50-inch caliber instead of 3 inches, and while the theory was plain enough, actually mass-producing such a complicated projectile in a half-inch diameter was a formidable task. They eventually succeeded, and then went on to develop the same thing in 30-caliber. The 50-caliber SLAP round has a muzzle velocity of 4010 ft/sec (1222 m/sec); its penetration is not revealed, nor its effective range, though it has been shown that at 2000 yards range the bullet is traveling at about 2500 ft/sec, so it should be capable of defeating most light armored vehicles at 1500 yards or so.

Unfortunately, it was found that the early SLAP ammunition did not take kindly to being fed into a machine gun at high speed, so two courses of action were begun; firstly to improve the ammunition and secondly to develop a 50-caliber gun which would happily accept

SLAP at the full normal rate of fire. Three guns eventually appeared from this effort.

The first two were American and gave rise to a new nomenclature: General Purpose Heavy Machine Gun or GPHMG. The first to appear was the 'Dover Devil', so-called from being developed by the US Army Armament Research and Development Command (AARADCOM) in their facility at Dover, New Jersey. It was the first to appear because it had a head start; AARADCOM had been working on a 20mm cannon design and simply adapted this to 50-caliber. The resulting machine gun was a full-automatic weapon, air-cooled, gas-operated and firing from an open bolt. It was modular in design, built up from six basic assemblies, and could be field-stripped in a matter of seconds without the use of tools. The receiver consisted of two aircraft-quality steel tubes, one above the other, with an aluminum end cap. The two tubes acted as gas cylinders and each held a piston and operating rod; as the round fired, gas pressure drive the rods back, taking with them the bolt carrier and cam-rotated bolt. Two springs in the tubes were compressed and drove the bolt carrier and bolt back at the end of their recoil stroke. Feed was by a disintegrating link belt feeding in from the left and propelled by a sprocket mechanism driven by the movement of the bolt.

The second GPHMG offering came from the AAI Corporation of Baltimore and was obviously influenced by the Dover Devil, being built upon a similar modular plan, but used three tubes for the receiver structure. There were two gas pistons driving a rotating three-lug bolt and carrier, feed was by a disintegrating-link belt which could be fed from either side so that two belts could be loaded and the firer could select which belt to fire. The selector also had a neutral position, which prevented either belt from feeding. The barrel was a quick-change design that required no headspace adjustment, and the makers claimed that it could be manufactured for 30 percent less cost than the contemporary 50-caliber M2HB Browning.

The US Army tested both guns in the early 1990s, but found neither to their satisfaction and both projects were closed down.

The next to appear was a total surprise; the Chartered Industries of Singapore company, who had been industriously making a 5.56mm rifle and the Ultimax

5.56mm machine gun for the Singapore Armed Forces suddenly announced the CIS-50 machine gun. Designed by a team led by A.C. 'Sandy' Cormack, a Scots ordnance engineer who had worked with Sterling and Mossberg, work had begun in 1983 and the gun appeared in 1988. As with the two American designs, it was of modular construction, split into five groups, the receiver having two tubes acting as gas cylinders. Feed was from either or both sides, selectable by the gunner, and firing was from the open bolt position. It was immediately taken into use by the Singapore forces, as an infantry support gun and as a close-defense weapon for armored vehicles.

All three of these guns had the ability to load and fire any kind of 50-caliber Browning cartridge, including the SLAP round; but while all this activity had been going on in the gunmaker's shops, Winchester had been busy sorting out the problem with their SLAP round and had come up with a modified design which fed quite satisfactorily into the normal M2 guns, so that the demand for a new design was no longer urgent.

One thing that had emerged from the GPHMG program was the desirability of a heavy machine gun with a quick-change barrel and a fixed

headspace. Various people began to work on this and by 1990 there were a number of designs available. New guns were being made with the 'QCB', and existing guns could be converted to QCB status by a simple kit. This varied from maker to maker but usually consisted of a new barrel, with a handle, new barrel extension assembly and new barrel support. The constant headspace was arrived at by shims inserted between the barrel and the barrel extension, and once the kit was fitted, usually by an armorer, no further adjustment was necessary and barrels could be changed whenever necessary.

But for all this activity, which certainly resulted in a more effectual 50-caliber Browning gun, the basic problem still remained: the 14.5mm KPV could still out-perform anything in the West.

Fabrique National now stepped in, and in 1984 announced their development of a new 15mm heavy machine gun firing an entirely new cartridge. Their object was to produce something between the 50-caliber machine gun and the 20mm cannon but keeping the size and weight to machine gun proportions so as to make it a practical field weapon. The gun itself was quite conventional in its design, a gas-operated weapon with a rotating bolt. The designer's aim was a

weapon which would use proven technology, available materials, and which would be capable, by means of adapters, of using existing mounts, tripods and other equipment already in use by various armies. It was provided with dual belt feed, allowing the gunner to select either belt at will.

However, at a later stage in the development it was found that the barrel was wearing out at an unacceptable speed, and investigation showed that this was due to the abrasive friction of the large bullet traveling at high velocity. The bullet was therefore redesigned, using a plastic rotating band similar in principle to the rotating band used with artillery shells. This necessitated redesigning the shape of the bullet and it was found that to obtain satisfactory ballistic performance the caliber had to be increased to 15.5mm.

The new cartridge, 15.5x106mm, gave a muzzle velocity of 3460 ft/sec (1055 m/sec) to the ball bullet, making it capable of defeating 19mm of rolled armor at 800 meters range; by comparison the Russian 14.5mm round could not defeat 19mm at 250 meters range. And in a more practical test, the bullet went through both sides of an ex-Soviet BMP armored personnel carrier at 1000 meters. AP and APDS (discarding sabot) bullets were also developed but no information of their armor-piercing performance was ever revealed.

A good deal of interest was aroused by the new gun, now called the FN BRG-15, but before very much more could be done there were various financial crises and upheavals in the European arms industry and when the smoke cleared away FN had been acquired by GIAT, the French 'privatized' government munitions consortium. GIAT had other plans for FN and proceeded to put the BRG-15 on the shelf. FN has since regained its independence but the BRG-15 is still shelved awaiting a more propitious time for its re-introduction.

Although the Russians were content with the KPV machine gun, they had to admit that it was scarcely a weapon for all purposes, and as the DShK 38/46 was beginning to show its age by the 1970s, there was a demand for a new 12.7mm gun which would be lighter, cheaper and easier to make - and with a better rate of fire. Design work began in 1989 by the three-man team of Nikitin, Sokolov and Volkov, the resulting weapon being known as the NSV-12.7. A gas-operated weapon, it uses an odd

Two Spanish soldiers with the Santa Barbara 40mm machine gun.

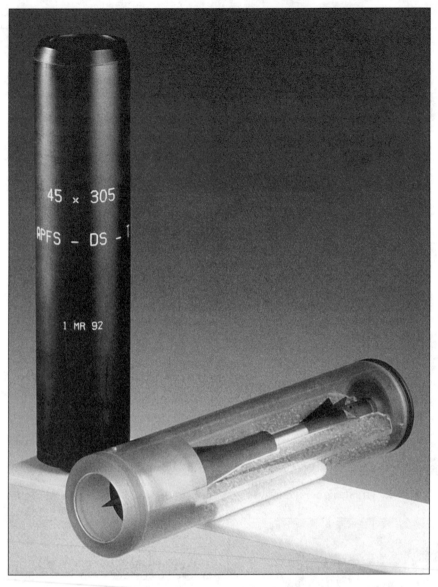

A round of cased telescoped ammunition. This is in 45mm and the projectile is a fin-stabilized armor-piercing shot, but the principle can be seen. The absence of a rim allows the fired case to be ejected forwards rather than being extracted rearwards and then ejected.

breech-locking system in which the breech-block is split into three parts that are moved laterally by the gas piston. This saves space that would otherwise be required for the axial movement of a conventional bolt and also speeds up the operating cycle, allowing a higher rate of fire. Construction is largely of metal stampings, riveted and welded, resulting in a saving of about 22 lbs.

The NSV has completely replaced the DShK in the Russian army and has also been adopted in several ex-Warsaw Pact forces, being built under license in Bulgaria, Poland and Serbia.

It has not, though, been adopted in China. For many years the Chinese have simply copied or licensed various Russian designs, but as China and Russia drifted apart ideologically the Chinese began developing their own designs, two of which are in the heavy class and fire the Russian 12.7mm cartridge. The Type 77 is a gas-operated weapon that uses the Degtyarev system of flaps to lock the breech, but, most unusually, uses a direct gas blast to propel the breech-block carrier. A pipe runs from the gas regulator at the midpoint of the barrel and the gas strikes the front face of the bolt carrier and drives it back. The initial movement of the carrier folds in the flaps and unlocks them, after which the carrier opens the bolt and carries out the usual cycle of operation before being returned by a spring, closing the bolt and then deploying the flaps to lock it.

Less has been divulged about the second model, the W-85. This is a remarkably light weapon, almost half the weight of the DShK, which

it replaced. The weapon is gas-operated and belt-fed, but the details of the breech locking system are not known.

The principal drawback to making better heavy machine guns is that they are very liable to become bigger heavy machine guns, and weight and bulk are important factors to the modern army, where more and more air mobility is being called for. One way to reduce the bulk of a gun is to reduce the bulk of the ammunition; with a conventional gas- or recoil-operated gun firing conventional ammunition, the length of the receiver is largely governed by the length of the cartridge and the size of the bolt. Reduce those and you can shrink the gun proportionately.

The latest move in this direction has been the development of Telescoped Ammunition, a cartridge in which the propellant is in the form of a cylinder with a blind hole in its center, into which the bullet is inserted. This can be caseless - simply a chunk of naked propellant with a combustible cap at the rear end, as used in the German G11 rifle - or enclosed in a case with a conventional primer, as in various experimental machine gun designs. Either way you end up with a shorter but fatter cartridge. But the slight gain in diameter is amply compensated by the considerable reduction in length, since the overall length of the cartridge is about one-third as long again as the bullet itself. Since the caseless cartridge introduces some considerable complications into the weapon design, very little has been done with it (but see below). Cased types, known collectively as CTA (Cased Telescoped Ammunition) guns, are a more practical proposition, but practical experience has shown that their advantages are not particularly marked until you get into the cannon calibers over 20mm.

Ares Inc., in the USA, produced TARG, the Telescoped Ammunition Revolver Gun, in 1989. Designed by Eugene Stoner of Armalite fame, TARG used a plastic cylindrical cartridge that contained propellant and a 50-caliber bullet, basically the same as that of the standard M33 ball round. The gun was gas-operated and used a four-chambered-revolving cylinder in the feed system. This allowed the feeding to be done in simultaneous phases, contributing to a rate of fire of about 2000 rounds per minute. The cylindrical and rimless case of the cartridge allowed the ejection phase to be a simple matter of pushing the fired case forward out of the chamber as the new case was pushed in from the rear, so that ejection did not demand a separate phase in the cycle of operation.

One of the problems with telescoping the bullet into the propellant is that if you simply light the propellant, quite a lot of gas will be wasted up the bore of the gun before the bullet gets seated. And since, obviously, the diameter of the cartridge is greater than the caliber, the bullet is positioned some small distance behind the rear end of the bore.

It is an interesting historical sidelight to find that this problem first made its appearance in the celebrated German 88mm Flak gun during World War II. The high temperatures and pressures in the chamber of this gun caused the initial few inches of the rifling to wear rapidly, increasing the apparent caliber in an erratic manner, so that when the gun fired a great deal of propellant was wasted, flowing past the shell before it was properly engaged in the rifling. The solution was to place a small gunpowder charge immediately behind the shell, in front of the normal smokeless powder charge, and extend a flash tube from the primer in the base of the case. When the primer fired, it immediately lit the gunpowder that exploded and blew the shell out of the mouth of the case and into the rifling, before the main charge exploded.

A similar solution has been adopted with CTA; a 'starter charge' behind the bullet explodes first and blows the bullet into the rifling, effectively sealing the bore by the time the main charge fires - and thus no propellant force is wasted.

The 50-caliber Ares TARG gun was 44.4 inches long and weighed 45lbs; the 50-caliber Browning M2HB is 65 inches long and weighs 84lbs. which indicates the measure of the saving in weight and bulk by a change of ammunition. Ares continued developing the gun for some years but in the late 1990s the company was taken over by Alliant Tech Systems and the project was closed down.

The torch was passed to a European consortium, CTA International, who have developed a 45mm cannon and a 50-caliber machine gun using CTA. The 50-caliber weapon was a four-barreled Gatling-type mechanical gun, with a rate of fire of 4000 rounds per minute, while the 45mm weapon uses a unique form of swinging chamber which turns transversely to allow a new round to be pushed in from one side and expels the spent case to the other. The chamber then swings back and the round is fired. Both these weapons were mere technology demonstrators and development is still in progress. It has been suggested that the 50-caliber design will not be followed up, since the size of the cartridge gives little scope for various improvements in propellant and projectile technology, and current development is concentrating upon cannon and artillery calibers.

The 40mm Machine Guns

In 1961 the US Army introduced the M79 40mm Grenade Launcher, a single-shot weapon firing a small grenade of 40mm diameter. Some 350,000 of them were made in the following decade after which the design was superseded by the M203, a clip-on device that fits under the M16 rifle.

Shortly after the 40mm weapon was introduced, one or two design agencies amused themselves by developing machine guns capable of firing the grenades; one advantage of this was that these weapons could fire a more powerful cartridge than the hand-held, shoulder-fired launchers, so the effective fighting range could be considerably increased. They met with short shrift; who on earth wanted a machine gun firing grenades?

In the late 1970s the Russians invaded Afghanistan and among the weapons that this revealed to the world was a machine gun firing 30mm grenades at about 65 rounds per minute to an effective range of about 12-1500 yards.

Immediately, every army in the west started clamoring for a similar weapon and the designers who had been slapped on the wrist for wasting time ten years previously were now assiduously sought out and given a free hand. Designs have since appeared in the USA, Spain, Germany, South Africa, Romania, Singapore and China. For my part, I prefer to call them 'grenade launchers' but their owners frequently classify them as machine guns, and I therefore include this short note on the species for those who might otherwise be mystified by references to the 'US Mark 19 machine gun', for example.

I do not intend to go into great detail on these weapons, since they are almost all alike and work on very simple lines. The western standard 40mm grenades fired by these weapons, while too potent to be comfortably fired from shoulder weapons, are still of relatively low power and low recoil force, due to their peculiar propellant system, known as the 'High-Low Pressure' system. Developed in Germany during World War II for a light anti-tank weapon, it relies upon holding the actual propellant in a small and strong compartment, forming part of the cartridge case directly in front of the primer cap. This compartment has a small vent (or vents) leading to the empty body of the cartridge case, and the grenade is fixed in the mouth in such a way that the effort needed to force it out is precisely fixed.

On firing, the propellant burns - at high pressure and therefore very quickly - in the small compartment, and the resulting gas is bled through the vent to expand in the body of the case at a much lower pressure which builds up to the figure specified for the release of the grenade. Once that pressure is reached (which only takes milliseconds), the grenade leaves the cartridge case and is launched at about 780 ft/sec to reach a maximum range of about 2000 yards. The use of this High-Low Pressure system allows the barrel to be much lighter and reduces the recoil force in comparison to a conventional system capable of producing the same performance.

The guns are invariably blowback, belt-fed, and capable of single shots or automatic fire at rates varying up to 300 rounds per minute. They can be tripod-mounted or mounted on armored vehicles, but when everything is considered, it has to be said that this is a very expensive and complicated method of throwing a small hand grenade a very long way. Their principal drawback is that they are relatively flat-trajectory weapons and are therefore useless against an enemy behind cover, however insubstantial that cover might be. A 60mm mortar is, in my opinion, far better value for money.

And Tomorrow?

Well, who knows? Not a lot is currently happening in the machine gun business; or if it is happening, it's taking place behind well-closed doors. The principal project in hand today appears to be the US development of the Objective Crew-Served Weapon (OCSW), which is officially defined as 'a two-man portable weapon system intended to provide high probability of suppression and incapacitation against light vehicles, slow-moving aircraft and water craft out to 1000 meters and pro-

An AGS-17 with the top cover open to show the belt feed mechanism.

the shell above the target with considerable precision, thus driving fragments down behind cover. We shall have to wait and see.

The other technology that has been lurking in the wings for some years is that of caseless ammunition. Removing the brass (or other metal) case from a round of ammunition saves a considerable amount of weight, but it brings a lot of problems in its train, not the least of which is the rapid heating of the gun chamber since there is no metal to absorb a large amount of the heat of the propellant explosion. A successful automatic rifle has been manufactured and is in limited service - the German G11 made by Heckler and Koch - and the obvious question, which then arose, was whether it was possible to make a machine gun working on the same principles. The answer appears to be 'Yes, but...' Both Heckler and Koch and GIAT, the French consortium, have displayed drawings of potential caseless weapons; but the difficulties of turning those drawings into practical weapons will be enormous, and neither company is in a position to bear the financial burden alone.

Which brings us firmly up against the bitter truth, which has already made itself obvious in the assault rifle field. It may be possible to develop a machine gun which is an advance upon what we already have; but will that advance be of sufficient magnitude to make it worth the enormous cost in time and money that the development of the weapon will demand? This, as I say, is not confined to the machine gun but it applies to every type of military weapon. A commercial designer has less of a problem; he can change the shape of the butt, give the gun some fancy handguard or engraving, or finish it in anodized green instead of chemical blue - there are always customers for something new. But armies are not seduced by such measures; they demand specific performance-related improvements. It must fire further, faster, produce better accuracy, more penetration of armor, and so forth and so on. And unless the designer and manufacturer can actually deliver that ten or fifteen percent improvement the customer will keep his wallet in his pocket.

So if you are contemplating designing that machine gun you dreamed up some time ago, all I can say is *Fine; go for it. But don't give up the day job.*

tected personnel up to a range of 2000 meters.' It is intended to replace both the M2HB Browning machine gun and the Mark 19 40mm machine gun in the infantry squad. Prototypes and technology demonstrators have been built, but it is not anticipated that the weapon will reach the hands of troops before 2015.

When all the persiflage and buzz-words are cleared away, what we are looking forward to appears to

be a shoulder-fired low-velocity 25mm cannon firing a high explosive projectile which may be purely anti-personnel or a dual-purpose anti-personnel and anti-materiel shell. The muzzle velocity will be about 1300 ft/sec, which will give it a somewhat flatter trajectory than the Mark 19, and the projectile will be fitted with an incredibly sophisticated fuse which will be linked to a laser rangefinder and a fire-control computer and be capable of bursting

A five-barrel Nordenfelt 65-caliber gun on a naval cone mounting.
(MoD Pattern Room/John Slough)

A five-barrel Gardner gun; it differs from the Nordenfelt by having five separate cartridge feeders and a rotary operating handle.
(MoD Pattern Room/John Slough)

An early British 45-caliber Maxim gun, with phosphor-Bronze water jacket and belt feed tray, on a heavy fortress-pattern tripod.

(MoD Pattern Room/John Slough)

A two-barrel Gardner gun has only one cartridge feeder, and there is a distribution mechanism, driven by the operating handle, that feeds the cartridges to each side alternately.

(MoD Pattern Room/John Slough)

The British XL73E2 light machine gun; the original 4.85mm version of what eventually became the 5.56mm L86E1 Light Support Weapon. It is fitted with the SUIT sight (Sight Unit, Infantry, Trilux) and is seen here complete with cleaning kit, sling, blank-firing attachment and sight cover, plus a bandolier of 4.85mm ammunition.

The French 'Tarasque' air defense gun mounts a 20mm M693 cannon, is fully power-operated and has an advanced electro-optical computing sight. The rate of fire is 900 rounds per minute.

All in one package; an FN MAG general purpose machine gun on a pintle mount, with roof brace and replacement side panel carrying a rocket launcher pod, ready to be bolted to a suitable helicopter to make an instant gunship.

50-caliber SLAP (Saboted Light Armor Penetrator) ammunition manufactured by Chartered Industries of Singapore (CIS) to accompany their CIS 50-caliber machine gun. The hard metal penetrator is held in a plastic sabot, which splits open and is discarded outside the gun muzzle.

A British soldier firing the L86A1 Light Support Weapon; this is really no more than a heavy-barrel version of the L85A1 5.56mm rifle, but had an additional girder support forend for the barrel, to which the bipod is attached. Note the use of a low-power optical sight; all infantry rifles and machine guns in British service now use this sight. Other arms of the service, less reliant upon personal weapons, use iron sights.

The M60D is not normally seen with a bipod. As might be gathered from the spade grips, it is intended to be pintle-mounted in helicopter doors or on vehicles.

The French Model 811 25mm cannon with dual feed. This is an externally-powered gun, using a rotating camshaft with a complex spiral groove cut in its surface. As it revolves, a lug attached to the bolt rides back and forth in the groove to perform the firing cycle. The mechanism is geared to deliver 150 or 650 rounds per minute at choice.

The range of projectiles available from Oerlikon in 20x128mm (KAA) caliber.
From left to right: APHC-I-T (Armor Piercing Hard Core, Incendiary, Tracer); SAP-HE-T (Semi-Armor Piercing, High Explosive, Tracer, with base fuze); AP-HE (Armor Piercing, High Explosive, with base fuze); HE-I (High Explosive, Incendiary, with base fuze); HE-I-T (High Explosive, Incendiary, Tracer, with nose fuze); HE-I (High Explosive, Incendiary, with nose fuze); TP-T (Target Practice, Tracer); TP (Target Practice).

The McDonnell Douglas ASP-30 30mm lightweight cannon demonstrates its ability to interchange with the 50-caliber machine gun by being mounted on the standard M3 tripod, ready for some desert firing. The sandbags suggest that the recoil might be substantial.

After their revolver failed to make an impression, Heckler & Koch went back to conventional designs and produced this '40mm Grenade Machine Gun' in the mid-1990s.

Below, a sectioned view of a 40mm HE grenade. This shows the high-pressure chamber over the primer, the vent holes and the low-pressure chamber. It also reveals just how little of the whole thing actually contains explosive.

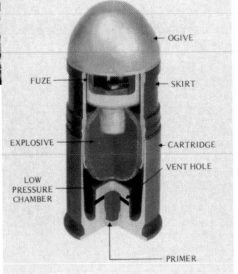

OGIVE

FUZE — SKIRT

EXPLOSIVE — CARTRIDGE

VENT HOLE

LOW PRESSURE CHAMBER

PRIMER

The most modern type of projectile for the 40mm machine guns is this HE Dual Purpose grenade. It is primarily a shaped charge for armor penetration, but the charge itself is surrounded by steel balls set in resin, so as to form lethal fragments around the point of burst when used in the anti-personnel role.

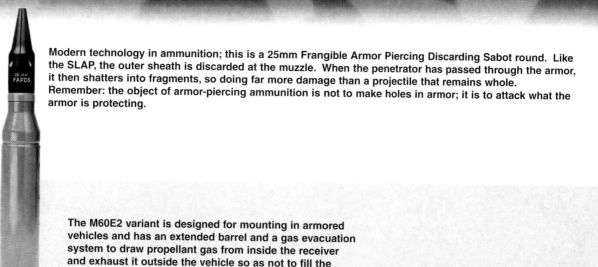

Modern technology in ammunition; this is a 25mm Frangible Armor Piercing Discarding Sabot round. Like the SLAP, the outer sheath is discarded at the muzzle. When the penetrator has passed through the armor, it then shatters into fragments, so doing far more damage than a projectile that remains whole. Remember: the object of armor-piercing ammunition is not to make holes in armor; it is to attack what the armor is protecting.

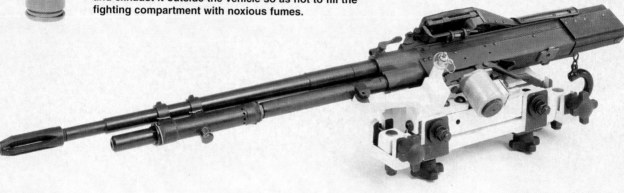

The M60E2 variant is designed for mounting in armored vehicles and has an extended barrel and a gas evacuation system to draw propellant gas from inside the receiver and exhaust it outside the vehicle so as not to fill the fighting compartment with noxious fumes.

A Norwegian soldier firing a 50-caliber M2HB Browning gun fitted into a Vinghøgs NM 152 Softmount. This type of mount began appearing in the late 1980s principally for air defense guns, as the mounting soaks up a great deal of the recoil force and vibration and allows more accurate control of the gun. The gun is also fitted with a 'red dot' type of collimating sight, which allows the gunner to keep both eyes open, and appears to project an aiming marking into the same plane as the target.

A 50-caliber M2HB with Quick Change Barrel, developed by Saco Defense of Saco, Maine, in the late 1970s. In addition to manufacturing complete guns, the company, like others, provides a conversion kit allowing any old-style M2HB to be converted to the QCB standard.

The basic M60 General Purpose machine gun. This is the original version with the bipod attached to the barrel, making things awkward when the time came to change the barrel.

The Spanish 'Merola' cannon is a 12-barrel 20mm weapon adopted by the Spanish Navy as a close-in weapon system for the destruction of anti-ship missiles. This rare picture shows experimental equipment in 1983, in which the Meroka gun battery was adapted for ground use.

Another view of the land-based Meroka, showing the control cabin with sights, the power unit behind it, and the ammunition supply. The idea was never pursued beyond this prototype model.

You never know what might fetch the customers. An air defense turret mounting a 20mm Gatling cannon plus four British 'Blowpipe' missiles, all ready to fit into your own armored car. Displayed at the Paris Air Show in 1985, it failed to reappear at later exhibitions.

The Spanish Ameli 5.56mm machine gun uses a roller-delayed blowback system of operation derived from the CETME rifles, which are used by the Spanish army and related to the Heckler and Koch rifles and machine guns.

When General Electric developed a 50-caliber Gatling gun; they called it the 'GECAL 50'. This is the six-barrel version. There was also a three-barrel model that the Army preferred, and this was taken into service as the GAU-19/A.

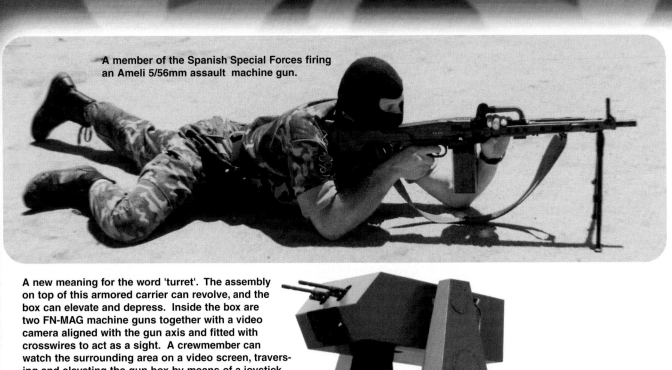

A member of the Spanish Special Forces firing an Ameli 5/56mm assault machine gun.

A new meaning for the word 'turret'. The assembly on top of this armored carrier can revolve, and the box can elevate and depress. Inside the box are two FN-MAG machine guns together with a video camera aligned with the gun axis and fitted with crosswires to act as a sight. A crewmember can watch the surrounding area on a video screen, traversing and elevating the gun box by means of a joystick, and should he see an enemy, he merely lays the crosswire on him and presses the *'fire'* button.

25mm Armor-Piercing, Fin-Stabilized Discarding-Sabot cartridges manufactured by Mecar of Belgium. The plastic nose cap and sabot conceal a finned tungsten alloy penetrator, which can go through 1.2 inches (30mm) of steel armor at 2000 meters range.

A rose by any other name . . . This is the Chinese Type 54 12.7mm machine gun. Look closely and you will soon realize it is actually a Russian DShK 38/46 in a recoil-absorbing mounting, atop a Chinese tank. But when made in China it becomes a Type 54.

Another air defense combination, this time seen at the AUSA display in Washington DC in the late 1980s; a 20mm M167 Vulcan Gatling gun fitted with auxiliary 'Stinger' missiles. Several similar proposals have been put forward over the past decade or so, but very few of them appear to have attracted any serious interest.

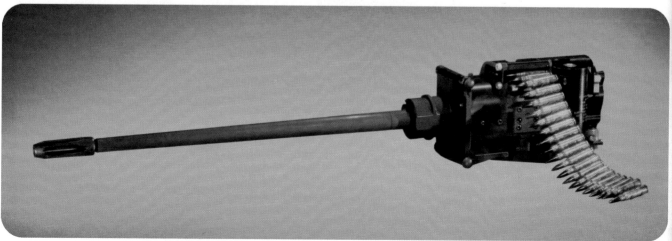

The 7.62mm Chain Gun. Originally developed by the Hughes Helicopter Company it now flies under the McDonnell Douglas flag and forms part of the armament of the McDonnell Douglas 500MD Defender light attack helicopter. Its principal user is the British Army who mount it as the co-axial turret gun in their Warrior infantry fighting vehicle.

The dual belt-feed system of the FN BRG15 heavy machine gun; a similar system can be seen on several Oerlikon cannons. Each belt enters the gun through its own 'gate' and either gate can be thrown out of action and the other brought into the 'feed' position by a simple lever.

Right, announced in June 1979, the Dover Devil was a proposed heavy machine gun that could be produced n any caliber from 50 to 20mm. This is the 20mm version, compared to a soldier of average stature. The project languished for some time before being revived, in 50-caliber, as a potential General Purpose Heavy Machine Gun (GPHMG).

Below, the component parts of the Dover Devil; the whole thing was built up around three 'chassis tubes', two of which also acted as gas pistons and carried the bolt. The receiver, at the top, was merely a lightweight dust cover instead of the more usual complex piece of machining. The Dover Devil had no success but it acted as a stimulant to designers in several countries.

What distinguishes this Bren gun from others is the slotted flash hider and the almost-straight magazine, indicating that it is chambered for the 7.62x51mm NATO cartridge. Being rimless, this cartridge no longer demanded the familiar curved magazine always associated with the Bren.

The Russian AGS-17 37mm grenade machine gun has a curiously top-heavy appearance, which is perhaps why the operator sits on the tripod leg.

The Winchester 5.56mm Penetrator: on the left, the complete bullet; next, a sectioned bullet with the steel front half of the core just distinguishable; then a bullet with the jacket peeled away to show the complete two-piece core; finally, another sectioned view.

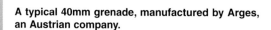

A typical 40mm grenade, manufactured by Arges, an Austrian company.

A closer view of the Spanish Santa Barbara AGL-40 machine gun, loaded with a belt of practice ammunition.

Even the small calibers can do damage; a sheet of typical 10mm steel APC armor which has been pierced by Winchester 5.56mm Penetrator ammunition

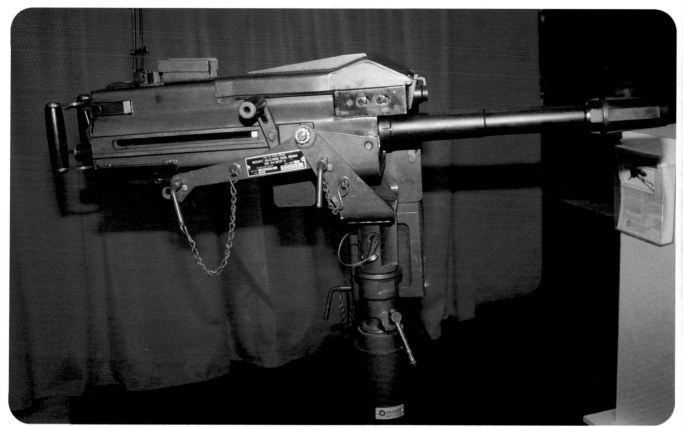

The U.S. Mark 19 40mm machine gun.

The FN BRG-15 heavy machine gun in 15.5mm caliber, on a test stand in the FN experimental range in Belgium.

The Belgian FN-MAG general-purpose machine gun demonstrating its versatility in a remote-controlled turret on top of an armored personnel carrier. It can be aimed and fired from the inside of the vehicle, using electronic sights. Note, though, that it still carries a bipod and has a pistol grip, so that if necessary it can be dismounted and taken into action by the squad on foot.

CHAPTER EIGHT

THE AUTOMATIC CANNON

CANNON CAN MEAN different things to different people, but for our purposes here cannon means the automatic weapon of a caliber between 16mm and 30mm. While in most respects they are similar to machine guns, they do have characteristics of their own and, due to their large caliber and powerful propelling charges, have some features not found in the lesser calibers of small arms.

The significant feature of cannon, in broad terms, is that they are capable of firing high explosive projectiles rather than just inert bullets, and their object is to be destructive towards materiel rather than against personnel. The cannon came into prominence as a means of arming aircraft against other aircraft, and this has been its major application ever since; it has also had a wide application in air defense, and in recent years has begun to achieve some prominence as the armament of light armored vehicles of the type variously called Infantry Fighting Vehicles (IFVs) or Mechanized Infantry Combat Vehicles (MICVs). This has led to more interest being taken in their potential for attacking light armor and some highly specialized ammunition has been developed for this purpose. Another byproduct of this role has been the development of weapons capable of feeding from two belts of ammunition at choice, so that one can be filled with ammunition suited to the weapon's primary role, such as air defense, while the other can be filled with ammunition more suited to a secondary role, for example armor-piercing ammunition for defense of the position against attack by armored vehicles. We might also note that the use of cannon in the air defense role, which had begun to decline in the late 1950s due to their ineffectiveness against high-speed modern aircraft, began to climb again in the 1970s with the adoption of modern radar, computer and electro-optical sighting technologies, which gave the

gun a far better chance of hitting than had hitherto been the case.

It might justifiably be argued that the principles upon which cannon work are the same as those upon which any other firearm works; this is quite true, but as already said, cannon have some features of their own which make them worth studying separately. Moreover there has been so little written on the subject of cannon that even if the following chapter becomes rather more descriptive of weapons than of principles, it is likely to be found useful in bringing all the cannon technology into one place and providing an overview of a somewhat neglected area of study.

Maxim and MacLean

The history of the automatic cannon is generally said to begin with the Becker design of 1915, but there are earlier contenders for the title, even though their weapons were of a caliber outside our immediate frame of reference.

When Hiram Maxim developed his machine gun in the 1880s he was already alert to the possibility of enlarging it so that it could fire explosive projectiles. The most receptive people for machine guns at that time appear to have been navies, who were concerned about the up-and-coming torpedo boat. This subject has already been explored in the chapter on early mechanical machine guns, and need not be gone over again except to remind you that 37mm became the smallest practical caliber capable of firing an explosive projectile. Maxim, however, appears to have set his sights rather higher than that, because there is a record in the Proceedings of the Department of the Director of Artillery for 1885 which records an application, on 17 July 1885, from the Maxim Gun Company for a supply of 47mm Hotchkiss cartridges to assist them in their development. At that time both the Royal Artillery and the Royal Navy were using the

3-pounder Hotchkiss single-shot gun of 47mm caliber and the Machine Gun Committee had encouraged Maxim develop an automatic gun to fire the 3-pounder round. But the cartridge case was not of a size that could be conveniently belt-fed in those early days, and Maxim was forced to adopt a vertical feed similar to that used by the Gardner gun. As can be seen from the illustration, this was not very practical, and Maxim eventually abandoned it and settled for 37mm and a more convenient size of cartridge.

Even though, as shown in the extracts quoted in Chapter Three, the Royal Navy was no longer interested in a large-caliber Maxim gun, the 37mm Maxim Automatic gun sold moderately well to other naval customers but received its biggest boost when a quantity purchased by the Boers were used as field army weapons against the British in the South African War. The rapid firing of the little gun caused it to acquire the nickname 'The Pom-Pom', which stuck thereafter. There is a story told of Maxim attempting to interest the King of Denmark in the weapon in the 1890s; on informing His Majesty that the ammunition cost 6s 6d per round (about $1.25 at the then rate of exchange) the King declined to order any guns on the grounds that "one gun would bankrupt my Kingdom in two hours."

The Pom-Pom was no different to any other Maxim machine gun in its mechanism, merely being bigger in all dimensions. It used the same toggle lock and method of belt feed, was water-cooled, and its rate of fire was originally 400 rpm but this was later slowed to 300 - probably more for economic reasons than for mechanical or tactical ones.

The Pom-Pom was followed by a second weapon, which more closely approximates to today's cannon. The McLean 37mm machine gun was a long-barreled weapon, much larger than the Maxim, and firing a

37x137mm US Navy one-pounder cartridge probably based on the Maxim/Hotchkiss projectile but with a larger cartridge to give higher velocity. Samuel McLean and O.M. Lissak, the inventors, whom we have already met in connection with the early days of the Lewis gun, developed this gas-operated weapon, which appeared in about 1905. What few accounts there are indicate that the weapon functioned well, but it was something which didn't fit current tactical ideas and it therefore met with very little interest in either the USA or Britain. However, it appears that the idea was accepted by the Russians, who either bought or manufactured under license a number of guns, which were used for close defense of harbors against torpedo-boat attack. Some were given to Finland in the 1920s and a one or two survive there in museums, while what is perhaps the only specimen remaining in the west is in the Royal Artillery Museum at Woolwich. Its presence there suggests that, like its companion the Lowell machine gun, it must have been submitted for test in Britain at some time, but we can find no record of it being put through its paces.

The original Becker cannon in use as an anti-aircraft weapon in 1918.

The Becker Cannon

The direct ancestor of all of today's automatic cannon is, without doubt, the Becker gun. It was developed with the intention of furnishing German Gotha bombers with a formidable defensive armament, and bearing in mind the fact that the St. Petersburg Declaration still had some force during the World War I, it is open to question how the inventors justified their choice of caliber, since the projectile was well below the prescribed figure of 400 grams. It seems probable that the argument advanced was that the gun was an anti-materiel weapon, with machines as its target, and not an anti-personnel weapon. I have also seen the suggestion that the inventors produced the first ammunition with solid ball bullets rather than explosive shells, thus avoiding the 400-gram issue, but if that was the case their good intentions didn't last very long and explosive ammunition was very soon on issue. Indeed, before the war ended, five types of ammunition - ball, tracer, HE, AP/T and Incendiary had been developed.

Two brothers named Cönders, employees of the Becker Stahlwerk of Reinickendorf, Germany in 1915-16, designed the gun. Of 20mm caliber, it worked on simple blowback action, using advanced primer ignition to obtain a delay before the breech opened. Feed was from a vertical 15-shot box and it could be fired

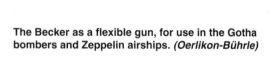

The Becker as a flexible gun, for use in the Gotha bombers and Zeppelin airships. *(Oerlikon-Bührle)*

When the Seebach company took over the Becker patents, they attempted to market the cannon as an infantry support and anti-tank gun, in the form shown here. *(Oerlikon-Bührle)*

by single shots or at 300 rounds per minute. Refinement of the design continued throughout the war, but weapons were issued for service use during the period of development. Records are no longer available to say how many were made, but they were certainly installed on some Gotha bombers, 131 were issued to German army anti-aircraft battalions, and the Allied Disarmament Commission records show that 392 guns were confiscated at the end of the war, most of which were destroyed forthwith.

It is interesting to speculate on whether either of the Cönders brothers was the 'Engineer Cönders' who managed to promote the multi-chambered long-range cannon known as the V-4 or the 'High Pressure Pump' during World War II. I have been unable to find any confirmation one way or the other.

A second, and generally forgotten, 20mm weapon developed in Germany during the war was the Erhardt cannon, produced by the *Rheinische Metallwaren und Munitionsfabrik* of Düsseldorf. It is believed that the German aviation corps approached Erhardt with a request for a potent machine gun, since (as we have seen) the Dreyse machine gun made by RM&M was widely used in German aircraft. Erhardt simply scaled-up the Dreyse machine gun and developed a suitable cartridge. Apparently he started with the Becker 20mm round but quickly dropped it in favor of a 20mm round of his own devising. About fifty prototypes were made but the project did not reach the series production stage before the war ended.

In the post-war years the Treaty of Versailles restricted the manufac-ture of weapons in Germany quite severely, and RM&M were, with Krupp, the only firms allowed to manufacture artillery, and they were further restricted in what calibers they could make. So RM&M (who soon adopted the name 'Rheinmetall') set up a company in Holland called HAIHA, an acronym for the *Hollandisch Artillerie Industrie en Handelsmaatschappij,* and began advertising the 20mm HAIHA cannon as a suitable infantry anti-tank weapon; this was, as you might imagine, the Erhardt cannon coming round for a second bite at the cherry, but it failed to make much impact. HAIHA managed to survive by selling war-surplus arms acquired from Germany, but when that supply ran out the company folded in the early 1930s, and so far as is known few, if any, of the 20mm weapons were made or sold. The design was passed to Solothurn AG of Switzerland, another Rheinmet-all off-shoot, went through some changes and re-appeared as the Solothurn S5-100, which we will encounter in due course.

After the war the Becker company were forbidden to manufac-ture weapons at all, and they therefore sold their patents to a Swiss firm, the *Maschinenbau AG* of Seebach. This company made some small improvements and placed it on the market as the Semag-Becker Cannon. It was on a light wheeled carriage and was offered as a light infantry support gun with possible applications in the anti-tank role. It failed to sell, and in 1924 the Maschinenbau AG went into receivership.

The Oerlikon Cannon

In 1923 the *Magdeburger Werkzeug-Maschinenfabrik* (Magdeburg Machine Tool Works) took over almost all the share capital of the *Schweizerische Werkzeug-Maschinenfabrik* (Swiss Machine Tool Works) of Oerlikon, a suburb of Zurich, which had been founded in 1906. In the following year they sent Emil Bührle to Oer-likon to examine their purchase and make proposals for reorganiza-tion. As a result of his proposals he was made manager, with about 80 men in his workforce. Since the firm was now in foreign ownership the 'Swiss' part of the title had to be dropped, and the company became the *Werkzeug-Maschinen-fabrik Oerlikon*. Bührle realized that the market for machine tools was, at that time, relatively depressed, and looking around for something else to occupy his fac-tory, his eye fell on the ailing Maschinenbau AG. In the summer of 1924 Oerlikon took over all the patents covering the Becker gun, together with the prototype anti-tank and anti-aircraft guns developed in Seebach, and also took on most of the weapon technicians of the defunct company. By the end of the year orders had been obtained from Finland and Mexico, and the Oerlikon gun had arrived. Bührle began buying shares in the company; by 1929 he held the majority and in 1937 he took over the company, renaming it the *Werkzeugmaschirieenfabrik Oer-likon, Bührle & Co.*

The original Oerlikon gun, as derived from the Becker design, was the Model L; it had a rate of fire of 150-170 rounds per minute and fired a shell with a muzzle velocity of 650 m/sec. Mechanically, it was a simple weapon; I once heard it described as 'a giant Sten gun' which was perhaps carrying things too far, but wasn't really far from the truth. It was a blowback gun, using advanced primer ignition (or differential recoil - the terms are interchangeable) to fire the cartridge before the working parts - in this case the bolt - have reached the fully-forward position. This led to an unusual cartridge, a case with a 'rebated rim' where the diameter of the rim is considerable less than the diameter of the bottom end of the case. In a submachine gun or rifle-caliber machine gun, advanced primer ignition means fir-ing the primer while the case is partly outside the chamber, but such is the speed of the moving parts and the momentum they have gathered, the case is invariably entirely inside the chamber before the pressure builds up inside it. But the cartridge case for a 20mm cannon is consider-ably larger, and firing it sufficiently far in advance becomes an imprecise

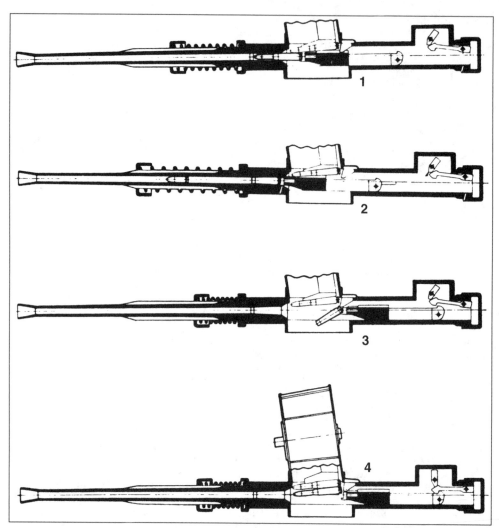

The blowback operation of the early Oerlikon cannons:
1) bolt moving forward, round being rammed into chamber;
2) cartridge is fired while the bolt is still moving forward, and this movement is resisted by the rearward explosion force; 3) the bolt is driven rearward by the gas pressure and the case is extracted;
4) bolt is stopped by the buffer and the cycle is ready to begin again. *(Oerlikon-Bührle)*

business if a rimmed case is used. By using a rebated rim the tip of the bolt and the extractor can grip the round and ram it into the chamber and continue ramming it in until the bolt entering behind the case closes the mouth of the chamber. Then, and only then, the primer fires - as the case is checked by friction as it meets the constricting chamber - and any minor variation in timing matters little since the whole round is enclosed in the chamber and perfectly safe. In effect we have exactly the same action as we would have in a submachine gun, but the chamber has been extended backwards to form a shroud around the cartridge.

The Model L was followed, in 1927, by the Model S with a rate of fire of 280 rpm and a muzzle velocity of 830 m/sec. This was the gun that really established the company's reputation, and it went into serious production in 1931. In the same year the Model SSG was produced, a heavy anti-tank machine gun for infantry use. This was not particularly successful, although it was continuously improved in the years that followed, and in 1932 the company turned again to the

The 20mm Oerlikon FF gun was taken into service by the German army as their '2cm Flak 28' in the early 1930s; most of these guns eventually went to the Navy, as they were replaced in field units by the later Flak 30, but the Flak 28 title was also used for 20mm Oerlikon guns taken from over-run countries in the war years.

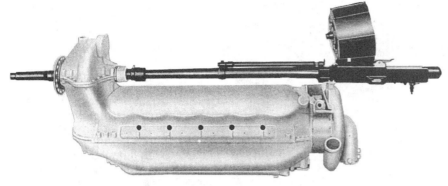

The Hispano-Suiza HS404 gun mounted on the Hispano-Suiza 12-cylinder Ycs engine for the French Dewoitine 501 fighter in 1935. *(Oerlikon-Bührle)*

also took some time to persuade designers that guns could be mounted in the wing, outside the propeller arc, and so avoid the complications of synchronization. It took even more time to convince pilots that they could have guns in the wings - they were used to having them inboard where they could (in theory, at any rate) take some action if they happened to jam. But more and more designers started putting guns out of reach of the pilot, and by this time the guns were becoming more reliable, so that eventually the objections were overcome. But even

aircraft field as having the greatest potential. They developed a new engine-mounted cannon, the Model FFS, which sat between the cylinder banks of a vee-type engine and fired through the propeller boss; this was licensed to the Hispano-Suiza company but after some experience with it they were not happy with its rate of fire and Mark Birgkit, the Hispano company's engine designer, turned his hand to gun designing and made some changes to the Oerlikon. Instead of being a pure blowback, the gun was modified to operate in a similar manner to the Scotti machine gun, using gas to unlock the breech after a short recoil movement, after which the operation reverted to blowback, the cartridge energy actually opening the breechblock. The recoil movement was used to drive the feed system, and the overall effect was to push the rate of fire from about 400 rds/min to about 700. This design sold quite well, in competition with the Oerlikon guns, and was to achieve considerable success during World War II as the Hispano HS404 cannon.

The next Oerlikon designs were the FF model for wing-mounting in fighter aircraft, and the SS for anti-aircraft use by field armies. This latter gun had the rate of fire stepped up to 450 rounds per minute and, being less restricted as to dimensions and weight, had a longer barrel and reached a muzzle velocity of 800 m/sec. The Model ISS (for Improved SS) came along in the early part of 1939 and provided a higher rate of fire than had the SS.

During the 1930s the adoption of cannon became more common; it could hardly be called 'widespread' since it was rarely possible to fit cannon into older designs of airplane, and the more general adoption had to wait for the late 1930s low-wing monoplane fighters. It

The HS404 could also be used as an anti-aircraft weapon and was widely adopted in that role by both the US and British navies during World War II. *(BMARC)*

Another view of the HS404, taken at the BMARC factory in Grantham as production began in 1942. (BMARC)

then there were some rather desperate adaptations of cannon to earlier-generation airplanes that, although they worked, tended to cut the speed and maneuverability of the machine.

It was this reluctance to set about a total re-design - because of the expense - that made other gunmakers reluctant to dip their toes into the cannon pool. An exception was the Madsen company who, in 1926 produced a 20mm weapon which was simply their well-tried Madsen machine gun scaled up. This, with a cartridge of Madsen's own design, was offered for sale as an aircraft weapon but found few takers, and in the early 1930s they re-launched it as an anti-aircraft or anti-tank gun, in which guise it did rather better, but the sales were not such as to encourage other makers to try their luck. Madsen were, though, quick to realize that an increase in caliber for their ground gun would provide them with a more potent weapon and they experimented with a new 23mm cartridge. They then re-entered the aircraft cannon field, and exhibited some 23mm guns in various aircraft in the Paris Air Show of 1936. But they do not appear to have found any buyers and the 23mm project was wiped out by the outbreak of war in 1939 and never heard of again.

The Hotchkiss company, which had developed a useful anti-tank gun in 25mm caliber in the early 1930s, took the cartridge, turned it from being rimmed into being rimless, and built an automatic cannon around it in about 1936. It had a useful performance - almost 3000 feet per second and 250-300 rounds per minute - but very few buyers.

If the aircraft manufacturers were slow to see the benefits of the cannon, then, said the gunmakers, let us try the other side of the coin - the anti-aircraft side. Here they were rather more successful.

Oerlikon had been promoting their cannons as anti-aircraft weapons ever since they began making them, but when the airplane was so flimsy that it could be brought down by rifle or machine-gun fire, there was little or no incentive to spend money on heavier weapons. By the beginning of the 1930s though, it was becoming obvious that those days were drawing to a close and some serious thought had to be given to air defense. This was the period when a British politician assured his audience that 'the bomber will always get through', and he wasn't far wrong at that time. The bomber was seen as the greatest threat, and even though funds were scarce, money was found for air defense. What most people failed to appreciate was the danger (at least to armies, if not the civil population) of the low-flying ground attack airplane, and consequently the category known as 'light air defense' was generally put to one side as being something that could be attended to as and when the

The French Hotchkiss 25mm as employed by the Japanese during World War II. This one was photographed after its capture by US troops on Saipan.

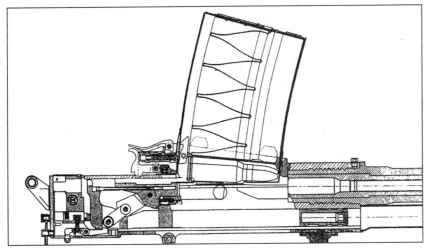

The mechanism is the Hotchkiss 25mm cannon; here the bolt is fully to the rear and held by the sear.

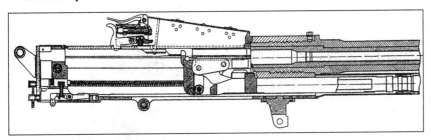

The Hotchkiss with the bolt closed, the locking link lifted, and the tail of the piston slide driving the firing pin into the cap.

major-caliber anti-aircraft artillery had been organized.

The success of Oerlikon led other manufacturers into the cannon field. Hispano-Suiza, who eventually became Oerlikon's principal competitor, came into the cannon business by accident, as we have seen. Other people with more gunmaking background, strangely enough did less well in the international market place, though they managed to satisfy their own national demands in many cases.

Solothurn (or Rheinmetall through Solothurn) became a major supplier to the German armed forces in 1934, with a powerful 20mm cannon that was adopted by the Navy, and then the Luftwaffe (who were responsible for anti-aircraft defense) as the 2cm Flak 30. It introduced a new belted cartridge of Solothurn design, which survived to become the popular 20x139mm round. Mechanically speaking the gun was little more than an enlarged version of the Solothurn MG30; it fired from an open bolt, and it even had two triggers, one for single shots and one for automatic fire. The gun had a cyclic rate of fire of 280 rounds per minute, but 120 rpm was considered the practical rate. The high explosive shell had a muzzle velocity of 2950 ft/sec and an effective ceiling of 6500 feet.

The Flak 30 made its combat debut in the Spanish Civil War, being taken to Spain by the Condor Legion, and experience there led the Luftwaffe to demand a higher rate of fire. By this time (1937) Rheinmetall-Borsig (as the company was now known) had enough on their plate manufacturing heavier weapons, and the Luftwaffe therefore went to Mauserwerke and asked if they would kindly double the rate of fire. Mauser simply took a leaf from the Rheinmetall book; if Rheinmetall could build a cannon by enlarging the MG30, then Mauser could improve it by enlarging the MG34, and that was precisely what they did, replacing the bolt and accelerator with their own components. Outwardly the gun remained the same, but the new Flak 38 had a cyclic rate of 480 and a practical rate of just over 200 rounds per minute. The mounting remained the same and it is virtually impossible to tell the difference between a Flak 30 and a Flak 38 without a close examination of the guns.

The Bofors company of Sweden also produced a useful 20mm automatic cannon for anti-aircraft use, but at more or less the same time they produced a 40mm automatic gun which virtually conquered the world and which put the 20mm out of the running, except in Sweden.

World War II finally gave the automatic cannon the chance to prove itself, which it did, handsomely. Navies relied upon cannon to deal with air attacks, armies used cannon for the same purpose, and aircraft designers gradually moved away from the machine gun

The 20mm Flak 30 in quadruple (*'Flakvierling'*) form, in action as a ground gun. This type of equipment, while primarily for air defense, delivered shattering firepower on to such obstacles as machine gun posts and small pillboxes. The gun was Rheinmetall design, sold under the Solothurn name, and was descended from the Dreyse machine gun.

to begin designing aircraft capable of carrying cannon.

What led to the more general adoption of aircraft cannon was the realization that rifle-caliber bullets were no longer sufficient to do lethal damage to a modern airplane. Machines now had metal structures, armor plating around the pilot, self-sealing gasoline tanks and various other features which made them relatively resistant to attack by simple ball bullets fired by anything less than a 50-caliber machine gun. The explosive projectile of a cannon, however, made nonsense of self-sealing gas tanks, and the armor-piercing shells made colanders of the pilot's protection; half-a-dozen well-placed 20mm HE-Incendiary shells could put paid to virtually any airplane in existence in 1941.

But the story of the airplane versus the airplane gun is rather like the story of the tank versus the anti-tank gun. For every advance by one side, the other would make a counter-advance. If the tanks got thicker, the guns got more powerful, so the tanks got thicker still, so the guns developed more specialized ammunition... and so on until the present day where the see-saw is still making regular movements. In just the same way, as soon as the 20mm cannon began shredding airplanes, the designers set about making them tougher, making them more powerful so that they could carry thicker armor and developing more efficient protection for the fuel tanks. At the same time aircraft speeds were increasing, so that engagement times were getting shorter.

By 1943 the Germans were being confronted with better-protected versions of the B-17 Flying Fortress, and it became a very difficult task to bring one of those down with a simple burst of 20mm fire. So the Luftwaffe did some experiments and decreed that they had to

The Mauser 25mm Model E feeds from both sides at will. This is a gas-operated weapon using double locking flaps, a modified Friberg-Kjellman system.

A single-feed version of the 30mm Mauser Model F cannon, which uses a similar system of operation to the Model E.

have a cannon capable of downing a B-17 with not more than five shots. The result of that was the development of the first 30mm cannon and, concurrently, the development of the 'mine shell' - a high-capacity high explosive shell filled with aluminized explosive.

In fact, Rheinmetall had foreseen this well before the war and had developed a 30mm cannon, the MK101, and demonstrated it to the Luftwaffe in 1939. At that time the Director-General of Equipment was General Erst Udet, a fighter pilot of

World War I, who knew that the rate of fire was of prime importance, and since the MK101 did not measure up to his standards in that respect, he turned it down. As a general rule, cannon fired at 350-400 rounds per minute, a leisurely rate by machine gun standards, though not really bad when you consider the size of the cartridge they had to shift. Even so, this was no excuse in the eyes of the users, and the designers were constantly being urged to improve the rates. Rheinmetall overhauled their design to become the MK103, increasing the rate of fire and giving it electric ignition, and limited numbers of this model were taken into service, more for the purpose of evaluation than anything else. The company kept on working on the design and by the end of the war had perfected the MK108, which in late 1944 began to appear in some numbers in fighter aircraft.

The bottleneck in speeding up the rate of fire lay principally in the time wasted while the bolt traveled back and forth; it needed a long movement firstly to try and absorb some of the recoil force, so as not to transmit it to the mounting on the

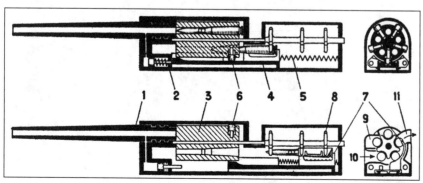

A simplified view of the revolver gun: 1) barrel; 2) receiver; 3) cylinder; 4) the piston slide; 5) return spring; 6) roller supporting the cylinder; 7) feed hook; 8) feed star; 9) ejector; 10) be lt entry; 11) belt exit. *(BMA RC)*

aircraft, and secondly because of the physical size of the cartridge. The average 20mm cartridge of the early war period was about six inches in length, so the bolt had to move just over a foot between each shot. As usual the German authorities turned to the Mauserwerke and, also as usual, they produced a solution - the revolver gun. Like the revolver pistol, the cartridge is held in a revolving cylinder and fired as the chamber comes into alignment with the barrel. But, unlike the revolver, a gas piston rotates the cylinder and the ammunition is fed continuously to the weapon by means of a belt. If we take a hypothetical gun with a four-chambered cylinder as our example, the cylinder is charged in stages by the action of a slide driven by the gas piston, which collects a round from the supply belt and rams it part-way into a chamber; on the next stroke, as the next shot is fired, the slide rams the round completely into the chamber, and on the next stroke the chamber is aligned with the barrel and fired, either electrically or by a percussion mechanism. At this point the rear end of the chamber is closed by a solid part of the receiver, which also carries the ignition system. On the next stroke the cylinder moves round again and the empty case is ejected, so that the loading can recommence as the slide goes forward for the fourth time.

Since there is no need to have a massive bolt flying back and forth

The Oerlikon 30mm KCA is described as a high-performance revolver cannon, and with a muzzle velocity of 3380 ft/sec, a 13-ounce shell and a rate of fire of 1350 rounds a minute, this would seem to be a well-founded claim.

the gun can be reasonably compact, and since the loading is carried out in stages the rate of fire is greatly increased. The only real drawbacks to this system are the need to have some external power to load the weapon initially, since, as shown above, it takes three operating cycles to bring the first round into the firing position. The high rate of fire leads to rapid barrel wear, but this is applicable to all weapons, and in the case of aircraft cannon it is something you simply have to accept unless you are prepared to go to a multiple-barrel solution, whereupon you lose the compactness. There is also a problem with overheating of the chambers and cylinder that could lead to a cook-off when the gunner releases the trigger, since there are always

three rounds in the cylinder when the gun stops firing. As with barrel wear, this is something you have to live with.

Mauser were still working on their revolver gun when the war ended; they did get early specimens into action, but they were far from reaching the complete solution in the spring of 1945. And it was the revolver gun that, more than almost anything else, caught the fancy of the gun designers in many countries when the principle became known. The British and French developed the Aden and DEFA guns, the Swiss developed the Oerlikon 20GRK and KCA, the Americans developed the Pontiac M39, and in later years the Russians got into the act as well. It has to be said, though, that some of the early development was pretty disheartening; in an effort to keep the rate of wear down and avoid the

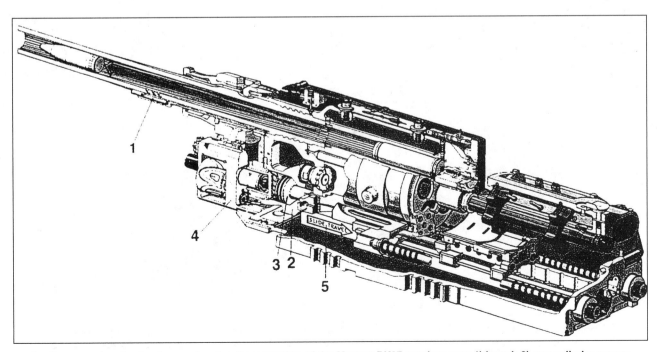

A rather more involved cutaway showing the operation of the Mauser BK27 revolver gun: 1) barrel; 2) gas cylinder assembly; 3) gas piston; 4) pyrotechnic recocking housing; 5) front slide. (Mauserwerke)

dreaded cook-off, some guns had velocities so low that the pilot of a high-speed jet was in danger of overtaking his shells and shooting himself down. Oerlikon were quick into the revolver field with their 20GRK gun in 1951, but the air forces of the world were still wary of the idea, and Oerlikon were also later to admit that they were ahead of their time in attempting to introduce it. They went away, put a great deal more effort into research, and re-appeared in 1970 with the 30mm KCA.

France and Britain both began studies based directly upon the Mauser MK213/30, with the result that they produced near-identical solutions, the British being the Aden (Armaments Development and ENfield being jointly responsible for the design) and the French the DEFA (Direction d'Etudes et Fabrication d'Armement) and both firing a short-cased round at a relatively low velocity. What was worse was that neither could fire the ammunition of the other, even though NATO standardization was, at that time, the flavor of the month. For once, common sense prevailed, the two establishments got together over a common drawing board, and while their guns still retain their own identities, they at least managed to standardize on a round of ammunition with reasonable performance.

Although the example of revolver working that I gave above was based (for the same of simplicity) on a four-chambered cylinder, other configurations are more generally used. The Aden/DEFA series used five-chambered cylinders, others use six or seven. A French derivative of the DEFA development, the GIAT (Groupement Indistrielle des Armements Terrestre) 30mm M791 uses seven chambers to produce 2500 rounds per minute out of a single-barreled gun, which is a quite startling performance. Mauser came back into the business in the 1980s and produced a five-chambered model in a new 27mm caliber, especially to arm the Multi-Role Combat Aircraft then being developed.

In the continuing search for high rates of fire the Gatling externally-powered type of gun began to surge ahead in the 1970s, but the demand for a source of electricity and problems with delays in getting the gun up to its maximum rate of fire tended to restrict its applications in the air-fighting field. One way round this, which has been most widely explored by Russian designers, is to retain the Gatling revolving barrel principle but drive the machinery by means of gas generated by the weapon's firing. This gets around both the objections, though some hybrid designs have appeared which demanded a 'kick-start' from an electric impulse or from a cocked spring, before the gas system came into operation. The Soviet GSh series of guns were the most successful of these self-powered Gatlings, but the complications of obtaining gas from a bundle of spinning barrels appear to be such that the design is unlikely to be perpetuated and a reversion to the simpler revolver gun is under way.

On the ground the cannon had been more or less forgotten after 1945. Aircraft now flew so fast that the hand-operated 20mm gun was no longer capable of reacting with sufficient speed to make it a valid form of defense, and as far as ground support went, who wanted a cannon anyway? What good would it do?

In the 1960s two developments began which were to change these assumptions very rapidly and very completely. In the first place transistors, solid-state circuitry, and computing technology began to make the calculation of firing data far faster and far more accurate than had ever before been possible and, at the same time, allowed radars and other electronic equipment to be smaller, more compact and more reliable. Allied to this, and stemming from it, came advances in electro-optical devices, image-intensifying sights, television cameras and displays, and above all in radar. Putting all these together produced a compact and relatively inexpensive system for acquiring, defining and tracking

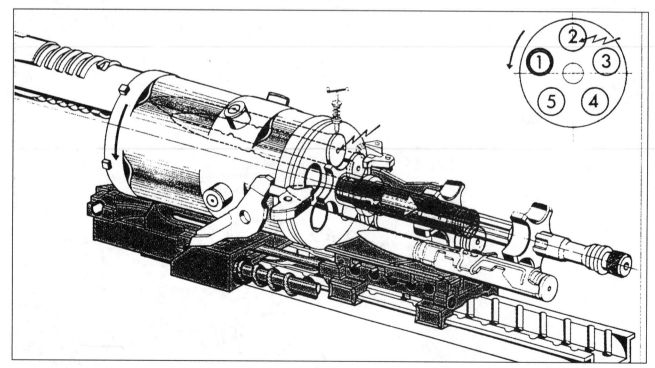

The feeding action of the BK27: the fired case *(with arrow)* is extracted and will be ejected during the forward movement of the slide. The next round *(top chamber)* is fired. The third cartridge *(3 o'clock chamber)* is in place and held by a retainer. The fourth cartridge *(5 o'clock chamber)* is partially rammed. The fifth cartridge is being removed from the belt, on the rear slide, and is about to take its place in the sequence,

Two KBB cannon in a French TA-25 turret with integrated radar and fire control computer–all mounted on an 8x8 Mowag Piranha armored car–constitutes a very formidable light air defense system.

aircraft at any speed and virtually any altitude, by day or night, and delivering the result to a power-driven gun mounting. Put two or four 20mm belt-fed cannons on such a mounting, drop the whole package into an armored car, and you have a three-man anti-aircraft battery, totally autonomous, capable of going anywhere, and capable of detecting an incoming target, calculating the firing data, pointing the gun and even telling the gunner when the aircraft is range and that he can open fire. Air defense of ground troops and field armies suddenly took on an entirely new and far more attractive appearance, and the cannon industry began to thrive.

The second tactical/technical development was the appearance of the armored infantry vehicle;

armored personnel carriers (APCs) had been around for a long time and they were generally considered as being simply 'battle taxis'. A means of getting the troops to where they were needed without getting them shot on the way. But now came the German army with their 'Marder' APC mounting a Rheinmetall Rh202 20mm cannon in the turret. It was followed by others, and suddenly we were into Armored Infantry Fighting Vehicles (AIFVs), or Mechanized Infantry Combat Vehicles (MICVs) and similar collections of initials, charging all over the battlefield and making thorough-going nuisances of themselves, firing machine guns in all directions. Obviously if you had an IFV then you had to be able to shoot at the

enemy's MICV with some hope of putting him out of action, and the obvious solution was - the cannon. So all these vehicles began to sprout cannon in their turrets, and as they did so, so there was the usual escalation, from 20mm to 25mm to 30mm - and even beyond in some cases. (Though really, once you get beyond 30mm, you are into the light tank category.)

One thing which was clearly seen from the outset was that a high rate of fire was really unnecessary in this context, though some feel that the British, even given their love of under-statement, carried it a bit too far in their Rarden 30mm cannon which is superbly accurate and highly destructive but which only fires single shots.

What was

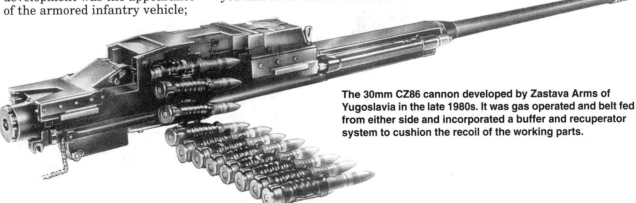

The 30mm CZ86 cannon developed by Zastava Arms of Yugoslavia in the late 1980s. It was gas operated and belt fed from either side and incorporated a buffer and recuperator system to cushion the recoil of the working parts.

The Rheinmetall Rh202 cannon, widely used in the German army as both an anti-aircraft weapon and as armament for their Infantry Fighting Vehicles.

more important than simple rate of fire, in many eyes, was the capability of rapidly changing the type of ammunition being fired. For dealing with enemy personnel in the open a simple HE/Fragmentation shell with impact fuze was quite satisfactory, but if their ranks parted to permit one of their MICVs to come to their aid, the gunner had to be able to switch to firing armor-piercing projectiles pretty quickly. Changing magazines was one solution, but today's cannon invariably use belts. Opening the feed cover, ejecting the round in the chamber, taking out the belt, putting a new belt in, closing the cover, re-charging the gun.... all that took time, during which the hostile would have doubtless played hell with your plans.

The solution was to build a cannon capable of being fed with two belts, one from each side. (Usually, that is; as we shall see there was one American design which had both belts on the same side, one behind the other.) The feed mechanism was arranged to feed from either side at the flick of a lever. Irrespective of what was in the chamber, whichever feed side was 'in gear', that was where the next round would come from. So to shift from armor to personnel, for example, meant that your first shot would be an AP round, followed by HE/Frag, but at 400+ rounds a minute, this was of no account.

At much the same period, the caliber began to move up; we have seen that the airmen more or less abandoned the 20mm cannon by the end of World War II, having found that it was incapable of doing sufficient damage in the time available. The stimulus to the ground gun designers was the need to

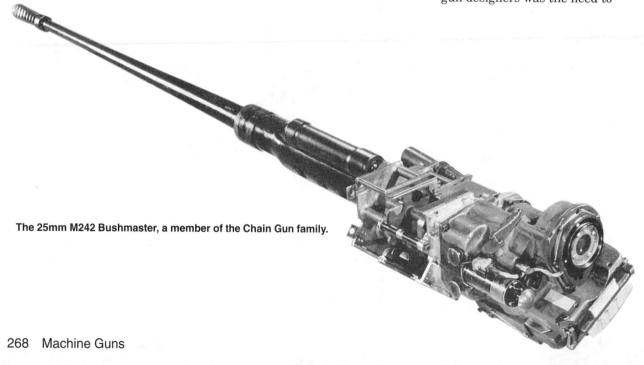

The 25mm M242 Bushmaster, a member of the Chain Gun family.

French 76/T2 twin 20mm anti-aircraft gun, using two M693 cannons.

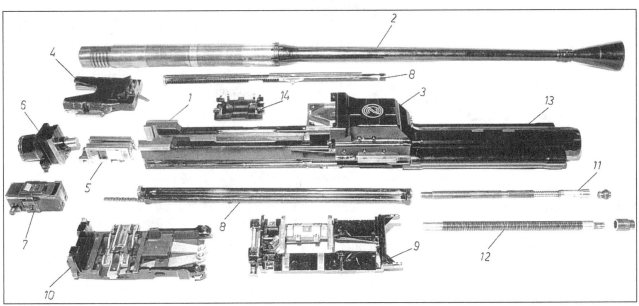

The component parts of the Zastava CZ86: 1) breech casing; 2) barrel assembly; 3) front slide; 4) rear slide; 5) breechblock; 6) buffer; 7) trigger assembly; 8) recoil buffer and recuperator assembly; 9) lower feeder; 10) upper feeder; 11) gas piston; 12) shock absorber; 13) barrel support; 14)link chute.

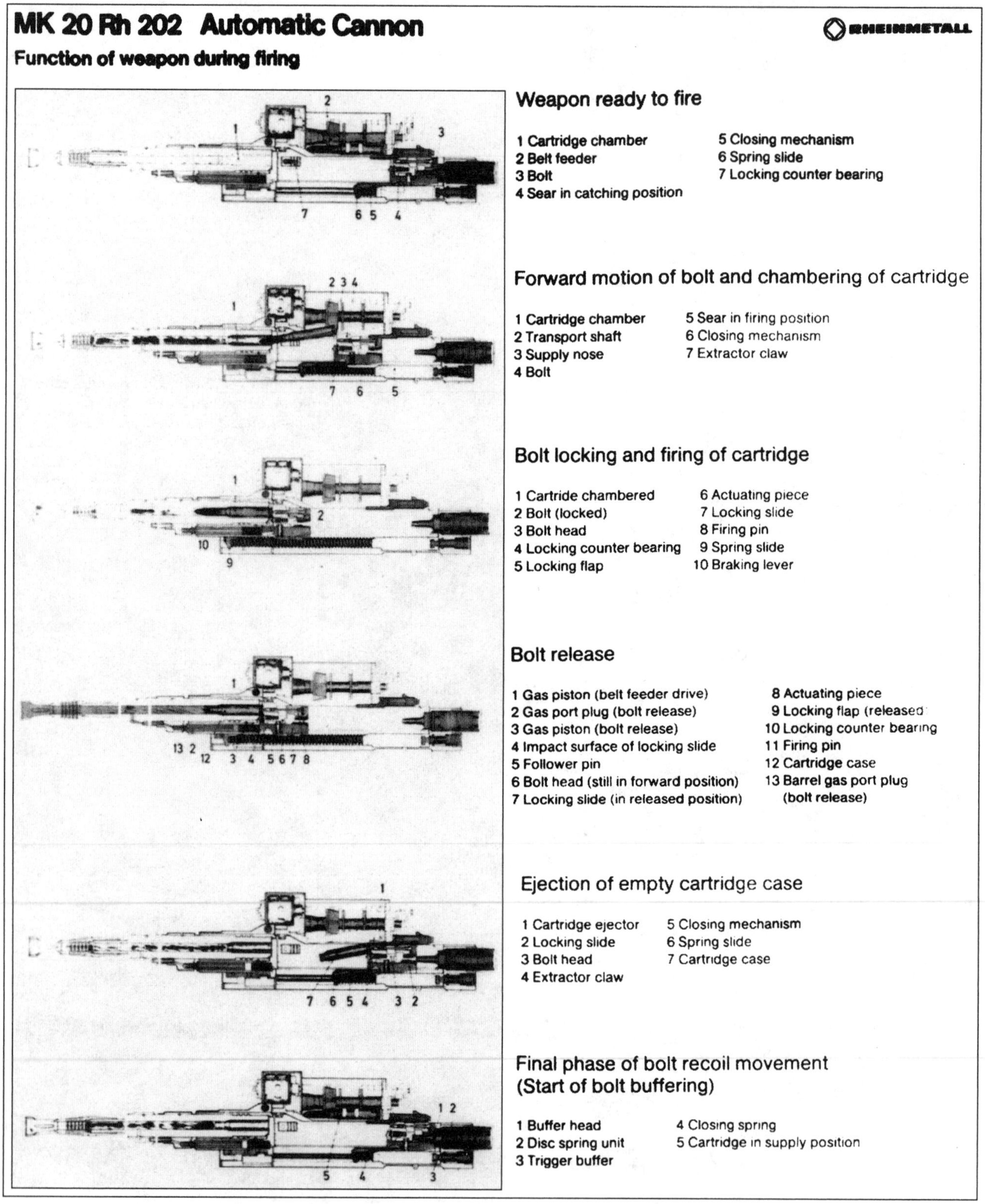

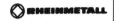

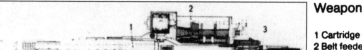

MK 20 Rh 202 Automatic Cannon
Function of weapon during firing
RHEINMETALL
Weapon ready to fire
1 Cartridge chamber
2 Belt feeder
3 Bolt
4 Sear in catching position
5 Closing mechanism
6 Spring slide
7 Locking counter bearing
Forward motion of bolt and chambering of cartridge
1 Cartridge chamber
2 Transport shaft
3 Supply nose
4 Bolt
5 Sear in firing position
6 Closing mechanism
7 Extractor claw
Bolt locking and firing of cartridge
1 Cartride chambered
2 Bolt (locked)
3 Bolt head
4 Locking counter bearing
5 Locking flap
6 Actuating piece
7 Locking slide
8 Firing pin
9 Spring slide
10 Braking lever
Bolt release
1 Gas piston (belt feeder drive)
2 Gas port plug (bolt release)
3 Gas piston (bolt release)
4 Impact surface of locking slide
5 Follower pin
6 Bolt head (still in forward position)
7 Locking slide (in released position)
8 Actuating piece
9 Locking flap (released)
10 Locking counter bearing
11 Firing pin
12 Cartridge case
13 Barrel gas port plug (bolt release)
Ejection of empty cartridge case
1 Cartridge ejector
2 Locking slide
3 Bolt head
4 Extractor claw
5 Closing mechanism
6 Spring slide
7 Cartridge case
Final phase of bolt recoil movement (Start of bolt buffering)
1 Buffer head
2 Disc spring unit
3 Trigger buffer
4 Closing spring
5 Cartridge in supply position

The sequence of operation of the Rheinmetall Rh202 gun. ***(Rheinmetall)***

defeat armor. Simple steel shot was no longer of much use except against the earlier types of APC, and it was necessary to consider such exotica as discarding sabot and fin-stabilized sabot ammunition, none of which was either effective or easy to manufacture inside the dimensional restrictions of the 20mm caliber. To go to 25mm may seem to be a small leap, but in terms of ammunition design it was a whole new world, and the designers took full advantage of it.

The 25mm round actually began in the USA in the 1960s with TRW's development of their 'Bushmaster' cannon, which was more or less a scale-up of the familiar gas-operated machine gun using a rotating bolt. Oerlikon developed suitable ammunition for this gun, but TRW were somewhat ahead of the market and the Bushmaster failed to take off. TRW put it on the back burner, and Oerlikon acquired rights to the design, which they then set about modifying until it eventually became the Oerlikon KBA cannon. By this time the world was more receptive to the 25mm idea, Bushmaster came back, and it eventually finished up

An Rh202 gun in its traveling mode.

in the turrets of 'Bradley', the US Army's MICV which appeared in the early 1980s.

'If 25mm is good, think how much better 30mm would be' was the next cry to be raised, and new and extremely powerful 30mm rounds were developed by Oerlikon for both air and ground use; the connection may not seem apparent, but the increasing use of helicopters has had an effect upon the increase in 30mm guns in the air defense role. The reason being that the best way to attack a low-hovering helicopter is to use a proximity fuse that is smart enough to distinguish between the rotating blades of the machine and the swaying tree-tops beneath it, and 30mm is the smallest caliber into which a viable proximity fuse can be built. And, of course, you could develop some very effective armor-piercing projectiles in that caliber.

The next cannon stimulator came in the Falklands War of 1982, when an Exocet missile, skimming the surface of the sea, demolished the principal British supply ship and this threw a sizable wrench into their logistic process. This put the fear of God up all the navies of the world who, until then, had scarcely realized just what damage a sea-skimming missile was capable of doing, and a frantic search for an antimissile Close-In Defense System began. A number of very exotic (and expensive) anti-missile-missiles were proposed, but the solution adopted by almost every navy has been the cannon. The difficult part of the solution was providing mountings which could track fast enough to keep up with the target, but since unlimited power and ample space were available on warships, this was simply an engineering problem and was fairly rapidly solved. Onto this mounting went the selected armament, either a Gatling-type or multiple conventional or revolver guns. Load these with a mix of armor-piercing, high-explosive and tracer

The 25mm Bushmaster cannon on the M2 Bradley Infantry Fighting Vehicle.

The Oerlikon KBA is a gas-operated weapon using a rotating bolt and with dual feed; note the similarity between the 'double gate' system used here and that of the Fabrique Nationale 15mm machine gun, described in the previous chapter.

An example of the current fashion for Close-in Weapon Systems is this Oerlikon-Contraves 'Seaguard', a very maneuverable turret carrying four 25mm KBB cannons which, as seen here, can spew out something in the order of 3200 rounds per minute at a velocity of 4450 ft/sec, which ought to be enough to catch any missile between wind and water.

The Oerlikon KBA is a versatile weapon; here four are used in a prefabricated turret unit, which can be fitted into a wide variety of vehicles to produce a self-propelled light AA gun.

The 30mm M230 Chain Gun on a 'chin mounting' underneath an AH-64 Apache helicopter makes a formidable anti-tank weapon.

This was quite a presentable airplane until it encountered a short burst from the KBA.

ammunition, provide a magazine big enough to permit sustained fire during the approach of the missile, and you have a virtually impervious system, spewing out six or seven thousand rounds per minute and detonating the target before it gets within lethal distance. (Well, that's the theory; so far as I am aware, nobody has yet had to try it for real.)

The cannon, like the submachine gun, is a product of the 20th century - as outlined above, the McLean and Maxim forebears were not really the same blood-line - and both were German children of World War I. Both went through a spotty adolescence in the 1920s and 1930s, both came into their estate in World War II and emerged with a good war record. But in the latter half of the century their ways diverged. The submachine gun has almost ceased to be a military weapon, replaced by the more versatile assault rifle at one end of the scale and the newcomer, the Personal Defense Weapon, at the other. The submachine gun lives on solely as a police weapon.

But the cannon goes from strength to strength. This chapter has only covered the high spots in their history, but sufficient had been written to show that no contemporary air force can expect to survive without cannon, and few armies are without light air defense cannon. No MICV, AIFV or IFV - and precious few APCs - would be seen in public without their cannon, and there are any number of promoters who will not rest until the infantryman carries, not a 50-caliber machine gun, but a 25mm or 30mm cannon into action as his company support weapon. As a study of the tables in the appendices will show, the number of cannon and the variety of cannon cartridges is quite surprising, and I think we can safely assume that there are a few more to come in the course of the next decade or two.

The 'Sea Zenith' mounting, with the four KBB guns and magazine and feed system, being lowered into position. This, together with radars, electro-optical sensors and sights, and fire control computers, forms the 'Seaguard' system.

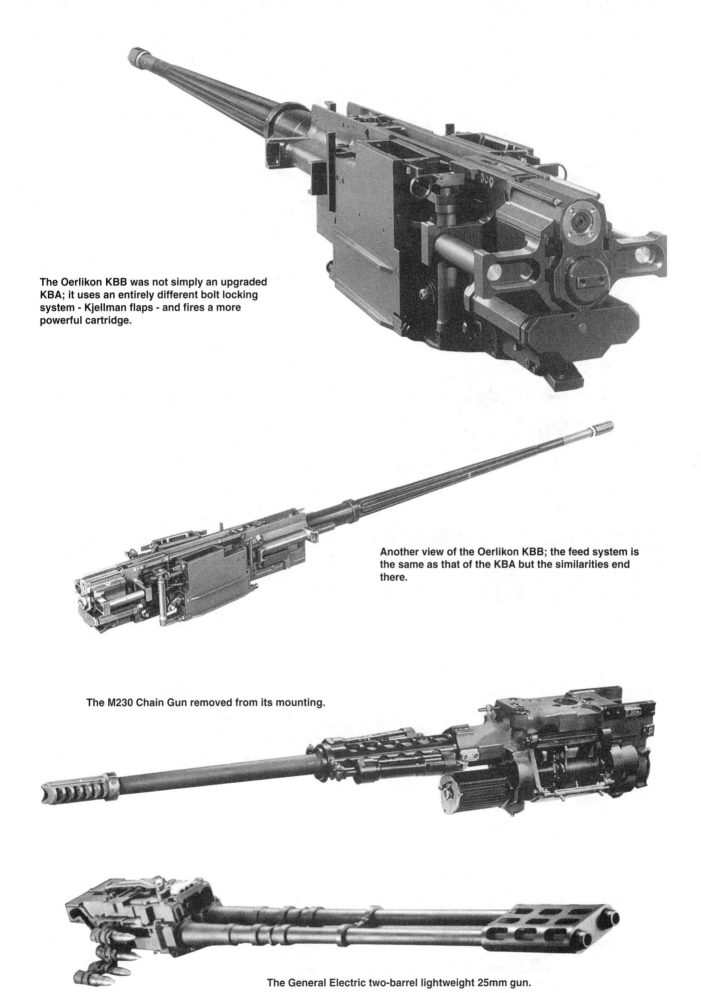

The Oerlikon KBB was not simply an upgraded KBA; it uses an entirely different bolt locking system - Kjellman flaps - and fires a more powerful cartridge.

Another view of the Oerlikon KBB; the feed system is the same as that of the KBA but the similarities end there.

The M230 Chain Gun removed from its mounting.

The General Electric two-barrel lightweight 25mm gun.

The KBB also serves at sea...

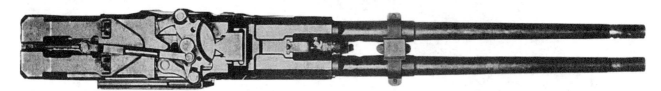

The Russian GSh-23 two-barrel 23mm gun.

The McDonnell-Douglas ASP-30; ASP for *A*utomatic, *S*elf-*P*owered, in order to distinguish it from the company's Chain Guns. The ASP-30 is gas operated, with a rotating bolt, and the object in view is to provide a lightweight compact but extremely powerful weapon which is interchangeable with the 50-caliber M2HB Browning machine gun so as to give an instant increment in firepower with the minimum of alteration.

AH-64 Apache

AN AH-64 Apache with its armament on display. The foremost commodity in the picture is 1200 rounds of 30mm ammunition for the Chain Gun. The rest of the line-up includes Hellfire missiles, Stinger missiles and 70mm rockets.

The ASP-30 mounted on a Hummer provides very mobile firepower.

APPENDIX ONE

'Strange-Sounding Names'
Some Less Well-Known Machine Guns And Cannon

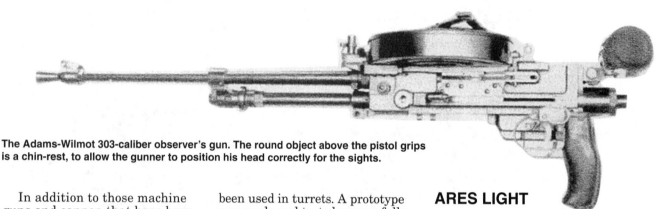

The Adams-Wilmot 303-caliber observer's gun. The round object above the pistol grips is a chin-rest, to allow the gunner to position his head correctly for the sights.

In addition to those machine guns and cannon that have been discussed in the body of the book, there are many more which made little impression upon the world, but which are occasionally encountered in memoirs or historical reports or minor campaign histories. In an attempt to provide as much information in as little space as possible, these guns, which are difficult to weave into a connected narrative without getting led down obscure side-tracks, and about which there is not a great deal to say anyway, are listed here with brief details. Dimensions and data, where known, will be found in the tables.

ADAMS

An experimental 50-caliber aircraft machine gun developed by the BSA Company in Britain during World War II and designed by the Adams of the Adams-Wilmot gun (below). Recoil-operated, belt-fed and air-cooled, with a prominent flash hider, it was principally intended as a fixed gun, though there appears to be no reason why it could not also have

been used in turrets. A prototype was made and tested successfully, but the development was then abandoned since the 50-caliber Browning became available and relieved BSA of the problem of finding the capacity to build an entirely new gun.

ADAMS WILMOT

A flexible machine-gun for use by aircraft gunners. Developed by the BSA company and offered to the Royal Air Force in 1934. It was tested, along with a number of other designs, but broke its firing pin early in the trial and then displayed numerous other methods of going wrong. The RAF rejected it and BSA abandoned the design. It was a gas-piston-operated weapon, using a tilting breechblock to lock, fed from a 99-round drum in 303 British and with a rate of fire about 900 rds/min. Sometimes referred to as the 'Adams-Wilmot-BSA' gun.

AL-QUDS

An Iranian heavy-barreled version of the Kalashnikov AKM rifle, used as the squad light machine gun.

ARES LIGHT

The Ares Corporation of Port Clinton, Ohio introduced their light machine gun in 1988. Gas-operated, with a rotating bolt in a carrier, it employed many of the elements of the Stoner 63 system. It normally fed from a 100-round belt in a box-carrier, but could be modified to use an M16-standard rifle magazine. It was designed on a modular basis, permitting rapid field-stripping and also assembly into various forms by the use of different barrels, sight mounts, sight, mountings and so forth. It was reported as being in 'low-volume production' for several years but manufacture appears to have been closed down in the latter 1990s.

ARMALITE AR-10

Eugene Stoner designed the Armalite AR-10 as an assault rifle in 30-06 before he joined the Armalite company and it was subsequently changed to 7.62x51mm in the hope of attracting NATO interest. Colt purchased a license to manufacture it, but at much the same time Stoner developed the

Adams 50-caliber aircraft gun, with top cover open to show the feed tray.

AR-15 in 5.56mm caliber, and when it became obvious that the 5.56mm rifle was a more marketable proposition, Colt dropped the AR-10.

It was then taken up by Artillerie Inrichtigen (AI) of the Netherlands, who hoped to attract European buyers, and under their guidance two machine gun variants were constructed, one magazine fed and the other belt fed. Both were gas-operated with a rotating bolt, on the Stoner system, and can be thought of as enlarged AR-15/M16 rifles with heavy barrels. AI had some degree of success with the rifle, selling it to Portugal, Burma, Sudan and Nicaragua, but the machine guns never got past the prototype stage.

BAILEY

American multiple-barrel mechanical gun submitted to the US Navy for test in 1874-6. A remarkable design, it was the first gun to use a flexible belt for feeding the ammunition, and the cartridge remained on the belt while being fired. The gun had six revolving barrels, similar to a Gatling gun, but the mechanism was much different. The ammunition belt carried upstanding brackets into which the center-fire cartridges were placed, and this was carried up into the gun and around a large driving wheel of the same diameter as the bundle of barrels. A cam caused the barrels to reciprocate back and forth as they revolved, so that as a round of ammunition entered the gun it was aligned with a barrel, which then gradually slid back until the chamber had completely enclosed the cartridge. At this point the barrel was at the 12-o'clock position and the cartridge was in front of a standing breech, through which a firing pin now came to fire it. Continued rotation took the barrel and spent case away from the firing position and the barrel was now cammed forward to leave the empty case to be carried down and out of the gun by the belt. It appears that when Bailey submitted the gun for firing trials in 1876 he did not supply sufficient pre-loaded belts to permit the Navy to test prolonged firing, and they therefore refused to continue with the tests. Bailey was permitted to fire the gun for demonstration, which he did, quite successfully, but there is no record of him ever going back with more belts.

BANG

Soren H. Bang was a Danish engineer who had something of a fixation with using muzzle blast to drive automatic weapons. Most of his energy was put into the development of automatic rifles, and some quite efficient models were tested by several armies in the 1930s. Operation was by means of a muzzle cone attached to a rod which locked and unlocked the breech. On firing, gas emerging from the muzzle into the cone caused the rod to be pulled forward, and a cam on the rear end rotated the bolt to unlock it. Opening the bolt was done by blowback action, the pressure in the chamber being sufficient to blow the case out and drive the bolt backwards. Whether Bang ever designed a machine gun is open to some doubt; the only known photograph claiming to be a Bang machine gun appears to be simply the mechanism of the Bang rifle lift out of its wooden stock, and the assertion that a Bang machine gun was tested by the RAF in the late 1920s has not been verified. It seems probable that Bang, conscious of his limitations, never strayed from his rifle designs and the Bang machine gun never existed.

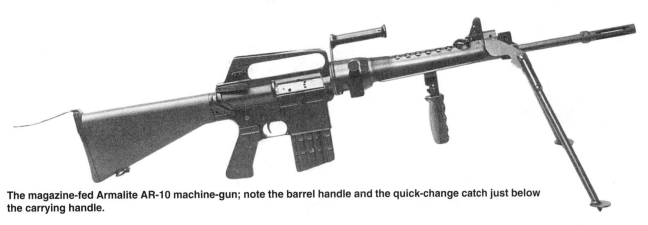

The magazine-fed Armalite AR-10 machine-gun; note the barrel handle and the quick-change catch just below the carrying handle.

The BSA Model 1924 50-caliber aircraft gun, without its ammunition drum.

A closer view of the BSA 1924, showing the magazine post and feedway.

The rate of fire was only 400 rounds per minute, far too slow for acceptability in the air role, and the small magazine capacity was another flaw. The slow rate of fire was due to an exceptionally long recoil stroke - almost three inches - that was chosen in order to try and absorb as much of the recoil energy as possible to avoid overstressing the mounting and the aircraft structures of the period. As a result, there was no way of speeding up the gun without a complete re-design and this would have introduced the recoil loads they had been seeking to avoid. The gun lingered for a short time, but the decision by the RAF to use power-driven turrets with belt-fed guns led to its abandonment.

CARR

An American design by a Mr. Carr of California, who enlisted the well-known Driggs-Seabury Ordnance Company to manufacture a prototype and promote it to the US Navy, to whom they had supplied several larger guns. It was tested in 1901. The Carr was an air-cooled, recoil-operated gun using a Maxim-type toggle to lock the breech and fed from an overhead drum magazine holding 248 30-40 Krag cartridges. Firing tests showed that the gun was wildly inaccurate and that it tore the heads off many of the cartridge cases during extraction. A subsequent test showed this to be due to faulty cartridge headspacing, but various other defects showed in the second test, notably a lack of power in closing the breech, and the gun was summarily rejected.

BSA M1924

This is often called the '50 Lewis', though its relationship with the Lewis is somewhat distant. It is obvious that BSA's long experience with manufacturing the Lewis gun had an influence on the design, which was an attempt to take a jump forward and equip the Royal Air Force with an observer's flexible gun of considerably greater power than the competition. However the operation was totally different, using recoil instead of gas, with a rotating bolt locking the breech by means of a spiral cam slot traveling over a stud in the receiver. Feed was from a Lewis-type drum but with a capacity of only 37 rounds, due to the large 0.50-inch Vickers cartridge being used. However, it was so designed that the drum could be 'topped up' with loose rounds at any time without having to remove it. Another feature was the ability to use either an air-cooled barrel, with radial fins rather like a Hotchkiss, or a water jacket fed by a pressure system installed in the aircraft, in a very similar manner to the system installed in some British tanks of the period to cool their Vickers guns.

Two guns were built and tested by the Royal Air force and the Royal Naval Air Service in 1928-29.

The Charlton, a New Zealand conversion of a Lee-Enfield rifle into a useful machine gun.

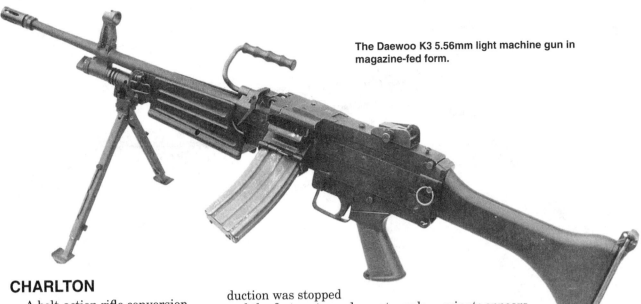

The Daewoo K3 5.56mm light machine gun in magazine-fed form.

CHARLTON

A bolt-action rifle conversion from New Zealand, dating from 1940, the Charlton was better thought-out than most conversions and actually worked well and went into production. It used the usual sort of gas cylinder and piston to propel an operating rod with a curved cam which rotated the bolt handle of a standard Short Lee-Enfield No 3 rifle and opened the bolt, after which a spring sent it back. A modified Bren magazine mounted underneath the receiver replaced the rifle box magazine, and a forward handgrip and a bipod were fitted. A contract to manufacture 4000 was given, the guns to be used for home defense within New Zealand, but after a few hundred had been made pro-duction was stopped and the factory turned over to making Owen sub-machine guns. So far as is known no Charlton was ever used outside New Zealand and specimens are therefore rare.

CLAXTON

American mechanical gun, ca 1867. It consisted of two barrels side-by-side, with a receiver behind them, on top of which was a handle capable of being swung from side to side and couple to the two breech-blocks of the two guns. One man pushed the handle back and forth, the other fed cartridges into the weapon. The faster they worked, the faster it fired, with too much speed generally leading to jams and other disasters, and about 80 rounds per minute appears to have been the maximum practical rate. Claxton raised no interest in the U.S.A. and is said to have taken his gun to Europe and sold the idea to the French; but the only illustra-tion I have ever seen of 'French troops manning a Claxton mitrailleuse' was quite obviously a picture of a Gatling gun, so I have my doubts about Claxton's salesman-ship.

COMMANDO

The Mark 23 Commando machine gun was a modified form of the Stoner 63 air-cooled, gas-operated weapon in 5.56mm caliber. The Mark 23 was the

And the same gun in belt-fed form. Comparison with the Minimi is inevitable.

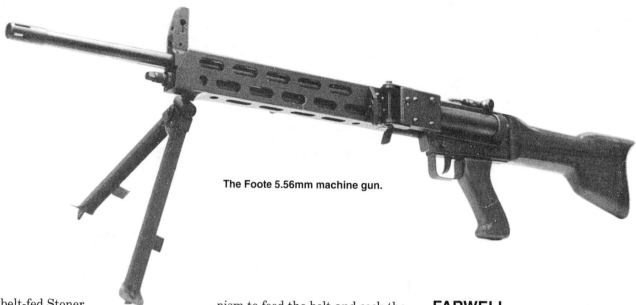

The Foote 5.56mm machine gun.

belt-fed Stoner 63A1 with the feed changed to the right side and numbers were purchased by the US Marine Corps for use by SEAL teams in Vietnam.

DAEWOO

Now widely known for their automobiles, Daewoo has various divisions, one of which came into the small arms business by manufacturing M16 rifles under license for the South Korean army. With this experience to guide them the company has since developed assault rifles, pistols and a light machine gun, all of which are in South Korean army service. The 5.56mm machine gun bears a striking resemblance to the FN Minimi.

DE KNIGHT

American water-cooled gas-operated and belt-fed gun patented in 1898 by Victor P. De Knight and a prototype made by Pratt & Whitney in 1902. In an attempt to circumvent various patents then still in force, De Knight had to produce a desperately complicated mechanism to feed the belt and cock the weapon. It worked; but proved to be so unreliable that no official test was authorized. It was revived in 1916 as war loomed over the horizon, and the US Army commenced a test on a fresh gun, also made by Pratt & Whitney. This failed so many times that the test was terminated and the gun withdrawn.

DROR

An Israeli design dating from the 1950s, when Israel was attempting to build up an indigenous arms industry. The Dror is always said to be identical to the Johnson M1944, but the only one I ever saw looked nothing like the Johnson, and I believe the similarity was confined to the operating system - short recoil - and the side-feeding magazine was changed to a bottom-feed. As might have been expected from a recoil-operated machine gun in the Middle Eastern deserts, its working life was relatively short due to excessive abrasive wear, and it did not remain in service for very long.

FARWELL

An American multi-barrel mechanical gun which appeared in 1870. It had four .45 barrels side by side and at a casual glance resembles a Nordenfelt. The mechanism is quite different, being operated by rotation of a crank handle on the right side, and the feed was from a large hopper above the breech end. The rotary crank drive was converted into a side-to-side movement of the breech assembly, in a similar manner to the Nordenfelt, though the loading and firing details were rather different.

The only known picture of the Farwell gun shows a great similarity to the Den Helder gun mentioned when dealing with the Nordenfelt gun in Chapter 2, and there is a distinct possibility that the Den Helder may have originated from Farwell's patent drawings.

FOOTE MG-69

American general-purpose machine gun designed by J.P. Foote. A prototype was built in 1969, which Foote offered to a number of companies but none were willing to manufacture it.

To those who know their machine guns, this is obviously a Heckler and Koch HK21, irrespective of the name 'Franchi' marked on it.

The Foote 5.56mm machine gun.

A gas-operated, belt-fed and air-cooled gun, using a rotating bolt, the design appeared to be clean and straight-forward, but insufficient firing was done to reach any conclusions about its durability. One notable feature was the side-opening feed cover that fed the belt in vertically rather than horizontally, as is the more general rule.

FRANCHI LF23

In the mid-1980s the Italian army was canvassing for a 5.56mm light machine gun. The Luigi Franchi company, best known for its shotguns, decided to make a bid for the contract and obtained a license to manufacture the Heckler & Koch 5.56mm HK23E machine gun. With some minor cosmetic modifications this was then entered for the contest as the Franchi LF23. The HK23E was simply a 5.56mm version of the HK21E, described elsewhere; belt-fed, air-cooled, delayed-blowback and with a quick-change barrel. The LF23 was duly tested against the Beretta and was turned down. Franchi advertised it on the export market for a short time but then gave up the project.

GECAL 50

GECAL-A 50-caliber gun made by General Electric, hence the name. A three or six-barrel Gatling type, it was eventually adopted by the US Army in the three-barrel configuration and is now known as the GAU-19/A.

GORGAS

American mechanical gun devised by General Gorgas, Chief of Ordnance of the Confederate Army. I say 'devised' since the principle he used was the well-known turret revolver system, and Gorgas' application was merely an enlargement of that. It consisted of a barrel behind which was a flat circular housing, so that from above it resembled a frying pan. Inside the flat housing was a revolving disc with 18 chambers bored in from the circumference and with 18 nipples at the inner end. A manual rammer was attached to one side of the gun, and the disc could be rotated by hand to bring each chamber opposite the rammer, when it could be charged with powder and shot. Percussion caps were placed on the nipples, and a hand crank operated to revolve the disc. As a chamber lined up with the barrel, a hammer fell and fired the cap. After 18 shots, the disc was removed and changed for a loaded disc, and firing would resume. That, at least, was the plan. But so far as is known only one gun was ever made and that was not completed before the Civil War had ended.

HUGHES LOCKLESS

Experimental American light machine gun developed by the Hughes Helicopter Company in the

A three-barrel GECAL 50 mounted in a helicopter.

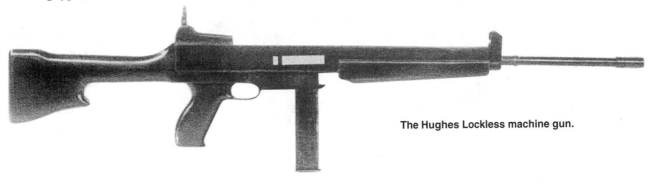

The Hughes Lockless machine gun.

Unlike the Charlton conversion, the Huon managed to conceal most of its machinery inside a light metal jacket.

late 1970s. It used a novel 'lockless' breech system involving a sliding sleeve instead of a conventional bolt, and fired a plastic-cased "telescoped" cartridge of Hughes' own design. The design was initially sponsored by DARPA (Defense Advanced Research Projects Agency) and subsequently became the subject of a U.S. Army developmental contract. Much useful research was done, but the eventual weapon was not considered suitable for military adoption as it stood. Other designers subsequently took up the telescoped ammunition idea.

HUON

A Canadian design, the Huon appeared in 1917 and was intended to be a conversion of the Ross bolt-action rifle, which had been withdrawn from service and replace by the Lee Enfield. A gas cylinder and piston was fitted, driving an operating rod connected to the rifle bolt. Since the Ross used a straight-pull bolt there was no need to use a cam to rotate the bolt handle, a hurdle at which many would-be conversions had fallen. The result was ungainly but it worked reasonably well and had the great advantage of being cheap - the conversion only cost $50. But by the time the design had been perfected and before trials were completed the war ended and the Huon was hurriedly discarded.

INSAS

INSAS stands for 'Indian Small Arms System' and applies to an assault rifle and a light machine gun, both in 5.56mm caliber, developed by the Indian Ordnance Factory organization in the late 1980s. The design is the now-familiar gas-operated rotating bolt, and the whole weapon is simply a heavy-barreled version of the INSAS assault rifle. This means that it is an amalgam of ideas from other weapons: pistol grip and receiver from the Kalashnikov, cocking handle from Heckler & Koch, gas regulator from the FN-FAL rifle and so on. Its introduction into service was delayed by funding problems until the late 1990s.

LADA

Light machine gun developed in the Czech Republic in the mid-1990s, this was a gas-operated air-cooled weapon, based upon the Kalashnikov rotating bolt and gas system, chambered either for the Soviet 5.45x39mm cartridge or the Western 5.56x45mm, as the potential customer might prefer. It was designed as part of a family of weapons, which also included an assault rifle and an assault carbine. The machine gun fed from a 75-round drum but could also accept the 30-round box magazines used with the rifle and carbine.

The name 'Lada' proved to be unfortunate; it was also the name of a Russian automobile that became

the butt of jokes all over Europe (e.g.: Why is the rear window of a Lada heated? To keep your hands warm while pushing it.) and inevitably the manufacturers of the machine gun found themselves catching the fallout. They therefore changed the name to 'CZ2000'. Under this title is in now being prepared for production in 5.56mm caliber when the Czechs join NATO.

LAHTI-SALORANTA

A 1926 design from Aimo Lahti, a noted Finn designer, this was a light recoil-operated gun feeding either from a box magazine beneath the receiver or, unusually, from a flat drum magazine also underneath the receiver. It had the usual perforated barrel jacket of the period, and a light bipod, and was taken into service by the Finnish army, who continued to use until they changed over to Soviet equipment in the late 1940s. There was little demand on the export market however, as the late 1920s were not a period when any army was spending money, and only China purchased a small number. So Lahti turned to designing a submachine gun, which did much better, after which he came back to the Saloranta and modified it to become an aircraft observer's gun, using only the underslung drum magazine. This was tested by a number of European air forces in the early 1930s but had no success outside Finland.

The INSAS is a combination of features taken from other weapons, but none the worse for that.

The Lahti-Saloranta was rather unusual in being recoil-operated at a time when gas operation was almost universal.

LAIRD-MENTAYNE

Based on patents taken out in 1908 by two Frenchmen, Mentayne and Degaille, and with some input from Laird, a British engineer who appears to have been responsible for the production engineering aspect, this gun, made by the Coventry Ordnance Works of England was offered to the British army in 1910. A long-recoil gun, it rested on a light bipod and had a quick-change barrel and, judging by various test reports of the period, it would seem to have been a reliable and light weapon which was, in fact, a good deal better than some of those which were adopted during World War I. (Though it has to be said that a test at Springfield Arsenal in 1909, of an early model, was something of a minor disaster.) But in 1910 it was fighting an uphill battle; machine guns were big things on tripods with water jackets, everybody knew that, so why was this company making a nuisance of itself with this ridiculous weapon? Exit the Laird-Mentayne.

MADSEN-SAETTER

This appeared in the 1960 and was the last attempt by Madsen to re-establish themselves in the small-arms world. The original Madsen was by then completely obsolete and manufacture had ceased; an excellent assault rifle had been developed just too late for the 1950s swing to automatic rifles and had therefore failed to find a market. So in 1959 the Madsen-Saetter machine gun appeared, a gas-operated magazine-fed air-cooled gun. Its only defect was that the design called for machined components at a time when the pressed-metal and wire-spring school of gunmaking was taking the stage. The Madsen-Saetter, for all is excellent quality and reliability and accuracy, well demonstrated in several trials, proved to be too expensive. A simplified and somewhat cheaper model was tried, but this went too far in the other direction and nobody was very impressed with it. Madsen saw the writing on the wall and left the firearms business, though they have kept a foot in the door by producing an excellent range of machine gun mounts for vehicles which have been widely sold in Europe and Africa. The company is now known as 'DISA Systems'.

MAREMONT DUAL FEED

A tank machine gun developed by the Maremont company in the USA as a possible replacement for the M73 tank gun. In 7.62mm caliber, it was designed to feed from two belts, so that alternative types of ammunition could be selected at will - the makers suggested armor-piercing in one belt and anti-personnel flechette ammunition in the other. Dual-feed guns are no novelty, but the Maremont was in a class of its own: the conventional method of dual feeding is to bring a belt up on each side and select which side to feed from. The Maremont design had the two belts arranged one behind the other, and they could feed from either or both sides.

The Madsen-Saetter machine gun on its tripod.

The Maremont Dual-Feed Tank machine gun complete with two belts.

The gun was short-recoil operated with a quick-change barrel.
On top of the receiver were two
feed trays, one behind the other,
and the bolt assembly was given a
long travel so that it could collect a
fresh round of ammunition from
either tray, the unused one being
simply thrown out of action and
thus not feeding a cartridge into
the bolt path. The gun was submitted for test in the mid-1970s but
was eventually rejected.

MAREMONT UNIVERSAL

Developed by the Maremont
Corporation in the mid-1970s,
this was postulated as a possible
replacement for both the M60 for
infantry use and the M73 for tank
use. The design was unusual in
that while 85 percent of the parts
were common to either application, it was possible to change a
few parts and convert the gun
from recoil to gas operation or
vice versa. Breech closure was by
a three-lug rotating bolt, and the
air-cooled gun was belt-fed from
either side. It was tested by the
U.S. Army but rejected.

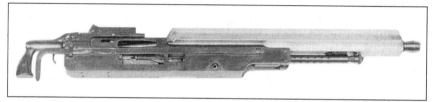

The tank version of the Marlin, with its aluminum radiator above the gas cylinder.

MARLIN

The Marlin-Rockwell Corporation
received a contract from the US Government in 1917 to manufacture several thousand Colt M1895
'Potato-Digger' machine-guns for
infantry use. At much the same time
they were advised of a requirement
for a suitable machine gun to be fitted into aircraft and synchronized to
fire through the propeller arc. Marlin
therefore adapted the Colt M1895 by
removing the swinging gas piston
system and substituting a conventional under-barrel gas cylinder and
piston assembly. This had to be carefully modified so as to duplicate the
gradual primary-secondary extraction phases, which came naturally to
the swinging-arm design, but it was

a complete success and became the
principal US synchronized gun for
several years. A version with a large
aluminum radiator was also adopted
as a tank machine gun. Numbers of
these latter guns were supplied to
Britain in 1940 and, with the radia-
tors removed, were used to arm fishing trawlers and small coastal
vessels against air attack.

MENDOZA

Rafael Mendoza was a Mexican
designer who produced a variety of
designs over a long period from the
early 1930s to the early 1960s.
Among them were three machine
guns, the Models of 1933, 1945 and
1955. The M1933 was gas-operated, fed from an overhead box
magazine, had a quick-change barrel and was basically a Lewis mechanism with some improvements. It
was quite advanced for its day and
the Mexican army used it until the
late 1940s. The M1945 was virtually the same gun but chambered
for the 30-06 cartridge. The final
RM2 model was completely different, more of a heavy-barrel rifle
than a machine gun, and did away
with the quick-change barrel. It
was not adopted in any quantity.

MEROKA

A Spanish naval anti-sea-skim-
ming missile Close-In Defense
System, Meroka is an interesting
reversion to the battery gun, but

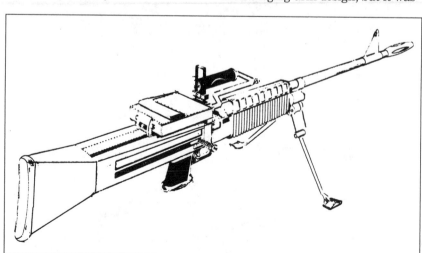

An artist's impression of the Maremont Universal gun.

The Mendoza M1945 in 30-06.

The Mendoza RM2 of 1955 was a simpler and no doubt cheaper weapon, but not so good as its predecessor.

with modern refinements. It consists of a two banks each of six 20mm barrels carried in a powered mounting directed by radar. Each rack of barrels has its own belt feed which move so as to deliver two sets of six rounds to the barrels, to be chambered, the breeches closed and the rounds fired in a 12-round salvo. This is repeated at one-eighth second intervals to produce a rate of fire of 3600 rounds per minute, sufficient to shred most types of missile long before they get close enough to do any damage.

MINIGUN (M134)

A six-barrel 'Gatling-type' 7.62mm machine gun based on the General Electric Company's 20mm Vulcan development, and specifically designed for use in helicopters in Vietnam. Due to its demands for power and ammunition, its application is limited to helicopters or vehicle mounts that provide the necessary space. The six barrels are revolved by an electric motor; they are normally parallel but can be clamped into various degrees of convergence if required. When the trigger is released, the ammunition feed is isolated so that there is no danger

Meroka's twelve 20mm barrels protrude from a turret packed with radar and computers.

The GE M134 Minigun on a test-firing stand.

of a cook-off during the short time the barrel and bolt assembly is coming to rest.

NTK

NTK is the abbreviated form of 'Nittoka Metal Industry Company Ltd', a Japanese engineering firm that, when the Japanese Self-Defense Force was established, obtained a number of contracts to refurbish Browning M1919 machine guns and other automatic weapons obtained from the USA. As a result of this, in 1965 they were approached by the JSDF and given a contract to develop a General Purpose machine gun. The resulting weapon was known as the NTK Model 7M and was a conventional gas-operated machine gun using a tilting bolt and capable of being tripod or bipod mounted, with heavy or light barrels respectively. Prototypes were made in 30-06, and generally resemble the FN-MAG except for having a heavily-finned barrel and a large conical flash hider.

The guns were not accepted by the JSDF and the company designer, Dr. Kawamura, then produced a second design, this time in 7.62mm NATO caliber and with a somewhat different gas system. The gas cylinder was above the barrel and the piston was a short-stroke tappet, which simply gave the bolt carrier an impulsive blow to throw it back and unlock the bolt. Less than half a dozen guns were made, and tests showed that the new gas system was unreliable. The JSDF indicated its preference for the design, which eventually became their Model 74, and the NTK company bowed out of the contest.

PIRAT

A Polish version of the Russian KPV mounted on a Polish-designed recoil-absorbing tripod, so turning what was originally an anti-aircraft machine gun into a somewhat cumbersome ground support weapon with good anti-armor properties.

POLSTEN

Poland had purchased a quantity of Oerlikon guns in the mid-1930s and then set a design team onto the task of simplifying the design to make it lighter, cheaper and easier

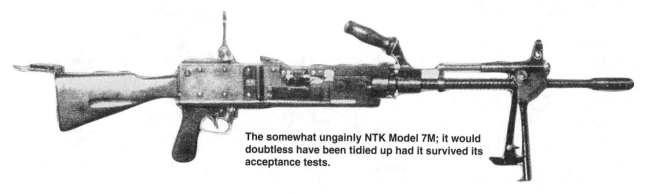

The somewhat ungainly NTK Model 7M; it would doubtless have been tidied up had it survived its acceptance tests.

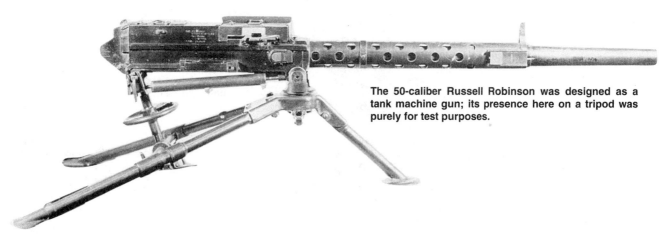

The 50-caliber Russell Robinson was designed as a tank machine gun; its presence here on a tripod was purely for test purposes.

to manufacture. Before the work was completed World War II broke out, and the Polish team fled to Britain where they finished up at the Royal Small Arms Factory, Enfield. Their drawings were studied, and in June 1941 they were given facilities to complete their design. This took rather more time than had been anticipated and it was not until the summer of 1944 that the Polsten gun went into production.

The Polsten was about 30lbs lighter than the Oerlikon, and manufacture was eased by the use of metal stampings and welded assembly instead of machining the receiver from the solid. It had 119 components, as opposed to 250 parts in the Oerlikon, required 900 machining operations to the Oerlikon's 3000, and cost $240 (£60) against the Oerlikon's $1280 (£320). It was widely used as a light air defense weapon by the British and other Allied forces in the latter months of World War II but was not retained in service after 1945.

RUSSELL ROBINSON

Russell Robinson was an Australian engineer who went to Britain and became a designer at the Royal Small Arms Factory, Enfield Lock, in the late 1940s. He developed a heavy machine gun which was recoil-operated, used a sliding-block breech mechanism, belt-fed and with a mechanical rammer to chamber the cartridge. The gun worked satisfactorily, but the British army was not in the market for a heavy machine gun and turned it down. Robinson

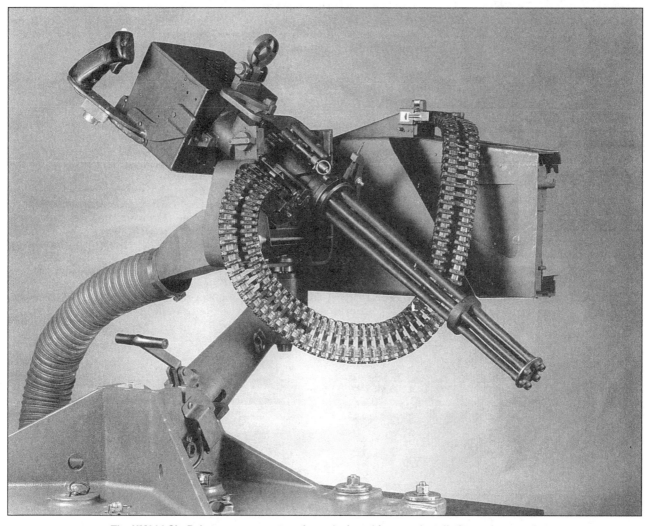

The XM214 Six-Pak was a compact package designed for easy installation and removal.

This model of the Soley-Lewis shows the aluminum radiator covering both barrel and gas cylinder.

then went to the U.S.A. and was later involved in the development of the U.S. M73 tank machine gun, using his sliding block and rammer system.

SISTAR

The Sistar machine gun appeared in Italy in the early 1930s and was vigorously promoted by its inventor, Niccolo Mancini. He engaged a public relations firm called Sistar to promote the gun, hence the name.

On close examination this gun has all the hallmarks of a confidence trick. Much play was made of the system of loading the fixed, side-mounted, magazine by hinging it forward and charging it from a special clip. This, of course, had already been put into service by the Breda company in their 1924 model. And the more you study the contemporary pictures the more you become convinced that the Sistar guns - one in 7.92mm Mauser and the other in 6.5mm Carcano calibers - were re-worked Breda guns with cosmetic additions to separate investors from their money. And after a couple of years of advertising the Sistar vanished as rapidly as it had appeared.

SIX-PAK

This was simply the General Electric Minigun (see preceding) rendered in 5.56mm caliber and provided with a complete package of magazine, power units, ammunition chutes and all the necessary add-ons to allow it to be fitted into any helicopter or vehicle with the minimum of alteration. A six-barreled Gatling, electrically powered, it was an effective and satisfactory weapon, but it was a considerable amount of machinery to propel a rather small caliber bullet, and as a result it appears that few armies took it seriously. Certainly none took it seriously enough to adopt it in any numbers, and by the late mid-1990s GE had dropped it from their inventory.

SOLEY LEWIS

This was marketed - or, at least offered - by the Soley Armament Company of London in the late 1930s, though who the actual inventor or designer was is difficult to determine. The weapon itself was simply a Lewis gun modified to fire from a top-mounted Bren magazine instead of the usual drum. Although it was a neat and workmanlike conversion, there was really very little point in it, and I rather think that Soley offered it simply as a

stop-gap until the British had sufficient Bren guns. But the army preferred to take their chance and wait for the Bren and the Soley-Lewis was never purchased in any quantity. Two versions have been seen, one with a Lewis-like aluminum finned heat radiator around the barrel and gas cylinder, the other with the barrel and cylinder exposed in similar fashion to the standard aircraft guns. The second version also does away with the familiar Lewis pinion casing and apparently reverted to a conventional return spring around the gas piston.

TAYLOR

American multi-barrel battery gun submitted for trial in 1878. It had nine barrels arranged in a curve, fed by a block containing a number of holes in nine columns, also arranged in a curve and filled with cartridges. This was dropped into the top of the gun body, and turning a hand crank fired each barrel in turn, then extracted the cartridge case from the block and ejected it. After a row of nine had been fired, the block dropped to align the next row of nine, and so on until the final row had been fired when the block would be removed for refilling. It worked, but appears to have been a cumbersome and

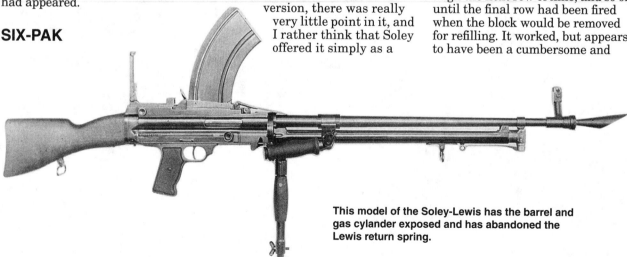

This model of the Soley-Lewis has the barrel and gas cylander exposed and has abandoned the Lewis return spring.

unnecessarily complicated system. Like the Bailey gun it was refused test because the feed arrangements prevented the sustained fire tests being properly carried out. It was never heard of again.

TUL-17

Heavy-barreled automatic rifle type light machine gun developed in Vietnam in the early 1970s and which appeared to be a copy of the Chinese Type 56 assault rifle but using a drum magazine similar to that used by the Soviet RPK machine gun.

VALMET

Valtions Metallehdas was a Finnish state engineering factory set up in 1917 and which made pistols, SMGs and rifles. The name was later condensed to Valmet, and in the 1990s it was taken over by the Sako company. It produced two light machine guns in the post-1945 period. The M62 was based on the action of the Czech ZB26, gas-operated with a rising block breech, but differed in being belt-fed from a belt box on the right side of the receiver. It was adopted by the Finnish army and also sold to the army of Qatar. The M78 was simply a Kalashnikov AKM with a longer and heavier barrel, firing

from either a 30-round box or a 75-round drum. This was the subject of trials by various armies but was not adopted. Sako then re-defined it as a heavy-barreled rifle, but to date it appears not to have had any takers.

VANDENBERG

American mechanical 'volley gun' used by Confederate forces in the American Civil War. It resembles the later Montigny Mitrailleuse in having multiple barrels (85 in one instance) arranged inside a casing resembling a cannon barrel. The rear end was closed by a large cylindrical screw-threaded block, which carried the appropriate number of chambers. There were charged with powder and ball, the breech closed, and a percussion cap placed on a central nipple. When this was struck, the flash passed down channels to all the chambers, igniting them more or less simultaneously and producing a massive volley. General Vandenberg, the inventor, failed to raise any interest in the USA, took the idea to Britain, had some guns made, and sent three back to the USA for trial by the Union Army in 1864. In some unexplained manner a number found their way to the Confederate army at more or less the same time. Nei-

ther side appears to have been impressed with the weapon; the Union army pointed out that simply cleaning the weapon after firing took one man nine hours.

VICKERS TYPE 'D'

The Vickers 'D' gun was a 50-caliber Vickers gun, of the standard pattern with water jacket and Maxim toggle action, but chambered for a very special cartridge never used by any other gun. The case was long (almost one inch longer than the 50-caliber Browning) and slender, the whole round about 6.2 inches long. It carried a 665-grain bullet and fired it at 2790 ft/second. For its day (the middle 1930s) it was a very formidable weapon, but it was also a big and heavy one, and most people were unable to see a tactical niche for it. Vickers found few takers, selling a handful to China and possibly to Japan (for both countries subsequently bought ammunition) but that was as far as the Type D ever got, and it made no showing in World War II. The ammunition has been a 'collector's item' for years.

WILDER

American mechanical machine gun developed in 1878. It resembled the Gatling in having multiple barrels, but in this case there

The Valmet M62 fires the 7.62x39 Soviet cartridge; note the absence of a trigger guard, to permit operation when wearing mitts in Arctic winters.

The Valmet M78 is a conventional Kalashnikov-clone heavy-barreled rifle.

were five fixed barrels mounted on the upper arc of a circle. Behind them was a large revolving drum with a cam, which controlled the action for the five bolts attached to the five barrels. There were five vertical magazines each holding fifty rounds. As the drum was revolved by the usual hand crank the bolts were withdrawn in succession; one bolt would open, a round would drop in from the overhead feed and the bolt would close. The drum would move on to operate the next bolt and the first one would fire. After the fifth barrel had fired, the action went back to the first barrel and began the sequence again.

The Wilder had a number of good points, but the early death of the inventor caused it to be abandoned. The patents were apparently purchased some years later, but by that time mechanical guns were obsolescent, the automatic gun having appeared, and nothing further was heard of the Wilder.

WILLIAMS

This was a mechanical gun developed by a Captain Williams of the Confederate Army during the American Civil War and is sometimes claimed as being the first machine gun ever to be used in battle. It cannot, however, be classed as a machine gun, since it was necessary to put each round into the feedway by hand. It was simply a quick-firing breech-loader, operated by a hand crank. Turning the handle operated a crank and connecting rod attached to the breechblock, so that, rather like the more successful Gardner gun, the block was opened and closed. Perhaps the 'machine gun' claim comes from the automatic firing device, which released the firing pin as soon as the breech was locked. About fifty of these guns were made and employed in several Civil War battles.

APPENDIX TWO
MACHINE GUNS
Arranged in alphabetical order

Name	Year	Caliber	Action	Length	Barrel	Weight	Feed	Velocity	Rate
AA-52 (France) (Light)	1952	7.5x54	DBB	45.08	19.68	22.00	Belt	2700	700
AA-52 (Heavy)	1952	7.5x54	DBB	49.00	23.62	25.06	Belt	2756	700
AA-T 7.62 F1		7.62x51	--------	------- as above -------				2720	900
AAI (USA) GPHMG	1982	.50 Brg	Gas	61.00	36.00	55.00	Belt	400	2900
Adams-Wilmot (UK)	1934	.303	Gas	n/a	n/a	20.00	D/99	2440	900
Alfa (Spain) Model 44	1944	7.92x57	Gas	57.08	29.53	28.62	Belt	2493	780
Alfa (Spain) Model 55	1955	7.62x51	Gas	43.30	24.00	28.56	Belt	2821	780
Al-Quds (Iran)	19993	7.62x39	Gas	40.35	21.34	11.02	B/30	2445	650
Ameli (Spain)	1980	5.56x45	DBB	38.19	15.75	11.44	Belt	2870	900
Ares (USA) Light	1987	5.56x45	Gas	42.24	21.65	10.81	Belt/B	3100	600
Ares (USA) Ext. Powered	1985	7.62x51	EP	31.81	23.50	27.62	Belt	2765	V/650
Ares (USA) TARG	1990	50 PCTA	Gas, Rev	44.40	36.50	44.97	Linkless	1800	2952
Beardmore-Farquhar (UK)	1920	.303	Gas	49.50	26.50	19.00	D/81	2440	500
Benet-Marcie (USA) M1909	1909	.30-06	Gas	46.75	23.50	27.00	S/30	2788	600
Berezin (USSR)									
UBT	1941	12.7x107	Gas	55.00	35.00	56.00	Belt	2800	1000
UBS	1941	12.7x107	Gas	53.0	35.0	47.0	Belt	2670	750
UBK	1941	12.7x107	Gas	53.0	35.0	47.0	Belt	2670	1050
Beretta (Italy) AR70/223	1978	5.56x45	Gas	37.60	17.71	11.69	B/40	3182	670
Beretta AR70-84	1984	5.56x45	Gas	37.60	17.71	11.69	B/30	3182	670
Beretta AS 70/90	1990	5.56x45	Gas	39.37	18.30	11.75	B/30	3215	800
Bergmann (Germany) MG10	1910	7.92x57	Recoil	n/a	n/a	36.00	Belt	2950	550
Bergmann MG15	1915	7.92x57	Recoil	44.13	28.20	28.38	Belt	2820	550
Bergmann MG15nA	1916	7.92x57	Recoil	44.13	28.50	28.50	Belt	2925	550

Name	Year	Caliber	Action	Length	Barrel	Weight	Feed	Velocity	Rate
Berthier US M1917	1916	.30-06	Gas	48.00	n/a	15.75	B/20	2625	500
Besa (UK) Mk 1	1939	7.92x57	Gas	43.50	29.00	47.00	Belt	2700	500
Besa (UK) Mk 1	1940	15x104	Gas	80.70	57.60	125.50	Belt	2700	450
Besa Mk 2	1940	7.92x57	Gas	43.50	29.00	48.00	Belt	2700	500
Besal (UK) Mk 1	1941	.303	Gas	48.00	22.00	15.75	B/20	2450	500
Besal Mk 2	1941	.303	Gas	46.63	22.00	21.50	B/30	2450	600
Breda (Italy)									
M1924	1924	6.5X52	Recoil			20.0	B/20	2080	500
M1930	1930	6.5x52	DBB	48.50	20.50	22.75	B/20	2065	500
M1931	1931	13.2x99	Gas	65.0	39.8	104.70	B/30	2590	500
M1935	1935	303	DBB			27.0	Belt	2400	650
M37	1937	8x59	Gas	50.00	25.00	42.50	S/20	2600	450
M38 Air	1938	12.7x81	Gas	63.93	54.72	31.50	Belt	2493	700
M38/7.35	1938	7.35x51	DBB	49.0	22.0	20.0	B/2-	2460	600
M38/Tank	1938	8x59	Gas						
Bren (UK) Mk 1, Mk 2	1938	.303	Gas	45.25	25.00	22.33	B/30	2400	500
Bren Mk 3	1944	.303	Gas	42.90	22.25	19.33	B/30	2400	480
Bren Mk 4	1944	303	Gas	42.90	22.25	19.12	B/30	2400	500
Britain									
Bren L4A1	1955	7.62x51	Gas	44.63	21.13	22.0	B/30	2700	500
L7A1 GPMG	1961	7.62x51	Gas	48.50	26.75	24.50	Belt	2750	800
L8A1 Tank MG	1965	7.62x51	Gas	43.25	29.00	23.0	Belt	2750	650
L19A1		7.62x51	Gas	------- Heavy-barrel variant of the L8A1 -------					
L20A1		7.62x51	Gas	------- Helicopter-mounted versionof L8A1					
L37A1		7.62x51	Gas	42.50	26.12	21.0	Belt	2750	650
L43A1		7.62x51	Gas	------- Ranging machine gun variant of L8A1 -------					
L86A1 LSW	1986	5.56x45	Gas	35.43	25.43	13.44	B/30	3182	700
L94A1 Chain Gun		7.62X51	EP	49.21	27.67	39.37	Belt	2870	520
Brixia (Italy) M1920	1920	6.5X52	Recoil	n/a	n/a	34.50	B/50	2080	500
Browning (USA)									
M1917	1917	.30-06	Recoil	37.50	24.00	32.62	Belt	2800	600
M1917A1	1930	.30-06	Recoil	38.64	24.00	32.57	Belt	2800	600
M1918 Aircraft	1918	.30-06	Recoil						

Name	Year	Caliber	Action	Length	Barrel	Weight	Feed	Velocity	Rate
M1919 tank	1919	.30-06	Recoil	35.10	18.00				
M1919A1	1931	.30-06	Recoil		18.00	40.00	Belt	2690	600
M1919A2	1927	.30-06	Recoil	------ As for M1919A1 but adapted to the M2 Tripod ------					
M1919A3	1927	.30-06	Recoil	------ As for M1919A2 but with modified sights; trials only. ------					
M1919A4	1934	.30-06	Recoil	41.11	24.00	31.00	Belt	2800	500
M1919A5	1941	.30-06	Recoil	40.80	24.00	30.50	Belt	2800	500
M1919A6	1943	.30-06	Recoil	53.00	24.00	32.50	Belt	2800	450
Aircraft M2 Fixed	1931	.30-06	Recoil	39.72	23.90	21.50	Belt	2800	1350
Aircraft M2 Flexible	1931	.30-06	Recoil	39.80	23.90	23.00	Belt	2800	450
M1927	1927	.50Brg	Recoil	56.00	36.00	66.00	Belt	2300	650
M2	1933	.50Brg	Recoil	66.00	45.00	100.00	Belt	2930	850
Aircraft M2	1928	.50Brg	Recoil	57.00	36.00	64.00	Belt	2840	575
M2HB	1933	.50Brg	Recoil	54.00	45.00	84.00	Belt	2930	600
M2HB-QCB (Ramo)		.50Brg	Recoil	65.00	45.00	84.21	Belt	3048	550
M2HB-QCB (FN)		.50Brg	Recoil	65.20	45.00	84.10	Belt	3005	500
M2HB-QCB (Manroy)		.50Brg	Recoil	65.00	45.00	84.87	Belt	2930	
M37 tank		.30-06	Recoil	------ As for M1919A5 but adapted for tanks, helicopters etc. ------					

Browning Automatic Rifle:

Name	Year	Caliber	Action	Length	Barrel	Weight	Feed	Velocity	Rate
Belgium FN M30	1930	7.65x53	Gas	45.27	22.00	20.50	B/20	189-	500
Belgium FN Type D	1947	7.92x57	Gas	45.10	19.70	20.31	B/20	2500	480
Poland M28	1928	7.92x57	Gas	47.83	24.00	20.93	B/20	2788	600
Sweden M21	1922	6.5x55	Gas	44.00	26.40	19.30	B/20	2460	500
Sweden M37	1937	6.5x55	Gas	46.10	24.00	20.88	B/20	2460	480
USA M1918	1918	.30-06	Gas	47.00	24.00	16.00	B/20	2905	550
USA M1918A1	1927	.30-06	Gas	47.00	24.00	18.50	B/20	2805	550
USA M1918A2	1939	.30-06	Gas	47.80	24.00	19.38	B/20	2805	450/650
USA M1922	1923	.30-06	Gas	41.00	18.00	19.20	B/20	2700	550
Browning: Saco Fifty/.50	1987	.50Brg	Recoil	61.41	36.00	58.88	Belt	2841	750
Browning: Ramo M2 Light	1991	.50Brg	Recoil	60.00	36.00	58.88	Belt	2841	750
BSA (UK) 1924	1924	.5 Vic	Recoil	46.3	53.93	37.80	D/37	2600	400
Chain Gun EX34	1975	7.62x51	EP	25.98	22.83	30.19	Belt	2828	520
Chain Gun M242	1981	25x137	EP	108.6	78.75	243.6	Belt	3610	500
Chatellerault M24/29	1929	7.5x54	Gas	42.60	19.70	20.25	B/26	2700	500

Name	Year	Caliber	Action	Length	Barrel	Weight	Feed	Velocity	Rate
Chatellerault M31	1931	7.5x54	Gas	40.50	19.70	21.25	D/150	2700	500
Chatellerault M34/39	1939	7.5x54	Gas			53.00	Belt	2700	1300
Chauchat (France) Mle 15	1915	8x50R	Recoil	45.00	18.50	20.00	B/20	2300	250
Chauchat (USA) M1918	1918	.30-06	Recoil	45.00	18.50	20.00	B/16	2700	300
China Type 24	1924	7.92x57	Recoil	48.00	23.80	52.50	Belt	2920	350
Type 26	1924	7.92x57	Recoil	48.00	23.80	52.50	Belt	2920	350
Type 53	1953	7.62x54	Gas	49.80	23.80	26.81	D/47	2700	55
Type 54	1955	12.7x107	Gas	62.50	42.00	78.50	Belt	2825	550
Type 56	1957	7.62x39	Gas	41.00	20.50	15.44	Belt	2410	700
Type 57	1958	7.62x54	Gas	44.09	28.35	30.44	Belt	2832	650
Type 58	1959	7.62x54	Gas	50.00	23.80	28.75	Belt	2750	650
Type 63	1963	7.62x54	Gas	44.09	28.35	29.88	Belt	2870	650
Type 67	1967	7.62x54	Gas	45.00	23.50	32.50	Belt	2740	650
Type 74	1974	7.62x39	Gas	43.62	20.80	14.12	D/101	2411	750
Type 77	1977	12.7x107	Gas	85.98	40.00	89.50	Belt	2625	800
Type 80	1980	7.62x54	Gas	46.93	26.57	17.37	Belt	2700	650
Type 81	1981	7.62x39	Gas	40.31	20.80	11.37	D/75	2411	
Type W-85	1985	12.7x107	Gas	78.05	40.00	40.75	Belt	2625	
Colt (USA) M1895	1895	.30-40	Gas	40.80	28.00	40.00	Belt	2000	430
Colt (USA) M1895	1895	.30-06	Gas	40.80	28.00	40.00	Belt	2800	450
Colt (USA) Model 715	1990	5.56x45	Gas	40.15	20.07	12.75	B/30	3035	625
Colt (USA) CMG-2	1975	5.56x45	Gas	41.90	20.00	14.62	Belt	3250	850
Czech CZ2000	1992	5.45x39	Gas	41.34	22.71	9.12	D/75	3150	800
Czech vz/52	1952	7.62x45	Gas	41.00	27.00	17.56	Belt/B	2450	1150
Czech vz52/57	1957	7.62x39	Gas	41.00	27.00	17.56	Belt/B	2477	1150
Czech vz/59 Light	1958	7.62x54	Gas	43.93	23.35	29.17	Belt	2657	750
Czech vz/59 Heavy	1959	7.62x54	Gas	47.83	27.28	42.37	B/30	2723	750
Czech ZGB33	1933	303	Gas	45.50	25.00	22.12	B/30	2450	500
Czech ZB vz/26	1926	7.92x57	Gas	45.78	23.70	21.33	B/20	2598	500
Czech ZB vz/30	1930	7.92x57	Gas	45.75	26.50	21.33	B/30	2500	600
Czech ZB vz/37	1937	7.92x57	Gas	43.50	26.70	41.00	Belt	2600	500/700
Daewoo K3	1990	5.56x45	Gas	40.55	21.00	15.12	Belt/B	3000	850
Darne (France) M1918	1918	8x50R	Gas	36.89	25.98	15.44	Belt	2300	1100
Darne Type 33	1929	7.5x	Gas			18.50	Belt	2700	1200

Name	Year	Caliber	Action	Length	Barrel	Weight	Feed	Velocity	Rate
Degtyarev DP	1928	7.62x54	Gas	50.80	23.80	20.50	D/47	2760	550
DT	1929	7.62x54	Gas	47.00	23.80	28.00	D/60	2700	650
DPM	1944	7.62x54	Gas	49.80	23.80	26.81	D/47	2700	55
DTM	1944	7.62x54	Gas	46.50	23.80	28.37	D/60	2700	600
DS39	1939	7.62x54	Gas	46.00	28.40	26.37	Belt	2650	550/1100
DShK38	1938	12.7x107	Gas	62.30	39.37	73.50	Belt	2805	575
DShK38-40	1940	12.7x107	Gas	62.50	42.00	78.50	Belt	2825	550
RPD	1953	7.62x39	Gas	41.00	20.50	15.44	Belt	2410	700
Dover Devil	1982	.50 Brg	Gas	52.30	36.00	50.00	Belt	400	2900
FIAT-Revelli M1914	1914	6.5x52	DBB	46.50	25.75	37.50	B/50	2100	400
FIAT-Revelli M1935	1935	8x59	DBB	50.00	25.75	40.00	Belt	2600	500
FN-BRG	1985	15x115	Gas	78.74	53.15	121.25	2 Belt	2952	700
FN-BRG15	1988	15.5x106	Gas	84.65	n/a	132.25	2 Belt	3460	600
FN-MAG	1955	7.62x51	Gas	49.20	21.50	22.25	Belt	2800	850
FN Minimi	1974	5.56x45	Gas	40.94	18.35	15.12	Belt/B	1000	850
FN Minimi Para	1982	5.56x45	Gas	35.15	13.66	15.65	Belt/B	2952	850
Foote (USA) MG-69	1969	5.56x45	Gas	41.70	20.0	14.50	Belt	3300	700
Galil (Israel) ARM	1974	7.62x51	Gas	40.94	18.35	15.12	B/50	2788	650
Gardner (UK) 5-bbl Mk 1	1882	.45	Hand	53.50	33.00	290.00	G/30	n/a	>800
Gardner, 2-bbl Mk 1	1884	.45	Hand	47.00	30.00	218.00	G/30	n/a	>250
Gardner (UK) 2-bbl Mk 1	1888	.402	Hand	45.00	28.50	88.00	G/20	n/a	>200
Gardner (UK), 2-bbl; Conv'd	1898	.303	Hand	45.25	28.25	92.00	G/20	n/a	400
Gast (Germany)	1918	7.92x57	Recoil	54.72	28.35	40.81	D/192	2700	1300
Gatling (UK)	1874	.45	Hand	59.41	31.95	444.00*	D/240	n/a	>800
Gatling (UK)	1875	.65	Hand	66.60	33.00	817.00	D/50	n/a	400
GE (USA) M134 Minigun	1963	7.62x54	EP	31.56	22.00	36.00	Belt	2850	6000
GE (USA) XM214 SixPak	1958	5.56x45	EP	28.80	20.14	22.50	Belt	3250	6000
Gebauer-Weich M1935	1935	7.92x57	EP				Belts	2700	1600
GECAL 50	1986	.50Brg	EP	46.50	36.00	96.12	Belt	2900	8000
Goryunov	1943								
SG-43		7.62x54	Gas	44.09	28.35	30.44	Belt	2832	650
SGM		7.62x54	Gas	44.09	28.35	29.88	Belt	2870	650
Heckler & Koch HK11		7.62x51	DBB	40.15	17.71	15.00	D/80	2560	850
HK11A1		7.62x51	DBB	40.55	17.71	16.94	B/30	2625	650

Name	Year	Caliber	Action	Length	Barrel	Weight	Feed	Velocity	Rate
HK11E		7.62x51	DBB	40.55	17.71	17.94	D/50	2625	800
HK13		5.56x45	DBB	38.58	17.71	13.19	B/40	3117	750
HK13E		5.56x45	DBB	40.55	17.71	17.62	B/30	3117	750
HK21		7.62x51	DBB	40.19	17.71	16.12	Belt	2625	900
HK21A1		7.62x51	DBB	40.15	17.71	17.62	Belt	2625	900
HK21E	1983	7.62x51	DBB	44.88	22.05	20.50	Belt	2756	800
HK23E		5.56x45	DBB	40.55	17.71	19.33	B/30	3117	750
HK G36 LSW	1995	5.56x45	Gas	38.98	18.90	7.69	B/30	3018	750
Hefah V Mk 1 (UK)	1942	.303	Gas	48.00	24.50	15.12	D/60	2500	600
Hotchkiss Mle 1897	1897	8x50R	Gas	n/z	n/a	55.00	S/30	2400	600
Hotchkiss Mle 1909	1909	8x50R	Gas	46.75	23.50	27.00	S/30	2180	500
Hotchkiss Mle 1914	1914	8x50R	Gas	51.60	31.00	55.69	Belt/S	2325	500
Hotchkiss (UK) Mks 1, 1*	1916	.303	Gas	46.75	23.50	27.00	S/30	2450	500
Hudson (US Navy)	1938	1.1in	Gas	119.60	81.89	-	B/8	2700	150
Hughes Lockless	1979	5.56mm	Gas	40.0	22.0	9.81	B/64	3100	420
INSAS Standard	1997	5.56x45	Gas	41.34	21.00	13.50	B/30	3130	650
INSAS Para	1997	5.56x45	Gas	40.35	20.07	13.44	B/30	3117	650
Japan: Model 62	1962	7.62x51	Gas	45.50	20.63	23.56	Belt	2400	600
Japan: Model 74	1974	7.62x51	Gas	42.72	24.60	44.94	Belt	2805	1000
Japan: Type 1	1941	7.7x58	Gas	42.40	23.23	77.00	S/30	2400	550
Type 1 Air	1941	12.7x81	Recoil	48.80	31.88	48.50	Belt	2400	900
Japan: Type 3	1914	6.5x51	Gas	45.50	29.52	62.00	S/30	2400	400
Japan: Type 11	1922	6.5x51	Gas	43.50	19.0	22.50	H/30	2300	500
Japan: Type 91	1931	6.5x51	Gas	42.00	19.20	24.44	H/50	2300	500
Japan: Type 92	1932	7.7x58	Gas	45.50	27.56	61.00	S/30	2400	450
Japan: Type 93	1933	13.2x99	Gas	95.00	65.00	87.00	B/30	2210	450
Japan: Type 96	1936	6.5x51	Gas	41.50	21.70	20.00	B/30	2400	550
Japan: Type 97	1937	7.7x58	Gas	46.50	28.00	24.00	B/30	2400	500
Japan: Type 99	1939	7.7x58	Gas	46.50	23.60	23.00	B/30	2350	850
Johnson (USA) 1941	1941	.30-06	Recoil	42.30	22.00	12.50	B/20	2800	600
Johnson 1944	1944	.30-06	Recoil	42.00	22.00	14.33	B/30	2800	900
Kalashnikov:									
RPK	1960	7.62x39	Gas	41.00	23.23	10.50	D/75	2400	600
PK	1963	7.62x54	Gas	45.67	25.90	19.81	B/30	2706	700

Name	Year	Caliber	Action	Length	Barrel	Weight	Feed	Velocity	Rate
RPK-74	1974	5.45x39	Gas	41.73	24.25	10.12	B/45	3150	650
Knorr-Bremse M/35	1933	7.92x57	Gas	51.48	27.25	22.06	B/20	2600	500
Lewis (UK) Mark 1	1914	.303	Gas	50.63	26.25	25.25	D/47	2450	550
Mk 2	1915	303	Gas			19.5	D/97	2440	50
Mk 3	1915	303	Gas			17.0	D/97	2440	700
Lewis (USA) M1917	1917	.30-06	Gas	51.75	26.25	25.25	D/47	2830	500
M1918	1918	30-06	Gas						
M1917 Air	1917	30-06	Gas			25.0	D/96	2750	500
M1918 Air	1918	30-06	Gas			23.0	D/97	2800	600
Madsen	1904-	7.92x57	Recoil	45.00	23.00	20.00	B/40	2460	450
Madsen-Saetter	1959	7.62x51	Gas	45.90	22.20	23.50	Belt	2800	1000
Madsen-Saetter Tank	1959	7.62x51	Gas	38.20	22.20	22.33	Belt	2800	750
Madsen-Saetter Heavy	1959	.50Brg	Gas	64.00	39.37	61.69	Belt	2850	1000
Maremont Dual Feed	1975	7.62x51	Recoil	34.40	n/a	n/a	Belts	2800	650
Maremont Universal	1975	7/62x51	Gas/Recoil	37.0	n/a	15.0	Belt	2800	650
Marlin (USA) M1917	1917	.30-06	Gas	40.00	28.00	22.50	Belt	2800	600
Maxim (USA) M1904	1904	.30-06	Recoil	48.00	28.54	68.50	Belt	2825	600
Maxim (UK) .45 Mk 1	1889	.45	Recoil	43.50	n.a	60.00	Belt	1350	400
Maxim (UK) .45 GG Mk 1	1892	.45	Recoil	43.75	n/a	60.00	Belt	1200	400
Maxim (UK) .303 Mk 1	1899	.303	Recoil	45.00	28.00	64.00	Belt	1800	400
Maxim (UK) .303 Conv'd Mk 1	1897	.303	Recoil	45.00	28.00	64.00	Belt	1800	400
Maxim (UK) .303 Conv'd Mk 2	1901	.303	Recoil	40.50	28.25	50.00	Belt	2750	600
Maxim (Germany) M1901	1901	7.92x57	Recoil						
Maxim (Russia) M1905	1905	7.62x54R	Recoil						
Maxim: (Germany) MG 08	1908	7.92x57	Recoil	46.25	28.35	58.33	Belt	2838	450
MG 1909	1909	7.92x57	Recoil						
Maxim (Russia) M1910	1910	7.62x54	Recoil	43.60	28.25	52.50	Belt	2830	550
Maxim (Germany):									
MG08/15	1915	7.92x57	Recoil	56.90	28.35	31.00	Belt	2840	450
IMG 08/15	1915	7.92x57	Recoil	46.25	28.35	28.65	Belt	2840	450
IMG 08/18	1918	7.92x57	Recoil	46.25	28.35	26.48	Belt	2940	450
Maxim (Belgium) légere	1920	7.65x53	Recoil	49.50	28.34	33.06	Belt	2025	450
Maxim: (China) Type 24	1924	7.92x57	Recoil	48.00	23.80	52.50	Belt	2920	350
Mendoza (Mexico) C-34	1934	7x57	Gas	46.00	25.00	18.50	B/20	2700	450

Name	Year	Caliber	Action	Length	Barrel	Weight	Feed	Velocity	Rate
Mendoza (Mexico) RM2	1960	.30-06	Gas	43.30	24.00	14.12	B/20	2750	650
MG3A1 (Germany)	1958	7.62x51	Recoil	48.22	20.90	24.37	Belt	2690	1100
MG13 (Germany)	1933	7.92x57	Recoil	57.75	28.25	23.94	D/75	2700	650
MG15 (Germany)	1932	7.92x57	Recoil	52.50	23.50	28.00	D/75	2700	850
MG 17	193?	7.92x57	Recoil	48.00		28.00	Belt	2550	1200
MG30 (Germany)	1930	7.92x57	Recoil	46.25	23.50	17.00	B/25	2500	800
MG34 (Germany)	1934	7.92x57	Recoil	48.00	24.75	26.69	D/75	2700	650
MG42 (Germany)	1942	7.92x57	Recoil	48.0	21.00	25.50	Belt	2480	1200
MG81 (Germany)	1938	7.92x57	Recoil	36.02	18.70	14.37	Belt	2592	1600
MG131 (Germany)	1936	13x64B	Recoil	46.25	21.75	40.00	Belt	2560	960
MG151 (Germany)	1935	15x95	Recoil	75.43	49.37	78.94	Belt	3150	700
MG151/20 (Germany)	1938	20x84	Recoil	69.52	43.40	93.50	Belt	2313	700
Negev (Israel) Light	1990	5.56x45	Gas	40.15	18.11	16.50	Belt/B	3280	1000
Negev Assault	1990	5.56x45	Gas	35.04	13.00	15.44	Belt/B	3280	1000
Nordenfelt (UK) 5-bbl Mk 1	1884	.45	Hand	46.00	28.50	154.00	H/50	1250	>300
Nordenfelt (UK) 5-bbl Mk 2	1886	.45	Hand	42.25	28.50	133.00	H/50	1250	>300
Nordenfelt (UK) 3-bbl Mk 1	1887	.45	Hand	41.50	28.50	93.00	B/27	1350	>300
Nordenfelt (UK) Conv'd Mk 1	1898	.303	Hand	41.25	28.50	98.00	B/27	1800	>300
NTK Model 5M Heavy (Japan)	1966	.30-06	Gas	51.20	23.80	35.80	Belt	2800	550
NTK Model 5M Light (Japan)	1966	.30-06	Gas	44.40	23.60	33.90	Belt	2800	550
NTK Model 7M (Japan)	1968	7.62x51	Gas	n/a	n.a	22.0	Belt	2720	650
Perino (Italy)	1908	6.5x52	Recoil	43.60	27.56	50.50	T/50	2000	600
Pirat (Poland)	1995	14.5x114	Recoil	77.95	53.00	115.00	Belt	3280	600
Puteaux (France)	1905	8x50R	Gas	49.21	30.70	54.00	S/23	2300	650
Rolls-Royce	1941	.50Brg	Recoil	50.00	40.00	49.00	Belt	2340	1000
Russell Robinson	1949	.50Brg	Recoil	n/a	n/a	43.00	Belt	2800	450
Russia: RP-46	1946	7.62x54	Gas	50.00	23.80	28.75	Belt	2750	650

SAWS:

Name	Year	Caliber	Action	Length	Barrel	Weight	Feed	Velocity	Rate
Maremont XM233	1976	6x45	Gas	42.00	n/a	25.30*	Belt	2500	450
Philco-Ford XM234	1976	6x45	Gas	42.0	n/a	22.50*	Belt	2500	500
ShKAS	1933	7.62x54	Gas	27.60	17.52	23.50	Belt	2750	600
St Etienne (France)	1907	8x50R	Gas	46.50	28.00	56.75	S/30	2300	400
Schwarzlose (Austria)									

Name	Year	Caliber	Action	Length	Barrel	Weight	Feed	Velocity	Rate
M1907	1907	8x50R	DBB	41.93	20.66	43.88	Belt	2050	400
M07/12	1913	8x50R	DBB	42.13	20.80	42.55	Belt	1885	400
M 1907/16	1916	8x50R	DBB			29.10	Belt	2050	500
M07/16nA	1917	8x50R	DBB				Belt		880
Scotti M1928	1928	7.7x56	Gas			22.0	Belt	2400	500
Scotti 12.7mm	1935	12.7x81SR	Gas/BB	55.5	33.8	50.7	Belt	2425	700
S.I.A. (Italy)	1913	6.5x52	Gas	n/a	n/a	23/50	S/25	2100	700
SIG (Switzerland): KE-7	1936	7.92x57	Recoil	46.87	23.63	17.25	B/20	2625	550
SIG MG51	1951	7.5x55	Recoil	50.00	22.20	35.37	Belt	2600	1000
SIG MG-710-1	1960	7.5x55	DBB	46.85	19.68	24.88	Belt	2600	800
SIG MG-710-2	1960	7.5x55	DBB	46.85	21.65	24.00	Belt	2600	800
SIG MG-710-3	1965	7.5x55	DBB	45.00	22.00	21.25	Belt	2600	900
Singapore; Ultimax	1982	5.56x45	Gas	40.31	20.00	10.81	D/100	3182	500
Singapore: CIS50	1988	.50Brg	Gas	70.00	45.00	66.12	Belt	2920	500
Skoda M1893	1893	8x52R	DBB	n/a	n/a	22.45	B/30	1805	350
Skoda M1909	1909	8x50R	DBB	41.15	22.44	34.21	Belt	1885	420
Steyr-Mannlicher: AUG LSW	1980	5.56x45	Gas	35.43	24.45	10.81	B/42	3280	680
Stoner 63 (USA)	1965	5.56x45	Gas	40.24	21.69	12.50	Belt/B	3250	700
Swiss M25	1925	7.5x55	Recoil	45.67	22.24	23.75	B/30	2460	450
Swiss M97	1987	7.5x55	Recoil	46.25	18.70	66.12	Belt	2625	1000
Tank und Flieger (Germany)	1918	13x92	Recoil	n/a	n/a	85.00	Belt	2600	400
TARG (USA)	1990	.50CTA	Gas	44.40	36.50	45.0	Linkless	2950	2000
TUL-17 (Vietnam)	1970	7.62x39	Gas	40.75	24.0	11.10	D/75	2410	600
Uirapuru (Brazil)	1988	7.62x51	Gas	51.18	23.62	28.60	Belt	2790	700
U.S. M60	1963	7.62x51	Gas	43.50	22.04	23.19	Belt	2838	550
U.S. M60E3	1986	7.62x51	Gas	42.00	22.00	18.94	Belt	2822	560
U.S. M60E4	1991	7.62x51	Gas	37.71	22.0	22.50	Belt	2800	600
U.S. M73	1962	7.62x51	Recoil	35.00	22.00	30.88	Belt	2800	600
U.S. M85	1963	.50Brg	Recoil	50.55	36.00	61.50	Belt	2842	400/1050
U.S. M240G	1995	7.62x51	Gas	48.03	24.68	25.81	Belt	2800	750
U.S. M249	1990	5.56x45	Gas	40.94	20.50	15.12	Belt/B	3000	750
U.S. GAU-19/A		.50Brg	EP	46.50	36.00	74.00	Belt	2900	1000/2000
Valmet (Finland) M62	1966	7.62x39	Gas	42.72	18.50	18.33	Belt	2395	1050
Valmet (Finland) M78	1978	7.62x39	Gas	41.73	n/a	10.36	B/30	2360	650

Name	Year	Caliber	Action	Length	Barrel	Weight	Feed	Velocity	Rate
Vektor (S.Africa): Mini-SS	1994	5.56x45	Gas	39.37	20.19	17.56	Belt	3210	800
Vektor (S.Africa) SS-77	1977	7.62x51	Gas	45.47	21.65	21.19	Belt	2750	750
Vektor MG-4	1980	7.62x51	Recoil	37.00	23.42	33.06	Belt	2756	700
Vickers (UK) Mk 1	1912	.303	Recoil	45.50	28.50	40.00	Belt	2450	450
Vickers, .5in Mark 1	1932	.5Vic	Recoil	54.00	31.10	52.00	Belt	2600	450/675
Vickers .5in Class D	1934	.5 Class D	Recoil	70.47	45.00	101.50	Belt	3040	450
Vickers GO (or Type K)	1937	.303	Gas	40.00	20.00	21.00	D/100	2450	1050
Vickers-Berthier Mk 3	1933	.303	Gas	46.50	23.50	22.00	B/30	2450	600
Vladimirov :									
KPV	1955	14.5x114	Recoil	78.98	53.00	108.25	Belt	3280	600
NSV	1971	12.7x107	Gas	61.42	44.50	55.12	Belt	2772	750
VYa (Russia)	1942	23x152B	Gas	84.53	60.60	150.0	belt	2975	700
Yugoslavia: M53	1953	7.92x57	Recoil	35.00	22.00	30.88	Belt	2800	600
Yugoslavia: M65	1965	7.62x39	Gas	43.10	18.50	12.00	B/30	2400	600
Yugoslavia: M72B1	1978	7.62x39	Gas	47.64	22.00	27.50	Belt/D	2340	1000
Yugoslavia: M77B1	1980	7.62x51	Gas	40.35	21.06	11.25	B/20	2750	600
Yugoslavia: M82	1982	5.56x45	Gas	40.15	21.34	8.81	B/30	3280	700
Yugoslavia: M84	1984	7.62x54	Gas	40.26	25.90	33.62	Belt	2706	700

NOTES:

* = weight with 200-round belt of ammunition

APPENDIX THREE
MACHINE GUNS

In ascending order of caliber

This table lists the various cartridges that have been used with machine guns. Data is given for weapons under the cartridge for which they were originally produced; where a change to another caliber has resulted in a considerable difference, then the gun will be noted under that caliber as well, but where the change has merely been a change of caliber with little or no dimensional - or other - change to the weapon, it is not specifically listed. For example, virtually every machine gun made in Europe in the 20th century has appeared in 7.92x57mm Mauser caliber at some time or other, but since this resulted in no more than a larger or smaller hole in the barrel and a few minor changes to the bolt face, they have not been treated as distinct different weapons. Such changes are merely noted under the relevant calibers.

Country	Title	Year	Operating System	Feed System	Gun length	Barrel length	Weight	Rate of Fire	Muzzle Velocity
5.45 x 39.5 Soviet									
Czech Rep.	CZ2000	1992	Gas	D/75	41.34	22.71	9.12	800	3150
Russia	RPK-74	1974	Gas	B/45	41.73	24.25	10.12	650	3150
5.56 x 45 M193 or NATO									
Austria	AUG LSW	1980	Gas	B/42	35.43	24.45	10.81	680	3280
Belgium	FN Minimi	1974	Gas	Belt/N	40.94	18.35	15.12	850	3280
Belgium	Minimi Para	1982	Gas	Belt/B	35.15	13.66	15.85	850	2995
Britain	L86A1 LSW	1986	Gas	B/30	35.43	25.43	13.44	650	3182
Germany	HK13		DBB	B/40	38.58	17.71	13.19	750	3117
Germany	HK13E		DBB	B/30	40.55	17.71	17.62	750	3117
Germany	HK23E		DBB	B/30	40.55	17.71	19.33	750	3117
Germany	G36 LSW	1995	Gas	B/30	38.98	18.90	7.69	750	3018
India	INSAS	1997	Gas	B/30	40.35	20.00	13.44	650	3117
Israel	Negev	1990	Gas	Belt/B	40.15	18.11	16.50	1000	3280I
Israel	Negev Assault	1990	Gas	Belt/B	35.04	13.00	15.44	1000	3280
Italy	AR70-78	1978	Gas	B/40	37.60	17.71	11.60	670	3182
Italy	AR70-84	1984	Gas	B/30	37.60	17.71	11.69	670	3182
Italy	AS 70/90	1990	Gas	B/30	39.37	18.30	11.75	800	3215

Country	Title	Year	Operating System	Feed System	Gun length	Barrel length	Weight	Rate of Fire	Muzzle Velocity
Singapore	Ultimax	1982	Gas	D/100	40.31	20.00	10.81	500	3182
South Africa	Mini-SS	1994	Gas	Belt	39.37	20.19	17.56	800	3210
South Korea	Daewoo	1990	Gas	Belt/B	40.55	21.00	15.12	850	3000
Spain	Ameli	1980	DBB	Belt	38.19	15.75	11.44	900	2870
USA	Ares Light	1987	Gas	Belt	42.24	21.65	10.81	600	3100
USA	Colt CMG-2	1975	Gas	Belt	41.90	20.00	14.62	850	3250
USA	Colt 715	1990	Gas	B/30	40.15	20.07	12.75	625	3035
USA	Foote MG69	1969	Gas	Belt	41.70	20.00	14.50	700	3300
USA	GE SixPak	1958	EP	Belt	28.80	20.14	22.50	6000	3250
USA	Stoner 63	1965	Gas	Belt/B	40.24	21.69	12.50	700	3250
USA	M249	1990	Gas	Belt/B	40.94	20.50	15.12	750	3000
Yugoslavia	M82	1982	Gas	B/30	40.15	21.34	8.81	700	3280
6 x 45mm SAWS									
USA	XM233	1976	Gas	Belt	42.00	n/a	25.30	450	2500
USA	XM234	1976	Gas	Belt	42.00	n/a	22.50	500	2500
6 x 59 Lee Navy									
USA	Colt M1895	1895	Gas	Belt	40.80	28.00	40.00	500	2550
6 x 51R Arisaka									
Japan	Type 3	1914	Gas	S/30	45.50	29.52	62.00	400	2400
Japan	Type 11	1922	Gas	H/30	43.50	19.00	22.50	500	2300
Japan	Type 91	1931	Gas	H/50	42.00	19.20	24.44	500	2300
Japan	Type 96	1936	Gas	B/30	41.50	21.70	20.00	550	2400
6.5 x 52 Carcano									
Italy	Brixia M1920	1920	Recoil	B/50	n/a	n/a	34.50	600	2080
Italy	Breda M30	1930	DBB	B/20	48.50	20.50	22.75	500	2065I
Italy	Fiat 1914	1914	DBB	B/50	46.50	25.75	37.50	400	210
Italy	Fiat M26								
Italy	Fiat M29								
Italy	Perino	1900	Recoil	T/50	43.00	27.65	50.00	600	2000
Italy	SIA	1908	Recoil	T/50	43.60	27.56	50.50	600	2000
7 x 57 Spanish Mauser									
Mexico	Mendoza	1934	Gas	B/20	46.00	25.00	18.50	450	2700

Country	Title	Year	Operating System	Feed System	Gun length	Barrel length	Weight	Rate of Fire	Muzzle Velocity
7 x 54 French Mle 29									
France	AA-52	1952	DBB	Belt	45.08	19.68	22.00	700	27
France	Mle 24/29	1929	Gas	B/26	42.60	19.70	20.25	500	2700
France	Mle 31	1931	Gas	D/150	40.50	19.70	21.25	500	2700
France	Mle34/39	1939	Gas	Belt	n/a	n/a	53.00	1300	2700
7.5 x 55 Swiss									
Switzerland	Fürrer M25	1925	Recoil	B/30	45.67	22.24	23.75	450	2460
Switzerland	SIG MG51	1951	Recoil	Belt	50.00	22.20	35.37	1000	2600
Switzerland	SIG MG 710	1960	DBB	Belt	46.85	19.68	24..88	800	2600
Switzerland	SIG MG 710-2	1960	DBB	Belt	46.85	21.65	24.00	800	2600
Switzerland	SIG MG710-3	1965	DBB	Belt	45.00	22.00	21.25	900	2800
Switzerland	M87	1987	Recoil	Belt	46.25	18.70	66.12	1000	2625
7.62 x 39 Soviet M1943									
China	Type 56	1957	Gas	Belt	41.00	20.50	15.44	700	2410
China	Type 74	1974	Gas	D.101	43.62	20.90	14.12	750	2411
China	Type 81	1981	Gas	D/75	40.31	20.80	11.37	750	2411
Czechoslovakia	vz/52/57	1957	Gas	Belt/B	41.00	27.00	17.56	1150	2477
Finland	Valmet M62	1962	Gas	Belt	42.72	18.50	18.33	1050	2395
Finland	Valmet M78	1978	Gas	B/30`	41.73	n/a	10.36	650	2360
Iran	Ak Quds	1993	Gas	B/30	40.35	21.34	11.02	650	2445
Russia	RPD	1953	Gas	Belt	41.00	20.50	15.44	700	2410
RussiaRPK	1960	1960	Gas	D/75	41.00	23.23	10.50	600	2400
Vietnam	TUL-17	1970	Gas	D/75	40.75	34.00	11.10	600	2410
Yugoslavia	M65	1965	Gas	B/30	43.10	18.50	12.00	600	2400
Yugoslavia	M72B1	1978	Gas	Belt/D	47.64	22.00.	27.50	1000	2340
7.62 x 45 Czech									
Czechoslovakia	vz/52	1952	Gas	Belt/B	41.00	27.00	17.56	1150	2450
7.62 x 51 NATO									
BelgiumFN-MAG	1955	GAS		Belt	21.50	22.25	Belt	850	2800
BrazilUirapuru	1988	Gas		Belt	51.18	23.62	28.60	700	2790
Denmark	Madsen-Saetter	1959	Gas	Belt	45.90	22.20	23.50	1000	2800
Denmark	Madsen-Saetter Tank1959		Gas	Belt	38.20	22.20	22.33	750	2800

Country	Title	Year	Operating System	Feed System	Gun length	Barrel length	Weight	Rate of Fire	Muzzle Velocity
France	AAT F-1	1958	DBB	Belt	49.00	23.62	25.06	700	2756
Germany	MG3A1	1968	Recoil	Belt	48.22	20.90	24.37	1100	2690
Germany	HK11		DBB	D/80	40.15	17.71	15.00	850	2560
Germany	HK11A1		DBB	B/30	40.55	17.71	16.94	650	2625
Germany	HK11E		DBB	D/50	40.55	17.71	17.94	800	2625
Germany	HK21		DBB	Belt	40.19	17.71	16.12	900	2625
Germany	HK21A1		DBB	Belt	40.15	17.71	17.62	900	2625
Germany	HK21E	1983	DBB	Belt	44.88	22.05	20.50	800	2756
Israel	Galil ARM	1974	Gas	B/50	40.94	18.35	15.12	650	2788
Italy	MG42/59	1959	Recoil	Belt	48.03	20.98	26.44	800	2690
Japan	Model 62	1962	Gas	Belt	45.50	20.63	23.56	600	2400
Japan	Model 74	1974	Gas	Belt	42.72	24.60	44.94	1000	2800
Japan	NTK 7M	1968	Gas	Belt	n/a	n/a	22/00	650	2820
South Africa	SS-77	1977	Gas	Belt	45.47	21.65	21.19	750	2750
South Africa	MG-4	1980	Recoil	Belt	37.00	23.42	33.06	700	2760
Spain	Alfa M55	1955	Gas	Belt	43.30	24.00	28.50	780	2821
UK	L4A1	1i955	Gas	B/30	44.63	21.13	22.00	500	2700
UK	L7A1	1961	Gas	Belt	48.50	26.75	24.50	800	2750
UK	L8A1	1965	Gas	Belt	43.25	29.00	23.00	650	2700
UK	L37A1		Gas	Belt	42.50	26.12	21.00	650	2750
UK	L96A1		EP	Belt	49.21	27.67	39.37	520	2870
USA	Ares EP	1985	EP	Belt	31.81	23.50	27.62	650	2765
USA	GE M134	1963	EP	Belt	31.56	22.00	36.00	6000	2850
USA	Maremont DF	1975	Recoil	Belt	4.40	n/a	n/a	650	2800
USA	Maremont U	1975	Gas/Rec	Belt	37.00	n/a	15.00	650	2800
USA	M60	1963	Gas	Belt	43.50	22.04	23.19	550	2838
USA	M60E3	1986	Gas	Belt	42.00	22.00	18.94	560	2822
USA	M60E4	1991	Gas	Belt	37.71	22.0	22.50	600	2800
USA	M73	1962	Recoil	Belt	35.00	22.00	30.00	600	2800
USA	M240	1995	Gas	Belt	48.03	24.68	25.81	750	2800
Yugoslavia	M77B1	1980	Gas	B.20	40.35	21.06	11.26	600	2750

7.62 x 54 Mosin-Nagant

Country	Title	Year	Operating System	Feed System	Gun length	Barrel length	Weight	Rate of Fire	Muzzle Velocity
China	Type 53	1953	Gas	D/47	49.80	23.80	26.81	550	2700

Country	Title	Year	Operating System	Feed System	Gun length	Barrel length	Weight	Rate of Fire	Muzzle Velocity
China	Type 57	1958	Gas	Belt	44.09	28.35	30.44	650	2832
China	Type 58	1959	Gas	Belt	50.00	23.80	28.75	650	2750
China	Type 63	1963	Gas	Belt	44.09	28.35	29.88	650	2870
China	Type 67	1967	Gas	Belt	45.00	23.50	32.50	650	2740
China	Type 80	1980	Gas	Belt	46.93	26.57	17.37	650	2700
Czechoslovakia	vz/59 Light	1959	Gas	Belt	43.93	23.35	29.12	760	2657
Czechoslovakia	vz/59 Heavy	1959	Gas	B/30	47.83	27.28	42.37	750	2723
Russia	DP	1928	Gas	D/47	50.00	23.80	20.50	550	2700
Russia	DT	1929	Gas	D/47	47.00	23.80	28.00	650	2700
Russia	DPM	1944	Gas	D/47	49.80	23.80	26.81	550	2700
Russia	DTM	1944	Gas	D/60	46.50	23.80	28.37	600	2700
Russia	DS39	1939	Gas	Belt	45.00	28.40	26.37	550/1000	2650
Russia	SG-43	1943	Gas	Belt	44.09	28.35	30.44	650	2832
Russia	SGM	1948	Gas	Belt	44.09	28.35	29.88	650	2870
Russia	PK	1963	Gas	Belt	45.67	25.90	19.81	700	2706
Russia	Maxim 1	1910	Recoil	Belt	43.60	28.25	52.50	550	2830
Russia	RP-46	1946	Gas	Belt	50.00	28.80	28.75	650	2750
Russia	ShKAS	1933	Gas	Belt	27.60	17.52	13.50	600	2750
Yugoslavia	M84	1984	Gas	Belt	40.26	25.90	33.62	700	2706

7.65 x 53 Belgian Mauser

Country	Title	Year	Operating System	Feed System	Gun length	Barrel length	Weight	Rate of Fire	Muzzle Velocity
Belgium	Maxim, light	1920	Recoil	Belt	49.50	28.34	33.06	450	2025

7.7 x 58 Arisaka

Country	Title	Year	Operating System	Feed System	Gun length	Barrel length	Weight	Rate of Fire	Muzzle Velocity
Japan	Type 1	1941	Gas	S/30	43.40	23.23	77.00	550	2400
Japan	Type 92	1932	Gas	S/30	45.50	27.56	61.00	450	2400
Japan	Type 97	1937	Gas	B/30	46.50	28.00	24.00	500	2400
Japan	Type 99	1939	Gas	B/30	46.50	23.60	23.00	650	2350

7.7 x 58SR Arisaka

Japan Type 89, Type 92?

7.92 x 57 Mauser

Country	Title	Year	Operating System	Feed System	Gun length	Barrel length	Weight	Rate of Fire	Muzzle Velocity
China	Type 24	1924	Recoil	Belt	48.00	23.80	52.50	350	2920
China	Type 26	1924	Recoil	Belt	48.00	23.80	52.50	350	2920
Czechoslovakia	vz/26	1925	Gas	B/20	45.78	23.70	21.33	500	2598

Country	Title	Year	Operating System	Feed System	Gun length	Barrel length	Weight	Rate of Fire	Muzzle Velocity
Czechoslovakia	vz/30	1930	Gas	B/30	45.75	26.50	21.33	600	2500
Czechoslovakia	vz/37	1937	Gas	Belt	42.50	36.70	41.00	500/700	2600
Denmark	Madsen	1904	Recoil	B/40	45.00	23.00	20.00	450	2460
Germany	MG 10	1910	Recoil	Belt	n/a	n/a	36.00	550	2950
Germany	MG 15	1915	Recoil	Belt	44.13	28.20	28.38	550	2820
Germany	MG 15nA	1916	Recoil	Belt	44.13	28.50	28.50	550	2925
Germany	Gast	1918	Recoil	D/192	54.72	28.35	40.81	1300	2700
Germany	Knorr-Bremse	1933	Gas	B/20	51.48	27.25	22.06	500	2600
Germany	MG '08	1908	Recoil	Belt	46.25	28.35	58.33	450	2838
Germanyl	MG '08/15	1915	Recoil	Belt	56.90	28.35	31.00	450	2840
Germanyl	MG '08/15	1915	Recoil	Belt	46.25	28.35	28.65	450	2840
Germanyl	MG '08/18	1918	Recoil	Belt	46.25	28.35	26.48	450	2940
Germany	MG 13	1933	Recoil	D/75	57.75	28.25	23.94	650	2700
Germany	MG 15	1932	Recoil	D/75	52.50	23.50	28.00	850	2700
Germany	MG 17	193?	Recoil	Belt	48.00	n/a	28.00	1200	2550
Germany	MG 30	1930	Recoil	B/25	46.25	23.50	17.00	800	2500
Germany	MG 34	1934	Recoil	Belt	48.00	24.75	26.99	650	2700
Germany	MG 42	1942	Recoil	Belt	48.00	21.00	25.50	1200	2480
German	MG 81	1938	Recoil	Belt	35.02	18.70	14.37	1600	2592
Hungary	Gebauer	1935	EP	Belt	n/a	n/a	n/	1600	2700
Spain	Alfa 44	1944	Gas	Belt	57.08	29.53	28.62	780	2493
Switzerland	KE-7	1936	Recoil	B/20	46.87	23.63	17.25	550	2625
UK	Besa Mk 1	1939	Gas	Belt	43.50	29.00	47.00	500	2700
Uk	Besa Mk 2	1940	Gas	Belt	43.50	29.00	48.00	500	2700
Yugoslavia	M53	1953	Recoil	Belt	35.00	22.00	30.88	600	2800

8 x 50R Lebel

Country	Title	Year	Operating System	Feed System	Gun length	Barrel length	Weight	Rate of Fire	Muzzle Velocity
France	St Etienne	1907	Gas	S/30	46.50	28.00	58.75	400	2300
France	Chauchat	1915	Recoil	B/20	45.00	18.50	20.00	250	2300
France	Darne	1918	Gas	Belt	36.89	25.98	15.44	1100	2300
France	Hotchkiss	1897	Gas	S/30	n/a	n/a	s/a	600	2400
France	Hotchkiss	1909	Gas	S/30	46.75	23.50	27.00	500	2180
France	Hotchkiss	1914	Gas	Belt/S	51.60	31.00	55.69	500	2325
France	Puteaux	1905	Gas	S/23	49.21	30.70	54.00	650	2300

Country	Title	Year	Operating System	Feed System	Gun length	Barrel length	Weight	Rate of Fire	Muzzle Velocity
8 x 50R Mannlicher									
Austria	Schwarzlose	1907	DBB	Belt	41.93	20.65	43.88	400	2050
Austria	Schwarzlose	1912	DBB	Belt				400	
Austria	Schw. 07/16	1916	DBB	Belt			29.10	500	2050
Austria	Schw. 07/16nA	1918	DBB	Belt				880	2050
8 x 56R Hungarian									
(Austria: MG30. Hungary: 21M, 34AM)									
8 x 58R Danish Krag									
(Krag: Madsen)									
8 x 59 Breda									
Italy	Breda M37	1937	Gas	S/20	50.00	25.00	42.50	450	2600
Italy	Fiat M1935	1935	DBB	Belt	50.00	25.75	40.00	500	2600
8 x 63 Swedish Browning									
Sweden	m/36	1936	recoil	belt	43.7	23.9	53.0	750	2460
Swedish	m/42	1942	recoil	belt	53.2	23.9	35.2	700	2460
10.15 x 61R Jarmann									
(Norway: Nordenfelt)									
10.4 x 38R Swiss Vetterli									
(Gatling 1867)									
10.4 x 47R Vetterli-Vitali									
(Italian Vetterli; Gardner M1886; Maxim M1887, M1906; Nordenfelt)									
10.6 x 57 Berdan									
(Russian Gorloff/Gatling)									
11 x 49R Egyptian Remington									
(Gatling)									
11 x 51R Beaumont									
(Holland; Gardner)									
11 x 53R Comblain									
(Brazil: Nordenfelt)									
11.15 x 57R Spanish Remington									
(Spain: Gatling; Nordenfelt)									

Country	Title	Year	Operating System	Feed System	Gun length	Barrel length	Weight	Rate of Fire	Muzzle Velocity
11 x 59R Gras									
(France: Hotchkiss; Vickers)									
11 x 70R Montigny									
(France: Montigny Mitrailleuse)									
11.35 x 62 Madsen									
(Denmark: Madsen)									
12.7 x 81 Breda									
Italy:	Breda M38	1938	Gas	Belt	63.93	54.72	31.50	700	2493
Italy:	Scotti	1935	Gas/BB	Belt	55.5	33.8	50.7	700	2425
Japan	Type 1 Air	1941	Recoil	Belt	48.80	31.88	48.50	900	2400
12.7 x 108 Soviet									
China	Type 54	1955	Gas	Belt	62.50	42.00	78.50	550	2825
China	Type 77	1977	Gas	Belt	85.98	40.00	89.50	800	2625
China	Type W-85	1985	Gas	Belt	78.05	40.00	40.75	625	2625
Russia	NSV	1971	Gas	Belt	61.4	44.5	55.2	750	2772
Russia	UBK	1941	Gas	Belt	53.0	35.0	47.0	1050	2760
Russia	UBS	1941	Gas	Belt	53.00	35.00	47.00	750	2670
Russia	UBT	1941	Gas	Belt	55.00	35.00	56.00	1000	2800
Russia	DShK 38	1938	Gas	Belt	62.30	39.37	73.50	575	2805
13 x 64B Rheinmetall									
Germany	MG131	1936	recoil	Bet	46.25	21.75	40.0	960	2500
(Germany: MG215. Japan Type 2)									
13 x 92SR Mauser									
Germany	TuF	1918	recoil	Belt	65.75	n/a	295.0*	300	2575
*with mounting									
13.2 x 99 Hotchkiss Long									
Italy	Breda M31	1931	Gas	B/30	65.00	39.40	104.70	500	2590
Japan	Type 93	1933	Gas	B/30	95.00	65.00	87.00	450	221
(France: Hotchkiss 1914)									
14.5 x 114 Soviet									
Poland	Pirat	1995	Recoil	Belt	77.95	53.00	115.00	600	3280
Russia	KPV	1955	recoil	Belt	78.98	53.00	108.25	600	3280

Country	Title	Year	Operating System	Feed System	Gun length	Barrel length	Weight	Rate of Fire	Muzzle Velocity
15 x 95 Mauser									
Germany	MG151	1935	recoil	belt	75.43	49.37	78.94	700	3150
15 x 104 Besa									
Czech	vz/60	1937	Gas	Belt	80.75	57.48	121.25	450	2700
U.K.	Besa	1940	Gas	Belt	80.70	57.60	125.50	450	2700
15 x 115 FN									
Belgium	BRG(1)	1985	Gas	Belts	78.74	53.15	121.25	700	2952
15.5 x106 FN									
Belgium	BRG-15	1988	Gas	Belts	84.65		132.25	600	3460
Machine gun ammunition; Imperial calibers									
.30-40 Krag									
USA (and Gatling)	Colt M1895	1895	Gas	Belt	40.80	28.00	40.00	430	2000
.30-06 Springfield									
Japan	NKT-5M (Hy)	1966	Gas	Belt	51.20	23.80	35.80	550	2800
Japan	NKT-5M (Lt)	1966	Gas	Belt	44.40	23.60	33.90	550	2800
Mexico	Mendoza	1960	Gas	B/20	43.30	24.00	14.12	650	2750
USA	Benet-Mercié	1909	Gas	S/30	46.75	23.50	27.00	600	2788
USA	Berthier	1916	Gas	B/20	48.00	n/a	15.75	500	2625
USA (Browning)	M1917	1917	Recoil	Belt	37.50	24.00	32.63	600	2800
USA (Brg)	M1919A1	1931	Recoil	Belt	35.10	18.00	40.00	600	2690
USA (Brg)	M1919A4	1934	Recoil	Belt	41.11	24.00	31.00	500	2800
USA (Brg)	M1919A5	1941	Recoil	Belt	40.80	24.00	30.50	500	2800
USA (Brg)	M1919A6	1943	Recoil	Belt	53.00	24.00	32.50	450	2800
USA (Brg)	Air M2	1931	Recoil	Belt	39.72	23.90	21.50	1350	2800
USA (BAR)	M1918	1918	Gas	B/20	47.00	24.00	16.00	550	2905
USA (BAR)	M1918A2	1939	Gas	B/20	47.80	24.00	19.38	450/650	2805
USA (BAR)	M1922	1923	Gas	B/20	41.00	18.00	19.20	550	2700
USA	Chauchat	1918	Recoil	B/16	45.00	18.50	20.00	300	2700
USA	Colt	1895	Gas	Belt	40.80	28.00	40.00	450	2800
USA	Johnson	1941	Recoil	B/20	42.30	22.00	12.50	600	2800
USA	Johnson	1944	Recoil	B/20	42.00	22.00	14.33	900	2800

Country	Title	Year	Operating System	Feed System	Gun length	Barrel length	Weight	Rate of Fire	Muzzle Velocity
USA	Lewis	1917	Gas	D/47	51.75	26.25	25.25	500	2830
USA	Marlin	1917	Gas	Belt	40.00	28.00	22.50	600	2800
USA	Maxim	1904	Recoil	Belt	48.00	28.54	68.50	600	2825
.303 British *(All weapons in this caliber originate in UK)*									
Adams-Wilmot		1934	Gas	D/99	n/a	n/a	20.00	900	2440
Beardmore-Farquhar		1920	Gas	D/81	49.50	26.50	19.00	500	2440
Besal Mk 1		1941	Gas	B/20	48.00	22.00	15.75	500	2450
Besal Mk 2		1941	Gas	B/30	46.60	22.00	21.50	600	2450
Bren Mks1 and 2		1938	Gas	B/30	45.25	25.00	22.33	500	2400
Bren Mk 3		1944	Gas	B/30	42.90	22.25	19.33	480	2400
Bren Mk 4		1944	Gas	B/30	42.90	22.25	19.12	500	2400
Czech ZGB33		1933	Gas	B/39	45.50	25.00	22.10	500	2450
Gardner, 2-bbl Converted		1898	Hand	G/20	45.25	28.25	92.00	400	1800
Hefah V Mark 1		1942	Gas	D/60	48.00	24.50	15.12	600	2500
Hotchkiss Mark 1, 1*		1916	Gas	S/30	46.75	23.50	27.00	500	2450
Lewis Mark 1		1914	Gas	D/47	50.63	26.25	25.25	550	2450
Maxim .303 Mark 1		1899	Recoil	Belt	45.00	28.00	64.00	400	1800
Nordenfelt .303 Converted Mk 1		1898	Hand	G/27	41.25	28.50	98.00	300	1800
Vickers Mark 1		1912	Recoil	Belt	45.50	28.50	40.00	450	2450
Vickers GO (Type K)		1937	Gas	D/100	40.00	20.00	21.00	1050	2450
Vickers-Berthier Mk 3		1933	Gas	B/30	46.50	23.50	22.00	600	2450
(.303 Browning Aircraft M2)									
.45-70 Government (USA: Gatling, Gardner)									
.450 Gatling									
UK Gatling .45 Mk 1		1874	Hand	D/240	59.41	31.95	444.00*	500	n/a
* = with wheeled carriage									
.450 Gardner & Gatling (UK: Gardners, Gatlings and Maxims)									
.50 Vickers									
BSA M1924		1924	Recoil	D/37	46.3	53.93	37.80	400	260
Vickers .5 Mark 1		1932	Recoil	Belt	54.00	31.10	52.00	450/675	2600

Country	Title	Year	Operating System	Feed System	Gun length	Barrel length	Weight	Rate of Fire	Muzzle Velocity
.50 Vickers Class D									
	Vickers Class D	1934	Recoil	Belt	70.47	45.00	101.50	450	3040
.50 Browning									
Belgium (FN)	M2HB-QCB	1988	Recoil	Belt	65.20	45.00	84.10	550	3005
Denmark	Madsen-Saetter1959	Gas	Belt	64.00	39.37	61.69	1000	2850	
Singapore	CIS50	1988	Gas	Belt	70.00	45.00	66.12	500	2920
UK (Manroy)	M2HB-QCB	1988	Recoil	Belt	65.00	45.00	84.87	500	2930
UK	Rolls-Royce	1941	Recoil	Belt	50.00	40.00	49.00	1000	2340
UK	Russell-Robinson1949	Recoil	Belt	n/a	n/a	43.00	450	2800	
USA	M85	1963	Recoil	Belt	50.55	36.00	61.50	400/1050	2842
USA	GAU-19/A	1988	EP	Belt	46.50	36.00	74.00	1000/2000	2900
USA	M1927	1927	Recoil	Belt	56.00	36.00	66.00	450	2300
USA	M2	1933	Recoil	Belt	66.00	45.00	100.00	650	2930
USA	M2 Air	1928	Recoil	Belt	57.00	36.00	64.00	850	2840
USA	M2HB	1933	Recoil	Belt	54.00	45.00	84.00	575	2930
USA (Ramo)	M2HB-QCB	1988	Recoil	Belt	65.00	45.00	84.21	600	3048
USA (Saco)	Fifty/50	1987	Recoil	Belt	61.41	36.00	58.88	750	2841
USA (Ramo)	M2 Light	1991	Recoil	Belt	60.00	36.00	58.88	750	2841
USA (GE)	GECAL 50	1986	EP	Belt	46.50	36.00	96.12	8000	2900
USA (AAI)	GPHMG	1982	Gas	Belt	61.00	36.00	55.00	400	2900
USA	Dover Devil	1982	Gas	Belt	52.30	36.00	50.00	400	2900
.50 PCTA (Plastic Cased Telescoped Ammunition)									
USA (Ares)	TARG	1990	Gas, Rev	Linkless44.40	36.50	44.97	1800	2952	
.577/450 Martini-Henry: (UK Maxim; some Gatling)									
.65 Gatling									
UK	Gatling	1875	Hand	D/50	66.60	33.00	817.00	400	n/a
1.1 inch US Navy									
USA	Hudson	1938	Gas	B/8	119.60	81.89	-	150	2700

APPENDIX FOUR
CANNON

In alphabetical order

TITLE	Caliber	Action	Feed System	Gun Weight (lbs)	Gun Length (in)	Barrel Length (in)	Rate of fire (rds/min)	Muzzle Velocity (ft/s)
Becker	20x70RB	BB	15-box	66.13	53.94	31.50	300	1610
2A38M (Sov)	30x165	gas	belt	439.0	135.80	-	2500	3182
2A42 (Sov)	30x165	gas/recoil	dual belt	253.5	120.8	-	650	3112
2A82 (Sov)	30x165	recoil	dual belt	185.2	118.5	-	330	31
2-M34, M8 (Sov)	25x218	recoil	belt	-	112.2	72.4	250	2950
25M-811 (France)	25x137	EP	dual belt	264.5	115.51	-	650	3610
Aden 25	25x137	gas revolver	belt	202.8	90.0	67.0	1850	3445
Aden Mark 4	30x86B	gas revolver	belt	191.8	62.20	42.52	1300	2560
Aden Mark 5	30x113B	gas revolver	belt	192.9	64.48	42.2	1400	2592
AK-306 (Sov)	30x165	Gatling	belt	397.0	85.4	-	3000	3112
AM-23 (Sov)	20x115	gas	belt	94.8	85.40	-	1300	2425
AN-M2 (USA)	20x110	gas/BB	60-drum	112.4	93.70	67.32	650	2850
ASP	30x113B	gas	belt	104.9	79.76	52.0	450	2750
B-20	20x99R	gas	belt	55.11	54.33	-	800	2650
Bofors m/32	25x205R	recoil	6-clip	275.5	70.86	56.10	240	2750
Bofors m/40	20x145	recoil	25-drum	92.60	80.71	57.10	360	2674
Bofors m/45	20x110	recoil	belt	108.0	84.25	51.0	700	2740
Bofors m/49	20x110	recoil	belt	130.0	83.1	55.1	775	2750
Breda M37	20x138B	gas	strip	147.7	82.28	51.18	220	2700
Erhardt	20x70RB(E)	recoil	20-box	79.4	59.05	39.75	250	1625
EX29	20x102	recoil	belt	126.3	126.30	48.0	500	3300
Fiat 1917	25x87R	recoil	8-box	99.20	52.36	26.37	150	1320

TITLE	Caliber	Action	Feed System	Gun Weight (lbs)	Gun Length (in)	Barrel Length (in)	Rate of fire (rds/min)	Muzzle Velocity (ft/s)
Flak 30	20x138B	recoil	20-box	141.10	90.55	51.18	280	2953
Flak 38	20x138B	recoil	20-box	125.60	88.62	51.14	480	2953
G12	20x139	gas/BB	dual belt	162.0	106.10	81.30	740	3445
GA1	20x82	recoil	belt	86.00	69.29	43.30	700	2363
BAU-8/A	30x173	Gatling	linkless	630.6	112.5	85.0	4000	3398
GAU-12/U	25x137	Gatling	belt	280.0	83.18	-	4200	3600
GAU-13/A	30x173	Gatling	linkless	339.5	109.84	84.25	3000	3398
GE-225	25x137	gas/EP	belt	189.5	87.0	65.0	2000	3600
GSh-30	30x165	gas	belt	231.5	116.5	91.0	2500	3112
GSh-301	30x165	recoil	belt	99.2	77.55	-	1800	3000
GSh-2-23	20x115	gas	belt	110.2	60.62	39.35	3000	2425
GSh-6-23	20x115	Gatling	belt	167.5	59.85	-	9000	2425
GSh-6-30	30x165	Gatling	belt	353.0	80.35	-	5000	3050
GSh-6-30K	30x165	Gatling	belt	441.0	85.8	-	6000	3112
Hispano Type 9	20x110	recoil	60-drum	105.80	81.59	-	400	2723
Hispano 804	20x110	BB	box/belt	99.2	100.0	66.9	800	2750
Hispano Mk 1	20x110	gas/BB	60-drum	110.2	98.4	66.9	600	2880
Hispano Mk 5	20x110	gas/BB	belt	92.6	86.6	55.2	750	2880
Ho-1, Ho-3	20x125mm	gas/BB	15-drum	99.2	68.9	47.25	400	2295
Ho0155 (Japan)	30x114	recoil	belt	132.25	73.2	44.9	600	2200
KwK 30	20x138B	recoil	10-box	138.90	76.38	43.31	280	3445
KwK 38	20x138B	recoil	10-box	123.50	76.38	43.31	480	3445
Lahti L/40	20x138B	gas	32-box	88.18	-	31.50	250	2500
M3/M24	20x110	gas/BB	belt	117.5	78.0	52.50	850	2840
M39A3	20x102	gas, revolver	belt	174.0	72.28	52.9	1800	3380
m/40 (Sov.Army)	25x205SR	recoil	7-clip	-	-	90.0	240	3035
m/40 (Sov.Navy)	25x218R	recoil	6-clip	275.5	70.86	56.9	300	2952
M53 (Czech)	30x220	recoil	10-rd clip	3853	128.0	82.7	450	3280
M61A1	20x102	Gatling	linkless	255.0	72.60	60.0	7200	3642
M86 (Serbia)	30x210B	gas	belt	330.6	120.7	82.7	750	3610
M89 (Serbia)	30x210B	gas	dual belt	474.0	120.7	82.7	750	3610
M139	20x139	gas/BB	belt	161.0	101.0	-	1050	3428

TITLE	Caliber	Action	Feed System	Gun Weight (lbs)	Gun Length (in)	Barrel Length (in)	Rate of fire (rds/min)	Muzzle Velocity (ft/s)
M168	20x102	Gatling	belt	300.0	72.0	60.0	3000	3380
M196	20x102	Gatling	belt	-	53.94	40.15	800	3300
M197	20x102	Gatling	belt	146.60	72.0	60.0	1500	3380
M230 (USA)	30x113B	chain	belt	123.2	64.48	42.0	624	2650
M242 (USA)	25x137	chain	belt	243.6	108.66	80.0	500	3610
M552 (France)	30x113B	gas, revolver	belt	176.36	66.90	55.12	1500	2684
M553 (France)	30x113B	gas revolver	belt	187.30	77.0	59.69	1350	815
M554 (France)	30x113B	gas revolver	belt	187.40	79.13	-	1800	820
M561 (France)	30x97B	gas, revolver	belt	185.20	65.35	43.41	1400	2198
M621 (France)	20x102	DBB	belt	100.3	86.88	61.0	740	3366
M693 (France)	20x139	DBB	dual belt	155.4	106.15	81.29	900	3445
M781 (France)	30x113B	EP	belt	143.3	73.62	-	750	3363
M791 (France)	30x150B	gas	belt	264.5	94.50	-	2500	3363
m/1922 (Swed)	25x87R	recoil	belt	275.5	53.9	30.0	150	1450
M1955	20x110	BB	60-drum	-	-	55.12	800	2740
Madsen m/35	20x120	recoil	belt/drum	116.8	78.75	47.25	400	2950
Mauser B	20x139	gas/BB	belt	137.0	96.61	75.0	800	3445
Mauser BK27	27x145	gas revolver	belt	204.6	90.94	66.9	1700	3445
Mauser E	25x137	gas dual	belt	246.9	2.67	82.67	900	3610
Mauser F	30x173	gas dual	belt	327.4	131.9	96.0	800	3363
Mauser MK212	30x90RB	gas	belt	-	-	-	600	1800
Mauser MK213	20x135	gas, revolver	belt	165.3	76.0	63.0	1400	1050
Mauser MK213/30	30x85B	gas, revolver	belt	165.3	64.17	51.18	1200	1740
Meroka	20x129	EP	belt	650	-	94.49	9000	42
MG-FF	20x72RB	BB	60-drum	52.10	52.75	32.28	520	1805
MG-FFM	20x80RB	BB	60-drum	61.72	52.75	32.28	540	1970
MG151/20	20x82	recoil	belt	92.60	69.68	43.30	700	2362
MG204	20x105B	recoil	20-drum	121.25	63.00	43.30	400	2395
Mk 11 Mod 1	20x110USN	rec/gas/rev	belt	240.00	78.50	56.50	4200	3200
Mk 12 Mod 1	20c110USN	gas/BB	belt	115.0	75.12	48.0	1000	3412
Mk 22 Mod 2	20x102	Rec/BB	belt	110.0	78.75	54.75	800	3400
NN-30 (Sov)	30x210B	gas/revolver	belt	341.7	105.1	76.0	1000	3610

TITLE	Caliber	Action	Feed System	Gun Weight (lbs)	Gun Length (in)	Barrel Length (in)	Rate of fire (rds/min)	Muzzle Velocity (ft/s)
NR-23 (Sov)	20x115	gas	belt	174.2	102.8	57.1	850	2425
NR-30 (Sov)	30x155B	gas	belt	145.5	85.0	71.25	900	2560
NS-23KM	20x115	recoil	belt	180.0	78.30	57.25	690	2425
Oerlikon F	20x70RB	BB	45-drum	66.13	53.94	29.92	450	1600
Oerlikon FFL	20x101RB	BB	100-drum	68.14	74.0	47.25	500	2290
Oerlikon FFS	20x110RB	BB	100-drum	86.0	83.5	55.10	470	2725
Oerlikon KAA	20x128	gas	belt	192.0	103.42	73.07	1000	3773
Oerlikon KAB	20x128	gas	50-drum	240.0	133.40	94.50	1000	3937
Oerlikon KAD	20x139	gas/BB	50-drum	134.51	117.20	91.18	1000	3412
Oerlikon KBA	25x137	gas	dual belt	247.0	105.50	78.75	600	4460
Oerlikon KBB	25x184	gas	dual belt	321.8	125.5	90.55	800	3805
Oerlikon KBD	25x184	Gatling	dual belt	352.7	-	-	5000	4215
Oerlikon KCA	30x173	Revolver	belt	300.0	105.9	77.8	1350	3380
Oerlikon KCB	30x170	gas	belt	298.7	138.7	88.6	650	3544
Oerlikon L	20x101RB	BB	45-drum	94.8	74.0	47.25	350	2290
Oerlikon Mk 1	20x110	BB	60 drum	147.7	85.0	55.2	450	2725
Oerlikon S	20x110RB	BB	45-drum	136.7	83.5	55.10	280	2725
Oerlikon SS	20x110RB	BB	60-drum	147.7	85.0	55.10	450	2725
Polsten	20x110	BB	30-box	121.2	85.8	57.1	450	2725
Rarden	30x170	recoil	3-shot clip	247.0	116.5	96.0	single	3527
Rh202	20x139	gas	dual belt	165.3	102.83	72.40	800	3445
Rh MK101	30x184	recoil	30-drum	396.8	102.0	61.0	250	2625
Rh MK103	30x184	gas/recoil	belt	310.8	92.5	52.75	400	2550
Rh MK108	30x90RB	BB	belt	132.7	41.38	17.32	650	1657
Scotti	20x138B	gas/BB	60 Drum	-	89.0	60.62	250	2730
ShVAK	20x99R	gas	belt	149.6	83.46	64.88	750	2820
Solothurn c/30	20x138B	recoil	100-drum	141.0	110.25	70.86	350	2600
SWC	30x113B	recoil	belt/mag	112.4	66.9	-	450	2650
Type 1 (China)	30x155B	gas	belt	145.50	-	-	850	2560
Type 1 (Ho-5) (Jap)	20x92	recoil	belt	81.57	57.1	35.43	800	2625
Type 2 (China)	20x115	gas	belt	209.0	-	-	1200	2426
Type 2 (Japan)	30x92R	BB	42-drum	110.2	82.67	53.15	400	165

TITLE	Caliber	Action	Feed System	Gun Weight (lbs)	Gun Length (in)	Barrel Length (in)	Rate of fire (rds/min)	Muzzle Velocity (ft/s)
Type 5 (Japan)	30x122	gas/BB	belt	154.3	81.5	56.7	450	2330
Type 98AA (Jap)	25x165	gas	15-box	253.5	90.55	59.0	220	2970
Type 97 A/Tk (Jap)	20x125	gas	7-box	152	82.5	47.0	350	2640
Type 98 A/Tk (Jap)	20x142	gas/BB	20-box	152	79.13	40.60	400	2725
Type 99-1 (Jap)	20x72RB	BB	60-drum	57.31	52.36	31.88	500	1805
Type 99-2 (Jap)	20x101RB	BB 100-drum	83.8	72.41	49.2	500	2295	
VYa	23x152B	gas	belt	147.0	84.48	65.0	720	3182
W+F FMK38	20x139	recoil	belt	121.3	100.4	72.0	400	2710
XM188E1 (USA)	30x113B	Gatling	belt	111.0	59.80	42.0	2000	2600
ZU-23	23x142B	gas	belt	165.3	100.60	74.0	1000	318

APPENDIX FIVE
CANNON

In ascending order of caliber

Country / TITLE	Action	Feed System	Gun Weight (lbs)	Gun Length (in)	Barrel Length (in)	Rate of fire (rds/min)	Muzzle Velocity (ft/s)
20 x 70RB (20mm Becker)							
Germany Becker	BB	15-box	66.13	53.94	31.50	300	1610
Switz Oerlikon F	BB	45-drum	66.13	53.94	29.92	450	1600
20 x 70RB (E) (20mm Erhardt)							
Germany Erhardt	recoil	20-box	79.4	59.05	39.75	250	1625
20 x 72RB (20mm Oerlikon FF)							
Germany MG-FF	BB	60-drum	52.10	52.75	32.28	520	1805
Japan Type 99-1	BB	60-drum	57.31	52.36	31.88	500	1805
20 x 80RB (20mm Oerlikon FFM)							
Germany MG-FFM	BB	60-drum	61.72	52.75	32.28	540	1970
20 x 82mm (20mm Mauser MG151)							
Germany MG151/20	recoil	belt	92.60	69.68	43.30	700	2362
S. Africa GA1	recoil	belt	86.00	69.29	43.30	700	2363
20 x 94mm (20mm Type 1)							
Japan Type 1 (Ho-5)	recoil	belt	81.57	57.1	35.43	800	2625
20 - 99R (20mm ShVaK)							
Russia ShVaK	gas	belt	149.6	83.46	64.88	750	2820
Russia B-20	gas	belt	55.11	54.33	-	800	2650
20 x 101RB (20mm Oerlikon FFL)							
Japan Type 99-2	BB	100-drum	83.8	72.41	49.2	500	2295
Switzerland Oerlikon L	BB	45-drum	94.8	74.0	47.25	350	2290
Switzerland Oerlikon FFL	BB	100-drum	68.14	74.0	47.25	500	2290
20 x 102 mm (20mm US Navy)							
France M621	DBB	belt	100.3	86.88	61.0	740	3366
USA M39A3	gas, revolver	belt	174.0	72.28	52.9	1800	3380
USA Mk 22 Mod 2	rec/blowback	belt	110.0	78.75	54.75	800	3400

Country	TITLE	Action	Feed System	Gun Weight (lbs)	Gun Length (in)	Barrel Length (in)	Rate of fire (rds/min)	Muzzle Velocity (ft/s)
USA	M61A1	Gatling	linkless	255.0	72.60	60.0	7200	3642
USA	M168	Gatling	linked	300.0	72.0	60.0	3000	3380
USA	EX29	recoil	belt	126.3	126.30	48.0	500	3300
USA	M196	Gatling	belt	-	53.94	40.15	800	3300
USA	M197	Gatling	belt	146.60	72.0	60.0	1500	3380
20 x 105Bmm (20mm Short Solothurn)								
Germany	MG204	recoil	20-drum	121.25	63.00	43.30	400	2395
20 x 110 mm (20mm HS404)								
Serbia	M1955	Blowback	60-drum	-	-	55.12	800	2740
Sweden	Bofors m/45	recoil	belt	108.0	84.25	51.2	700	2740
Sweden	Bofors m/49	recoil	belt	130.0	83.1	55.1	775	2750
Switzerland	Hispano 804	gas/BB	box, belt	99.2	100.0	66.9	800	2750
UK	Hispano Mk 1	gas/BB	60-drum	110.2	98.4	66.9	600	2880
UK	Hispano Mk 5	gas/BB	belt	92.6	86.6	55.2	750	2880
UK	Oerlikon Mk 1	BB	60 drum	147.7	85.0	55.2	450	2725
UK	Polsten	BB	30-box	121.2	85.8	57.1	450	2725
USA	AN-M2	gas/BB	60-drum	112.4	93.70	67.32	650	2850
USA	M3/M24	gas/blowback	belt	117.5	78.0	52.50	850	2840
20 x 110RB (20mm Oerlikon S)								
France	Hispano Type 9	BB	60-drum	105.80	81.59	-	400	2723
Switzerland	Oerlikon S	BB	45-drum	136.7	83.5	55.10	280	2725
Switzerland	Oerlikon FFS	BB	100-drum	86.0	83.5	55.10	470	2725
Switzerland	Oerlikon SS	BB	60-drum	147.7	85.0	55.10	450	2725
20 x 110USN (20mm Mark 100)								
USA	Mk 11 Mod 5	recoil/gas	belt	240.00	78.50	56.50	- 4200	975
USA	Mk 12 Mod 0	gas/blowback	belt	115.0	75.12	48.0	- 1000	3412
20 x 120mm (20mm Madsen)								
Denmark	Madsen m/35	recoil	belt/drum	116.8	78.75	47.25	400	2950
20 x 125mm (20mm Type 97)								
Japan	Ho-1, Ho-3	gas/BB	15-drum	99.2	68.9	47.25	400	2500
Japan	Type 97 A/Tk	gas	7-box	152	82.5	47.0	350	2640

Country	TITLE	Action	Feed System	Gun Weight (lbs)	Gun Length (in)	Barrel Length (in)	Rate of fire (rds/min)	Muzzle Velocity (ft/s)
20 x 128 mm (20mm OerlikonKAA)								
Spain	Meroka	Power	belt	650	-	94.49	9000	4265
Switz.	Oerlikon KAA	gas	belt	192.0	103.42	73.07	1000	3773
Switz.	Oerlikon KAB	gas	20, 50- drum	240.0	133.40	94.50	1000	3937
20 x 135mm								
Germany	Mauser 213C	gas, revolver	belt	165.3	76.0	63.0	1400	1050
20 x 138B (20mm Long Solothurn or Breda)								
Finland	Lahti L/40	gas	32-box	88.18	-	31.50	250	2500
Germany	Solothurn c/30	recoil	100-drum	141.0	110.25	70.86	350	2600
Germany	Flak 30	recoil	20-box	141.1	90.55	51.18	280	2953
Germany	Flak 38	recoil	20-box	125.6	88.62	51.14	480	2953
Germany	KwK 30	recoil	10-box	138.9	76.38	43.31	280	3445
Germany	KwK 38	recoil	10-box	123.5	76.38	43.31	480	3445
Italy	Breda M37	gas	strip	147.7	82.28	51.18	220	2700
Italy	Scotti	gas/BB	60 Drum	-	89.0	60.62	250	2730
20 x 139mm (20mm HS820)								
France	M693	DBB	dual belt	155.4	106.15	81.29	900	3445
Germany	Rh 202	gas dual	belt	165.3	102.83	72.40	800	3445
Germany	Mauser	B gas/blowback	belt	137.0	96.61	75.0	800	3445
S Africa	G12	gas/blowback	dual belt	162.0	106.10	81.30	740	3445
Switzerland	Hispano 804	gas 60-drum	-	-	1510	-	800	825
Switzerland	Oerlikon KAD	gas/BB	50-drum	134.51	117.20	91.18	1000	3412
Switzerland	W+F FMK38	recoil	belt	121.3	100.4	72.0	400	2710
USA	M139	gas/blowback	belt	161.0	101.0	-	1050	3428
20 x 142 (20mm Type 98)								
Japan	Type 98 AA-A/Tk	gas/BB	20-box	152	79.13	40.60	400	2725
20 -145R (20mm Bofors)								
Bofors	M40	recoil	25-drum	92.60	80.71	57.10	360	2674
23 x 115 mm (23mm Soviet NS)								
China	Type 2	gas	belt	209.0	-	-	1200	2426
Russia	AM-23	gas	belt	94.8	85.40	-	1300	2425
Russia	GSh-2-23	gas	belt	110.2	60.62	39.35	3000	2425

Country	TITLE	Action	Feed System	Gun Weight (lbs)	Gun Length (in)	Barrel Length (in)	Rate of fire (rds/min)	Muzzle Velocity (ft/s)
Russia	GSh-6-23	Gatling	belt	167.5	59.85	-	9000	2425
Russia	NR-23	gas	belt	174.2	102.8	57.1	850	2425
Russia	NS-23KM	recoil	belt	180.0	78.30	57.25	690	2425
23 x152B (23mm Soviet VYa)								
Russia	VYa	gas	belt	147.0	84.48	65.0	720	3182
Russia	ZU-23	gas	belt	165.3	100.60	74.0	1000	3182
25 x 87R (25mm Fiat)								
Italy	Fiat 1917	recoil	8-box	99.20	52.36	26.37	150	1320
Sweden	m/1922	recoil	belt	275.5	53.9	30.0	150	1450
25 x137 mm (25mm Oerlikon KBA)								
France	25M811	Mech. cam	dual belt	264.5	1-5.51	-	650	3610
Germany	Mauser E	gas	dual belt	246.9	112.67	82.67	900	3610
Switz.	Oerlikon KBA	gas	dual belt	247.0	105.50	78.75	600	4460
U.K.	Aden 25	gas revolver	belt	202.8	90.0	67.0	1850	3445
USA	M242	Mech. chain	belt	243.6	108.66	80.0	500	3610
USA	GE 225	gas/ext pwr	belt	189.5	87.0	65.0	2000	3600
USA	GAU-12/U	Gatling	belt	280.0	83.18	-	4200	3600
25 x 165 (25mm Type 96)								
Japan	Type 96 AA	gas	15-box	253.5	90.55	59.0	220	2970
25 x 184mm (25mm Oerlikon KBB)								
Switz.	Oerlikon KBB	gas dual	belt	321.8	125.5	90.55	800	3805
Switz.	Oerlikon KBD	Gatling dual	belt	3527	-	-	5000	4215
25 x 205R (25mm Bofors)								
Sweden	Bofors m/1932	recoil	6-clip	275.5	70.86	56.10	240	2750
25 x 205SR (25mm Soviet m/40)								
Russia	Army m/40	recoil	7-clip	-	-	90.0	240	3035
25 x 218R (25mm Soviet Navy)								
Russia	Naval m/1940	recoil	6-clip	275.5	70.86	56.9	300	2952
25 x 218m m (25mm Soviet 2-M3)								
Russia	Naval 2-M3, -M8	recoil	belt	-	112.2	72.4	250	2950
27 x 145B (27mm Mauser MRCA)								
Germany	Mauser BK27	gas revolver	belt	204.6	90.94	66.9	1700	3445

Country	TITLE	Action	Feed System	Gun Weight (lbs)	Gun Length (in)	Barrel Length (in)	Rate of fire (rds/min)	Muzzle Velocity (ft/s)
30 x 85B								
Germany	Mauser 213/30	gas revolver	belt	165.3	64.17	51,18	1200	1740
30 - 86B (30mm Aden 3M) -								
UK	Aden Mk IV	gas revolver	belt	191.8	62.20	42.52	1300	2560
30 x 90RB (30mm MK108)								
Germany	Rh MK 108	BB	belt	132.7	41.38	17.32	650	1657
Germany	Mauser MK212	gas	belt				600	1800
30 x 92R (30mm Type 2)								
Japan	Type 2	BB	42-drum	110.2	82.67	53.15	400	1650
30 x 97B (30mm DEFA M541)								
France	DEFA M561	gas, revolver	belt	185.20	65.35	43.41	1400	2198
30 x113B (30mm Aden/DEFA)								
France	DEFA M552	gas, revolver	belt	176.36	66.90	55.12	1500	2684
France	DEFA 553	gas revolver	belt	187.30	77.0	59.69	1350	815
France	DEFA 554	gas revolver	belt	187.40	79.13	-	1800	820
France	GIAT 30-554	gas, revolver	belt	187.40	79.13	-	1800	2684
France	M781	Mech. cam	belt	143.3	73.62	-	750	3363
UK	Aden Mk 5	gas revolver	belt	192.9	64.48	42.2	1400	2592
USA	M230	Mech. chain	belt	123.2	64.48	42.0	624	2650
USA	ASP-30	gas	belt	104.9	79.76	52.0	450	2750
USA	SWC	recoil	belt/mag	112.4	66.9	-	450	2650
USA	XM188El	Gatling	belt	111.0	59.80	42.0	2000	2600
30 x 114mm (30mm Ho-155)								
Japan	Ho-155	recoil	belt	132.25	73.2	44.9	600	2297
30 x 122 (30mm Type 5)								
Japan	Type 5	gas/BB	belt	154.3	81.5	56.7	450	2330
30 - 150B (30mm GIAT)								
France	M791	gas	belt	264.5	94.50	-	-	2500
30 x 155B (30mm Soviet NR-30)								
China	Type 1	gas	belt	145.50	-	-	850	2560
Russia	NR-30	gas	belt	145.5	85.0	71.25	900	2560

Country	TITLE	Action	Feed System	Gun Weight (lbs)	Gun Length (in)	Barrel Length (in)	Rate of fire (rds/min)	Muzzle Velocity (ft/s)
30 x 165mm (30mm Soviet GSh)								
Russia	2A38M	gas	belt	439.0	135.80	-	2500	3182
Russia	2A42	gas/recoil	dual belt	253.5	120.8	-	650	3112
Russia	2A72	recoil	dual belt	185.2	118.5	-	330	3112
Russia	GSh-30	gas	belt	231.5	116.5	91.0	2500	3112
Russia	GSh-301	recoil	belt	99.20	77.55	-	1800	3000
Russia	GSh-6-30	Gatling	belt	353.0	80.35	-	5000	3050
Russia	GSh-6-30K	Gatling	belt	441.0	85.8	-	6000	3112
Russia	AK-306	Gatling	belt	397.0	85.4	-	3000	3112
30 - 170 mm (30mm HS831 or Rarden)								
Switz.	Oerlikon KCB	gas	belt	298.7	138.7	88.6	650	3544
UK	Rarden	recoil	3-shot clip	247.0	116.5	96.0	single	3527
30 - 173 mm (30mm Oerlikon KCA or GAU-8A)								
Germany	Mauser F	gas	dual belt	327.4	131.9	96.0	800	3363
Swiz.	Oerlikon KCA	Revolver	belt	300.0	105.9	77.8	1350	3380
USA	GAU-8/A	Gatling	linkless	630.6	112.5	85.0	4000	3398
USA	GAU-13/A	Gatling	linkless	339.5	109.84	84.25	3000	3398
30 x 184B (30mm MK103)								
Germany	Rh MK 101	recoil	30-drum	396.8	102.0	61.0	250	2625
Germany	Rh MK103	gas/recoil	belt	310.8	92.5	52.75	400	2550
30 x 210B (30mm Soviet NN-30)								
Russia	NN-30	gas/revolver	belt	341.7	105.1	76.0	1000	3610
Serbia	M86	gas	belt	330.6	120.7	82.7	750	3610
Serbia	M89	gas dual	belt	474.0	120.7	82.7	750	3610
30 x 220 (30mm Czech M53)								
CZ	M53	recoil 1	0-rd clip	385.3	128.0	82.7	450	328

APPENDIX SIX

AMMUNITION

MACHINE GUN AMMUNITION DIMENSIONAL DATA

NOTES: Case Type (shape of cartridge) is defined as: **RN** - rimmed necked; **RS** - rimmed straight; **RLN** - rimless necked; **RLS** - rimless straight; **SRN** -semi-rimmed necked; **SRS** -semi-rimmed straight; **RB** -rebated rim; **B** - belted. All dimensions are in thousandths of an inch; bullet weights in grains.

Name and Metric Caliber	Case Type	Length Round	Length Case	Diameter Rim	Diameter Head	Diameter Neck	Diameter Bullet	Bullet Weight
4.85 x 49 Enfield	RLN	2456	1929	414	415	220	195	55
5.45 x 39.5	RLN	2224	1555	394	394	244	221	53
5.56 x 45mm M193	RLN	2256	1752	375	375	253	223	55
5.56 x 45mm NATO	RLN	2260	1760	378	378	253	223	62
6 x 45 SAWS	RLN	1708	1134	311	311	249	224	23
6 x 59mm Lee USN	RLN	3110	2345	446	445	246	244	112
6.5 x 51R Arisaka	RN	2992	1996	480	450	288	259	138
6.5 x 51SR Arisaka	SRN	3003	1995	471	450	293	260	137
6.5 x 52mm Mannlicher-Carcano	RLN	3004	2067	448	445	295	265	161
6.5 x 54R Dutch/Romanian Mannlicher	RN	3102	2110	527	450	294	263	156
6.5 x 54mm Mannlicher-Schoenauer	RLN	3035	2112	454	452	295	264	159
6.5 x 55 Swede Mauser & Norway Krag	RLN	3150	2165	480	476	281	263	156
7 x 57mm Spanish Mauser	RLN	3063	2240	474	470	320	284	154
7.5 x 54 French M1929	RLN	2992	2115	482	480	340	308	190
7.5 x 55 Swiss M1911	RLN	3062	2180	496	494	334	304	174
7.5 x 58 French M1924	RLN	3157	2275	486	484	336	307	139
7.62 x 39mm M1943	RLN	2193	1510	445	443	340	310	123
7.62 x 45mm Czech	RLN	2364	1770	441	442	334	311	130
7.62 x 51mm NATO	RLN	2750	2010	470	466	338	308	150

Name and Metric Caliber	Case Type	Length Round	Length Case	Diameter Rim	Diameter Head	Diameter Neck	Diameter Bullet	Bullet Weight
7.62 x 54R Russian	RN	3020	2110	564	489	335	310	185
7.65 x 53mm Belgian Mauser	RLN	3063	2105	470	470	338	311	226
7.7 x 58mm Arisaka	RLN	3138	2275	472	472	338	311	200
7.7 x 58SR Arisaka	SRN	3134	2283	500	470	340	313	200
7.92 x 57mm Mauser	RLN	3173	2244	473	469	353	323	198
7.92 x 57R Schwarzlose	RN	2642	2240	530	471	382	356	197
7.92 x 61RB Norwegian Browning	RBN	3295	2389	468	484	340	319	220
8 x 50R Austrian/Bulgarian Mannlicher	RN	3000	1980	553	492	351	323	240
8 x 50R Lebel	RN	2948	1980	621	535	350	323	200
8 x 52R Siamese Mauser	RN	2940	2045	560	506	348	320	180
8 x 56R Hungarian Mannlicher	RN	3000	2196	554	491	348	329	205
8 x 58R Danish Krag	RN	3014	2280	575	503	355	322	198
8 x 59mm Breda	RLN	3161	2320	470	491	360	326	210
8 x 63mm Swedish Browning	RLN	3338	2477	479	485	256	321	220
10.15 x 61R Jarmann	RN	3070	2360	613	548	430	405	337
10.4 x 38R Swiss Peabody rimfire	RN	2232	1520	620	540	437	415	312
10.4 x 47R Vetterli-Vitali	RN	2366	1840	626	537	437	411	308
10.6 x 57.5R Russian Berdan Rifle	RN	2937	2268	598	515	451	430	365
11 x 49R Egyptian Remington	RN	2543	1921	653	578	463	438	401
11 x 51R Beaumont	RN	2708	2010	665	576	484	457	375
11 x 53R Brazilian Comblain	RN	2768	2100	673	575	460	436	380
11 x 59R Gras	RN	3020	2350	667	544	468	445	388
11 x 70R Montigny	RN	3185	2752	598	589	466	451	
11.15 x 58R Spanish Remington	RN	2976	2240	642	520	457	439	387
11.35 x 62 Madsen	RLN	3276	2433	627	628	492	457	306
12.7 x 81SR Breda	SRN	4220	3200	775	720	545	496	565
12.7 x 108R ShVAK	RN	5587	4244	992	854	548	511	790
12.7 x 108mm DShK	RLN	5776	4170	852	855	547	510	790
13 x 64B MG131	BN	4130	2520	672	(belt 705)	546	533	1150
13 x 92SR Tankpatrone (TuF)	SRN	5232	3614	910	863	574	522	965
13 x 94mm PzB	RLN	4645	3724	864	823	575	520	226
13.2 x 99mm Hotchkiss Long	RLN	5366	3898	797	792	567	530	802
14.5 x 114mm Soviet	RLN	6114	4500	1060	1061	640	570	968

Name and Metric Caliber	Case Type	Length Round	Length Case	Diameter Rim	Diameter Head	Diameter Neck	Diameter Bullet	Bullet Weight
15 x 95mm Mauser MG 151	RLN	5783	3760	790	793	626	614	880
15 x 104mm Besa	RLN	5820	4085	975	975	664	587	1160
15 x 115mm FN	RLN	6283	4519	970	972	643	604	1080
15.5 x 106mm FN	RLN	6925	4173	1055	1055	650	610	1203

Name and Imperial Caliber	Case Type	Length Round	Length Case	Diameter Rim	Diameter Head	Diameter Neck	Diameter Bullet	Bullet Weight
.280 (7mm) Enfield	RLN	2540	1700	460	467	312	284	130
.30-40 Krag	RN	3078	2314	545	461	338	309	220
.30-06 Springfield	RLN	3320	2490	470	470	338	308	150
.303 British, Marks I - VI	RN	3050	2151	530	460	330	311	215
.303 British, Marks VII-VIII	RN	3050	2211	530	460	330	311	174
.402 Enfield-Martini (and Gardner MG)	RN	3280	2740	677	586	432	404	384
.45-70 Government	RS	2700	2100	600	500	475	457	405
.577/450 Martini-Henry Rolled Case	RN	3150	2320	750	660	490	450	480
.577/450 Martini-Henry Solid Case	RN	3150	2355	757	666	496	450	480
.450 Gardner & Gatling	RN	3305	2450	662	580	484	450	480
.450 Gatling	RN	3000	2343	661	580	483	470	480
.5 Vickers	RLN	4340	3160	715	723	545	514	580
.5 Vickers Class D	RLN	6200	4732	871	822	546	511	665
.50 (12.7 x 99mm) Browning	RLN	5425	3910	800	800	557	510	662
.55 Boys	BN	5310	3950	795	[belt 850]	616	563	735
.65 Gatling (UK Mk I)	RN	4662	3815	955	785	707	650	1422
1 inch Nordenfelt	RS	6255	5655	1220	1107	1100	1011	3480

CANNON CARTRIDGES

In ascending order of caliber.

NOTE: *Case Types:* **R** - rimmed straight; **RN** - rimmed necked; **RL** rimless straight; **RLN** - rimless necked; **RB** - rebated rim; **B** - belted

Caliber and designation	Case Type	Length Round	Length Case	Diameter Rim	Diameter Head/belt	Diameter Neck	Diameter Bullet	Bullet Weight
20 x 70RB Becker	RB	5.590	2.755	0.787	0.862	0.807	0.767	4.58
20 x 70RB (E) Erhardt	RB			0.827	0.905			

Caliber and designation	Case Type	Length Round	Length Case	Diameter Rim	Diameter Head/belt	Diameter Neck	Diameter Bullet	Bullet Weight
20 x 72RB Oerlikon F	RB	5.394	2.834	0.748	0.882	0.811	0.783	2.82
20 X 80RB Oerlikon FFM	RB	5.748	3.150	0.760	0.854	0.815	0.783	4.69
20 x 82 Mauser MG151	RLN	5.787	3.217	0.988	0.984	0.814	0.783	4.09
20 x 94 Japan Ho-5	RLN	5.787	3.700	0.976	0.984	0.827	0.783	4.23
20 x 99R ShVa	RS	5.787	3.897	0.992	0.862	0.815	0.779	3.42
20 x 101RB Oerlikon FFL	RB	6.850	3.976	0.748	0.870	0.811	0.779	2.82
20 x 102 US Navy	RLN	6.692	4.015	1.161	1.150	8.811	0.783	3.56
20 x 105B Short Solothurn	B	6.692	4.133	0.984	1.035	0.815	0.783	4.94
20 x 110 HS 404	RLN	7.244	4.334	0.964	0.980	0.811	0.783	4.58
20 x 110RB Oerlikon S	RB	7.126	4.323	0.874	0.972	0.811	0.783	4.30
20 x 110 USN Mark 100	RLN	7.283	4.311	0.807	1.142	0.811	0.783	3.88
20 x 113 Lahti	RLN	6.890	4.437	1.102	1.102	0.823	0/783	4.94
20 x 120 Madsen	RLN	7.322	4.705	1.142	1.142	0.827	0.787	5/15
20 x 125 Japan Type 97	RLN	7.378	4.901	1.122	1.130	0.799	0.783	5.50
20 x 128 Oerlikon KAA	RLN	7.992	5.067	1.260	1.267	0.834	0.783	4.41
20 x 135 Mauser	RLN		5.315	1,260	1.260			3.95
20 x 138B Long Solothurn or Breda	B	8.070	5.425	1.055	1.125	0.819	0.797	4.33
20 x 139 HS 820	RLN	8.386	5.059	1.118	1.118	0.846	0.783	4.41
20 x 142 Japan Type 98	RLN	8.386	5.591	1.314	1.314	0.807	0.780	4.55
20 x 145R Bofors RLS	RS	8.661	5.709	1.161	1.000	0.825	0.787	5.11
23 x 115 Soviet NS	RLN	7.819	4.520	1.061	1.059	0.941	0.898	6.17
23 x 152B Soviet VYa	B	9.250	5.950	1.305	1.362	0.941	0.898	6.53
25 x 87 Fiat-Revelli	RLN	6.023	3.425	1.189	1.189	1.000	0.961	7.05
25 x 137 Oerlikon KBA	RLN	8.780	5.394	1.489	1.496	1.027	0.976	6.35
25 x 165 Japan Type 96	RL	8.267	6.476	1.685	1.692	1.086	1.003	8.89
25 x 184 Oerlikon KBB	RLN	11.338	7.244	1.496	1.504	0.980	8.11	8.82
25 x 205R Bofors	RN	12.125	8.070	1.653	1.456	1.047	0.964	8.82
25 x 205SR Soviet m/40	SRN	11.102	8.051	1.653	1.453	1.012	0.980	10.15
25 x 218R Soviet Navy	RN	11.690	8.583	1.574	1.266	1.039	0.968	9.87
25 x 218 Soviet 2-M3	RLN	11.496	8.610	1.374	1.370	1.027	0.972	10.15
27 x 145B Mauser MRCA	B	9.448	5.709	1.342	1.358	1.130	1.063	8.82
30 x 85B Mauser	B		3.346	1.248	1.260			11.65
30 x 86B Aden	B	7.874	3.386	1.315	1.327	1.224	1.177	11.64

Caliber and designation	Case Type	Length		Diameter				Bullet Weight
		Round	Case	Rim	Head/belt	Neck	Bullet	
30 x 90RB MK108	RB	8.031	3.543	1.023	1.275	1.220	1.177	11.64
30 x 92RB Japan Type 2	RB	6.652	3.622	1.094	1.299	1.238	1.181	9.31
30 x 97B DEFA	B	7.795	3.783	1.307	1.331	1.220	1.173	10.44
30 x 113B Aden/DEFA	B	7.874	4.382	1.311	1.330	1.232	1.181	8.64
30 x 114 Japan Ho-155	RLN	7.520	4.466	1.476	1.496	1.240	1.181	8.29
30 x 122 Japan Type 5	RLN	8.110	4.811	1.518	1.518	1.236	1.181	12.17
30 x 150B GIAT	B	9.842	5.905			1.220	1.173	9.70
30 x 165 Soviet GSh	RLN	11.023	6.496	1.574	1.574	1.272	1.173	13.75
30 x 170 Rarden	RLN	11.181	6.693	1.689	1.689	1.240	1.173	10.58
30 x 173 Oerlikon KCA	RLN	11.417	6.811	1.732	1.732	1.240	1.173	14.46
30 x 184B MK103	B	11.733	7.244	1.496	1.555	1.212	1.173	12.35
30 x 210B Soviet NN-30	B	12.010	8.268	1.811	1.870	1.268	1.173	12.70
30 x 220 Czech	RLN	13.58	8.661	1.889	1.889	1.270	1.173	15.87

GLOSSARY

AAT
Arme Automatique Transformable. French term analogous to General Purpose Machine Gun.

ACCELERATOR
Component of an automatic or self-loading firearm that increases the velocity of the opening breechblock or bolt.

ADVANCED PRIMER IGNITION
A system of operation commonly found in automatic weapons in which the cartridge primer is struck and fired while the breech bolt is still moving forward and loading the cartridge into the weapon's chamber or, in the case of a recoil-operated weapon, while the moving parts, having closed and locked the breech, are still moving forward into battery. The explosion force must therefore arrest the moving mass before it can make it recoil. In the case of a simple blow-back weapon such as a submachine gun, this introduces a slight delay that allows the bullet to leave the barrel and the chamber pressure to drop before the bolt begins to open, and it also allows the bolt to be smaller and lighter thus permitting a more compact weapon. In the case of recoil-operated weapons with locked breeches, it reduces the recoil force felt by the firer or the gun mounting and, as a rule, improves the accuracy and reliability of the weapon.

AGS
Avtomaticeski Granatomojot Stankovy. A Russian automatic grenade launcher. The AGS-17 is an automatic weapon of 37mm caliber, resembling a heavy machine gun.

ASP
Automatic, Self-Powered. Descriptive name used by McDonnell Douglas (USA) for a 30mm automatic cannon.

AUG/HB
Armee Universal Gewehr - Heavy Barrel. Austrian machine gun version of the AUG assault rifle manufactured by Steyr-Mannlicher, which is of modular construction and capable of being configured in various barrel lengths, firing modes and tactical applications.

AUTOMATIC
An automatic weapon is one which, when the trigger is pressed, will fire and continue to reload and fire so long as the trigger remains pressed and the supply of ammunition is maintained.

BALL
Term used to describe an inert bullet for small arms, having kinetic energy only. The term is derived from antiquity, when bullets from smooth-bore muskets were actual balls of lead.

BALLISTIC
Pertaining to the study of the flight of projectiles.

BARREL
That component of a firearm through which the projectile is launched and which gives direction to it. If rifled, it also imparts spin to the projectile.

BARREL EXTENSION
A frame attached to the barrel of a recoil-operated firearm and carrying the breech-block or bolt and also usually carrying or controlling the means of locking the breech.

BELTED CASE
A cartridge case having a prominent raised belt around the body, close to the base or extraction groove. This belt serves to locate the case accurately in the chamber and also reinforces the case against high internal pressure. Found on high-powered sporting rifle ammunition and on some types of machine gun and automatic cannon ammunition.

BELT FED
An automatic weapon in which the ammunition feed system takes the form of a flexible belt in which the cartridges are carried.

BENT
A notch cut into the weapon's firing pin, striker or hammer into which the sear engages to hold the component ready to fire.

BERDAN PRIMER
A type of primer cap used with small arm ammunition, named for Colonel Hiram Berdan, US Ordnance Department, who invented it in the 1860s. The principal feature is that the anvil forms part of the cartridge case, there being a number of flash holes alongside the anvil to permit the passage of flame from the cap to the propelling powder. The Berdan primer is used in almost all military ammunition. *Cf.* Boxer Primer.

BFA
Blank Firing Attachment. A device which can be fitted to the muzzle of a self-loading or automatic firearm and which causes an obstacle to the gases escaping from the firing of a blank cartridge. This permits pressure to build up in the weapon's operating system so that it can fire blank cartridges automatically.

BLOWBACK
A system of operation for self-loading and automatic weapons in which the breech is not locked at the instant of firing and the only resistance to the rearward movement of the cartridge case is the inertia of the breechblock or bolt. Once this resistance is overcome, the breech opens and the loading cycle is performed. The design of the weapon ensures that the bolt is of sufficient mass to resist opening until the bullet has left the weapon's barrel and the chamber pressure has dropped to a level at which it is safe to open the breech.

BK
Bord-Kanone. German term for cannon carried 'on board' an aircraft.

BLOW-FORWARD
A system of operation for self-loading and automatic weapons which is analogous to 'blow-back' *(above)* but in which the breechblock remains stationary and the breech pressure blows the barrel forward. Rarely encountered.

BOAT-TAILED
American term for projectiles in which the rear portion is tapered, so as to reduce base drag. Known in British terminology as 'streamlined'.

BOLT
That part of a small arm that closes the breech. Use of the word usually indicates a rotary locking movement; where no rotary movement is involved, the component is often called a breech-block.

BORE
The interior of a gun barrel, extending from the muzzle face to the rear of the chamber - including both the chamber and the rifled portion.

BOTTLE-NECKED
A cartridge case in which the mouth is sharply reduced in diameter to hold the bullet or projectile. It allows the case to hold the desired amount of propellant without being excessively long.

BOXER PRIMER
Primer cap for small arm cartridges invented by Col. Edward Boxer, Superintendent of the Royal Laboratory at Woolwich Arsenal in the 1860s. It is distinguished from the Berdan Primer *(qv)* by having the anvil as a separate component that is fitted into the cap before insertion into the cartridge case. There is a single central flash hole in the case, leading from the cap chamber to the interior of the case and the propellant charge. The Boxer primer is preferred for sporting ammunition since it is easy to push out the fired cap from a used case, using a thin rod through the central flash hole, so allowing the case to be reloaded. Military ammunition is now never reloaded, so that the Berdan Primer is preferred as being an easier manufacturing and assembly proposition.

BOX MAGAZINE
A method of ammunition supply in the form of a metallic or plastic box, either detachable from the weapon or integral with it—below, above, or to one side of the weapon. The cartridges are held inside the box and impelled to the mouth of the magazine by a spring, from where they are fed into the weapon's chamber.

BREECH
The rear end of the barrel; the area of the gun chamber.

BUFFER
A resilient unit at the rear of the body of a machine gun or other automatic weapon, against which the recoiling bolt or breechblock comes to rest, absorbing some of the recoil energy and assisting in controlling the rate of fire. The resilience may be due to springs, rubber, oil or pneumatic media.

BULLPUP
Colloquial term for a rifle in which the mechanism is set well back in the stock so that the end of the receiver is against the firer's shoulder. This design permits the use of a full-length barrel in a weapon that is shorter in overall length than a rifle of the conventional stocked type. The term, of American sporting origin, is of unknown derivation.

BUTT
That part of a rifle or other shoulder firearm which is placed against the firer's shoulder and which transfers the recoil force to his body.

CARTRIDGE CASE
A metallic or plastic case containing the propellant charge for a round of ammunition or a blank charge, and carrying the means of ignition–and possibly carrying the projectile.

CASELESS CARTRIDGE
A small arm cartridge that dispenses with the conventional metallic or plastic case and has the propellant formed into a solid mass attached to the bullet. It may or may not incorporate the means of ignition.

CHAMBER
That portion of the gun bore in which the cartridge is exploded.

CHANGE LEVER
A lever or switch on a firearm which allows the firer to choose between modes of fire, *eg* single shots or automatic fire. Also called a 'selector lever'.

CLOSED BOLT
A weapon in which the bolt is closed, though not necessarily locked, when the firing impulse is applied, is said to 'fire from a closed bolt'. *cf* 'Open Bolt'.

COOK-OFF
Colloquial expression for the premature ignition of the propelling charge of a small arm cartridge caused by induced heat from the gun chamber walls after prolonged firing.

CORIOLIS EFFECT
A component of "drift" *(qv)*. The Coriolis Effect is an error due to the projectile's motion in flight being considered as being fixed in space, when in fact it refers to the rotating Earth.

CYCLE OF OPERATION
A term used in connection with small arms and referring to the successive processes involved in firing one shot; *ie* feeding, chambering, firing, extraction, ejection, cocking and storing energy in the return spring. Also called the 'Firing Cycle'.

CYCLIC RATE
The theoretical rate of fire for an automatic weapon supposing it to be operated continuously with an infinite and uninterrupted ammunition supply; *ie* the rate of fire, disregarding the need to change magazines or fit new belts.

DANGEROUS SPACE
That part of a bullet's flight between the *first catch* and the *first graze*, *ie* the period when it is close enough to the ground to strike a human target.

DELAYED BLOWBACK
System of operation used with small arms. The breech of the weapon is not locked, and the breechblock or bolt is driven back by the effect of the cartridge explosion inside the chamber. However, the movement of the block or bolt is resisted by some arrangement, which slows or delays it, so keeping the cartridge in the chamber until the pressure has dropped to a safe level.

DISINTEGRATING LINK BELT
A belt *(qv)* of ammunition for an automatic weapon in which the actual rounds of ammunition

hold the individual metal links together. Thus, when the round has been pulled out of the belt to be loaded into the gun the link falls free. Developed originally during WWII for use in aircraft guns in order to avoid the need to provide space in which to collect and store the empty belt, its use later spread to all types of machine guns and cannons.

DOUBLE TRIGGER

A type of firing mechanism used with some selective fire weapons in which there are two triggers, one providing single shots and the other automatic fire. In some cases the triggers may be combined into a single unit, pivoted in the center; pulling back on the top section provides single shots and on the bottom section produces automatic fire.

DP

Degtyarova Pulyemet - Degtyarev machine gun (Russia).

DRIFT

The sideways movement of a projectile during flight, caused by a combination of yaw, Coriolis effect and Magnus effect. Drift is always in the direction of the twist of rifling, and is constant for any given combination of gun, projectile and propelling charge, allowing it to be calculated and corrections incorporated in firing tables or in the construction of sights.

DRUM MAGAZINE

A circular magazine into which the rounds are loaded axially or radially and propelled towards the feed lips by a spring or by a mechanism driven by the gun. The spring system is more usual, being employed on the Thompson, Lahti and other submachine guns; the mechanical system is less common, and was used on the Lewis machine gun

DShK

Degtyarova, Shpagina, Krupnokalibernyi; heavy machine gun designed by Degtyarev and Shpagin (Russia).

DT

Degtyarova Tankovyi; Degtyarev tank machine gun (Russia).

EJECTOR

The component in a small arm that throws the expended cartridge case clear of the weapon after extraction.

EXTRACTION

The process of removing the cartridge case from the chamber of a gun after firing. Ideally it should be divided into two phases: primary and secondary. The primary phase sees the exertion of a *(comparatively)* slow but powerful pull on the base of the case by the extractor *(qv)* so as to loosen the case from its close contact with the chamber walls. The secondary phase is much faster and demands less power, since it is merely a matter of pulling the now-loosened case from the chamber and expelling it from the gun. However, blowback and delayed-blowback weapons frequently omit the primary phase and apply the fast pull with heavy pressure, which unless steps are taken can lead to damaged cartridge cases and a jammed gun.

EXTRACTOR

A claw-like device that removes the empty cartridge case from the chamber of a weapon by engaging with a rim or groove forming part of the case. The extractor is operated by the opening movement of the breechblock or bolt and may form part of the block or bolt (in small arms) or be a separate component (in artillery).

FEED

That portion of the firing cycle of a weapon in which the cartridge is removed from the ammunition supply and loaded into the chamber.

FEED TRAY

Area of the receiver of a belt-fed automatic weapon across which the belt is laid and where the cartridge is separated from the belt and delivered to the feedway.

FEEDWAY

The area of a weapon mechanism in which the cartridge is removed from the ammunition supply and aligned before loading into the chamber.

FERMETURE NUT

A system of locking the breech of a light machine gun, used in some Hotchkiss and Benet-Mercié designs from about 1910 to the 1930s. It consists of a collar with interrupted lugs that surrounds the weapon's chamber. Operated by a gas piston, it is given a part- revolution that disengages the interrupted lugs from similar lugs on the breechblock, which is then free to be withdrawn by further movement of the gas piston. When the breech block returns and re-loads the chamber, the fermeture nut is rotated back and the lugs secure the block to the barrel.

FIRING MECHANISM

That part of the breech mechanism of a gun that delivers the firing impulse to the cartridge. It may be 'percussion', in which case the firing pin delivers a blow to a sensitive cap; or 'electric', in which case a contact delivers an electric current to the cap.

FIRST CATCH

That point in the trajectory of a small arm bullet when it falls close enough to the ground to strike the head of a standing man. The beginning of the *'Dangerous Space'.*

FIRST GRAZE

That point in the trajectory of a small arm bullet where it will strike the ground or a prone man. The end of the *'Dangerous Space'.*

FLASH ELIMINATOR

A device fitted to the muzzle of a small arm to cool the emergent propellant gases so that they do not enflame on contact with the air.

FLASH HIDER

A conical muzzle attachment to a gun designed to conceal the weapon's flash from the firer and thus not dazzle him at night. May also serve as a flash eliminator, though a hider is usually less efficient than a properly designed eliminator.

FLASHLESS

A term used to classify propellant powders. A flashless artillery propellant has been defined as one which, when fired from a gun, does not attract the attention of the naked eye at 3000 yards range, but for use with small arms a much lesser flash is demanded. *Flashlessness* depends upon the weapon; a powder that is flashless in one type or caliber may not be flashless in a different type or caliber, and each gun/cartridge combination has to be determined by trial.

FLUTED CHAMBER

(1) The chamber of a small arm that has longitudinal grooves cut into most of its length and beyond the mouth of the cartridge case when a round is loaded. When the cartridge is fired a proportion of the propellant gas flows down these flutes and equalizes the pressure inside and outside the case, floating the case on a layer of high-pressure gas and thus easing extraction. Usually found in weapons operating on the blowback or delayed blowback principle and using bottle-necked cartridges that, in a plain chamber, display a tendency to stick due to the mouth expanding rather more than the body. The grooves do not extend to the mouth of the chamber, so that obturation is not affected. An example of this system can be found in the French 7.62mm AA-52 machine gun.

(2) In distinction to the system outlined above, which is by far the commonest form of fluted chamber, two other systems must be described. The first, occasionally found in light, blowback-operated automatic pistols, has a number of shallow grooves incised in the chamber but not extending to either the chamber entrance or the cartridge mouth. On firing, the case expands and these flutes offer an increased amount of friction to the rearward movement of the case which is tending to open the breech, so giving a degree of delay to the opening. This is advantageous where the slide of the pistol is light and might otherwise open too quickly. This system is used in the Chinese Type 64 7.62mm pistol, and the flutes in this case are helical, in order to obtain a greater friction surface within the length of the cartridge case. The third fluted system uses a fluted chamber of the first type described but has one or two flutes extended to the mouth of the chamber so that a small amount of high-pressure gas escapes and is directed at the face of the breech block, where it passed through a small hole and impinges on the internal locking system and assists in starting the unlocking movement; this system can be found in the Swiss StuG57 service rifle.

FN

Fabrique Nationale SA, Herstal, Belgium; formerly known as *Fabrique Nationale d'Armes de Guerre.* Established in 1889 to manufacture Mauser rifles under license for the Belgian Army, it later obtained the services of John Browning and made several of his pistol and shotgun designs. In more recent times the company has been famous for the Browning Hi-Power pistol, the FAL rifle, the MAG general-purpose machine gun, the FNC assault rifle and several other military weapons. In 1989 it was purchased by GIAT, the French munitions consortium, and became known as FN Herstal SA. It 1998 it was sold back to the Walloon government and became an independent company once more.

FOLLOWER

The spring-driven platform in a small arm magazine upon which the cartridges rest and which pushes them towards the feedway.

FURNITURE

Those parts of a small arm which are solely for facilitating its handling, *ie* the stock, pistol grip, butt and forend, sling swivels, bipod, muzzle cap and similar items.

GPHMG

General Purpose Heavy Machine Gun. (USA) A development program for a heavy machine gun to replace the 50-caliber Browning which began in about 1980 but was placed in suspended animation in 1986 due to lack of funding.

GPMG

General Purpose Machine Gun. A machine gun capable of being employed either as a bipod-mounted squad automatic weapon or as a tripod-mounted sustained-fire weapon.

GRIP SAFETY

A safety device on a firearm that forms part of the pistol grip or other handgrip and which, unless pressed by the hand in the act of correctly holding the weapon, prevents the weapon from firing.

HANGFIRE

An ignition failure in a propelling charge, resulting in a delay between applying the firing impulse and having the charge explode. Invariably due to a defect in the ammunition.

HB

Heavy Barrel; item of nomenclature used with some machine guns and machine rifles to indicate the use of a heavier barrel than standard so as to be able to deliver sustained fire.

HE/I

High explosive, incendiary. Term descriptive of large-caliber small arm bullets and small-caliber artillery projectiles - especially cannon shells - with a filling designed to produce blast and fragmentation and also an incendiary effect against fuel and similar materials.

HE/I/T

High explosive, incendiary, tracer. As HE/I above, but with the addition of a tracer element to the bullet.

HIGH-LOW PRESSURE SYSTEM

A ballistic system developed in Germany in 1944 and which used a cartridge case of considerable strength in which the propellant is exploded, and a nozzle plate through which the explosive gas is bled so as to pass into the gun chamber and so propel the projectile. The system allows the charge to be burned at high pressure, for efficiency, but to develop a much lower pressure inside the gun barrel, allowing the barrel to be much lighter than would otherwise be possible. It was originally used with an 8cm anti-tank gun firing a fin- stabilized shaped-charge projectile. It has since been used by the Soviets in a similar 73mm gun fitted to an armored fighting vehicle, by naval forces for anti-submarine mortars, and by the various manufacturers of 40mm projected grenades.

HIT PROBABILITY

The chance, expressed as a percentage, of a round fired by any weapon hitting the target. Hit probability, usually contracted to *Ph*, is the product of the effect of a number of factors: the accuracy of the weapon; the accuracy of the sighting or fire control system; the accuracy of the ammunition; the skill of the firer. Thus, if the accuracy of the weapon is assessed as 95% and the accuracy of the firer at 50%, then the overall Ph will be .95 x .50 = .475% and if the accuracy of all four factors is 95%, then the Ph of the system will be .08 percent; in other words only 8 shots out of every hundred can be expected to hit the target. A few minutes with a calculator will show that to have a 90 percent chance of hitting, you require all four elements to be of the order of 98% or better. Since the flight of the bullet is governed by the standard laws of probability, it follows that there is not—nor ever will be—a weapon with a Ph of 100.

HMG
Heavy Machine Gun; usually implies a caliber of 12.7mm/0.50-inch or greater.

KPV
Krupnokalibernyi Pulemyot Vladimirova (Russia). A heavy machine gun designed by Vladimirov.

LANDS
The portion of a gun barrel left between the rifling grooves.

LEAD (Pronounced 'leed')
(1) The angular offset between the axis of the gun bore and the axis of the sight, which is designed to point the gun ahead of a moving target so that the projectile will hit it.
(2) The conical front end of the chamber of a small arm that directs the bullet into the rifling. Sometimes called the 'forcing cone'.

LINKLESS FEED
A system of supplying ammunition to heavy machine guns or cannon used in aircraft in which the ammunition is expelled from a fixed magazine by spring or other power and delivered down a flexible chute to the gun as individual rounds, not connected in any way. It eliminates the need to remove cartridges from a belt or to dispose of belt links. In some cases the empty cartridge cases are returned to the magazine and stored there so as to avoid the dangers of ejecting cartridge cases from supersonic aircraft.

LMG
Light machine gun; a generally-used abbreviation to describe the infantry squad automatic weapon. A machine gun capable of being carried and operated by one man.

LOCK TIME
The interval between applying the firing impulse - eg, pulling the trigger - and the ejection of the bullet or projectile from the muzzle of a gun. It is shortest in closed bolt weapons, where the firing pin or hammer is cocked and merely needs to be released; longest in weapons firing from an open bolt where the bolt must move forward and chamber the cartridge before firing can take place.

LONG RECOIL
A system of operating an automatic or self-loading weapon in which, after firing, the barrel and bolt recoil locked together for a distance greater than the length of a complete round of ammunition. The bolt is then unlocked and held, while the barrel runs forward, so opening the breech. During this forward movement the empty cartridge case is extracted and ejected. After the barrel has regained its forward position, the bolt is released to run forward, chamber a fresh round and lock to the barrel. Currently used on the 30mm Rarden cannon, its principal advantage is that the long movement of the recoiling mass reduces the load on the weapon's mounting.

LSW
Light Support Weapon. A heavy-barreled automatic rifle used as the infantry squad automatic weapon.

MACHINE GUN
An automatic firearm capable of delivering continuous fire. May be a 'Light Machine Gun', capable of being carried by one man and used by the infantry squad; or a 'Heavy Machine Gun.' Usually of 12.7mm or greater caliber, used for long-range support fire and for the attack of aircraft and light armored vehicles. The 'General Purpose Machine Gun' is capable of being used on a bipod as the squad weapon or on a tripod as the company or battalion support weapon. The category of 'Medium Machine Gun' was used in the past to classify the rifle-caliber company or battalion (*usually water-cooled*) support weapon but is no longer in common use.

MACHINE RIFLE
An obsolescent term used to describe a heavy-barreled automatic rifle capable of being used as a light machine gun. It differs from the 'true' light machine gun in not having an interchangeable barrel and by being based directly upon an existing automatic rifle design.

MAG
Mitrailleuse d'Appui Generale: a general-purpose machine gun developed and manufactured by Fabrique National Herstal SA of Belgium and widely adopted from 1955 onward.

MAGAZINE
(1) A store in which ammunition is kept, under special conditions and precautions.
(2) A feed system for a firearm in which cartridges are kept in an integral or attachable container. May be a 'Box Magazine', rectangular in shape and holding ammunition in a column or columns; or a 'Drum magazine', circular in shape and holding the ammunition radially, feeding it by rotation or spring power to the feedway of the weapon. A 'Saddle Drum magazine' consists of two drums connected by a unit that contains the feed exit, so that the whole sits across the top of the weapon with one drum on each side. Magazines may be of metal or plastic; the disposable magazine has yet to find military approval.

MAGAZINE HOUSING
That part of the receiver of the weapon into which a removable magazine fits so as to present the cartridges to the feedway.

MAGNUS EFFECT
The generation of a sideways force in a spinning cylinder in any fluid medium - eg air in the case of bullets. It forms a component of drift (*qv*).

MEAN POINT OF IMPACT
The arithmetical center of the points of impact of a group of projectiles.

MISFIRE
Total failure of a propelling charge to ignite. In guns is often due to a defect in the ammunition, but it can also be caused my mechanical defects in the weapon, particularly faults in the protrusion of the striker or firing pin, a weak or broken firing pin spring, or excessive cartridge-head clearance.

MK
Maschinen Kanone (German)

MMG
Medium Machine Gun. Obsolescent term referring to rifle-caliber machine guns used in the sustained-fire support role. Generally water-cooled, eg the Vickers, Maxim and Browning M1917 patterns.

MRBF
Mean Rounds Between Failures. The average number of rounds that a weapon might be expected to fire before a major defect occurs.

MUZZLE BRAKE
A device fitted to the muzzle of a gun and designed to deflect some of the emergent gas and direct it against surfaces so as to produce a pull on the muzzle and thus reduce the recoil force. Widely used on artillery weapons, less common on small arms since an efficient brake will direct too much gas to the sides and rear, thus inconveniencing the firer and his companions.

MUZZLE ENERGY
The kinetic energy possessed by a projectile as it leaves the gun. Calculated in foot-pounds or Joules for small arms, foot-tons or kilo-Joules for larger weapons, it is based on the formula $\frac{1}{2}\mathbf{M}\mathbf{V}^2$ and is calculated by multiplying the projectile weight by the square of the muzzle velocity and dividing by a factor which compensates for the different units of measurement and for gravity.

MUZZLE VELOCITY (MV)
The speed at which the projectile leaves the muzzle of a weapon. Also referred to as **'Vo'**, the Velocity at zero distance from the weapon. Expressed either in feet per second (ft/sec) or meters per second (m/sec).

OPEN BOLT
A weapon is said to fire 'from an open bolt' when the bolt is held back from the empty chamber in the cocked condition, and when the trigger is pressed, the bolt runs forward propelled by a spring to load a round into the chamber and fire it. On releasing the trigger the bolt is again held back. This system, used with automatic weapons, allows air to circulate through the barrel between bursts of fire for cooling purposes, and it is usually simpler to design and manufacture than a weapon which 'fires from a closed bolt'. Its principal drawback is the shift of balance experienced by the firer as the bolt runs forward for the first shot, which usually disturbs the aim. For this

reason some selective-fire weapons are designed so that in automatic fire they operate from an open bolt, but for single-shot, deliberate, fire they fire from a closed bolt.

PANORAMIC SIGHT
An optical sight used with heavy machine guns in the indirect-fire role. It has a fixed eyepiece mounted for the convenience of the gunlayer and a rotating head, which allows the layer to look in any direction through the full 360 degrees without moving his eye. Angular scales are geared to the head so as to measure the angular displacement from the axis of the gun bore in the horizontal plane and also the displacement of the optical line of sight in the vertical plane where this is provided. Also known as a 'goniometric' or 'dial' sight.

PARABELLUM
Term used to identify certain cartridges and weapons that were originally developed by the *Deutsche Waffen & Munitionsfabrik* of Germany in the early years of the 20th century. The word was taken from 'Parabellum Berlin', their telegraphic address.

PROPELLANT
A low explosive used to fire a projectile from a weapon by the rapid generation of gas. Usually a nitro-cellulose compound, though other types appear from time to time.

REBATED RIMLESS
A form of small arm and cannon cartridge case in which the extraction rim is smaller in diameter than the base of the case. Adopted in blowback weapons where it is desirable that the entire case be inside the chamber before being fired, or in weapons of unusual caliber so that the extracting rim conforms to a standard bolt face dimension.

RECEIVER
The action body of a small arm; the casing covering the breech and breech mechanism; the housing for the bolt or breechblock.

RECOIL
The rearward movement of a gun or other firearm due to reaction to the ejection of the projectile from the muzzle.

RECOIL INTENSIFIER
A device attached the muzzle of a recoil-operated machine gun that impedes the muzzle blast and thus amplifies the rearward thrust on the barrel, so giving greater impulse to the automatic mechanism. Sometimes called a recoil booster or muzzle booster.

RECOIL OPERATED
A term descriptive of automatic and self-loading weapons that depend upon the recoil of the weapon to actuate the automatic or self-loading mechanism. In general, the barrel is permitted to recoil so as to deliver impetus to the mechanism; the recoil may be long (*qv*) or short (*qv*), the latter being more common.

RECOIL SPRING
The spring in an automatic weapon which returns the bolt or slide after firing; sometimes, and perhaps more accurately, called the 'return spring'.

REGULATOR
A valve on a gas-operated automatic weapon through which a proportion of the propellant gas is diverted to the actuating mechanism. It is provided with an adjustment, usually a number of different-sized ports, so that more or less gas can be admitted to the system so as to give extra power to overcome stiffness from lack of lubrication, heat expansion, dirt or other causes. In some weapons the regulator may permit the gas to be entirely shut off so as to allow the weapon to be used for launching grenades; in such cases the automatic action is not required and all the gas can be applied to the grenade.

RETARDED BLOWBACK
A blowback (*qv*) automatic weapon in which the rearward movement of the bolt or breech-block is mechanically impeded so as to slow down its initial movement and thus permit the chamber pressure to drop to safe limits before the breech begins to open. Often used to permit the firing of a more powerful cartridge than would be advisable in a simple blowback mechanism—but without adding the complication and expense of a locked breech. Also called 'delayed blowback'.

RETURN SPRING

A spring in an automatic or self-loading weapon which is compressed by the recoiling bolt and which then drives the bolt forward to reload and recommence the cycle of operation.

RIFLING

The helical grooves cut into the interior of a gun barrel that cause the projectile to rotate and thus attain a state of gyroscopic stability in flight.

RIMLESS

A cartridge case in which the extraction rim is the same diameter as the base of the case and is separated from it by a prominent extraction groove.

RIMMED

A cartridge case in which the extraction rim is greater in diameter than the base of the case.

ROUND

A complete item of ammunition, comprising all the components necessary for one effective shot; eg, cap, cartridge case, propellant charge, projectile and fuse.

SAWS

Squad Automatic Weapon System (USA). Acronym that applied to a development program for a light machine gun in the 1970s but since loosely applied to any proposal for a light machine gun.

SEAR

A component of the firing mechanism of a small arm or gun, linked to the trigger and which engages the hammer, striker or firing pin, keeping it cocked against the pressure of a spring. When the trigger is operated, the sear is withdrawn from engagement, allowing the hammer & components to move forward and fire the cartridge. Occasionally spelt *scear* in old documents.

SELECTIVE FIRE

Term used to describe small arms that are capable of firing single shots semi-automatically or of firing full automatic; the choice being governed by some form of switch or controller.

SEMI-RIMMED

Cartridge case which has an extraction groove like a rimless case, but in which the rim so exposed is slightly larger than the head of the case. This means that the rim can position the case correctly in the chamber but is not sufficiently large to interfere with feeding from the magazine. Invented by John Browning and first used with the 7.65mm ACP cartridge.

SG

Stankovy Gorynuova. (Russia); heavy machine gun designed by Goryunov.

ShKAS

Shpitalny, Komaritsky, Aviatsionnyi, Skorostrelnyi A Russian aircraft machine gun, now obsolete.

SIGHTS

Apparatus attached to a firearm or gun so as to direct fire accurately at a target. 'Iron Sights' are the metal sights used with small arms, as opposed to 'Optical Sights'. 'Night Sights' are used to engage targets in darkness and are usually some form of image-intensifying or thermal imaging device. 'Telescope (or Telescopic) Sights' are optical sights with some degree of magnification to give an enhanced view of the target. "Unit Power Optical Sights' are telescopes with a magnification of 1 or slightly more, giving better definition of the target but without distorting the scale in comparison to the naked-eye view of the same area. 'Collimating Sights' are quasi-optical sights that allow fast alignment by projecting an image of the sighting mark into the same apparent plane as the target.

SLAP

Saboted Light Armor Penetrator (USA). A discarding sabot, armor-piercing (APDS) small arm bullet.

SPIN STABILIZATION

The method of keeping a projectile nose-first in flight by spinning it, usually accomplished by firing from a rifled gun. Imparting spin to a mass gives it gyroscopic stability, the tendency to resist any attempt to displace it from its flight attitude; an elongated projectile fired from a smooth-bored gun, and thus not given spin, would tumble end-over-end in flight

SSKP

Single Shot Kill Probability. A more fashionable way of saying 'Hit Probability' *(qv)*.

STRIKER

A firing pin of generous proportions that is driven by a spring, and thus has sufficient momentum to fire the cartridge cap.

TERMINAL VELOCITY

The velocity of a projectile at the instant it strikes its target or reaches the end of its trajectory.

TOGGLE LOCK

A method of locking the bolt or breechblock of an automatic weapon by using a two-lever linkage. One end is attached to the barrel extension, the other to the bolt, and in the middle is a hinge. With the bolt closed, the two levers lie flat, and any thrust is resisted. As the weapon recoils, some mechanism is used to raise the central hinge, and once this occurs the strut-like resistance fails and the two levers can fold up, allowing the bolt to move backwards and open the breech. First used on the Maxim machine gun, most famously used on the Parabellum pistol, and found on a variety of Swiss automatic weapons designed by Col Fürrer, Superintendent of the Thun arsenal 1925-45, who had a predilection for this mechanism. It is rarely seen otherwise, since it demands fine machining and very consistent ammunition performance.

The toggle may also be used as a delaying mechanism for a delayed blowback weapon, either by positioning the hinge points above the line of recoil so that the recoil force tends to open the toggle, though at a considerable mechanical disadvantage (the Pederson rifle) or by having the toggle folded in the closed position and making the recoil force unfold it (the Schwarzlose machine gun).

TRACER

A pyrotechnic device in the rear of a projectile which burns during flight, emitting light and smoke, so that the trajectory is defined and can be used as an aid to fire control.

TRAJECTORY

The path described by a projectile as it passes through the air. In a vacuum this would be a parabola, but due to the effects of air drag and gravity it becomes a compound curve, steeper at the target end than at the gun end.

TWO-PART BOLT

A mechanism to provide delayed blowback action of an automatic weapon. It consists of a bolt in two parts, the front light and the rear heavy, together with some delaying element between the two - eg, a lever or rollers engaging in a recess in the receiver. On firing, blowback action of the cartridge case forces the light forward section backwards; the lever or rollers must then be disengaged from their lodgment by this pressure before the rearward movement can be imparted to the heavy section of the bolt which, by reason of its inertia, adds a further delay before it begins to move back, taking the forward section and the locking device with it. The first application of this principle appears in a 1912 patent by Kiraly, and it was used by him in a variety of weapons in the 1930-40 period, notably the Hungarian Danuvia submachine guns and the SIG-Neuhausen submachine gun. It has since been used in improved form in the Heckler & Koch and CETME rifles and machine guns, in the French FA-MAS rifle and AAT-52 machine gun, and the Stgw57 Swiss rifle and 510 machine gun.

VERTEX

The highest point reached by a projectile on its trajectory. An approximation of the vertex height in feet can be made by squaring the projectile's time of flight and multiplying the result by four.

VULCAN

A multi-barreled 20mm cannon with very high rate of fire developed by the General Electric Co of the USA on the Gatling principle and used for the armament of fighter aircraft and also as a light air defense weapon.

WINDAGE

(1) The difference in diameter between the caliber of a gun and the external diameter of the projectile.

(2) Lateral adjustment of a weapon's sight in order to compensate for a cross-wind blowing across the trajectory. *(Principally an American usage).*

YAW

The deviation of the axis of the projectile from its theoretical trajectory during flight. On leaving the muzzle, yaw will develop because of the disturbing effects of the propellant gas rushing past the bullet. This initial yaw is relatively slight in a rifled weapon but can be considerable in smooth-bored weapons, such as mortars. Later in flight the bullet, gyroscopically stabilized by its spin, tends to maintain its flight attitude while the trajectory it is following adopts a curve, so that the nose of the bullet deviates from the trajectory. This allows air to strike the side of the nose, pushing the bullet even further from the trajectory. Any irregularity in the balance of the bullet due to faulty manufacture will set up a centrifugal force, which will add to the yaw. The initial yaw at the muzzle will also form a component of the drift of the projectile, due to the variations in pressure at the nose arising from the other two components allowing air pressure to exert a sideways thrust on the nose of the bullet.

ZEROING

The act of adjusting the sights of the weapon to the axis of the gun barrel so that, when fired, the bullet strikes at the point of aim. The term is largely confined to small arms. When the adjustment has been performed, the weapon is said to be 'zeroed'. Correctly done, it will take into account not only the idiosyncrasies of the weapon but also the eyesight defects of the firer. With cannon the term 'bore-sighting' is more usually used.

INDEX